Myroblytes and Miracles in Europe

Clarissa Gleason

ABSTRACT

In medieval European society, holy oil played a seminal role in defining individual sanctity and

legitimate political authority. In the *Glossa Ordinaria,* exegetes presented oil as a sign of divine

election. Within the oil-rich liturgy, medieval Christians celebrated their beloved saints, some of

whose bodies produced quantities of oil. The saints who oozed miraculously are known as *myroblytes*

– from the Greek, meaning "myrrh-gushing" or "myrrh-flowing." In the early medieval period oil

flowed predominantly from the bodies of male saints who were members of the ecclesiastical elite.

In the later medieval period, however, oil flowed mainly from the bodies of laywomen, including

penitents. With the rise of Catherine of Alexandria's cult in the eleventh century, authors began to

envision female saints as sources of holy oil. Mendicants in particular took an interest in

disseminating the cults of female myroblytes, in order to bring women and their devotional practices

into the fold of the institutional Church. The appearance of female myroblytes coincided with a

development in Rome's *fons olei* legend. Prior to the High Middle Ages, authors interpreted the *fons*

olei as a portent of Christ's birth, which providentially coincided with Caesar Augustus' reign and the

pax romana, an unprecedented era of peace. In the eleventh and twelfth centuries, however, medieval

authors claimed the *fons olei* flowed from Santa Maria in Trastevere, a church dedicated to the

Blessed Virgin. Mary became the myroblyte of myroblytes. This development reflected greater

devotion to female figures such as the Blessed Virgin and Mary Magdalene as well as a new emphasis

on Christ's humanity. In the early thirteenth century, the *fons olei* served as a powerful symbol in

papal discourse as Innocent III sought to combat the Cathar heresy and to bring marriage more

firmly within the purview of the Church. The "oil of gladness" flowing from the *fons olei* symbolized the papacy's *plenitudo potestatis* – the divine source of power from which all other earthly powers flowed. Myroblyte *vitae* and the legend of the *fons olei* demonstrate how miraculous oil defied gender binaries and shifted from being mainly a sign of powerful male monarchs and ecclesiastical elites (both of whom were anointed with oil) to signifying the miraculous and divine nature of more ordinary human beings, including laywomen and children.

TABLE OF CONTENTS

INTRODUCTION

When monks sitting in choir sang about fragrant nard flowing from Mary Magdalene's jar or oil dripping down Aaron's beard, what were they thinking about? When a medieval Christian made a pilgrimage to the oozing tomb of St. Nicholas, what did she hope to find? When Innocent III processed to Santa Maria in Trastevere during the Fourth Lateran Council and consecrated the church surrounding the legendary *fons olei,* what message did he send to Latin Christians and the wider world? Holy oil played a salient role in the religious culture of the medieval Latin West, and yet it remains largely overlooked as a key to understanding medieval mentalities, devotional practices and political discourse. In particular, the saints whose bodies produced holy oil merit further exploration, as does the legend of Santa Maria in Trastevere's *fons olei.* Did producing holy oil make a saint more Christ-like? Were only those smeared with holy or miraculous unguent Christians? Was oil a sign of new life? Was oil a sign of eternal life? Why was an oily, miraculous fountain a powerful symbol for divinely given authority?

Imagery of oil and unguents permeates both the Hebrew and Christian Scriptures. Close to two hundred references to oil or anointing appear in the Hebrew Scriptures alone – from Jacob anointing the stone at Bethel (Genesis 28:10-22) to the Prophet Samuel anointing Saul and David as kings (1 Samuel 10 & 16). In Psalm 132, the psalmist compares fraternal love with the unguent poured on the head of Aaron, the unguent which drips down Aaron's beard and rolls to the very edge of his robe – which incidentally Augustine interpreted as a symbol for God's grace spreading to the farthest reaches of the Church.[1] The opening line of the Song of Songs speaks of the name of the beloved being like oil poured out: *oleum effusum nomen tuum.* In the Christian Scriptures, references to oil are fewer but nevertheless potent: Jesus's disciple Mary (later called the Magdalene) anoints

---

[1] Psalms are referenced according to their numbering in the Latin Vulgate.

1

Jesus' feet with precious, perfumed unguent, breaking her alabaster jar in the process. In the parable of the Wise and Foolish Virgins, only those with oil in their lamps are allowed entrance to the wedding feast. The Good Samaritan heals the wounds of a beaten and abandoned victim with oil and wine. And, when Jesus gives his disciples authority over unclean spirits, he commissions them to cast out demons and anoint the sick with oil.

Medieval Christians did not simply encounter oil through private readings of the Bible. Stories and images made their way into the liturgy to such an extent that – metaphorically speaking – oil slipped from the lips and tongues of medieval choristers when they sang in choir. Holy oil had a sacramental function within the liturgy, particularly in the rites of Christian initiation. Starting in the mid-ninth century bishops alone had the power to consecrate holy oils, which they did once each year on Holy Thursday before Easter. These oils were then used to anoint catechumens and neophytes and to anoint the sick. Medieval prelates used chrism, the holiest of the three holy oils, in the anointing rituals of baptism, episcopal ordinations, and royal coronations. While very much in the hands of the ecclesiastical elite, holy oil was also a focus of great popular devotion. Within the context of the oil-rich liturgy, medieval Christians celebrated their beloved saints. The saints whose bodies produced oil are known as *myroblytes* – from the Greek, meaning "myrrh-gushing" or "myrrh-flowing" – myrrh being an aromatic plant resin that was used in the ancient Near East and medieval Latin West as incense and as perfume when combined with oil. Oil mixed with fragrant balsam or myrrh was also known as chrism. Furthermore, from Late Antiquity through the Counter Reformation, a legend proliferated about a fountain of oil gushing from the ground beneath Santa Maria in Trastevere, one of Rome's earliest Marian churches. In a sense, this legend made the Virgin Mary the myroblyte of myroblytes.

In order to understand the significance of oil in medieval culture, we must understand how medieval people's minds worked and the intellectual landscape they inhabited. In her studies of music and the liturgy, Margot Fassler observed that memory and intertextuality were fundamental to medieval religious culture, particularly the liturgy and music making. Medieval people had prodigious memories, in which they stored vast arrays of music and texts. Hearing a phrase or a series of notes could conjure a memorized piece, either textual or musical, bringing it to the fore.[2] This "art of memory" allowed for the creation of meaning through intertextuality, a "web of interrelationships" within and between works of art. If a monk memorized a melody for an antiphon about the Blessed Virgin Mary but then later sang that same melody to a text about Mary Magdalene, the juxtaposition of text and music led to a new combination of figures, images or ideas. Even in the singing of a single hymn "the poetic images pile up in the memory" and play off one another, creating multiple levels of meaning.[3] Intertextuality thus allowed for a kind of exegesis. By juxtaposing certain melodies, chant texts, biblical pericopes or even images within sacred spaces, medieval people could effectively create a multifaceted commentary on, or interpretation of, ideas, images or texts.

In addition to words and sounds, smells also brought memories to life. Like tastes, scents possessed the power to conjure the past. Saint Paul reminded his readers of the correlation between smells and the lingering impressions left in peoples' minds, impressions that cumulatively contributed to the fame or reputation of early Christians: "For we are the aroma of Christ to God among those who are being saved."[4] For early and medieval Christians, a pleasant fragrance signaled

---

[2] Margot Elsbeth Fassler, *Music in the Medieval West*, Western Music in Context : A Norton History (New York: W.W. Norton & Company, 2014), 4–12.

[3] Ibid., 4.

[4] 2 Cor.2: 15-16.

the presence of a holy person.[5] Saints' bodies often emitted a flower-like fragrance that testified to

the incorruptible nature of their flesh. In the medieval period, the scent of chrism flowing on the

heads of kings, bishops, or the newly baptized would have evoked not only the "odor of sanctity"

floating from relics but also the fragrance filling the house where Mary Magdalene anointed Jesus'

feet. A chant sung on the feast of Mary Magdalene and on Holy Thursday, during the foot washing

rite, described the smell of nard filling the house, which glossators interpreted as a symbol for the

Church: "Maria then anointed Jesus' feet and wiped them with her hair and the house was filled with

the scent of unguent."[6] Two of the gospels recorded Jesus as saying the whole world would

remember Mary Magdalene for having anointed him with fragrant nard.[7] Another chant sung for

Marian feasts credited the Virgin Mary with producing the odor of sanctity, a symbol perhaps for

Christ: "Just like choice myrrh, you gave the odor of sweetness, Holy Mother of God."[8] Fragrant

chrism would have also conjured nuptial imagery in the minds of those familiar with the Song of

Songs. A chant for the feast of the Assumption as well as other feasts honoring virgins told of myrrh

permeating the bridegroom's clothing: "In the aroma of your unguents we run; young maidens loved

you exceedingly."[9]

In my analysis of the role of oil in medieval culture, I limit my study to texts and images,

leaving aside the musical and olfactory dimensions for the moment. The texts and images alone,

---

[5] Béatrice Caseau, "Syméon Stylite Entre Parfum et Puanteur," *Revue Des études Byzantines* 63 (2005): 71–96; Béatrice Caseau, "Christian Bodies: The Senses and Early Byzantine Christianity.," in *Desire and Denial in Byzantium. Papers from the Thirty-First Spring Symposium of Byzantine Studies, University of Sussex, Brighton, March 1997*, ed. Liz James (Aldershot: Ashgate, 1999) 101–9; Susan Ashbrook Harvey, *Scenting Salvation: Ancient Christianity and the Olfactory Imagination*, The Transformation of the Classical Heritage 42 (Berkeley: University of California Press, 2006).

[6] "Maria ergo vnxit pedes iesu et extersit capillis suis et domus impleta est ex odore unguento." For further discussion of this chant, see Chapter 3.

[7] "She has done what she could; she has anointed my body beforehand for its burial. Truly I tell you, wherever the good news is proclaimed in the whole world, what she has done will be told in remembrance of her." Mark 14:8-9; "By pouring this ointment on my body she has prepared me for burial. Truly I tell you, wherever this good news is proclaimed in the whole world, what she has done will be told in remembrance of her." Matt 26:12-13.

[8] The chant text reads: "Sicut mirra electa odorem dedisti suavitatis sancta dei genetrix." Debra Lacoste (Project Manager and Principal Researcher) and Jan Koláček (Web Developer), Cantus: A Database for Latin Ecclesiastical Chant – Inventories of Chant Sources, available from <http://cantus.uwaterloo.ca/>, July 31, 2015, Can 004942.

[9] "In odore unguentorum tuorum currimus adolescentulae dilexerunt te nimis." Can 003261.

however, provide a rich trove of overlapping concepts that allow us to see how, throughout the centuries, authors embellished or reinterpreted ideas about holy oil. Biblical passages, Patristic commentaries, medieval glosses and chants created the intellectual framework that informed medieval thought and ritual involving holy oil. Authors of biblical glosses, sermons, saints' biographies, and church chronicles drew on their audiences' memories and knowledge of the established corpus of texts and images to explain the significance of anointings or to perpetuate legends about miraculous oil. To understand the meaning of holy oil in myroblytes' vitae or the art, pageantry and political discourse surrounding Santa Maria in Trastevere's fons olei, we must first understand the conceptual foundation of medieval beliefs and practices involving oil and anointing.

Medieval thought and ritual did not emerge *ex nihilo*. Beliefs and legends did not spring into existence, *sui generis*. The intellectual traditions and ritual practices of ancient Near Eastern cultures served as a cradle for Christianity, directly informing medieval rites and beliefs. Early Christianity inherited perceptions of oil and anointing rituals from ancient Mesopotamian, Hebraic and Greco-Roman cultures. Early Christian writings, including Patristic exegesis and mystagogy, in turn influenced the medieval methods of interpreting sacred texts, historical figures and events of the past. Medieval authors received specific ideas about oil from their intellectual forbearers as well as modes of thinking and interpreting. The major themes surrounding oil in the medieval period first surfaced centuries earlier in classical and late antiquity. In looking at the role of oil in pre-Christian and early Christian cultures, we find early evidence of belief in the power of oil to divinize an individual, the interpretation of oil as a sign of fecundity, abundant life or divine favor and the use of oil in marriage rituals and legal contracts. Furthermore, examining the significance of oil in these early cultures reveals oil was not the exclusive domain of any one gender, but played a role in the lives of both men and women, who often had distinct gender roles. Men alone, for example, consecrated oil for use in the temple liturgy. Women alone carried oil and spices to anoint the bodies of the dead. The ambiguity of oil endured for generations, resurfacing again and again within the medieval period. Oil consistently escaped the confines of gender binaries.

The perceptions of holy oil inherited from the ancient Near East found their way into medieval culture in part via the Glossa Ordinaria, the standard biblical commentary that took shape in northern France in the mid-twelfth century. The ideas enshrined in the Glossa Ordinaria both reflected the intellectual past of the medieval Church and influenced its future. In the High Middle Ages, as Europe shifted from a diffuse agrarian culture to an increasingly urban populace, cathedral schools surpassed monasteries as centers of learning. When literacy increased and master teachers taught a growing student population, questions arose regarding methods of biblical interpretation. Master teachers read biblical texts aloud to students and explicated the texts' meanings. The masters did not always rely on their own insights and ingenuity for biblical interpretation, but drew largely on commentaries passed down from Patristic and early medieval authors, namely Augustine, Jerome, Gregory the Great, Cassiodorus, and Isidore of Seville. Compilers or glossators, such as Anselm of Laon, codified diverse glosses for biblical texts, making a *glossa ordinaria* – a standard gloss. The development of the *Glossa Ordinaria* in northern France coincided with a parallel development in Bologna, where standard glosses emerged for legal texts.

The *Glossa Ordinaria* became central to the intellectual framework of the Latin West, directly informing how people in the High and Later Middle Ages viewed oil and anointing. As a standard reference work in any library or scriptorium in the later medieval period, the *Glossa* would have informed the thinking of countless authors, including saints' biographers describing miraculous oozings, cantors composing liturgies, chroniclers retelling Church history and even popes composing sermons. For this reason, understanding the meaning imputed to oil in the *Glossa Ordinaria* is key to explaining the significance of miraculous oil in popular devotions as well as political or ecclesiastical discourse. A single verse from Psalm 44, for example, appeared as a gloss for nearly every pericope about oil or anointing: "Therefore God, your God, has anointed you with the oil of gladness in the presence of your companions."[10] Readers were so well acquainted with the verse that glossators abbreviated the phrase instead of writing the text out in full. The *Glossa* also often reproduced Augustine's commentary on this psalm, such that Augustine's ideas and the psalm verse itself became a familiar refrain in numberless contexts in which oil appeared, both within the *Glossa Ordinaria* and in the wider medieval society. Psalm 44's image of a king being anointed with oil before his companions became a template for medieval thought, ritual, and legend. The king's fragrant, myrrh-scented clothes and his desire for a young girl's beauty would circulate throughout medieval texts and within the liturgy, suffusing people's imaginations with unguent and ideas about royalty, marriage, and immortality.

The *Glossa Ordinaria* worked in tandem with the liturgy to disseminate ideas about holy oil within medieval culture. The Bible, including the Hebrew and Christian Scriptures, acted as the fundamental text giving life to every liturgical celebration. Readings, chants, and ritual reenactments of biblical scenes brought the ancient Scriptures back to life, day in and day out, within countless religious communities. Each week monks recited the Psalter in its entirety (one hundred and fifty psalms) from memory during the Divine Office. Antiphons, responsories, responsory verses, and hymns all elaborately embroidered new meanings on old biblical texts, giving fresh life to ancient verses, placing them within new contexts or altering them through innovative juxtapositions. Within this soundscape, the drama of the liturgy unfolded in sacred spaces, where ritual actions communicated to the faithful participants and observers their roles within the cosmos and within salvation history. In these highly ritualized contexts, bishops consecrated holy oils, distributed holy oils to the faithful, and anointed the newly baptized. Kings and bishops also received precious chrism on their heads at their coronations or ordinations. Saints, famed for their heroic martyrdoms

---

[10] "dilexisti iustitiam et odisti iniquitatem propterea unxit te Deus Deus tuus oleo laetitiae prae consortibus tuis." Psalm 44:8.

or impeccable virginity, appeared in processions or under the altars where priests consecrated hosts. Choristers lauded these saints in song, sometimes singing of fragrant oil flowing from the limbs of the holy ones.

Inquiramus: Historiographical Questions

Myroblytes

While saints and their cult have garnered ample attention from scholars in the last three decades, historians of medieval sanctity have cast only a passing glance at one of the cult's most unusual phenomena: myroblytes. Myroblytes were holy men and women whose bodies produced oil in their own lifetimes or whose entombed bodies did so after death. The circumstances in which oil appears in myroblyte *vitae* vary, reflecting sundry uses of oil and perceptions of the liquid as an expression of holiness. The earliest and most common use of myroblytes' unguent was for healing. Menas, a fourth-century martyr from Egypt, may have been the earliest saint whose liquid wielded restorative powers. In the ancient Near East pilgrims traveled far and wide to pour holy oil into saints' tombs and then collect the oil once it had made contact with the holy relics. Pilgrims also collected oil from lamps hanging near saints' tombs, believing that anything in proximity to holy bodies absorbed the saints' *praesentia*. The pilgrims would carry the sanctified oil back to their homelands as souvenirs or for healing purposes. In the Latin West in the early medieval period, clerics began circulating stories about oil spontaneously gushing from the tombs of holy men. Gregory of Tours' account of Andrew the Apostle's tomb appears to be the paradigm for later myroblytes' oozing. Andrew's oil distinguished itself, however, by possessing augural qualities: the amount of oil pouring from his tomb corresponded to the relative abundance or dearth of crops in a given year. A small number of saints exuded holy oil while still alive, such as Lutgard of Aywières and Christina the Astonishing, both thirteenth-century holy women from the Low Countries. Miraculous unguent flowed from their fingertips and breasts, respectively.

While myroblytes' oil miracles number among the more curious religious phenomena of the medieval period, myroblytes *qua* myroblytes remain an understudied segment of the medieval population. When scholars discuss oil miracles, they generally do so only in small measure, within the larger context of a saint's life or cult, giving little explanation to the meaning of oil within the *vitae* or how these miracles reflect the larger role of holy oil in medieval religious culture. In *Holy Feast, Holy Fast: the Religious Significance of Food to Medieval Women* (1987), Caroline Walker Bynum coupled the miracle of oil production with extreme female asceticism, arguing that flowing oil was characteristic of a peculiarly feminine spirituality. In her study of female sanctity, Bynum argued that spirituality, like so many other aspects of human society, was subject to gender distinctions.[11] She stated that the spiritual concerns and practices of medieval women were fundamentally different from those of men.[12] Bynum contended, moreover, that female myroblytes' oil was a by-product of food asceticism and Eucharistic devotion, the central and preeminent religious practices of medieval women, but not men. Ostensibly this distinctly feminine piety, so physical in nature, led to the excretion of healing liquid, often post-mortem.[13] If in female *vitae* oil appeared as the result of a carnal, food-oriented spirituality, how are we to interpret the nature of oil production in male *vitae?* If men did not produce oil because of their devotion to the Eucharist, why did they? Moreover, how

---

[11] For an overview of the subject of gender and history see Joan Wallach Scott, "Gender: A Useful Category of Historical Analysis," *American Historical Review* 91, no. 5 (1986): 1053-75; "AHR Forum: Revisiting 'Gender: A Useful Category of Historical Analysis'" AHR 113, no.5 (2008): 1344-1430. An extensive body of literature now exists on saints and gender. See Caroline Walker Bynum, *Holy Feast and Holy Fast: The Religious Significance of Food to Medieval Women*, New Historicism (Berkeley: University of California Press, 1987); Caroline Walker Bynum, *Fragmentation and Redemption: Essays on Gender and the Human Body in Medieval Religion* (New York : Cambridge, Mass: Zone Books ; Distributed by the MIT Press, 1992); Caroline Walker Bynum, *Jesus as Mother: Studies in the Spirituality of the High Middle Ages*, Publications of the Center for Medieval and Renaissance Studies, UCLA 16 (Berkeley: University of California Press, 1982); Catherine M Mooney, ed., *Gendered Voices: Medieval Saints and Their Interpreters*, The Middle Ages Series (Philadelphia: University of Pennsylvania Press, 1999); Samantha Riches and Sarah Salih, *Gender and Holiness : Men, Women, and Saints in Late Medieval Europe* (London; New York: Routledge, 2002).

[12] In response to Bynum's study of female sanctity, Richard Kieckhefer took up the question of whether there existed a male counterpart to female Eucharistic devotion. In his study of what might constitute characteristic male piety, Kieckhefer examined the lives of male saints only to conclude that while their *vitae* indicate certain spiritual tendencies, no single, over-arching form of devotion was common to all. See Richard Kieckhefer, "Holiness and the Culture of Devotion: Remarks on some Late Medieval Male Saints" in *Images of Sainthood in Medieval Europe*, eds. Renate Blumenfeld-Kosinski and Timea Szell (Ithaca: Cornell University Press, 1991), 288-305.

[13] Bynum, *Holy Feast and Holy Fast*, 93.

do we explain near-identical accounts of oil excretion in the lives of Nicholas and Catherine, two of the most widely venerated saints in Christendom?

Although Bynum's thesis certainly applies to a number of female saints, mainly ascetics of the thirteenth and fourteenth centuries, I argue that saints' miraculous oozing was a much broader phenomenon that transgressed temporal and geographic boundaries as well as gender binaries. Bynum estimated that roughly fifty percent of myroblytes were women. My findings, however, suggest that men outnumbered women two to one. Although as many as sixty saints may have been myroblytes, only twenty were women.[14] By studying the lives of both male and female myroblytes over the *longue durée*, which is to say from the early to late medieval period, demographic shifts as well as changes in the nature of myroblytes' miracles become evident.

This research answers a question Bynum posed regarding why the gender of myroblytes changed over the course of the Middle Ages. In a footnote Bynum observed that in the early medieval period, myroblytes were almost entirely male but that by the late Middle Ages, the majority of myroblytes were female.[15] I propose the shift from male to female myroblytes began in the eleventh century with the rise of Catherine of Alexandria's cult, when increased trade and travel to the Near East sparked an interest in relics that had enjoyed proximity to the Holy Land. Prior to the eleventh century, myroblytes were male clerics with one exception, Segolena (d. circa 769), abbess of the Troclar monastery in the Pyrenees. Amidst crusading fervor, Catherine's cult emerged in tandem with, or just after, the cult of Nicholas of Myra, who also hailed from the Near East. Nicholas and Catherine's offices contain near-identical accounts of pilgrims with insatiable desires for the myroblytes' holy oil. When Catherine's cult, including the singing of her office, spread throughout

---

[14] This number is based on lists assembled by Bynum and the Catholic Encyclopedia as well as other sources listed by Bynum. I have yet to examine the *vitae* of every saint on these list, however, and in some instances when I examined the *vitae* of saints on the list, I was unable to locate miraculous oil. These lists are therefore only estimates and admittedly incomplete. See Ibid., 392n85; "Oil of the Saints," *New Advent Catholic Encyclopedia*, accessed March 6, 2017, http://www.newadvent.org/cathen/11228d.htm.

[15] Bynum, *Holy Feast and Holy Fast*, 392n85.

Europe, biographers began to imagine female saints as potential sources of holy oil. After 1200, the number of female myroblytes more than doubled, while far fewer male myroblytes appeared. With one exception, the only new myroblytes to appear after the mid-thirteenth century were women.

The shift from male to female myroblytes coincided with two pivotal developments in Latin Christianity. Instead of representing Christ as an omnipotent king, august ruler, or omniscient judge, medieval authors increasingly depicted Christ as a baby or a vulnerable human being, emphasizing his humanity, susceptibility to pain and mortality.[16] This change coincided with the rise of the cult of the Virgin Mary and devotion to female figures, such as Mary Magdalene, as well as an elevated estimation of "feminine" characteristics, such as nurturing and caring for the young. Rather than appearing as a regal Queen of Heaven, Mary herself became a mother looking after her baby.[17] In the early medieval period, the Church in the Latin West predominantly associated oil with secular and ecclesiastical authorities, who were anointed with oil at ordinations or coronations. The power of bishops expanded and the consecration of oils became an increasingly regulated feature of liturgical rites. In the religious culture of the early medieval period, holy oil became largely a male attribute, with miraculous oil appearing almost exclusively in the vitae of male clerics. When stories began to circulate that the virginal members of Catherine of Alexandria's body oozed oil, such an anomaly was not without precedent. A Carolingian iconic tradition depicted Mary with a beard – "the mother of God with a male attribute."[18] Was oil seeping from the body of a woman like a beard on the Virgin Mother? Did biographers wish to endue female saints with male *virtus?* In his *Dialogue of Miracles* Caesarius of Heisterbach (1180-post 1240) explained that the oil ceaselessly issuing from Catherine's bones was a sign of her virtues, perhaps intending to play on the idea of male *virtus.*[19]

---

[16] Caroline Walker Bynum, *Jesus as Mother: Studies in the Spirituality of the High Middle Ages*, Publications of the Center for Medieval and Renaissance Studies, UCLA 16 (Berkeley: University of California Press, 1982), 16–17.

[17] Ibid., 137.

[18] Ibid., 139.

[19] Caesarius, *Die Wundergeschichte des Caesarius von Heisterbach Bd. 3*, ed. Alfons Hilka (Bonn: Hanstein, 1937).

Oil, after all, had appeared as a sign of *virtus* in the lives of a number of male myroblytes, including

Andrew the Apostle (1stc.), Eligius (588-660), and Willibrord (658-739). By the late twelfth century,

however, fragrant oils evidently had become a female attribute. In *The Art of Courtly Love* (circa 1184-

86), Andreas Capellanus (late 12th century) claimed that a man of "praiseworthy character" would

never anoint himself "all over like a woman" echoing Catullus' claim over a millennium before.[20]

Although the question regarding myroblytes' gender is certainly essential to understanding

the importance of miraculous oil in medieval culture, we must also look beyond a male-female

binary to understand what is happening in myroblytes' *vitae* and grasp the larger significance

medieval Christians imputed to saints' holy oil: as representative of the invisible Holy Spirit. Without

abandoning the question of gender, I propose to read myroblyte miracles in light of the medieval

proclivity for allegory and multivalent symbols, which pervaded the liturgy, sermons and biblical

exegesis. So often in these texts, oil appears as a symbol of grace. Reading saints' *vitae* as legends that

play on their readers' knowledge of both the Bible and liturgical chants, we can better see into the

hearts and minds of medieval people and ascertain what oil meant for them. Although authors of

myroblyte *vitae* often appear inspired by oil's rich, symbolic potential, they were also keenly aware of

the popular and practical demand for oil. Since oil was a principal means of healing a sick or

damaged body, holy oil was a precious commodity in a culture rife with disease and wanting basic

infrastructures that facilitated physical longevity. Oil issuing from a myroblyte's tomb could thus

draw pilgrims from far and wide. Holy oil was not only useful for the preservation of individuals'

corporeal bodies. Oil figured in discourse about the health and preservation of the body politic and

the mystical "body of Christ," the Church.

---

[20] Andreas Capellanus, *The Art of Courtly Love*, trans. John Jay Parry, Reprint edition (New York: Columbia University Press, 1990), 34; "C. Valerius Catullus, Carmina, Poem 61," accessed July 19, 2016, http://www.perseus.tufts.edu/hopper/text?doc=Perseus%3Atext%3A1999.02.0006%3Apoem%3D61; Ole Thomsen, *Ritual and Desire: Catullus 61 and 62 and Other Ancient Documents on Wedding and Marriage* (Aarhus, Denmark: Aarhus University Press, 1992).

The *Fons Olei*

The first modern scholar to address the origin of the *fons olei* legend was Carlo Cecchelli, who located the origin of the *fons olei* legend among the Jewish population of Trastevere.[21] Since according to Cassius Dio (c.164-c.229) and Eusebius (c.260-339/40) (translated by Jerome) the oil exploded before the birth of Christ, the *fons olei* legend at its origin did not locate the fountain in or near the basilica dedicated to Mary.[22] In her doctoral thesis "S. Maria in Trastevere from Its Founding to 1215" (1975), Dale Kinney argued that although Marian devotion was present in Rome in as early as the seventh century, the earliest evidence to attribute the *fons olei* to the church of Santa Maria in Trastevere dated to the late eleventh century.[23] In *Fons olei: Abelard, sermon 4 et hymne 34* (1976), L.J. Engels questioned if the association of the *fons olei* with Santa Maria in Trastevere was of Roman or extra-Roman origin, given that the earliest texts (to his knowledge) were Abelard's Hymn 34 and Sermon 4, which dated to the 1130s.[24] Engels' study of the *fons olei* in these two texts examined the miraculous *fons* in terms of how Christian authors in the High Middle Ages sought to explain God's providence throughout history: while non-Christian classical texts attested to the grandeur of Caesar Augustus, medieval Christian authors reinterpreted the miracles and wonders pagans associated with the emperor as heralding the birth of Christ, the Anointed Savior. Engels observed that the spread of the legends about Augustus and his relationship with early Christianity were not without complications.[25] In "Fons Olei e Anastasio Bibliotecario" (1990), however, Karen Einaudi traced the connection between the *fons olei* legend and Santa Maria in Trastevere to Anastasius Bibliotecarius (c.810 – c.879), the papal librarian and abbot of Santa Maria in Trastevere's

---

[21] Carlo Cecchelli, *S. Maria in Trastevere* (Roma: Danesi-Editore, 1930), 8–10.

[22] Cassius Dio Cocceianus, *Dio's Roman History*, The Loeb Classical Library 82 (Cambridge, Mass: Harvard University Press, 1954); Eusebius of Caesarea, *Eusebius Werke* (Leipzig: J.C. Hinrichs, 1902).

[23] Dale Kinney, "S. Maria in Trastevere from Its Founding to 1215" (Ph.D., New York University, 1975). See also Chapters 8-9.

[24] L. J. Engels, "Fons Olei: Abelard, Sermon 4 et Hymne 34," *Festoen* (1976) 235–47.

[25] "L'éboration de ces légendes s'étendit sur plusiers siècles et ne s'est pas déroulée sans complications." Ibid., 236.

monastery during the reign of Pope Nicholas I (r.858–867).[26] Einaudi convincingly argued that in the midst of a papal struggle in Rome, Anastasius wished to invoke the *fons olei* to bolster his authority and that of Pope Nicholas I given that since Charlemagne's (748-814) coronation in Rome in 800, oil functioned as a sign of legitimate authority. The Latin text of Anastasius' letter does not make absolutely clear, however, whether the librarian meant to suggest the oil flowed from Santa Maria in Trastevere or simply from the region of Trastevere, an area that Romans had associated with the legend since ancient times.[27] As Aristotle (384-322 B.C.E.) said, one swallow does not make a spring.[28] Given that the preponderance of eighth and ninth-century sources discuss the *fons olei* as issuing from the *taberna meritoria* without any mention of the Blessed Virgin Mary or her church *Transtyberim*, the preponderance of evidence indicates that only in the twelfth century did a consistent legend emerge locating the *fons olei* within Santa Maria in Trastevere. Thus, the attribution of the *fons olei* to Santa Maria in Trastevere coincided with the proliferation of female myroblytes and the shift toward greater devotion to female figures.

Scholars have overlooked two additional related factors that arguably influenced Innocent III's decision to consecrate Santa Maria in Trastevere at the opening of the Fourth Lateran Council: his wishes to combat the Cathar heresy and to bring marriage more firmly within the purview of the Church.[29] By 1215, when Innocent III consecrated Santa Maria in Trastevere during the Fourth Lateran Council, the Marian church, with her *fons olei* and apse mosaic of Mary and Christ as bride and groom, served as a potent symbol of conjugal union. By processing to Santa Maria in Trastevere

---

[26] Karin Einaudi, " 'Fons Olei' E Anastasio Bibliotecario," *Rivista dell'Istituto Nazionale d'Archeologia E Storia Dell'arte* 3, no. s.13 (1990): 179–222.

[27] "Anastasius exiguus abbas monasterii sanctae dei genitricis mariae virginis siti trans tiberim, ubi olim circa domini nativitatem fons olei fluxit." Kinney, "S. Maria in Trastevere from Its Founding to 1215," 165n202. See also Chapter 8 below.

[28] Aristotle, "Nicomachean Ethics," in *The Complete Works of Aristotle: the Revised Oxford Translation*, trans. Jonathan Barnes, vol. 2 (Princeton, N.J.: Princeton University Press, 1984), 1735.

[29] Stephan Kuttner and Antonio García y García, "A New Eyewitness Account of the Fourth Lateran Council," *Traditio* 20 (January 1, 1964): 115–78; Brenda Bolton, *Innocent III : Studies on Papal Authority and Pastoral Care* (Aldershot, Hampshire, Great Britain; Brookfield, Vt., USA: Variorum, 1995); John C Moore and Brenda Bolton, *Pope Innocent III and His World* (Brookfield, Vt.: Ashgate, 1999).

and consecrating her altar, Innocent III sought to solidify the papacy's power in the Latin West. In making marriage a sacrament, Innocent III effectively brought marriage, progeny, and property transfers related to both firmly within the domain of the Church. Moreover, by sacralizing carnal marriage and the offspring that would issue from such unions, Innocent III effectively confronted the Cathar heresy, which reviled the body, human sexuality and offspring as well as the institutional Church as the "body of Christ." Whether fundamentally feminine or masculine in character, for Innocent III, the *fons olei* might have symbolized the papacy's *plenitudo potestatis* – the divinely given source of power from which the power and authority of all other earthly authorities flowed.

Chapter Summaries

Chapter One

Chapter One establishes a foundation for understanding the role of holy oil in the medieval Latin West by examining the significance of oil in ancient beliefs and rituals. This chapter draws largely on the work of previous scholars who analyzed the use of oil in ancient Mesopotamian, Greco-Roman, Hebrew and early Christian culture as well as primary sources that demonstrate the use of oil in Late Antique Christianity. In several ancient cultures, oil hallowed and divinized select individuals, conferring immortality and making a person the beloved elect of God. Oil not only signified the presence of divinity but also human flourishing. Ancient Mesopotamians, Hebrews and Christians associated oil with abundant life, health, and fecundity. Perhaps as a result, oil played a salient role in marriage rituals as well as other legal contracts. Oil also figured prominently in rituals surrounding hospitality in the ancient Near East as well as banqueting and burials.

Did these ancient culture associate oil with any one gender? Women carried oil mixed with spices to the bodies of the dead and oversaw embalming and burial rites. Men alone, however, consecrated holy oils for use in the Hebrew temple liturgy. Within the early Christian culture, oil appears to have transcended gender distinctions in belonging to clearly defined gender roles of both men and women. Early Christian exegetical interpretations of oil drew largely on pagan and Hebrew precedents while also tailoring the meaning of oil for new Christian audiences. Patristic exegetes first interpreted oil as having a spiritual or symbolic meaning within the liturgy. Through anointing, early Christians became "kings, priests and prophets." Oil revealed that an individual had renounced Satan and absorbed Christ's divinity, physically, mentally and spiritually. In the mystagogy of the early Church, nascent parallels emerged between holy oil and the Eucharist. Exegetes presented both the Eucharistic host and holy oil as sacraments that imparted an invisible power to the individual who absorbed them, effectively internalizing God's divine presence.

Chapter Two

Recent scholarship on the *Glossa Ordinaria*, the twelfth-century compilation of biblical glosses, has generally focused on the origin and authorship of a particular book of the *Glossa Ordinaria*. In Chapter Two, I depart from the work of previous scholars by examining a particular theme across multiple biblical books. Inspired by patristic exegesis, medieval biblical commentators read the biblical narratives as replete with symbolic language. Twelfth-century glosses of biblical pericopes involving oil indicate a medieval belief in "spiritual oil" that could enlighten the mind as well as cure the body. Biblical stories conveyed visible and invisible realities; images pointed beyond themselves to the invisible world of the spirit, perceivable only through faith. Those who were anointed were able to see "interior things." The *Glossa* stated that Scripture itself was full of "oil" – to read and pray with scripture was to be anointed or to have God's spirit permeate one's mind or soul.

Biblical glosses on oil offer insights into the various cultural and religious uses of oil in medieval culture. In biblical glosses, oil often appeared where the boundary between heaven and earth were permeable, such as Bethel, where Jacob anointed the stone after dreaming of angels ascending to and descending from heaven. The medieval celebration of the dedication of a church often included chants alluding to Jacob's anointing of the stone, reinforcing the image of the Church as a rock. The image of the Church as the source of holy oil becomes particularly relevant when we consider the legend of Santa Maria in Trastevere's *fons olei*. Passages from the *Glossa Ordinaria* would help authors interpret or explain the significance of the *fons olei,* such as in Abelard's Sermon 4 (on the Epiphany), in which he borrowed directly from Augustine's commentary on Psalm 44. Oil was closely associated with prophecy, which the Holy Spirit inspired. Ideas of divine election, secrecy, mystery, and the precarious nature of medieval kingship surfaced in biblical glosses. Glossators often characterized those who were anointed - royal or not - as the beloved elect of God or like Christ.

Chapter Three

Chapter Three explores the role oil played in the medieval liturgy through an analysis of the prayers and liturgical rites surrounding the consecration of holy oils on Holy Thursday before Easter. The medieval liturgy was an essential means for expressing and disseminating ideas about holy oil within medieval culture. The meaning of oil in saints' lives and in the legend of Santa Maria in Trastevere's *fons olei* can only be understood in light of the significance of oil within liturgical rites. The liturgy shows that oil transcended gender binaries as well as divisions within the hierarchy of the Church. Oil pertained to both the highest and lowest echelons of medieval society though the Pope and his bishops alone were invested with the authority to consecrate holy oils, which they did during the Chrism Mass (*Missa chrismatis*). On the same day at Vespers, during a rite known as *Ad mantatum,* bishops and other prelates assumed the role of humble servants during the washing of feet (*pedilavium*), which sometimes included washing the feet of the poor.

The *Ad mandatum* rite included the chanting of antiphons that retold the story, not just of Jesus washing his disciples' feet, but of Mary Magdalene washing and anointing Jesus' feet before he could perform this service for others. The liturgy created an oblique parallel between Mary Magdalene and those who, like Christ, would cleanse and sacralize religious communities. Prayers, chants, and sermons for the Chrism Mass and the *pedilavium* rite reveal that holy oil signalled the presence of the Holy Spirit, who, by its unpredictable and non-material nature, reflected the ambiguous and mutable nature of divinity, calling into question the fixity of gender and authority within medieval religious culture. Although Mary Magdalene was a source of sanctifying water and oil, medieval authors seldom interpreted her to be a symbol for the Church itself, a privilege more often reserved for the Blessed Virgin Mary. Nevertheless, the Magdalene prefigured Jesus' gesture of humility and love. Given the correlation between Mary Magdalene, repentance and oil, we can better understand why, in the later Middle Ages, myroblytes were predominantly women penitents.

Chapter Four

Chapter Four examines how medieval liturgists interpreted the significance of oil within the liturgy from the ninth through the fourteenth centuries. The liturgical commentaries of Amalarius of Metz (c.780-850), Rupert of Deutz (1075-1129), and Guillaume Durand the Elder (c.1230-1296) reveal how the significance of oil shifted from a symbol of peace to one of repentance, perhaps as a result of the expanding episcopal powers, the sharper delineation between clergy and laity, and the emerging popularity of Mary Magdalene's cult. For Amalarius of Metz, the olive and its oil signified peace, gave succor to the body while also imparting grace, wisdom and knowledge to the mind and soul. Plain oil was a symbol for wisdom while balsam was a symbol for knowledge. Thus chrismal anointing imparted wisdom and knowledge necessary for peace. Rupert of Deutz, in contrast, emphasized the hidden and mysterious significance of holy oils, which were known only to a few (clerics). Rupert depicted oil as a female servant dispensing light, perhaps alluding to the parable of

the wise virgins. He also described how Christ's Spirit-filled body issued from the Virgin's womb,

making Mary the ultimate source of holy oil. This image of Mary as the source of oil echoed the

legend of the *fons olei*. Durand, in contrast with Amalarius and Rupert, associated oil more closely

with sin and repentance than with peace or female virginity. Emphasizing the power of an individual

to enact law, the holiness of bishops and the remission of sins through reconciliation, Durand

minimized the role of oil as a conduit for wisdom and knowledge. Anointing became a symbol for

the grace and forgiveness imparted to a penitent. By the late thirteenth century, Durand had aligned

oil and anointing more closely with mercy and penance than had his predecessors, although

Augustine's long-established preface to the psalms spoke of the "oil of mercy." The close correlation

between oil and the sacrament of reconciliation in the Late Middle Ages is perhaps partially

explained by the emergence of the cult of Mary Magdalene. Her cult likewise sheds light on why in

the thirteenth and fourteenth centuries, myroblytes were predominantly women whose *vitae*

emphasized repentance.

Chapter Five

This chapter explores the origin of myroblytes, holy men and women whose bodies

produced oil in their own lifetimes or whose entombed bodies did so after death. To date, scholars

of medieval sanctity have largely overlooked the oil miracles of these saints. No scholar has

sufficiently explained when and where the myroblyte phenomenon originated or how and why oil

miracles proliferated. The popularity of myroblytes in Europe appears to have begun in Merovingian

Gaul with Gregory of Tours' (538-593) accounts of the miraculous tombs of Andrew the Apostle

(1st c.) and Martin of Tours (316-397). Carolingian biographers later interpolated oil miracles into

older *vitae* or fashioned new myroblytes from Merovingian saints. Merovingian and Carolingian

Gaul, which may have been the birthplace of physical rather than merely spiritual anointings of kings and bishops, was home to a curiously high concentration of myroblytes. The appearance of predominantly male myroblytes coincided with developments in the ritual use of oil in coronation and ordination rituals. During this period, Merovingian biographers infused oil into the lives of their Gallic saints. Beyond merely producing a liquid capable of healing the sick, the oil miracles of these male myroblytes demonstrated the clerics' status as beloved elect, their intimacy with God, and their divine favor, which God bestowed on them so that they might heal "the people." While a number of early medieval female myroblytes existed, biographers did not compose these women's' *vitae* or offices until centuries later, suggesting that few women were famed for oil prior to the High Middle Ages.

Chapter Six

While the majority of myroblytes from the sixth through the eighth centuries were male clerics, in the twelfth and thirteenth centuries, the number of female myroblytes rose considerably. Before this shift in the thirteenth and fourteenth centuries, however, a pair of myroblytes appeared in Europe who heightened the presence of oil in the imaginations of medieval biographers and temporarily made oil production a gender-neutral miracle. Nicholas of Myra and Catherine of Alexandria were allegedly fourth-century saints from the Near East whose cults became wildly popular in the tenth and eleventh centuries. Perhaps as a result of increased trade routes and pilgrimage to the Near East, the cults of these two saints spread in Europe. Their oil might have particularly appealed to medieval Christians who associated fragrant oil with spices from the Greek East. In the Latin West, the cults of Nicholas and Catherine proliferated with near-identical stories of miraculously oozing tombs, revealing how during the High Middle Ages, miraculously producing oil became a gender-neutral expression of sanctity. In addition to examining the biographical dossiers of Nicholas and Catherine including their offices within the liturgy, I explain how their

popularity led to a proliferation of myroblytes in the eleventh and twelfth centuries. These saints

include Eligius (588-660), Bishop of Noyon, and Babolenus (d.670), Abbot of St. Maur-des-Fossés.

Monks sought to establish the cults of these two Gallic myroblytes by associating them more closely

with Nicholas in particular, whose fame was universal by the early twelfth century.

Chapter Seven

The rise of the cult of Mary Magdalene appears to have contributed to the proliferation of

female myroblytes in the Latin West from the thirteenth through the fourteenth centuries. With the

increase of devotion to Mary Magdalene in the late medieval period, medieval ecclesiastics placed

greater emphasis on the correlation between holy oil and repentance, as echoed in the liturgical

commentary of Guillaume Durand the Elder. As Mary Magdalene's cult spread, primarily through

the efforts of mendicant preachers, the number of female myroblytes also increased. Late medieval

female myroblytes often had close ties with Cistercians, Franciscans, or Dominicans. In some

instances, mendicants composed myroblyte lives; a glistening trail of oil spread from the pens of

Dominican biographers in particular. Thomas de Cantimpré (1201-1272) and Jacob de Voragine

(1228-1298) circulated oily legends about both female saints and Santa Maria in Trastevere's *fons olei*.

In several instances, the myroblyte *vitae* heavily emphasized the importance of repentance and were

evidently intended to inspire female audiences to become tertiaries of the Dominican or Franciscan

orders. The *vitae* Lutgard of Aywières (1182-1246), Christina the Astonishing (1150-1224), Franca

Visalta of Piacenza (1170-1218), Humility of Faenza (1226-1310), Agnes of Montepulciano (1268-

1317), Margaret of Città di Castello (1287-1320), Rose of Viterbo (1233-1251), Zita of Monte Sagrati

(1212-1272), Elizabeth of Hungary (1207-1231) and Hedwig of Silesia (1174-1243) demonstrate the extent to which miraculous oil was increasingly characteristic of holy women and mendicants' efforts

to bring women, particularly laywomen, more firmly within the fold of the church.

Male myroblytes from this period were outliers, both in terms of their gender and their

geographical location. All male myroblytes from the late medieval period hailed from either Spain or

England: Peter Gonzales (1190-1246), Hugh of Lincoln (c.1135-1200), Robert Grosseteste (c.1175-

1253) and William of York (d.1154). From the late thirteenth through the fifteenth century, the

number of myroblytes dwindled to a scant three, all of whom were women. Following this shift, the

appeal of saints producing holy oil waned, despite the fact that in Rome the popularity of the

miraculous *fons olei* never ceased.

Chapter Eight

Chapter Eight examines the origin of one of the most extraordinary stories about holy oil to

circulate in the Latin West in the medieval period. Medieval authors claimed that Santa Maria in

Trastevere, one of Rome's earliest Marian shrines, contained a fountain of oil that gushed for an

entire day, running all the way to the Tiber River. Marian devotion in Rome had its roots in the

pagan fertility cults of the ancient Near East where flowing liquids were characteristic of life and

fecundity. Ancient Trastevere, with its natural springs, streams, pools and shrines dedicated to water

nymphs was the ideal setting for a cult dedicated to the Mother of God. The development of the *fons

olei* legend began in Rome during the Late Republican period and dispersed throughout Europe well

into the eighteenth century.

While scholars have partially explained the origin of Marian devotion in Trastevere and the

advent of the *fons olei* legend, this chapter considers a number of additional eighth- and ninth-century

texts that scholars have thus far overlooked. These sources reveal how in the early medieval period,

authors transposed the date of the eruption of the *fons olei* from before Christ's birth such that the oil was an omen, to occurring simultaneously with the birth the Anointed One, such that oil was a wondrous sign of the Incarnation, like the star above Bethlehem. To a greater degree than the Late Antique sources, Carolingian sources stress the nature of leadership at the time of the *fons olei* and Christ as the ruler of spiritual and temporal realms. Carolingian authors told of how the oil appeared during the reign of Augustus, such that both Christ and the *fons olei* appeared within the context of the *Pax Romana*. These authors consistently said the oil flowed from a *taberna meritoria* and never mentioned oil flowing from a shrine or church dedicated to Mary.

Chapter Nine

This chapter examines how the legend of the *fons olei* spread across the Latin West in the High Middle Ages, as the popularity of myroblytes also grew. I argue holy oil's connection to Marian devotion in Rome resulted largely from high medieval developments: the shift to presenting both Mary and Christ as ordinary human figures rather than divine rulers, the increased role of holy oil in the liturgy, evolving concept of the Holy Land as the ultimate source of sanctity, and the spread of the cults of Nicholas of Myra and Catherine of Alexandria. A single piece of evidence exists that potentially suggests that Anastasius Bibliotecarius (c.810-c.878) was the first author to claim that Santa Maria in Trastevere was the original site of the *fons olei*. I support Engels' thesis that the widespread association of the *fons olei* with Mary was a twelfth-century development. An eleventh-century martyrology belonging to Santa Maria in Trastevere, for example, includes no mention of the *fons olei*. Santa Maria in Trastevere's widespread popularity as a source of miraculous unguent appears to have followed the reconstruction of its edifices from 1140-43 by Innocent II (d.1143) after the papal schism brought about by his rival Anacletus II (d.1138).

The circulation of the *fons olei* legend in connection with Santa Maria in Trastevere resulted, I argue, from the rise of devotion to feminine figures and the dispersion of richly symbolic discourses on the meaning of oil and concerns about political and papal legitimacy. Santa Maria in Trastevere's

holy oil assumed a significance that was both like and unlike other oils; the *fons olei* became a sign of

divine election, perpetual kingship and perhaps more importantly, conjugal union. Oil was closely

linked with marriage, as evidenced in the Songs of Songs, the Psalms, and the parable of the Wise

and Foolish Virgins. By the High Middle Ages, when oil had become a symbol for both legitimate

authority and extraordinary sanctity, friction increased between secular and ecclesiastical rulers;

bishops and kings claimed to be "married" to their churches and kingdoms, respectively. Santa Maria

in Trastevere, a source of holy oil and a symbol for the Church, was mystically united with the Pope,

the elect "Anointed One."

Chapter Ten

Chapter Ten argues that in thirteenth-century papal discourse, the *fons olei* evidenced the

corporeal, material aspect of Christian existence, the power of the Church to offer salvation through

the sacraments (particularly the Eucharist and anointings) and the perception of Rome as the new

Jerusalem. While previous scholars have partially explained why Innocent III processed to Santa

Maria in Trastevere at the opening of the Fourth Lateran Council to consecrate the church, their

explanations, in my estimation, are incomplete. I argue that the procession and consecration of Santa

Maria in Trastevere within the context of Lateran IV resulted from Innocent III's desire to combat

Cathar heretics, to firmly establish marriage as a sacrament, and to reinforce the doctrine of the

Incarnation. Innocent III's *Second Sermon on the Nativity,* interpreted the *fons olei* as divine revelation of

the Prince of Peace and a triumphant disruption of the natural order, which accompanied the

Messiah's birth. In comparing Christ, the Anointed One (human and divine), to the commingling of

spouses in a conjugal union, Innocent III clarified the meaning of oil: the divine presence of God

comingled with human flesh through anointing. The themes of marriage and holy oil also played out in the cult surrounding the Uronica, an icon of Christ that oozed oil. I discuss how holy oil related to the processional pageantry of medieval Rome, in which the Uronica (i.e. the Christ) processed through the city to join his mother-spouse, the Blessed Virgin, on the feast of the Assumption.

In seeping oil, the Christ and Santa Maria in Trastevere both resembled myroblytes. Not coincidentally, Jacob de Voragine, the thirteenth-century Dominican, discussed the miraculous *fons olei* in his *Legenda Aurea*, reaffirming that Dominicans had a seminal hand in the proliferation of myroblytes in the High Middle Ages. Franciscans were similarly influential. During the papacy of the Franciscan Nicholas IV (r.1288-1292), Cardinal Bertoldo Stefaneschi commissioned Pietro Cavallini (1259-c.1330) to create a series of mosaics – Scenes from the Life of the Virgin – that clearly depict the church as the source of the *fons olei*, which coincided with Christ's birth. The lower apse mosaics show a river of oil flowing from the *taberna meritoria* as the Virgin gave birth. Another mosaic in the same series shows the oil flowing from the church, not the *taberna meritoria*, when the Magi present their gift to the Christ-child. The images pictorially represent the power of holy oil to transform a pagan house of ill repute into a shrine dedicated to the Blessed Virgin, the Mother of God, the anointer.

CHAPTER 1

OIL, ANOINTING AND EXEGESIS IN
HEBRAIC, GRECO-ROMAN & EARLY CHRISTIAN CULTURE

"QUO OLEO, NISI SPIRITALI?" – ST. AUGUSTINE

OIL AND ANOINTING IN THE HEBRAIC AND PAGAN TRADITIONS

In the medieval Latin West, when monks chanted in choir, they often chanted Psalm 132, which tells of oil running down the beard and tunic of Aaron, the Hebrew prophet, when he was anointed High Priest: "How very good and pleasant it is when kindred live together in unity! It is like the precious oil on the head, running down upon the beard, on the beard of Aaron, running down over the collar of his robes."[30] In this psalm, oil is a symbol for brotherly love: the unguent runs from the priest's head down to the very edge of his robe, which Augustine of Hippo (354-430) interpreted as a symbol for the furthest reaches of the Church. The Psalmist says the oil is like the "dew" (likely literally the snow) that falls on Hermon, a snow-capped mountain range on the border of Syria, Lebanon and Israel: "It is like the dew of Hermon, which falls on the mountains of Zion. For there the Lord ordained his blessing, life for evermore."[31] The "dew of Hermon" is reminiscent of the Ten Commandments descending on Mount Sinai.[32] Like brotherly love or the divine commandments, the oil finds its way to the edge of the known world, symbolized by Aaron's robe. Like snow, which melts and becomes a living river, feeding the dry landscape, oil imparts life and is a sign of the divine. Christianity became a religion based on the belief that the all-powerful, all-knowing and all-loving God had become Incarnate, assuming human form as the 'Anointed One.' A

---

[30] Psalm 132:1–2.

[31] Psalm 132:3.

[32] The Hebrew word here is כְּטַל kə·ṭal. The same word also appears in Micah 5:7: "Like dew from the Lord."

central tenant of ancient Judaism was the belief in the eventual appearance of a saviour, born from the Davidic line.[33] For Christians, the long awaited Messiah had finally arrived. Early Christians were Hebrews who believed Jesus of Nazareth was the "hope of all nations," whom the Hebrew Scriptures had foretold. The word 'Messiah' derives from the Hebrew *mashach* (מָשַׁח) 'to anoint.'[34] Thus, the Messiah was the Lord's anointed. The Greek equivalent of *mashach*, Χριστός gives us the word 'Christ.'[35]

In order to understand the role of holy oil in medieval religious culture, we must first briefly look at oil's pre-Christian and early Christian roots in the ancient Near East. This chapter will examine how oil entered the Christian cult by way of Judaic and Greco-Roman beliefs and practices in the central and eastern Mediterranean, as well as the Christian exegetical tradition that emerged in that region the first half of the first millennium. Since the times of the Hebrew kings, Hebrews and Christians associated oil with the spirit of God or divine presence; it was a means by which a community set a person apart, consecrated him or made him holy.[36] Holy oil did not simply signify the presence of God's spirit within the confines of the religious cult. Beyond the sacred realm of the temple, oil represented life, health, fecundity and abundance. Oil was a cure for illness and thus a prophylactic against death. By playing a role in the rituals surrounding marriage, oil was also instrumental in the creation of new life. For early Christians, oil was a mark of being prepared to enter spiritual combat with spiritual foes as well as being worthy to receive the Holy Spirit – to be anointed, like Christ.

---

[33] Regarding the issue of perpetual kingship, see Chapters 9 & 10.

[34] Geoffrey Rowell, *Anointed with Fresh Oil* (Colchester: Centre for the Study of Theology in the University of Essex, 1996), 15,18. Also in the OED: "Messiah, N.," *OED Online* (Oxford University Press), accessed May 18, 2016, http://www.oed.com.proxy.library.georgetown.edu/view/Entry/117116.

[35] Rowell, *Anointed with Fresh Oil*, 15,18. In the OED: "Christ, N.," *OED Online* (Oxford University Press), accessed May 18, 2016, http://www.oed.com.proxy.library.georgetown.edu/view/Entry/32427#eid9362019.

[36] In the Hebrew tradition, putting on ritual vestments was another means of consecration. See Lev 21:12.

In the Hebrew tradition, the process of hallowing people and the accoutrements of the cult had a distinctly corporeal dimension: the Hebrew word for "anoint", *mashach,* meant "to rub or stroke with the hand."[37] Hebrews saw holiness as having a physical quality, which could be transferred to both people and material things. Hebrews anointed high priests by pouring holy oil on their heads.[38]

The concoction of sacred unguent took place within the temple cult. Priests compounded oil and aromatic spices expressly for ritual purposes. The recipe for holy anointing oil consisted of a mixture of liquid myrrh, cinnamon, aromatic cane, cassia, and olive oil.[39] Christians would later simplify the recipe, using only balsam mixed with olive oil to make chrism, the most precious of the three oils used in Christian ritual. Hebrew priests used their precious aromatic unguent to consecrate the physical objects associated with their cult: "...you shall make of these a sacred anointing-oil blended as by the perfumer; it shall be a holy anointing-oil...you shall consecrate [the objects of the temple and altar], so that they may be most holy; whatever touches them will become holy."[40] The same unguent that sanctified the ark and the altar sanctified the priests who worshipped there: "You shall anoint Aaron and his sons, and consecrate them, in order that they may serve me as priests. You shall say to the Israelites, 'This shall be my holy anointing-oil throughout your generations.'"[41] Hebrews considered this oil so sacred that they forbid the laity to make or apply the substance. If anyone unlawfully used the holy unguent on a human body, the penalty was death.[42]

---

[37] J. Roy Porter, "Oil in the Old Testament," in *Oil of Gladness: Anointing in the Christian Tradition,* eds. Martin Dudley and Geoffrey Rowell (London: S.P.C.K., 1993), 36.

[38] Ibid.

[39] Ex 30:22-24.

[40] Ex 30:25-29. Regarding the similarity between the anointing of the Hebrew Temple and the anointing of Mesopotamian temples, see Hector Avalos, "Daniel 9:24-25 and Mesopotamian Temple Rededications," *Journal of Biblical Literature* 117, no. 3 (September 1998): 507–11.

[41] Ex 30:30-31.

[42] Porter, "Oil in the Old Testament," 36.

The purpose of ritual anointing was not to cleanse, but rather to make holy – to consecrate,

setting the individual apart as someone sacred.[43] The individual no longer belonged to the realm of

ordinary life. Through anointing, a particular, intimate bond was forged between the individual and

God.[44] The anointed priest was unlike other members of his community; having been sanctified, he

was required to abstain from activities in which others were free to engage.[45] While placing

limitations on the anointed one, the consecration designated him as divinely chosen. According to

Judaic belief, God established and expressed the bond between Himself and his anointed, in part,

through oil. Leviticus states: "the consecration of the anointing-oil of his God is upon him: I am the

Lord."[46] In some cases, however, the Hebrew Scriptures refer to the "anointed ones" in a

metaphorical sense, since these individuals (patriarchs and possibly prophets) were not literally

anointed with oil.[47] To "anoint" may have meant simply to set apart, to consecrate or to make holy,

not to physically smear with oil.[48] Hebrews believed God performed the anointing himself,

---

[43] Ibid., 37. In Leviticus 8:10–13, Moses used oil to consecrate Aaron along with the material objects relating to ritual worship: "Then Moses took the anointing-oil and anointed the tabernacle and all that was in it, and consecrated them. He sprinkled some of it on the altar seven times, and anointed the altar and all its utensils, and the basin and its base, to consecrate them. He poured some of the anointing-oil on Aaron's head and anointed him, to consecrate him. And Moses brought forward Aaron's sons, and clothed them with tunics, and fastened sashes around them, and tied head-dresses on them, as the Lord commanded Moses."

[44] Ibid.

[45] See Leviticus 21:10-15: "The priest who is exalted above his fellows, on whose head the anointing-oil has been poured and who has been consecrated to wear the vestments, shall not dishevel his hair, nor tear his vestments. He shall not go where there is a dead body; he shall not defile himself even for his father or mother. He shall not go outside the sanctuary and thus profane the sanctuary of his God; for the consecration of the anointing-oil of his God is upon him: I am the Lord. He shall marry only a woman who is a virgin. A widow, or a divorced woman, or a woman who has been defiled, a prostitute, these he shall not marry. He shall marry a virgin of his own kin, that he may not profane his offspring among his kin; for I am the Lord; I sanctify him."

[46] Lev 21:12.

[47] Regarding the covenant between God and his people, Israel, Psalm 105:15 states: "he allowed no one to oppress them; he rebuked kings on their account, saying, 'Do not touch my anointed ones; do my prophets no harm.' " The elect status of the patriarchs, prophets, kings and then priests in Hebraic society was later reflected in the formula recited at the consecration of holy oils within the Christian ritual: "unde unxisti sacerdotes, reges, prophetas, et martires chrisma tuum perfectum." The correspondence between this formula and Hebrew ideas of anointing will be discussed in greater detail below.

[48] Paul F Bradshaw, *Ordination Rites of the Ancient Churches of East and West* (New York: Pueblo Pub. Co., 1990); Porter, "Oil in the Old Testament," 39. In the early Christian tradition, to "anoint" meant only a spiritual anointing. See Paul F Bradshaw, "Medieval Ordinations," in *The Study of Liturgy*, ed. Cheslyn Jones (London: Oxford University Press, 1992), 126. Bradshaw's conclusions about the direction of influence regarding anointings is problematic, however, given the lack of evidence that Frankish kings were anointed prior to 800. The earliest manuscript witnesses of clerical anointings with oil date to circa 700 while earliest evidence of royal anointings date to circa 800. See Cornelius Adrianus Bouman,

conferring his spirit on the individual and thus changing that individual's role within the community.[49]

The presence of oil in the ancient Hebraic cult may have stemmed from the widespread use of oil in ancient Mesopotamian pagan culture, where oil played a prominent role in sacred religious and social rituals as well as ordinary life. Ancient Mesopotamians rubbed oil into their flesh after washing and before dressing, effectively smoothing the skin and making it shine.[50] Sometimes such anointings took place as signs of hospitality; servants would feed, bathe and anoint the guests.[51] After death, women washed the bodies of the beloved dead and anointed them in preparation for burial and the afterlife, in order that the assuaged spirit of the dead person was well disposed toward the living.[52] In addition to anointing bodies, ancient Mesopotamians rubbed oil into divine statues, anointed objects used in the cultic worship and solemnized legal contracts with oil. After eating and drinking, men concluded a contractual process by rubbing oil into their flesh and taking an oath, which might include a magical spell or curse, to guard against the contract being broken.[53] When people forged a legal contract within the context of a meal, anointing became a symbolic action with legal consequences.[54] Sometimes participants would swear by their king or city god to keep the contract. They could also say magic spells over food, water and oil; once the oath-taker absorbed these materials, he held the potential curse within himself. Breaking the oath would "activate the curse," unleashing divine retribution. The anointing of the body with oil was likened to putting on a

---

"Sacring and Crowning: The Development of the Latin Ritual for the Anointing of Kings and the Coronation of an Emperor before the Eleventh Century" (Groningen: J.B. Wolters, 1957), 2–4.

[49] 1 Sam 12:12. Also: "...it is the endowment with Yahweh's spirit that is determinative: the gift of the spirit, which anointing confers, is the sign that the prophet truly possesses the status that anointing brings." Porter, "Oil in the Old Testament," 39.

[50] Stephanie Dalley, "Anointing in Ancient Mesopotamia," in *Oil of Gladness: Anointing in the Christian Tradition*, eds. Martin Dudley and Geoffrey Rowell (London: S.P.C.K., 1993), 19.

[51] Evidence of such practices is also present in Homer's *Iliad* and *Odyssey*. See below.

[52] Dalley, "Anointing in Ancient Mesopotamia," 20.

[53] Ibid., 19.

[54] Ibid., 21.

garment or smearing an oath-curse into one's flesh.[55] A similar phenomenon appears in Psalm 108,

in which a fondness for curses is likened to both a garment and oil covering the body: "He clothed

himself with cursing as his coat, may it soak into his body like water, like oil into his bones."[56] Thus,

oil had the potential to hold these ritual prayers or curses, physically transmitting them to the

anointed.

In ancient Mesopotamia, oil also played a significant role in marital ritual and contract

making: a man poured oil on the head of the girl chosen for marriage.[57] In contrast with other

anointings, in which all parties rubbed oil into their bodies, in marital (and royal) anointings, the

head of only one person was anointed; through anointing, the marital contract became binding.[58]

Similarly, female slaves and prostitutes were released from their status as such through anointing.[59]

The texts recording such rituals, however, are ambiguous: the anointing could signal either a

marriage or a manumission.[60] The ambiguity may be due to the fact that once a girl was released

from slavery or prostitution, she was free to marry. The idea that oil signaled a passage from slavery

to freedom was present in the Hebrew Psalms and would appear as a recurrent theme in Christian

exegesis. Thus oil, which was fundamental to daily life and legal contracts as well as the

establishment of a political and religious hierarchy, was present in both the sacred and profane

---

[55] One spell from a Hittite text from circa 1200 – 1180 BCE states: "[Just as] you rub yourself down with oil, [thus also]
let these oath-curses be rubbed down onto [you]! Just as you put on a garment, so also put on these oath-curses!" Anne
Marie Kitz, "An Oath, Its Curse and Anointing Ritual," *Journal of the American Oriental Society* 124, no. 2 (April 1, 2004):
316.
[56] Psalm 108:18. See Ibid., 319–20. Kitz notes the significance of agency in anointing and oath-cursing: the individual
anoints himself and similarly assumes the responsibility of activating the curse by violating the oath. The self-anointing
and agency of the anointed in Mesopotamian culture is inverted in Christian initiation, where the catechumen is anointed
by a presbyter and is similarly passive in the reception of grace or the activation of the spirit in the anointed Christian.
[57] Dalley, "Anointing in Ancient Mesopotamia," 19.
[58] Ibid., 22–23. Anointings accompanied not just marriage contracts but other legal agreements which included the
transfer of property. "Various changes in legal relationships in Mesopotamia and Syria may be marked by anointing:
women upon betrothal, both parties in property transactions, a woman released from status as a prostitute, and
merchants from royal obligations." See Daniel E. Fleming, "The Biblical Tradition of Anointing Priests," *Journal of
Biblical Literature* 117, no. 3 (October 1, 1998): 406.
[59] Fleming, "The Biblical Tradition of Anointing Priests," 406.
[60] Dalley, "Anointing in Ancient Mesopotamia," 23. See also Daniel E Fleming, *The Installation of Baal's High Priestess at
Emar: A Window on Ancient Syrian Religion* (Atlanta, Ga.: Scholars Press, 1992), 407.

realms of life in the ancient Near East and Mesopotamia. Although ancient, pre-Christian religious traditions differed in their understanding what god or deity exercised power through the anointing, they universally regarded oil as possessing a sacred potency that could transform both individuals and communities.

The Anointing of Ancient Priests & Kings

The earliest ritual anointing of a cultic figure appears to have been the anointing of a woman: NIN.DINGIR, the high priestess of the ancient Mesopotamian storm god.[61] A "diviner" anointed the woman's head with oil taken from the temple of the storm god, thus making the woman the god's priestess.[62] The woman's installation as priestess and head of the god's household was comparable to both a wedding and the initiation of a slave into service of a master.[63] The anointing with oil was, however, only one of several aspects of the installation ritual and not the defining characteristic of assuming the priestly office.

When and how the Hebrew rituals for the anointing of kings and priests evolved is a matter of scholarly debate. R. de Vaux, R. Williams, and H. Fischer endorsed the thesis that the practice of anointing Hebrew kings likely derived from Canaanite practice, which they conclude was of Egyptian origin if Egyptian officials installed their vassals in Syria-Palestine through anointing.[64] The king or the king's representative would either anoint the vassal or give him a jar of ointment as a sign that the vassal possessed the authority to act in the king's name.[65] Stephanie Dalley argued that no evidence exists showing the use of oil in the coronation rituals of Babylonian and Assyrian kings, which in turn led scholars to believe the anointing of kings pertained solely to Israelites and

---

[61] Fleming, "The Biblical Tradition of Anointing Priests," 403.

[62] Ibid.

[63] When the priestess-to-be left her father's house to move into her new temple quarters, she was treated like a bride. Ibid., 404.

[64] Stephen E. Thompson, "The Anointing of Officials in Ancient Egypt," *Journal of Near Eastern Studies* 53, no. 1 (January 1, 1994): 16.

[65] Ibid.

Hittites.[66] In Syria and Egypt, overlords may have anointed vassal kings. A letter from a king to the

Pharaoh reads: "Nobody shall [depose] anyone whom the king of Egypt has installed as king, and on

whose head he has put [oil]."[67] Stephen Thompson, however, rejects the thesis based on the paucity

of evidence that such was the practice for investing officials in Syria-Palestine.[68]

Fragmentary evidence suggests that Hittites asked their Sun-god to directly anoint the Hittite

kings.[69] According to Ilya Yakubovich, this practice of anointing priestly kings and other priests

directly influenced anointings among ancient Hebrews and early Christians; the Hittite king was

similarly "raised" or "exalted" through the anointing.[70] Zeev Weisman distinguished the nature of

Hebraic kingly anointings with those in Assyrian myth and ritual, in which kings received unction

from spiritual beings without human intermediaries.[71] Assyrian archeological evidence suggests,

according to Weisman, an ancient mythology of divine kingship. The ritual anointing of the king

took place in a supernatural locale, where mythological winged figures anointed the king, suggesting

the king's divinity and union with divine beings.[72] The prophetic tradition of the Hebrew Scriptures,

in contrast, emphasized the humanity of the anointed king, who was God's representative but not

himself a divine being, creating the tradition of charismatic, but not divine, kingship.[73]

Some scholars, including J. Roy Porter, argued that the Hebrew kings were the Lord's

anointed before the Babylonian exile, but that with their disappearance, in postexilic Judaism the

high priests and other priests received the anointings previously conferred on kings.[74] Daniel

---

[66] Dalley, "Anointing in Ancient Mesopotamia," 23.

[67] Ibid.

[68] Thompson, "The Anointing of Officials in Ancient Egypt," 25.

[69] Ilya Yakubovich, "Were Hittite Kings Divinely Anointed?: A Palaic Invocation to the Sun-God and Its Significance for Hittite Religion," *Journal of Ancient Near Eastern Religions* 5 (2005): 107.

[70] Ibid., 114.

[71] Zeev Weisman, "Anointing as a Motif in the Making of the Charismatic King," *Biblica* 57, no. 3 (1976): 392.

[72] Ibid., 393.

[73] The charismatic Hebrew king was imbued with the spirit of YHWH but was not himself a god. Ibid., 394.

[74] "...we only hear of the anointed highpriest after the exile and the reason for this, as is now generally recognized, is that, with the disappearance of the monarchy, the chief priest of the Jerusalem Temple assumed many of the characteristics of the old Israelite king, including anointing." Porter, "Oil in the Old Testament," 37. For other passages from the Hebrew Scriptures which describe royal anointings, see 1 Sam 16:1,13; 2 Kings 9:1-3; Ps 89:20; Heb 21; 1 Kings 1:39.

Fleming, however, contended that two very different rites for anointing priests evolved simultaneously prior to the Babylonian exile; they did not emerge in the postexilic period sequentially from pre-exilic anointing of kings.[75] Fleming argued that in fact the ritual anointing of priests, as having been chosen by God for divine service, may have been the precedent for royal anointings.[76] The horn, a symbol for power in ancient Hebraic culture, held the oil used to anoint kings.[77] Before and after battle, Hebrews anointed their weapons with oil. They likewise anointed the leather sheath or shield that held the sword. When Saul fell in battle, David lamented that his shield was not anointed, a symbol perhaps of neglect or death.[78] If the unoiled shield was a symbol for Saul's body devoid of God's spirit, we can see how for ancient Hebrews, being anointed signified being imbued with life.

Oil and Divinization

What exactly transpired when someone received the "spirit of the Lord" through anointing? Ancient Hebrews thought a human being, as a material, mortal body received the divine spirit, bringing him into "the divine sphere of holiness."[79] Anointing, not just of people, but material objects such as stones, marked the indwelling of divine presence. In Genesis, after Jacob dreams of

---

[75] Daniel Fleming argues: "The supposed evolution of these rites from the anointing of kings treats the second as a development from the first, but the considerable contrast between the two methods suggests that they did not originate by a linear process of this sort. Instead, we should suspect that the Jerusalem cult tradition had incorporated side by side two independent procedures for anointing that probably came from separate origins. Neither the specific settings nor the dates of these origins can be retrieved from current evidence, but there is no reason to insist that either anointing rite came into Hebraic practice only after the Babylonian exile." Fleming, "The Biblical Tradition of Anointing Priests," 402.

[76] "The hypothetical development from anointing Israelite kings to unction for all Second Temple priests forces evidence for a widespread ancient custom into Israelite cult through the narrowest of passages, an unlikely scenario. From a purely theoretical perspective, furthermore, the particular association of royal anointing with designation by God, however early, may itself be rooted in the old practice of consecrating 'priests' for divine service, set apart as sacred to the god." Ibid., 408.

[77] Porter, "Oil in the Old Testament," 42. "The anointing endues the king with splendour and might which exalts him above his 'fellows' – perhaps, in view of verse 8...anointing is related to the wedding festivities: the subject of the two verses is anointed 'both as king and as lover'." See also Canticles 3:6,4:14; Ezek 16:9; Ruth 3:3; Esth 2:12; Judith 10:5, 16: 8-9.

[78] 2 Sam 1. Alan Ralph Millard, "Saul's Shield Not Anointed with Oil," *Bulletin of the American Schools of Oriental Research* 230 (April 1978): 70.

[79] Porter, "Oil in the Old Testament," 39.

seeing a ladder leading up to heaven, where angels ascend and descend, he recognized the presence

of the divine in the place where he slept. He referred to the location as the "house of God" and the

"gate of heaven."[80] To mark the presence of divinity in that place, he anointed the stone that served

as his pillow.[81] This anointing was consistent with the ritual practice of anointing stones in

Mesopotamia.[82] Centuries later in medieval Christian Europe, anointed stones became symbols for

consecrated churches.[83] Oil marked the presence of God in a particular physical location, where the

earthly and heavenly spheres were permeable. Oil was also expressive of the covenant: God spoke to

Jacob (a prefiguration of Christ), promising him land, offspring, and God's abiding fidelity for

generations.

In certain parts of the Hebrew scriptural tradition, being anointed signalled the conferring of

immortality: the super-terrestrial origin of the anointing meant that a human being, having received

God's spirit, became a heavenly being.[84] Zeev Weisman argued that the supernatural, divine origin of

kingly anointing derived from Mesopotamian mythology, in which winged beings or genii directly

anointed kings, imparting a "magic virtue" without human intermediaries.[85] This model of royal

kingship did not necessarily translate to the anointing of Hebrew kings, since they remained human

beings acting as God's representatives, who were invested with power by fellow human beings.[86]

Nevertheless, several passages from the Hebrew Scriptures elucidate the correspondence between oil

and heavenly presence, describing how divinization took place through anointing. In the apocryphal

accounts of the patriarch Enoch, Enoch told of the presence of oil in the liminal realm of Paradise,

---

[80] See Chapter 2 for medieval exegetical interpretations of this pericope.

[81] Gen 28:10-19.

[82] "Continuity in ritual practice between inland northern Syria and the Israelite hill country is evident in the related consecration of upright stones for identification with the divine presence. The NIN.DINGIR anoints an upright *sikkānu* stone to stand for the goddess Hebat in the storm god's temple precincts...and Jacob anoints the stone he used for a pillow at Bethel to be a ... shrine for Yahweh (Gen 28:18). Both rites are performed by oil poured on the 'top' (literally, 'head') of the stone." Fleming, "The Biblical Tradition of Anointing Priests," 405.

[83] See Chapter 3.

[84] Porter, "Oil in the Old Testament," 39.

[85] Weisman, "Anointing as a Motif in the Making of the Charismatic King," 390–93.

[86] Ibid., 393–94.

where oil flows continuously from a spring along with wine, milk and honey.[87] Paradise, as the

source of this ever-flowing oil, was associated with fruit, sweetness, and fragrance – qualities the

Greeks imputed to ambrosia. Angelic music also emanated from the garden along with oil, which

belonged to this heavenly realm that was at once invisible and spiritual and yet perceived by the

human senses. Once Enoch beheld Paradise and saw the face of God, God anointed him with oil.

The author of Enoch described this mystical experience as being anointed with heavenly unguent:

the encounter with God, exceeded the bounds of verbal expression and intellectual comprehension.

Through heavenly anointing, God transformed the prophet into a heavenly being. As the Lord's

anointed, Enoch traded his earthly, human garments for a glorified raiment: the ointment itself.

In ancient Judaism, oil was not only a sign of divinity, but also a sign of happiness. Hebrews

associated anointing with weddings and other joyful events such as banquets.[88] Anointing was the

mark of celebration, not mourning: "who drink wine from bowls, and anoint themselves with the

finest oils, but are not grieved..."[89] Nowhere is the cultural association between oil and joy more

evident than in the Psalms. Psalm 22 in particular illustrates the connection between oil and

happiness: "you anoint my head with oil; my cup overflows. Surely goodness and mercy shall follow

me all the days of my life..."[90] Oil also indicated justice, joy and opulence, all signs of God's favor:

"you love righteousness and hate wickedness. Therefore God, your God, has anointed you with the

oil of gladness beyond your companions; your robes are all fragrant with myrrh and aloes and cassia.

From ivory palaces stringed instruments make you glad..."[91] Psalm 103 illustrates how, by extension,

---

[87] James H Charlesworth, *The Old Testament Pseudepigrapha* (Garden City, N.Y.: Doubleday, 1983). In Classical Greece, oil was also grouped with honey, milk, water and wine in religious ritual. See Angus Bowie, "Oil in Ancient Greece and Rome," in *Oil of Gladness: Anointing in the Christian Tradition*, eds. Martin Dudley and Geoffrey Rowell (London: S.P.C.K., 1993), 27.

[88] Porter, "Oil in the Old Testament," 41. Hersh explores the question of whether Roman weddings were in fact joyful affairs for the bride. See Karen K. Hersch, *The Roman Wedding: Ritual and Meaning in Antiquity* (Cambridge; New York: Cambridge University Press, 2010), 61–65.

[89] Amos 6:6.

[90] Ps 22:5-6.

[91] Ps 44:7-8.

oil was associated with fecundity and abundance: "You cause the grass to grow for the cattle, and plants for people to use, to bring forth food from the earth, and wine to gladden the human heart, oil to make the face shine, and bread to strengthen the human heart."[92] Thus oil was emblematic of physical, material needs that, when met, led to happiness and physical strength. Drawing on Hebrew traditions and yet provocatively inverting cultural norms, Jesus urged his followers who fasted to anoint themselves, so that they would not appear sullen: "...when you fast, put oil on your head and wash your face, so that your fasting may be seen not by others but by your Father who is in secret..."[93] Generally a person who mourned, fasted or did penance was not anointed, since oil on a living, human body was a mark of joy. Oil also, however, played a role in rituals surrounding death.[94] In the scene of the anointing of Jesus at Bethany by Mary Magdalene, Jesus announces that the woman anointed him in preparation for burial.[95] At the end of Luke's Gospel, the female disciples of Jesus prepare his body for burial: "The women who had come with him from Galilee followed, and they saw the tomb and how his body was laid. Then they returned, and prepared spices and ointments."[96] While in ancient Judaism, oil and unguents were predominantly associated with joy, abundance and fecundity, they also evoked death and the loss of life. In the Christian tradition, oil would signify both, heralding death which led to new life.

---

[92] Ps 103:14-15.

[93] Matthew 6:16-18.

[94] See Daniel 10:3; 2 Sam 14:2. "Anointing (*aleiphō*) seems to signify good health and happiness, and its lack suggests sickness, sadness, and death. *Murizō* is similar to *aleiphō* but emphasizes the use of fragrant oil; it may thus be translated 'pour perfume' rather than 'anoint.' This term is absent from the LXX, and in the New Testament it appears only in Mark 14:8: after the woman 'pours' (*katacheō*) expensive oil on Jesus' head, he proclaims that she has 'anointed' (*murisai*) his body for the tomb." Teresa Hornsby, "Anointing Traditions," in *The Historical Jesus in Context*, eds. Amy-Jill Levine et al. (Princeton: Princeton University Pres, 2006), 340.

[95] Mark 14:8; Matt 26:12; John 12:7.

[96] Luke 23:55-56.

In part through their ritual use of oil, early Christians developed a religious and cultural identity that distinguished them from other Hebrews and Romans. The Gospels first tell of Jesus becoming the Lord's anointed when John the Baptist baptized him in the Jordan River: the Spirit of God descended upon him. All three synoptic Gospels present the baptism as the moment of Jesus' election as the beloved Son, as the Anointed One; the Spirit rushed upon him, descending from heaven like a dove.[97] Jesus was not anointed with oil, however, until the Last Supper when Mary breaks her alabaster jar, in anticipation of Jesus' death or as an expression of love for having her sins forgiven. How can one explain how a man who was never anointed within the Hebrew temple cult became known as 'The Anointed One'? Cyril of Jerusalem (c. 313-386) argued that on account of his divinity, Christ was not anointed with "human oil" but rather directly with the Holy Spirit by God the Father.[98] The oil that Christians poured on new initiates, who were ordinary mortals, was "the sacramental sign of the anointing which Christ received."[99]

While in ancient Judaism and early Christianity oil was a sign of the presence of God's spirit, as well as divine favor and election, paradoxically in the Gospels, oil sometimes appears in contexts relating to marginalized members of society, who are sometimes responsible for carrying out the sacred anointing. In the Gospel of Mark, Jesus commissions the disciples to cast out demons and anoint the sick with oil.[100] In the Gospel of Luke, a Samaritan heals a beaten man by pouring oil on

---

[97] See Mark 1:9–11; Matthew 3:13–17; Luke 3:21–23. In medieval Europe, the dove and then the eagle were associated with holy oil. The chrism used at the baptism of Clovis (circa 466-511) was said to have been brought from heaven by a dove. In 1318 some people claimed Thomas Becket (c.1118-1170) had received an eagle-shaped vial of holy oil from the Virgin Mary while he was in exile. In 1399 Richard II requested to be anointed with oil from Becket's eagle vial. See Michel Rouche, ed., *Clovis: Histoire & Mémoire: Actes Du Colloque International D'histoire de Reims, 19-25 Septembre 1996* (Paris, France: Presses de l'Université de Paris-Sorbonne, 1997); T. A. Sandquist, "The Holy Oil of St. Thomas Becket," in *Essays in Medieval History Presented to Bertie Wilkinson,* eds. T.A. Sandquist and M.R. Powicke (Toronto: University of Toronto Press, 1968), 330–44; Walter Ullmann, "Thomas Becket's Miraculous Oil," *The Journal of Theological Studies* VIII, no. 1 (1957): 129–33.

[98] Cyril, *Cyril of Jerusalem*, trans. Edward Yarnold (London; New York: Routledge, 2000), 176.

[99] Ibid. Cyril's explanation of the absence of oil at Jesus' anointing will be discussed further below.

[100] Mark 6:13.

the victim's wounds.[101] All four Gospels contain pericopes of a (potentially sinful) woman anointing

Jesus at Bethany, prior to his crucifixion in Jerusalem.[102] Each version of this story differs in certain

details, including the day of the anointing and whether the woman anointed Jesus' head or feet,

which had great implications later for medieval exegetes.[103] In three Gospels, Jesus says the woman

prepared his body for burial.[104] Finally, the Gospel of Luke tells of women coming to Jesus' tomb

with spices and ointments, in order to prepare his body for burial.[105] When the woman from

Bethany used costly unguent to anoint Jesus either a few days before or on the eve of his crucifixion,

she anointed Jesus with physical, visible, tangible oil – not just with the invisible Holy Spirit.[106] The

Gospels refer to the woman as either "Mary" or "a woman in the city, who was a sinner."[107] The

Gospels of Mark and Matthew say she anointed Jesus' head, while the Gospels of Luke and John

claim she anointed his feet.[108] Popular tradition began to refer to this woman as Mary Magdalene; in

the later Middle Ages, she became the most widely venerated female saint after the Virgin Mary.[109]

To a degree, Jesus' anointing at Bethany was consistent with hospitality practices of the time.

Like in the pagan culture of ancient Mesopotamia, in the Hebrew tradition oil was a sign of peace

and friendship, and thus the necessary requisites for establishing any kind of legal contract or social

bond. Anointing often took place, therefore, within the context of a shared meal, since eating and

drinking together were likewise signs of trust and unity. Thus, within the context of a ritual meal,

when Jesus is anointed, he gives his disciples "a new commandment" – a legal contract of sorts – to

---

[101] Luke 10:34.

[102] Mark 14:3–4; Matt 26:6–13; Luke 7:37–38; John 12:1–8.

[103] See Chapter 2.

[104] Mark, Matthew and John.

[105] Luke 23:56. For additional discussion of this periscope, see Chapter 2.

[106] See Dominika A. Kurek-Chomycz, "The Fragrance of Her Perfume: The Significance of Sense Imagery in John's Account of the Anointing in Bethany," *Novum Testamentum* 52, 4 (2010): 334-54; Robert Holst, "The One Anointing of Jesus: Another Application of the Form-Critical Method," *Journal of Biblical Literature* 95, 3 (Sep., 1976): 435-46; Charles F. Nesbitt, "The Bethany Traditions in the Gospel Narratives," *Journal of Bible and Religion* 29, 2 (Apr., 1961): 119-24.

[107] John 12:3; Luke 7:37.

[108] See Mark 14; Matt 26; Luke 7; John 12.

[109] On the development of the figure of the Magdalen and her significance in medieval religious culture, see Katherine L. Jansen, *The Making of the Magdalen: Preaching and Popular Devotion in the Later Middle Ages* (Princeton, N.J.: Princeton University Press, 2000).

love one another.[110] The washing and anointing of a guest's feet was a sign of hospitality throughout

the Mesopotamian, Hebraic and Greco-Roman world in the first century C.E.[111] The practice

appears in both the Hebrew Scriptures as well as in Homer's *Odyssey* and other works of Greek and

Roman literatures, where oil was associated not only with hospitality, but also with fragrant

ambrosia, the only unguent worthy of the gods (who sometimes disguised themselves as strangers in

need of hospitality).[112] In *The Odyssey*, Odysseus received oil from Nausicaa, the unmarried nubile

daughter of the Phaeacian king. Having been swept ashore after a shipwreck, Odysseus emerged

from the bushes sea-battered and brined. Nausicaa, having gone out to bath with her maidens prior

to her wedding, found Odysseus and offered him the oil her mother gave her: "soft olive oil in a

flask of gold." Odysseus insisted the maidens leave him while he washed and anointed himself:

"Maidens, stand yonder apart, that by myself I may wash the brine from my shoulders, and anoint

myself with olive oil; for of a truth it is long since oil came near my skin. But in your presence will I

not bathe, for I am ashamed to make me naked in the midst of fair-tressed maidens."[113] When

Odysseus first returns to his native Ithaca as a beggar, his wet-nurse Eurykleia washes and anoints

him with oil.[114] Later, when Odysseus prepares to battle Penelope's suitors in Ithaca, Athena anoints

Odysseus with ambrosia, giving him an immortal, god-like appearance. First, however, Penelope's

house-maid, Eurynome, washes and anoints Odysseus with oil, after which Athena pours on a

beautifying substance that was possibly ambrosia: "Meanwhile the housewife Eurynome bathed the

great-hearted Odysseus in his house, and anointed him with oil, and cast about him a fair cloak and a

---

[110] "I give you a new commandment, that you love one another. Just as I have loved you, you also should love one another. By this everyone will know that you are my disciples, if you have love for one another." John 13:34–35.

[111] "Of the Evangelists, only Luke uses *christō* for 'anoint', but the context is not the woman's ministrations to Jesus. Rather, it is Jesus' quotation from Isaiah in the Nazareth synagogue: 'The Spirit of the Lord is upon me because he has anointed me to bring good news to the poor" (Luke 4:18). The words *aleiphō* and *murizo*, which appear in Luke 7, can be used for anointing kings and priests, but they also are used for the anointing that one performs to adorn oneself, to soothe tired feet, to heal, or to mask offensive odors." Hornsby, "Anointing Traditions," 340.

[112] Genesis 18:4, 19:2; 1 Samuel 25:41. Also, *The Iliad*, 19.385 – 402.

[113] Homer, *Odyssey*, trans. W. Walter Merry et al. (Oxford: Clarendon Press, 1886-1901), Book 6, Line 211, accessed July 19, 2016, http://www.perseus.tufts.edu/hopper/text?doc=Perseus%3Atext%3A1999.01.0136%3Abook%3D6%3Acard%3D211.

[114] Homer, *Odyssey*, Book 19, Line 499.

tunic; and over his head Athena shed abundant beauty, making him taller to look upon and mightier, and from his head she made locks to flow in curls like the hyacinth flower."[115] Mario Telò argues that the liquid (literally: "beauty") Athena poured on Odysseus' head was ambrosial in nature, given the likeness of the scene to an anointing in the *Homeric Hymn to Demeter* (235-38), in which Demeter bestows divinity on a man, causing him to grow "like a god" by anointing him with ambrosia.[116] According to Telò, by pouring ambrosia on Odysseus, Athena anointed the wanderer with a supernatural unguent that augmented the oil poured out by the mortal housemaid.[117] Thus, for the ancient Greeks, the use of oil in rituals surrounding hospitality demonstrate a link between oil and female figures, both mortal and immortal.

OIL AND FEMININITY

What can we make of the fact that a woman anointed Jesus with perfumed unguent during a meal? In ancient Greek and Roman culture, which influenced early Christian thought and ritual, oil was often indicative of women and femininity. Among the ancient Greeks, oil was closely associated with two feminine deities: Athena, whose symbol was the olive, and Aphrodite, who was associated with fragrant unguent.[118] Athena, the goddess of war and wisdom, was said to have good sense, signified by simple, plain olive oil.[119] Aphrodite, the goddess of love and physical beauty, was characterized by oil mixed with spices; fragrant unguent represented the pleasures that accompanied

---

[115] Homer, *Odyssey*, Book 23, Line 129.

[116] Mario Telò, "Aristophanes, Cratinus and the Smell of Comedy," in *Synaesthesia and the Ancient Senses*, eds. Shane Butler and Alex C. Purves (Durham, UK ; Bristol, CT: Acumen, 2013), 63.

[117] "It is thus evident that based as it is on the bestowal of ambrosia, Athena's beautification of Odysseus reads as a supernatural supplement to the unguent that Eurynome uses to cleanse Odysseus' body…Notwithstanding the emphasis laid by the Homeric narrator upon the visual consequences of Odysseus' rejuvenation, it is an eminently olfactory process that engenders his metamorphosis, for not only is fragrance ambrosia's chief characteristic but ambrosia was also originally assimilated to pure odour 'as the only thing good enough for gods.' "Ibid., 63–64.

[118] Nevertheless, as we have just seen, Athena anointed Odysseus with fragrant ambrosia in preparation for battle, perhaps to suggest a parallel between post-ablution anointing oil and the fragrant unguent associated with *eros* and Aphrodite. Given that Odysseus was preparing to confront his wife for the first time after a twenty-year absence, perhaps the Homeric narrator sought to conceptually conflate the battle scene and the marriage bed.

[119] See Chapter 8 regarding the role of the olive in the founding myth of Athens.

erotic desire.[120] In the Roman marriage ritual, the bride anointed her future husband's doorposts (either the exterior entrance of the house or the entrance of the bedchamber itself) with oil, wolf fat or pig fat, before entering his home or the bridal chamber for the first time.[121] Some Roman authors claimed that *uxor* (wife) was derived etymologically from *ungere* (to anoint) because of this ritual anointing of the groom's doorposts.[122] Likewise, the similitude between the Latin word for 'wife', *uxor* and 'anointress', *unxor* expressed, for some Romans, the conceptual link between marriage and anointing.[123] One author claimed that the Roman goddess Unxia, who presided over weddings, likewise received her name from the ritual anointing of doorposts on the wedding day.[124] Similarly, the Latin verb "to anoint" *ungere* is almost identical to the verb "to join or unite" *iungere*, from which our English word "conjugal" derives.

Perfumed oils were, perhaps not surprisingly, the accouterment of the Roman bride rather than the groom.[125] The narrator of Catullus' poem 61 urges the bridegroom to enter the bridal chamber and perform his conjugal duties, lest rumors spread calling his masculinity into question: "They will say when the bridegroom has been anointed that you can scarce abstain from your hairless boys."[126] In his analysis of Catullus' poem, Ole Thomsen observed that Roman men likely eschewed fragrant unguents, believing them to be effeminate. The "perfumed bridegroom" was, according to Thomsen, a paradox given that scented oils were exclusively the embellishments of

---

[120] Bowie, "Oil in Ancient Greece and Rome," 29.
[121] Ibid., 30. Also Hersch, *The Roman Wedding*, 177–79.
[122] Hersch, *The Roman Wedding*, 177–78.
[123] Bowie, "Oil in Ancient Greece and Rome," 30.
[124] Hersch, *The Roman Wedding*, 178n188. According to Hersch, the gods and goddesses who were said to preside over weddings varied according a "poet's literary designs and Roman poetic conventions" rather than "actual Roman religious practices." Ibid., 232–33.
[125] Hersch, 137n7.
[126] Gaius Valerius Catullus, *The Carmina of Gaius Valerius Catullus*, trans. Richard Francis Burton (London: 1894), Poem 61, accessed July 19, 2016, http://www.perseus.tufts.edu/hopper/text?doc=Perseus%3Atext%3A1999.02.0006%3Apoem%3D61.

women.[127] Furthermore, by imputed feminine qualities to the bridegroom, Catullus may have sought

to call not only the bridegroom's masculinity into question, but also his authority as a civic leader.

How would Roman citizens have interpreted Jesus being anointed with perfumed unguent in

Bethany by a sinful woman? In saying he was being anointed for burial, did they also suggest he was

being anointed for a wedding banquet? Was his anointing at Bethany the basis for the idea of death

as an eschatological wedding banquet? Could Christians separate the presence of oil and the

Eucharist as signs of the heavenly banquet? Given the Greco-Roman cultural associations between

fragrant oil and femininity, we must consider how early Christians conceptualized and explained

Jesus' anointing at Bethany. In subsequent chapters, I will discuss how medieval Christians did not

disassociate oil from femininity, but nevertheless interpreted oil as a polysemous symbol: oil also

represented masculine authority, including male clerics and divinely chosen kings.

Oil in Hebraic, Greco-Roman and Early Christian Exegesis

How did early Christians interpret the appearance of oil in these biblical scenes and how did

they incorporate anointing into their nascent rituals? How did oil express and ritualize the great

commandment to love God and one's neighbor? The Christian tradition of scriptural exegesis grew

directly from both Judaic exegesis and Greco-Roman rhetorical practices. The Hebraic exegetical

tradition was based on the fundamental assumption that God created the Bible and, as such, the

Bible possessed an underlying unity that precluded self-contradiction.[128] The complexities of biblical

interpretation derived from the belief that God, as the author of the Bible, spoke a language that was

---

[127] Thomsen observed: "It is well known that the Greeks and Romans were sceptical of men using scent: the man who uses scent – that is, as a permanent part of his *corpus cura* rather than on singular occasions, symposia, for example – is *effeminatus*, which in the sexual area means *adulter* and/or *pathicus/cinaedus*." Both *pathicus* and *cinaedus* carry the meaning of 'sodomite.'" Ole Thomsen, *Ritual and Desire: Catullus 61 and 62 and Other Ancient Documents on Wedding and Marriage* (Aarhus, Denmark: Aarhus University Press, 1992), 64.

[128] On "the 'unicity' of the scripture, its wholeness and its lack of self-contradiction" see Benjamin D. Sommer, "Introduction: Scriptures in Jewish Tradition, and Traditions as Jewish Scriptures," in *Jewish Concepts of Scripture: A Comparative Introduction,* ed. Benjamin Sommer (New York: New York University Press, 2012), 3-4.

essentially different from human language. While human beings' words usually carry a limited

number of meanings, God's language was believed to be superabundantly full of meaning.[129]

The midrashic literature of the first centuries C.E. reveals the influence of rabbinic thought

on early Christian exegesis.[130] The most prominent figures in the development of the Christian

exegetical tradition, namely Origen (185-253/4), Jerome (c. 347-420) and Eusebius (c. 260-339/40),

demonstrated an awareness of the midrash literature and may have even contributed to the

development of the midrash tradition as Hebrews sought to counter Christian interpretations of the

Hebrew Scriptures.[131] Some early Christian writings, which were of a polemic nature, claimed that

Hebrews had failed to grasp the full meaning of Scripture, whose true sense had not been lost on

Christians: their minds had been newly enlightened by the Spirit.[132] This early Christian view of the

Hebrew Bible gave rise to the "typological" sense of Scripture.[133]

In the Near East during the first millennium, Christian exegesis emerged not only from

Hebraic literature but from Greco-Roman writings. Patristic exegesis, as it was handed down to the

medieval Latin West, was a synthesis of pagan and Hebraic literary techniques.[134] A firm grounding

in rhetoric was essential in the education of an early Christian. Not only did training "in harmony

with the spirit of the times" raise the (relatively low) social status of a Christian, but being schooled

---

[129] "The challenge, then, is to find keys to unlock some of the additional meanings that are not so obvious at first reading." Benjamin D. Sommer, "Concepts of Scriptural Language in Midrash," in *Jewish Concepts of Scripture: A Comparative Introduction* (New York: New York University Press, 2012), 66.

[130] Michael Singer and Susan Graham note the existence of "remarkable parallels in hermeneutical method between midrashim and Greek and Syriac patristic literature." Michael A. Singer and Susan L. Graham, "Rabbinic Literature," in *Handbook of Patristic Exegesis: The Bible in Ancient Christianity*, vol. 1 (Leiden: Brill, 2006), 130.

[131] Ibid.

[132] Charles Kannengiesser, *Handbook of Patristic Exegesis: The Bible in Ancient Christianity*, The Bible in Ancient Christianity, v. 1 (Leiden ; Boston: Brill, 2006), 185.

[133] Regarding the difference "senses" of Scripture, see Henri de Lubac, *Exégèse médiéval: les quatres sens de l''ecriture* (Paris: Aubier, 1959).

[134] These techniques ranged from explaining the etymological origins of names (as found in Homer and Hesiod) to the formalized rhetorical methodology of the Sophists and other Athenian orators. Early Christian exegetes were aware of Plato's (428/7-348/7 BCE) critique of rhetoric in favor of philosophy (as dedicated to the truth rather than mere persuasion) and Aristotle's (384-322 BCE) conception of rhetoric as "the capacity of discovering what, in each case, is the most convincing," a tool which would come in handy in Christian discourse. Cicero (106-43 BCE) and Quintilian (35-100 CE) likewise projected an influence on early Christian authors, as did the tradition of writing commentaries on a range of scientific, legal and philosophical texts. See Christoph Schäublin, "The Contribution of Rhetorics to Christian Hermeneutics," in *Handbook of Patristic Exegesis: The Bible in Ancient Christianity*, vol. 1 (Leiden: Brill, 2006), 145-47.

in rhetoric gave a Christian the means necessary to be an effective apologist, proselytizer and

catechist of the faith.[135] Like rabbinic exegetes who presumed an underlying unity to the Bible,

Christian exegetes presumed the existence of a divine message in the Scriptures, a *res* that was

"disguised" in various linguistic forms (also known as *verba*).[136] The exegetes' job was to make the *res*

manifest, the divine message.[137] Given that this *res*, however, was often far from evident, the

exegetes elucidated what would otherwise remain hidden in the obscure language of Scripture. Since

the divine message was cloaked in "signs," the interpreter needed to determine how to read the

"sign": as having a "proper" (literal) sense or "figurative" meaning that it carried a typological

(allegorical), tropological or anagogical meaning.[138] The "literary sensitivity" of the early Christian

exegetes, which developed through formal training in rhetoric, allowed them to interpret sacred texts

in a way that was highly methodical rather than arbitrary.[139] The divine message, ensconced in

Scripture, was not beyond the reach of the human mind; divine mystery was accessible through

careful reading and through reason.

Exegetes from Antioch were more attentive to the literal sense of scripture and less prone

than Alexandrines to interpret the Hebrew Scriptures allegorically; the same is true of their

mystagogy, exegesis of liturgical rites rather than sacred texts. Antiochians saw liturgical mysteries as

portrayals of the historical events of salvation history. In the mystagogy of Cyril of Jerusalem, John

of Chrysostom (347-407), and Theodore of Mopsuestia (c. 350-428) we find the liturgy is a kind of

mirror of history; the sacraments imitate the salient moments of Christ's life and point toward the

Resurrection.[140] The Alexandrians, on the other hand, stressed a moral, individual eschatology: the

---

[135] Ibid, 151.

[136] Ibid., 156–57.

[137] Matt 22:37-40. Ibid., 156.

[138] See Lubac, *Exégèse Médiéval.* Also Schäublin, "The Contribution of Rhetorics to Christian Hermeneutics," 158.

[139] Ibid, 163.

[140] "Prefigured in Old Testament types, the sacramental rites are an 'imitation'…of the saving acts of Christ's life, and an anticipation of the heavenly liturgy." Robert F. Taft, *Beyond East and West: Problems in Liturgical Understanding,* 2nd ed. (Rome: Edizioni Orientalia Christiana, 2001), 21.

true Christian was not waiting "Passover" of the *parousia* but was "passing continuously from the things of this life to God, hastening towards his city."[141] The Byzantine approach to the liturgy prior to Germanus of Constantinople (circa 634-733/740) was predominantly Alexandrian, based on the writing of a Neo-Platonist, Pseudo-Dionysius the Areopagite (late 5th or early 6th century), and Maximus the Confessor (circa 580-662).[142] The notion of the earthly liturgy representing the heavenly things dominated interpretations of the Christian liturgical rites. Alexandrians perceived the liturgy to be an ascent to the kingdom of heaven as well as an image of the soul's conversion and ascent to union with God, for which the Incarnation served as a model. Germanus, in contrast with his predecessors, added some Antiochene perspectives, by focusing on the human ministry of Christ and the historical dimension of his life.

Mystagogy: Oil in the Early Christian Liturgy

Medieval liturgical commentary is a genre with its roots in the fourth century, when figures such as Cyril of Jerusalem (313-386), Ambrose of Milan (337-397), and John of Chrysostom (347-407) attempted to explain the Christian mysteries to the faithful through mystagogy – exegesis applied to the liturgy, which consisted in "reading in the rites the mystery of Christ and in contemplating beneath the symbols the invisible reality."[143] For these early exegetes, the liturgy was like scripture: a direct channel to God and a means of experiencing divine life during earthly existence. Despite the presence of oil in Mark's gospel (Mark 6:13), in which Jesus commissioned the disciples to cast out demons and anoint the sick with oil, oil entered the Christian liturgy by way

---

[141] Ibid.

[142] Paul Meyendorff, "Introduction," in *On the Divine Liturgy* (Crestwood, N.Y: St. Vladimir's Seminary Press, 1984).

[143] Robert F. Taft, *Beyond East and West: Problems in Liturgical Understanding*, 2nd ed. (Rome: Edizioni Orientalia Christiana, 2001), p. 11, Jean Daniélou quoted in Taft; Paul Germanus, *On the Divine Liturgy* (Crestwood N.Y.: St. Vladimir's Seminary Press, 1984).

of initiation rituals rather than the anointing of the sick.[144] Cyril of Jerusalem explained the presence

of oil at Christian initiation by way of 1 John: "the anointing from the Holy One" preserved the

Christian in truth following baptism.[145] Though initiation rituals varied during the first centuries of

Christianity, by the third century baptism was never unaccompanied by anointing.[146] Through the

writings of early Christians authors who interpreted the significance of oil within the liturgy, we can

see how early Christians perceived oil, including its literal and symbolic significance.

Hippolytus' *Apostolic Tradition*

Hippolytus (d. 236) recorded the early use of oil in the Christian cult in his *Apostolic Tradition*,

a commentary that had lasting impact on later liturgical developments.[147] Hippolytus' text testified to

the early consecration rites for oils, both baptismal oil blessed by a bishop, which was referred to as

the 'oil of thanksgiving,' and oil to be blessed and then consumed. The blessing of the second oil

occurred between the blessing of bread, wine, cheese and olives.[148] In this early prayer we see an

early appearance of the formula 'kings, priests and prophets' which would carry through into

consecration prayers (with the addition of 'martyrs') in the High Middle Ages. Given that this

formula relates to anointing, Alistair Stewart-Sykes notes the oddity of its inclusion in the blessing of

foods. Nevertheless, the apparent intended use of this oil was consumption, not anointing: "If

anyone offer oil, [the bishop] shall render thanks in the same manner as for the offering of bread

and wine, not saying it word for word, but to the same effect, saying 'O God, sanctify this oil: grant

holiness to all who use it and who receive it, and as you anointed kings, priests and prophets, so may

---

[144] John Halliburton, "Anointing in the Early Church," in *Oil of Gladness: Anointing in the Christian Tradition* (London: S.P.C.K., 1993), 78. Halliburton notes: "...for many years, oil, liturgically, belongs to the font and not the bedside."
[145] Ibid.
[146] Ibid.
[147] Alistair Stewart-Sykes, "Introduction," in *The Apostolic Tradition* (Crestwood, N.Y.: St. Vladimir's Seminary Press, 2001), 18–19.
[148] Hippolytus, *On the Apostolic Tradition*, trans. Alistair Stewart-Sykes (Crestwood, N.Y.: St. Vladimir's Seminary Press, 2001), 77.

it give strength to all who consume it and health to all who use it."[149] Given the reference to anointings in the Hebrew Scriptures (kings, priests, prophets), Stewart-Sykes argues that this blessing is an adaptation of the prayer for baptismal oils.[150] Since the prayer for the blessing of the oil for consumption directly followed the prayer for the blessing other foods, including cheese and olives, these prayers offer insight into how early Christian perceived material things, including their foods, as revelatory of God's presence in the material world: "Sanctify this milk which is congealed, and congeal us with your love. Let this fruit of the olive, which is an example of your richness, not depart from your sweetness, which you poured out from the tree into the life of those who hope in you."[151] Divine presence dwelt within the olive and its oil, whether people consumed the oil as a comestible or absorbed the oil topically through anointing.

The use of oil for anointing occurred within the Christian cult in the context of ritualized initiation: before and after baptism. The appearance of oils in connection with baptism on Holy Saturday, however, was a relatively later development in the Roman rite; the *Apostolic Tradition* preserves a primitive form of this practice.[152] The blessing of the two oils used for baptism, the oil of exorcism and the oil of thanksgiving, appears to have taken place just before baptism. A renunciation of Satan accompanied the oil of exorcism, which in turn drove all evil spirits from the catechumen just before baptism:

> …when the presbyter takes hold of each of those who are to be baptized he should bid him renounce saying: 'I renounce you Satan, and all your service and all your works.' And when

---

[149] Hippolytus, *Apostolic Tradition.*, trans. Burton Scott Easton ([Hamden, Conn.: Archon Books, 1962), 76. Alistair Stewart-Sykes notes that Hippolytus' text is problematic in that there are conflictual readings: *sanitatem* (health) is an emendation of *sanctitatem* (holiness).

[150] Hippolytus, *On the Apostolic Tradition*, 77.

[151] This prayer for the cheese is reminiscent of the practice of some early heretics, who included cheese and maybe yogurt among the foods consumed as Eucharist. The prayer for the olive, however, is suggestive of another prayer regarding the blood and water flowing from Christ's side. See Ibid., 79.

[152] Stewart-Sykes, "Introduction," 18.

he has renounced all this he should anoint him with the oil of exorcism saying to him: 'Let all evil spirits depart from you.'[153]

Following baptism, the presbyter would then anoint the neophyte with the 'oil of thanksgiving' just after he or she emerged from the water. Once anointed, dressed, and inside the church, the neophyte received blessings from the bishop, in the form of the laying on of hands. The bishop forgave sins and invoked the Holy Spirit, whom the new Christian was now worthy to receive.[154] After invoking or "anointing" the neophyte with the invisible spirit, the bishop then anointed him or her with oil:

> After this, pouring the sanctified oil from his hand and putting it on his head he shall say: 'I anoint you with holy oil in God the Father Almighty and Christ Jesus and the Holy Spirit.' And signing him on the forehead he shall give him the kiss and say: 'The Lord be with you.' And he who has been signed shall say: 'And with your spirit.'[155]

The earliest witness of post-baptismal anointing in Rome is found in Tertullian (155-240), who described how the followers of Marcion of Sinope (circa 85-160) were baptized, anointed, and fed with milk and honey.[156] Some scholars have tried to find in Hippolytus' record of post-baptismal anointings the origins of confirmation, in which individuals receive the Holy Spirit. Stewart-Sykes argued, however, that Hippolytus indicated that following baptism neophytes were well disposed or

---

[153] Hippolytus, *On the Apostolic Tradition*, 110-111. The exorcism of evil spirits, however, began in the days leading up to baptism: "From the time they [catechumens] are set apart, a hand is laid on them daily whilst they are exorcized. When the day of baptism draws near the bishops should exorcize each of them so that he may be sure that they are pure...when [the bishop] lays his hand on [the catechumens] he shall exorcize them of every foreign spirit and they shall flee away from them and shall not return. And when he has finished exorcizing them he should blow on their faces; and when he has sealed their forehead [sic], their ears and their noses he should make them stand up." Ibid., 106.

[154] "And the bishop, laying his hand on them invokes, saying: 'Lord God, you have made them worthy to deserve the remission of sins through the laver of regeneration: make them worthy to be filled with the Holy Spirit, send your grace upon them that they may serve you in accordance with your will; for to you is glory, to the Father and the Son with the Holy Spirit in the holy church both now and to the ages of ages. Amen." Hippolytus, *On the Apostolic Tradition*, 112.

[155] Ibid., 112.

[156] Ibid., 122. Stewart-Sykes notes that this practice may not have been a native Roman practice, but nevertheless occured in Rome at the time of Marcion.

"worthy" of receiving the Holy Spirit but did not necessarily do so.[157] Even if the second post-baptismal anointing was a later interpolation, Hippolytus' text demonstrated the close correlation between oil and the indwelling of the Holy Spirit for early Christians.[158]

Cyril of Jerusalem's *Mystagogical Catechesis*

Cyril of Jerusalem (c. 313 – 386) became the Bishop of Jerusalem in 350, as Christianity gained a more secure foothold in the Roman Empire, including in the Near East. At this time, internal conflicts, including the Arian heresy, divided the Church. Cyril may have aligned himself with Arians to a degree, but nevertheless repudiated some Arian beliefs in his writings.[159] After his deposition and exile, Cyril espoused a moderate, anti-Arian stance, maintaining that the Son was of *like* substance as the Father (*homoiousios* rather than *homoousios*).[160] After having been exiled and exonerated a number of times, late in life Cyril returned to Jerusalem, then torn by schism and widespread social decay.[161] Within this context, Cyril delivered his *Mystagogical Catechesis*, which he intended as instruction for newly initiated Christians. By this point in his career and theological development, he adopted a *homoosian* position: the Son was of the same substance as the Father. Nowhere in his writings did Cyril deny or question the divinity of the Holy Spirit, as did some.[162] Regarding Cyril's approach to scriptural exegesis, he followed the practices of Antioch, in which historical interpretation was given a priority, while not entirely excluding spiritual readings, which were more prevalent in Alexandria where authors approached Scripture allegorically.[163] For Cyril, the Hebrew Scriptures contained prophecies regarding Jesus and the Church. The people and events

---

[157] "The candidates may merit being filled with the Spirit at a later point, perhaps in their reception of the eucharistic gifts, but more probably in the subsequent episcopal unction." Ibid., 122–23.

[158] Ibid., 123.

[159] Edward Yarnold, "Introduction," in *Cyril of Jerusalem* (London; New York: Routledge, 2000), 3–7.

[160] Ibid., 6.

[161] Ibid., 7.

[162] Ibid.

[163] Regarding Cyril's exegetical and theological positions, see Ibid., 56–64.

that preceded the birth of Christ were symbols (*tupos*), of future things, which is to say, Christ or elements of the Christian faith, including holy oil.[164]

In Cyril's *Mystagogical Catechesis* we see a full flowering of a typological interpretation of holy oil. Cyril found precedent for the baptism and anointing in the Hebrew Scriptures, which prefigured the reality brought about by Christ.[165] During Cyril's lifetime, catechumens received full-body anointing prior to baptism. Having recited the Creed to the Bishop by heart, those hoping to be received into the Church renounced Satan. In darkness, deacons or presbyters then stripped catechumens of all their clothing and anointed the catechumens' naked bodies with the oil of exorcism.[166] Following baptism, which symbolized Christ's death, descent into the tomb and subsequent resurrection, neophytes were anointed with perfumed oil, known as *muron* or chrism.[167] In Orations 2, 3, and 4 of the *Mystagogical Catechesis*, Cyril explicated the meaning of the oil and anointing that accompanied this salvific drama.

According to Cyril, the Holy Spirit entered the bread and wine during the *epiclesis*, transforming them into the body and blood of Christ. Similarly, the prayers blessing oil transformed the liquid into a medium by which the Holy Spirit was conveyed to human beings: "...just as after the invocation of the Holy Spirit the bread of the Eucharist is no longer ordinary bread but the body of Christ, so too this holy *muron* is no longer ordinary or, so to say, common ointment, but Christ's grace which imparts to us his own divinity through the presence of the Holy Spirit."[168] By being anointed with oil infused with the Holy Spirit, Christians assumed a likeness with Christ and became

---

[164] Ibid., 58.

[165] Cyril states: "For when Moses passed God's command on to his brother and installed him as high priest, he first made him bathe and then anointed him. Thus he was called the 'christ' – a word derived from the anointing. So too when the high priest made Solomon king, he anointed him after making him bathe in the Gihon. These rites were performed for them as a prefiguration, but for you not as a prefiguration but in reality, because your salvation began with the one who was anointed in reality by the Holy Spirit." Cyril, *Cyril of Jerusalem*, 178.

[166] Yarnold, "Introduction," 40. Paul W. Harkins notes that the exact words for the exorcism of oil are not to be found in Cyril of Jerusalem, Theodore of Mopsuestia, nor John of Chrysostom. See John Chrysostom, *Baptismal Instructions*, trans. Paul W Harkins (Newman Press: Westminster, Md.; Longmans, Green & Co.: London, 1963), 219n29.

[167] Yarnold, "Introduction," 40.

[168] Cyril, *Cyril of Jerusalem*, 63.

themselves conduits of God's presence, which descended from heaven like a dove and was at work through the ages. The removal of clothing prior to baptism corresponded to the removal of "the old man with his deeds" and the nakedness symbolized "Christ naked on the cross."[169] Cyril likened the naked catechumen to a shameless Adam in the Garden of Eden and the bride of the Song of Songs who says "I have taken off my tunic. How could I put it on?"[170] Cyril told the neophytes that in their nakedness, when they were anointed from head to toe, they became like Jesus, "the true olive": "...once you had removed your clothes, you were anointed with exorcized oil from the topmost hairs of your head to the lowest parts of your body, and became shares in Jesus Christ, the true olive. You were cut from the wild olive and grafted to the true olive, and began to share in the richness of the genuine olive."[171] Having been cut from the "wild olive" the neophyte could ward off the powers of darkness, drive away demons, and defend against sin, bringing about a kind of rebirth. Having emerged from a paradoxical transformation, in which "your birth coincided with your death" the Christian was ready for anointing with chrism.

According to Cyril, having received the Holy Spirit, new Christians, like Christ himself, acquired a new mission that determined their identities as Christians: "The Holy Spirit has come upon me; that is why he has anointed me and sent me to announce the good news to the poor."[172] Christ's anointing, however, was unlike that of other Christians: "Christ did not receive a human anointing with bodily olive-oil or *muron*; it was the Father who anointed him with the Holy Spirit in proclaiming him Saviour of the whole world."[173] Cyril emphasized the divine or heavenly origin of

---

[169] Ibid., 173.

[170] Chrysostom likewise compares the naked catechumen to Adam in Paradise. See Chrysostom, *Baptismal Instructions*, 170. Also Cant 5:3; Gen 2:25.

[171] Cyril, *Cyril of Jerusalem*, 173–74.

[172] Is 61:1.

[173] Cyril, *Cyril of Jerusalem*, 176.

Christ's anointing to which human beings were not privy.[174] Augustine echoed this idea in his exposition of Psalm 44 when he posed the question, "with what oil is Jesus anointed if not spiritual oil?"[175] Cyril equated the Holy Spirit with 'the oil of gladness' (Psalm 44) with which Jesus was anointed; Christians were anointed with a like – not identical – substance: "He [Christ] was anointed with the spiritual 'oil of gladness', that is with the Holy Spirit, which is called the oil of gladness because it causes spiritual gladness; you were anointed with *muron* and became partners with Christ and began to share with him."[176] Without saying so directly, Cyril suggested that while Christ was anointed with invisible, immaterial Spirit, Christians were anointed with a visible, physical substance, *muron*, which nevertheless brought about similar results and established a kinship or likeness between all the anointed ones.

Despite the fact that Christians were anointed with physical oil, they experienced a spiritual transformation as new Christs. Cyril likened *muron* to the Eucharist; the material appearance did not correspond to the spiritual reality:

> Beware of imagining that this is ordinary ointment. For just as after the invocation of the Holy Spirit the bread of the Eucharist is no longer ordinary bread but the body of Christ, so too with the invocation this holy *muron* is no longer ordinary or, so to say, common ointment, but Christ's grace which imparts to us his own divinity through the presence of the Holy Spirit. To symbolize this truth you are anointed on your forehead and on your other senses. Your body is anointed with the visible *muron*, while your soul is sanctified by the life-giving Spirit.[177]

---

[174] To show the heavenly versus human nature of Christ's anointing, he cited the following scriptural passages: "Jesus of Nazareth, whom God anointed with the Holy Spirit" (Acts 10:38) and "God, your God has anointed you with the oil of gladness beyond your fellows" (Ps 44:7-8). Ibid., 177.

[175] "Quo oleo, nisi spiritali?" "Augustinus Hipponensis - In Psalmum 44 Enarratio," accessed May 24, 2016, http://www.augustinus.it/latino/esposizioni_salmi/esposizione_salmo_059_testo.htm. Augustine's interpretations of the significance of oil will be further discussed in Chapter 2, given the omnipresence of his writings within the *Glossa Ordinaria*.

[176] Cyril, *Cyril of Jerusalem*, 177.

[177] Ibid.

God imparted his divinity to human beings through their bodies. For this reason, Cyril explained which body parts received the anointing: the forehead, the ears, the nose and the breast.[178] Cyril referred to the anointing as a "sacred gift" and warned his neophytes to not lose or undo what had been bestowed on them for physical and soteriological protection.[179] Curiously, Cyril closed his catechesis by again urging the neophytes to keep their anointing immaculate, as if its nature were corruptible: "Now that you have been anointed with this holy *muron*, keep it pure and spotless within yourselves by making progress in good works and becoming pleasing to the 'pioneer of your salvation' Jesus Christ..."[180] Cyril's final discussion of oil emphasized the spiritual dimension of anointing, looking to the anointings in the Hebrew Scriptures as foreshadowing the anointings Christians received. *Mystagogic Catechesis 4 (Concerning Christ's body and blood)* dealt with oil only briefly, within a discussion of Psalm 22: " 'You have anointed my head with oil.' He anointed your head on the forehead with oil, by means of the seal which you receive from God, to make you 'the engraving of a signet: 'Holy to the Lord'." In Ecclesiastes, Cyril found hints of the anointing of Christians with chrism: "It is in reference to this grace that Solomon says enigmatically in Ecclesiastes: 'Come, eat your bread with gladness' (this spiritual bread). 'Come' (the author issues the saving invitation that offers happiness), 'and drink your wine with a good heart' (the spiritual wine), 'and let oil be poured over your head' (do you notice that the author is hinting at the mystic anointing with chrism?)."[181] In the Hebrew Scriptures, Cyril found the essential elements of Christian initiation and worship: bread, wine and oil, all of which possessed spiritual dimensions that affected not only the bodies but the souls of Christians.

---

[178] The forehead corresponds to Exod 34:29 and 2 Cor 3:18: "First you are anointed on the forehead so as to be released from the shame which the first sinner carried around everywhere, and to reflect the glory of the Lord with face unveiled." The ears refer to Isaiah 50:4 – "And the Lord has given me an ear to hear" and Matthew 11:15: "He that has ears to hear, let him hear." The nose is anointed to indicate "We are Christ's sweet fragrance before God among those who are saved" (2 Cor 2:15). The breast corresponds to Ephesians 6:14 and 11: "put on the breastplate of righteousness" against the "devil's wiles." Ibid.

[179] Ibid., 178.

[180] Ibid.

[181] Ibid., 180.

John of Chrysostom (c. 347 – 407) wrote his *Baptismal Homilies* in Antioch circa 390 C.E., in the wake of the Arian, Manichean, Gnostic, Apollonarian and Messalian controversies, prior to his election as bishop. Addressing catechumens, Chrysostom explained the significance of the two pre-baptismal anointings the catechumens would receive.[182] In describing the first anointing, Chrysostom depicted oil as a powerful prophylactic against evil; once anointed, the catechumen was prepared to engage in spiritual combat. Chrysostom depicted the Christian as engaging in a public spectacle, in which good was pitted against evil:

> After that contract of renunciation and attachment, after you have confessed His sovereignty and by the words you spoke have attached yourself to Christ, in the next place, as if you were a combatant chosen for the spiritual arena, the priest anoints you on the forehead with the oil of the spirit and signs you [with the sign of the cross], saying: 'So-and-so is anointed in the name of the Father, and of the Son, and of the Holy Spirit.' The priest knows that henceforth the enemy is furious, grinds his teeth, and goes about like a roaring lion when he sees those who were formerly subject to his sovereignty in sudden rebellion against him, not only renouncing him, but going over to the side of Christ...Henceforth from that day there is strife and counterstrife with him, on this account the priest leads you into the spiritual arena as athletes of Christ by virtue of this anointing.[183]

The anointing of the catechumen who will then "wrestle" with the devil may stem from the Greco-Roman tradition of anointing wrestlers before a match. The Christian being oiled in preparation for battle with a spiritual foe appears in the narrative of the Passion of Perpetua, in which Perpetua has a vision of being anointed with oil before entering combat with her foe in the ampitheatre of Carthage in 203:

---

[182] Harkins notes: "Unlike Cyril [of Jerusalem] and Theodore [of Mopsuestia], Chrysostom recognizes two anointings: first, on the forehead, and second, of the entire body." Chrysostom, *Baptismal Instructions*, 224n49.
[183] Ibid., 51–52.

The day before we fought, I saw in a vision that Pomponius the deacon had come hither to the door of the prison, and knocked hard upon it…we came to the amphitheatre, and he led me into the midst of the arena. And he said to me: Be not afraid; I am here with you and labour together with you. And he went away. And I saw much people watching closely. And because I knew that I was condemned to the beasts I marvelled that beasts were not sent out against me. And there came out against me a certain ill-favored Egyptian with his helpers, to fight with me. Also there came to me comely young men, my helpers and aiders. And I was stripped naked, and I became a man. And my helpers began to rub me with oil as their custom is for a contest; and over against me saw that Egyptian wallowing in the dust….[She fights the Egyptian and wins.] And I awoke; and I understood that I should fight, not with beasts but against the devil; but I knew that mine was the victory.[184]

In Chrysostom's explanation of the second anointing, this time a full-body anointing, the imagery of combat remains, but a heavenly reward is imminent: "…in the full darkness of the night, he strips off your robe and, as if he were going to lead you into heaven itself by the ritual, he causes your whole body to be anointed with that olive oil of the spirit, so that all your limbs may be fortified and unconquered by the darts which the adversary aims at you."[185] In Chrysostom's address, the combat imagery extends to neophytes following their baptism; oil becomes the sign of Christ's favor and victory. God anoints the Christian but binds the enemy in chains: "How true it is that Christ does not stand aloof but is entirely on our side you may see from this: He anointed us as we went into combat, but He fettered the devil; He anointed us with the oil of gladness, but He bound the devil with fetters that cannot be broken to keep him shackled hand and foot for combat."[186] For Chrysostom, oil was a sign of God's favor and, in a sense, a preordained triumph of the Christian over the forces of evil.

---

[184] Perpetua, "The Passions of Saint Perpetua and Felicity," accessed May 24, 2016, http://legacy.fordham.edu/halsall/source/perpetua.asp. See also Thomas J Heffernan, *The Passion of Perpetua and Felicity* (New York: Oxford University Press, 2012).
[185] Chrysostom, *Baptismal Instructions*, 52.
[186] Ibid., 58.

During the reign of Constantine (r. 312-337), the persecution of Christians ceased as

Christianity became the most favored cult in the Roman empire. Nevertheless, even in the late

fourth century Christian identity retained elements of a persecuted minority. Following initiation

into the Christian faith, neophytes would gather at the tombs of martyrs, who were their

predecessors and spiritual models. Chrysostom speaks of the "blessing" which was reaped from the

presence of the holy dead:

> Beloved, when you stand beside these tombs and your mind considers that this whole
> throng hastens with such speed to gather here that they may clasp the dust and reap the
> blessing which comes from these tombs, how will your mind fail to be lifted aloft, how will
> you fail to be eager to show the same zeal for the martyr, so that you may yourself be judged
> worthy of the same reward?[187]

The "blessing" (*eulogia*), which neophytes gathered at the tombs, may have in fact been oil taken

from the lamps burning near the martyrs' bodies.[188] In his homily *In martyres*, Chrysostom described

how oil from the tombs was to be used for ritual anointing:

> Do you wish to live a life of luxury? Remain beside the martyr's tomb, pour forth there your
> streams of tears, berate your mind, take up the blessing (*eulogian*) from the tomb. Having
> taken this blessing as your advocate in your prayers, spend your time in [reading] the
> accounts of his contests. Embrace his coffin and fasten yourself to his casket; for not only
> the martyrs bones but also their tombs and coffins are rich with abundant blessing (*eulogian*).
> Take the holy oil and anoint your whole body, your tongue, your lips, your neck, and your
> eyes, and you will never fall into the shipwreck of drunkenness. For the fragrance of the oil
> recalls to your mind the martyrs' contests, it curbs your lack of temperance, it holds you in
> perseverance, and it overthrows the ailments of your soul.[189]

---

[187] Ibid., 105.

[188] See Paul W. Harkins regarding Antoine Wenger's argument: "As well as here, Chrysostom speaks twice again (Stav. 8.1 and 16) of the *eulogia*, the blessing, which comes from the martyr's tombs, and the question arises as to the nature of this blessing. Wenger…holds that it was the holy oil which was kept burning before the shrine and which the faithful used for their devotional anointings. Ibid., 230n3.

[189] Ibid., 230n3.

Rather than being anointed by oil blessed by a bishop, early Christians could anoint themselves with oil sanctified by the presence of martyrs. In this ritual, we see an echo of devotional practices surrounding oil gathered from the tombs of martyrs and saints themselves, not simply the lamps burning nearby.

In his last address to catechumens before their baptism, Chrysostom introduced imagery of oil-filled lamps, drawing a parallel between Christian initiation and marriage. The catechumens were likened to the wise virgins of Matthew's parable,[190] whose oil-filled lamps allow them to enter to the wedding banquet with the Messiah:

> Today is the last day for your instruction. And I, the last of all men, have come to the last of my instruction. I have come as the last to tell you that after two days the Bridegroom is coming. Arise, kindle your lamps, and by their shining light receive you the King of heaven. Arise and keep watch. For not during the day but in the middle of the night the Bridegroom comes to you. This is the custom for the bridal procession – to give over the brides to their bridegrooms late in the evening.[191]

The likeness between a bride and those seeking redemption through Christian initiation corresponds to the marital imagery in Chrysostom's Exposition of Psalm 5: "Hence, after He came into her dwelling and found her filthy, unwashed, naked, and befouled with blood, He bathed her, anointed her, nourished her, and clothed her with a garment, the like of which could never be found."[192] Chrysostom further elucidated the nuptial dimension of initiation by evoking the perfumed unguent worn by the bride as well as the oil (for wrestling purposes) worn presumably by the groom in other contexts. When contemplating the anointing he or she was to receive, the catechumen was to remember that oil had a fragrant dimension (associated with the bride in need of redemption) and a

---

[190] Matt 25:3-8.

[191] Chrysostom, *Baptismal Instructions*, 161.

[192] Harkins notes that the three sacraments of initiation (baptism, anointing, and Eucharist) correspond to gestures of hospitality (bathing, anointing and feeding). See Ibid., 315–316n7.

slippery dimension (associate with the groom who would wrestle in combat with a foe): "...God

anoints your countenance and stamps thereon the sign of the cross. In this way does God hold in

check all the frenzy of the Evil One...for through the chrism the cross is stamped on you. The

chrism is a mixture of olive oil and unguent; the unguent is for the bride, the oil is for the athlete."[193]

Chrysostom further impressed upon his audience the idea that God Himself anointed them; the

transformation which transpired was of divine and not human origin: "And that you may again

know that it is not a man but God Himself who anoints you by the hand of the priest, listen to St.

Paul when he says: *It is God who is warrant for us and for you in Christ, who has anointed us*. After He

anoints all your limbs with this ointment, you will be secure and able to hold the serpent in check;

you will suffer no harm."[194] In Chrysostom's homilies, we see oil as a conduit of divine presence

which shielded the anointed from spiritual harm. The anointing brought about a kind of spiritual

purity, characteristic of a bride at marriage, which was itself a mark of salvation.

THEODORE OF MOPSUESTIA'S *BAPTISMAL HOMILIES*

Like John of Chrysostom, Theodore of Mopsuestia (350 – 428) composed his *Baptismal*

Homilies in the midst of religious conflict, as Christians sought to resolve doctrinal disputes and

establish the legitimacy of their religion. In his discussion of the renunciation of "Satan and his

angels" by the initiates, Theodore explained that these angels included pagan poets, philosophers,

and heretics.[195] When the catechumen renounced the powers of evil, a priest appeared in fine

garments. Theodore explained that priest was dressed in "clean and radiant linen," to signify "the joy

of the world to which you will move in the future, and the shining colour of which designates your

---

[193] Ibid., 169.

[194] Ibid. Here Chrysostom speaks of using chrism (fragrant unguent) prior to baptism. In the Latin West in the Middle
Ages, chrism (oil mixed with spices) was only used after baptism, not before. See Chapter 3.

[195] Theodore of Mopsuestia, *Commentary of Theodore of Mopsuestia on the Lord's Prayer and on the Sacraments of Baptism and the
Eucharist*, trans. Alphonse Mingana, vol. VI, Woodbrooke Studies (Cambridge: Heffer, 1933), 40–41.

own radiance in the life to come, while its cleanness indicates the ease and happiness of the next

world."[196] The shining garments were intended to inspire fear and love in the catechumen. In this

state of awe, the uninitiated received chrism on the forehead, in the sign of the cross accompanied

by an invocation of the Godhead. According to Theodore, the tracing of the cross in chrism marked

the individual as belonging to the Church or Christ. This sign was comparable to a lamb branded to

designate its owner or a soldier stamped to designate his king.[197] With the application of chrism, the

catechumen was set apart: "When the priest performs these things for you and signs you with a sign

on your forehead, he separates you from the rest as a consequence of the aforesaid words, and

decides that you are a soldier of the true King and a citizen of heaven."[198] Having received this

"stamp which is the sign of your election to the ineffable military service," the catechumen was

"invested with the complete armour of the Spirit" by which Theodore means full-body anointing

with chrism.[199]

Having been freed from earthly things, and prepared to turn his vision heavenwards (toward

the heavenly Jerusalem), the catechumen received oil all over his body. First the catechumen

removed his clothing, which according to Theodore, was a sign of mortality and the sin of Adam.[200]

The catechumen exchanged clothing and mortality for oil and immortality, an idea reminiscent of

the vision of Enoch:

> After you have taken off your garments, you are rightly anointed all over your body with the
> holy Chrism: a mark and a sign that you will be receiving the covering of immortality, which
> through baptism you are about to put on….And you are anointed all over your body as a
> sign that unlike the covering used as a garment, which does not always cover all the parts of
> the body, because although it may cover all the external limbs, it by no means covers the
> internal ones – all our nature will put on immortality at the time of the resurrection, and all

---

[196] Ibid., 45.
[197] Ibid., 46.
[198] Ibid., 47.
[199] Ibid.
[200] Ibid., 54.

that is seen in us, whether internal or external, will undoubtedly be changed into

incorruptibility according to the working of the Holy Spirit which shall be with us.[201]

The oil, according to Theodore, pertains not simply to the external, material body but to the

internal, spiritual dimension of the human being. The idea of oil permeating the human being all the

way to the *viscera*, the bowels or internal parts of the body, which were believed to be the seat of the

emotions, appeared often in medieval discourse on oil.[202] Saying that oil penetrated to the body's

interior, Theodore suggested a unity of the body and the spirit; the physical anointing with oil had

affected the condition of the soul or spirit. Moreover, according to Theodore, the anointing

foreshadowed the resurrection itself, by encompassing the human being in his or her entirety.

Having been baptized, the newly initiated received the sign of the cross, in chrism, on the

forehead, symbolizing the anointing Jesus received in the Jordan River, when the Holy Spirit

descended upon him in the form of a dove. The anointment, according to Theodore, was

permanent: "…the Holy Spirit is never separated from Him, like the anointment with oil which has

a durable effect on the men who are anointed, and is not separated from them."[203] According to

Theodore, the invocation of the Trinity and the chrism indicated the reception of grace and the

inseparability of divinity from the human being following baptism. The oil, moreover, offered a

glimpse of future heavenly things: "Indeed, at present you only receive symbolically the happiness of

the future benefits, but at the time of the resurrection you will receive all the grace, from which you

will become immortal, incorruptible, impassible and immutable; even your body will then remain

forever and will not perish, while your soul will be exempt from all inclination, however slight,

---

[201] Ibid.

[202] See Chapter 3.

[203] Theodore of Mopsuestia, *Commentary of Theodore of Mopsuestia on the Lord's Prayer and on the Sacraments of Baptism and the Eucharist*, 68.

toward evil."[204] Thus oil permeated the entirety of the human being, suffusing the material body with divine presence. The presence of God, within the mortal frame, suggested a more perfect and complete divinization after death.

AMBROSE OF MILAN'S *DE SACRAMENTIS & DE MYSTERIIS*

Ambrose, Bishop of Milan, (340 – 397) composed *De Sacramentis* & *De mysteriis* on the Italic peninsula, a fair distance from his contemporaries in the Near East. In Ambrose's addresses to new Christians, we see how the secretive dimension of Christianity at the time influenced the significance of holy oil: those not initiated into the Christian cult were prohibited from knowing its mysteries and rituals.[205] Ambrose's texts offered an explanation to those being initiated into the mysteries of the cult. *De Sacramentis* consists of speeches given during Easter Week; *De mysteriis* was intended for an indeterminate time. These texts reveal the extent to which Ambrose, like Chrysostom, associated holy oil with the spiritual struggle that preceded salvation.

As in the writings of John of Chrysostom and Theodore of Mopsuestia, we find Ambrose likening the anointed catechumen to a wrestler preparing for a match:

> Thou wast anointed as Christ's athlete; as about to wrestle in the fight of this world, thou didst profess the objects of thy wrestling. He who wrestles has something to hope for; where the contest is, there is the crown. Thou wrestlest in the world, but thou are crowned by Christ, and thou art crowned for contests in the world; for though the reward is in heaven, yet the earning of the reward is placed here.[206]

Ambrose emphasized the dichotomy between the heavenly and earthly spheres; the oil allowed the catechumen to engage in earthly combat, which had heavenly rewards – and so the catechumen was

---

[204] Ibid., 68–69.

[205] Ambrose, *St. Ambrose On the Sacraments and On the Mysteries*, ed. J. H Srawley, trans. T Thompson (London; New York: S.P.C.K., 1950), 4.

[206] Ibid., 49.

to concern himself with those heavenly, rather than earthly, things. After undergoing a symbolic death in baptism, the neophyte received chrism on the forehead, which Ambrose claimed was the place of wisdom. In *De Sacramentis*, Ambrose stated: "…you receivest *myron*, that is, *ointment upon the head.* Why upon the head? Because *the* senses *of a wise man are in his head,* says Solomon. For wisdom is lifeless without grace; but when wisdom has received grace, then its work begins to be perfect. This is called regeneration."[207] In *De Mysteriis*, the Bishop of Milan explained post-baptismal anointing by invoking Psalm 132 – the anointing of Aaron as High Priest: "Was it not that which David said, *It is like the ointment upon the head, that ran down unto the beard, even unto Aaron's beard?* This is the ointment of which Solomon also says, *Thy name is as ointment poured forth, therefore did the maidens love thee and draw thee.* How many souls regenerated to-day have loved thee, Lord Jesus, saying, *Draw us after thee, we run to the odour of thy garments,* that they may drink in the odour of the resurrection!"[208] Finally, Ambrose explained that the reason for the anointing was to suffuse the Christian with wisdom and to make the anointed the elect or beloved of God: "Understand why this is done, because *the wise man's eyes are in his head.*[209] It flowed down *unto the beard* – that is, unto the grace of youth – *even unto Aaron's beard,* for this purpose, that thou mayest become *a chosen generation,* priestly, *precious;* for we are all anointed with spiritual grace unto the kingdom of God and the priesthood."[210] Thus, in Ambrose, we see the seeds of ideas about oil which would take root in the Latin West: that oil is a sign of election, of being God's beloved, of being a member of a sacred priesthood, and a citizen of heaven.

Conclusion

In ancient Mesopotamian culture, oil was closely associated with the sacred, playing a central role in legal and marital contracts as well as in the bestowal of kingly authority. Oil was also a means

---

[207] Ibid., 70.

[208] Ibid., 135. Ambrose references Psalm 132:2 and Cant. 1:3.

[209] Eccles. 2:14.

[210] Ambrose, *St. Ambrose On the Sacraments,* 135–36.

by which an individual could be consecrated to a sacred office, such as the priesthood. The use of oil

carried over into ancient Hebraic ritual where both kings and priests were consecrated through

anointing. Oil was a mark of election and a covenant with God; God Himself anointed the human

being. The Hebraic belief that in receiving God's spirit, the anointed was divinized influenced the

beliefs and practices of early Christianity. As "the Anointed One" Christ was God's elect: the

beloved Son, the Messiah. The Gospels reflect the power of oil to heal both the body and spirit. For

early Christians, oil was a sign of both wisdom and divine love. In the early Christian liturgy, oil

became central to initiation rites, preparing catechumens for spiritual battle and strengthening them

for Christian discipleship, which often meant embracing death through self-sacrifice. These early

Christian texts reveal the paradoxes of the Christian faith; oil was a sign of death and new life,

sorrow and joy, masculine authority and feminine divinity. While some of the meanings attributed to

oil by early Christian authors carried over into the medieval period, as the next chapter on the *Glossa

Ordinaria* will show, oil was reinterpreted by medieval Christians, who placed a greater emphasis on

the typological dimension of oil as foreshadowing Christ and as being an instrument through which

the Church and its ministers saved both bodies and souls.

Chapter 2

Reading Between the Lines:

Oil in the Glossa Ordinaria

Introduction

Allegory – *allegoria* in Latin, ἀλληγορία in Greek: Speaking otherwise than one seems to

speak. Saying one thing in terms of another. In the medieval period, symbolic thought dominated

the intellectual and spiritual landscape.[211] Medieval exegetes drew on the writings of Patristic authors

and adapted their view of the world and Scripture as having multiple senses as well as a visible and

invisible reality. Before approximating a meaning for oil in the medieval period, we must consider

the symbolic framework or *mentalité* that permeated the thought of the Middle Ages. Johan Huizinga

characterized the spirituality of late-medieval Christianity as spirituality based predominantly on

symbols and allegory. Many medieval Christians believed physical realities, as well as historical

events, possessed a higher meaning, which was accessible through faith, but not necessarily through

reason.[212] The reality or signification that reason could neither attain nor conceptualize belonged to

mystery or the divine nature of God.[213] Symbols disclosed the interconnectedness of things human

and divine, of the creature and the creator.[214] Biblical exegesis involved discerning the multiple

"senses" of Scripture, including the literal or historical, allegorical, tropological and anagogical. Not

only were the people and events of the Christian Scriptures prefigured by the Hebrew Scriptures, but

biblical texts contained images which pointed to things beyond themselves and beyond the things of

this world; visible realities revealed the invisible. Symbols disclosed the bonds uniting the material

---

[211] See Johan Huizinga, *The Autumn of the Middle Ages* (Chicago: University of Chicago Press, 1996); Marie Dominique Chenu, "The Symbolist Mentality," in *Nature, Man, and Society in the Twelfth Century; Essays on New Theological Perspectives in the Latin West* (Chicago: University of Chicago Press, 1968). Chenu states: "In the whole range of its culture, the medieval period was an era of the symbol as much as, indeed more than, an era of dialectic." See Ibid., 102–3.

[212] Chenu, "The Symbolist Mentality," 102–3.

[213] Ibid., 102.

[214] "These symbols claimed to disclose certain intimate relationships…which the art of ascertaining multiform truth could not fail to take into consideration." Ibid., 103.

and spiritual worlds, bonds that could only be partially grasped.[215] Just as in Platonic thought, the

material world reflects the world of Forms, so for medieval exegetes the natural world and the texts

of the Bible were a *speculum*, or mirror, through which the well-tuned mind or faithful soul might

perceive the *vestigia Dei* and so possess the *imago Dei* within himself or herself.[216]

The manifold reading of the "sense" of Scripture, which permeated early Christian exegesis,

found its way to the medieval Latin West, in part through the *Glossa Ordinaria*, a collection of

patristic and medieval *glossae* (glosses) on the Bible, which became the standard biblical commentary

in the twelfth century. Scholars have investigated the origin and evolution of the *Glossa ordinaria*, in

its seemingly infinite variations. Beryl Smalley's *The Study of the Bible in the Middle Ages* (1941) first

substantively addressed the role of the Bible and its gloss in medieval society, arguing that the Bible

was the most widely read book in the Latin West. As such, it had tremendous influence not only as a

religious text, but also as a tool for teaching and learning in the liberal arts. In eleventh and twelfth-

century classrooms, master teachers would read aloud to their students.[217] The master would

expound on a primary text, be it legal or biblical, by reading an interpretive gloss. These glosses,

---

[215] "Scientific analysis by theologians would soon define the limitations inherent in the very nature of such metaphors; nonetheless, they concealed, in dialectical suspension between likeness and disparity, the intrinsic bond uniting the material and spiritual realms, here conjoined in a single stroke of thought." Chenu, "The Symbolist Mentality," 114.

[216] Ibid., 116.

[217] Students would sometimes have the primary text or the gloss in front of them, which they would have copied by hand. The system of acquiring texts for medieval universities or schools is known as the pecia system. See Louis-Jacques Bataillon, "Les Textes théologiques et philosophiques diffusés à Paris par exemplar et pecia" in *La Production du livre universitaire au Moyen Âge: exemplar et pecia. Actes du symposium tenu au Collegio S. Bonaventura de Grottaferrata en Mai 1983* (Paris: Centre National de la Recherche Scientifique, 1988), 155–63; Leonard E. Boyle, "Peciae, Apopeciae, Epipeciae," in *La Production du livre universitaire au Moyen Âge: exemplar et pecia. Actes du symposium tenu au Collegio S. Bonaventura de Grottaferrata en Mai 1983* (Paris: Centre National de la Recherche Scientifique, 1988), 39–40; D. L. D'Avray, *The Preaching of the Friars: Sermons Diffused from Paris before 1300* (Oxford : New York: Clarendon Press ; Oxford UniversityPress, 1985); Alan J. Piper and Meryl R. Foster, "Evidence of the Oxford Booktrade, about 1300," *Viator: Medieval and Renaissance Studies* 20 (1989): 155–59; Graham Pollard, "The Pecia System in the Medieval Universities," in *Medieval Scribes, Manuscripts and Libraries. Essays Presented to N.R. Ker* (London: Scolar Press, 1978), 145–61; James Patrick Reilly, "A Preliminary Study of a Pecia," *Revue d'histoire des textes* 2 (1972): 239–50; Richard H. Rouse and Mary A. Rouse, "The Dissemination of Texts in Pecia at Bologna and Paris," in *Rationalisierung der Buchherstellung im Mittelalter und in der Frühen Neuzeit: Ergebnisse Eines Buchgeschichtlichen Seminars, Wolfenbüttel 12.-14. November 1990* (Marburg an der Lahn: Institut für Historische Hilfswissenschaften, 1994), 69–77; Chiara Ruzzier, "Quelques observations sur la fabrication des bibles au XIIIe siècle et le système de la pecia," *Revue Bénédictine* 124, no. 1 (2014): 151–89; Hugues V. Shooner, "La Production du livre par la pecia," in *La Production du livre universitaire au Moyen Âge: exemplar et pecia. Actes du symposium tenu au Collegio S. Bonaventura de Grottaferrata en Mai 1983* (London: Centre National de la Recherche Scientifique, 1988), 17–37.

which accompanied widely-reproduced texts such as the Bible or works of Roman and canon law,

became increasingly standardized, taking shape as *glossae ordinariae* (ordinary glosses).[218] The primary

text occupied the page's center, usually as one large column. Exegetical expositions surrounded the

primary text, appearing both in the margins and between the lines; they are known as marginal and

interlinear glosses, respectively. No surviving manuscript contains an entire glossed Bible; rather,

glossed biblical books appear in independent codices.[219]

The *Glossa Ordinaria* emerged from the cathedral schools of Paris and Laon, which eclipsed

the monasteries as centers for learning and intellectual innovation by the twelfth century.[220] A

handful of eleventh and twelfth-century figures, who expounded on the meaning of scripture to

their students, collectively contributed to the emergence of the *Glossa Ordinaria*. These figures

included Fulbert of Chartres (d. 1028), Berengar of Tours (d. 1088),[221] Lanfranc of Bec (d. 1089),

Bruno of Chartreux (d. 1101), Master Manegold (d. 1110), Anselm of Laon (d. 1117), his brother

Ralph (d. 1134/6), Gilbert de la Porrée (d. 1154), and Peter Lombard (d. 1160-64). These masters of

the 'sacred page'[222] produced two kinds of texts that led to the eventual distillation of biblical

commentary: text-books or study aids and independent exegesis.[223] Smalley's claim that the Bible's

Glossa emerged from the cathedral schools of the twelfth century challenged the then-prevalent view

that Walafrid of Strabo ('the Squinter') (d. 849), a Swabian poet and theologian who studied under

Rabanus Maurus (d. 856), authored the *Glossa*.[224] Smalley proved that Anselm of Laon was the

---

[218] Beryl Smalley, *The Study of the Bible in the Middle Ages* (Notre Dame: University of Notre Dame Press, 1964), 52.

[219] Mary Dove, *The Glossa Ordinaria on the Song of Songs* (Kalamazoo, Mich.: Medieval Institute Publications, Western Michigan University, 2004), x.

[220] Smalley, *The Study of the Bible in the Middle Ages*, 47–66. Jean Leclercq, *L'amour des lettres et le désir de Dieu; initiation aux auteurs monastiques du Moyen Âge* (Paris: Éditions du Cerf, 1957).

[221] Berengar of Tours' glosses on the Pauline Epistles are ascribed to 'Drogo' and 'Lanfranc.' Smalley, *The Study of the Bible in the Middle Ages*, 47.

[222] Ibid., 49.

[223] Ibid., 51.

[224] Smalley, *The Study of the Bible in the Middle Ages*, 56; Smalley's conclusions were based in part on the work of J. de Blic, "L'oeuvre exégétique de Walafrid Strabon et La Glossa Ordinaria," *Recherches de théologie ancienne et médiévale* vi (1949): 5–28. For authors who disseminated the Strabo thesis see: J. de Ghellinck, *Le Mouvement théologique du XII siècle. Sa préparation lointaine avant et autour de Pierre Lombard, ses rapports avec les initiatives des canonistes. Etudes, recherches et documents.* (Bruges:

central figure in the production of the *Glossa Ordinaria* and probably authored (or compiled) the glosses for the following books: Psalms, Matthew, John, and the Pauline Epistles.[225] The glosses for the books of Genesis, Job, Proverbs, Ecclesiastes, the Minor Prophets, the Canonical Epistles, Luke and the Apocalypse may have also originated in Laon.[226]

In the mid-twelfth century, glossed bibles became a common feature of monastic and secular libraries in northern Europe.[227] Scholars have yet to determine if the phenomenon was equally prevalent on the Italian peninsula.[228] The peak period for the composition of glossed bibles was just over a hundred years: roughly 1130 – 1250.[229] The work of the twelfth-century glossators was an extension of the work begun by Carolingian compilers, who amassed running biblical commentaries based upon patristic commentary. Not surprisingly, the centers of *Glossa* production in the twelfth century, namely Laon and Auxerre, were also *loci* of biblical scholarship during the Carolingian period.[230] In the tenth century, Laon briefly became the capital of the West Frankish kingdom. The fruits of the Carolingian cathedral libraries remained for centuries, becoming the basis for the

---

Editions de Tempel, 1948), 104–12; Samuel Berger, *De l'histoire de la Vulgate en France leçon d'ouverture* (Paris: Fischbacher, 1887).

[225] Dove, *The Glossa Ordinaria on the Song of Songs*, xii.

[226] Ibid.

[227] See Margaret T. Gibson, "Introduction" in *Biblia Latina Cum Glossa Ordinaria Facsimile Reprint of the Editio Princeps Adolph Rusch of Strassburg 1480/81*, Karlfried Froehlich, ed. (Turnhout: Brepols, 1992).

[228] Ibid., 1:vii.

[229] Ibid., 1:vii. Regarding the origin of the *Glossa Ordinaria*, see Veronika von Büren, "Auxerre, lieu de production de manuscrits?," in *Etudes d'exégèse carolingienne: autour d'Haymon d'Auxerre. Atelier de recherches, Centre d'études médiévales d'Auxerre 25-26 Avril 2005*. Sumi Shimahara, ed., Collection Haut Moyen Age, 4 (Turnhout: Brepols, 2007), 167–86; Marcia L. Colish, "Psalterium Scholasticorum: Peter Lombard and the Emergence of Scholastic Psalms Exegesis," *Speculum* 67, no. 3 (1992): 531–48; Franklin T. Harkins, "'Following with Unequal Step': Andrew of St Victor, the *Glossa Ordinaria*, and Compilatory Exegesis in the Northern French Schools of the Twelfth Century," in *Transforming Relations: Essays on Jews and Christians throughout History in Honor of Michael A. Signer*. Franklin T. Harkins, ed. (Notre Dame: University of Notre Dame Press, 2010), 150–78; E. Ann Matter, "The Legacy of the School of Auxerre: Glossed Bibles, School Rhetoric, and the Universal Gilbert," *Temas Medievales* 14 (2006): 85–98; Giuseppe Mazzanti, "Anselmo di Laon, Gilberto l'Universale e la *Glossa Ordinaria* alla Bibbia.," *Bullettino dell'Istituto italiano per il Medio Evo* 102 for 1999 (2001): 1–19; Beryl Smalley, "La *Glossa Ordinaria*. Quelques prédécesseurs d'Anselme de Laon," *Recherches de théologie ancienne et médiévale*, no. 9 (1937): 365 – 400; Lesley Smith, *The Glossa Ordinaria the Making of a Medieval Bible Commentary* (Leiden; Boston: Brill, 2009); Patricia Stirnemann, *Où ont été fabriqués les livres de la glose ordinaire dans la première moitié du XIIe siècle ?* (Paris: Le Léopard d'or, 1994); Jenny Swanson, "The *Glossa Ordinaria*," in *The Medieval Theologians*, G.R. Evans, ed., 2000, 156-67.

[230] Margaret T. Gibson, "Introduction," 1:x.

twelfth-century *Glossa*.[231] By 1150, Paris became the heart of glossed bible production.[232] The Abbey of St. Victor in particular may have been responsible for the production and dissemination of a "complete and definitive" version of the *Glossa Ordinaria*.[233] By the second half of the twelfth century, the *Glossa* was the standard reference for authors expounding on the Bible, including Peter Comestor, Peter the Chanter, and Stephen Langton.[234] In subsequent centuries, this same *Glossa* served the exegetical needs of figures such as Thomas Aquinas, John Wyclif, and Martin Luther.[235]

When the *Glossa Ordinaria* first appeared in print in 1480/1 under the title *Biblia cum glossis ordinariis*, its editor, Adolph Rusch of Strassburg, made no claims about its authorship.[236] His edition of the *Glossa Ordinaria*, which was based on a selection of manuscripts, served as the basis for later printed editions of the text, the last of which appeared in Antwerp in 1634.[237] J.P Migne's *Patrologia Latina* (1841 – 1855) contains the most recent printed version of the *Glossa*, based on Rusch's 1480/1 edition. Migne, however, misattributed the marginal glosses to Strabo and claimed the interlinear glosses were a twelfth-century interpolation by Anselm of Laon.[238] In 1992, Karlfried Froehlich oversaw the publication of a facsimile of Rusch's 1480/1 edition. Under the leadership of Margaret T. Gibson, a group of scholars, including Froehlich as well as John Cavadini, Ann Matter, and Mark Zier, sought to create the first modern edited edition of the *Glossa Ordinaria*, based on the *editio princeps* as it appeared in 1480/81. Following Gibson's untimely death, however, the researchers never brought the project to completion. Subsequently, a handful of scholars have published critical

---

[231] Ibid.

[232] See Christopher De Hamel, *Glossed Books of the Bible and the Origins of the Paris Booktrade* (Woodbridge, Suffolk; Wolfeboro, N.H., USA: D.S. Brewer, 1987).

[233] Margaret T. Gibson, "Introduction," 1:xi.

[234] Ibid.

[235] Ibid.

[236] Karlfried Froehlich, "An Extraordinary Achievement: The *Glossa Ordinaria* in Print," in *The Bible as Book: The First Printed Editions*, Paul Saenger and Kimberly van Kampen, eds. (London: British Library, 1999), 15–21.

[237] Dove, *The Glossa Ordinaria on the Song of Songs*, x.

[238] J.P. Migne, ed., *Patrologia Latina the Full Text Database* (S.l.: Chadwyck-Healey, Inc, 1996), CXIII, 67-1316 ; CXIV, 9-752., http://proxy.library.georgetown.edu/login?url=http://pld.chadwyck.com. Smalley claims this edition is "worthless." Smalley, *The Study of the Bible in the Middle Ages*, 56.

editions of particular books of the *Glossa*, including the Book of Ruth, the Song of Songs and Gospel of John.[239]

Scholars generally agree that Rusch's 1480/1 edition of the *Glossa Ordinaria* is the most reliable version available. This text will therefore serve as the basis for my analysis of oil in the *Glossa Ordinaria*. I will compare Rusch's edition of the *Glossa* with a selection of manuscripts in an attempt to find variant interpretations of oil's meaning. My study departs from the work of previous scholars in that I focus on the exegesis of a particular subject (oil) rather than the development of the *Glossa* for a particular biblical book, historical figure or religious order associated with *Glossa* production.[240] To my knowledge, scholars have not traced a single theme throughout multiple books of the *Glossa*, with one exception.[241] I limit my study to interpretations of pericopes about oil and anointing, asking why glossators chose the glosses they did. My goal is to assess what significance the glossators impute to oil and explain how the glosses reflect their historical contexts. Since the *Glossa Ordinaria* provided interpretations that became standard in medieval Europe, the ideas contained therein

[239] Lesley Smith, *Medieval Exegesis in Translation: Commentaries on the Book of Ruth* (Kalamazoo, Mich.: Medieval Institute Publications, 1996); Dove, *The Glossa Ordinaria on the Song of Songs*; Alexander Andrée, "The *Glossa Ordinaria* on the Gospel of John. A Preliminary Survey of the Manuscripts with a Presentation of the Text and Its Sources," *Revue Bénédictine* 118, no. 1 (2008): 109–34.

[240] See Andrée, "The *Glossa Ordinaria* on the Gospel of John. A Preliminary Survey of the Manuscripts with a Presentation of the Text and Its Sources"; Constance B. Bouchard, "The Cistercians and the *Glossa Ordinaria*," *Catholic Historical Review* 86, no. 2 (2000): 183–92; Mary Dove, "Sex, Allegory and Censorship: A Reconsideration of Medieval Commentaries on the Song of Songs," *Literature and Theology: An Interdisciplinary Journal of Theory, Criticism and Culture* 10: 4 (1996): 317–28; Dove, *The Glossa Ordinaria on the Song of Songs*; Robert J. Karris, "A Comparison of the *Glossa Ordinaria*, Hugh of St. Cher, and St. Bonaventure on Luke 8:26-39," *Franciscan Studies* 58 (2000): 121–236; Atria A. Larson, "The Influence of the School of Laon on Gratian: The Usage of the Glossa Ordinaria and Anselmian *Sententiae* in *De Penitentia*," *Mediaeval Studies* 72 (2011): 197–244; Suzanne Lavere, "From Contemplation to Action: The Role of the Active Life in the Glossa Ordinaria on the Song of Songs," *Speculum: A Journal of Medieval Studies* 82, no. 1 (2007): 54–69; Frans A. van Liere, "Andrew of St Victor and the Gloss on Samuel and Kings.," in *Media Latinitas: A Collection of Essays to Mark the Occasion of the Retirement of L.J. Engels*. R.I.A. Nip et al., eds. (Turnhout: Brepols, 1996), 249–53; E. Ann Matter, *The Voice of My Beloved: The Song of Songs in Western Medieval Christianity* (Philadelphia: University of Pennsylvania Press, 1990); E. Ann Matter, "Gregory the Great in the Twelfth Century: The *Glossa Ordinaria*," in *Gregory the Great: A Symposium*. John C. Cavadini, ed. (South Bend, Ind.: University of Notre Dame Press, 1995), 216–26; E. Ann Matter, "The Church Fathers and the Glossa Ordinaria," in *The Reception of the Church Fathers in the West: From the Carolingians to the Maurists*. Irena Backus, ed. (Leiden: Brill, 1997), 1:83-111; Mazzanti, "Anselmo di Laon, Gilberto l'Universale e la *Glossa Ordinaria* alla Bibbia."; Beryl Smalley and Roland E Murphy, *Medieval Exegesis of Wisdom Literature: Essays* (Atlanta, Ga.: Scholars Press, 1986); Smith, *Medieval Exegesis in Translation*; Patrizia Stoppacci, "Le Glossae continuae in psalmos di Pietro Lombardo. Status quaestionis: studi pregressi e prospettive di ricerca," in *Pietro Lombardo: Atti del XLIII convegno storico internazionale, Todi 8-10 Ottobre 2006*. Enrico Menestò, ed. (Spoleto: Centro Italiano di Studi sull'Alto Medioevo, 2007), 20:289–331.

[241] Signer, "The *Glossa Ordinaria* and the Transmission of Medieval Anti-Judaism."

would have made their way into the minds and writings of other medieval authors and may have even influenced the beliefs and practices of the unlettered faithful. In particular, I hope to clarify how medieval people may have understood miraculous events involving oil, including oil seeping from saints' bodies and tombs, as well as oil flowing from the foundation of a church dedicated to Mary. To understand the meaning of oil in medieval religious culture, we can begin with the meaning of oil in the *Glossa Ordinaria*.

OIL IN THE MEDIEVAL BIBLE

Oil permeates the Hebrew and Christian Scriptures. Close to two hundred references to oil or anointing appear in the Hebrew Scriptures alone. An examination of each of these passages is beyond the scope of this chapter. I will limit my study to passages that are of greatest import to oil's role in the medieval Latin West, given how they served as a basis for medieval thought and ritual. In many instances, biblical pericopes about oil or anointing reverberate through the liturgy of the medieval Church, either in chants or in prayers for the consecration of oils, or are invoked in diverse contexts within biblical commentaries. These passages include: Jacob's dream at Bethel, where he anoints a stone (Genesis 28: 10 – 22); the anointing of Saul and David (1 Samuel 10 & 16); Psalms 22, 44, 132;[242] the Book of Job (29:6); and the Song of Songs.[243] In the Christian Scriptures, the references to oil and anointing are fewer but nevertheless potent, since these passages served as fundamental elements of the medieval Christian imagination and discourse. I examine the following pericopes: the casting out of demons and anointing with oil (Mark 6:13); the Parable of the Good Samaritan (Luke 10: 34); the Parable of the Wise & Foolish Virgins (Matthew 25: 3-4; 7-8); the anointing of Jesus at Bethany (Mark 14, Matthew 26, Luke 7, John 12); and the anointing of Jesus

---

[242] Other psalms include 4, 54, 88, 103, 108, 140.
[243] Cant. 1:1-2; 3:6; 4:10; 4:14; 5:5-6; 5:13.

after his death (Luke 23: 56).[244] This analysis of these glosses reveals a distinct variance of

interpretation of oil in the Hebrew Scriptures and the Gospels. Glosses for oil and anointings in

Genesis, 1 Samuel, Job, and the Psalms invariably described the thing or person anointed as being

like Christ – or as being a typological foreshadowing of Christ. Glosses of oil and anointings in the

Gospels, however, do not interpret the anointed as being Christlike. Rather, these glosses

emphasized the role of clerics as ministers of salvation, the power of the Church to consecrate oil

and the non-material dimension of oil as a conduit of the Holy Spirit.

Oil in the Hebrew Bible

Jacob's Dream

"Quam terribilis est locus iste" – Genesis 28:17.

In Genesis 28, Jacob leaves his home, setting off for a foreign land to find a wife. Between

Beer-sheba and Haran, he spends the night in the open, resting his head on a stone. In this place,

Jacob has a remarkable dream: he sees angels ascending and descending from heaven on a ladder. In

the dream, Jacob also sees God standing besides him and hears his voice: God promises Jacob the

land on which he rests, blessings upon his offspring, and his faithful presence and protection. When

Jacob awakes, cognizant of God's presence, he declares: "This is none other than the house of God,

and this is the gate of heaven."[245] To mark God's presence, Jacob raises the stone that served as his

pillow, makes it a pillar and anoints it with oil, naming the place "Bethel," which means "House of

God."

---

[244] English translations of biblical passages borrow from the Douay-Rheims translation of the Vulgate or the New Standard Revised Version (NSRV). I provide my own Latin transcriptions of Rusch and diverse manuscripts in the footnotes, noting disparities between these texts and the standard Vulgate text or texts as they appear in modern edited editions (PL, CCC, etc.) Transcriptions and translation of glosses, unless otherwise noted, are my own.
[245] Gen 28:17.

The glosses for this pericope draw on the standard set of authors who feature frequently in the *Glossa Ordinaria*: Augustine (354-430), Isidore of Seville (c.560-636), Gregory the Great (540-604), and Jerome (340/2-420). Most of the glosses are from Gregory the Great, namely *The Book of the Morals (Moralia in Job)* and *Register of Letters (Registrum epistularum)*. The gloss on the anointing of the stone, however, is drawn from Augustine's *City of God (De ciuitate Dei)*. Since the oil follows a dream, which naturally occurs in sleep, Gregory explained what it meant for someone to sleep on a journey: to close the "eyes of the mind" to earthly, temporal things in order to see heavenly things.[246] Gregory's interpretation of the angels ascending and descending the ladder to heaven reveals the medieval perception of the heavenly and earthly spheres as distinct yet permeable. Gregory also suggested that heaven, like earth, was a civic community, a diocese populated by divine citizens, just as earth below was *respublica christiana* populated by Christians: "Angels ascending and descending' is to mark the citizens of the patria above, either with what love they cleave to their Creator above them, or with what fellow-feeling in charity they condescend to aid our infirmities."[247] The ability to see the "citizens" of heaven depended upon one's proximity to Christ, the Anointed One. According to Gregory, the anointed stone signified Christ; the head lying on the stone was a symbol for an inward, invisible activity – contemplating the image of Christ in one's mind: "Moreover it is noteworthy that the one who sees angels while sleeping is the one who puts his head on the stone. For on the stone, resting from exterior things, he penetrates internal things; he eagerly observes the

---

[246] "Lectionary Central," Accessed on 14 October 2014. The Latin text, as published in Rusch reads: "In itinere dormire, est in hoc praesentis uitae transitu a rerum temporalium amore quiescere. et in dierum labentium cursu ab appetitu uisibilium mentis oculos claudere. quos primis parentibus seductor aperuit, qui dixit: Culpa oculos concupiscentiae aperuit: quos innocentia clausos tenebat." Froehlich, *Biblia Latina Cum Glossa Ordinaria Facsimile Reprint of the Editio Princeps Adolph Rusch of Strassburg 1480/81*, 1:73.

[247] "Lectionary Central," accessed on October 14, 2014, http://www.lectionarycentral.com/GregoryMoralia/Book05.html. "Angelos descendentes et ascendentes cernere, est ciues supernae patriae contemplari: quanto amore auctori suo inhaereant. uel quanta compassione charitatis. nostris infirmitatibus condescendant." See also Froehlich, *Biblia Latina Cum Glossa Ordinaria Facsimile Reprint of the Editio Princeps Adolph Rusch of Strassburg 1480/81*, 1:73. According to Ken Pennington, beginning in the eleventh century, dioceses were referred to as *patriae*. Ken Pennington, "Bishops and Their Dioceses," accessed April 11, 2017, http://legalhistorysources.com/Canon%20Law/Pennington%20-%20Bishops%20and%20their%20Dioceses.pdf.

image of the redeemer, because who puts his head on the stone adheres to Christ with his mind."[248]

Furthermore, those who rested their attention on Christ rested in mind as well as body: "For those who are distant from the action of the present life and do not strive for things above, may sleep, but they are unable to see angels because they disdain keeping one's head on the stone and they sleep in body, not in zeal, because they do not lay the head on the stone, but on the earth."[249] To lay one's head on the stone was to rest one's attention on Christ, which brought the peace of mind required to see the internal, otherwise invisible angels of God, the citizens of heaven. A gloss attributed to Isidore further interpreted the anointed stone as prefiguring Christ:

> The sleep of Jacob on the journey is the death of Christ on the cross. The stone placed for the head is 'Christ according to humanity' which Jacob anointed, to signify Christ. That is to say, 'christus' in Greek, 'unctus' in Latin. The head of Christ is God. The stone therefore placed for Jacob's head signifies the humanity of Christ united with God, who has taken it upon himself. For the head of man is Christ, the head of Christ is God.[250]

The next gloss, drawn from Gregory's *Registrum epistularum,* also appeared in Gratian's *Decretum* (*Concordia discordantium canonum*), the twelfth-century compilation of ecclesiastical canons. This passage compared the ascending and descending angels to Moses entering and exiting the tabernacle. Within the tabernacle (the heavenly realm), the prophet contemplated sacred mysteries, leaving behind the things of this world. The analogy is four-fold: Jacob, the angels, Moses and the Church's preachers all share a likeness.

---

[248] "Notandum autem quod ille dormiens angelos conspicit qui in lapide caput ponit. In lapide enim ab exterioribus cessans, interna penetrat: qui intenta mente imitationem redemptoris obseruat. quod caput ponit in lapide: qui Christo inhaeret mente." Froehlich, *Biblia Latina Cum Glossa Ordinaria*, 1:73.

[249] "Qui enim a praesentis uitae actione remoti sunt, et ad superna nullo intendunt dormire possunt, sed uidere angelos nequeunt: quia caput in lapide tenere contemnunt. et corpore non studio dormiunt: quia caput non in lapide. Sed in terra posuerunt." Ibid., 1:73.

[250] "Dormitio iacobi itinere mors christi in cruce. Lapis capiti supositus. christus est secundum humanitatem. quem iacob vnxit: ut christus significaretur. Christus enim grece vnctus latine. Caput autem Christi deus. Lapis ergo capiti iacob suppositus. Significat humanitatem christi coniunctam deo assumenti caput enim uiri christus caput christi deus." Ibid.

> Jacob signifies the preachers who not only seek to contemplate the head of the Church, which is Christ, but who lower themselves with compassion to the members of the church, whom the angels ascending and descending reveal. Hence Moses frequently enters and exits the tabernacle. Within he is carried off in contemplation; without, he is beset by the pain of weakness. Within he reflects on mysteries; without he carries the burdens of the flesh.[251]

By highlighting the likeness of Jacob, the angels, and Moses to ecclesiastical preachers, the passage evidently sought to instruct members of the Church to turn away from "the burdens of the flesh" toward heavenly mysteries. How were medieval readers to see divine things? Instead of resting their heads on anointed stones, they were to rest their eyes on the sacred page in *lectio divina*. Through anointing, the divine presence permeated the stone in the same way the spirit of God saturated the sacred page. Through the contemplation of scripture, a reader could enter into sacred mysteries, ascending to the heavenly realm, like Moses returning to the tabernacle. Moses served as an example for teachers whose actions diverged from their teachings or who lost sight of the truth:

> From doubt [Moses] always returns to the tabernacle. He consults the Lord in the presence of the Ark of the Covenant, showing an example to teachers, such that when they go outside of what they prescribe, may they return to the mind as if to the tabernacle and consult the Lord, as if in the presence of the Ark of the Covenant, concerning the things about which they doubt. May they seek within themselves the pages of sacred eloquence.[252]

The gloss admonished the reader to turn inward and contemplate an interior world rather than live in the external world of the flesh. The anointed stone was like the sacred page, where one was to rest one's eyes to see things beyond the material, earthly realm. Just as Jacob saw the angels in his sleep, a

---

[251] "Jacob praedicatores significat qui non solum caput ecclesiae id est christum contemplando appetunt: sed ad membra illius miserando descendunt: quod angeli ascendentes descendentes demonstant. Hinc moyses crebro tabernaculum intrat et exit: et qui intus ad contemplationem rapitur: foris infirmantium negociis vrgetur. Intus arcana considerat, foris onera carnalium portat." Ibid., 1:73-74.

[252] "Qui de dubiis semper ad tabernaculum recurrit, coram testamenti arca dominum consulit, exemplum doctoribus praebens: ut cum foris ambigunt quid disponant: ad mentem quasi ad tabernaculum redeant. et uelut coram testamenti arca dominum consulant, de quibus dubitant apud se intus sacri eloquii paginas requirant." Ibid., 1:74.

medieval Christian could see divinity within himself. Such dream-like visions returned the reader to paradise, restoring the mind to a sinless state. A gloss from Gregory's *Moralia* returned to the theme of closing one's eyes to temporal things, and opening one's internal vision to heavenly things:

> For to sleep on a journey is to rest on the journey of this age from the hindrance of worldly activity. Sleeping, Jacob saw angels, because they who gaze upon divine beings close their eyes to a desire of temporal things. Those eyes which were well closed the devil opened saying: 'on whatever day you will eat, your eyes will be opened,' etcetera.[253]

The oil on the stone signified that human minds were open to divine presence, or that God's presence inhabited human minds.

A gloss attributed to Isidore of Seville, drawn from his *Mysticorum expositiones sacramentorum seu questiones in uetus testamentum*, addressed the role of the Church's preachers, like the gloss drawn from Gregory's *Registrum epistularum*.[254] Isidore's text borrowed directly from Augustine's *Contra Faustum* (circa 400) in which the Bishop of Hippo addressed the heresies espoused by Faustus of Mileve, the prominent Manichaean, who opposed orthodox Christianity and wrote a polemic against the Hebrew and Christian scriptures. In Augustine's response, reproduced first in Isidore's *Mysticorum*, and then in the *Glossa Ordinaria*, we see an allegorical interpretation of the ladder in Jacob's dream as Christ himself:

> The angels denote the evangelists, or preachers of Christ. They ascend when they rise above the created universe to describe the supreme majesty of the divine nature of Christ as being in the beginning God with God, by whom all things were made...Christ is the ladder reaching from earth to heaven, or from the carnal to the spiritual...He is the ladder, for He says, 'I am the way.' We ascend to Him to see Him in heavenly places; we descend to Him

---

[253] "In itinere dormire est in via huius saeculi ab impedimento actionum saecularium quiescere. Jacob dormiens angelos vidit: quia illi diuina conspiciunt qui ab appetitu temporalium rerum oculos claudunt. Quos bene clausos diabolus aperuit dicens: In quacumque die comederitis aperientur oculi vestri et cetera." Ibid. See LLT: Gregorius Magnus – Moralia in Job (CPL 1708) SL 143, lib.:5, par.:31, linea: 24.

[254] See LLT: Isidorus Hispalensis – Mysticorum expositiones sacramentorum seu Quaestiones in Uetus Testamentum (CPL 1195) In Genesim, cap.: 24, par.:2, col.: 258, linea: 23.

for the nourishment of His weak members. And the ascent and descent are by Him as well as to Him. Following His example, those who preach Him not only rise to behold Him exalted, but let themselves down to give a plain announcement of the truth.[255]

The interlinear glosses for this pericope likewise draw a direct parallel between Jacob and Christ. When Jacob lays his head on the stone, he signifies Christ, whose head is God.[256] The glossator further extended the parallel, stating that Jacob's sleep signified Jesus's death on the cross: "[Jacob] slept in that same place" is interepreted to be "Just as Christ died on the cross."[257] The stairs Jacob saw in his dream were Christ himself: "Christ who is life."[258] The physical earth where Jacob slept was the future tabernacle.[259] By calling the place "the house of God," Jacob spoke of the "future temple and cult of God."[260] Moreover in this gloss oil, Christ's birth, and prophecy converge: "Christ was born in Bethlehem as the Spirit foresaw."[261]

When Jacob raised the stone and made it a pillar, he foreshadowed the resurrection of Christ.[262] For the medieval glossator, Jacob's anointing of the stone mirrored the anointing of Christians. The gloss above "and pouring oil over [the stone]" was an allusion to Psalm 44:8: "Therefore God, your God, has anointed you with the oil of gladness in the presence of your

---

[255] "Angeli per scalam ascendentes et descendentes euangelistae sunt et praedicatores christi. Ascendentes ad intelligendam diuinitatem omnem creaturam excedentes: vt inueniant in principio verbum apud deum per quem omnia fact sunt. Descendentes vt inueniant cum factum ex muliere. factum sub lege et cetera. In illa enim scala a terra vsque ad spiritum. quia in illa carnales proficiendo. quasi ascendendo spirituales fiunt. Ad quos lacte nutriendos spirituales descendunt: quia non possunt eis loqui quasi spiritualibus. sed quasi carnalibus. Iste est sursum in capite Ipse deorsum in corpore suo id est ecclesia. Ipse scala ergo ait: Ego sum via. Ad ipsum ascenditur: vt in excelsis intelligatur. et descenditur. vt in membris paruulis nutriatur. per illum se erigunt: vt sublimes expectent. et humiliant. vt enim sublimiter et temperanter annuncient." Froehlich, *Biblia Latina Cum Glossa Ordinaria*, 1:74. English translation from *Contra Faustum, Book XII,* accessed on November 14, 2014, http://www.newadvent.org/fathers/140612.htm.

[256] "et supponens capiti suo" and "caput christi deus." Froehlich, *Biblia Latina Cum Glossa Ordinaria*, 1:74.

[257] "dormiuit in eodem loco" and "Sic christus in cruce mortuus." Ibid.

[258] "Christum qui est vita." Ibid.

[259] "ibi futurem erat tabernaculum." Ibid.

[260] "templum et cultum dei futurum significat." Ibid.

[261] "quia ibi natus est christus in bethleem quod spiritu[s] preuidebat." Ibid. See Chapters 8-10 for a discussion of the correlation between oil, the savoir's birth and Messianic prophecy vis-à-vis Santa Maria in Trastevere's *fons olei.*

[262] "Christi resurrectionem significat." Ibid.

companions."[263] This psalm verse was central to medieval Christian identity; it appears frequently as a gloss in pericopes about oil and was evidently so familiar to readers that glossators simply provided an abbreviation for the verse rather than the verse in its entirety, as we shall see.

Intermingled with the gloss from Isidore/Augustine are a few lines of text whose author I have yet to identify. These glosses emphasize the centrality of the Church, not just Christ, as the mediator of grace and the gate of heaven. The first unidentified gloss quotes Psalm 2, promising the earth's inheritance to the Church and to his "seed," the Christian people: "Ask of me, and I will make the nations your heritage, and the ends of the earth your possession."[264] The second unidentified gloss refers to Jacob's awaking from sleep, saying good works rouse the torpid soul from a sleep of sloth and ignorance. The good works were ostensibly accomplished through the Church, the locus of grace and the gate of heaven: "Whoever will have been awakened after the torpor of inertia and truly will have risen through the exercise of good works – he will understand the supreme grace of God and the entrance of the heavenly kingdom [to be] in the Church."[265] The place where Jacob slept and anointed the stone was a locus of divine presence. This place, recorded in the Hebrew Scriputre, had a counterpart in medieval Europe: the Church itself was the anointed "House of God" for Christians in the medieval Latin West.[266]

After Jacob wakes and returns to a conscious state, he rises to anoint his stone pillow. The gloss on Jacob's physical rising from his earthly, makeshift bed is drawn from Augustine's *De civitate*

[263] "dilexisti iustitiam et odisti iniquitatem propterea unxit te Deus Deus tuus oleo laetitiae prae consortibus tuis." Ibid. The gloss contains a few words, then a string of letters, suggesting the phrase was well-known to readers, a stock phrase in their mental repertoire: "Secundum illud vnxit te deus d.t.o.l." English translations differ as to how to translate "prae consortibus tuis." The Douay-Rheims translates this phrase as "above thy fellows." The NSRV translates the same phrase: "beyond your companions." Whether the preposition merely indicates "in the presence of" or designates the anointed one as superior to his companions remains a question.

[264] "Distice designat mandatum diuinitatis ad humanitatem christi directum cui terra[e] in ecclesia promittitur. et semini illius id est christiano populo. Unde postula a me .et dabo tibi gentes haereditatem tuam et p.t.t.terrae." Froehlich, *Biblia Latina Cum Glossa Ordinaria*, 1:74. Psalm 2:8 reads: "Postula a me, et dabo tibi gentes haereditatem tuam, et possessionem tuam terminos terrae."

[265] "Cumque euigilasset et cetera. Quisquis post torporem inertiae euigilauerit: et per exercitium boni operis vere exsurrexerit: in ecclesia supereminentem gratiam dei et introitum regni caelestis intelliget." Froehlich, *Biblia Latina Cum Glossa Ordinaria*, 1:74.

[266] Regarding the use of oil medieval church dedications, see Chapter 3.

Dei: "Jacob raised the stone on which he rested his head, setting it as a pillar, and anointed it with

oil, not in idolatry, for neither then nor afterwards did he frequent the stone, adoring it or sacrificing

to it, but he made a sign and prophecy about the anointing from which one is called Christ."[267] The

medieval glossator chose to emphasize the fact that in anointing the stone, the Israelite did not

engage in the worship of idols like a pagan, but rather testified to Christ's presence. Indeed, oil was a

prophetic "sign and prophecy," foreshadowing the advent of the "Anointed One."

The final two glosses for this pericope come from Jerome's *Liber quaestionum hebraicarum in

Genesim*. The first gloss from Jerome pertains to Jacob's exclaiming, "*quam terribilis est locus iste*" –

"How awesome is this place,"[268] where he encountered the divine presence and named the location

"House of God."[269] The second and final gloss was brief, yet alluded to the correspondence between

oil and prophecy: "[The place] was called the House [of God]. The prophecy [concerned] the House

of God, which was to be erected there. On his way back [i.e. later in his journeys], he sacrificed to

God there."[270] For Jerome, the physical location where the heavenly and earthly realms proved

permeable represented the Church, perhaps both as an institution and as a physical aedifice. The

single anointed stone became emblematic of the universal Church, in addition to the many stone

edifices that would appear in Latin Christendom. As we shall see in Chapter 3, the prayers sung

---

[267] "erexit iacob lapidem quem capiti supposuerat in titulum et superfudit oleum nihil fecit ydolatrie simile quia non vel
tunc vel postea frequentauit lapidem adorando .aut ei sacrificando .sed signum fuit et prophetia pertinens ad vnctionem
vnde christus dicitur." Froehlich, *Biblia Latina Cum Glossa Ordinaria*, 1:74. The text in LLT reads: "hoc ad prophetiam
pertinet; nec more idololatriae lapidem perfudit oleo iacob, uelut faciens illum deum; neque enim adorauit eundem
lapidem uel ei sacrificauit; sed quoniam christi nomen a chrismate est, id est ab unctione, profecto figuratum est hic
aliquid, quod ad magnum pertineat sacramentum." LLT: Augustinus Hipponensis – De ciuitate Dei (CPL 0313) SL 48,
lib.:16, cap.:38, linea:38.

[268] Gen 28:17.

[269] Jerome notes that the place that Jacob names Bethel, House of God, was former called *Luz*, adding that *Luz* means
"nut" or "almond." "Ab eo quod dictum est. quam terribilis est locus iste et cetera .loco nomen imponit bethel id est
domum dei .qui ante luza vocabatur id est nux vel amigdalum." What follows is a little discourse on place names: "Unde
ridicule quidam verbum hebraicum vlam nomen vrbis esse putant cum vlam interpretetur prius. Ordo ergo iste est
lectionis vocavit nomen loci illius bethel et prius luza . vocabulum civitatis. Anti[?] vero scripturae verbo vlam .vel elam
plenae sunt .quod nichil significat .nisi prius vel ante vel vestibulum. Vel superliminare vel postes et cetera." Froehlich,
Biblia Latina Cum Glossa Ordinaria, 1:74.

[270] "Vocabitur do[mus]. Prophetia est domus dei ibi futurae. Ibi et ipse rediens deo sacrificauit." Ibid.

during the consecration of a church invoked Jacob's anointing of the stone; the medieval faithful saw the anointed stone as representing churches, which clerics consecrated with holy oil.[271]

The Anointing of Saul

Since in the minds of medieval exegetes Jacob's anointed stone represented both Christ and the Church, we must explore the extent to which Christ, as the Anointed One, embodied the characteristics of a ruler of both temporal and spiritual realms. In the Hebrew Scriptures, the prophet Samuel anoints two men as royal leaders: Saul and David.[272] In Rusch's *editio princeps* of the *Glossa Ordinaria*, 1 Samuel (1 Kings) is sparsely glossed. The moments of the story in which oil appeared, however, merited commentary.[273] A glossator noted the meaning of Saul's anointing: "Saul anointed signifies Christ, who is himself called 'the Anointed.'"[274] The interlinear gloss tells us God anointed Saul in order to save his people from the enemies of God, who were neither heretics or infidels, but rather demons.[275] The glossator emphasized both the mysterious nature of the anointing, which was done in secret in a remote locale, where Samuel took Saul to speak "of the kingdom" in secret.[276] Sacral kingship was not simply about having dominion over earthly territory, but about knowledge of divine mysteries. The medieval glossator may have placed an emphasis on the secrecy surrounding Saul's anointing because of the precarious nature of medieval kingship. The anointing oil was held in an earthen vessel (*lenticular*), whose spout, according to the glossator, symbolized the vulnerability of kings: "*Lenticula* – a square, earthen vessel, which has on one side an

---

[271] Regarding the ritual use of holy oil to consecrate medieval churches, see Méhu, *Mises en scène et mémoires de la consécration de l'Église dans l'Occident médiéval*; Neuheuser, "Materialiter Aedificare, Spiritualiter Coaedificari"; Sevestre, "La Liturgie de La dédicace et ses hymnes."; Thomas, "Le Sermon V de Saint Bernard Pour La Dédicace."

[272] 1 Sam 9-10 and 1 Sam 16 respectively.

[273] For studies of the glosses on these periscopes, see Liere, "Andrew of St Victor and the Gloss on Samuel and Kings"; Vogüé, "La *Glossa Ordinaria* et le commentaire des rois attribué à Grégoire le Grand."

[274] "Saul vntus christum significat: qui et ipse christus appellatus est." Froehlich, *Biblia Latina Cum Glossa Ordinaria*, 2:15.

[275] "christus saluet populum suum de potestate demonum." Ibid.

[276] "Cumque descenderent. Descenderunt de excelso: vt in aliquo secretiori loqueretur de regno et vngeret eum." Froehlich, *Biblia Latina Cum Glossa Ordinaria*, 2:15.

opening, which signifies the fragility of royal power."[277] For the medieval exegete, the opening of the

vessel, through which oil flowed, symbolized the vulnerability of the king who, like the vessel, could

be emptied of the life-giving Spirit. Before Saul died, however, he devolved into a madness soothed

only by David's music, which wielded restorative powers akin to those often imputed to holy oil.

The Anointing of David

Samuel recognized David, the ruddy shepherd, to be the next king of Israel, the chosen one

and the Lord's anointed, despite his non-royal bearing. God instructed Samuel to go to Jesse's house

and promised to show the prophet which of the sons would be king.[278] The gloss for David's

anointing correlated him with Christ, whom the glossator noted was anointed with the 'oil of

gladness,' again making reference to Psalm 44: "Christ was anointed with the oil of gladness before

his companions."[279] When God instructs Samuel to "Rise and anoint him; for this is the one", the

gloss alluded again to Psalm 44 in abbreviated form: "vnxit te deus. deus t.o.l.p.c.t."[280] This line was

evidently so well known to medieval readers, the glossator or scribe needed only invoke the text in

abbreviated form. The anointing David received, according to the gloss, was "to condemn Saul."[281]

The glosses correlated David with Christ and highlighted his role as the Messiah.[282] Thus, the

---

[277] "Lenticula vas fictile quadrangulum: in latere habens foramen per quod fragilitas regni designatur." Froehlich, *Biblia Latina Cum Glossa Ordinaria*, 2:16.

[278] "Et vocabis Isai ad victimam et ego ostendam tibi quid facias: et vnges quemcumque monstrauero tibi fecit ergo samuel sicut locutus est ei dominus vnges quemcumque monstrauero tibi fecit ergo samuel sicut locutus est ei dominus. Venitque in bethleem et ad mirati sunt seniores ciuitatis occurentes ei." Froehlich, *Biblia Latina Cum Glossa Ordinaria*, 2:26.

[279] "christus vnctus est oleo laeticie pre consortibus suis." Ibid. The full line of text in the Latin Vulgate reads: "Dilexisti justitiam, et odisti iniquitatem; propterea unxit te Deus, Deus tuus, oleo laetitiae, prae consortibus tuis," Ps 44:8. The "prae" of "Prae consortibus suis" can be translated as "beyond", "above" or "before."

[280] "Surge et vnge eum." Ibid. Psalm 44:8: "unxit te Deus, Deus tuus oleo laetitiae prae consortibus tuis."

[281] "Et directus est spiritus domini in dauid a die illa et deinceps"..."reprobato saule." Froehlich, *Biblia Latina Cum Glossa Ordinaria*, 2:26.

[282] "upon Christ by the strength of his hand, because he conquered the devil, the world and desires, whereby he will come, the one longed for by all nations." "christum qui manu fortis quia diabolum et mundum vicit et desiderabilis. vnde veniet desideratus cunctis gentibus." Ibid.

glossator drew a parallel between David and Christ as anointed ones – Christ being the fulfillment of the prophecy that the Messiah would stem from the Davidic line.

Although he was the Lord's anointed, David was both the smallest and youngest of Jesse's clan, creating yet another contrast with Saul, who was taller than his peers. The glossator said Christians, like David, were the *minimus,* meaning of a younger faith than the Hebrews. The glossator in no way implied Christians were inferior to non-Christians, but made a vituperative claim that God favored Christians over Jews: "In rejecting the Jesse's elder sons, [God] chose the smallest for king, because in scorning the Judaic priesthood and the reign of the earlier people [i.e. Jews/the Synagoge], Christ the head was made king and priest of the lesser people [i.e. Christians/the Church]."[283] According to the glossator, David was the shepherd of Jewish people but Christ was the shepherd "of all nations."[284] David's strength as a divinely chosen leader extended to his power over evil spirits, which manifested in his ability, as a musician, to soothe Saul's madness with music. A gloss drawn from Gregory the Great distinguished between the two spirits at work in the human being: the spirit of God that was a "just power" acting in freedom, and the evil spirit that instilled a "wrongful wish" in the human heart.[285] Saul's madness potentially posed a challenge to belief in the efficacy of oil and anointing. Although both kings were anointed with holy oil, two different spirits

---

[283] "Reprobatis maioribus filiis Isai. minimus ad regnum eligitur . quia spreto iudaico sacerdotio. et regno prioris populi christus caput minoris populi rex et sacerdos factus est." Ibid. The Latin adjective *minor, minoris* carries the meanings: smaller, less, inferior; younger; descendants (in the plural form). The gloss plays on the connotation regarding physical stature, age, rank (inferior) as well as the idea of Christ/Christians being descendants of the Judaic people.

[284] "De officio pecorum factus est dauid rex hominum. christus autem ab ouili iudaicae plebis ad regnum gentium translatus est." Ibid.

[285] "Diabolus licet ad destructionem iustorum semper appetat: tametsi a Deo potestatem non accipit, ad temptationis articulum non convalescit. Unde omnis voluntas eius iniusta. Ex se enim temptare appetit, sed eos, qui temptandi sunt, et prout temptandi sunt: Deus iuste temptari permittit. Ideo idem spiritus et Domini appellatur, et malus: Domini - per licentiam iustae potestatis, malus - per desiderium iniustae voluntatis. Formidari ergo non debet qui nihil nisi permissus valet. Quamuis enim malignitas a domino non sit, potestas nisi a deo non est." My English translation is as follows: "The devil, to be sure, always desires the destruction of the just. Nevertheless, he does not receive the power from God and one would not recover from the moment of temptation. Hence every wish of his [the devil's] is wrongful. For by his nature he seeks to tempt, but only those who may be tempted and to such extent as they may be tempted, for God allows temptation provided that it is just. Therefore, both the spirit of the Lord and the evil spirit are called spirits: the one of the Lord through the freedom of just power, and the evil through the desire of the wrongful wish. Therefore, no one should fear the one [the Devil] who can do nothing unless he is permitted. For although the malice does not come from the Lord, there is no power unless it is given from God." Ibid.

worked within them: Saul was tormented by a "filthy spirit" that could only be allayed by David's

music, whose harmony and melodic order possessed the power to conquer demonic forces and to

soothe the spirit, allay suffering, heal wounds, and restore health to the mind and body.[286]

Job's Lament

The Book of Job contains a salient pericope that tells of oil miraculously pouring forth from

a rock, signifying a time of happiness, prosperity, and divine favor: "Who will grant me, that I might

be according to the months past, according to the days in which God kept me? … When I washed

my feet with butter, and the rock poured out for me rivers of oil?[287] The interlinear gloss for this

pericope draws a clear parallel between the miraculous flowing of oil and Christ: "Christ by whose

teaching, rivers flowed everywhere."[288] Another interlinear gloss for "rivers of oil" emphasized that

the oily rivers of Christ's speech (his teachings), anointed listeners, an idea consistent with the

glosses which appeared for the pericope of Jacob's ladder: Christ's words "flow quickly and

anoint."[289] The glossator drew from Gregory the Great's *Moralia in Iob*,[290] which included a long

exposition of the line: "When I washed my feet with butter and the rock poured out for me rivers of

oil."[291] The idea of Job's feet being washed with butter and anointed with oil may have been of

particular interest to medieval readers given the central role of footwashing in the liturgy of the

medieval Latin West.[292]

---

[286] For the music as *pharmakon*, something with the power to heal the sick, see Ciabattoni, *Dante's Journey to Polyphony*, 109–136; Froehlich, *Biblia Latina Cum Glossa Ordinaria*, 2:27.

[287] Job 29:2-6: "Quis mihi tribuat ut sim juxta menses pristinos, secundum dies quibus Deus custodiebat me? Quando lavabam pedes meos butyro, et petra fundebat mihi rivos olei." This image, of oil pouring forth from a rock, set the precedent for the oil flowing from Santa Maria in Trastevere (the Church as a rock). This parallel is most evident in Pietro Cavallini's mosaics. See Chapter 10.

[288] "Christus quo docente riui vbiquam manauerunt." Froehlich, *Biblia Latina Cum Glossa Ordinaria* 2:424.

[289] "predicamenta in tunc vnctionis quia currunt et vngunt." Ibid.

[290] Book 19, Ch.14-16.

[291] Job 29:6.

[292] As we will see in Chapter 3, the ritual footwashing took place on the first evening of the *Triduum* leading up to Easter. On Holy Thursday, after bishops consecrated holy oils in the afternoon and following the Mass celebrating the institution of the Eucharist and the Last Supper (*In Cena Domini*), prelates washed the feet of the members of their

In Gregory's *Moralia*, we see an image that would dominate medieval political and papal discourse: the body politic and the Church as a body of Christ with Christ as the head.[293] Gregory's text is noteworthy in how it depicted Christ and the Church as male and female components: the head and body, respectively. These two body parts unite, like spouses, to form one person.[294] Earliest Christian writers depicted the relationship between a cleric and his church as being like a marriage; the cleric or bishop was to remain in one place.[295] Discourse on medieval kingship likewise characterized the king as being united to his kingdom like to his spouse.[296] Rather confusingly, although Gregory depicted Christ as the head, he also said the whole person (head and body) was Christ's body. Gregory said that in the body of Christ, in which the feet were preachers: "Therefore whom do we understand to be the feet of the Lord, if not holy preachers?"[297] According to Gregory, the feet of these preachers were washed with oil because "the holy preachers are replete with the oiliness [*pinguedine*] of good works."[298] Again, we encounter the word *pinguedo,* which encompassed a range of meaning, including fat, fatness, oiliness, richness, abundance, fecundity, fullness, and exuberance.[299] This quality characterized the preachers of the Church, according to Gregory, insofar as their lives were full of good deeds, which washed away the "dust" that accumulated in preaching. By "dust" Gregory meant sins of expressing indignation toward others, furthering one's own self-

---

community during a rite called *Ad mandatum*, a ritual gesture of humility and self-sacrifice. The ritual actions imitated Jesus washing his own disciples' feet, after he himself had been washed and anointed with perfumed unguent by Mary Magdalene.

[293] See Chapter 9 for further discussion of this topic. Regarding the metaphor of the body politic, see John of Salisbury, *Policraticus*; de Pizan, *The Book of the Body Politic*.

[294] "Christum et Ecclesiam unam esse personam crebro jam diximus, illum videlicet hujus corporis caput, hanc autem illius capitis corpus." PL 76: Col.0110C.

[295] Ken Pennington, "A Short History of Canon Law," accessed on April 11, 2017, http://legalhistorysources.com/Canon%20Law/PenningtonShortHistoryCanonLaw.pdf

[296] Regarding the similarities and differences between secular and ecclesiastical rulers vis-à-vis being "wed" to a particular geographic domain, see Pennington, "Bishops and Their Dioceses." French kings later appropriated the image of marriage between the king and his kingdom. See James B. Collins (forthcoming book, Chapter 6).

[297] "Quos ergo pedes Domini, nisi sanctos praedicatores accipimus." PL 76: Col.0110C.

[298] "quia praedicatores sancti bonorum operum pinguedine replentur." Ibid.

[299] The verb *pinguesco, pinguescere* can likewise mean "to grow fat, become fertile" or "to become strong."

glorification or cultivating the favor of one's audience.[300] Gregory noted that the Apostles

themselves were also subject to such error and in need of foot washing, alluding of course to Jesus

washing the disciples' feet at the Last Supper.[301]

Rearranging Gregory's exposition on the meaning of the feet as preachers, the gloss for Job

29:6 initially omitted the discussion of the feet as preachers, but instead drew on a later section in

which Gregory interpreted the feet as the minor works carried out by the Lord's ministers. The

glossator, however, inverted the order of Gregory's exposition by first addressing the feet as minor

works of ministers and then moving on to the sins of the preachers and the need to wash their feet

of "dust":

> But those who are in charge [i.e. at the head], ought [to pay heed to] the voice of constant
> admonition to minister with so great a flowing of oiliness [*pinguedinis*], because even Job did
> so for his own. Indeed, the feet should be accustomed to being lacerated by the roughness
> of the path. The feet of the preachers of God, who are not without sin, are washed with
> butter, because the accumulated dust or glory in preaching is doused with the oiliness
> [*pinguedine*] of good works. Or, as it were, the wearied feet are anointed [*unguntur*] with butter,
> as long as the preachers, by good works, are pampered in ministering to one another, that is
> by delighting in [doing good works] more than by being given rewards.[302]

---

[300] "Nam quilibet praedicans, aut ad quantulamcunque indignationem trahitur, si contemnitur; aut ad aliquantulamcunque gloriam, si ab audientibus veneratur." PL 76: Col.0110C.

[301] "Unde et apostolis pedes loti sunt, ut a quamlibet parvo contagio in ipsa praedicatione contracto, quasi a quodam itinere collecto pulvere mundarentur." PL 76: Col.0110C-D.

[302] "Pedes ecclesiae sunt inferiorum operum ministri: qui domino ad vsus necessarios ea quae sunt exterius exercent: per extremum ministerium: velut pedes terrae inherent. Sed debent qui praesunt crebrae admonitionis voce infusionem pinguedinis talibus ministrare: quod et iob suis fecit. Solent enim pedes itineris asperitate lacerari. Pedes dei praedicatores qui non sine culpa: sed lauantur butiro, quia pinguedine boni operis infunditur et mundatur collectus puluis vel gloria praedicationis. Vel quasi fessi pedes butiro unguntur: dum praedicatores bonis operibus sibi ministrantium fouentur id est fructu magis quam dato. ita ex uoce capitis: Ex voce corporis pedes sunt qui exteriora ministrant." Froehlich, *Biblia Latina Cum Glossa Ordinaria* 2:424. The last few phrases are a distillation of a longer passage in the *Moralia*: "Datum quippe est res ipsa quae impenditur; fructus vero dati est, si benigna mente futurae mercedis studio aliquid impendatur. Ergo datum in re accipimus, fructum in corde. Et quia discipulorum suorum Apostolus mercede potius quam munere pascebatur, nequaquam datum, sed fructum se quaerere fatetur. Unde et subdidit protinus, dicens: *Habeo autem omnia, et abundo.* Butyro ergo lavantur pedes, cum praedicatores sancti, ut diximus, ipsa praedicatione fatigati, auditorum suorum bonis operibus foventur. Fessos namque pedes butyro unxerat ille qui audiebat: *Viscera sanctorum requieverunt per te, frater* (Philem. 7). Hoc butyro unctus fuerat pes qui in catena tenebatur, dicens: *Det misericordiam Dominus Onesiphori domui; quia saepe me refrigeravit, et catenam meam non erubuit* (I Tim. II, 16). Si ergo ex voce capitis haec verba pensamus, recte pedes, sicut dictum est, praedicatores accipimus." PL 76: Col.0111B-C.

For Job, having one's feet anointed with butter was a sign of great prosperity and divine favor.

Gregory does not suggest, however, that the ministers of the Church should seek to be indulged

with luxury, but rather should serve one another – the central theme of the medieval *Ad mandatum*

foot-washing ritual. Following the gloss about the feet being the ministers of God or the good

works carried out by those ministers, the glossator turned to clarifying the meaning of the

miraculous oil pouring forth from Job's rock. Drawing again on the *Moralia*, the glossator briefly

noted that the rivers of oil were symbols for the outpouring of Christ's words: "because in [the

rivers of oil] preaching about Christ's interior anointing flows outward. The rivers of oil spouting

from this rock [are] the books of the evangelists – or the rivers of oil mean the gifts of the Spirit."[303]

This gloss is a condensation of a longer exposition by Gregory on the meaning of the oil, which

would have likely been familiar to medieval readers and glossators.

> In the Church the rivers of oil are either sacred dogma or the grace of the Holy Spirit …
> From this rock, a river of oil gushed forth: the book of Matthew, the book of Mark, the
> book of Luke, and the book of John. In diverse parts of this world the Lord spread the
> preachings. This rock poured out, through the mouths of all the Apostles, so many rivers of
> oil…Anyone who is dipped in these [rivers] is anointed; whoever is anointed [*ungitur*], is
> strengthened [*impinguatur*] within.[304]

Gregory's text established how reading scripture was akin to being anointed with holy oil from

within. Instead of receiving a physical anointing, readers were anointed invisibly or spiritually.

---

[303] "Et petra fundebat michi ri.o.[sic] quia in ea christi praedicamenta intimae unctionis emanant De hac petra riui olei exierunt euangelistarum libri. Vel riuos olei dona spiritus dicit." Ibid.

[304] "*In Ecclesia rivi olei sunt vel sacra dogmata, vel sancti Spiritus gratia.*---Quia petrae nomine Christus accipitur, praedicator egregius fatetur, dicens: *Petra autem erat Christus* (I Cor. X, 4). Quae videlicet petra nunc ad usum sanctae Ecclesiae olei rivos fundit, quia in ea loquens Dominus, praedicamenta unctionis intimae emanat. De hac petra olei rivus exiit, liber Matthaei, liber Marci, liber Lucae, et liber Joannis. In diversis hujus mundi partibus quod praedicamenta edidit, tot petra haec per ora apostolorum omnium olei rivos fudit. Toties adhuc de petra hac olei rivus funditur, quoties a sancto Spiritu [Col.0112D] ungendis mentibus auditorum ea quae in libris veteribus de Christo dicta sunt explanantur. Et rivi vocantur olei, 617 quia decurrunt et ungunt. In quibus quisquis tingitur ungitur, quisquis ungitur interius [Col.0113A] impinguatur [*Vet. XIII*]." PL 76: Col. 0112D – 0113A. One could also say that anointing "oiled" the anointed interiorly. *Impinguatur*, however, carries the meaning of strengthening, which corresponds to the sacraments of confirmation, or strenthening.

Gregory found a source of oil, not just in the Gospels, which flowed like rivers of oil, but also in the

Hebrew Scriptures, which were themelves textual *fontes olei*. According to Gregory, contemplating

Scripture had the power to liberate the oppressed, who could be cognizant of God's providential

care:

> Without doubt, concerning such oiliness [*pinguedine*], the Psalmist said: In the same way, let
> my soul be filled with fat and oiliness [*pinguedine*]. By 'oil,' the unction of the Holy Spirit can
> be signified, about which was said by the prophet: "the yoke decays through the presence of
> oil." (Isaiah 10:27) Naturally the yoke decays through the presence of oil when we are
> anointed by the grace of the Holy Spirit. We are liberated from the slavery of our captivity,
> provided that the overbearing domination of the evil spirit is repelled. The yoke, by which
> the neck of our liberty was pressed down, is crushed."[305]

The people freed from the oppressive yoke of tyranny were, according to Gregory, 'sons of oil' –

those had been liberated from earlier trials or oppressions:

> About this streaming of oil is written: 'My beloved made a vineyard in a fertile place
> (literally: 'son of oil').[306] (Isaiah 5:1) Of course, 'the son of oil' means the people of faith,
> created for faith in God through the internal anointing of the Holy Spirit. Therefore the holy
> Church, then oppressed by many tribulations, now has the preaching gifts and miracles of
> the Spirit, that she may recall in memory, and may lament her silence, saying: *The rock poured
> out rivers of oil for me.*[307]

---

[305] "De qua nimirum pinguedine Psalmista ait: *Sicut adipe et pinguedine repleatur anima mea* (Psal. LXII, 6). Potest nomine olei ipsa sancti Spiritus unctio designari, de qua per prophetam dicitur: *Computrescit jugum a facie olei* (Isai. X, 27). Jugum quippe a facie olei computrescit, quia dum sancti Spiritus gratia ungimur, a captivitatis nostrae servitute liberamur: dumque maligni spiritus dominatio superba repellitur, jugum conteritur, quo libertatis nostrae colla premebantur." PL 76: Col. 0112D – 0113A

[306] In the Latin Vulgate, this line reads: "Vinea facta est dilecto meo in cornu filio olei." The Douay-Rheims translates this phrase: "My beloved had a vineyard on a hill in a fruitful place." The NSRV translates it as: "My beloved had a vineyard on a very fertile hill." No direct mention of oil is made in these translations. The 'son of oil,' nevertheless, appears to represent fecundity or fruitfulness.

[307] "De hoc cursus oleo scriptum est: *Vinea facta est dilecto meo in cornu filio olei* (Isai. V, 1). Filius quippe olei, fidelis populus dicitur qui ad fidem Dei interna sancti Spiritus unctione generatur. Multis ergo tunc sancta Ecclesia tribulationibus depressa, dona Spiritus, et mira quae nunc habet praedicamenta, ad memoriam revocet, et suum silentium deploret, dicens: *Petra fundebat mihi rivos olei.* PL 76: Col. 0113A-B.

For Gregory, the oil brought about a distinct interior strengthening that accompanied liberation –

symbolized by the dissolved yoke. The sermons of preachers were, like oil itself, conduits of the

power that pacified and allayed suffering within the human body and the human soul. The words of

preachers spread faith throughout the Latin West during periods of tribulation. Oil was a sign of

God's providential care and presence in the midst of desolation.

Oil in the Psalms

In the medieval Latin West, no biblical texts would have been more familiar to medieval

Christian authors than the Psalms, which monks chanted in choir each day, singing through the

entire Psalter each week. The Psalms contain rich imagery of oil and anointing that convey a sense

of God's providence and the fulfillment of a promise foretold through prophecy. Glossators

invoked some verses, such as Psalm 44:8, in disparate glosses of biblical pericopes. Sung within

monastic communities during the liturgy of the hours, the Psalms were foundational texts for

medieval perceptions of oil and anointing.[308]

The *prothemata* (introductory themes) to the Psalms in Rusch's *Glossa Ordinaria* consisted of

an amalgamation of Augustine (354-430), Jerome (347-420), Cassiodorus (c. 485-585) and Remigius

of Auxerre (c.437-533).[309] These *prothemata* differ, however, from a text that evidently also served as a

preface to the Psalms in numerous medieval psalters. This second text attests to the "power of the

---

[308] For the development of medieval psalm exegesis see Marcia L. Colish, "Psalterium Scholasticorum: Peter Lombard
and the Emergence of Scholastic Psalms Exegesis," *Speculum* 67, no. 03 (1992): 531–48; Patrizia Stoppacci, "Le *Glossae
Continuae in Psalmos* di Pietro Lombardo. *Status Quaestionis*: studi pregressi e prospettive di ricerca," in *Pietro Lombardo: Atti
del XLIII Convegno Storico Internazionale, Todi 8-10 Ottobre 2006.* Enrico Memestò, ed. Atti Dei Convegni Del Centro
Italiano Si Studi Sul Basso Medioevo, n.s.20 (Spoleto: Centro Italiano di Studi sull'Alto Medioevo, 2007), 289–331;
Andrew B. Kraebel, "John of Rheims and the Psalter-Commentary Attributed to Ivo II of Chartres," *Revue Bénédictine*
122, no. 2 (2012): 252–93; Thomas J. Renna, "The Psalms in Early Medieval Theology," *Michigan Academician: Papers of the
Michigan Academy of Science, Arts, and Letters* 28, no. 1 (1996): 1–10.
[309] In the introduction to Rusch's *editio princeps*, Froehlich notes: "The prolegomena to the Psalter belong to a complex
and ancient tradition, some form of which normally precedes any twelfth-century Psalter. Both series of prolegomena
are thus appropriate to their context, but not peculiar to the Glossed Bible." Gibson, "Introduction" in *Biblia Latina Cum
Glossa Ordinaria*, 1:ix.

Psalms" according to Augustine.[310] Minge attributed the text to Bruno of Würzburg.[311] The litany

does not appear in Augustine's *Enarrationes in Psalmos* or in the *prothemata* for Rusch's *editio princeps*.

Nevertheless, whoever penned or compiled the text described the power of the Psalms as being,

among other things, like "the oil of compassion." Both the *prothemata* in Rusch and the litany

attesting to the Psalms' power reveal a conceptual link between oil, prophecy and salvation.

The *prothemata* to the Psalms in Rusch drew a correlation between oil and prophetic vision

induced by the Holy Spirit.[312] Prior to a discussion of oil, the *prothemata* addressed how prophecy, as

inspiration or divine revelation, was given to human beings through human works, human births,

angelic speech, prophetic sight, dreams, a heavenly voice from a cloud, or through the Holy Spirit.[313]

Following this discussion of the nature of prophecy, the author of the *prothemata* turned to a

discussion of holy oil. Drawing on Jerome's *Commentary on the Minor Prophets,* the glossator cited the

Hebraic origin of chrism, the methods of anointing Hebrew kings and the spiritual anointing that

superceded these previous royal anointings.[314] The author of the *Glossa* text claimed, however, that

royal anointings preceded priestly anointings, all of which originated with Christ.[315] First, however,

the author of the *prothemata* described the Hebrews who fled Egypt as Christians (by virtue of having

---

[310] "Incipiunt dicta sancti augustini de virtute psalmorum canticum psalmorum." This introductory litany appears in PL, as well as "BAV Arch.S.Pietro E 14"; "BSB Clm 13067."

[311] See PL 142: Col.0046A. I have yet to determine if he is really the author.

[312] See Chapters 8-10 regarding prophecies of Christ's birth and Santa Maria in Trastevere's *fons olei*.

[313] "Prophetia est inspiratio vel reuelatio diuina quae euentus rerum vel per facta. vel per dicta. immobili veritate pronunciat. vnde prophetia visio propheta videns. Multis autem modis haec gratia data est. vel per operationes hominum vt fuit arca noe. et sacrificium abrae et transitus maris rubri. Vel per natiuitates: vt esan et iacob qui futura significabant. Vel per loquentes angelos: sicut locuti sunt abrae. loth. et aliis. Vel provisiones: sicut ysaiae et ezechieli. et caeteris. Vel per somnia: sicut salmoni ioseph et danieli. Vel pro nubem et vocem de caelo: vt moysi. Vel adhuc aliis modis. Dauid autem nullo horum. sed caelesti aspiratione intus edoctus spiritu in eo loquente completus est. vt in libro regum: directus est spiritus domini in dauid. et dominus. si dauid in spiritu vocat eum dominum. quomodo filius eius est. Spiritus autem sanctus sic datus est prophetis vt aliquando pro peccatis recederet: et placatus rediret. Et sicut ait petrus non voluntate humana allata est aliquando prophetia: sed spiritu sancto inspirati locuti sunt sancti homines dei. non sunt autem illi a munere prophetiae alieni quibus data est facultas intelligendi vel interpretandi scripturas."
Froehlich, *Biblia Latina Cum Glossa Ordinaria* 2:457.

[314] LLT: CPL 0589.

[315] Regarding the question of whether priestsly anointing preceeded or followed royal anointing see Chapter 1; Fleming, "The Biblical Tradition of Anointing Priests"; Jacobson, *"Sicut Samuel Unxit David"*; Bouman, "Sacring and Crowning"; Ellard, *Ordination Anointings in the Western Church before 1000 A.D*; Nelson, "National Synods, Kingship as Office, and Royal Anointing"; Enright, *Iona, Tara, and Soissons.*

been anointed) and distinguished between the kinds of vessels used to anoint various figures in the

Hebrew Bible, suggesting perhaps a controversy in the author's own time regarding a variety of

anointing rituals or oils. According to the glossator, the kings David and Salomon were anointed

with the horn of oil while Jehu and Hazael are anointed with an earthen vessel.

> Many born of Christian patriarchs were called of Christ, thus 'do not touch my anointed.'[316]
> The parables tell of all the Christians who came out of Egypt. Chrism [*chrisma*] may be in
> Exodus, from which priests are anointed. Kings are anointed with another ointment, but
> these two manners [exist] because even if David has a strong arm and Salomon is peaceful,
> each is anointed with the horn. If Jehu and Hazael [are anointed] with the *lenticula*, it is
> because it is an earthen vessel...[317]

After addressing the anointing of kings, the author described the "prophetic ointment" with which

the prophet Elijah anointed Elisha and stated that Christ was anointed with a superior "spiritual

unguent.."[318] Alluding to the anointing of the king *prae consortibus suis* described in Psalm 44:8, the

author of the *prothemata* stated: "Above all things is the spiritiual unguent, because it is called the 'oil

of exaltation' by which Christ was anointed in front of the participants who have the chrism of

baptism..."[319] The passage about the genealogy of oil concludes with a discussion of the oil used to

---

[316] This is an allusion to Psalm 104: "Nolite tangere christos meos, et in prophetis meis nolite malignari." English translation: "Do not touch my anointed and do no evil to my prophets."

[317] "'Multa genera sunt christorum Patriarchae dicti sunt christi. vt nolite tangere christos meos. In parabolis dicuntur christi omnes qui de aegipto egresssi sunt. Chrisma in exodo sit. vnde sacerdotes vncti. Est aliud vnguentum quo reges inunguntur: sed hoc duobus modis. quia si dauid est et salomon id est fortis manu et pacificus: vngitur cornu. Si hieu et azael lenticula. quod est vas fictile." The anointing of David and Solomon with the horn of oil (*cornu*) appears in 1 Kings (1 Samuel) 16:13: "Tulit ergo Samuel cornu olei, et unxit eum in medio fratrum ejus" and 3 Kings (1 Kings) 1:39: "Sumpsitque Sadoc sacerdos cornu olei de tabernaculo, et unxit Salomonem et cecinerunt buccina, et dixit omnis populus: Vivat rex Salomon!" The anointing of Jehu the son of Jehoshaphat appears in 4 Kings (2 Kings) 9:1-3 includes a *lenticula*, a lentil-shaped earthen vessel mentioned above instead of a horn (*cornu*): "Tenensque lenticulam olei fundes super caput ejus, et dices: Haec dicit Dominus: Unxi te regem super Israel." God commands Elijah to anoint Hazael and Jehu, the son of Namsi, as kings of Syria and Israel respectively in 3 Kings (1 Kings) 19:15-16. This passage also includes instructions for Elija to anoint Eliseus son of Saphat of Abelmeula prophet. No mention is made, however, of the vessel: "Et ait Dominus ad eum [Elija]: Vade, et revertere in viam tuam per desertum in Damascum: cumque perveneris illuc, unges Hazael regem super Syriam Et Jehu filium Namsi unges regem super Israel: Eliseum autem filium Saphat, qui est de Abelmeula, unges prophetam pro te."

[318] 3 Kings 19:16-19.

[319] "Sed cyrus rex persarum et medorum qui israel relaxauit. christus est. secundum illud. haec dicit dominus christo meo cyro. quod non sinunt sequentia de saluatore accipi. vt quidam putant. Est vnguentum propheticum quo precipitur

anoint lepers, interpreting the oil of baptism as an extension of the oil once used by the Hebrew priests to cure lepers of leprosy as recorded in the Book of Levitius.[320] If the oil failed to cure the leper on the first try, he could always be anointed again. From the oil of lepers, the author traced the origin of the anointing oil back through time to Christ himself, the source or origin of all oils:

> [The leper] himself may be called the Lord's Anoited {Christ of God}...the same man who is frequently anointed may not be the occasion of ruin through negligence. For it suffices for the leper that even if after the first anointing he is lost, he may be anointed again. The person anointed often always benefits. And from the oil of lepers, we come to the unguent of the people, from thenceforth to the priesthood, whence to the chrism of the pontiff, from the pontiff to the king, from the king to the patriarchs, from the patriachs to Christ.[321]

Thus in tracing the hierarchy of anointings from low to high, the author began with lepers and ended with Christ. Worthy of note are the different kinds of oil attributed to the different groups: lepers were anointed with plain oil (*oleo leprosi*), the people with unguent (*unguentum populi*), and pontiffs with chrism (*chrisma pontificis*), the most precious of the oils.

The *prothemata* to the Psalms then further elaborate the relationship between anointing, prophecy and Christ. Directly following Jerome's discussion of the geneology of anointings, the glossator returned to a discussion of prophecy, using salvific births to illustrate the various kinds of prophecy which exist: "...another kind of prophecy exists according to the foreknowledge of God, which must of necessity be fulfilled in every manner, such as 'behold the virgin will conceive etc.'"[322]

---

haeliae vt vngat heliseum in prophetam. Super omnia est vnguentum spirituale. quod dicitur oleum exultationis. quo christus vnctus est prae participibus. qui habent chrisma baptismi..." Froehlich, *Biblia Latina Cum Glossa Ordinaria,* 2:457.

[320] Lev 14:10-18.

[321] "quod si perdat quis non desperet: quia de reparando chrismate scribitur in leuitico. quod cum lepra alicuius fuerit mundata. mittat ei sacerdos oleum in manu sinistra. et caetera quae ibi dicuntur. et ipse vocetur christus. dei. hoc autem restat quod idem homo frequenter vngitur ne sit occasio ruinae negligenti. Sufficit enim leproso vt post primum vnguentum perditum vngatur secundo. Hoc ille saepe vngitur: qui semper proficit: et de oleo leprosi venit ad vnguentum populi. inde ad sacerdotale. de quo ad chrisma pontificis. a pontifice ad regem. a rege ad patriarchas. a patriarchis ad christum." Froehlich, *Biblia Latina Cum Glossa Ordinaria,* 2:457.

[322] "Sicut prophetia sit diversis modis. ita et diuersis temporibus. Est igitur alia de praesenti. vt elizabeth unde mihi hoc vt veniat mater domini etcetera. De praeterito vt moyses. In principio c.d.c. et t. De futuro: vt ecce virgo concipiet

An excerpt drawn from Cassiodorus addressed the ambiguity inherent in prophecy and the absence

of temporal distinctions where the Holy Spirit was concerned.[323] If prophecy was given through the

Holy Spirit and one was imbued with the Holy Spirit through anointing, the conceptual link between

oil and prophecy in the minds of medieval exegetes is clear. The sayings about the Psalms attributed

to Augustine further corroborate the correlation between oil and prophecy in the minds of medieval

Europeans:

> Here begin the sayings of Saint Augustin concerning the power of the Psalms: it adorns the
> soul; invites angels to help; drives away demons; expels darkness; brings about sanctity...
> flows like the throne [soothes like oil]; offends the devil; extinguishes carnal desire [reveals
> God; extinguishes carnal pleasures]; is the oil of compassion; oracle of joy; elect portion of
> angels...similar to honey; musical song of psalms, chosen in the presence of God. Expels
> every sin...grants royal power over the earth; draws the soul high...[324]

The coupling of the "oil of compassion" with "oracle of joy" reveals the correspondence between

anointing and prophecy. Furthermore, since prophecy also coincided with predictions about salvific

births, we can better understand why medieval Christians believed that the oil flowing from the *fons

olei* in Rome was a prophetic sign of Christ's birth. Oil, whose power was akin to that of the Psalms,

manifested God's presence in the world and restored right order to chaotic, sinful earthly existence,

fulfilling the prophecy of old.

---

etcetera. Item prophetia alia est secundum praescientiam dei quam necesse est omnibus modis impleri. vt ecce virgo
concipiet etcetera. Alia secundum comminationem. vt quadraginta dies et ninine subuertetur." Ibid.

[323] "Note, therefore, that the prophet speaks differently, sometimes concerning future things as if concerning present
things, sometimes concerning past things and even sometimes particularly regarding the future, because he says
everything according to the consecrating Holy Spirit, for whom all things are known without respect to the past or the
future, as if in the present." "Notandum igitur quod propheta aliquando loquitur in discrete de futuris quasi de
praesentibus. Aliquando de proteritis. Aliquando etiam proprie de futuris. quod ideo sit quoniam omnia dicante spiritu
sancto dicit: cui sunt omnia nota sine proterita sine futura tanquam praesentia." Ibid.

[324] "Incipiunt dicta sancti augustini de virtute psalmorum. animas decorat. Inuitat angelos in adiutorum. Effugat
demones. Expellit tenebras. Efficit sanctitatem. Homini peccatori refectio mentis est. Delet peccata. Similis est
elemosinis. Sanctorum auget fidem. Sic sol illuminat. Sic aqua sanctificat. Sic ignis esurit. Sic solium defluit [oleum
lenificat]. Diabolum offendit. Voluntatem carnalem extinguit. [Deum ostendit, voluptates carnales exstinguit] Oleum
misericordie est. Sors laetitiae. Pars angelorum electa....Similis est melli. Canticum psalmorum carmen electum est apud
deum. Omne peccatum expellit...[fol.10v] Regnum super terram dat. edium anime trabit..." "Arch.S.Pietro E 14," n.d.,
fol.10r-v. NB: text in brackets appears in PL but not in Arch.S.Pietro E 14.

Psalm 22

While the Psalms do not always testify to the prophetic powers imparted through oil, they

consistently portray oil as a sign of God's presence and providential care. The glosses reinforced the

idea of a spiritual anointing affecting the mind more than the body. Psalm 22 contains the well-

known verse: "You prepare a table before me in the presence of my enemies; you anoint my head

with oil; my cup overflows."[325] In Rusch, the interlinear glosses for this psalm emphasized the

spiritual nature of the oil and the mental joy that accompanied anointing. The glossator interpreted

"You anointed my head with oil" as "you delighted the mind with spiritual joy."[326] The oil signified

"spiritual grace" which God bestowed, not on the physical body, but on the "mind."[327] As if echoing

Gregory the Great's idea that the words of Christ anointed the minds of readers or listeners, the

glossator for this psalm interpreted the "head" as the mind, which received spiritual grace (oil). The

glossator further interpreted the anointed head to be the head of Christ, which in turn nourished the

other members of the "body" – presumably the Church.

The gloss for Psalm 22 also alluded to Augustine's gloss of Psalm 132, which extols the

beauty of people living together in unity and depicts oil as a life-giving liquid. For Psalm 132, the

Psalmist used the image of holy oil to convey the nature of religious harmony among the Israelites:

"Behold, how good and pleasant it is for brethren to dwell together in unity! It is like the precious

oil upon the head that ran down upon the beard, the beard of Aaron, running over the collar of his

robes."[328] Oil runs down Aaron's beard to the edge of his robe, like the "dew of Hermon"

descended on Mount Sion.[329] Just as the snow that descends on a snow-capped mountain

---

[325] "Parasti in conspectu meo mensam, adversus eos qui tribulant me; impinguasti in oleo caput meum; et calix meus inebrians quam praeclarus est!" Psalm 22:5.

[326] "Impinguasti in oleo caput meum" Froehlich, *Biblia Latina Cum Glossa Ordinaria,* 2:481. "Letificasti spirituali leticia mentem." Ibid.

[327] "spirituali gratia" and "mentem." Ibid.

[328] Psalm 132:1-2.

[329] Hermon is a snow-capped mountain on the border between Syria, Lebanon and Israel. The "dew of Hermon" likely refers to snow which was the only precipitation in an otherwise parched region. The "dew of Hermon" might also

transforms into water that flows through rivers to water a dry land, so the love between individuals

could extend outward to society at large. In his commentary on the Psalms, *Enarrationes in Psalmos*,

Augustine interpreted the oil of Psalm 132 to be the divine nature of God, which flowed first to

priests and then to the entire Christian community.[330] The oil, like the unity among brothers,

imparted "blessing and life forevermore."[331]

The medieval gloss for Psalm 22 picked up on the theme of oil as a nourishing, hydrating

liquid that eliminated the spiritual dryness created by sin or discord: "The…anointing of the head

evidently is of Christ, who did not dry up through the drought of sin. From Christ the other

members flourished, because the ointment descended to the beard of Aaron and to the edge of his

vestments."[332] The idea that salvation was characterized by the presence of moisture rather than

dryness also appeared in the writings of Bonaventure (1221-1274), who explained the great quantity

of liquid gushing from the *fons olei* in Rome as consistent with a God who saves through an

abundance of liquid rather than drought.[333]

Medieval glossators, however, were not simply interested in moisture in a material sense.

Two manuscripts, both glossed psalters, echo the interlinear glosses found in Rusch with some

significant additions and variations. Vat.lat. 4946, an eleventh or twelfth century glossed psalter of

Italian provenance, includes a gloss in which the oil represents the "grace or compassion of the Holy

Spirit."[334] According to the glossator, the grace of the Holy Spirit manifested God making his

---

suggest the descent of the Ten Commandments on Mount Sinai or Mount Horeb, neither of which have been definitively defined geographically.

[330] J.P. Minge, *Patrologia Latina*, Col.1218B-C, 1219A.

[331] Psalm 132.

[332] "Octaua vnctio capitis scilicet christi quod nulla ariditate peccati exaruit. vnde caetera laetantur membra. quia a capite descendit vnguentum in barbam aaron et in oram vestimenti eius." Froehlich, *Biblia Latina Cum Glossa Ordinaria*, 2:481. The "eighth anointing" (octaua vnctio) may refer to the anointing of David, the eighth son of Jesse.

[333] See Chapter 10.

[334] "per oleum spiritus sancti gratiam uel misericordiam figuramus. " "BAV Vat.lat. 4946," fol.26v. For a catalog description of Vat.lat.4946, see Salmon, *Les manuscrits liturgiques latins de la Bibliothèque vaticane*. No.91 (Psalterium Glossatum).

faithful fruitful or full of delight.[335] The gloss for "my chalice which inebriates me, how goodly it is"
further emphasized the spiritual nature of oil and wine.[336] Holy men became drunk through
imbibing scripture: "The chalice of the Lord is understood to be divine scripture; moreover in this
spiritual men become inebriated."[337] Regin.lat.33, a twelfth-century glossed psalter elaborated on the
effects of spiritual inebriation: the wine of scripture infuses the minds of holy men with an oblivion,
in which they forget vain pleasures.[338] Thus for the medieval Christian, tangible liquids, such as wine
and oil, represented non-material forces that had the power to transform the individual who was the
beloved elect or anointed.

Psalm 44

The glosses for Psalm 44 likewise cast oil as a sign of God's providential care and further
emphasized the status of the anointed as divinely chosen. Psalm 44 includes the line of text which
glossators disseminated throughout *Glossa Ordinaria* when oil appeared: "You loved justice and
hated iniquity; therefore God, your God, anointed you with the oil of gladness beyond your
companions."[339] A number of glossed psalters present interpretations of this line which differ from
the glosses in Rusch.[340] In Rusch, the interlinear gloss of "You loved" (*delixisti*) referred to the
previous line, "Thy throne, O God, is for ever and ever: the sceptre of thy kingdom is a sceptre of
uprightness," correlating "love" with "truly of rightness."[341] The gloss asserted that God delighted
not only in justice among his own but also among others: "You love justice not only among one's

---

[335] "spiritus sancti gratiam intende meam letificasti" "BAV Vat.lat. 4946," fol. 26v. Like *impinguare*, the Latin verb
laetificare has a range of meanings, including: fertilize, enrich, make fruitful, delight, cheer, gladden, rejoice.
[336] English translation from Douay-Rheims.
[337] "Calix domini diuinae scripturae intelliguntur. Hic autem spirituales uiri inebriantur." "BAV Vat.lat. 4946," fol.26v.
[338] "dans oblivionem vanarum delectationum." "BAV Regin.lat.33," 28r. Then the glossator adds: "Non a calix Christi
sanguis qui sic inebriat ut sobrio{s} reddat." "Regin.lat.33," fol.28r.
[339] "Dilexisti justitiam, et odisti iniquitatem; propterea unxit te Deus, Deus tuus, oleo laetitiae, prae consortibus tuis."
Psalm 44:8. This line was evidently so well-known to medieval readers it often appeared in abbreviated form. See notes
above.
[340] "BAV Reg.lat.13"; "BAV Regin.lat.33"; "BSB Clm 22017"; "BSB Clm 14501."
[341] Psalm 44:7: "*Sedes tua, Deus, in saeculum saeculi; virga directionis virga regni tui.*" Froehlich, *Biblia Latina Cum Glossa
Ordinaria*, 2:509.

own, in you, but also in others."[342] Hating iniquity was a requisite for loving justice: "otherwise justice is not perfectly loved."[343] Furthermore, hate directed toward men was distinct from hate directed toward iniquity itself. Reg.lat.33 likewise included such a gloss, distinguishing hatred of iniquity from hatred of iniquitous human beings.[344] God anointed people so they themselves might love and hate as God did.[345] Those who received the anointing were among the elect. God anointed human beings so they could be God-like, since in the Incarnation, God became human: "God is man...'man' signifies 'king and priest.'"[346] Repeating ideas of Augustine regarding anointing and the Trinity, the gloss said the God who anointed his elect was not Jesus, the human being, but rather the omnipotent "Father."[347] Having thus addressed the roles of the first two Persons of the Trinity, the gloss explicated the role of the Third Person: the Holy Spirit was oil itself.

As in other glosses we have seen, "oil" in this context indicated a spiritual anointing. The "oil of gladness" [*oleo laetitiae*] has a distinctly non-material effect: one was anointed "for purity of conscience and fullness of grace."[348] Reg.lat. 13 included an interlinear gloss above "oleo laetitiae" indicating that the oil was distinctly spiritual: "spirituali oleo."[349] According to the psalm, God anointed his beloved amidst or in front of companions [*prae consortibus tuis*].[350] The Douay-Rheims translation interprets this phrase to mean "above thy fellows," emphasizing the elect character of the anointed rather than the communal context in which the anointing took place. The gloss, however, prioritized the presence of Jesus' disciples, who received the spiritual benefits of Christ from whom grace flowed like oil. In the gloss, the companions signify "the Apostles or others on whom the

---

[342] "non solum in suis in te. sed etiam in aliis diligis iusticiam." Ibid.

[343] "Aliter non perfecte diligitur iusticia." Ibid.

[344] "BAV Regin.lat.33," fol.58v.

[345] "unxit - vt diligeres iusticiam et odires iniquitatem." Froehlich, *Biblia Latina Cum Glossa Ordinaria*, 2:509.

[346] "te - Quia homo deus. Secundum hominem regem et sacerdotem significat." Ibid.

[347] The glosses corresponding to "Deus deus tuus" correlate the first "Deus" with "O" meaning "omnipotens," while "Deus tuus" signifies "Pater" alluding to the formula "Pater omnipotens aeterna deus." Ibid.

[348] "pro puritate conscienti[a]e et plenitudine grati[a]e." Ibid.

[349] "spirituali oleo." "BAV Reg.lat.13," fol.20r.

[350] Psalm 44:8.

unction of grace may have flowed from him [Christ]."[351] Furthermore, Reg.lat.33 interpreted the

companions to signify "man, king, and priest."[352] Thus, Christ was not the only "Anointed One" - so

too were his companions, reaffirming the idea set forward in the gloss of Psalm 132: the oil which

flowed from the head of the High Priest (Aaron/Christ) spread outward to the other members (the

companions).

The grace bestowed by unction allowed an individual to transcend the material, physical

realm. The next line of the psalm, one of most sumptuous in the psalter, speaks of the clothes of the

anointed elect as being fragrant with precious perfumes: "your robes are all fragrant with myrrh and

aloes and cassia."[353] Myrrh, which emanated from the anointed's clothes, represented "mortification

of the flesh," alluding perhaps to the use of myrrh in burial customs or asceticism that entailed dying

to physical pleasures while still alive. The gloss corresponding to "aloes" [*gutta*] said the aromas

signified "the good odors of the virtues, whence we are the odor of Christ through good [works]."[354]

This reference was to 2 Corinthians 2:15-16: "For we are the aroma of Christ to God among those

who are being saved and among those who are perishing; to the one a fragrance from death to

death, to the other a fragrance from life to life."[355] Furthermore, the fragrances wafting from the

anointed one also correspond to "humility" and "faith" which ideally emanated from Christians as

God's anointed ones.[356]

In Rusch's edition of the *Glossa*, the marginal gloss on the meaning of the anointing in Psalm

44 was brief, yet tied in with other glosses, indicating that perhaps the *Glossa Ordinaria* may have

---

[351] "Apostolis et aliis in quos ab eo vnctio gratie efflueret." Froehlich, *Biblia Latina Cum Glossa Ordinaria*, 2:509.

[352] "sed hominem regem et sacerdotem significat." "BAV Regin.lat.33," fol.59r.

[353] NSRV Psalm 44:9.

[354] "boni odores virtutum his aromatibus signantur vnde .christi boniis odor sumus." Froehlich, *Biblia Latina Cum Glossa Ordinaria*, 2:509.

[355] "Quia Christi bonus odor sumus Deo in iis qui salvi fiunt, et in his qui pereunt. Aliis quidem odor mortis in mortem: aliis autem odor vitae in vitam." 2 Cor. 2:15-16. English translation from NSRV.

[356] The marginal gloss in Reg. lat. 13, however, suggests something different: "istis dico difluentibus a vestimentis tuis id est apostolis qui orant deum [agendibus?] eburneis. Exposino exquibus id est ex mirra et gutta et ceteris. delectauerunt te filiae regum." "BAV Reg.lat.13," fol.20r.

been a trigger for the memory or a tool pointing toward other texts (either memorized or in familiar

codices) rather than a self-standing work of exegesis. The gloss included just two points from

Augustine's exposition on Psalm 44. The first made an obsure reference to Greek naming and

signification.[357] In Augustine's exposition of this line from the psalm, he stressed the spiritual nature

of anointing and argued that the person anointed was none other than Christ. This passage

influenced later authors' interpretations of oil and served as the basis for medieval biblical and

liturgical commentary.

> Therefore, God, Your God, has anointed You...observe in what way he expresses
> himself. Therefore, God, Your God, has anointed You: i.e. God has anointed You,
> O God. God is anointed by God...Who then is the God that is anointed by God? Let
> the Jews tell us; these Scriptures are common to us and them. It was God, who
> was anointed by God: you hear of an Anointed one; understand it to mean Christ.[358]

Augustine then explicated the origin of the name 'Christ,' attributing the name to the anointing Jesus

received. Furthermore, Augustine explains that not coincidentally were kings and prophets anointed

in the place where prophesies had predicted the advent of a messiah:

> For the name of "Christ" comes from "chrism"; this name by which He is
> called "Christ" expresses "unction": nor were kings and prophets anointed in any kingdom,
> in any other place, save in that kingdom where Christ was prophesied of, where He was
> anointed, and from whence the Name of Christ was to come. It is found nowhere else at all:
> in no one nation or kingdom.[359]

---

[357] "His ponitur in greco aperte alter vocatinus. alter nominatinus." Froehlich, *Biblia Latina Cum Glossa Ordinaria* 2:509. This gloss may correspond to Augustine's line: "Etenim in latino putatur idem casus nominis repetitus: in graeco autem evidentissima distinctio est, quia unum nomen est quod compellatur, et alterum ab eo qui compellat: *Unxit te, Deus.* O tu *Deus, unxit te Deus tuus.*" Augustine, *Enarrationes in Psalmos,* Psalm 44, accessed on February 18, 2015, http://www.augustinus.it/latino/esposizioni_salmi/index2.htm.

[358] Augustine, *Expositions on the Psalms,* Psalm 44 (45), English translation by J.E. Tweed, accessed on April 11, 2017, http://www.newadvent.org/fathers/1801045.htm.

[359] Ibid.

Finally, in his discussion of Christ as the Anointed One, Augustine set forward nascent ideas

regarding the sacramental nature of anointing and the dual nature of God Incarnate, ideas which

would appear time and again in discourse on the meaning of oil and anointing, particularly in

medieval liturgical commentaries.[360]

> God, then, was anointed by God; with what oil was He anointed, but a spiritual one? For the
> visible oil is in the sign, the invisible oil is in the mystery; the spiritual oil is within. "God"
> then was "anointed" for us, and sent unto us; and God Himself was man, in order that He
> might be "anointed": but He was man in such a way as to be God still. He was God in such
> a way as not to disdain to be man. "Very man and very God;" in nothing deceitful, in
> nothing false, as being everywhere true, everywhere "the Truth" itself. God then is man; and
> it was for this cause that "God" was "anointed", because God was Man, and became
> "Christ."[361]

Thus we see that anointing was fundamental to Augustine's conception of both humanity and

Christianity. To be human and to be Christian was to be anointed.

Psalm 132

As previous discussed, Psalm 132, though brief, contains some of the most vivid oil imagery

in the Bible. In this psalm, the Psalmist compares the love of brothers living in community to the oil

used to anoint Aaron, the High Priest. Fraternal love is likened to this unguent, running down the

beard of the priest to the hem of his robe.

> How very good and pleasant it is
>   when kindred live together in unity!
> It is like the precious oil on the head,
>   running down upon the beard,
> on the beard of Aaron,

---

[360] See Chapter 4.

[361] Augustine, *Expositions on the Psalms*, Psalm 44 (45), English translation by J.E. Tweed, accessed on April 11, 2017, http://www.newadvent.org/fathers/1801045.htm. For the Latin text, see Augustine, *Enarrationes in Psalmos*, Psalm 44, accessed on February 18, 2015, http://www.augustinus.it/latino/esposizioni_salmi/esposizione_salmo_059_testo.htm.

> running down over the collar of his robes.
> It is like the dew of Hermon,
>   which falls on the mountains of Zion.
> For there the LORD ordained his blessing,
>   life for evermore.[362]

As we have already seen in the gloss for Psalm 22, Augustine interpreted the oil to be the divine

nature of God, which extended from the priest to the entire Christian community. The glosses for

this psalm allude to the discord extant among Christians despite being ostensibly united by a single

God. The interlinear gloss for the first line of this psalm, [ostensibly] from Augustine, remarked that

what was "good" was "useful"[363] and what is "pleasant" was "delightful"[364] with the caveat that

"Good are the things that do not delight."[365] The gloss corresponding to "to live" [*habitare*] spoke of

the unity of heart and soul that was possible despite the members of a community one finds

unpleasant: "The heart was one and the soul was one in God through those people."[366] By "unity"

the glossator intended: "Through the right arrangement of each according to diverse offices."[367] The

psalm likens this unity to the ointment poured on the head of Aaron, the High Priest.[368] The gloss

reminded the reader that the ointment signified "The anointing of the Holy Spirit which was

previously on Christ's head, through a likeness of kings and priests who are the image of Christ.

Thus it is good and pleasant for brethren to live in unity."[369] Predictably, according to the gloss, the

head of Aaron signified Christ, and the oil that descended, descended "from the head of Christ."[370]

---

[362] "Ecce quam bonum et quam jucundum, habitare fratres in unum! Sicut unguentum in capite, quod descendit in barbam, barbam Aaron, quod descendit in oram vestimenti ejus; sicut ros Hermon, qui descendit in montem Sion. Quoniam illic mandavit Dominus benedictionem, et vitam usque in saeculum." Psalm 132. English translation from NSRV.

[363] "Quod ostendentis est vtile." Froehlich, *Biblia Latina Cum Glossa Ordinaria*, 2:631.

[364] "id est delectabile." Ibid.

[365] "Quia sunt bona que non delectant." Ibid.

[366] "Erat illis cor vnum et anima vna in deum." Ibid.

[367] "Recte dispositis singulorum diuersis officiis." Ibid.

[368] See Chapter 1.

[369] "inunctio spritius[sic] sancti qu[a]e prius fuit in capite christo. A similitudine regum et sacerdotum qui figura sunt christi. Ita bonum et iocundum est habitare fratres in vnum" Froehlich, *Biblia Latina Cum Glossa Ordinaria*, 2:631.

[370] "a capite christo." Ibid. Regarding Aaron's beard: "determinat in cuius barbam subdens bar[bam] a[aron]."

The beard of Aaron signified "Christ the true priest."[371] The glossator interpreted the spatial

elements of the psalm temporally: the descent of the unguent across Aaron's robe suggested the

spreading of Christ's priesthood through time.[372] The oil reached all the way to the edge of Aaron's

garment, which the glossator noted represented the prelates of the Church living in harmonious

unity.[373] Indeed, the glossator observed that peaceful cohabitation led to spiritual anointing: "The

comparison may [be made] between fraternal cohabitation and spiritual anointing as between cause

and effect."[374] The glossator thus saw peace and concord among Christians as a prerequisite for the

anointing that would impact blessing and mark them as true Christians.

An interlinear gloss, attributed to Augustine, noted that Mount Hermon was like Mount

Sion, thus suggesting that the oil was like the law (Ten Commandments) given to the Jews on Mount

Sion.[375] The gloss for *quoniam* explained that the grace, which oil symbolized, was bestowed so that

the people could praise God rather than live in discord: "among brothers who received the blessing

as one, that those in concord may praise God. Truly, those in concord praise God, those in

discord do not."[376] The glossator interpreted "his blessing, life for evermore" as an eschatological

promise: eternal life rather than mortality.[377]

Oil in the Gospels

Casting Out of Demons

The Gospel of Mark contains a reference to Jesus bestowing on the disciples "authority over

unclean spirits."[378] He sent them out two by two, charging them with the power to cast out demons

---

[371] "veri sacerdotis christi." Ibid.
[372] The gloss corresponding to "descendit" is "postea," suggesting the descent of oil continued well after the anointing of Aaron. Ibid.
[373] "oram...id est in illos praefectos qui in vnum habitant." Ibid.
[374] "sit comparatio inter cohabitationem fraternam et spiritualem vnctionem tanquam inter causam et effectum." Ibid.
[375] "Mons pascualis sicut et mon syon. gratia quam gentes receperunt prius descendit in syon id est super iudeos." Ibid.
[376] "in fratribus qui in vnum precepit benedictionem. ut concordes benedicent deum. Concordes enim benedicunt deum. discordes non." Ibid.
[377] "vitam...in futuro duraturam" and "saeculum...in eternum." Ibid.

and to anoint the sick with oil: "So they went out and proclaimed that all should repent. They cast

out many demons, and anointed with oil many who were sick and cured them."[379] In Rusch's *editio*

princeps, only one gloss, drawn from the Venerable Bede, corresponds to this line of text. In contrast

with glosses of anointings in the Hebrew Scriptures, which depicted the anointed as Christ-like, for

anointings in the Gospels the glosses emphasize an apostolic tradition and the role of clerics in

consecrating the oil, not the Christ-like nature of the anointed:

> The apostle James said: the sick person among any of you may bring in priests of the church,
> and they may pray over him, anointing him with oil in the name of the Lord and if he has
> committed sins, they will be forgiven. Whence is it known that this custom [*morem*] of the
> holy Church was bequeathed from the apostles themselves, that those possessed by the devil
> or that any other diseased people may be anointed with oil consecrated through pontifical
> benediction.[380]

In this twelfth-century context, we see the need to link the anointing of the sick to a more ancient

tradition instituted by the apostles during Jesus' lifetime. We also see the invocation of ecclesiastical

control over oil, as rules reguling the sacraments became more stringent in the twelfth century:

priests must administer the anointing and a pontiff or bishop must consecrate the oil. The glosses

on the Hebrew Scriptures interpreted anointed figures like Jacob, Saul and David as prefigurations

of Christ. In the gloss of this Gospel, however, the anointed sick were not Christlike. Rather, the

---

[378] Mark 6:7.

[379] Mark 6: 12-13. NSRV translation. The Latin vulgate in Rusch reads: "Et exeuntes praedicabant vt paenitentiam agerent et daemonia multa eiiciebant. et vngebant oleo multos egros et sanabantur." Froehlich, *Biblia Latina Cum Glossa Ordinaria,* 4:106.

[380] "Jacobo dicit. Infirmatur quis in vobis: indu.p.ec.et o super e.vn.e.o...Unde patet ab apostolis hunc morem esse traditum vt energumini et alii egroti vngantur oleo a pontifice consecrato." Ibid. This gloss is drawn from Bede: "Dicit apostolus iacobus: infirmatur quis in uobis inducat presbiteros ecclesiae, et orent super ipsum ungentes eum oleo in nomine domini et, si in peccatis sit, dimittentur ei. Vnde patet ab ipsis apostolis hunc sanctae ecclesiae morem esse traditum ut energumeni uel alii quilibet aegroti ungantur oleo pontificali benedictione consecrato." See LLT Beda Uenerabilis - In Marci euangelium expositio (CPL 1355), lib. : 2, cap. : 6, linea : 685-687. This text also appears in Thomas Aquinas' *Catena aurea in Marcum:* "Beda. Unde patet ab ipsis apostolis hunc sanctae Ecclesiae morem esse traditum, ut energumeni, vel alii quilibet aegroti, ungantur oleo, pontificali benedictione consecrato. Glossa. Post praedicationem discipulorum Christi, et miraculorum operationem convenienter Evangelista subiungit de fama quae consurgebat in populo; unde dicit et audivit Herodes rex." See LLT: Thomas de Aquino - Catena aurea in Marcum cap.: 6 , lectio: 2, linea: 173, pag.: 475, linea: 61-66.

glossator emphasized the sinfulness of the sick, the presence of demonic possession and the need for salvation that was accomplished through the ministers of the Church and her sacraments.

Oil on Wounds: the Good Samaritan

For the gloss on the parable of the Good Samaritan, the glossator drew on Bede's Commentary on the Gospel of Luke and emphasized the sacramental nature of the oil used to heal the poor man's wounds. Luke's Gospel states: "a Samaritan while travelling came near [the beaten man]; and when he saw him, he was moved with pity. He went to him and bandaged his wounds, having poured oil and wine on them. Then he put him on his own animal, brought him to an inn, and took care of him."[381] The interlinear gloss above *alligauit* (he bandaged) says *in baptismo*, suggesting that healing the wounds of the body was like baptism, which removed original sin, and thus served a spiritual and soteriological function.[382] Moreover, acording to the gloss, the Samaritan assumed a distinctly priestly function. The gloss for the oil and wine further elucidates the likeness between the Samaritan and a priest. Tending to the beaten man's wounds was like administering sacraments of initiation. The oil that the Samaritan poured on the man's wounds was said to be "the chrism of the Holy Spirit."[383] The wine was "the cup of his passion," alluding to both the Eucharist and the crucifixion.[384] The marginal gloss for this passage showed how just as oil cured physical wounds, hope was a salve for the wounded soul, allowing sinners to return to heaven:

> He bandaged his wounds…He pours oil while he gives hope to the repentants, saying 'Away penance!' because he will approach the kingdom of heaven. He pours wine while the Lord instills fear of punishment in sinners, saying 'Every tree that does not bear good fruit is cut down and thrown into the fire.'[385] The mule is his own flesh [Christ's] in which he [Christ]

---

[381] Luke 10:25-34. Translation from the NSRV.

[382] Froehlich, *Biblia Latina Cum Glossa Ordinaria*, 4:180.

[383] "crisma sancti spiritus." Ibid.

[384] "calicem sue passionis." Ibid. Regarding the cup as a symbol for Jesus' sacrifice, see Mark 10:38; Matt 20:22, 26:39,42; Luke 22:42; John 18:11.

[385] Matt 7:19.

came to us, on which he puts the wounded, because he carried our sins on his body. He himself was truly afflicted, trusting in the Incarnation. The inn is the Church of the present, where travelers are restored, returning to the eternal native land.[386]

Instead of interpreting the beaten man as the Lord's Anointed or the wounded man as being like Christ, Christ is the one who proffers salvation in form of the sacraments offered through the Church. The Samaritan, according to the glossator, was like a priest who healed those wounded by sin. Being anointed with oil infused hope in those doing penance for their sins.

Wise and Foolish Virgins

While in the parable of the Good Samaritan oil represented hope of salvation and the forgiveness of sins, in the parable of the wise and foolish virgins, oil becomes a symbol for internal or spiritual light. In Matthew's gospel, Jesus likened the kingdom of heaven to women who were waiting, ready to receive the bridegroom at the moment of his arrival. Jesus admonished his listeners to live in the present, in anticipation of death, symbolized by marriage.[387] The Gospel text states: "Then the kingdom of heaven will be like this. Ten bridesmaids took their lamps and went to meet the bridegroom. Five of them were foolish, and five were wise. When the foolish took their lamps, they took no oil with them; but the wise took flasks of oil with their lamps...."[388] According to the interlinear gloss in Rusch, the foolish virgins lack an interior, spiritual or mental condition that is pleasing to God. The oil they lack represents this spiritual quality, since the oil was said to be "glory

---

[386] "Alligauit v.e. peccata redarguendo cohibuit. Infundit oleum dum paenitentibus tribuit spem dicens .Paenitentiam agite. quia appropinquabit regnum caelorum. Infundit vinum dum peccantibus terrorem paenae incutit dominus dicens .Omnis arbor quae non facit fructum bonum excidetur et in ignem mittetur. Iumentum caro ipsius est in qua ad nos venit in quam saucium imponit quia peccata nostra portauit in corpore suo. Imponitur vero qui ipsam incarnationem credit. Stabulum est praesentis ecclesia. vbi reficiuntur viatores in aeternam patriam redeuntes." Froehlich, *Biblia Latina Cum Glossa Ordinaria*, 4:179. For the passage from Bede, see LLT: Beda Uenerabilis – In Lucae euangelium expositio (CPL 1356) lib.: 3, cap.:10, linea: 2245-2269.
[387] Regarding marriage as a symbol for death, see Long, "The Origin of the Eschatological Feast as a Wedding Banquet in the Synoptic Gospels."
[388] Matt 25:1-13. English translation from the NSRV.

of conscience or oil is the joy of the mind, which the one who is pleasing to God has within."[389] The

oil within the lamps of the wise virgins was "the brightness of glory."[390] The wise virgins carried a

store of oil within vessels that, according to the glossator, represent "their consciences."[391] The

lamps themselves, through which the light of the burning oil shined, were said to exhibit good

works.[392] The glossator of this pericope further interpreted the virgins to be all people who abstained

from worldly concerns, including the pleasures of the flesh.[393]

Unguenti Pretiosi: the Anointing at Bethany

In all four of the gospel narratives, a dramatic event takes place leading up to Christ's

crucifixion in Jerusalem.[394] While Jesus reclines at table during a dinner party in Bethany, a woman

approaches him and anoints him with costly unguent. The stories differ regarding several details,

including whether the woman anoints Jesus' head or feet, but all four narratives include the

anointing. According to the Gospels of Mark and Matthew, the woman breaks the alabaster of costly

unguent and pours it on Jesus' head, in anticipation of Jesus' burial. The Gospel of Luke emphasizes

that the woman is a sinner from the city and claims that she wept, washing Jesus' feet with her tears,

drying them with her hair and anointing them with her unguent. Rather than saying the woman

prepared his body for burial, Jesus explains that she showed great love because he forgave her sins.

The Gospel of John names the woman (Mary), rather than just referring to her as a sinful woman

from the city. This gospel further explains that Jesus is in the home of Mary and her brother

Lazarus, whom Jesus resurrected earlier, suggesting a parallel between the forgiveness of sins and

---

[389] "gloriam intra conscientiam. vel oleum est letitia mentis quam habet qui intus deo placet." Froehlich, *Biblia Latina Cum Glossa Ordinaria,* 4:76.

[390] "Nitorem glorie." Ibid.

[391] "Id est in consciis suis." Ibid.

[392] "ostensione bonorum operorum." Ibid.

[393] "Decem virginea sunt omnes qui se a {?} saeculi continent. Quinquorum quia quimquam pertita est continentia in carnalibus ille {?} videlicet vt in quinquam sensibus contineant se a voluptatibus." Ibid.

[394] Mark 14; Matt 26; Luke 7; John 12.

being brought back to life. John's gospel also includes the detail of Mary's house being filled with the fragrance of the unguent, which exegetes would interpret to mean the "good aroma of Christ" filling the Church.

The *Glossa Ordinaria* presented the woman anointing Jesus as a symbol for the "Church having faith."[395] Mary's devotion signified faith and piety.[396] The alabaster jar represented "carnal desire," which was destroyed.[397] The pure unguent served to protect the anointed.[398] According to the *Glossa,* the anointing of Jesus' head symbolized the quelling of physical desires, since the body was joined to the head (mind).[399] Furthermore, Jesus' head anointed with precious ointment signified the Incarnation, in which God became human, imparting divine spirit to corporeal materiality.[400] The anointing Jesus' feet, in contrast, represented the outpouring of truth for the faithful.[401] The *Glossa* cited Jerome's interpretation of the fragrant nard filling the house (*domus*) as a symbol for "the good aroma of Christ" filling both heaven and earth.[402] This image of Mary's fragrant nard filling the house of God would appear in the chants of the liturgy, as Mary Magdalene appeared as a symbol for the Church, which dispensed water (tears) and chrism (unguent) for the sanctification of the body of Christ.

---

[395] "Ecclesia habens fidem." Froehlich, *Biblia Latina Cum Glossa Ordinaria,* 4:126.
[396] "Devotio mariae fidem et pietatem designat ecclesiae." Ibid.
[397] "Carnale desiderium." Ibid.
[398] "Unguenta nicorrupta [sic] servat." Ibid.
[399] "Fractum alabastrum carnale est desiderium quod frangitur ad caput ex quo omne corpus compaginatum est." Ibid.
[400] "cum humanitatem digna reverentia suscipit." Ibid.
[401] "In pedes unguentum pisticum id est fidele et verum perfundit: quia illam naturam eius qua terram contingere id est inter homines conversari dignatus est: pia praedicatione et deuotis venerator obsequiis." Ibid.
[402] "christi bonus odor sumus deo"; "Domus impleta odore: caelum et terra est." Ibid.

CHAPTER 3

THE ALABASTER JAR: OIL IN THE LITURGY

INTRODUCTION

The medieval liturgy was an essential means for expressing and disseminating ideas about

holy oil within medieval culture. More than any other feast within the liturgical calendar (perhaps

with the exception of certain myroblytes' feast days,) Holy Thursday (*In Cena Domini*) reveals that in

the Church in the Latin West, holy oil was a sign of both penance and self-sacrificing love. The

liturgical rites for this feast shows that oil pertained to both the highest and lowest echelons of

medieval society. The Pope and his bishops alone were invested with the authority to consecrate

holy oils, which they did on Holy Thursday during the Chrism Mass (*Missa chrismatis*). On the same

day, however, at Vespers, following the Chrism Mass, during a rite known as *Ad mantatum*, bishops

and other prelates assumed the role of humble servants during the washing of feet (*pedilavium*),

sometimes including washing the feet of the poor. This rite included the chanting of antiphons,

some of which retold the story of a woman washing and anointing Jesus' feet, potentially suggesting

a parallel between the woman and those invested with power to cleanse and sacralize religious

communities. This analysis of the prayers, chants, and sermons for the Office of Holy Thursday and

the Chrism Mass, as well as the chants and ritual actions accompanying the *pedilavium* rite,

demonstrates that oil was a distinct sign of divine presence in the medieval material world. More

particularly, sanctified oil signalled the presence of the Holy Spirit, who, by its unpredictable and

non-material nature, reflected the ambiguous and mutable nature of divinity, calling into question

the fixity of gender, authority and sanctity within medieval religious culture. As a prominent feature

of the Holy Thursday rites, oil was emblematic of both penance and charity. Beyond Holy Thursday,

oil featured prominently on the feast days of both virgins and sinners, including the Blessed Virgin

Mary and Mary Magdalen. Although on Holy Thursday, references to Mary Magdalen were often

107

oblique or peripheral, she was present in the liturgy as a symbol for the Church as a source of both

purifying water and sanctifying oil.

Within the great drama of Holy Week, when the Church reconciled sinners with God and

initiated unbelievers into the mysteries of the Christian faith, bishops consecrated holy oils on the

Thursday before Easter, during the celebration of *In Cena Domini* (The Lord's Supper).[403] The

celebration of *In Cena Domini* was the first of the great liturgical rites of the *Triduum*, the three days

preceding Easter: Holy Thursday (*In Cena Domini*), Good Friday (*Parasceve*), and Holy Saturday

(*Sabbatum Sanctum*).[404] On Holy Thursday, following the consecration of oils during the celebration

of the Lord's Supper (the Last Supper), at Vespers a bishop, abbot or priest would wash the feet of

the members of his religious community, or the feet of the poor, after which the altars were stripped

bare.[405] Good Friday followed, commemorating the crucifixion of Jesus. During the great Easter

vigil of Holy Saturday, the Church baptized catechumens and anointed them twice with oil. During

these three days, the faithful symbolically underwent the drama of death and rebirth. The liturgical

texts evoke images of night, darkness, and sin. The bright light of the Resurrection and the power of

the living Christ dispelled the darkness, bringing new life. The Church imparted this new life to the

newly initiated through baptism and strengthened them with the fragrant chrism. At the Easter Vigil,

since roughly the fifth century, a deacon sang the *Exultet*, an extended resurrection prayer, which

marked the culmination of the Lenten season and the apex the *Triduum* rites: *Exultet iam angelica turba*

---

[403] Thursday of Holy Week is now known as "Holy Thursday" or "Maundy Thursday." The appellation "Maundy" is an abbreviation of *Mandatum novum*, "a new commandment," which refers to an antiphon sung on this day, commemorating Jesus' exhortation to his disciples to love one another. John 13:34: "Mandatum novum do vobis: ut diligatis invicem: sicut dilexi vos, ut et vos diligatis invicem." Harper, *The Forms and Orders of Western Liturgy from the Tenth to the Eighteenth Century*, 144.

[404] Tyrer, *Historical Survey of Holy Week*; Pierce, "Holy Week and Easter in the Middle Ages."

[405] For an overview of the history of the *pedilavium* rite, see Peter Jeffery, "Mandatum Novum Do Vobis: Toward a Renewal of the Holy Thursday Footwashing Ritual," *Worship* 64, no.2 (1990), 107-142.

caelorum.[406] The singer proclaimed the passage of believers from death to eternal life: "Nox in qua ex

orta est resurreccio in aeternum"[407] The *Exultet* proclaims that "on this night" the things of heaven

and earth unite, as do things human and divine: *O vere beata nox, in qua terrenis caelestia, humanis divina

iunguntur!* (O truly blessed night, when earthly and heavenly things, human and divine things are

joined!)

In medieval manuscripts, particularly in Gothic script, the words "are joined" and "are

anointed" are nearly indistinguishable: "*iunguntur*" and "*unguntur*." Only a single minim distinguishes

the two words. Since the word *iunguntur* meant not only to join, but also to wed, the joining of

heaven and earth on the vigil of Easter evoked nuptial imagery. Easter, in a sense, was a great

wedding feast.[408] To be wed and to be anointed were akin substantially, and not simply linguistically.

At the Easter vigil, new initiates were anointed with holy oil – first with the oil of catechumens

before their baptisms and then with the more precious chrism (oil mixed with balsam) directly

following baptism. In becoming Christians (anointed ones) the newly initiated were, in a sense, wed

to the Church, in the same way Christ himself was wed to the Church in a mystical marriage. Before

these anointings could take place, however, bishops consecrated the oils on Holy Thursday.

While the liturgy of the Church in the Latin West became increasingly standardized over the

course of the medieval period, particularly in the eighth and ninth centuries with Carolingian

reforms, in the tenth century with the compilation of the Romano-Germanic Pontifical, and with

reforms by the Roman Papal Curia in the thirteenth and fourteenth centuries, the rites of the

Triduum continued to exist with manifold variations well into the High Middle Ages.[409] The

---

[406] Vogel, *Medieval Liturgy*, 171.

[407] BAV Reg.lat. 317, fol. 168v.

[408] John of Chrysostom makes a direct comparison between the initiation ritual for catechumens and a marriage. See Chrysostom, *Baptismal Instructions*, 161-64.

[409] "The timetable for these three days was exceptionally crowded. At various times in the Middle Ages this led to omissions...or elisions...or to some curious timings...It is impossible to generalize: Uses differed from place to place and from century to century." Harper, *The Forms and Orders of Western Liturgy from the Tenth to the Eighteenth Century*, 140-41. For

manuscripts recording *In Cena Domini* in the Roman Rite present a variety of liturgical practices that are often confounding in their ambiguity and complexity.[410] Despite the labyrinthine manuscript tradition for this liturgical celebration, however, some generalizations are in order regarding how the Latin Church celebrated *In Cena Domini*. To date, Peter Maier's *Die Feier der Missa Chrismatis: die Reform der Ölweihen des Pontificale Romanum vor dem Hintergrund der Ritusgeschichte* (1990) constitutes the most thorough study of the development of the Chrism Mass and the attendant liturgical rites of Holy Thursday. Christopher A. Jones's article "The Chrism Mass in Later Anglo-Saxon England" (2005) expanded upon Maier's findings with his research on the Chrism Mass in the Sarum Rite.[411] This chapter explores the themes and imagery contained in the liturgical readings, chants, prayers for the consecration of holy oils and *pedilavium* rite to understand how oil was perceived and what role holy oil played in the sanctification of individuals and communities. Understanding the role oil played in the medieval liturgy will reveal how medieval Christians understood otherwise elusive legends about miracles involving holy oil.

TENEBRAE: THE TRIDUUM BEGINS

Before sunrise on Holy Thursday, the *Triduum* began with the *Tenebrae*, a name given to Matins and Lauds during the *Triduum* because of the dark and gloomy character of the readings on those days.[412] Shortly after midnight, the Divine Office (also known as the Liturgy of the Hours) started as it would on all other days: with the sound of a bell. And yet, this day was unlike other

---

an overview of the spread of the Roman rite throughout the Latin West and in particular the development of the Divine Office see Fassler and Baltzer, *The Divine Office in the Latin Middle Ages*, 128-34.

[410] See Hughes, *Medieval Manuscripts for Mass and Office a Guide to Their Organization and Terminology*, 260. The music for the rites for Holy Thursday are not recorded predominantly in Graduals nor Missals but in Processionals: "The chants for the service do not appear in Graduals and are only rarely given in Noted Missals: Processionals are the most likely source for the music." Ibid.

[411] Jones, "The Chrism Mass in Later Anglo-Saxon England."

[412] Originally the *Tenebrae* service occurred on the nights preceding the three days before Easter Sunday (Holy Thursday, Good Friday, and Holy Saturday), but shifted at some point to Matins and Lauds. See Tyrer, *Historical Survey of Holy Week*, 81. According to Pierre Batifoll, this particular form of the Divine Office for the *Triduum* was in place in Rome during Charlemagne's reign. See Batiffol, *Histoire du bréviaire romain*, 142-44.

days; the holiest time of the year was approaching. For three days, the liturgy would blend into one immense ritual celebration. After the ringing of the bell in the dark on Thursday morning, Matins and Lauds unfolded in a way that would have struck participants as highly unusual: many aspects of the daily Office were absent. The service was reduced to the bare minimum.[413] In this regard, the Divine Office during the *Triduum* resembled the Office of the Dead.[414] During Matins twenty-four candles were lit. Over the course of the Matins and Lauds, all but one candle would be gradually extinguished, signifying, perhaps, the "apparent victory of the powers of evil and the apparent failure of God's plan of salvation at our Lord's crucifixion."[415] A single burning candle would be hidden behind the alter until Holy Saturday, a sign that the "light of the world was extinguished, the Christ was dead, and that darkness covered the earth."[416] The readings on these days would speak of pain and sorrow, shame and disgrace. As the candles were extinguished one by one, the participants in the liturgy would hear the Psalmist plead with God for mercy and deliverance.[417]

These dark hours before Easter represented, according to Pierre Batiffol, the "sorrowful mystery of the passion, death and resurrection of the Savior and the heart-felt regrets of penitent humanity."[418] The readings or lessons during *Tenebrae* helped to create the somber atmosphere in which holy oils were then consecrated on Holy Thursday afternoon.[419] Of all the hours of the Divine Office, Matins had the highest concentration of scriptural readings; the other hours of the day were

---

[413] Regarding the structure of Matins, see Tyrer, *Historical Survey of Holy Week*, 81–82.

[414] Harper, *The Forms and Orders of Western Liturgy from the Tenth to the Eighteenth Century*, 141.

[415] Tyrer, *Historical Survey of Holy Week*, 84.

[416] "L'office nocturne de ces trois jours devenait la grande représentation du mystère douloureux de la passion, de la mort, de l'ensevelissement du Saveur, et des pathétiques regrets de l'humanité pénitente." Batiffol, *Histoire du bréviaire romain*, 142.

[417] Psalms (Vulgate) 68, 69, 70; 71, 72, 73; 74, 75, 76.

[418] Batiffol, *Histoire du bréviaire romain*, 144.

[419] Regarding medieval lectionaries, the codices containing the reading for the Mass and Office, see Grégoire, *Les homéliaires du moyen âge; inventaire et analyse des manuscrits.*, 3–11. The earliest lectionaries appear to date to the fifth century, and would have been contemporary with the first sacramentaries. This would mean a lectionary system or its structure existed prior to Gregory the Great. See Ibid., 4. Beginning in the sixth century, lectionaries for the Divine Office began to appear. Ibid., 5. The lectionary and homiletic tradition "solidified" with the production of homiliaries such as those of Cîteaux and la Grand-Chartreuse. See Ibid., 9.

primarily sung prayer in the form of recitations from the Psalter.[420] The *Tenebrae* service consisted of

three nocturns. The first nocturn included lessons (readings) from the Lamentations of Jeremiah; the

second nocturn drew from Augustine's commentary on the Psalms; the third nocturn included a

lesson from 1 Corinthians or the gospel reading of the day.[421]

The first nocturn of *Tenebrae* on Holy Thursday might have included Psalms 68 – 70

followed by readings from Jeremiah.[422] A twelfth century monastic lectionary, Vat.lat.1271,

potentially of Beneventan provenance, includes a reading from the Jeremiah 1:1-19, which tells of

Jerusalem's downfall: like a woman abandoned by her husband, the city is desolate with mourning.[423]

How lonely sits the city
  that once was full of people!
How like a widow she has become,
  she that was great among the nations!
She that was a princess among the provinces
  has become a vassal.[424]

...

I called to my lovers
  but they deceived me;
my priests and elders
  perished in the city

---

[420] Regarding the structure of the Divine Office, see Harper, *The Forms and Orders of Western Liturgy from the Tenth to the Eighteenth Century*, 73–108.

[421] Matins begins with opening versicles, introductory psalms and a hymn, followed by three nocturns. Each nocturn consists of psalms, a prayer and blessing, and a reading with *responds*. Matins then ends with *Te Deum laudamus*. The reading for the first nocturn was generally scriptural; the reading for the second nocturn was patristic or hagiographical; the third reading was from a homily on the Gospel for that day. In secular Use, each nocturn consisted of three lessons; in monastic Use, four lessons made up each nocturn. During the Triduum, monastic Use followed secular Use for the Office. See Ibid., 76–77, 81, 104. Fassler notes the Gospel reading for the day is key to the rest of the liturgy (mass and office) for that day – everything emanates from it. See Fassler, *The Divine Office in the Latin Middle Ages*, 27.

[422] Lectionaries differed according to geographical regions, religious order and particular communities. They were not universally fixed or "figée" as Grégoire says, until a later period. For studies on particular lectionaries, see for example Boyle, "Dominican Lectionaries and Leo of Ostia's *Translatio S. Clementis*."; Carmassi, "Feria V in Authentica, Mane"; Chavasse, "Les Lectionnaires Romains de La Messe Du VIIe Siècle, Au *Missale Romanum* (1570)"; Etaix, "Le Lectionnaire de l'Office à Cluny."; Krochalis and Matter, "Manuscripts of the Liturgy"; Parkes, "The Compilation of the Dominican Lectionary"; Ramis, "Il Triduo Sacro Nella Liturgia Gallicana"; Smith, "The Roman Origin of Two Sections of the Sarum Lectionary."

[423] "BAV Vat.lat.1271," fol.148v–150v.

[424] English translation from the NSRV. The Douay-Rheims translation reads: "How doth the city sit solitary that was full of people! how is the mistress of the Gentiles become as a widow: the princes of provinces made tributary!" The Latin Vulgate: "Quomodo sedet sola civitas plena populo! Facta est quasi vidua domina gentium; princeps provinciarum facta est sub tributo." Lam 1:1.

while seeking food
   to revive their strength.[425]

The second reading listed in Vat.lat.1271 may have been intended as the reading for the

second nocturn, since it is an excerpt from Augustine's commentary on Psalm 63, which tells of the

faithful seeking refuge from their enemies: "*Hearken, O God, to my prayer, while I am troubled; from fear of*

the enemy deliver my soul. Enemies have raged against the Martyrs: for what was that voice of Christ's

body praying? For this it was praying, to be delivered from enemies, and that enemies might not

have power to slay them. Were they not therefore hearkened to...?"[426] The second nocturn would

have included Psalms 71 to 73 followed by a reading from Augustine's commentary on the psalms.

These psalms likewise spoke of God's judgement, the willful disobedience of sinners and divine

wrath. Bonaventure would use Psalm 71:6 to explain the miracle of Santa Maria in Trastevere's *fons*

olei.[427] The third nocturn consisted of Psalms 74 – 76 with the reading from either 1 Corinthians 11

or the Gospel (John 13:1-15). 1 Corinthians 11 dealt with a range of issues, including women's

subordination to men, the significance of hair and headcoverings, and the sacred nature of the

Eucharistic meal. The reading from John 13, which told of Jesus' washing his disciples' feet at the

Last Supper, was clearly in anticipation of the *pedilavium* ritual to be enacted later in the day.

Following Matins, just before sunrise, Lauds sometimes seamlessly began, as presumably it

did on Holy Thursday since the gradual extinguishing of candles concluded at the end of Lauds, not

Matins.[428] During Lauds on Holy Thursday the choir might have sung psalms of praise, including

---

[425] Translation from the NSRV. The Douay-Rheims translation reads: "I called for my friends, but they deceived me: my priests and my ancients pined away in the city: while they sought their food, to relieve their souls." The Latin Vulgate: "Vocavi amicos meos, et ipsi deceperunt me; sacerdotes mei et senes mei in urbe consumpti sunt, quia quaesierunt cibum sibi ut refocillarent animam suam." Lam 1:19.

[426] "BAV Vat.lat.1271," fol.150r. "Exaudi deus orationem meam, a timore inimici eripe animam meam. Seuierunt inimici in martyres. Quid orabat ista uox corporis christi. hoc orabat ut eruentur ab inimicis et non eos possent occidere inimici. Ergo exauditi non sunt..." Augustine, Expositions on the Psalms, Psalm 64, English translation by J.E. Tweed, accessed on June 3, 2015, http://www.newadvent.org/fathers/1801064.htm.

[427] Bonaventure quoted Psalm 71:6 as evidence that God's salvific activity was accompanied by an abundance of moisture or flowing liquids: "Descendet sicut pluvia in vellus, et sicut stillicidia super terram." Douay-Rheims: "He shall come down like rain upon the fleece; and as showers falling gently upon the earth."

[428] Vogel, Elze, and Andrieu, *Le Pontifical romano-germanique du dixième siècle*, 55–57.

Psalms 1, 62, and 89, a passage from Exodus 15:1-19, which told of the Pharoah's chariots being cast into the sea, and Psalm 148-150 (chanted continuously as one).[429] On Holy Thursday there was also a brief commemoration of Passion with the Gradual *Christus factus est pro nobis obediens usque ad mortem.*[430] In some parts of Christendom (in the eastern Church and Gallican churches), catechumens would recite the Creed, known as the *Redditio Symboli*, to the bishop or his deputy on Holy Thursday morning; in Rome this recitation look place at the Easter Vigil.[431] After Lauds, the church's walls or pavement were washed, as were the utensils for the Eucharist. Then a new fire, which was to illuminate the hearts and minds of those celebrating the paschal mysteries, was blessed and placed within the church, to remain as the sole light within the church until the Easter vigil.[432]

MISSA CHRISMATIS: THE CHRISM MASS

A mournful atmosphere of the *Tenebrae* service pervaded Matins and Lauds in the last hours of the night, leading up to sunrise. Beginning in the eighth century, religious communities celebrated the feast of *In Cena Domini* (The Lord's Supper) in the afternoon, after None; this celebration would include a Chrism Mass if a bishop were present. The evolution of the Chrism Mass in the Latin West was a highly complex, non-uniform process. The rites for consecrating holy oils, including chrism, transformed over the course of roughly nine centuries (from the fifth to the fourteenth) and varied considerably from one region to another throughout Europe.[433] Local variations in practices abounded even as late as the twelfth and thirteenth centuries.[434] The great variety of rites and instability of liturgical forms offer a rich source-base for exploring how ideas about oil emerged in medieval religious culture.

---

[429] Tyrer, *Historical Survey of Holy Week*, 83.
[430] Ibid.
[431] Ibid., 84.
[432] Vogel, Elze, and Andrieu, *Le Pontifical romano-germanique du dixième siècle*, 57.
[433] For the meaning of "chrism" in the oldest Roman sacramentaries, see Maier, *Die Feier der Missa chrismatis*, 50–53.
[434] Jones, "The Chrism Mass in Later Anglo-Saxon England."

The sources for studying the Chrism Mass consist mainly of sacramentaries, *ordines romani,* and pontificals. Sacramentaries are liturgical books containing mainly prayers for the celebration of the Mass and other services.[435] The Roman *ordines* or *ordines romani* are some of the earliest compilation of Roman rites.[436] Pontificals are liturgical books used by the celebrants of liturgical rites, usually bishops, from which they derive their name.

In fifth and sixth-century Gaul, chrism oil was blessed sometime during Lent, prior to the Easter solemnities.[437] The earliest sacramentary, the Verona or Leonine Sacramentary (*Veronensis* or *Leonensis),* dates from the sixth century, but contains no prayers for the consecration of oils on Holy Thursday.[438] At the Diocesan Synod of Auxerre (561-605), the Fourth Sunday of Lent was established as the day on which oils would be consecrated. According to the Pseudo-Germanus, however, at the end of the seventh century oils were consecrated on Palm Sunday. The Gregorian Sacramentary, a mid-seventh century Roman mass book that circulated north of the Alps, is key to understanding the development of oil in the liturgy of the Latin West in Rome, particularly at the Lateran basilica and the stational churches throughout the city, prior to implementation of a composite Gallo-Roman rite in the ninth century.[439] The consecration of oils on Holy Thursday became customary in the eighth-century, as shown in the Gelasian Sacramentary, which exists in several manuscript witnesses that reflect the convergence of Roman and Gallican rites. Over the course of the ninth century, the Roman liturgy incorporated the practice of consecrating oils on Holy Thursday.[440] Why were holy oils consecrated in tandem with the celebration of *In Cena Domini,*

---

[435] For an overview of the development and function of pontificals, see Vogel, *Medieval Liturgy,* 225–256. For a general overview of sacramentaries and their use for liturgical studies, see Fassler and Baltzer, *The Divine Office in the Latin Middle Ages,* 22–27. Also Vogel, *Medieval liturgy,* 61–134.

[436] Andrieu, *Les "Ordines romani" du haut Moyen Âge.*

[437] Jacobson, "Sicut Samuel Unxit David," 280.

[438] Maier, *Die Feier der Missa chrismatis,* 35.

[439] On the Gregorian Sacramentary, see Vogel, *Medieval Liturgy,* 79–102; Baldovin, *The Urban Character of Christian Worship.* Santa Maria in Trastevere was one of the stational churches in Rome, visited on the last Thursday of Lent before Holy Week. The connection between Santa Maria in Trastevere's *fons olei* and Holy Thursday will be addressed in Part III.

[440] Jacobson, "*Sicut Samuel Unxit David,*" 280.

which included the washing of feet? Were medieval liturgists influenced by the image of Mary

Magdalen breaking her alabaster jar and anointing Jesus' feet after washing them with her tears? Was

the sinful woman somehow a model for the Church washing and anointing newly initiated

Christians?

The Gelasian Sacramentary of the eighth century, which contains the earliest appearance of

rites for consecrating holy oils on Holy Thursday, was a Gallic adaptation of the Roman Gelasian or

'Old Gelasian' Sacramentary (circa 750), whose "prototype" appeared in Rome in the seventh

century.[441] The Gelasian sacramentary effectively introduced a new liturgical tradition in the Latin

West: Roman and non-Roman (i.e. Gallic) texts and customs became a composite rite in Gaul which

liturgists then reintroduced in Rome, such that this new composite rite became the universal Roman

rite.[442] Maier identified three features of Holy Thursday that are found in all versions of the Gelasian

Sacramentary: reconciliation of penitents, the consecration of oil, and the commemoration of the

Lord's Supper.[443] In addition to the composite Gelasian sacramentary, the *Ordines Romani,* some of

the oldest descriptions of Roman liturgical practices from the eighth century, also bear witness to the

development of the Chrism Mass and rites for consecrating holy oils.[444] Pontificals, which began to

---

[441] Vogel, *Medieval Liturgy,* 31. On the Old Gelasian Sacramentary, see Ibid., 64–70. The Old Gelasian Sacramentary is found in BAV Reg. lat. 316, fol. 3–245. In his survey of the Gelasian sacramentary, Maier uses five manuscripts dating from the mid to late eighth century as his source base. See Maier, *Die Feier der Missa chrismatis,* 36.

[442] Jeffery, "Eastern and Western Elements in the Irish Monastic Prayer of the Hours," 128. On the Frankish Gelasian Sacramentary (a.k.a. the Gelasian or 8th century Gelasian), see Vogel, *Medieval liturgy,* 70–78.

[443] Maier, *Die Feier der Missa chrismatis,* 36. The Chrism Mass in the Gelasian Sacramentary is structured as follows: it begins with "Domine deus qui in regenerandis"; before the gift-prayer (Gabengebet) comes the formula: "Da nobis omnipotens deus remedias"; the prayer closes with a Super Oblata, for example: "Huius sacrificii potentia"; some of the Gelasian sacramentaries then include a prayer like: "Clementiam tuam suppliciter obsecrare"; then the "kings, priests & prophets" formula. In the "Hanc igitur" things differ: most Gelasian sacramentaries have the formula: "Hanc igitur oblationem famulorum famularumque" while the Mass for the Reconciliation of Sinners states: "Hanc igitur oblationem domine cunctae familiae." For the consecration of oil, the text in the Gelasian sacramentary is consistent. There is the prayer: "Emitte quaesumus domine spiritum"; "Deus incrementorum et profectuum spiritalium…qui uirtute"; "UD Qui in principio"; "Exorcizo te creatura olei in nomine"; "UD. Qui mysteriorum tuorum secreta" Maier, *Die Feier der Missa chrismatis,* 39. According to Maier, one cannot know with certitude over which oil and at what point in the liturgy these prayers were spoken.

[444] For a compilation of these rites in a modern critical edition, see Andrieu, *Les "Ordines romani" du haut Moyen Âge.* Also, Maier, *Die Feier der Missa chrismatis,* 58–74. For a useful diagram giving overview of these sources and their interrelationship, see Vogel, *Medieval Liturgy,* 402–403. For a re-evaluation of the origin and nature of the PRG, see Parkes, *The Making of Liturgy in the Ottonian Church.*

appear in the tenth century, are by far the most numerous sources containing the rites for the

consecration of oils.[445]

PRAYERS FOR CONSECRATING HOLY OILS

The themes and imagery embedded in the prayers for the consecration of oils reveal how in

the early medieval period, Christians perceived the transformation of oil into something holy.[446] In

the tenth-century compilation, known as the Pontificale Romano-Germanicum, we see that an

elaborate ritual for consecrating the oils evolved in the High Middle Ages.[447] At the end of Lauds,

when a single lamp burned within the church, the sacristan would arrange all that was necessary for

consecrating the chrism later in the afternoon: "three ampullas full of the purest oil placed in the

sacristy, one for the oil of the sick, another for chrism, the third for the oil for anointing

catechumens. The greatest ampulla, which is for chrism, should be wrapped with white silk, but the

other ampullas should be wrapped in a different silk. The bishop should provide the balsam."[448]

Following the reconciliation of penitents at Terce, the *In Cena Domini* took place in the afternoon,

between None and Vespers. If a bishop was present, the Mass was the Chrism Mass (*Missa

chrismatis*), at which the bishop consecrated holy oils for the whole year. These oils would then be

used for baptism, confirmation and the anointing of the sick.[449]

On that day the bells are wrung for the mass and at other hours as is the custom on solemn

days, that all may come to the church in which it is customary to consecrate the chrism, and

---

[445] Maier, *Die Feier der Missa chrismatis*, 16–27.

[446] I limit my analysis here to the prayers as they appear in the tenth century compilation known as the Pontificale Romano-Germanicum.

[447] Henry Parkes challenged Michele Andrieu's argument regarding the origin of the PRG. Nevertheless, the prayers as they appear in Vogel and Elze's edition will serve as the basis for this analysis. See Vogel, Elze, and Andrieu, *Le Pontifical romano-germanique du dixième siècle*; Parkes, *The Making of Liturgy in the Ottonian Church*.

[448] "ampullas III de oleo mundissimo plenas ponentes in sacrario, unam ad oleum pro infirmis, alteram ad chrisma, teriam vero ad oleum ad catechuminos unguendos, maximam illam quae ad chrisma, debet fieri de albo serico, alias autem de alio serico coopertas. Et pontifex provideat de balsamo." Vogel, Elze, and Andrieu, *Le Pontifical romano-germanique du dixième siècle*, 59. PRG 222.

[449] Harper, *The Forms and Orders of Western Liturgy from the Tenth to the Eighteenth Century*, 142. NB: Since the Chrism Mass was only celebrated by a bishop, these rites are found in Pontificals rather than Missals.

then the bells are silent until Holy Saturday. Indeed at Terce let the priests and other clerics dress themselves in solemn vestments and the deacons in the vestments of deacons (*dalmaticis*) and the sub-deacons dress in silk albs and let them stand in their orders, individually in church, waiting until the Lord Bishop arrives with a full procession for the Mass, just as should happen on solemn days, with seven deacons and all the sub-deacons and candle bearers and seven candles [*cereostatis*] and two thuribles with incense.[450]

After invitatory prayers, readings from 1 Corinthians 11 and John 13:1-15, and an extended prayer for the consecration of the Eucharist, the consecration of oils began.

THE OIL OF SICK: AD EVACUANDOS DOLORES

First the bishop consecrated oil for the anointing of the sick. The bishop would first say: "Through all these things, Lord, you always create what is good."[451] Then the bishop would exorcize the oil, driving out all evil spirits: "I exorcize you, most filthy spirit and every incursion of Satan and every phantasm, in the name of the Father and Son and Holy Spirit, so you may withdraw from this oil, so that it may bring about spiritual anointing for strengthening the temple of God the Father omnipotent..."[452] Following the exorcism, the bishop blessed the oil by calling down the Holy Spirit, which had the power to restore health and strength to the mind and body:

Send forth, Lord, your spirit the paraclete from heaven into this oiliness [*pinguedinem*] of the olive, which you deemed worthy to produce from fresh wood for the restoration of the

---

[450] "Ipso die sonentur campanae ad missam et ad ceteras horas sicut mos est diebus sollempnibus, ut omnes veniant ad ecclesiam in qua chrisma mos est consecrari, et sic sileant usque in sabbatum sanctum. Presbiteri vero et ceteri clerici, hora tertia, induant se vestimentis sollemnibus et diaconi dalmaticis atque subdiaconi albis sericis induantur et stent in ordine suo, singuli in ecclesia, expectantes usquedum veniant domnus pontifex cum processione pleanria ad missam, sicut diebus sollemnibus solet, cum VII diaconibus et totidem subdiaconibus et ceroferariis et VII cereostatis et duobus turibulis cum incenso." Vogel, Elze, and Andrieu, *Le Pontifical romano-germanique du dixième siècle*, 67. PRG 252.

[451] "Per quem haec omnia, domine, semper bona creas." Ibid., 70. PRG 259.

[452] "Exorcizo te, inmundissime spiritus, omnisque incursio sathanae, et omne fantasma, in nomine patris et filii et spiritus sancti, ut recedas ab hoc oleo, ut possit effici unctio spiritalis ad corroborandam templum Dei patris omnipotententes et per nomen dilectissimi filii eius domini nostri Iesu Christi." Ibid. PRG 260.

body, so that your holy benediction might be, for everyone touched, the salubrious unguent

of heavenly medicine, the means of protection of the mind and body, for purging all pains

and all sicknesses and every disease of the mind and body, from which [unguent] you

anointed priests, kings, prophets and martyrs, your perfect unction [*chrisma*], Lord, blessed by

you for us, remaining in our innermost parts [*visceribus*], in the name of our Lord Jesus

Christ.[453]

After the blessing of the oil of the sick, the bishop led the recitation of the *Pater noster*, followed by a

short prayer for a liberation from evil, invoking the Virigin Mary and the apostles Peter, Paul and

Andrew. Then the bishop pronounced a series of blessings that explain why oils were consecrated

on the day celebrating the Lord's Supper.[454]

The Chrism: In Oleo Exhilarandos

The consecration of chrism began with a solemn procession of twelve presbyters and other

clerics, carrying the remaining oils to be consecrated, including the chrism and the oil for

catechumens. First two acolytes processed forward with candles burning. Then two more acolytes

processed, each carrying a cross. Between the crosses, an acolyte solemnly carried the chrism

ampulla, swathed in silk. Two acolytes then followed, swinging thuribles filled with burning incense.

Between the incense-bearers, another acolyte carried the ampulla for the oil of catechumens.

Following the oils, an acolyte processed carrying the codex containing the Gospel, followed by the

---

[453] "Emitte, domine, spiritum tuum paraclitum de caelis in hanc pinguedinem olivae quam de viridi ligno producere dignatus es ad refectionem corporis, ut tua sancta benedictione sit omni tangenti unguentum salubre medicinae caelestis, tutamen mentis et corporis ad evacuandos omnes dolores omnesque infirmitates omnemque aegritudinem mentis et corporis, unde unxisti sacerdotes, reges, prophetas et martires, chrisma tuum perfectum, domine, nobis a te benedictum permanens in visceribus nostris, in nomine domini nostri Iesu Christi." Ibid. PRG 261.

[454] " Benedicat vos deus qui per unigeniti sui passionem vetus pascha in novum voluit converti, concedatque vobis, ut expurgato veteris fermenti contagio, nova in vobis perseveret conspersio. Amen. Ut qui ad celebrandam redemptoris nostri cenam, mente devota, convenistis, aeternarum dapium vobiscum epulas reportetis. Amen. Ipsiusque opitulante clementia, mundemini a sordibus peccatorum, qui ad insinuandum humilitatis exemplum pedes voluit lavare discipulorum. Amen. Quod ipse praestare dignetur. Amen." Ibid., 71. PRG 266.

twelve presbyters, processing two by two. Boys would then sing out: "Listen, Judge of the Dead, the only hope of mortals, listen to the prayers of those bringing forward the gift of peace, leading the way."[455] The choir responded with the *O Redemptor* hymn, in which the choristers addressed God conflating the identity of God, the bishop and a king. The hymn reveals how the secular and sacred concerns of medieval Christians intertwined, as the language of the verses allude to law (*iura*), pecuniary matters (*debitum*), and the equality of the sexes (*sexus*) concerning sin and redemption.

> O Redeemer…standing at the altar, the suppliant pontifex, vested with the mitre, pays every debt (*debitum*) with the consecrated chrism. O Redeemer…King of the Everlasting Homeland (*patriae*), You deigned to consecrate this olive oil, a living sign, justice (*iura*) against the demon. O Redeemer…that every sex may be renewed by the anointing of chrism and the wounded glory of grace (*dignitatis*) be healed. O Redeemer…with the mind washed in the sacred fonte, offenses are put to flight, with the forehead anointed, the consecrated spiritual gifts flow. O Redeemer…[456]

Following the hymn, in which the choristers praised the chrism's power to heal the wounds of sin and human nature, the ritual continued as the members of the procession gathered around the altar, bringing the chrism ampulla and the balsam to the bishop, who then read the sermon for the consecration of chrism, surrounded by the crosses, the candles and the smoking thuribles.

---

[455] "Audi iudex mortuorum, Una spes mortalium, Audi voces proferentum Donum pacis praevium." Vogel, Elze, and Andrieu, *Le Pontifical romano-germanique du dixième siècle*, 72. PRG 269.

[456] "O redemptor sume carmen Temet concinentium…/ Stans ad aram immo supplex Infulatus pontifex / Debitum persolvit omne Consecrato chrismate / O redemptor…Consecrare tu dignare, Rex perennis patriae, / Hoc olivum signum vivum Iura contra demonum. / O redemptor…Lota mente sacro fonte Aufugantur criminal / Uncta fronte sacrosancta Influunt chrismata. / O redemptor…" Vogel, Elze, and Andrieu, *Le Pontifical romano-germanique du dixième siècle*, 72. PRG 269.

Within the medieval liturgy, the sermon was a central and stable feature that allowed celebrants to interpret biblical texts and communicate essential ideas to their communities.[457] Liturgists constructed the meaning or significance of feast days and their rites through juxtaposing chants, liturgical readings and sermons, which were often excerpts from Patristic writings.[458] The early sermon literature of the early medieval period in particular was essential for later liturgical developments. Margot Fassler observed that the fifth and sixth century sermons were, "the foundation upon which all future liturgical development took place, especially in the Office, where readings from early sermon literature shaped feasts and seasons as they were introduced in later periods."[459] Examining medieval compilations of sermons, known as homiliaries, can take one to the heart of these celebrations.[460]

Medieval collections of sermons or homilies (*homiliarium*) demonstrate that celebrants delivered a range of homilies on Holy Thursday, due the non-uniformity of a homiletic tradition as well as the fact that within a single community, a variety of sermons were available on certain feast days.[461] While no two homiliaries are identical, two principle traditions existed, which bore considerable influence on subsequent collections of homilies. The homiliary of Alain of Farfa (d.769), which belonged to the Basilica of St. Peter in Roman, testifies to the early Roman homiletic tradition. The homiliary of Paul Diacre (720-799), which was commissioned by Charlemagne, later

---

[457] In most of the medieval period the Latin words corresponding with "sermon" and "homily" were used interchangeably. See Kienzle, *The Sermon*; Fassler and Baltzer, *The Divine Office in the Latin Middle Ages*, 46n.65; Grégoire, *Les homéliaires du moyen âge; inventaire et analyse des manuscrits.*, 6n26; Grégoire, *Homeliaires Liturgiques Medievaux*, 18–24. The secondary literature on medieval sermons is vast. Some starting points for this aspect of medieval religious practices include: Kienzle, *The Sermon*; Fassler and Baltzer, *The Divine Office in the Latin Middle Ages*, 18, 33–36.
[458] Fassler and Baltzer, *The Divine Office in the Latin Middle Ages*, 21.
[459] Ibid., 18–19.
[460] "…the homiliaries and their traditions are both as complicated and as important to liturgical history as the sacramentaries and Gospel books, and…they are the first great body of liturgical book prepared specifically for the Office use, taking the researcher to the heart of this subject more directly than any other body of early liturgical materials." Ibid., 33.
[461] Réginald Grégoire's inventories and analyses of medieval homiliaries are invaluable references for determining what homilies were delivered on a given day. See Grégoire, *Les homéliaires du moyen âge; inventaire et analyse des manuscrits.*; Grégoire, *Homeliaires Liturgiques Medievaux*.

became the basis for the Roman breviary.[462] An array of homiliaries, which do not conform to either

of these traditions demonstrate, according to Réginald Grégoire, the "suppleness" of the liturgical

practices in the medieval period.[463]

On Holy Thursday, if a bishop was present to celebrate a Chrism Mass, the celebrant

potentially read one of two sermons: either the *Sermo generalis de confectione chrismatis* or a sermon

known only by its incipit, *Chrismate unguendum primum Moyses*.[464] Neither of these sermon texts appear

in the homiliaries inventoried in Grégoire's *Les homéliaires du moyen âge; inventaire et analyse des manuscrits*

(1966)[465] nor in the homiliaries listed in his second inventory *Homeliaires liturgiques médiévaux* (1980).[466]

The sermon texts or references to them appear mainly in pontificals, not homiliaries. One mention

of this sermon appears in an eleventh-century letter by Peter Damien (1007-1071).[467] At least twenty

manuscripts (mainly pontificals), dating from the tenth to the thirteenth centuries, contain either one

or both sermons.[468] The sermon texts first appeared in print in the late eighteenth century, when

Edmund Martène, a French Benedictine monk in the Congregation of St. Maur, published the

sermons in his *De antiquis ecclesiae ritibus* (1737), based on a small number of manuscripts of uncertain

---

[462] Grégoire, *Les homéliaires du moyen âge; inventaire et analyse des manuscrits.*, 7.

[463] Ibid.

[464] Vogel appends the text of this sermon after the *Sermo generalis*, at the end of the rites for *In Cena Domini*. Vogel, Elze, and Andrieu, *Le Pontifical romano-germanique du dixième siècle*, 82–85. PRG XCIX, 255. Peter Maier, however, makes no mention of this sermon in his study of the Chrism Mass. Furthermore, Reginald Grégoire does not list the *Sermo generalis* as one of the sermons traditionally delivered for *In Cena Domini*.

[465] Grégoire, *Les homéliaires du moyen âge; inventaire et analyse des manuscrits.*

[466] Grégoire, *Homeliaires Liturgiques Medievaux*, 158–160.

[467] "Sacrosancto itaque baptismatis lavacro ego iuxta morem Romanae aecclesiae solum crisma semper inmiscui , vinum vero permisceri vel oleum nunquam vidi . Nam et illa scriptura , quae in die coenae Domini legitur , quae etiam sic attitulatur: Sermo generalis de confectione crismatis, hoc videtur exprimere , ut nil praeter sanctum crisma debeamus fonti baptismatis admiscere . Ait enim inter caetera : Oleo vero sacri crismatis conficitur aqua baptismatis , et efficitur fons gratiae coelestis. Nam cum ille sermonis istius auctor de oleo sanctificato sufficienter superius eloquatur , quando vero ad baptisma descendit , tacito oleo solo illud perhibet crismate confici." See LLT: Petrus Damiani – Epistulae CLXXX, vol.:4, epist.:177, pag.: 285, linea: 11 and Peter Damian, "Die Briefe des Petrus Damiani. Teil 4," Monumenta Germaniae Historica, accessed on April 11, 2017, http://www.mgh.de/dmgh/resolving/MGH_Briefe_d._dt._Kaiserzeit_4,4_S._285.

[468] See Appendix I for a list of manuscripts containing the sermons. Thanks to Henry Parkes for bringing several of these manuscripts to my attention.

date and provenance.[469] More recently, Andrieu (posthumously) published the texts in his *Les Ordines romani,* as OR L. His edition, however, was based on only ten manuscripts, which were not the earliest known manuscript witnesses. The sources consulted for Andrieu's edition of the chrism sermons thus do not account for the earliest codices, which are of disparate provenance and thus call into question not only the dissemination of the sermon, but the evolution of the PRG as Andrieu conceived it.

To date, scholars have not substantively studied the chrism sermons and how they became part of the PRG. No scholar has created a *stemma codicum* for all the manuscripts containing the sermon texts, and thus have not sufficiently explained the possible evolution and dissemination of the chrism sermons throughout Europe.[470] Peter Maier's *Die Feier der Missa chrismatis: die Reform der Ölweihen des Pontificale Romanum vor dem Hintergrund der Ritusgeschichte* remains the most in-depth study of the evolution of medieval Chrism Mass. Maier did not, however, address how and why these sermons became a stable feature of the Chrism Mass or who their author(s) might have been. In his article "The Chrism Mass in Later Anglo-Saxon England" (2005), Christopher A. Jones traced developments in the Chrism Mass in England and argued the changes corresponded to the ascent of the episcopacy. Like Maier, however, Jones did not include an investigation of the chrism sermons in his study. Most recently, Henry Parkes' *The making of liturgy in the Ottonian Church: books, music and ritual in Mainz, 950-1050* (2015) observed that the chrism sermons were an amalgamation of authoritative texts, including Amalarius of Metz's (c.780-850) *De ecclesiasticis officiis* and the Pseudo-Isidorian Decretals; he conceded that further analysis of the sermons' origins was beyond the purview of his study.

---

[469] Martène, *De antiquis ecclesiae ritibus.*
[470] This research is beyond the scope of this chapter. Here I base my analysis of the sermon text on Andrieu's edition as it appears in the PRG/OR L.

The *Sermo generalis de confectione chrismatis* begins with the bishop addressing his fellow clerics, as opposed to the laity: "…my brothers, O you priests of the Lord and other clerics, not laity…"[471] In keeping with the theme of Holy Thursday, in which Jesus makes a gesture of serving his disciples, the chrism sermon spoke of the role of clerics as ministers, particularly of the sacraments. Echoing the Apostle Paul, Augustine and, in turn, Amalarius of Metz (who may have authored the sermon), the sermon spoke of how God had the power to heal the sick and drive away demons without oil. The oil was a visible sign, provided by God, on account of the fragility (weakness) of human nature, which has need of visible things in order to grasp the invisible or spiritual.[472] The consecration of the chrism brings about an ontological change in the oil, like the consecration of the Eucharist. The appearance of the liquid and its actual substance no longer correspond: "Truly, when offered by the bishop, the oil is, and has the physical appearance of, a simple liquid, but after the benediction of priests, the oil is transformed into a sacrament."[473] According to the *Sermo generalis*, the consecrated oil had the power to impart peace, which was the "work of divine grace, so that peace and concord might reign among us."[474] Like Amalarius of Metz, the author of the sermon quoted Isidore of Seville's interpretation of the olive tree as a sign of peace.[475] The sermon also correlated the sweet smell of balsam with the good reputation of Christians and then explained the symbolic meaing behind the rites of Christiantian initiation, including the transformation of the baptismal font into a "fountain of heavenly grace" (*fons gratia caelestis*) once it was anointed with chrism. The fonte brought about regeneration, functioning as a portal of death and rebirth.

---

[471] "fratres mei, o vos sacerdotes domini et ceteri clerici necnon et laici." Vogel, Elze, and Andrieu, *Le Pontifical romano-germanique du dixième siècle*, 82. PRG 301. I am translating "necnon" as "and not" rather than as "and also" since the bishops appears to only address his fellow clerics.

[472] "Potest enim Deus sine oleo sanare infirmos sanctificareque suos, et daemones effugare, sed propter fragiles et animales aguntur haec visibilia, ut spiritualia et invisibilia facilius capiantur." Vogel, Elze, and Andrieu, *Le Pontifical romano-germanique du dixième siècle*, 83. PRG 301.

[473] "Oleum vero, quando offertum pontifici, simplex liquor est et speciem habet corporalem, sed post benedictionem sacerdotum transfertur in sacramentum." Ibid.

[474] "hoc est opus gratiae divinae ut pax et concordia regnent in nobis." Ibid.

[475] See Chapter 4. If the author of the sermon was not Amalarius himself, he evidently borrowed directly from Amalarius' expositions on the liturgy.

The second chrism sermon, known by its incipit, *Christmate unguendum primum Moyses*, appears to have likewise beeen directed toward clerics. The sermon traces the Christian anointing tradition back to Hebrews, whose priests and kings prefigured Christ. According to the sermon, God first commanded Moses to anoint Aaron and his sons, whose "mystical anointing" foreshadowed Christ, whose name means anointed "by anointing."[476] After citing the royal and priestly nature of anointing among the Hebrews, the sermon explained that all Christians received holy unction due to the spiritual rather than physical nature of their anointing: "But after our Lord, the true king and eternal priest, was anointed (*delibutus*) with a celestial and mystical unguent by God the Father, now not only high priests (*pontifices*) and kings but everyone in the Church is consecrated with the unction of anointing through the imposition of hands."[477] The sermon then traces the tradition of anointing with literal oil, as opposed to with the spirit through the imposition of hands, one of the most ancient ritual practices in the church. Throughout the discourse on anointing, the sermon emphasized the exclusive role of clerics in administering anointings with actual physical oil (as opposed to spiritual oil), which had the power to fortify the anointed.

The Consecration of Chrism

When the bishop concluded the chrism sermon, he turned toward the east, the symbolic location of resurrection and new life. An archdeacon then processed forward holding the oil ampulla, wrapped in silk, in his left hand. The bishop then mixed the balsam with the oil, invoking the powers of God Omnipotent, whose Son assumed human nature while remaining eternal: "cooperating with the grace of the Holy Spirit, [God the Father] smeared (*linivit*) [Jesus] with the oil

---

[476] "…in regibus et sacerdotibus mistica unction qua Christus figurabatur, unde et ipsum nomen a chrismate dicitur." Vogel, Elze, and Andrieu, *Le Pontifical romano-germanique du dixième siècle*, 84. PRG 302.
[477] "Sed postquam dominus noster, verus rex et sacerdos aeternus, a Deo patre, caelestis ac mistico unguento est delibutus, iam non soli pontifices et reges, sed omnis ecclesia unctione chrismatis per impositionem manuum consecratur." Ibid.

of exaltation before his partakers."[478] The prayer presents a curious variation on the much-quoted verse from Psalm 44; instead of being anointed *prae consortibus suis,* "before his companions" the Christ is anointed "before his partakers" (*prae participibus*). Those who partake or participate in Jesus' anointing (i.e. those who are anointed), receive an interior as well as an exterior anointing that divinizes the anointed. According to the consecration prayer, the interior anointing had the power to free the anointed from "all the filth of corporeal matter" such that anointed might rejoice as "a partaker of the kingdom of heaven."[479] The bishop would then pronounce another prayer promising eternal health and protection for the anointed, and then breathe over the ampulla, reciting prayers of exorcism, acknowledging the material nature of the olive as God's creation and putting demonic spirits to flight. A benediction followed, in which the bishop traced the role of the olive in salvation history.

OTHER SERMONS FOR HOLY THURSDAY

If a bishop was not present to celebrate a Chrism Mass on Holy Thursday, following the reading from the gospel (John 13:1-15) the celebrant might have delivered any number of sermons, drawing from both patristic texts and the early sermon literature of the fifth and sixth-centuries. This analysis of the sermons for *In Cena Domini* will include sermons from ten codices dating from the tenth through the thirteenth centuries as well as the homilies listed in Grégoire's first homiletic inventory, *Les homéliaires du moyen âge; inventaire et analyse des manuscrits* (1966) and his second inventory, *Homeliaires Liturgiques Medievaux* (1980).[480] Some codices list a number of sermons for the same feast day, indicating that either celebrants delivered more than one sermon on that day – if, for instance,

---

[478] "gratia cooperante sancti spiritus, oleo exultationis prae participibus suis linivit." Vogel, Elze, and Andrieu, *Le Pontifical romano-germanique du dixième siècle,* 73. PRG 272.

[479] "quicumque exterius inde perunctus fuerit, ita interius liniatur, quo omnibus sordibus corporalis materiae carens, se participem regni caelestis effici gratuletur." Ibid.

[480] From Grégoire, *Les homéliaires du moyen âge; inventaire et analyse des manuscrits.*; *Homeliaires Liturgiques Medievaux.*

three Masses were celebrated instead of one – or that celebrants may have had a range of sermons to choose from. The sermons may have also been used for short readings during other offices besides those in which Mass was celebrated.

Perhaps not surprisingly, the gospel reading for *In Cena Domini* was never the pericope of Jesus' anointing at Bethany. This reading did appear, however, close to Holy Week and was often accompanied by sermons from Augustine, Gregory the Great, the Venerable Bede and Héric of Auxerre. A tenth or eleventh-century *homiliarium* (Palat.lat.431) contains a homily on the anointing at Bethany, which was read for Lauds on the last Friday of Lent, just before the beginning of the great pageantry of Holy Week. The gospel reading was drawn from John 12, in which the anointing takes place six days before the Passover, when Jesus washed his disciples' feet. Thus, the reading of Mary Magdalene's anointing of Jesus was positioned six days before the celebration of the Last Supper on Holy Thursday. In the pericope, the anointing took place at the home of Mary, Martha and their brother Lazarus, whom Jesus raised from the dead.[481] The sermon following this gospel was drawn from Augustine's *Tractatus 49*, in which the Bishop of Hippo dwelt on the resurrection of Lazarus rather than the anointing of Jesus.

On Holy Thursday, the gospel text for Lauds and Vespers was likewise the anointing at Bethany, although this time the pericope was from Luke's Gospel, accompanied by Gregory the Great's Homily 33 (circa 591-592), in which the *peccatrix* plays a central role.[482] Two manuscripts contain Gregory's Homily 33: Palat.lat.431, the tenth or eleventh-century *homilarium* and Arch. S

---

[481] "In illo tempore. Erat quidam languens lazarus abethania decastello mariae et marthe sororis eius. Maria autem erat quae unxit dominum unguento et extersit capillis suis pedes eius cuius frater lazarus infirmabatur et rel[iqua]." "BAV Pal.lat.431," fol.79v.

[482] The manuscript reads: "LV Fer. V. EBD.V. IN XL Lec. Sci. Eug. Scd. Lucam In illo tempore Rogauit iesum quidam phariseus ut manducaret cum illo. Et ingressus domum pharisei discubuit. Et ecce mulier quae erat in ciuitate peccatrix ut cognouit quod iesus accubuit in domo pharisei [fol.84r] adtulit alabastrum unguenti et rel[iqua]." Ibid., fol.83v–84r. According to Harper, the Gospel reading for Matins was the identical to the reading for the Mass that day: "In the monastic Use the longer form of Matins also included the Gospel after *Te deum laudamus*. The text was that of the Mass of the day, and also corresponded with the Gospel verse before the lessons from the homily, but here it was recited in full." Harper, *The Forms and Orders of Western Liturgy from the Tenth to the Eighteenth Century*, 82. Perhaps on Holy Thursday, however, the Gospel reading for Lauds and Vespers differed from the Gospel read during the Mass (John 13).

Pietro B 42, a thirteenth-century *homilarium*.[483] The texts of these two manuscripts, however, show

variations of Gregory's text, as is evident from their opening lines.[484] David Hurst observed that in

the medieval period, Gregory's writings were greatly influential among monastic communities not

only because they were reproduced in their own right, but also because they were widely reproduced

in the biblical commentaries of the Venerable Bede (672-735).[485] Naturally, the proliferation of a text

meant attendant textual variations, due either to scribal error or deliberate alteration. In the late sixth

century, when Gregory composed his homilies on the Gospels, of which Homily 33 is one, an

allegorical reading of scripture had largely eclipsed a literal or historical reading.[486] In Homily 33,

Gregory first offered a literal interpretation of the anointing, then a mystical reading.[487] In the

exposition of the literal meanings, Gregory gave an explanation of alabaster and the woman herself.

In the mystical reading, Gregory presented fragrant oil as a means of pursuing the pleasures of the

flesh, rather than spiritual sanctification. First Gregory addressed the more earthly, material nature

of the unguent, briefing his brothers on the historical-critical context for nard and alabaster:

> Alabaster is a kind of marble for storing the best ointment. Evidently, brothers, the woman
> who earlier was intent on illicit actions, used the unguent on herself for the fragrance of her
> flesh. What therefore she had earlier used for concupiscence of the flesh, this she now

---

[483] The opening lines of Arch. S Pietro B 42 more closely resembles the version of the text found in PL and LLT, than Palat.lat.431: "Cogitanti mihi de marie penitentia flere magis libet quam aliquid dicere..." "BAV Arch. S Pietro B 42," fol.60v.

[484] The homily in Pal.lat.431, dating from the tenth or eleventh century, opens with the following lines: "Lectio sancti euangelii fratres karissimi quam audistis de mariae paenitentia salutaris nobis remedii contulit exemplum...Dominus uero iesus ideo ad conuiuia peccatorum uocatus uenire non rennuit. ut occasionem haberet docendi et spiritales inuitatoribus suis praeberet cibos et Humility eius eundo ad peccatores et potentia doctrinae in poenitentum conuersatione monstraretur." "BAV Pal.lat.431," fol.84r. Arch. S Pietro B 42, however, begins: "Cogitanti mihi de marie penitentia flere magis libet quam aliquid dicere..." "BAV Arch. S Pietro B 42," fol.54v.

[485] Gregory, *Forty Gospel Homilies*, 4.

[486] David Hurst states: "...like many of his predecessors and contemporaries [Gregory] is also given to expounding the import of a particular passage, especially of the New Testament, by referring to a verbal or mental resemblance to another part of either the Old or New Testament. This is the basis of allegorical interpretation – explaining one statement or place or event in the scriptures by alluding to a suggestive or similar account or name or happening of an earlier instance." Gregory, *Forty Gospel Homilies*, trans. David Hurst (Kalamazoo, Mich.: Cistercian Publications, 1990), 1-2. Fassler notes that Gregory's homilies are based upon a particular lectionary and thus pertain directly to the Gospel readings themselves. Fassler and Baltzer, *The Divine Office in the Latin Middle Ages*, 21.

[487] "Haec, fratres charissimi, historica expositione transcurrimus; nunc vero, si placet, ea quae dicta sunt mystico intellectu disseramus." PL, Col.1242A. This phrase is missing from the edition of the text in Pal.lat.431.

laudably offered to God. Earlier with her eyes, she had ardently desired earthly things but now she cried, exhausting her eyes with penance. She had exhibited the beauty of her hair to compliment her face but she [later] dried tears with that hair. With her mouth, she had spoken arrogant things, but this mouth dissolved, kissing the feet of the Lord. The pleasures she possessed within herself were as many as the sacrifices she discovered. She converted so great a number of crimes into virtues that she entirely served God in penance, as she had disdained the Lord himself in sin.[488]

In the subsequent mystical exposition of the pericope, Gregory explained that the woman symbolized the Gentiles who had been converted to Christianity, which included Gregory himself and his audience. In this interpretation, the woman's unguent represented the good reputation of Christians, who dispersed their aroma (goodness) throughout the Church, symbolized by the Lord's body.[489]

> Whom does the Pharisee, who relies on his spurious righteousness, represent but the Jewish people? And whom the sinful woman, coming to the Lord's feet and weeping there, except the Gentiles who have been converted? She came with an alabaster flask, she poured out the ointment, she stood behind [Christ] at his feet, she wet his feet with her tears, she wiped with her hair the feet she had moistened, and she did not cease to kiss the feet she had wiped. That woman represented us, if we return to the Lord wholeheartedly after we have sinned, if we imitate the distress of her repentance. And what is indicated by the ointment

---

[488] "Alabastrum genus est marmoris ad seruanda unguenta obtimum. Liquet fratres quod[488] in licitis actibus prius mulier intenta unguentum sibi pro odore suae carnis exibuit. Quod ergo sibi antea per carnis concupiscentiam ad hibuerat. hoc nunc deo laudabiliter offerebat. Per occulos antea terrena concupierat sed hos iam per paenitentiam conterens flebat; Capillorum decorem ad compositionem uultus exibuerat sed illis capillis lacrimis tergebat. Ore superba dixerat sed hoc pedes domini osculans diluebat; quot ergo in se habuit oblectamenta tot de se inuenit holocausta conuertit ad uirtutum numerum criminum ut totum seruiret deo in paenitentia quicquid ex se dominum contempserat in culpa." "BAV Pal.lat.431," fol.84r. The LLT text presents a few variations: "Liquet, fratres, quod illicitis actibus prius mulier intenta, unguentum sibi pro odore suae carnis adhibuit. Quod ergo sibi turpiter exhibuerat, hoc iam Deo laudabiliter offerebat. Oculis terrena concupierat, sed hos iam per paenitentiam conterens flebat. Capillos ad compositionem uultus exhibuerat, sed iam capillis lacrimas tergebat. Ore superba dixerat, sed pedes Domini osculans, hoc in Redemptoris sui uestigia figebat. Quot ergo in se habuit oblectamenta, tot de se inuenit holocausta. Conuertit ad uirtutum numerum numerum criminum, ut totum seruiret Deo in paenitentia, quidquid ex se Deum contempserat in culpa." LLT: Gregorius Magnus – Homiliae in euangelia (CPL 1711), Cl 1711, lib.:2, homilia: 33, par.: 4, pag.: 291, linea: 25ff.
[489] Regarding the role of fragrance or a fine odor as a sign of sanctity in Christianity, see Béatrice Caseau, "Syméon Stylite Entre Parfum et Puanteur" *Revue des études byzantines* 63 (2005): 71-96; Susan Harvey, *Scenting Salvation: Ancient Christianity and the Olfactory Imagination* (Berkeley: University of California Press, 2006).

except the aroma of a good reputation? So Paul says, *We are the aroma of Christ to God everywhere.* If then we do what we ought to do, by spreading the aroma of a good reputation throughout the Church, what are we doing except pouring out ointment on the Lord's body?[490]

The homily then described the ways in which penitents' acts of contrition mirrored those of the woman. Gregory identified Christ's feet as the "lowliest members" of the Church, an echo of the glosses in the *Glossa Ordinaria* drawn in *Moralia in Job.*

> And the woman stood at his feet. We have stood over against his feet when we were in a state of sin and resisting his ways. If we turn to him in true repentance after we have sinned, we are standing behind Jesus at his feet, since we are following in the footsteps of him we opposed. The woman wet his feet with her tears. We do this in actuality if we are moved by compassion toward any of the Lord's lowliest members, if we are compassionate to his holy ones in their tribulations, if we consider their sorrows our own.[491]

---

[490] The above English translation is David Hurst's, which is based on an assortment of manuscripts not printed in a single edited edition. See Gregory, *Forty Gospel Homilies,* 3, 272. The text from Pal.lat.431, which is a variation of Gregory's text, reads: "Nos ergo nos illa mulier expraesit si toto corde ad dominum post peccata redeamus. si eius penitentiae luctus imitemus. Cum Vunguentum igitur boni odoris in sancta aecclesia flagrare facimus quid aliud quam in dominum corpus unguentum fundimus. Nam si post pecca ad ueram paenitentiam conuertimus quasi retro secus pedes domini ut mulier stamus quia eius uestigia sequimur. Pedes eius lacrimis rigamus si quibus libet ultimus in aecclesia quia membra sunt domini." "BAV Pal.lat.431," fol.84v–85r. The most definitive modern edition of Gregory's Homily is Raymond Étaix's edition in Corpus Christianorum v. 141, reproduced in the LLT: "Quem namque pharisaeus de falsa iustitia praesumens nisi iudaicum populum, quem peccatrix mulier, sed ad uestigia Domini ueniens et plorans, nisi conuersam gentilitatem designat? Quae cum alabastro uenit, unguentum fudit, retro secus pedes stetit, lacrimis pedes rigauit, capillis tersit, eosdem que quos infundebat et tergebat pedes osculari non desiit. Nos ergo, nos illa mulier expressit, si toto corde ad Dominum post peccata redeamus, si eius paenitentiae luctus imitemur. Quid namque unguento, nisi bonus odor opinionis exprimitur? Vnde et Paulus dicit: Christi bonus odor sumus Deo in omni loco. Si igitur recta opera agimus, quibus opinionis bonae odore ecclesiam respergamus, quid in Domini corpore nisi unguentum fundimus?" LLT: Gregorius Magnus – Homiliae in euangelia (CPL 1711), Cl 1711, lib.:2, homilia: 33, par.: 4, pag.: 291, linea: 104-113. The PL text reads: "Quem namque Pharisaeus de falsa justitia praesumens nisi Judaicum populum, quem peccatrix mulier, sed ad vestigia Domini veniens et plorans, nisi conversam gentilitatem designat? Quae cum alabastro venit, unguentum fudit, retro secus pedes Domini stetit, lacrymis pedes rigavit, capillis tersit, eosdemque quos infundebat et tergebat, pedes osculari non desiit. Nos ergo, nos illa mulier expressit, si toto corde ad Dominum post peccata redeamus, si ejus poenitentiae luctus imitemur. Quid namque unguento nisi bonae odor opinionis exprimitur? Unde et Paulus dicit: *Christi bonus odor sumus Deo in omni loco* (II Cor. II) Si igitur recta opera agimus, quibus opinionis bonae odore Ecclesiam respergamus, quid in Domini corpore nisi unguentum fundimus?" PL 76, Col.1242A-B.

[491] Gregory, *Forty Gospel Homilies,* 273. Étaix's text reads: "Sed secus pedes mulier stetit. Contra pedes enim Domini stetimus cum in peccatis positi eius itineribus renitebamur. Sed si ad ueram paenitentiam post peccata conuertimur, iam retro secus pedes stamus, quia eius uestigia sequimur quem impugnabamus. Lacrimis mulier pedes rigat. Quod nos quoque ueraciter agimus, si quibuslibet ultimis membris Domini per compassionis affectum inclinemur, si sanctis eius in tribulatione compatimur, si eorum tristitiam nostram putamus." LLT: Gregorius Magnus – Homiliae in euangelia (CPL 1711), Cl 1711, lib.:2, homilia: 33, par.: 4, pag.: 291, linea: 116-120. The PL text is nearly identical. See PL 76, Col.1242B.

Gregory goes on to explain that Jesus' feet represent not only the "lowliest members" but also the

Incarnation. Anointing those divine feet meant preaching about the Incarnation itself: "We kiss our

Redeemer's feet when we love the mystery of his incarnation with our whole heart. We anoint his

feet with ointment when we preach the power of his humanity by the good repute of our holy

speech."[492] The homily ends by exhorting listeners to imitate the woman: "Dearly beloved, bring

back to your mind's eye, bring before you the repentant sinful woman as an example for you to

imitate."[493] Instead of *imitatio Christi*, we see an early exhortation to *imitatio peccatricis*.

The Gospel reading for the Mass on Holy Thursday, according to Pal.lat.431, was the

standard pericope from John 13 in which Jesus, not the woman, washes feet. The homily for this

gospel reading was drawn from the Venerable Bede's Homily 5. In this text, Bede makes no mention

of Mary having washed Jesus' feet and anointed them with oil. Instead, like Augustine, Bede focused

on the theme of resurrection: Jesus' paschal passage from this life to the next. Bede also offered a

mystical interpretation of foot washing: the forgiveness of sins and washing away of spiritual

impurities.[494] Never, however, did Bede apply this mystical interpretation of footwashing to the

ablution of Jesus' own feet.

Arch. S. Pietro C.105, a partially mutilated tenth-century codex, ends with the sermons for

Holy Thursday. The manuscript is a *homilarium* reflecting the sixth-century usage of the Vatican

---

The text for Pal.lat.431 presents a highly abbreviated version: "per affectum compassionis inclinemur. Sanctis uiris in tribulatione eorum conpatimur si eorum tristiciam quasi nostram doleamus." "BAV Pal.lat.431," fol.85r.

[492] English translation from Gregory, *Forty Gospel Homilies*, 274.

[493] Ibid., 278. Pal.lat.431's text reads: "Festinate ergo adtantae pietatis sinum considerate apertum uobis misericordiae gremium ad uos {met ipsios} mentis occulos redu cite et paenitentiam peccatricis mulieris in exemplum uobis imitationis ante ferte." "BAV Pal.lat.431," fol.85r–85v.

[494] "Fer .V. In cena domini Lec. Sci. Eug. Scd. Ioh. In illo tempore Ante diem festum pasche sciens iesus quia uenit eius hor ut transeat ex hoc mundo ad patrem. Cum dilexisset suos quierant in mundo in finem dilexit eos et reliqua." "BAV Pal.lat.431," fol.88v. For the Latin text of Bede, see LLT: Beda Uenerabilis - Homeliarum euangelii libri ii (CPL 1367) lib. : 2, hom. : 5. The text in Palat.lat.431 includes: "Sacro sanctam ac uenerabile ministerium quod fecit dominus et saluator noster fratres karissimi...Ipse post custodiant mandatorum suorum ad beatitudinem nos suae perpetuae uisionis inducat." Ibid., fol.88v–90r.

basilica ("ad usum basilicae vaticanae").[495] Unfortunately, the Arch. S. Pietro C.105 codex ends with

the opening lines of the first homily for *In Cena Domini*. The text was drawn from Augustine's

Tractatus 55, a commentary on John 13:1-5, which Thomas Aquinas later reproduced in his *Catena

aurea in Iohannem* (circa 1261-1265).[496] Reg.lat.195, an eleventh-century *homiliarium* likewise includes

this text as one of several sermons for *In Cena Domini*, suggesting both codices might stem from

Alain of Farfa's homiliary.[497] Based on this codex, we can determine that the sermon, if it was

roughly identical to that of Arch. S. Pietro C.105, largely dealt with the theme of passing from

earthly life to eternal life, rather than anointing.[498] Augustine's commentary focused on the pericope

in which Jesus washes his disciples' feet, knowing that he would soon leave them. Augustine's text,

however, makes no reference to oil. The commentary focused instead on Jesus assuming the role of

servant, itself a symbol for the humanity assumed by God, a humanity that would soon be

transformed once again into pure divinity. Augustine drew a parallel between the washing of feet

and the crucifixion: both bring about purification, one physical, the other spiritual.

A second sermon for Holy Thursday in Reg.lat.195, drawn from Augustine's *Tractatus 56*, is

an exposition of the next few lines of the gospel, John 13:6-10, in which Jesus urges Peter to let him

wash his feet.[499] This sermon also focused on foot washing, omitting any direct mention of oil or

---

[495] "Incipiunt sermones in caena domini." "BAV Arch. S. Pietro C.105," fol.281v. Regarding this MS, Fassler notes: "Vatican, BAV San Pietro C 105 is a liturgical homiliary from the Basilica of St. Peter's itself, the handwriting dating from the second half of the tenth century. This fragmentary book, the surviving contents of which represent the first part of the church year, is very close to the homiliary from Alan of Farfa..." Fassler and Baltzer, *The Divine Office in the Latin Middle Ages*, 34. Grégoire notes: "Cet homéliaire reproduit, avec quelques interpolations postérieures (notamment les fêtes mariales) celui de Saint-Pierre de Rome, du VIᵉ siècle. Ainsi qu'il a été dit ci-dessus, il a été repris par Alain de Farfa; le manuscrit date du IX-X siècle." Grégoire, *Les homéliaires du moyen âge; inventaire et analyse des manuscrits.*, 8.

[496] All that remains of the sermon is: "Pascha non sicut quidam aestimant grecum nomen est. sed hebreum. Oportunissime tamen occurrit in hoc nomine quaedam congruentia utrarumque linguarium. Qui enim." "BAV Arch. S. Pietro C.105," fol.281v.

[497] "Incipiunt sermones in cena domini". "BAV Reg.lat.195," fol.31r.

[498] For the full Latin text of Augustine's commentary on the Gospel of John, see Augustine, *Tractatus 55*, "S. Aurelii Augustini OPERA OMNIA - Editio Latina," accessed on April 11, 2017, http://www.augustinus.it/ricerca/index.htm. The excerpt included in Reg.lat.195, fol.31r-33v, includes roughly the text from "Pascha non sicut aestimant grecum nomen est sed haebreum..." through "illi qui eum fuerat" with some omissions and textual variations. Sometimes the sermons included only excerpts from a patristic text rather than the text in its entirety. Pal.lat.431, for example, reproduces roughly 40% of Gregory the Great's Homily 33 as a sermon for *In Cena Domini*.

[499] "BAV Reg.lat.195," 34v–38v.

anointing. Augustine alluded, however, to a passage from the Song of Songs in which myrrh appears amidst nuptial imagery.[500] The bride wonders how she will let her lover into her room without dirtying her newly washed feet. Despite the risk of sullying her soles, the young woman rises to open the door. Doing so, her fingers drip with myrrh. Citing this same passage in his next commentary, *Tractatus 57*, Augustine claimed: "O admirabile sacramentum! O grande mysterium!" Given the role of memory in the medieval period, upon hearing Augustine's first the reference clean feet in the Song of Songs while commenting on Jesus washing Peter's feet, listeners may have very likely also recalled the pericope, including the presence of myrrh, especially given the prominence of myrrh in antiphons sung in the Liturgy of the Hours. One such antiphon, *Sicut myrrha electa odorem*, was popular for Marian feasts, but particularly the feast of the Purification of the Virgin (February 2).[501] Within the context of the Chrism Mass on *In Cena Domini*, prior to the *pedilavium* rite, Augustine's discussion of clean feet and (indirectly) hands dripping with myrrh would have imputed to the feast and its rituals a new meaning. By drawing a connection between the *pedilavium* ritual, oil, myrrh, and the Song of Songs, medieval Christians could further contemplate the *Mandatum novuum* – the great exhortation to love.

A partial *homilarium* from the twelfth century (Regin.lat.115) of French provenance contains two relevant homilies for *In Cena Domini* by Héric of Auxerre (841-876).[502] The homilies are part of

---

[500] Cant.5:1-5.

[501] The chant text reads: "Sicut mirra electa odorem dedisti suavitatis sancta dei genetrix." Lacoste (Project Manager and Principal Researcher) and Koláček (Web Developer), "Cantus Database: Inventories of Chant Sources | CANTUS Database," Can. 004942. For a further discussion of chants with myrrh or oil, see subsequent chapters.

[502] Salmon attributes these to Haimo of Auxerre (d. circa 878) but the LLT attributes to Héric of Auxerre. Salmon notes: "Homélaire de Pierre Quentell, composé des homélies d'Haymon d'Auxerre, sauf des ff. 65 – 114v, qui contiennent la collection *In quaresima*, d'Héric. Provient de France." See Salmon, *Les livres de lectures de l'office, les livres de l'office du chapitre, les livres d'heures*, no. 81. The homilies found on fol.130v-135v (Feria II) and fol.135v-144v (In Cena Domini), however, are attributed to Héric of Auxerre, by the LLT: Homiliae per circulum anni pars hiemalis, 63 and 64, respectively. For other Carolingian homiliaries, see Grégoire, *Les homéliaires du moyen âge; inventaire et analyse des manuscrits.*, 9–11. Grégoire notes that many of these Carolingian homiliaries present innovative composite arrangements of previous homiliaries: "Ces collections seront reprises, interpolées et altérées, et formeront ainsi de nouvelles collections plus ou moins composites, dont subsisten aujourd'hui encore plusieurs manuscrits. L'oeuvre la plus originale de l'homilétique carolingienne est sans conteste celle d'Héric d'Auxerre." Ibid., 11.

Héric's larger work, *Homiliae per circulum anni pars hiemalis*.[503] The homily for Monday of Holy Week (Feria II) was Homily 63 on the Anointing at Bethany from John 12.[504] The next homily in the collection, Homily 64, commented on John 13, in which Jesus washed his disciples feet, suggesting a close correlation between the washing and anointing of Jesus' feet and Jesus' subsequent washing of the disciples' feet.[505] In Homily 63, Héric borrowed from one of Bede's homilies, which Alcuin subsequently reproduced in an epistle.[506] Héric began by explaining the mystical significance of the meal in Bethany, at which Mary anointed Jesus: "Mystically this dinner which is prepared by the Lord signifies the faith of the holy Church."[507] Héric noted that one ought not overlook the fact that the meal took place on the Mount of Olives, which itself signified mercy:

> Rightly this dinner is celebrated in Bethany, which is a city situated on the side of the Mount of Olives, which signifies the house of obedience, foreshadowing the holy Church, which faithfully complies with the commands of her founder. The house is built on the Mount of Olives, that is, of mercy, because the Church was founded on Christ.[508] It is also fitting that the house is on the side of the same mountain, because the holy Church was soaked with the

---

[503] "BAV Regin.lat.115," fol.130v–135v; fol.135v–144v. For modern edited edition of Héric of Auxerre's works, see Heiric of Auxerre, *Heirici Autissiodorensis Homiliae per circulum anni*, Riccardo Quadri, ed. (Turnholt: Brepols, 1992). For secondary literature, see Joyce Hill, "Ælfric and Heiric of Auxerre" *Poetica: An International Journal of Linguistic-Literary Studies* 75 (2011): 103-23; Veronika Büren, "Auxerre, lieu de production de manuscrits?" in *Etudes d'exégèse carolingienne: Autour d'Haymon d'Auxerre. Atelier de recherches, Centre d'études médiévales d'Auxerre 25-26 avril 2005*, Sumi Shimahara, ed. (Turnhout: Brepols, 2007), 167-86 ; Edouard Jeauneau, "Dans le sillage de l'Erigène" in *The Mind of Eiugena: Papers of a Colloquium, Dublin, 14-18 July 1970*, John O'Meara and Ludwig Bieler, eds (Dublin: Irish University Pres for the Royal Irish Academy, 1973), 113-124; Pierre Janin, "Heiric d'Auxerre et les Gesta Pontificum Autissiodorensium," *Francia: Forschungen zur Westeuropäischen Geschichte* 4 (1997): 89-105; Cantelli, "L'esegesi al tempo di Ludovico il Pio e Carlo il Calvo" in *Giovanni Scoto nel suo tempo. L'organizzazione del sapere in età carolingia. Atti del XXIV Convegno internazionale (Todi, 11-14 ottobre 1987)*, Claudio Leonardi and Enrico Menestò, eds. (Spoleto: Centro italiano di studi sull'alto medioevo), 261-336.

[504] "In illo tempore Ante sex dies paschae uenit iesus bethaniam ubi lazarus fuerat mortuus quem suscitauit iesus [in] Ierusalem [Irl.]." "Regin.lat.115," fol.130v. John states the anointing at Bethany took place six days before the Passover meal. Monday of Holy Week would, however, only be three days before Passover (Holy Thursday).

[505] "Ante diem festum paschae sciens iesus quia uenit eius hora ut transeat ex hoc mundo ad patrem..." "Regin.lat.115," fol.135v.

[506] See LLT: Beda Venerabilis – Homeliarum euangelii libri ii (CPL 1367) lib.: 2, hom.: 4, linea 75 ff; Alcuinus – Commentaria in sancti Iohannis Euangelium ep. Ad Gislam et Rodtrudam, col.: 907, linea: 8.

[507] "Mystice autem haec cena quae domino praeparatur, fidem designat sanctae ecclesiae." LLT: Héric of Auxerre, *Homiliae per Circulum Anni Pars Hiemalis, Homilly 63*, linea 64.

[508] "Oleum misericordiae" appears in an enumeration of the power of the psalms (attributed to Augustine) in which their power is likened to, among other things, the 'oil of mercy.' "BAV Arch.S.Pietro E 14," fol.10r.

water of ablution and the blood of purification, which flowed from the side of Christ

hanging on the cross.[509]

After stating the correspondence among olives, mercy, Christ (the Anointed One) and the Church,

Héric goes on to explicate the meaning of Mary's nard.

> 'Mary took a pound of precious, pure nard and anointed Jesus' feet and dried his feet with
> her hair.' Nard is a kind of aromatic ointment, which is considered to be preeminent among
> ointments. Pure ointment moreover is said to be trustworthy and true, because the unguent
> was uncorrupted and therefore was of great price, and because it was worthily prepared for
> anointing the feet of the Lord, or if we follow Matthew, for the head [of the Lord].[510]

Noting the disparity among the gospels regarding which part of Jesus' body Mary anointed, Héric

observed that in pouring out her nard, Mary showed not only her love, but the piety of other faithful

souls: "Truly in this deed Mary strove and gave evidence, not only of her great love for the Lord, but

also truly signaled the compliance of other faithful, pious souls. On the other hand, with the pound

of unguent, the perfection of justice was made prefigured."[511] Héric's exposition of this Gospel

passages contains two noteworthy references to the law or judgement – first in this instance

(*unguenti, perfectio iustitiae figuratur*), in which the unguent is the image of perfect law (presumably the

law of love) – and then later when he refers to the treatment of the lowest members of society as

------

[509] "Bene autem haec cena in Bethania celebratur, quae est ciuitas in latere montis Oliueti sita et interpretatur domus oboedientiae, sanctam praemonstrans ecclesiam quae fideliter iussis sui conditoris obtemperat. Est super montem Oliueti, hoc est misericordiae, constituta, quia ecclesia super Christum fundata est; aptissime quoque in latere eiusdem montis, quia ecclesia sancta ablutionis aqua et sanguine purificationis quae de latere Christi in cruce pendentis manauerunt imbuta est." LLT: Héric of Auxerre, *Homiliae per Circulum Anni Pars Hiemalis, Homilly 63*, linea 71-75.
[510] "Maria autem accepit libram nardi pistici pretiosi et unxit pedes domini Ihesu, et extersit capillis suis pedes eius. Nardus aromatica species est, quae fertur principalitatem tenere in unguentis; pisticum autem unguentum, id est fidele et uerum dicitur, quia incorruptum et ideo pretiosissimum erat, quod que unguendis domini pedibus, siue secundum Matheum perducendo capiti, dignissime praeparatur." Héric of Auxerre, *Homiliae per Circulum Anni Pars Hiemalis, Homilly 63*, linea 80–82.
[511] "Verum Maria in hoc facto, non solum suae magnae dilectionis qua erga dominum certabat dedit indicium, uerum etiam aliarum fidelium animarum pietatis signauit obsequium; per libram namque unguenti, perfectio iustitiae figuratur." LLT: Héric of Auxerre, *Homiliae per Circulum Anni Pars Hiemalis, Homilly 63*, linea 86.

pertaining to *iudicio* – the Last Judgement, with its connotation of a trial, legal action, a court, or a

tribunal. The interjection of legal terms into Héric's exegesis of Mary's anointing of Jesus suggests,

perhaps, a perception of justice residing with religious authorities in Carolingian Gaul. Mary, like the

Church, was a source of unguent, which represented law or justice. Héric continued his exposition

by invoking the 2 Corinthians 2:14-15, in which the role of Christians in their society is likened to a

fragrant aroma that would, presumably, be pleasing to all people.[512] According to Christ, Christians

were to live according to a new commandment or divine law: self-sacrifice. Instead of a fragrant

aroma emanating from the flesh of sacrificial victims at the temple, Christians offered themselves

instead, for the redemption or sanctification of others.

> Truly beautifully this unguent, made from pure nard, is remembered, for the unguent
>
> suggests the aroma of good opinion, with the apostle testifying, who said: We are the good
>
> aroma of Christ for God in every place.[513] And this unguent was made from pure, faithful
>
> nard, because without faith it is impossible to please God, nor is it possible to exist with a
>
> good reputation without the catholic faith. What should we understand by 'the Lord's feet' if
>
> not his lowliest members in the Church?[514]

Borrowing from Gregory the Great's Homily 33, Héric then elaborates on the meaning of the

woman's hair and the necessity of giving one's superfluous material possessions to the poor:

> The hair, truly, is superfluous to the body and being cut, it does not feel pain. What
>
> therefore does hair mean if not exterior things?[515] Therefore we dry the feet of the Lord with
>
> hair, when we possess superfluous things and busy ourselves with giving certain things to the

---

[512] The original inspiration for Paul's image may have been the smell released by the burning flesh of the temple sacrifices. Christians, who offered themselves as sacrificial victims as Jesus had, became the 'good aroma' – which is to say, they became sacrificial victims through their suffering and a redemptive spirit (i.e. fragrance) was released into the world for the benefit of others.

[513] 2 Cor 2:14-15.

[514] "Pulchre uero hoc unguentum ex nardo pistico factum memoratur; unguentum namque bonae odorem opinionis insinuat, apostolo testante qui ait: Christi bonus odor sumus Deo in omni loco. Et hoc unguentum ex nardo pistico, id est fideli, confectum erat, quia sine fide impossibile est placere Deo, nec potest esse bona fama sine fide catholica. Quid uero per pedes domini, nisi humilia membra eius in ecclesia accipere debemus?" LLT: Héric of Auxerre, *Homiliae per Circulum Anni Pars Hiemalis, Homilly 63*, linea 90–96.

[515] See Gregory the Great's Homily 33. See Gregory, *Forty Gospel Homilies*, 273.

poor and the least, about whom [the Lord] in the [Last] Judgement will say: 'As long as you did this to one of my least, you did so to me.'[516]

After his exhortation to his listeners to view the lowliest members of the Church or society as part of God Himself (Christ's body), Héric explained the meaning of the aroma filling Mary's house:

> Furthermore, the house is filled with the aroma of unguent when the Church is sprinkled with the good fame of religious life. Hence the Church is spoken of in the Song of Songs: when the king was reclining at his table, my nard gave off its fragrance.[517] Thus by the deed of Mary, who did this only once, it is expressed what the holy Church and any faithful soul must do every day.[518]

While the authors of the gospels sometimes observed the instances in which Jesus' words or actions fulfilled what had previously been written about the messiah in the Hebrew Scriptures, none of the Evangelists made such an observation when Mary anointed Jesus in Bethany; none of the gospel authors noted that, in being anointed with Mary's unguent, Jesus was like the king or bridegroom mentioned in the Song of Songs. Héric, however, saw the correspondence but did not make the parallel explicit. Only obliquely did he suggest that the anointed messiah was *rex*.

Pedilavium: The Washing of Feet

After the homily on Holy Thursday, when listeners were invited to dwell in their imaginations on the scenes of biblical anointings, the Chrism Mass proceeded. Once the bishop had

---

[516] "Capilli uero superfluunt corpori, et incisi non dolent: quid igitur per capillos, nisi exterior substantia designatur? Capillis ergo pedes domini tergimus, cum ea quae superflua possidemus pauperibus et quibusdam minimis erogare satagimus, de qualibus in iudicio dicturus est: Quamdiu fecistis uni ex minimis meis, michi fecistis." LLT: Héric of Auxerre, *Homiliae per Circulum Anni Pars Hiemalis, Homily 63*, linea 97–99. Here Héric alludes to Matthew 25:40: "Truly I tell you, just as you did it to one of the least of these who are members of my family, you did it to me."
[517] Cant. 1:11.
[518] "Domus autem impletur ex odore unguenti, cum ecclesia respergitur religiosae uitae fama bona; hinc in Canticis canticorum ecclesia loquitur: Cum esset rex in accubitu suo, nardus mea dedit odorem suum, ubi apertissime per hoc quod semel Maria fecerat, quid cottidie sancta ecclesia uel unaquaeque fidelis anima agat exprimitur." LLT: Héric of Auxerre, *Homiliae per Circulum Anni Pars Hiemalis, Homily 63*, linea 103. NB: "in accubitu suo" can be translated any number of ways, including "on his cushion" etc.

consecrated the oils, the Mass proceeded to Communion and the deposition of the host. Since no

Mass would be celebrated again until Easter, the bishop consecrated two hosts, one of which was

consumed by the celebrant and one of which was held in a special reliquary or sepulcher, until it was

divided; part was consumed the celebrant on Good Friday and part was raised on the cross on

Easter Sunday.[519] Following the deposition of the host, the altars of the church were stripped:

ornaments, candles, and clothes were removed. The high altar was washed with water and wine, "a

symbol of Christ's blood washing the world clean."[520] Then, the *pedilavium* rite began: the actual

washing of feet in imitation of the gospel reading of that day.[521] The footwashing rite belonged to

early church, when the initiates had their feet washed at their baptisms. From its inception, the

footwashing ritual was a sign of both hospitality and humble service.[522] In the medieval Latin West,

ritual footwashing became prominent through the Rule of St. Benedict, which stated that the feet of

all guests or strangers should be ceremoniously washed by monks, who also regularly washed one

anothers' feet.[523] In medieval Europe, two rites evolved: the *Mandatum Pauperum,* in which monks or

clerics washed the feet of the poor or pilgrims, and the *Mandatum Fratrum,* in which the members of

a religious community washed one anothers' feet, sometimes on a daily or weekly basis.[524] Since Holy

Thursday commemorated the Last Supper, when Jesus washed his disciples' feet, the ritual

celebrations on that day naturally included footwashing as well, sometimes to a more elaborate

degree.[525] In secular contexts, Mass was followed by Vespers, a meal, the stripping of the altars, and

---

[519] Harper, *The Forms and Orders of Western Liturgy from the Tenth to the Eighteenth Century,* 143.

[520] Ibid.

[521] Regarding the origin and development of the *pedilavium* rite, see Jeffery, "Mandatum Novum Do Vobis: Toward a Renewal of the Holy Thursday Footwashing Rite"; Thomas Schäfer, *Die Fusswaschung im monastischen Brauchtum und in der lateinischen Liturgie. Liturgiegeschichtliche Untersuchung* (Beuron: Beuroner Kunstverlag, 1956); Pier Franco Beatrice, *La lavanda dei piedi: contributo alla storia delle antiche liturgie cristiane* (Roma: C.L.V.-Edizioni liturgiche, 1983).

[522] Jeffery, "Mandatum Novum Do Vobis: Toward a Renewal of the Holy Thursday Footwashing Rite," 114.

[523] Ibid., 114-15; Harper, *The Forms and Orders of Western Liturgy from the Tenth to the Eighteenth Century,* 143-44.

[524] Jeffery, "Mandatum Novum Do Vobis: Toward a Renewal of the Holy Thursday Footwashing Rite," 116.

[525] Harper, *The Forms and Orders of Western Liturgy from the Tenth to the Eighteenth Century,* 143-44.

the washing of feet.[526] In monastic contexts, Mass was directly followed by the stripping of altars,

the washing of feet, followed by Vespers and then a meal.[527] As the poor or lowly clerics removed

their sandals or shoes, and prelates poured water into basins, their minds were newly saturated – not

just with the image of Jesus washing his disciples feet – but also of Mary Magdalene, a sinner,

washing and anointing the feet of God Incarnate. As medieval Christians celebrated Jesus' new

commandment - his *mandatum novum* – to love one another through self-sacrifice and humble

service, they often heard or sang chants, not only about Jesus washing the disciples' feet, but about

Mary Magdalene washing and anointing Jesus.

During the *pedilavium* rite, the choir sang an assortment of antiphons, which varied according

to local traditions. The number of antiphons sung would depend on how many people had their feet

washed. Almost invariably the antiphon *Mandatum novum* was sung: "I give you a new

commandment: that you love one another as I loved you, says the Lord."[528] The psalm verses

chanted during the washing of the feet often ended with the refrain, *Ubi caritas et amor, Deus ibi est.*[529]

In the *pedilavium* rite, some of the first antiphons told of Jesus washing his disciples feet, revealing

what he wanted the disciples to do for one another.[530] The sequence of events is important to note:

before the disciples could serve others, Jesus had to first be their servant by washing their feet. Before

Jesus washed his disciples feet, however, Mary Magdalen washed and anointed his feet.[531]

---

[526] Ibid., 143.

[527] Ibid.

[528] Lacoste (Project Manager and Principal Researcher) and Koláček (Web Developer), "Cantus Database: Inventories of Chant Sources | CANTUS Database," Can.003688.

[529] Harper, *The Forms and Orders of Western Liturgy from the Tenth to the Eighteenth Century*, 144.

[530] "Dominus iesus postquam cenauit cum discipulis suis lauit pedes eorum et ait illi scitis quid fecerim uobis ego dominus et magister exemplum dedi uobis ut & uos ita faciatis"; "Si ego dominus & magister laui uestros pedes quanto magis & uos debetis alter alterius lauare pedes"; "Postquam surrexit dominus a cenam missit aquam in peluem cepit lauare pedes discipulorum hoc exemplum reliquid eis." "Vat.lat.4770", fol.85vA. See also the feast "Ad Mandatum" in CANTUS Lacoste (Project Manager and Principal Researcher) and Koláček (Web Developer), "Cantus Database: Inventories of Chant Sources | CANTUS Database." Can.001431: "Ante diem festum paschae"; Can.002392: "Domine tu mihi lavas pedes"; Can.002413: "Dominus Jesus postquam cenavit"; Can.004340: "Postquam surrexit dominus."

[531] An aspect of the cult of Mary Magdalen that I do not explore here is the popular (and potentially bawdy) devotion to the saint, which certain merits further study. Another dimension to her cult includes the Gnostic tradition, in which

In addition to love and charity, oil and anointing were central themes of the antiphons and psalms sung during the *pedilavium* rite. In some liturgical contexts, Psalm 132 was chanted twice, with a reprise of the text sandwiched in between.[532] *Ecce quam bonum*, of course, tells of fraternal love being like the oinment running down Aaron's beard and robe.[533] After singing the *Ecce quam bonum* antiphon, the choristers would sing another version of the same psalm, giving a slightly different emphasis to the text, this time stressing the divine blessing that descends on a people praising God in unity: *Ubi fratres in unum glorificant Deum, ibi dabit dominus benedictionem*. Singers would then return to *Ecce quam bonum*, singing once again about the oil descending on Aaron's head: *Ecœ quam bonum et quam jocundum habitare fratres in unum, sicut unguentum in capite, quod descendit in barbam, barbam Aaron*. An antiphon then told of the oil poured on the head: *Sicut unguentum in capite*.[534] The weaving together of biblical texts had the effect of introducing a theme and then embellishing the theme with successive variations.

A partial pontifical (Vat.lat.4770) of unknown provenance, likely dating from the eleventh century, contains antiphons and psalms that juxtapose the two washing scenes from John 12 and John 13 in an extraordinary way.[535] Of the fourteen psalms and antiphons listed for the *pedilavium* rite, four pertain to a woman anointing Jesus. Most often, during the *pedivalium*, only a few antiphons spoke of Mary anointing Jesus. These might include *Maria ergo unxit, In diebus illis, Dimissa sunt ei*

Mary Magdalen appeared as Jesus' wife. See Elaine Pagels, *The Gnostic Gospels* (New York: Random House, 1979); Pagels, *Beyond Belief: the Secret Gospel of Thomas* (New York: Random House, 2003).

[532] "Psalmus. *Ecce quam bonum*. Antiphona. *Ubi fratres in unum glorificant Deum, ibi dabit dominus benedictionem*. Psalmus. *Ecce quam bonum*." Vogel, Elze, and Andrieu, *Le Pontifical romano-germanique du dixième siècle*, 78.

[533] Psalm 132.

[534] Lacoste (Project Manager and Principal Researcher) and Koláček (Web Developer), "Cantus Database: Inventories of Chant Sources | CANTUS Database," Can.005261zb.

[535] Salmon, *Les manuscrits liturgiques latins de la Bibliothèque vaticane ...*, no.100. Salmon classifies this codex as "Pontificalis Partes."

peccata multa, and *Accessit ad pedes peccatrix,* but rarely all.[536] Vat.lat.4770, however, places an extraordinary emphasis on a woman washing and anointing Jesus' feet with unguent, and moreover, interweaves several antiphons with chants about Jesus washing the feet of his own disciples and urging them to do likewise for others.

The antiphon, *Maria ergo unxit,* most commonly found as an antiphon for the Feast of Mary Magdalen (22 July), was a stable feature of the *pedilavium* rite by the tenth century, and can be found in antiphoners manuscripts dating as late as the fourteenth century.[537] Vat.lat.4770 presents an unusual variation of the foot-washing ritual, effectively reinterpreting the sign of the new commandment: "I give you a new commandment, that you love one another. Just as I have loved you, you also should love one another."[538] In Vat.lat. 4770, the chanting Psalm 118 followed the dispensation of the new commandment: "Happy are those whose way is blameless, who walk in the law of the Lord."[539] Then a citation from 1 John 4:7 followed the psalm: "Beloved, let us love one another, because love is from God; everyone who loves is born of God and knows God."[540] Following the quote from 1 John 4:7, Psalm 132 was sung again, making the relationship between love, unity and oil even more evident. The participants and observers of the ritual ablution would have heard about Jesus washing the disciples' feet, the new commandment to love, Aaron's head being anointing with oil, and then another biblical scene which would bring the imagery of washing

---

[536] See Anne B. Yardley, "The Sonic Presence of Mary Magdalene at the Last Supper" in *Magistra Doctissima: Essays in Honor of Bonnie Wheeler,* ed. Dorsey Armstrong et al. (Kalamazoo: Medieval Institute Publications, 2013), 169-182; Lacoste (Project Manager and Principal Researcher) and Koláček (Web Developer), "Cantus Database: Inventories of Chant Sources | CANTUS Database." Also included here are related chants for *Ad Mandatum,* even if they do not mention oil: "In diebus illis mulier quae erat in civitate peccatrix ut cognovit quod Jesus accubit in domo Simonis leprosi attulit alabastrum unguenti et stans retro secus pedes domini Jesu lacrimis coepit rigare pedes ejus et capillis capitis sui tergebat et osculabatur pedes ejus et unguento ungebat" Can. 003224; "Dimissa sunt ei peccata multa" Can.003224za; "Maria optimam partem elegit." Can.003224zb; "Beata immaculati in tua qui ambulant in lege domini" Can.003224zc; "Accessit ad pedes peccatrix mulier Maria et osculata est et lavit lacrimis et tersit capillis et unxit unguento" Can.200068.
[537] Vogel, Elze, and Andrieu, *Le Pontifical romano-germanique du dixième siècle,* 77.
[538] John 13:34: "Mandatum novum do vobis: ut diligatis invicem: sicut dilexi vos, ut et vos diligatis invicem." Vat.lat. 4770, fol.85v
[539] "Beati Inmaculati in uia qui ambulant in lege domini." Vat.lat. 4770, fol.85v
[540] 1 John 4:7: "Diligamus nos in inuicem quia caritas ex deo est & qui diligit fratrem suum ex deo natus est & uidit deum." Vat.lat. 4770, fol.85v

feet into sharp relief: a woman washing Jesus' feet and anointing him with oil. Directly following the chanting of Psalm 132, the antiphon *In diebus illis* recounted how a sinful woman washed Jesus' feet and anointed them with oil: "In those days a woman who was a sinner in the city and who knew that Jesus was reclining at table in the house of Simon the Leper brought an alabaster jar of ointment and standing behind him, took the feet of the Lord Jesus, to wash his feet with tears and anointed them with unguent."[541] Notably, this version of the chant omits any mention of Mary Magdalen kissing the feet of Jesus, a detail that appears in other versions of the same chant text.[542] The manuscript, within the span of a few folia, refers to the woman in two ways: first as a sinful woman (*peccatrix*), then as 'Maria,' then twice more as *peccatrix*. The text weaves back and forth between these two identities: "The woman in the city who was a sinner" (*Mvlier quae erat in civitate peccatrix*) and "Maria then anointed Jesus' feet and wiped them with her hair and the house was filled with the scent of the unguent" (*Maria ergo vncxit pedes iesu et extersit capillis suis et domus impleta est ex odore unguento*).[543]

What accounts for this disparity? The discrepancy found in the Gospel texts and names for the woman may have led to a form of exegesis, by which those constructing the liturgy cast light on the ritual and personages – both biblical figures and those participating in the ritual. Were the monks (or whomever recorded this rite) somehow suggesting that Maria, well-known to be the Mother of God, was somehow akin to the "sinner from the city"? The juxtaposition of these texts and names may have been a reflection of the medieval approach to the gospels themselves: though varying slightly in concrete details, they communicated a unified truth (albeit paradoxical).[544] Indeed, during the *pedilavium,* these antiphons exhort listeners to live in unity despite plurality – or to embrace a

---

[541] "In diebus illis mulier que erat in ciuitate peccatrix ut cognouit quod iesus recubuit in domo symonis leprosi attulit alabastrum unguenti et stans retro pedes domini iesu lacrimis cepit rigare pedes eius & unguento ungebat." Vat.lat. 4770, fol.85v. *Rigare* - literally: "wet" or "moisten." In the CANTUS database, a variation of this chant appears as Can. 003224.

[542] Lacoste (Project Manager and Principal Researcher) and Koláček (Web Developer), "Cantus Database: Inventories of Chant Sources | CANTUS Database," Can. 003224.

[543] Vat.lat.4770, fol.85v.

[544] Regarding the role of paradox in medieval Christianity, see Caroline Walker Bynum, *Christian Materiality: An Essay on Religion in Late Medieval Europe* (New York; Cambridge, MA: Zone Books; MIT Press, 2011).

truth despite apparent contradiction. Oil was characteristic of both the sinner and the namesake of the Mother of God.

In the chants of the medieval Church of the Latin West, unguent and anointing feature prominently on the feast days of both the Blessed Virgin Mary and Mary Magdalen. The antiphon *In odore unguentorum tuorum* was a stable feature of the multiple Marian feasts including a Votive Office for Mary, the Immaculate Conception (8 December), the Visitation (2 July), the Purification (2 February), the Assumption (15 August), and the Nativity (8 September). This antiphon was a reprise of Canticles 1:3, which tells of adolescent girls vowing to chase after the fragrant anointed one: "In the aroma of your unguents we run; young maidens loved you exceedingly."[545] This antiphon was also universal for the feasts of the Common of Several Virgins and appeared on the feast of the Eleven Thousand Virgin Martyrs of Cologne (21 October), the feast of Lucy (13 December), the feast of Elisabeth of Hungary (19 November) and the Common of Holy Matrons. The text, however, did not only bespeak virginal or marital purity. The antiphon was also emblematic of penance and was sung for the feast of Mary of Egypt the Penitent (2 April) as well as Mary Magdalen (22 July).

Several other antiphons featured prominently on Marian feasts and feasts for other virgins as well as the feast of Mary Magdalen. One chant drawing on the Song of Songs (1:1) saturated the liturgy on feasts for women: "Your name is like oil poured out, therefore the young maidens loved you exceedingly."[546] This chant appeared on the Assumption, the feasts of Elisabeth of Hungary (19 November) and Catherine of Alexandria (25 November), the Eleven Thousand Virgin Martyrs of

---

[545] "In odore unguentorum tuorum currimus adolescentulae dilexerunt te nimis" Lacoste (Project Manager and Principal Researcher) and Koláček (Web Developer), "Cantus Database: Inventories of Chant Sources | CANTUS Database," Can.003261.

[546] "Unguentum effusum nomen tuum ideo adolescentulae dilexerunt te nimis." Can.005273.

Cologne, and the Common of Holy Matrons.[547] Another chant for the feast of the Assumption

elaborated on the theme of oil poured out, this time speaking of a female beloved, drawing on both

Canticles 1:1 and Psalm 44:12: "The Lord greatly desired the daughter of Jerusalem richly adorned

with a necklace and seeing her, the most beautiful of the daughters of Sion, they proclaimed saying,

'Your name is oil poured out.'"[548] The chants for the feast of Mary Magdalen which mention oil or

anointing are even more numerous; circa 30 different chants vividly commemorated the breaking of

the alabaster jar and powerful nard that flowed alongside with the penitents' tears, an image echoed

in the legend of Santa Maria in Trastevere's *fons olei*: the oil flowed all the way to Tiber and flowed

into the water of the river.

Was the ambiguity of female identities (virgin and sinner) not sustainable within most

medieval Christian communities? Carolyn Walker Bynum has drawn attention to the centrality of

paradox in Christianity: virgin mother, word made flesh, etc. Vat.lat.4770 presents an incidence of

another paradoxical blending of two female figures: the Virgin and the sinner. Were some paradoxes

perhaps more viable than others in the minds of medieval Christians? After recounting how the

woman washed and anointed Jesus' feet, the text returns to the initial theme of Jesus washing his

disciples feet: after having been washed an anointed by the woman, Jesus washed the disciples feet

and urged them to do likewise for each other. This is the *mandatum novum* – that the disciples of Jesus

love and serve each other through self-sacrifice. Jesus tells his disciples that before they can truly

love and serve each other, however, he must first have their feet washed by him. Before Jesus can

minister to his disciples, however, the woman (both saint and sinner) must cleanse and anoint him.

The juxtaposition of the scenes (a woman washing and anointing Jesus before he washes his

---

[547] See Chapters 6 & 7 regarding the appearance of this chant on the feasts of female myroblytes.

[548] "Ornatam in monilibus filiam Jerusalem dominus concupivit et videntes eam filiae Sion beatissimam praedicaverunt dicentes unguentum effusum nomen tuum." Can.007340. See Isaiah 61:10 regarding the necklace as a symbol of the bride and the crown as the symbol of the bridegroom. See Chapter 9 regarding the relationship between oil, crowning and spousal imagery.

disciples) presents a provocative idea: before Jesus can fulfil his role as servant and Messiah, a

woman must first sacrifice herself (symbolized by the alabaster jar) for him. Before the disciples can

emulate his own humility and self-sacrifice, Jesus emulates the woman with the alabaster jar. Before

Jesus can commission the disciples to do for others as he has done for them, he has to be anointed.

Again, he becomes the *christus,* the Lord's anointed. Instead of being anointed by God, however,

directly before his crucifixion Jesus is anointed by a woman.

While one might interpret the woman anointing Jesus as suggestive of hospitality within the

context of a convivial meal, the ablution and unction of a man by a woman also signalled death. In

three of the Gospels, Jesus himself told those present at the dinner that the woman prepared his

body for burial.[549] The gospels differ regarding how far in advance of the crucifixion the anointing

took place. Mark's and Matthew's Gospels say the woman anoints Jesus two days prior to the

Passover meal. Luke's Gospel, which includes the text that most closely resembles the text in

Vat.lat.4770,[550] does not specify when the anointing took place.[551] In the Gospel of John, the

anointing at Bethany (John 12) takes place six days before the Passover (John 13). Directly after the

anointing, Jesus entered Jerusalem, where he celebrated the Passover with his disciples and washed

their feet. In John's gospel, the two events appear in temporal and narrative proximity: in the

narrative, the woman washed and anointed Jesus' feet not long before Jesus washed his disciples'

feet and commanded them to do likewise for each other. In John's gospel the woman who anointed

Jesus' feet was Mary, the sister of Martha and Lazarus, whom Jesus raised from the dead.[552] The text

in Vat.lat.4770, however, combines this figure with the "woman in the city, who was a sinner" from

---

[549] Mark, Matthew and John.

[550] The Vulgate text reads: "Et ecce mulier, quae erat in civitate peccatrix, ut cognovit quod accubuisset in domo pharisaei, attulit alabastrum unguenti: Et stans retro secus pedes ejus, lacrimis coepit rigare pedes ejus, et capillis capitis sui tergebat, et osculabatur pedes ejus, et unguento ungebat." Luke 7:37-38.

[551] The anointing happens in Chapter 7 while the Passover meal appears considerably later, in Chapter 22.

[552] John 12:1-8: "Six days before the Passover Jesus came to Bethany, the home of Lazarus, whom he had raised from the dead. There they gave a dinner for him. Martha served, and Lazarus was one of those at the table with him."

Luke's gospel, the only text to refer to the woman as "a woman in the city, who was a sinner."[553]

Directly after singing about Maria anointing Jesus, the monks sang: "If I your Lord and Master

washed your feet, how much more should you wash one another's feet."[554] And then: "By this

everyone will know that you are my disciples, if you have love for one another."[555] The oil, like the

washing of the feet, was a sign of divine presence and divine love embodied, not only in Jesus, but

also in the figure of Mary Magdalen. On the eve of the Easter celebrations, when inititates would be

baptized and anointed, Mary Magdalen appeared, even if only obliquely. She was a sign of

reconciliation and the forgiveness of sins. But she was also a source of cleansing, life-giving water

and ointment, making her effectively a symbol for the Church itself. Mary Magdalen was not,

however, the only source of sanctifying liquids. The bodies of saints, like the alabaster jar, would

pour forth perfumed unguent to sanctify medieval Christians.

---

[553] The Vulgate texts reads: "Et ecce mulier, quae erat in civitate peccatrix." Luke 7:37.

[554] "Si ego dominus et magister uester laui uestros pedes quanto magis uos debetis alter alterius lauare pedes." Vat.lat. 4770, fol.85v.

[555] John 13:35: "In hoc cognoscent omnes quia mei estis discipulis si dilectionem habueritis in inuicem." Vat.lat. 4770, fol.85v.

CHAPTER 4

OIL IN THE LAW AND LITURGY OF THE MEDIEVAL CHURCH

INTRODUCTION

No aspect of medieval life was more laden with symbol than the liturgy. The Divine Office

brought symbols to life or became "performed symbol."[556] Medieval theologians and liturgists

elucidated the symbolic dimensions of the liturgy in commentaries intended for monks, canons and

clerics who celebrated the Divine Office on a daily basis.[557] Allegorical commentaries, which drew

on the methods of Scriptural exegesis, were not simply manuals explaining the mechanics of

liturgical rites. Rather, the authors envisioned their works as devotional texts that might renew the

spiritual dispositions of their readers.[558] In providing explanations of the interior or spiritual meaning

of rituals, mystical commentaries unveiled the sacred rites practiced daily by members of the

church.[559] Although liturgical commentators also composed and circulated non-allegorical

expositions of the medieval liturgy, those commentaries were not nearly as influential as the ones

that dwelt on the mystical or spiritual meaning of words and gestures.[560]

This chapter will explore interpretations of oil in a selection of liturgical commentaries from

the ninth through thirteenth centuries, composed by three seminal liturgists and jurists: Amalarius of

Metz (circa 775 – 850), Rupert of Deutz (1075 – 1129), and Guillaume Durand the Elder (c. 1230 –

1296). This analysis will consider how legal developments, such as the appearance of Gratian's

Decretum in the twelfth century, affected the promulgation of liturgical norms for oil. This study will

---

[556] Liturgical rites as performed symbol gave "symbolic representation to the mystery accomplished once by Christ and preserved effectively in the church." Chenu, "The Symbolist Mentality," 12.

[557] Timothy Thibodeau, "Les sources du Rationale de Guillaume Durand" in *Guillaume Durand: évêque de Mende* (v.1230-1296), canoniste, liturgiste et homme politique, ed. Pierre-Marie Gy (Paris: Editions du Centre National de la Recherche Scientifique, 1992), 145.

[558] Timothy Thibodeau, "Enigmata Figurarum: Biblical Exegesis and Liturgical Exposition in Durand's Rationale," *Harvard Theological Review* 86, no.1 (1993): 68.

[559] Ibid.

[560] Thibodeau, "Les sources du Rationale de Guillaume Durand," 144.

show that the *Decretum* influenced the mystagogical interpretation of oil and anointing by expanding

the source base of legal, liturgical, and theological texts as well as by resolving contradictions or

inconsistencies in liturgical practice through dialectic reasoning. As an initially liminal and then

increasingly well-established part of the medieval liturgy, holy oil further discloses the process

whereby liturgists established ecclesiastical norms by drawing on the authority of patristic authors

and other liturgists as well as the popular devotional practices of the time. These liturgical

commentaries demonstrate how in the High Middle Ages, holy oil became a sign of an individual's

power to dispense law, thus placing oil within the domain of the ecclesiastical elite to a much greater

extent. As episcopal authority expanded and the division between clerics and the laity became more

distinct, commentators increasingly interpreted oil as remedy for sin and a sign of penance rather

than a conduit of peace, divine grace, knowledge and wisdom.

This study is situated at the confluence of several streams of historical developments:

changes in the liturgy during the Carolingian period, from the Gallican to the Roman rite;

development of the *Glossa Ordinaria* and an increasingly mystical approach to historical events and

biblical texts; advances in canon law including the appearance of Gratian's *Decretum* as well as the

advent of jurists who reasoned about justice by going beyond the letter of the law. The symbolic

mentality that prevailed in the medieval period was not without its detractors. Biblical interpretation

based on delving into the multiple senses of Scripture, a method adopted by monks such as Bernard

of Clairvaux, did not find favor in all corners of the medieval Latin West. Peter Abelard, as an

adamant opponent of Bernard and his exegetical method, heralded the era of Scholasticism through

his use of dialectical reasoning.[561] Historians have often associated mystical exegesis with recluse

monastics and dialectic with Scholastics populating cathedral schools and universities. Liturgical

---

[561] "All creation and all biblical history were transparent to that faith [that made use of metaphoric analogy]. It dwelt
fondly, it got carried away as it read, discovered, and divined at the heart of the most lowly things and the most simple
events those signs and invitations and direct messages which came to it out of the most hidden recesses of love." Chenu,
Nature, Man, and Society in the Twelfth Century; Essays on New Theological Perspectives in the Latin West, 133.

commentaries challenge such distinctions. Individuals such as Amalarius, Rupert, and Durand were actively engaged in society beyond the monastery walls and yet produced liturgical commentaries that expounded on the mystical meanings of liturgical symbols, including oil and anointing.

While scholars have written extensively about the relationship between the liturgy and the Bible, they have devoted less attention to how legal developments shaped interpretations of ecclesiastical rituals, including the sacraments, with a few exceptions.[562] Roger Reynolds drew scholarly attention to the relationship between law and liturgy by revealing how ritual, far from existing in isolation from political and legal controversies and innovations, stood at the center of all things ecclesiastical.[563] Indeed, the liturgists who composed liturgical commentaries also made laws and negotiated with secular powers as politicians or diplomats.[564] Thus liturgical commentaries challenge the idea that there existed in medieval society a distinct dichotomy between monastic and Scholastic approaches to Scripture, and by extension, exegesis and mystagogy. Timothy Thibodeau noted instances in which medieval and early modern authors' positions regarding allegorical readings of texts were "out of place" given their time, notably Albert the Great's expressed dislike for allegorical explanations, evident in his *Liber de sacrificio missae* and Thomas More's mystical discourse in *De tristitia Christi*.[565] Peter Comestor's *Historia Scholastica* can also be added to the list.[566] Joseph Jungmann argued that the allegorical method of liturgical exposition survived the onslaught of Scholasticism in the thirteenth century; metaphorical interpretations of the liturgy triumphed over

---

[562] For studies on the relationship between the Bible and the liturgy, see Cushing and Gyug, *Ritual, text, and law*; Chazelle and Edwards, *The Study of the Bible in the Carolingian era*; Gy, "La Bible dans la liturgie au Moyen Âge"; Daniélou, *Bible et Liturgie; La Théologie Biblique Des Sacraments et Des Fêtes D'après Les Pères de l'Eglise*; Lubac, *Exégèse Médiéval*; Smalley, *The Study of the Bible in the Middle Ages*, 1964.

[563] See Reynolds, "Liturgical Scholarship at the Time of the Investiture Controversy: Past Research and Future Opportunities."

[564] Ibid.

[565] Thibodeau, "Enigmata Figurarum: Biblical Exegesis and Liturgical Exposition in Durand's Rationale," 66n7; 67n8.

[566] Pickering, "Exegesis and Imagination," 33.

literal or historical interpretations.[567] This chapter will demonstrate, however, that the influence of

Scholasticism in the thirteenth century ought not be separated from the influence of jurisprudence in

the twelfth; both utilized the dialectical method and relied on human reason to ascertain

transcendental norms or truths. The style of liturgical commentary that emerged at the end of the

thirteenth century, exemplified by Guillaume Durand's *Rationale divinorum officiorum*, was a synthesis

of the quintessentially "monastic" predilections for allegorical exposition and the rational, dialectical

method emblematic of medieval Scholasticism and jurisprudence. A close reading of the mystical

significance ascribed to oil in the commentaries of Amalarius, Rupert, and Durand reveals the

mutability of attitudes towards oil as well as attendant changes in the ritual practices of the church in

the high Middle Ages.

AMALARIUS OF METZ

Known as the grandfather of allegorical exposition of the medieval liturgy, Amalarius of

Metz was a student of Alcuin and schooled in biblical exegesis.[568] Alcuin had been a liturgist in his

own right; he was instrumental in instituting the Roman liturgy in lands where the Gallican rite had

prevailed, with myriad local variations, in the Frankish church at the beginning of Charlemagne's

reign. As a canon regular, Amalarius was not limited to a monk's cloistered experience of the liturgy.

Rather, he fostered close ties with Charlemagne's court, traveled widely and actively participated in

enacting liturgical reforms throughout the realm.[569] In an effort to consolidate and extend royal

power, Charlemagne sought to stabilize his kingdom by establishing a uniform liturgy; this meant

---

[567] "The allegorical method of contemplating and explaining the liturgy had to face a *crisis* in the thirteenth century, and it is really a matter of wonder…that the old method should survive unscathed in the period to follow." See Jungmann, *The Mass of the Roman Rite*, 74–127; Thibodeau, "Enigmata Figurarum: Biblical Exegesis and Liturgical Exposition in Durand's Rationale," 66n7.

[568] Thibodeau, "Enigmata Figurarum: Biblical Exegesis and Liturgical Exposition in Durand's Rationale," 66.

[569] Schnusenberg, *The Relationship between the Church and the Theatre*, 175.

enacting numerous reforms, including the substitution of the Roman rite for the Gallican.[570]

Charlemagne also looked to Rome where legal matters were concerned. Pope Hadrian sent the

emperor a copy of the *Collectio Dionysiana,* the earliest canonical collection, which contained eastern

conciliar canons and papal decretals, and which served as the basis for law in the Latin Church.

While Charlemagne did not view such a collection as authoritative in his own realm, he utilized the

Collectio to establish some norms among the Franks. In the ninth century, the establishment of law

under Charlemagne was fluid; jurists adopted or rejected canonical norms as they saw fit.[571]

A similar phenomenon took place in the liturgical sphere during Charlemagne's reign. Less

than a hundred years after receiving the Gregorian Sacramentary from Rome, the Gallican church

made substantial additions to the Roman rite. For example, while the Roman prayer for the

ordination of a bishop involved an anointing with the "dew of heavenly unction," the unguent was

to be taken figuratively rather than literally.[572] Nevertheless, the liturgists of the "barbarian north"

interpreted the dew literally and physically anointed bishops.[573] Paul Bradshaw argued this literal

interpretation of the Roman rite, which included the physical anointing of clergy, was attributable to

the fact that prior to the eighth century, the kings of Gaul were anointed with actual oil.[574] No

liturgical evidence exists, however, for the anointing of kings with actual oil prior to circa 800. Roger

Reynolds argued that Visigothic rites continued to influence the liturgy of the Carolingian Empire,

despite attempts to establish the Roman rite.[575] What had become *consuetudo* (custom) among the

people became the law of the church.

---

[570] Brundage, *Medieval Canon Law*, 29.
[571] Pennington, "A Short History of Canon Law."
[572] Bradshaw, *Rites of Ordination*, 369–390.
[573] Bradshaw, "Medieval Ordinations," 126.
[574] Ibid. See also Bouman, "Sacring and Crowning," 2–4.
[575] Reynolds, "The Visigothic Liturgy in the Realm of Charlemagne." The role of oil and anointing in the Visigothic liturgy and its influence on Gallic and Roman rites is beyond the scope of this study. A starting point for such research would be: Zapke and Mundó, *Hispania Vetus*; Gros, *Les Wisigoths et les liturgies occidentales*; Reynolds, "The Visigothic Liturgy in the Realm of Charlemagne"; Reynolds, *Studies on Medieval Liturgical and Legal Manuscripts from Spain and Southern*

The first edition of Amalarius' *Liber officialis* dates to 823, after the bishop had traveled to

Constantinople and Rome and been influenced by both the Byzantine and Roman rites.[576]

Amalarius' discussion of oil is scattered throughout the *Liber officialis*. Amalarius quotes liberally from

both the *Liber sacramentarium* (Gelasian Sacramentary) and the *Sacramentarium greogorianum* as well as

the Acts of the Apostles, Augustine, and the Venerable Bede. Both sacramentaries figure

predominantly in his exposition of the anointing of neophytes, the imposition of hands, and the

consecration of oil by a bishop. Amalarius began his exposition of oil in a chapter on the six

varieties of the Lord's Supper, wherein he proposed to explain the meaning and significance of oil:

proferre de ratione olei (to advance arguments about oil). The bishop began his allegorical reading of oil

by quoting Isidorus of Seville's *Etymologies*; he saw a three-fold material nature of the olive (*olea*)

which then also bore a greater signification: "The olive is moreover herself a tree, the olive fruit, oil

juice. The tree is also a sign of peace."[577] As a sign of peace, oil manifested a duality; it had both a

physical quality (*pinguedinem*) which succored those suffering physical ailments and a non-tangible

quality (*gratia*) that Isidore implicitly suggested could affect the soul: it displayed the grace of light.

Having distinguished between the physical and spiritual dimensions of the oil, Amalarius proceeded

to explain the visible and invisible workings of God. According to Amalarius, oil was not necessary

for accomplishing the works of salvation; God superfluously bestowed oil on human beings so they

might perceive what would otherwise remain invisible: "For without oil, God is able to heal the sick

and sanctify his own, and drive out demons."[578] Amalarius cites the "ambrosial" Apostle Paul as

having said: "For we know both the Holy Spirit is given by God without the imposition of the hand

---

Italy; Díaz, "Monasticism and Liturgy in Visigothic Spain"; Fontaine, *L'Europe héritière de l'Espagne visigothique (Reseña)*; Ferreiro, *The Visigoths*.

[576] Schnusenberg, *The Relationship between the Church and the Theatre*, 174, 176.

[577] "Olea autem ipsa arbor est, fructus oliva, sucus oleum. Est autem arbor pacis insignis; habet et pinguedinem qua lassi atque infirmi artus recreantur, et gratia praestatur luminis." Amalarius of Metz, *Amalarii Episcopi Opera Liturgica Omnia 2*, 66.

[578] "Sine oleo enim potest Deus sanare infirmos, santificareque suos et daemones effugare. Unde Ambrosius in epistola ad Corinthios prima: 'Scimus enim et Spiritum Sanctum sine manus impositione datum a Deo, et non baptizatum consecutum remissionem peccatorum." Ibid., 67.

and subsequently the non-baptized is given remission from sins."[579] Since oil was, in a sense,

gratuitous, its function was to point toward what lay beyond the material world. Amalarius observed

that while human beings could believe in what they could not apprehend with their physical senses,

the created things of this world were the means by which the invisible or imperceptible became

intelligible.[580]

Since such matters touched upon the nature of the Trinity itself, Amalarius demonstrated

how Augustine's commentary of Psalm 40 echoed Isidore's tripartite depiction of the olive: "For oil

is visible in a sign, oil is invisible in a sacrament, spiritual oil is invisible."[581] Elaborating on the

significance of Augustine's observations about oil's material and spiritual character, Amalarius

emphasized the non-corporeal nature of God, who became Incarnate so that He might be known:

"God is able to bestow spiritual oil through himself without a body, but on account of animals

visible things are made, so that invisible things can be easily grasped."[582] Amalarius' discussion of

signs and sacraments, of the visible and the invisible, revealed not only how medieval thinkers

perceived oil, but also how they viewed the relationship between the body and the immaterial world.

Amalarius elucidated the means by which God made Himself known; he also revealed how the

material and spiritual nature of God affected the establishment of laws for the Church.

Following his invocation of the Apostle Paul and Augustine regarding the visible and

invisible manifestations of the divine, Amalarius turned to a discussion of circumcision. Here we see

clues about how the ninth-century liturgist understood the relationship between religious authority

and the creation of ecclesiastical law. Likening oil to circumcision, Amalarius posed a rhetorical

question regarding the *cultus consecrationis olei*: "If it is possible, how can the cult of the consecration

---

[579] Ibid.

[580] "Olei naturam audivimus, quae habilis est ad recreandos artus fessorum et luminis gratiam praestat. Animales enim haec possunt cognoscere; credant etiam quod non possunt videre." Ibid.

[581] "Oleum enim visibile in signo est, oleum invisibile in sacramento est, oleum spiritale invisibile est." Ibid.

[582] "Potest Deus per se oleum spirituale tribuere sine corporali, sed propter animals aguntur visibilia, ut invisibilia facilius capiantur." Ibid.

of oil be observed with such great zeal?" According to Amalarius, circumcision was a visible sign of God's covenant and of the faithful's obedience to the commandments. While circumcision was the old, visible sign of the covenant, oil was the new sign; just as circumcision marked the Israelites, oil marked Christians. The replacement of Hebraic ritual and tradition with new Christian ritual was evident also in iconography of Ecclesia's triumph over Synagogue, in personified form. Amalarius highlighted how the apostles brought neophytes into the fold through healing them and visibly making them followers of Christ through consecration with oil: "For the apostles made use of this art, that is of oil, renewing the sick; the apostolic men [did so] in sealing the neophytes."[583] In addition to quoting Mark 6:12-13, Amalarius cited the Venerable Bede, who quoted the apostle James instructing early members of the church about how to heal the sick: the presbyters of the church were to pray over them, anointing them with oil in the name of the Lord.[584] Bede then added that this custom (*morem*) of the Church was handed down by the apostles. Moreover, the presbyter anointed the sick "with oil consecrated with the pontifical blessing."[585] From Bede's discussion of the *mos* and the pontifical blessing, Amalarius explained that the cult of oil, despite its apparently tenuous authority, derived its legitimacy from the practices of the people. To support his argument for the validity of oil rites, Amalarius cited Augustine, who claimed that in the absence of scriptural authority, the legitimacy of a religious practice was derived from the customs of the majority:

> Concerning this oil, which is poured over the neophytes, we do not read about it to such a great degree, but we have the apostolic custom and the authority which we accept from the Roman *ecclesia*, which it is necessary to maintain on behalf of the law, for Augustine says to Casulanum, the presbyter, concerning the Sabbath fast: 'In these things, about which sacred

---

[583] "Apostoli enim hac arte, id est olei, utebantur in redintegratione infirmorum, apostolici viri in consignatione neofytorum." Amalarius of Metz, *Amalarii Episcopi Opera Liturgica Omnia 2*, 68.
[584] "Infirmatur quis in vobis, inducat presbiteros ecclesiae, et orent super eum, unguentes eum oleo in nomine Domini." Ibid.
[585] "ungantur oleo pontificali benedictione consecrato." Ibid.

scriptures establishes nothing certain, the custom of the people of God or the habits of the majority are held as law.'[586]

Amalarius' text weaves together the instructions about how to conduct oil rites with a legal defense of custom and more lofty ruminations about the spiritual dimensions of holy unguent. In part, the persuasiveness of Amalarius' argument about oil rests on his symbolic rhetoric, which includes a lengthy exposition about the moral dimensions of oil as representative of righteousness, wisdom and knowledge:

> Through oil we understand right conduct, which is controlled in the mind through the ripeness of wisdom, and through balsam we understand doctrine, which outwardly displays a good aroma. Likewise in another place in the same book[587] the author says of wisdom: 'Wisdom pertains to life, knowledge truly pertains to doctrine.' The chrismal anointing that we discussed pertains to the two gifts of the Holy Spirit, wisdom and knowledge: oil pertains to wisdom; balsam, with its spacious and boundless aroma dispersing outwards, to knowledge.[588]

In the ninth century, to bolster the apparently liminal status of oil in the rites of the church, Amalarius of Metz drew on both established ecclesiastical authorities and his own allegorical exposition of oil. By citing authorities who testified to the legitimacy of anointing practices which, though absent from scripture, were customary among the faithful, Amalarius defended and reinforced rites that were apparently questionable at the time. The bishop sealed his argument, as it

---

[586] "De eo oleo, quod infunditur super neofytos, non tale aliquid legimus, sed tenemus apostolicam consuetudinem, et auctoritatem quam accepimus a romana ecclesia, quam pro lege tenere oportet, dicente Agustino ad Casulanum presbyterum de ieiunio sabbati: "In his enim rebus, de quibus nihil certi statuit scriptura divina, mos populi Dei vel instituta maiorum pro lege tenenda sunt." Ibid.

[587] Ibid., 147. See Gregory the Great, *Homiliarum in Ezechielem* 1.II, hom.6, 2, pl 76.

[588] "Ut per oleum intellegamus rectam conversationem, quae moderatur in mente per maturitatem sapientiae, et per balsamum doctrinam, quae bonum odorem praestat foris, idem in alio loco in eodem libro dicit de sapientia: 'Sapientia ad vitam, scientia vero pertinet ad doctrinam.' Chrismalis unction, ut praetulimus, pertinet ad duo dona Spiritus Sancti, id est ad sapientiam et scientiam: oleum ad sapientiam, balsamus [sic], odorem suum longe lateque spargens, ad scientiam. Haec duo, id est vita et doctrina, sibi conexa inveniuntur in septem donis. Sapientia primum et intellectus: sapientia ad vitam, intellectus ad doctrinam; consilium ad doctrinam, fortitudo ad vitam; scientia ad doctrinam, pietas ad vitam." Ibid., 148.

were, by explicating the material and spiritual dimensions of oil and by elucidating its function and

power as a conduit of wisdom and knowledge.[589]

While few liturgical commentaries appeared from the mid-ninth through the mid-eleventh

centuries, the period was nevertheless one of active growth for the liturgy.[590] Monks and clerics

created new liturgical forms, including liturgical drama, and composed salient texts such as the

Ordines romani and the *Pontificale romanogermanicum*.[591] Reynolds notes that while Germanic and

Frankish emperors shaped liturgical norms leading up to the late eleventh century, the reigns of

Popes Alexander II and Gregory VII marked a decided shift in liturgical governance: a Roman

liturgy was imposed by papal authority in Rome.[592] The ascendant papal interest in the liturgy led to

the creation of fresh commentaries, in which liturgists interpreted ecclesiastical ritual anew.[593]

By the time Rupert of Deutz composed his *De Divinis Officiis* in 1111 or 1112, liturgical

commentaries had become a well-established genre. Caught in the nexus between nascent

Scholasticism and the monastic milieu of the early twelfth century, Rupert of Deutz exhibited a

predilection for allegorical interpretation of the liturgy reminiscent of his predecessor Amalarius of

Metz. He was unlike previous biblical and liturgical exegetes, however, in his mystical approach to

the events of the Christian past. Rupert sought not simply to augment understanding of the biblical

narrative by interpreting the events allegorically by reading Christ's life in light of Old Testament

prophecies, but endeavored instead to "displace" the literal, historical reading of the Gospels with a

"Testament of the Spirit," which transcended biblical *historia* by offering a mystical narrative of

---

[589] Regarding the division of Charlemagne's Empire into north-south parcels to allow each new kingdom access to the Mediterrean, which was a key source of both wine and oil, see Collins, *From Tribes to Nation.*
[590] Reynolds, "Liturgical Scholarship at the Time of the Investiture Controversy: Past Research and Future Opportunities," 111.
[591] Ibid.
[592] Ibid., 112.
[593] Ibid., 113.

Christ's life.[594] Frederick Pickering suggested that, rather than dubbing Rupert an "aberrant historian," one might view the abbot as an "imaginative exegete" regarding "what really happened."[595]

Rupert's exposition of oil appears in the fifth book of his *De divinis officiis*. In addition to a raft of citations from the Hebrew and Christian Scriptures, Rupert drew extensively from the *Ordo romanus*, Jerome's *De interpretatione nominum hebraicorum*, Maurus Rabanus' *De natura rerum*, the *Liber Pontificalis*, and Amalarius of Metz's *De ecclesiasticis officiis*. Rupert's exposition of the rites surrounding the consecration of oil emphasized the mysterious and exclusive dimensions of the ritual that were not accessible to all, but only to those initiated in the art of spiritual seeing.[596] While many members of the church witnessed the *ordo consecrationis*, few understood the *causae* or reasons behind the rite:

> Venerable and holy is the ceremony of consecration, but if you will delicately examine the reasons behind the ceremony, which are likewise performed at the consecration, you will take much greater pleasure in the innermost beauty of piety. The ceremony itself is indeed seen by everyone, but we investigate the reasons alongside the practices. What therefore the chrism signifies, or what is accomplished by chrism within us, or why chrism is consecrated on this day, which the same ceremony of the mysteries of consecration contains, we desire to contemplate through the gracious dispensation of true light.[597]

To investigate the reasons accompanying the practices (*iuxta propositum causas*) surrounding the consecration of oil, Rupert first reminds readers that Christ is the Anointed One. He then turns to

---

[594] Pickering, "Exegesis and Imagination," 31. Regarding the allegorizing of historical events, Chenu notes: "Consideration of sacred history involved a biblical interpretation which took literal history (*littera*) as the basis for continuous reference to supra-historical realities figured in terrestrial events." Chenu, *Nature, Man, and Society in the Twelfth Century; Essays on New Theological Perspectives in the Latin West*, 110.

[595] Ibid.

[596] Rupert's vision of an exclusive minority enjoying the more mystical dimensions of the liturgy is consistent with his desire to exclude certain members of the *ecclesia* from the sacraments or expel them altogether from the church, as recorded by John Van Engen. See Van Engen, *Rupert of Deutz*.

[597] "Venerabilis et pius est ordo consecrationis, sed si causas eorum, quae in eadem consecratione aguntur, vel tenuiter inspexeris, multo amplius intima pietatis pulchritudine delectaberis. Ordo quidem ipse ab omnibus videtur, sed nos iuxta propositum causas inquirimus. Quid ergo chrisma significet, aut quid illo in nobis agatur, vel cur hac die consecretur, qui die mysterii consecrationis eius ordo contineat, veri luminis largitore praeeunte considerare cupimus." Rupert, *Ruperti Tuitiensis Liber de divinis officiis*, 169.

the past, citing a long tradition of oil in the Christian tradition, beginning with Exodus, when Moses

institutes chrism and Aaron and his sons are anointed.[598] Rupert's treatment of oil in the Christian

tradition is not entirely original but rather a composite drawn from three sources: Jerome's *De

interpretatione nominum hebraicorum*, Rabanus' *De natura rerum*, and the *Ordo romanum*. Rupert testifies to

how anointing with oil evolved into the imposition of hands and baptism; all three "anointings"

appear to have served the same sacred function:

> By means of God himself Christ the Son of God comes from God the heavenly Father and
>
> is smeared with the true ointment. Now not only high priests and kings, but also the whole
>
> church is consecrated with unction of chrism through the imposition of hands, which is
>
> destined for use by bishops alone, in order that they might seal and bequeath the Paraclete
>
> Spirit. This demonstrates not only the church custom, but also that reading of the Acts of
>
> the Apostles, which asserts the Holy Spirit was given to whomever was baptized in the name
>
> of the Lord Jesus through the imposition of hands by Paul the Apostle.[599]

Like Amalarius, Rupert emphasizes the importance of the church's *consuetudo*, which works in

tandem with the authority of the Acts of the Apostles to justify rituals imparting the Holy Spirit, be

they anointings with oil or otherwise. In addition, Rupert refers to the *gestis pontificabilus* of Pope

Sylvester regarding the institution of a rule that the newly baptized be smeared with oil by a

presbyter: the newly baptized are anointed by a presbyter, not on account of the absence of a bishop

and the attendant difficulty of his imposing of hands from a distance, but because of occasions in

which death might directly follow baptism.[600] Presbyters, however, were not to anoint the crown of

---

[598] "Dominus noster Christus id est *unctus* nuncupatur. Chrismate ungendum primum Moyses instituit in Exodo, quod et iubente Domino composuit, et eo primum Aaron et filii eius uncti sunt." Ibid.

[599] "…per seipsum veniens Christus Dei filius a Deo pater caelesti et vero unguento est delibutus iam non soli pontifices et reges sed et omnis ecclesia unctione chrismatis per impositionem manuum consecratur. Quod solis debetur episcopis, ut consignent et Spiritum Paraclitum tradant, non solum consuetudo ecclesiastica demonstrat, verum et illa lectio Actuum apostolorum, quae asserit quibusdam in nomine Domini Iesu baptizatis per impositionem manuum Pauli apostolic datum esse Spiritum sanctus." Ibid., 169–70.

[600] "Legitur autem in gestis pontificalibus, quod Sylvester Papa constituit, ut baptizatum liniat presbyter chrismate leuantum de aqua propter occasiones transitus mortis, ne propter absentiam episcopi et difficultatem eum consequendi

the head, a privilege reserved for bishops. Rupert's reference to a privilege reserved for the bishop and as well as his concern for the more esoteric meanings hidden within liturgical mysteries further evidences the increasing separation between clerics and the laity as well as the expanding powers of the episcopate during the twelfth century.

In addition to explaining the historical background to oil anointings, Rupert interjects passages that appear to stand *extra historiam* by evoking the mystical dimensions of olives and the substance they exude:

> Therefore chrism is a sign of the Holy Spirit and contains its power. And beautifully, through its own splendor, the Holy Spirit was pleased for us to give thanks. A fruit and indeed *pinguedo*[601] is the olive, which is a tree of peace and a handmaid of light, intermingled with balsam, whose fragrant tree is single and particular among the fragrant trees. The Holy Spirit of divine substance is also *pinguedo*. Therefore whoever was restored as a result of it says: 'You anoint my head with oil.'[602]

Rupert's exposition of oil echoes Amalarius' in several respects. Apart from its close association with the Holy Spirit, Rupert uses an identical word employed by Amalarius to describe the olive: *pinguedo*. Moreover, both authors speak of the olive tree as a sign of peace, likely because of the appearance of the olive branch and the dove in Genesis 8. Rupert surpasses Amalarius' discussion of the olive tree, however, by personifying the tree as a female servant who dispenses light. Oil dispensing light was a reference, naturally, to oil lamps which hung not only by tombs of saints but provided lighting on a daily basis. Like in Amalarius's exposition, Rupert noted the importance of another tree, the balsam,

---

sine manus impositione baptizati migrent. Presbyteris itaque chrismate baptizatos ungere licet, sed quod ab episcopo fuerit consecratum, non tamen frontem, quod solis debetur episcopis, sed uerticem." Ibid., 170.

[601] *Pinguedo* is better left translated, as no single English word captures the varied Latin meanings: fat/fatness; oiliness; richness/abundance; fullness; exuberance.

[602] "Igitur chrisma Spiritus sancti signum est, cuius et virtutem continet. Et pulchre Spiritui sancto per hac speciem suam nobis placuit dare gratiam. Fructus namque et pinguedo est oleo, quae arbor pacis et luminis ministra est commixto balsamo, cuius arbor odorifera una est et praecipua arborum aromaticarum. Sanctus autem Spiritus divinae substantiae pinguedo est, ita ut quicumque ex eo refectus fuerit, dicat: *Impinguasti in oleo caput meum*." Rupert, *Ruperti Tuitiensis Liber de divinis officiis*, 170.

which he maintained had a mystical power all of its own. Rupert embroidered Amalarius'
understanding of the significance of balsam through yet another personification: the balsam tree is
like a peerless maiden who releases an especially lovely fragrance, setting her apart from her nice-
smelling cohort of fragrant trees. Rupert depicted the balsam tree's scent as having a power (or
meaning perhaps) which only fine-tuned senses could perceive, making the things perceptible
through the body (scents) similar to those perceived by the mind (*causae*). More so than Amalarius,
Rupert emphasized the role pleasure played in leading souls to the divine:

> And the scent of the balsam in the oil signifies the sweetness of the Holy Spirit, which all
> together entices the nose (that is for those who have the power of discernment) with a good
> scent and of itself causes desiring. Whoever receives the scent of balsam says with the
> apostle: *We are the good aroma of Christ for God in every place.* Therefore the Holy Spirit rightly
> performs visible things for our sake, so through these things we might be able to readily
> understand spiritual things. Through this likeness, he pours out his pleasant and fragrant
> grace on us.[603]

Just as the balsam mingles with the oil, so the Holy Spirit mingles with the minds of those who

receive it. Similarly, the odor of the balsam enters the nose and interacts with the body,

demonstrating how physical things, or the senses, commingle with the spiritual or invisible. Rupert's

personification of trees was of a piece with his larger purpose – to explain the invisible causes

behind the visible ritual. Such an explanation sheds light on the mystery of the Godhead: the

invisible Father makes Himself known as a person: a visible Son. God revealed Godself both in flesh

and in metaphor. The Holy Spirit communicated His essence through likeness to a mellifluous scent.

Taking a simple line of instruction from the *Ordo Romanus* about the ampoule which housed

consecrated oil, Rupert spun an elaborate chrysalis of symbols in which holy oil represented not a

---

[603] "Et balsami odor in oleo suauitatem eiusdem Spiritus sancti significat, qua cunctos, qui nasum, id est virtutem habent
discretionis, bono odore allicit et suimet appetentes efficit. Quem quicumque accipiunt, cum apostolo dicunt: *Christi
bonus odor sumus Deo in omni loco.* Bene ergo Spiritus sanctus, qui propter nos idcirco agit visibilia, quo per haec facilius
capere invisibilia, per hoc simile suam nobis suavem et odoriferam infundit gratiam." Ibid., 170–71.

fragrant maiden, but Christ himself who issued forth from the Virgin. Concerning the consecration of chrism, Rupert cited the "little book of Roman orders" as saying: "At once two acolytes hold the ampoules wrapped in white silk muslin with their right hands, so that they may be seen by the community."[604] From this simple instruction, Rupert unfolded something greater: "The ampoule, before it comes before the bishop up to the altar, is half covered and half naked. The ampoule with sacred oils in a certain way signifies the body of Christ taken from the Virgin, corporally dwelling in her and containing the fullness of the Holy Spirit."[605] The partially clad ampoule signified Christ, filled with the Holy Spirit. The ampoule is also a symbol for the Virgin's body: a vessel carrying the divinity. Like a good historian, Rupert brought the parallels between the past and the present into sharp relief; he explained how the liturgy of his present day corresponded to the past. He did so by explaining that the partially covered ampoule was like the outward, physical appearance of Jesus of Nazareth, which belied his divine nature:

> The body of Christ, which previously passed over to the altar of the cross, was in another time completely covered and in another time naked. Thus the first time it was covered was when he fled into Egypt as if he were not the king of kings, and when he was brought to the temple as if he were not omnipotent and when thus he was placed under his parents as if he were not the author of parents. In these and similar instances, covered, he lay hidden. He was naked after he began to work miracles and simultaneously preach and reveal God Himself, such that he said, 'The Father and I are one.' In these and in other instances, he was naked.[606]

---

[604] "Dicit libellus Romani ordinis de consecratione chrismatis: *Continuo duo acolythi involutas ampullas cum sindone alba de serico teneat in brachio dextro, ita ut videri possint a medio.*" Ibid., 172.

[605] Ibid.

[606] "Quod antequam transiret ad altare cruces, aliquo tempore erat coopertum, et aliquo nudum. Primaevo tempore erat coopertum, quandoo ita fugit in Aegyptum, quasi non esset rex regnum, et quando ita portatus est ad templum, quasi non esset omnipotens, et quando ita subditus erat parentibus, quasi non esset auctor parentum. In his et similibus coopertum latebat. Nudum erat postquam miracula coepit facere simulque praedicare et se Deum demonstrare, ut *Ego et Pater*, inquit, *unum sumus.* In his et aliis nudum erat." Ibid., 173.

The ritual of transporting the ampoules of holy oil to the altar to be blessed by the bishop was an occasion for Rupert to explicate the nature of divinity itself, which was partially hidden and partially revealed throughout salvation history and in the sacraments. According to Rupert, to bless was to undress; the transformation accomplished through consecration revealed rather than concealed divinity, suggesting a parallel between the human body and God. The ritual of consecration effectively transformed the ampoule from something human to something divine. Similarly, Rupert's commentary imparted a significance or meaning to the ampoule, transforming an inanimate object into something human – if not in actuality, at least in the minds of his readers.

Rupert described the twelve presbyters who surrounded the bishop at the blessing of the oil as witnesses of a sacred mystery; to them, Christ appeared as he did to the disciples after the Resurrection: "after the ampoule is blessed and returns to the altar, naked and visible, it will be hailed by the pontiff and by the ministers of the altar. This signifies that Christ, after going to the altar of the cross, showed his corporeal presence to the same people who wished to be witnesses of his resurrection."[607] Since, according to Rupert, to be dressed was human and undressed divine, the cross was the ultimate shedding of humanity. In offering himself as a sacrifice, Christ removed not only his clothing, but his mortal body. After the crucifixion, he was most fully naked and divine in the Resurrection. The transformation from the physical to the spiritual was also a transformation from the visible to the invisible. For Rupert, oil aptly represented the slippery or paradoxical nature of God, who was at once visible and invisible; on the one hand, Christ was naked and visible as oil after consecration. On the other hand, Christ remained hidden within the ampoule: daily the faithful worshipped what they did not see.[608] As a product of the early part of the twelfth century, Rupert's *De Divinis Officiis* falls at the mystical end of the spectrum of liturgical commentaries. It manifests

---

[607] "Ampulla vero postquam benedicta fuerit et ab altari redit, a pontifice et ministris altaris visibiliter et nuda salutatur. Hoc significat, quod Christus, postquam ab altari crucis transivit, praesentiam suam corporalem eis praebuit, quos testes suae resurrectionis esse voluit." Ibid.

[608] "Nos vero, quamuis corporalem eius praesentiam non videamus, tamen venerando eum quotidie salutamus." Ibid.

few, if any, qualities characteristic of Scholastic or legal thought. While investigating the *causae* or

reasons underlying oil rituals, Rupert's commentary did so without the rigorous use of logic. Rather,

the author relied on his imagination and those of his readers. Delving deeply into the parallels

between the present and the past, Rupert elucidated the mystical significance of oil and revealed a

liturgy replete with hidden mysteries, mysteries that could only be glimpsed from aloft, on the

iridescent wings of metaphor.

GRATIAN'S DECRETUM

The late eleventh and early twelfth centuries witnessed meteoric developments in both

biblical exegesis and canon law, which had lasting impact on liturgical commentaries. The exegetical

work and compilation of the biblical *Glossa Ordinaria* begun in the monasteries shifted to the

cathedral schools.[609] Simultaneously, school masters such as Irnerius began teaching law in Bologna

and Paris. Gratian's *Concordia discordantium canonum*, later known as the *Decretum*, appeared in Bologna

between the 1120's the 1140's, radically altering the study and promulgation of secular and

ecclesiastical law. Gratian's *magnum opus*, which was intended as a textbook for teaching canon law in

emergent universities, called on nascent jurists to resolve conflicting *canones* by apprehending

transcendental norms through reason.[610] Organizing his canonical collection around *causae*, Gratian

posed a series of questions regarding each *causa* and asked students to reconcile conflicting norms

contained within diverse texts. In this regard, Gratian's work and that of jurists shared in the

dialectical method employed by the early Scholastics of the twelfth century, namely Peter Lombard

---

[609] See Leclercq, *L'amour des lettres et le désir de Dieu; initiation aux auteurs monastiques du Moyen Âge*; Smalley, *The Study of the Bible in the Middle Ages.*Constance Bouchard challenged a well-established thesis that the majority of developments in the biblical exegesis of the twelfth-century and the development of the *Glossa Ordinaria*, took place among the first 'Scholastics' – clergy populating cathedral schools and emergent universities. Bouchard also challenges the notion of a clear demarcation between 'monastic' and 'Scholastic' thought. See Bouchard, "The Cistercians and the *Glossa Ordinaria*."
[610] Pennington, *Gratian,* accessed on October 21, 2014, http://faculty.cua.edu/pennington/law111/gratiandma.htm.

in his *Sentences* and Peter Abelard, most notably in *Sic et non*.[611] Using dialectical reasoning, law

masters taught students to go beyond the literal meaning of laws to extract a kernel of truth or

justice. In their search for transcendental norms, young jurists resembled biblical exegetes in search

of the hidden meaning in symbols. It was only fitting that Gratian, as a teacher who encouraged his

students to see beyond the letter of the law, should start his *Decretum* by citing Isidore of Seville's

Etymologies, which presents multiple readings or "senses" of Scripture and divine law. The *Etymologies*

stated:

> Divine law should be looked at in three ways. In the first place, let it be understood
> historically, in the second place, tropologically, and in the third place, mystically. For the
> historical sense is geared to the letter, tropological sense is geared to moral science, and the
> mystical sense is geared to a spiritual understanding, etc.[612]

As the twelfth century witnessed the birth of jurisprudence, jurists interpreted laws as if they were

biblical texts: laws could not only be read literally. While liturgical commentaries teased out the

meanings of rituals to rejuvenate faith or heighten an awareness of mystery, medieval jurists weighed

and assessed laws to determine what was just.[613] To find answers to legal problems and to legitimize

a new legal system, jurists often turned to the Bible and derived authority for procedural norms

through biblical exegesis. For example, the emergence of the *ordo iudiciarus* was partially dependent

on an allegorical reading of Genesis 3:8-13.[614] Canonists interpreted the events taking place in

Paradise as a reflection of the first legal procedure: a transgression, an accusation of entrapment, and

---

[611] Like Gratian's *Decretum*, Lombard's *Sentences* were broken up into *distinctiones*, intended originally as pauses in the readings or moments for reflection. These *caesurae* later became chapter divisions.

[612] Isidore of Seville, as quoted in Lubac, *Exégèse Médiéval*, 106. Chenu noted that for the "symbolist mentality" of the twelfth century, Isidore's *Etymologies* was especially influential on the medieval perception of numbers which were believed to be "like the thoughts of God" and of names, which "revealed the realities they stood for." Chenu, *Nature, Man, and Society in the Twelfth Century; Essays on New Theological Perspectives in the Latin West*, 107.

[613] Kenneth Pennington noted: "As any student of statutory interpretation learns very quickly, laws cannot just be read literally; they must be interpreted." See Kenneth Pennington, "The 'Big Bang': Roman Law in the Early Twelfth Century," accessed on October 21, 2014, http://faculty.cua.edu/pennington/BigBangRomanLaw.htm.

[614] Kenneth Pennington, History of Canon Law lecture. Catholic University of America. Washington, DC. December 6, 2010.

a legal defense or pleading. The legitimacy of the *ordo* was derived from an allegorical interpretation of the Genesis text, which served as the model for just procedure adopted by ecclesiastical courts.

Just as exegetes discerned a spiritual meaning in Scripture, jurists discerned the presence of natural law or transcendental norms. In the case of God summoning a naked Adam from the bushes, a jurist perceived an individual's inalienable right to a court summons. The implications of such allegorical readings of Scripture in legal contexts were substantial. Johannes Monachus, the late thirteenth and early fourteenth-century canonist and bishop of Meaux, used such allegorical reasoning to establish an argument for the pope being subject to natural law, if not positive law: the pope could not abrogate an individual's right to a court summons (as an integral step in the procedure established by natural law in the Garden of Eden) and the right to be present in court at the time of judgement.[615] The trial in the Garden, according to Monachus, even suggested an individual was innocent until proven guilty and that law ought first to seek to absolve rather than to condemn.[616]

In the thirteenth century, further influences of allegorical expositions and biblical glosses surfaced in the legal realm. Glosses of Gratian's *Decretum* and Gregory's *Decretals* assumed the form of biblical glosses composed a century earlier. The manuscripts containing biblical and legal commentaries mirrored one another: glosses were written into the margins of manuscripts, forming a wide border of exposition around the given text. Apart from the physical similarities of their manuscripts, legal and liturgical texts both manifested a predilection for allegorical interpretation. Elaborate metaphors characteristic of biblical and liturgical commentaries appeared in expositions about the ecclesiastical hierarchy and canon law itself. The Italian jurist Henricus de Segusio, known as Hostiensis, greatly influenced the development of canon law by recasting the language of

---

[615] See Kenneth Pennington, "Due Process, Community, and the Prince in the Evolution of the *Ordo Iudiciarius*, accessed on 21 October 2014, http://faculty.cua.edu/pennington/law508/procedure.htm.
[616] Ibid.

ecclesiastical and secular authority.[617] He presented the arts or disciplines which apprehended divine

law as parts of the human body, with the church itself personified as a human being: theology was

the head, canon law the hand, Roman law the feet and the prince the mouth, from which divine law

issued.[618] While the primary concern of law was the establishment of justice, the goal of the liturgy

was sanctity. Although law and liturgy used allegorical methods of exegesis for apparently different

ends, their purpose was singular: to impart to each individual his or her *ius* or the divine nature of

God.

GUILLAUME DURAND

The seismic changes effected by Gratian *Decretum* are abundantly evident in the liturgical

expositions of the thirteenth-century liturgist and jurist, Guillaume Durand the Elder. Like

Amalarius of Metz, Durand enjoyed an active apostolate. After being educated at cathedral schools

in his native Provence, Durand studied law at the University of Bologna, where he received a

doctorate in canon law sometime between 1260-1263. He went on to serve as a papal lawyer,

diplomat and advisor to Pope Gregory X in 1274 at the Second Council of Lyon. Elected bishop of

Mende in 1285, Durand composed his liturgical commentaries and *Pontificale* (c.1296), which would

have lasting impact on the liturgy. Durand's *Pontificale* or the "Bishop's Book" was the most

authoritative pontifical of the later medieval period and remained unchallenged until the Second

Vatican Council.[619] Durand's epic work on the medieval liturgy, the *Rationale divinorum officiorum*, in

addition to being the most expansive and comprehensive liturgical commentary, was the definitive

---

[617] Kenneth Pennington, "Politics in Western Jurisprudence", accessed on October 21, 2014,
http://faculty.cua.edu/pennington/law508/PoliticsWesternLaw.htm.
[618] "Hostiensis did not create a new jurisprudence of law but outfitted traditional definitions with remarkable
metaphors." Ibid.
[619] Thibodeau, and Durand, *The Rationale Divinorum Officiorum of William Durand of Mende (A New Translation of the Prologue
and Book One)*, xviii.

distillation of the church's understanding of its liturgy in the late thirteenth century.[620] Indeed, the

Rationale carried great weight up to the Reformation and beyond; it was the second non-biblical book

printed by Gutenberg's press (1459) and was reprinted 104 times before 1859.[621]

The *Rationale* embodies both the monastic and Scholastic approaches to Scripture. Like

Amalarius and Rupert's expositions, Durand attempts a reasoned explanation of the liturgy.[622]

Aiming to undercover the fundamental rationale underlying ecclesiastical rites, he compiled and

evaluated diverse texts containing canon laws and liturgical norms. His work was akin to jurists

searching for *concordia* among divergent canons or Scholastics engaged in dialectic debate: seeking a

rational explanation of the transcendental norms or truths governing human practices. Just as

Gratian's *Decretum* was a survey of the canonical tradition in its entirely, Durand's *Rationale* was an

all-inclusive compendium of the Christian liturgy. Durand distinguished himself as a compiler and

synthesizer of texts, not as an author of an original exposition.[623] And yet, it was precisely the

composite nature of Durand's work that lent it such authority.[624]

Durand's interpretations of the church, including its physical structure and its liturgy, were

founded on the work of early Gothic liturgists, including Honorius "of Autun" (c.1075/1080-1156)

and Sicardus of Cremona (c.1150-1215).[625] Later authors who figure prominently in the *Rationale*

include Lothaire de Segni (Pope Innocent III) (1160/1161-1216), Guillaume d'Auxerre (d. 1231),

---

[620] "From the time of its appearance at the end of the thirteenth century to the Catholic Restorationist liturgical revival in mid-nineteenth-century France, it was hailed by admirers as the quintessential expression of the medieval church's understanding of the divine offices." Thibodeau, "Enigmata Figurarum: Biblical Exegesis and Liturgical Exposition in Durand's Rationale," 65–66.

[621] Timothy Thibodeau "Introduction" in *The Rationale Divinorum Officiorum of William Durand of Mende (a New Translation of the Prologue and Book One)*, xxii.

[622] Thibodeau notes the aptly multivalent meaning of *rationale*: on the one hand, *rationale* indicated a "preoccupation with making manifest the hidden or deeper meaning of the divine offices"; on the other, *rationale* meant "an actual liturgical vestment called the *rationale* which was worn in place of the *pallium* by some archbishops, primarily in Germanic lands." Durand's own *Rationale* offers a commentary on the *rationale iudicii*, a pectoral described in Exodus 28:15-30 and worn by high priests of the ancient Israelites, who used the garment "as an oracle for determining God's will." Thibodeau, "Enigmata Figurarum: Biblical Exegesis and Liturgical Exposition in Durand's Rationale," 70.

[623] Timothy Thibodeau, "Introduction" in *The Rationale Divinorum Officiorum of William Durand of Mende (a New Translation of the Prologue and Book One)*, xx.

[624] Ibid.

[625] Ibid., xix.

and Prévostin of Crémone (ca. 1150-1210).[626] Durand gleaned his interpretations of the liturgy not

only from prior liturgists. As a faithful pupil of canon law, Durand supplemented his allegorical

expositions of ritual with a plethora of legal material, including excerpts from Gratian's *Decretum*,

Gregory IX's *Liber Extra*, and Justinian's *Corpus Iuris Civilis*.[627] Durand's knowledge of papal and

conciliar prescriptions for the liturgy resulted from his encounters with legal texts in Bologna.[628]

Indeed, Gratian's *Decretum* was so exhaustive a repository of texts that it served as Durand's source

base for Scripture as well as the writing of Greek and Latin theologians, canonists and exegetes.[629]

Durand's original contributions to commentary on the liturgy, though perhaps few, derived from his

expansive exposure to the *Decretum* and his own training as a jurist; he had the ability to evaluate

points of dispute or seemingly contradictory practices.[630] Richly adorned with references to legal,

theological and liturgical texts, Durand's *Rationale* reveals the impact of legal reasoning on the

liturgical practices of the late medieval Roman Church, including its norms for the use of oil.

In the eighth chapter of the *Rationale*, entitled *De Consecrationibus et Unctionibus*, Durand

discussed the various uses of oil and what they signified. Like Amalarius and Rupert, Durand began

with a reference to the importance of oil in the Christian tradition. His purview extended back to

Moses, the Tabernacle and the Ark of the Covenant.[631] The opening paragraph of Durand's chapter

on consecrations and unction stems from Gratian's *De Consecratione*, ironically from a portion of the

text likely authored by someone else.[632] Durand's opening passage on consecrations and unctions

---

[626] Thibodeau, "Les sources du Rationale de Guillaume Durand," 147–48.

[627] Thibodeau, "Introduction" in *The Rationale Divinorum Officiorum of William Durand of Mende (a New Translation of the Prologue and Book One)*, xxi.

[628] Thibodeau, "Les sources du Rationale de Guillaume Durand," 151.

[629] Ibid.

[630] Thibodeau, "Introduction" in *The Rationale Divinorum Officiorum of William Durand of Mende (a New Translation of the Prologue and Book One)*, xxi.

[631] Ibid., 89, 119n1.

[632] This portion of the *Decretum* appears to be one of the last additions to the text and was likely authored by a jurist other than Gratian himself. Later redactions of the *Decretum* were double the size of the original text and included quantities of Roman law in addition to the appended section on the sacraments. The four manuscripts containing the first recession of the *Decretum* do not include *De Consecratione*: Admont, Stiftsbibliothek 23 and 43; Barcelona, Arxiu de la Corona d'Aragó, Ripoll 78; Florence, Biblioteca Nazionale Centrale, Conventi soppressi A.I.402; Paris, Bibliothèque

states: "We read that the Lord commanded Moses to make a chrism with which he would anoint the

Tabernacle as well as the Ark of the Covenant, the table, and the vessels on the day of dedication,

and with which he could also anoint the priests and kings."[633]

What portions of the *De Consecratione* did Durand choose to omit or to include? While

Gratian's text states that the commandment to anoint Israelite kings is found "in the law of the

Lord," Durand omitted this legal invocation. He also skipped a detailed discussion of Hebrew

practices and the Levite kings who were the first recipients of holy oil.[634] Durand proceeded directly

to contrasting Moses with Jesus by interjecting his own observation that while Moses was not

himself anointed with oil, Christ was anointed, hence the physical anointing of Christians: "Christ

wished for us to be anointed with a material unction so that we could attain the spiritual unction that

is attached to the material."[635] Durand's justification for actual physical anointing was radically

different from that of either Amalarius or Rupert. Rather than deferring to the authority of the

Apostles or *consuetudo*, Durand simply stated that anointing with oil was the will or the wish of

Christ: *voluit itaque Christus*. Such an argument subtly but unmistakably reflects one of the most

important legal developments of the thirteenth century: "what pleases the prince has the force of

law" – "*sed et quod principi placuit, legis vigorem habet.*"[636]

By the thirteenth century, the authority of the pope and his power to promulgate law

reached an unprecedented height. Innocent III's interpretation of the pope as the "vicar of Christ"

coupled with the notion of *plenitudo potestatis* (fullness of power) established an individual as the

---

nationale de France, nouv. acq. lat. 1761. While John Van Engen rejected the thesis that Gratian was not the author of
De Consecratione, Anders Winroth argued for its validity. See Van Engen, "Observations on the De Consecratione";
Winroth, *The Making of Gratian's Decretum*, 12.

[633] Ex. 30:22-29. See Thibodeau, and Durand, *The Rationale Divinorum Officiorum of William Durand of Mende (a New Translation of the Prologue and Book One)*, 89.

[634] See De cons. D.1 c.1-2.

[635] Ibid.

[636] Kenneth Pennington, "Innocent III and the Divine Authority of the Pope", accessed on October 21, 2014,
http://faculty.cua.edu/pennington/canon%20law/POPEBISHOPSChaptOne.htm. Regarding the dissemination of the
term "princeps" for the King of France and the concept of the will of the prince as the source of law in Gaul, see
Collins, *From Tribes to Nation*.

source of law. In Durand's commentary on liturgical rites, we see that the power of an individual to bestow law replaced authority previously enjoyed by the Apostles and the *mos populi* (custom of the people). Following the excerpt taken from *De Consecratione*, Durand turned to the Decretals of Gregory IX; Gregory's *De sacra unctione* begins with Innocent III's legislation on unction.[637] Innocent began with a nod to the authority of the Apostles and custom of the church, but then interpreted oil and balsam in a way that emphasized individual authority and the importance of reputation.[638] First Innocent stated that the efficacy of a sacrament was dependent on the spirit in which it was bestowed or received: "Visible and exterior anointing is a sign of interior and invisible unction. Moreover, invisible and interior unction is not only a sign, but also a sacrament because, if worthily accepted or done or honored without doubt, unction indicates a sacrament."[639] After noting that chrism was "made from oil and balsam for a mystical reason" (*ex oleo fit et balsamo mystica ratione*), Innocent proceeded to explicate the symbolic or mystical significance of oil.

Innocent III's explanation of the mystical meaning of oil was quite unlike that of Rupert; rather than emphasizing the interior experience of an individual delighting in a fragrance, Innocent emphasized a correlation between conscience, fame or reputation, and episcopal authority. First and foremost, oil indicated the splendor or brightness of the conscience, which Innocent associated with the wisdom exhibited by the wise virgins with their lamps full of oil: "The prudent virgins accepted oil in their vessels with their lamps."[640] According to Amalarius, balsam represented doctrine and knowledge graciously dispensed by the Holy Spirit. For Rupert, balsam represented the Holy Spirit, who was like a fragrant maiden sweetly inciting desire for spiritual things among the learned.

---

[637] See X 1.15.1

[638] Innocent quotes the same passage from James 5:14 quoted by Amalarius and Rupert: "De prima Iacobus Apostolus ait: 'Infirmatur quis in vobis, inducat presbyteros ecclesiae, et orent super eum, ungentes eum oleo in nomine Domini, et oratio fidei salvabit infirmum." See See X 1.15.1.

[639] "Unctio visibilis et exterior signum est interioris et invisibilis unctionis. Unctio vero invisibilis et interior non solum est signum, sed etiam sacramentum, quia, si digne sumitur, vel agit vel auget absque dubio quod designat." X 1.15.1.

[640] "Per oleum enim nitor conscientiae designatur, iuxta quod legitur: "Prudentes virgines acceperunt oleum in vasis suis cum lampadibus;" per balsum autem odor famae exprimitur, propter quod dicitur: "Sicut balsamum aromatizans, odorem dedi." X 1.15.1.

Innocent's concerns were far worldlier; they were tied directly to the role of ecclesiastical authority in the church. Innocent interpreted balsam to be the "aroma of fame": "Through balsam, however, the aroma of fame is expressed (*exprimitur*), on account of which it is said: Like aromatizing balsam, fragrance is given."[641] While Innocent's choice of words delicately and playfully suggested the olive, which was pressed to extract oil, he was nevertheless more concerned with the role of bishops than the mystical meaning of scents and oily substances. The "aroma of fame" is clearly an illusion to the "aroma of Christ" discussed by previous liturgists. According to Innocent III, sanctification through oil was not simply about imparting holiness to an individual. Rather, oil marked the sanctification of the church through its bishops. Bishops were anointed with chrism not only "in body, but in their hearts" so that interiorly they would have the "brightness of conscience" while exteriorly they would exhibit the aroma of good repute, by which Innocent meant the "aroma of Christ."[642] Innocent III's discourse on oil as a guarantor of episcopal strength and reputation further demonstrates the expansion of episcopal power in the High Middle Ages, when the papacy reached the height of its influence in both secular and ecclesiastical realms.

Durand, in his commentary on oil and balsam, partially adapted Innocent III's exposition as found in Gregory IX's decretal. Durand appropriated Innocent's language of the exterior and interior anointings but then he did not apply these terms to the conscience and reputation of bishops. Drawing on a pseudo-Augustinian text, Durand interpreted anointing with the "good odor of Christ" to mean "we are fully prepared to hear the faith."[643] Those who were anointed with oil received faith rather than wisdom or knowledge. Like Innocent III, Durand's discussion of the

---

[641] "Per balsamum autem odor famae exprimitur, propter quod dicitur: 'Sicut balsamum aromatizans, odorem dedi." X 1.15.1. *Exprimitur* suggests something is expressed or squeezed out, like oil from an olive.

[642] "Hoc ergo chrismate ungi debet episcopus, non tam in corpore, quam in corde, ut et interius habeat nitorem conscientiae, quantum ad Deum et exterius habeat odorem famae, quoad proximum…De odore famae idem Apostolus ait: 'Christi bonus odor sumus in omni loco, et aliis sumus odor vitae in vitam, aliis odor mortis in mortem.' Debit enim episcopus bonum habere testimonium, et ab iis, qui sunt intus, et ab iis, qui sunt foris, ut cortina cortinam trahat, et qui audit dicat: veni." X 1.15.1.

[643] Thibodeau, and Durand, *The Rationale Divinorum Officiorum of William Durand of Mende (a New Translation of the Prologue and Book One)*, 92.

symbolic significance of sweet-smelling oil was far less fanciful than Rupert of Deutz. Durand is

less concerned with profusions of knowledge and spiritual insight than with sin and good works.

Durand began with a rhetorical question, reflecting the dialectical method of question and answer,

common among both the Scholastics and jurists: "But we should ask: why do we anoint the sick and

the catechumens with oil? I respond: it is because invisible things are more easily grasped through

visible things, just as the oil, while putting sickness to flight, rejuvenates the limbs of the weary, and

on account of its own nature, sheds its light."[644] This passage was clearly an adaptation of

Amalarius' exposition on oil, to which Durand made additions and omissions that reflected

theological and liturgical peculiarities of his time.

In describing the anointings of the newly baptized, Durand gave an explanation for the

legitimacy of liturgical practices not found in Scripture, like Amalarius had done some 400 years

earlier. Whereas Amalarius referred to the "*mos populi Dei*" which granted authority to non-

Scripturally-based rituals, Durand spoke of usage rather than mores or customs: "According to

Augustine the first three anointings were introduced more through usage than through any

Scripture."[645] Entirely missing from Durand's account is the interpretation of oil as an extension of

the imposition of hands, which played such a prominent role in Amalarius' exposition. By the

thirteenth century, oil had evidently supplanted the imposition of hands as the means by which the

Holy Spirit was imparted to the faithful. Moreover, while Durand made a passing reference to "the

authority of the apostles" regarding the healing of the sick with oil, gone was the need to justify

practices regarding neophytes or catechumens, as was the case with Amalarius. Durand simply

referred to the established authority of the Apostles' successors.[646]

---

[644] Ibid., 90.

[645] "…secundum Augustinum prime tres unctions potius introducte sunt usu quam per aliquam Scripturam." Ibid., 98.
Thibodeau translates *usu* as custom rather than usage. Nevertheless, it's important to note Durand employs neither *mos*
nor *consuetudo*.

[646] "De oleo infirmorum auctoritatem accepimus ab apostolis, de oleo catechumenorum ab apostolicis." Ibid.

In his explanation of oil's power to heal and revive the bodies of the sick, Amalarius made

no explicit reference to sin nor did he overtly suggest a moral component to illness. Durand's

explanation of oil's power, however, included the ability to take away sin and restore the health of

the soul: "it must be believed that an unction with consecrated oil, which is a sign of faith, while

putting sin to flight provides health to the soul and shows its light to it."[647] Moreover, Durand's

discussion is minimal. He noted oil "warms weary limbs and provides light, as was noted above, and

balsam gives off a sweet scent."[648] Rather than emphasizing the mystical meaning of balsam or

describing the ability of the mind and body to perceive spiritual things, Durand was concerned with

penance and sin:

> Seeing that the soul's members are weary when one does penance for having turned against
> God, the Holy Spirit comes to it, and illuminates its understanding, and shows it the sins that
> have been remitted or must be remitted, and the Spirit gives him good works which provide
> a good odor for others, which is designated by the fragrant balsam. This anointing is also
> done on the crown of the head, where the seat of pride [*superbia*] is seen, which always seeks
> after higher things [*superiora*], so therefore, it is done in the form of the cross and in the name
> of humility.

For Rupert, balsam signified the spiritual things that enticed and evoked desire among the holy and

faithful who possessed the virtue of discernment. For Durand, balsam represented the good works,

done for the sake not of pleasure but for the remission of sins and the good of others. Whereas

Rupert gave no explanation for why bishops anoint the crown of the head with oil, Durand

provided a moral explanation, which emphasized human sinfulness and exhorted readers to seek

humility and contrition rather than delight. Durand's exposition of the liturgy certainly relied on the

---

[647] "Sic credendum est quod unctio olei consecrati, quod est signum fidei, peccata fugando, sanitatem anime confert et lumen ei prestat." Ibid.
[648] Ibid.

allegorical methods used by previous liturgists, but the thirteenth-century bishops' approach to oil displays an attenuation of mystical rumination.

Conclusion

Although scholars have duly noted that liturgical commentaries did not lose their allegorical nature over the course of the thirteenth century, the advent of Scholasticism and jurisprudence did not leave liturgical commentaries unchanged. Bernard of Clairvaux could not have rightly accused Guillaume Durand of misapplying cold reason to the sacred mysteries expressed in the liturgy. Durand was, nevertheless, guilty of adapting a style of commentary that, if not completely rational, was far less mystical than that of his predecessor, Rupert of Deutz. Trained as a jurist, Durand authored commentaries on the liturgy that were a synthesis of allegorical and Scholastic thought; he revealed the mystical parallels between the visible and invisible realms while also rationally harmonizing an extensive body of discordant texts. Medieval jurists uncovered the transcendental norms incarnate in extant laws as medieval liturgists similarly sought eternal truths, which were partially veiled and partially naked in ritual. While the medieval period can be aptly characterized as an age of symbol and symbolic thought, liturgical commentaries demonstrate how allegorical exposition could rigorously serve "worldly" ends, as evinced by Amalarius of Metz's defense of Frankish *consuetudo* and Innocent III's concern for the consciences and reputations of bishops. Although some medieval liturgical expositions engaged in rapturous flights of metaphorical fancy, they existed alongside highly rational texts, deeply rooted in the Scholastic and legal traditions. These commentaries demonstrate that over the course of the High Middle Ages, oil paradoxically became a symbol for both worldly episcopal power and otherworldly, esoteric knowledge of the sacred mysteries. As the ecclesiastical elite sought to further their control over holy oils, which they maintained belonged to the privileged domain of the *ecclesia*, oil lost its feminine nature (dispenser of light, grace and fragrance) but nevertheless became a symbol for penance and the forgiveness of

sins.

Chapter 5

Late Antique and

Early Medieval Myroblytes

Introduction

This chapter investigates the origin of the myroblyte phenomenon and explains how oil-

producing saints became widely venerated in the Latin West. Although the earliest saints whose

tombs produced oil hailed from the Late Antique Near East, the accounts of their miraculously oily

tombs often appeared centuries later. The lives and offices of Demetrius of Thessaloniki (4th c.),

Nicholas of Myra (4th c.) and Catherine of Alexandria (4th c.), for example, date to the High Middle

Ages.[649] The popularity of myroblytes in Europe appears to have begun in Merovingian Gaul with

Gregory of Tours' (538-593) accounts of the miraculous tombs of Andrew the Apostle (1st c.) and

Martin of Tours (316-397). Carolingian biographers later interpolated oil miracles into older *vitae* or

fashioned new myroblytes from Merovingian saints. Merovingian and Carolingian Gaul, which may

have been the birthplace of physical rather than merely spiritual anointings of kings and bishops,

was home to a curiously high concentration of myroblytes. The appearance of predominantly male

myroblytes coincided with developments in the ritual use of oil in coronation and ordination rituals.

During this period, Merovingian biographers infused oil into the lives of their Gallic saints. Beyond

merely producing a liquid capable of healing the sick, the oil miracles of these male myroblytes

demonstrated the clerics' status as beloved elect, their intimacy with God, and their divine favor,

which God bestowed on them so that they might heal "the people." While a number of early

---

[649] See Chapter 6.

medieval female myroblytes existed, biographers did not compose these women's *vitae* or offices

until centuries later, suggesting that few women were famed for oil prior to the High Middle Ages.[650]

FELIX OF NOLA

What accounts for the preponderance of male myroblyte *vitae* in the early medieval Latin

West? One of the earliest male saints associated with miraculous oil in the Latin West was Felix of

Nola (d. circa 250), a martyr from Nola, in the Campania region outside of Naples. In the early fifth

century, Paulinus, the Bishop of Nola (354-431) established the cult of his predecessor Felix,

composing songs (*carmina*) in praise of the saint and building an elaborate cemetery around the

martyr's grave.[651] Later biographers rewrote Felix's life, including Marcellus the Presbyter (dates

unknown), Gregory of Tours (c. 538-594), and the Venerable Bede (672/3-735). None of these

biographers, however, describe miraculous oil flowing from Felix's tomb. Paulinus' account of the

tomb, however, provides insight into how Late Antique Christians poured fragrant oil into the

tombs of saints, so the oil might acquire the saints' power through material contact. The tombs of

martyrs greatly influenced the character of Late Antique Christianity and the development of the cult

of the saints.[652] In contrast to the suffering and uncertainties human beings faced while alive, the

saints enjoyed enduring peace and safety in their heavenly abode. Their tombs both wielded

extraordinary powers and reflected this blessed state of the saint in heaven, as evidenced by Paulinus'

discovery of Felix's bones resting in perfect peace.[653]

---

[650] Carolyn Walker Bynum observed that overall, the number of female saints increased dramatically in the High Middle Ages and that in the early medieval period "virtually all saints were male." The increase of female myroblytes in the High Middle Ages reflects the trend toward a higher number of female saints, including those who oozed oil. See Caroline Walker Bynum, *Holy Feast and Holy Fast: The Religious Significance of Food to Medieval Women* (Berkeley: University of California Press, 1987), 391n85.

[651] Regarding the Paulinus' establishment of Felix's cult, see Peter Robert Lamont Brown, *The Cult of the Saints: Its Rise and Function in Latin Christianity* (Chicago: University of Chicago Press, 1981), 8, 40, 53–57, 59–60, 63–64, 67.

[652] Brown, *The Cult of the Saints.*

[653] Brown states: "The tombs of the very special dead were exempt from the facts of death. This was not only because the souls of the occupants are in Paradise: the deep peace of their sleep before the resurrection shows in their bones. It

The first account of oil flowing from Felix's tomb appears in *Carmen 21,* which Paulinus composed in 407 for Felix's *Natalicium* – birthday or feast day – in mid January.[654] The poet began by praising the passing of a tumultuous period of Roman history; with the advent of the new year and the imminent return of spring, peace also arrived in the Roman Empire: "With the welcome change of season, bright peace ushers in for us the new year with placid light after our experience of winter, and unfolds this day, stamped with the honour paid to St. Felix, for a now carefree people."[655] Not only had winter passed, but also a period of war, which was brought to an end by the secular ruler and the Prince of Peace. Paulinus' poem coupled the birth of Christ with the reign of Caesar Augustus, a motif that later medieval authors would replicate in their dissemination of the *fons olei* legend:

> So now that fear is driven out like a spent storm, it is pleasant to look back at the clouds dispelled and to compare our present condition with what is past...Now look in turn at the powerful gifts of Christ the Peace-bringer. The enemy and their unholy king alike are slaughtered, and the victory of the boy Augustus has restored peace.[656]

According to Paulinus, Felix had been concerned with "Roman safety and the existence of the state."[657] Throughout Latin Christendom, many holy ones begged for peace, not just Felix. Nevertheless, the Bishop of Nola played a seminal role in the establishment of peace. Perhaps greater than his participation in the collective petitioning for peace were the wonders worked at his tomb.

---

is the repose of the body of Saint Felix that moves Paulinus so deeply. Dust pouring from the sarcophagus had made him fear that an animal had disturbed Felix's bones; but on lifting the lid, he saw them for the first time, lying in an awesome stillness." Ibid., 76.

[654] Paulinus, *The Poems of St. Paulinus of Nola*, trans. P.G. Walsh (New York: Newman Press, 1975), 385n1.

[655] Ibid., 173.

[656] Ibid. The king here refers to Radagaesus, as recorded in Orosius 7.37 and Augustine, *De civitate Dei* 5.23. The emperor Augustus Honorius, a youth in his mid-twenties, reigned from 395-423. See Ibid., 386n.4-5. Regarding the Messianic nature of the first Roman emperor Augustus, see Chapter 8.

[657] Paulinus, *The Poems of St. Paulinus of Nola*, 174.

Felix distinguished himself (according to Paulinus) with the supreme care and attention he lavished on his followers at Nola. The saint's generosity consisted in offering his entire being, which was to say, his tomb: "For it was nothing other than the depths of your heart, dear saint, which you offered us when you deigned to expose for us the recesses of your tomb."[658] The saint exposed himself and conferred on his followers his "heart" by unexpectedly discharging a large quantity of ash from his tomb. In so doing, the holy Felix indicated to Paulinus and his companions their election or privileged status: "Our purposes were awakened by your buried dust. You wished to demonstrate the unique love of your attachment to us by so great a sign that you determined to open during our lifetime the abode of your body, so silent and unmoved for many previous generations, with the sudden emergence of your ashes, kindly father."[659] Paulinus gave the best of all possible interpretations to a clogged hole. Where others might have seen divine disfavor, Paulinus saw the potential for abundant grace.

In the Near East and on the Italic peninsula, the devotional needs of the faithful were met, in part, through pouring oil into the tombs of the beloved dead. The oil, having physically encountered the saint's body, acquired the saint's power and emerged from a hole at the bottom of the tomb, replete with *praesentia*. Pilgrims collected this oil, applying it to their bodies or carrying it home for their loved ones. Some holy women in the Near East distributed the oil to large crowds on feast days.[660] In *Carmen 21*, Paulinus described the ritual pouring of oil into the saint's tomb and how, at a certain point, the oil providentially failed to pass through.

> This table [a marble slab] set over the tomb has twin holes, allowing perfume to be poured into the recesses below. From the holy ashes stored there comes a healing breath and a hidden fragrance, conferring a sacramental quality on the pouring vessels. For after they had

---

[658] Ibid., 191.

[659] Ibid.

[660] Alice-Mary Talbot, ed., *Holy Women of Byzantium: Ten Saints' Lives in English Translation*, Byzantine Saints' Lives in Translation 1 (Washington, D.C.: Dumbarton Oaks Research Library and Collection, 1996); *Byzantine Saints' Lives in Translation* (Washington, DC: Dumbarton Oaks Research Library and Collection, 1996).

poured in the liquid perfume, and at once as usual scooped it from the tomb lying below in the earth, and those who had bestowed the nard on the tomb prepared to draw it up to apply it to themselves, they found the vessels miraculously filled not with nard but with a heap of dust which burst from below. They fearfully withdrew their hands, covered with heaps of dust, from the aperture of the tomb. This strange event affected everyone, and they were fired with eagerness to discover the reason for this sudden prodigy.[661]

Rather than interpreting the dust as a sign of divine disfavor or condemnation, Paulinus and his fellow priests decided to investigate the tomb. Rather than recoiling at the unexpected "prodigy," the priests sought to determine the cause of the dust. Paulinus reasoned that perhaps "some creature enclosed in a hidden den below was throwing up the ashes from the saint's body."[662] The poet elaborately described dismantling the sacred tomb of the beloved dead to get to the bottom of the mystery. The men found a body perfectly intact. Paulinus reflected that the tomb and body were proof that "living grace abides in the tombs of saints, proving that those who expired in Christ are buried but not dead, for their bodies are temporarily in tranquil sleep."[663] The state of the dead man's bones mirrored the state of his soul in heaven: "So the same peace which awaits his holy soul in the heavens possesses also his revered body in the earth."[664] The poet, however, appears to have forgotten the question of what plugged the hole and prevented the oil from passing through. Instead, Paulinus turned to a rapturous praise of Felix, through whose intercession the people of Nola diverted water from a neighboring town to the aqueduct of Nola, successfully creating a living spring of water in the shrine of the blessed saint (at the expense of the neighboring town that was subsequently deprived of water).[665] Rather than offering a perhaps mundane explanation of why dust

---

[661] Paulinus, *The Poems of St. Paulinus of Nola*, 192.
[662] Ibid., 193.
[663] Ibid., 194.
[664] Ibid.
[665] Ibid., 195–201.

instead of oil issued from the holy man's tomb, Paulinus praised Felix as a saint who made abundant liquid (albeit water) flow.

In *Carmen 23,* once again the poet waxed eloquent about liquids, this time about the intermingling of oil and water in a lamp.[666] While P.G. Walsh observed that this passage was a "long-winded irrelevance unfortunately inserted at the dramatic moment of the story," the passage reveals the poet's perception of oil as a source of light, a metaphor for divinity.[667] At the beginning of the poem, Paulinus invoked God as a source of divine liquid: "Christ God, pour into my heart and slake my thirst with heavenly waters. Even a drop from You sprinkled into my heart will be a stream."[668] The dramatic action, which Walsh observed was so unnecessarily interrupted, entailed a man getting a lamp hook caught in his eye, depriving him of sight on the vigil of Felix's birthday. Unable to safely remove the hook painfully lodged in his eye, the man cried out to Felix: "If you wish to pass judgment in my case according to the rights of justice, I deserve to be deprived not merely of one eye, but of both, for then my face would correspond with the darkness of my heart which causes me to misuse my bodily eyes, which makes me blind to justice and alert for wickedness. I admit it is fitting for a sinner to lose an eye."[669] The saint naturally complied with the request and assisted the man in safely removing the hook from the eye with no lasting harm. Paulinus described the eye as "all healed and shining through the kindness of the undying Christ. In fact, I believe it may shine brighter now than it did before, because the feast day that restored it lends it additional lustre."[670] Understanding the eye to be a kind of lamp that shines when not darkened by sin, we can better understand what significance the poet imputed to oil.

---

[666] Regarding the miraculous healing of a demoniac woman who drank oil from a lamp in Byzantium, see Alice-Mary Talbot, "Holy Springs and Pools in Byzantine Constantinople" in *Istanbul and Water*, ed. Paul Magdalino and Nina Ergin, Supplement 47 of *Ancient Near Eastern Studies* (Leuven; Paris; Bristol, CT: Peeters, 2015), 167; "Constantinople: City of Miraculous Healings" in *Life is Short, Art Long: The Art of Healing in Byzantium* (Istanbul: Perma Museums Publication, 2015), 81.

[667] Paulinus, *The Poems of St. Paulinus of Nola*, 393n11.

[668] Ibid., 209.

[669] Ibid., 217.

[670] Ibid., 218.

The water at the base [of the lamp] shows white, and above it the oil gleams yellow. Fluid stands on liquid, the smooth solution floating on the water beneath without the two uniting or intermingling. Remarkably, the fatty liquid floats. The thick matter does not force its way down through the liquid water, but the light element supports the thick substance, the water (which is thinner than the treacly fluid) lying below the oil and acting as foundation for the liquid above it. The inner repulsion by each of the other is so clear when they associate with each other that you can see the mingled liquids separating out. Lying inside the same cup they are clearly distinct for the natural quality of each preserves each liquid's colour. The triple base of lead is joined at the centre, from which the hollow top rises, filled with fuel for the oily wick. The dripping tow ignites to form a slender torch. Spreading round the surface of the still oil, the tiny wick shines in the shallows of the glass. The [flame] flickers keenly from its trembling tip, and gently throws a shadowy light into the inner part of the house, diffusing the thick darkness with its tranquil brightness.[671]

The discussion of these two liquids, which were separate and yet united, may have been an indirect discussion of the two natures of Christ (human and divine), an aspect of Christian theology which had not been definitively resolved by the early fifth century. This was the central question debated in the Council of Chalcedon in 451, which maintained that Christ (the Anointed One), was true God and true man, consubstantial with the Father.[672] In his retelling of the life of Felix, Gregory of Tours included this tale of the oil lamp's hook getting stuck in the sinner's eye; the story took up approximately one fourth of Gregory's account of Felix's *vita* in *De Gloria Beatorum Martyrym* of the *Libri Miraculorum*.[673] Felix did not, however, miraculously produce oil from his tomb, according to Gregory's account. Another anonymous account of Felix's life which, according to the Bollandists was drawn *ex veteribus mss* includes a mention of benediction of oil for healing, but no account of the injurious oil lamp or miraculous oil from the tomb.[674] Nor did Bede's account of Felix's life and

---

[671] Ibid.
[672] Henry Chadwick, *The Early Church* (New York: Dorset Press, 1986).
[673] AASS Jan I, Dies 14. BHL 2872 & BHL 4541.
[674] AASS Jan I, Dies 14. BHL 2885.

miracles include a mention of oil flowing from the saint's tomb. In the first half of the sixth century Marcellus, the Presbyter from Nola, wrote another account of Felix's life, which he dedicated to Leo, Bishop of Nola during the reign of Pope Agapetus (r. 535-536).[675] According to the Bollandists, the manuscripts containing the life of Felix belonged to the Church of Saint Audomar (d. ca 670), also known as Saint Omer, which may refer to the Cathedral of Saint-Omer in the Pas-de-Calais region of northern France. Audomar was formerly a monk of the Luxeuil monastery, whom King Dagobert appointed as bishop of Terouenne in 637. Audomar subsequently founded the Abbey of Saint Peter (later Saint Bertin's) in Sithiu as well as the Church of Our Lady in Sithiu, which may have been Audomar's burial place; the cathedral later bore his name. Marcellus' account of Felix's life does not tell of miraculous oil, suggesting that his miracle was not attributed to the Italic bishop-saint in early medieval Gaul. By that point, myroblytes were an increasingly popular phenomenon reserved, perhaps, for Gallic rather than Italian bishops.

MENAS OF EGYPT

The first saint to acquire widespread fame for his miraculous oil was a Late Antique martyr from the Near East.[676] Menas (285 – c. 309) was a Roman soldier who enjoyed widespread popularity following his death at the hands of Roman officials. Menas may owe his name to the Phrygian god Men, a god commonly depicted with a crescent moon who presided over months. The oil from his tomb, or from the lamps burning nearby, became a highly prized substance for pilgrims. Near Eastern Christians believed in the efficacy of contact relics, material objects or substances (including liquids), which came into contact with a saint's dead body. In the centuries following Constantine's reign (306-337), particularly in Syria, the faithful poured oil into sarcophagi containing

---

[675] AASS Jan. I, Dies 14. BHL 2874. Pope Agapetus is also known as Agapitus.
[676] See Mary-Ann Talbot, "Pilgrimage to Healing Shrines: the Evidence of Miracle Accounts," *Dumbarton Oaks Papers* 56 (2002): 153-173.

the relics of saints; having passed over or through the relics, the oil was deposited in flasks, which

pilgrims carried home.[677] Oil as a contact relic, however, was not the only oil coveted by pilgrims in

Byzantium.

Pilgrims visited Menas' tomb to collect his oil for either personal use or mercantile purposes.

The focal point of Menas' cult was Abu Mina, a sanctuary-city built over and around Menas' tomb.

Abu Mina lies approximately 45 kilometers west of Alexandria, an urban center on the

Mediterranean coast, in the Nile delta of north central Egypt.[678] The sanctuary was a thriving locus

of international pilgrimage until the seventh century, when the Islamic conquest of the region

brought an end to the town's trade in religious tourism.[679] While the majority of Menas' ampullae

were unearthed in Egypt and the Levant, some turned up around the Black Sea and Western

Europe, as far away as England.[680] The wide geographic dispersion of Menas' ampullae may be

explained in part by the Roman imperial economy's long-distance trade of bulk goods, including oil

and other basic commodities.[681] During the sixth century, as deep-sea travel became possible

through new nautical technology, pilgrimages and the transportation of goods across larger bodies

of water increased.[682] During this same period, as the Roman Empire declined, Christianity spread,

in part due to innovations in technology that facilitated the transportation of ideas as well as material

<hr>

[677] Christopher Walter, *The Warrior Saints in Byzantine Art and Tradition* (Aldershot, Hants, Burlington, VT: Ashgate, 2003), 80–81. See also Ann Marie Yasin, *Saints and Church Spaces in the Late Antique Mediterranean : Architecture, Cult, and Community* (Cambridge, UK; New York: Cambridge Univ Press, 2009).

[678] Regarding Abu Mina as a center of Late Antique religious devotion and its attendant archeological excavation, see Peter Grossmann, *Abū Minā 1: die Gruftkirche und die Gruft* (Mainz am Rhein: P. von Zabern, 1989); Peter Grossmann, *Abū Minā II*, (Mainz am Rhein: Von Zabern, 2004).

[679] Susanne Bangert, "Menas Ampullae: A Case Study of Long-Distance Contacts," in *Incipient Globalization?: Long-Distance Contacts in the Sixth Century*, ed. Anthea Harris (Oxford: Archaeopress, 2007), 28. See also Monica Gilli, *Le Ampolle di San Mena: religiosità, cultura materiale e sistema produttivo*, Tardoantico e Medioevo 5 (Roma: Palombi, 2002).

[680] Bangert, "Menas Ampullae: A Case Study of Long-Distance Contacts," 29. Regarding the reliability of the archeological evidence of ampoules in northern Europe, see Ibid., 29–33.

[681] K.R. Dark, "Globalizing Late Antiquity: Models, Metaphors and the Realities of Long-Distance Trade and Diplomacy," in *Incipient Globalization?: Long-Distance Contacts in the Sixth Century*, ed. Anthea Harris (Oxford: Archaeopress, 2007), 3.

[682] Ibid., 1.

goods.[683] Gregory the Great, for example, commissioned the sixth-century Benedictine monk,

Augustine of Canterbury (d. 604), to traverse Europe and establish a Christian presence in

England.[684]

Late Antique trade across the Mediterranean and Europe was both diplomatic and

mercantile in nature. According to K.R. Dark, the trade routes connecting the Near East, including

Syria and Constantinople, to the Latin West established "Byzantine mercantile communities" in

places like Italy, Gaul, Spain, North Africa, and maybe Britain, all of which served diplomatic and

economic functions.[685] Trade routes from the Mediterranean to Europe included a passage either up

the Rhône river or through the Italian Alps to the Rhineland or, alternatively, a sea-route through

the Straits of Gibraltar to the Atlantic seacoast of northern Europe.[686] Susanne Bangert has argued

that the presence of Menas' ampullae in the far reaches of Europe does not necessarily imply that

pilgrims journeyed across Europe to Abu Mina to collect the holy oil.[687] While such long distance

devotion was possible, it was more probable that merchants traded the ampullae along with other

goods from the Near East, such as amulets.[688] Alternatively, southern Europeans (either merchants

or missionaries) may have brought the ampullae to northern Europe.[689] Menas' ampullae fall into the

category of *eulogia*, objects seen as desirable given their physical proximity to the saint or the holy

power imparted to the object (i.e. the ampoule) because of their contents, which came into contact

---

[683] Ibid.

[684] Bangert, "Menas Ampullae: A Case Study of Long-Distance Contacts," 30–31.

[685] Dark, "Globalizing Late Antiquity: Models, Metaphors and the Realities of Long-Distance Trade and Diplomacy," 7.

[686] Bangert, "Menas Ampullae: A Case Study of Long-Distance Contacts," 30.

[687] England in particular illustrates the improbability that pilgrims from northern Europe returned home from pilgrimage with ampoules from Abu Mina in tow; if England was ostensibly Christianized in the late sixth century by Augustine of Canterbury, and if the Islamic conquest of Egypt in the seventh century curtailed Abu Mina's life as a center of international pilgrimage, the scant 100 intervening years could hardly give rise to such devotion to Menas, which might account for the presence of so many ampullae in England. See Ibid., 32.

[688] Ibid., 31. Banger notes the impracticality of the ampoules as vessels for transporting oil long distances: "...their properties as liquid containers are very dubious, so it is inconceivable that they could be in use because of their actual contents for long after they left Abu Mina, although their perceived contents and their former proximity to the shrine may have enhanced their value." An argument might be made, however, for the precious nature of oil in northern Europe given its scarcity. See Andrea Brugnoli and Gian Maria Varanni, eds., *Olivi e olio nel medioevo italiano.*, Biblioteca di storia agraria medievale 29 (Bologna: Clueb, 2005), 3–100.

[689] Bangert, "Menas Ampullae: A Case Study of Long-Distance Contacts," 32.

with the saint.[690] The contents of the ampullae could include oil spread over a saint's body, oil drawn from a lamp burning near the saint's tomb, or water from a spring flowing near the site of martyrdom or the tomb itself.[691] As a patron of pilgrims and merchants, Menas could protect Late Antique Christians traveling long distances.[692]

ANDREW THE APOSTLE

By the time the shrine of Menas in Abu Mina declined in popularity due to Islamic invasions, the cults of other myroblytes were on the rise in the Latin West. Gregory of Tours appears to be the first author to have circulated stories about myroblytes within Gaul, imputing the miraculous production of oil to the tombs of Andrew the Apostle and Martin of Tours. Although Gregory said nothing about oil oozing from Felix's tomb, in his *Libri Miraculorum, De Gloria Beatorum Martyrum* he told of manna, like flour, emanating from the tomb of John the Evangelist and oil flowing from the tomb of Andrew the Apostle. Writing in the sixth century, Gregory claimed that when Andrew died and was buried in Patras, Greece, his tomb miraculously produced oil. According to Gregory, the miracles happened in Patras, Greece rather than Constantinople, where the Apostle's relics were translated in 357. In the thirteenth century, the relics were moved yet again to Amalfi.[693]

---

[690] Gilli, *Le Ampolle di San Mena*, 9.

[691] Ibid. See also Chapter 1, on the *eulogia* of martyrs.

[692] Christopher Walter, *The Warrior Saints in Byzantine Art and Tradition* (Aldershot, Hants, Burlington, VT: Ashgate, 2003), 181–90.

[693] Further study of the cult of Andrew is beyond the scope of this study. See Robert Boenig, *Saint and Hero: Andreas and Medieval Doctrine* (Lewisburg: Bucknell University Press, 1991); Paul Devos, "Saints garants de la foi jurée: André, Ménas, Nicolas.," *Analecta Bollandiana: Revue Critique D'hagiographie / A Journal of Critical Hagiography* 104, no. 3–4 (1986): 315–26; Francis Dvornik, *The Idea of Apostolicity in Byzantium and the Legend of the Apostle Andrew*, Dumbarton Oaks Studies 4 (Cambridge: Harvard University Press, 1958); Edward G. Farrugia, ed., *Amalfi and Byzantium: Acts of the International Symposium on the Eighth Centenary of the Translation of the Relics of St Andrew the Apostle from Constantinople to Amalfi (1208-2008), Rome, 6 May 2008*, Orientalia Christiana Analecta 287 (Rome: Pontificio istituto orientale, 2010); J Flamion, *Les Actes Apocryphes de l'Apôtre André: les Actes d'André et de Mathias, de Pierre et d'André et les textes apparentés* (Louvain: Bureaux du Recueil, 1911); Peter M. Peterson, *Andrew, Brother of Simon Peter: His History and Legends*, Novum Testamentum : Supplement, v. 1 (Leiden: E. J. Brill, 1958); Jean-Marc Prieur, ed., *Acta Andreae*, Corpus Christianorum 5–6 (Turnhout: Brepols, 1989).

According to the *Martyrologium Hieronymianum*, Andrew's feast day was celebrated on 30

November. When a number of new myroblytes, including Nicholas of Myra (4th c.), Eligius of

Noyon (588-660), and Babolenus of St. Maur-des-Fossés (d.670), entered the liturgical calendar they

were - perhaps not surprisingly - placed in temporal proximity to Andrew, who was potentially the

original myroblyte.[694] Before discussing Andrew's oil, Gregory credited the "manna" from John's

tomb with miraculously restoring health to the diseased: "Nowadays his tomb noisily discharges

manna in the form of flour, from which the blessed relics, having been carried throughout the whole

world, bring about health from diseases."[695] Curiously enough, between the narrative descriptions of

John and Andrew's miraculous tombs, Gregory mentioned Mary Magdalene was buried in the same

town as John the Evangelist, but said nothing about miracles at her tomb. Unlike her alabaster jar,

Mary Magdalene's tomb was evidently not famous for producing unguent.[696] The tomb of Andrew

the Apostle, like John's tomb, produced flour but also oil, which augured the fertility of land in a

given growing season:

> Andrew the apostle brings forward a great miracle on the day of his solemnity, that is manna
> in the form of flour or oil with the fragrance of nectar, which gushes from his tomb. By this
> miracle, the fruitfulness of the subsequent year is revealed. If a small [amount of oil] flowed,
> the earth brings forth little fruit. Truly if it was a copious [amount of oil], it signifies the
> arable land [*arva*] will have an abundance of crops.[697]

---

[694] AASS Nov. II, Pars 1, 148. See Chapter 6. Further study of Merovingian versions of Jerome's martyrology would shed light on exactly when myroblytes such as Eligius, Nicholas and Babolenus entered liturgical calenders. See Felice Lifshitz, *The Name of the Saint: The Martyrology of Jerome and Access to the Sacred in Francia, 627-827* (Notre Dame, Ind.: University of Notre Dame Press, 2006).

[695] "Cujus nunc sepulcrum manna in modum farinae hodieque eructat, ex qua beatae reliquiae, per universum delatae mundum, salutem mordibis {sic} praestant." PL 71, Col.0730B.

[696] "In ea urbe Maria Magdalene quiescit, nullum super se tegumen habens." PL 71, Col.0731A.

[697] "Andreas apostolus magnum miraculum in die solemnitatis suae profert, hoc est manna in modum farinae, vel oleumcum odore nectareo, quod de tumulo ejus exundat. Per id enim quae sit fertilitas anni sequentis ostenditur. Si exiguum profluxerit, exiguum terra profert fructum; si vero fuerit copiosum, magnum arva proventum fructuum habere significat." PL 71, Col.0731A-B.

Using phrases that read like the template for later authors writing about Santa Maria in Trastevere's

legendary *fons olei*, Gregory described how sometimes Andrew produced so much oil he flooded the

basilica in Patras, in Greece, where he lay buried: "For in some years they tell of so much oil gushing

from the tomb that the stream [of oil] flows all the way to the middle of the basilica. These things

happened in the province Greece, in the city of Patras, in which the Blessed Apostle or

Martyr...died."[698] The miraculous oil was not only abundant, but also fragrant. The magnitude of the

fragrance attested to the greatness of the gift the Apostle bestowed on the people: "Nevertheless,

when the oil flowed, so much fragrance prevailed upon the nostrils that you might think a heap of

many aromatic spices was scattered there, such that the people were not without a miracle and

favor."[699] Gregory emphasized the use of the oil for the people - the *populus* - a motif that other

biographers would repeat, including those who composed the life and office of Nicholas, Bishop of

Myra. In describing the great benefits the oil bestowed on the people, Gregory told of how the oil

cured many ailments, a trope that subsequent biographers would replicate.[700]

MARTIN OF TOURS

According to Gregory of Tours, oil from the tomb of Martin of Tours possessed great

powers to heal the sick, like oil from the tomb of Andrew the Apostle. Gregory observed that

Martin's oil was particularly efficacious in warding off demons who ravaged the bodies and minds of

medieval Christians. In naming the powerful liquid that cured the sick, Gregory made a point of

saying the oil was taken from the tomb of the "blessed bishop" (*beati Antistitis*) rather than "Martin,"

---

[698] "Nam ferunt in aliquibus annis, in tantum e tumulo oleum exundare, ut usque ad medium basilicae profluat rivus ille. Haec autem aguntur apud provinciam Achalam, in civitate Patras, in qua beatus apostolus sive martyr, pro Redemptoris nomine crucifixus, praesentem vitam gloriosa morte finivit." PL 71, Col.0731B.

[699] "Tamen cum oleum defluxerit, tantum odorem naribus praestat, ut putes ibi multorum aromatum sparsam esse congeriem, quod non sine miraculo ac beneficio habetur in populis." PL 71, Col.0731B.

[700] " Nam ex hoc seu inunctiones factae, sive potiones datae, plerumque languentibus commodum praestant. Post cujus gloriosam assumptionem multae virtutes vel ad hoc sepulcrum, vel per loca diversa in quibus ejus reliquiae collocatae sunt, feruntur ostensae. De quibus pauca memorari non putavi absurdum, quia aedificatio est Ecclesiae gloria martyrum virtusque sanctorum." PL 71, Col.0731B-C.

even though Gregory used that appellation elsewhere in his narrative. The bishop's power, even

while dead, was mighty. Moreover, drawing a clear distinction between the cleric's oil and the laity's

illness, Gregory singled out a woman (*mulier*) who lost her senses through demonic possession; she

was miraculously cured by the bishop's holy oil. An abbot also restored sight to a blind person with

Martin's oil. Moreover, the exorcism of one particularly harsh demon required that someone be

anointed with oil on the head, as if conveying the sanctity of the head and the extraordinary nature

of that form of anointing. According to Gregory, that demon promptly fled, gushing out from the

belly of the afflicted.[701] Gregory's stories about oil healing the sick and liberating the insane echoed

throughout the *vitae* of later Gallic myroblytes.

Stories about saints' miraculous oil appear to predate the emergent role of oil in ordination

and coronation rites. The first evidence of the ritual use of oil for anointing clerics and kings in the

Latin West dates to Merovingian and Carolingian Gaul, respectively. Not coincidentally, male

myroblyte *vitae* proliferated during this period. Beginning in the eighth and ninth centuries, Gallic

priests, bishops and kings were consecrated with oil at ordinations and coronations. The earliest

liturgical text to testify to the use of oil at a clerical ordination is the Merovingian *Missale Francorum*,

which dates to circa 700. This codex includes prayers for anointing the hands of presbyters.[702] The

Sacramentary of Angoulême, a later eighth-century adaptation of Gelasian Sacramentary, contains a

---

[701] "Conversus vero ad oratorium in quo beati Antistitis reliquiae tenebantur, deductaque in vigiliis nocte, mane de oleo quod attulerat, locum infirmitatis inunxit, sedatoque dolore convaluit. Post haec quidam manum inflatam ab spina percussam detulit, quae protinus ut de oleo delibuta est, incolumitati donatur. Mulier quae sensum perdiderat, et quibusdam horis daemonium putabatur habere, de hoc oleo tacta, sanata est. Nam et alius abbas ejusdem cellulae proximus, de hoc oleo caeci oculos attigit, qui protinus visum recepit. Sed et cum multos energumenos exinde restituisset sanitati, uni qui atrociorem, ut credo, daemonem habebat, super caput de oleo posuit: illico daemonem per fluxum ventris egessit; et alteri in ungula pollicis daemonium descendit. Quo viso presbyter super digitum oleum infudit, moxque disrupto corio, sanguine defluente, discessit. Haec ille de oleo retulit." PL 71, Col.0836A-B.

[702] Paul F Bradshaw, "Medieval Ordinations," in *The Study of Liturgy*, Rev. ed (London : New York: SPCK ; Oxford University Press, 1992), 126, 129–31.

composite Roman and Gallic rite, which includes prayers for anointing the hands of bishops as well as presbyters. The tenth-century composite compilation known as the Pontificale Romano-Germanicum (PRG) includes prayers for the anointing of a bishop's head as well as his hands. According to Paul Bradshaw, the Romans interpreted the prayers for anointed bishops mystically or metaphorically; Gallic liturgists, however, interpreted the "dew of heavenly unction" literally and physically anointed bishops in imitation of royal anointings.[703] C.A. Bouman, however, argued that the direction of influence was the reverse.[704] The first manuscript witnesses of royal anointings postdate the *Missale Francorum* by approximately a hundred years. Scholars have speculated about whether Pippin the Short was the first Frankish ruler to be anointed with oil or if he was simply carrying on an established Frankish tradition.[705] The Benedictional of Freising, the Sacramentaries of Gellone and Angoulême, and a liturgical compilation from St. Emmeram near Ratisbon, all composed circa 800, contain prayers for royal anointings that emulate the *Unguantur manus istae* prayer found in the *Missale Francorum*.[706] In the mid-ninth century a new prayer for anointing the heads of kings appeared: *Deus electorum fortitudo et humilium celsitudo*. The formula was largely based, however, on the formula bishops used to consecrate chrism.[707] The practice of anointing the bishops' heads may have been subsequent to the anointing of kings' heads, however, since the first

---

[703] Ibid., 126.

[704] Cornelius Adrianus Bouman, "Sacring and Crowning: The Development of the Latin Ritual for the Anointing of Kings and the Coronation of an Emperor before the Eleventh Century" (J.B. Wolters, 1957), 1-8. More recently Paul Jacobson observed: "'Whether regal anointings preceded clerical anointings, or vice versa, has long been argued. Such debates, generally centered in legal and political history, miss the point. There must certainly have been mutual relationships between regal and clerical anointings, but the search for a causal relationship between the two is doomed to failure." Paul A. Jacobson, "*Sicut Samuel Unxit David*: Early Carolingian Royal Anointings Reconsidered," in *Medieval Liturgy: A Book of Essays*, ed. Lizette Larson-Miller (New York: Garland, 1997), 270.

[705] Jacobson, "*Sicut Samuel Unxit David*," 267.

[706] The prayer for the anointing of the king reads: "Unguantur manus istae oleo sanctificato, unde uncti fuerunt reges et prophetae, sicut unxit Samuhel David in regem: ut sis benedictus et constitutes rex in regno isto, quod dedit tibi Dominus Deus tuus super populum hunc ad regendum vel gubernandum. Quod ipse." The prayer for clerical anointing found in the *Missale Francorum* reads: " Unguantur manus istae de oleo sanctificato et crismate sanctificationis: sicut uncxit Samuhel David in regem et prophetam, ita unguantur et consummentur in nomene Dei Patris et Filii et Spiritus sancti, facientes imaginem sanctae crucis salvatoris Domini nostri Iesu Christi, qui nos a morte redemit et ad regna caelorum perducit." Bouman, "Sacring and Crowning," 108–9.

[707] Ibid., 109–10.

liturgical formulas for anointing bishops' heads appear in the tenth-century PRG.[708] Beginning in the second half of the ninth century, the ritual anointing of queens as well as kings became a fixed feature of the accession liturgies of France and England.[709] Nevertheless, within the church, only male clerics were anointed with oil for ordination. Perhaps as a result, few female myroblytes emerged during this period.

HIC LOCUS EST: OIL AS A SIGN OF A HOLY PLACE

In the earliest Gallic myroblyte biographies, oil demonstrated the sanctity of male ecclesiastical figures who, in the minds of their biographers, succeeded apostles and martyrs like Andrew. Reverianus of Autun (d. 274), a bishop martyr who left Rome to Christianize Gaul in the late third century, was one of the earliest saints to have miraculous oil spill from his tomb, although his *passio* was likely composed centuries after his death.[710] According to the Bollandist, the account was composed "long after" the discovery of his body in the third or fourth century. Reverianus's *passio* explained why a certain church was built in a certain location in Gaul and even suggested, obliquely, that that particular church was not dependent on holy oils consecrated by a local living bishop.

Reverianus' *passio* illustrates how the saint was a valiant martyr, unwilling to yield to Roman threats and arguments against the Christian faith. Subsequently, a Gallic presbyter constructed a church over his remains. Reverianus, along with his companion, Paul the Presbyter, and ten other followers faced their Roman opposition without fear; the biographer described Reverianus as "stripped of fear and dressed with the passion of faith."[711] This steadfastness led to the Christians'

---

[708] Gerald Ellard, *Ordination Anointings in the Western Church before 1000 A.D* (Cambridge, Mass: Mediaeval Academy of America, 1933).

[709] Bouman, "Sacring and Crowning," 16.

[710] Regarding the Christianization of Gaul, see Brigitte Beaujard and André Vauchez, *Le culte des saints en Gaule: les premiers temps : d'Hilaire de Poitiers a la fin du 6. siecle* (Paris: Editions du Cerf, 2000); Paul Fouracre, "Merovingian History and Merovingian Hagiography," *Past & Present*, no. 127 (May 1, 1990): 3–38.

[711] "Reverianus Episcopus, timore nudus, fidei fervore vestitus." AASS, Jun. I, Dies 1, Col.0040D.

torture and eventual decapitation.[712] After the Roman commander Aurelius ordered his soldiers to toss the martyrs' bodies into a vast wilderness where they would be devoured by beasts, a woman named Maxima, "having been inflamed by the love of Christ," noted where the bodies lay and later buried them.[713] Initially no one took notice of the grave, but "God Almighty" did not wish for the martyrs to remain hidden and so began to show the "hidden treasure."[714] Seven monks from Rome, carrying relics of saints Peter and Paul, happened upon the place where the martyrs lay buried.[715] Tired from their journey, the monks decided to spend the night near the grave, unaware that they were sleeping near martyrs' remains.[716] During the night, the monks had an experience akin to the apostle Paul's vision on the road to Damascus.[717] The heavenly vision, however, also resembles Jacob's angelic experience while sleeping in the wild with his head against the stone:

> In the middle of the night they heard a loud sound, like a multitude of angels fervently praising God. When they stood up, a great light appeared to them with great brilliance. The monks were stunned by so immense a brilliance, they began to think about what they were to do. Shaken by so great a fear, they decided to flee into the wilderness. But there in the middle of the road two dazzling men appeared and the monks could by no means continue on the way they had set out on. Indeed, realizing that the aforementioned relics of the saints [of Peter and Paul] ought not to be taken thence, the monks left them in that place and an oratory was built there by Abolenus the Presbyter.[718]

---

[712] Tunc impiissimus Aurelianus, verba illius ferre non valens, [& flagellatus capite plectitur, cum S. Paulo & aliis,] jussit eos a præsentia sua omnes amoveri, & a lictoribus flagellis torqueri, & diversis tormentis affligi, postmodum capita singulis amputari." Ibid.

[713] "amore Christi accensa." Ibid., Col.0040D-Col.0041B.

[714] "Sed omnipotens Deus noluit ut manerent incogniti, sed in consolatione fidelium pro illo certantium manifestare præcepit thesaurum occultum." AASS, Jun. I, Dies 1, Col.0041B.

[715] Regarding the importation of foreign relics to Gaul, see Beaujard and Vauchez, *Le culte des saints en Gaule*, 248–51.

[716] Ignorance of the true whereabouts of saint's relics also appears in Eligius' vita: "Among the other miracles of [Eligius'] virtue it was conceded to that most holy man from the Lord that the bodies of holy martyrs, which had until then been hidden from the people through many ages, were brought to light when he investigated and searched with the great ardor of his faith. Some had formerly been venerated by people in places where they were not while being completely ignored in the places where they were certainly buried." Book II, 6. English translation from Jo Ann McNamara, trans., Medieval Sourcebook, "The Life of St. Eligius, 588-660," accessed on October 21, 2015, https://sourcebooks.fordham.edu/basis/eligius.asp.

[717] "Et cum iter faceret, contigit ut appropinquaret Damasco: et subito circumfulsit eum lux de caelo." Acts 9:3.

[718] "Cum inibi ad hospitium declinassent, fatigati ex itinere, media nocte audierunt quasi sonitum Angelorum multorum, sublime Deum laudantium. Exurgentes vero, apparuit illis claritas magna, cum magno splendore. Illi autem stupefacti de tam immensa claritate, secum cogitare, quidnam agerent, cœperunt. Timore concussi nimio, fugere per eremum

Whether the two men on the road were the apostles Peter and Paul or their third-century successors Reverianus and Paul, is unclear. Whoever the men were, they inspired the monks to build a church in that very place, just as Jacob had erected the stone on which he slept, naming it the "The House of God," and anointing it with oil. Despite the best of intentions, Abolenus the Presbyter, who erected the church, failed to notice that the martyrs' bodies were lying buried in the ground outside the church rather than inside the church itself.[719] Nevertheless, the presence of the saints became visible. Light flashed from the earth and oil dripped:

> But because the protections of Reverianus himself had not reached the notice of Abolenus, the martyrs' precious bodies lay next to the very same oratory. When the monks diligently kept watch in that place, the love of God did not allow the precious bodies to remain hidden for long in the earth: the bodies shone more brightly than the sun with the brightness of the Most High. The earth was opened through the will of Christ and the precious bodies of the saints appeared, without any decay of the members: because neither beast nor vermin could corrupt any of the saints, whom the protection of the Most High encircled. Truly at that time, the church was built in that place over the saints with God's blessing. From that day, on which the precious body of Blessed Reverianus appeared, He who created everything from nothing, caused a liquid of oil to drip continually in that same place, such that oil was never brought into that place from another place by human beings. Truly thereafter whoever among the sick drew from that oil with faith was immediately restored to perfect health.[720]

---

decreverunt. In media itaque via steterunt duo splendidissimi viri devoluti, ut nullatenus viam quam destinaverant in itinere arripere possent. Agnoscentes vero quod prædicta pignora Sanctorum exinde ferre non valerent, ea in eodem loco reliquerunt; & oratorium ab Aboleno Presbytero desuper fuit ædificatum." AASS, Jun. I, Dies 1, Col.0041B-C.

[719] Abolenus ought not be confused with Babolenus, another Gallic monk, who will be discussed in turn.

[720] "Sed quia ad notitiam ipsius, S. Reveriani præsidia non pervenerunt, juxta ipsum oratorium pretiosa corpora latebant. Cumque inibi attentius excubarent, pietas Dei non sinebat diutius terra pretiosa corpora occultari: quia in claritate Altissimi splendidiores sole fulgebant. Aperta est vero terra per imperium Christi, & apparuerunt Sanctorum corpora pretiosa, absque ulla diminutione membrorum: quia non potuit bestia nec vermis quidquam ex illis contaminare, quos protectio Altissimi circumdabat. Tum vero desuper per misericordiam Dei ecclesia fuit ædificata. Ab eo die quo pretiosum B. Reveriani apparuit Corpus, qui omnia creavit ex nihilo, liquorem olei in eodem loco ita jugiter perstillare fecit, ut numquam aliunde ibidem ab hominibus fuisset oleum illatum. Quicumque vero ægrotantium fideliter exinde detulerint, statim pristinam recipiunt sanitatem." AASS, Jun. I, Dies 1, Col.0041C-D.

Reverianus' *passio* concludes with a description of the Christ-like power of the martyrs' bodies to heal: oil enlightened the blind, allowed the lame to walk, made the deaf hear, the mute speak and effectively ejected demons from many besieged bodies. The saints also may have liberated the church from dependence on the local bishop by producing all the holy oil needed to meet the needs of the faithful.

Electus Est: Oil as a Sign of a Holy Person

While the *passio* of Reverianus suggested that a church could rely on the oil produced by ancient martyrs bones instead of oil consecrated by a local bishop, another bishop myroblyte's *vita* emphasized the intimate link between a bishop and chrism. Eligius, the Bishop of Noyon, from 588 – 660, was of a humble background and practiced the goldsmith's craft before being elevated to the bishopric. His feast was celebrated on December 1ˢᵗ, between the feasts of two other famous myroblytes, Andrew the Apostle (30 November) and Nicholas, the Bishop of Myra (December 6ᵗʰ). While in the Late Antique period biographers often described the heroic martyrdoms of bishops who attempted to lead their nascent flocks, in seventh-century Gaul, bishops could no longer distinguish themselves as martyrs who died for their faith.[721] Since the role of bishops in this period was highly secular and since martyrdom was unlikely, biographers such as Dado (609-686), who composed Eligius' *vita*, often searched for other evidence of sanctity.[722] Rather than being at odds with secular authorities, sixth and seventh-century Gallic bishops were courtiers to kings. Kings, rather than the *vox populi*, appointed bishops such as Eligius, who represented royal families and carried out administrative work also done by lay nobility. Eligius' friend Dado composed Eligius' *vita*

---

[721] Regarding the role of bishops in seventh-century Gaul, see Jo Ann McNamara, trans., "Dado of Rouen, Life of St. Eligius of Noyon," in *Medieval Hagiography: An Anthology* (New York: Routledge, 2001), 137–39.

[722] Jo Ann McNamara observed that for Dado, this involved drawing on the previous hagiographical tropes of the saintly monk and the saintly queen. Ibid., 138.

shortly after the saint's death.[723] The earliest extant manuscript containing Eligius' *vita*, however, dates to the Carolingian period and was likely edited or embellished for liturgical purposes.[724] The miraculous oil that appears in Eligius' *vita* could thus have been a Carolingian interpolation. Whether of seventh or ninth-century origin, Eligius' miraculous oil revealed the saint's election as a leader of both the spiritual and temporal realms.

Early in Eligius' *vita*, Dado tells of the miraculous appearance of chrism in connection with the saint's experience of adolescent desire. Undertaking penances to quell his youthful longings, Eligius sought a sign that his mortifications were pleasing to God. In response, God poured chrism upon the bishop's head:

> When as usual he lay prostrate in that place one night, praying on his haircloth, he was weighed down by descending sleep and dropped off for a moment and suddenly he saw someone standing before him who said: 'Behold, Eligius! Your prayers have been heard and the sign you asked for in the past will now be given to you.' As soon as he heard this, he sensed a sweet odor, and the softest drops from the chrism of the reliquaries flowed smoothly upon his head.[725] Exceedingly astonished by this, he swiftly arose and careful investigation disclosed chrism like balsam distilled on the blanket that covered him. And such a sweet fragrance spread from there that it filled the room so that he could scarcely remain there.[726] And then, mindful of his petition, and exceedingly amazed by the generosity

---

[723] Bruno Krusch, ed., *Passiones vitaeque sanctorum aevi Merovingici* [4.] (Hannover [u.a.]: Hahn, 1913), 731. Dado, also Audoen or Ouen. Dado had been a member of the court before becoming the Bishop of Rouen. With his two brothers Ado and Rado, Dado founded Iotrum, a monastery for virgins as well as the monastery Rebais in Brie in 635.

[724] McNamara, "Dado of Rouen, Life of St. Eligius of Noyon," 139.

[725] While the reliquary that anointed Eligius on the head with drops of liquid that could have been chrism, the reliquary might have also potentially contained myroblytes' remains, thus anointing the saint with a saint's oil rather than chrism. Bruno Krusch notes that the liquid flows from a *chrismarium* – a container for relics or amulets (a phylactery): "Idem quod infra chrismarium dicitur, theca reliquiarum seu phylacterium." Krusch, *Passiones vitaeque sanctorum aevi Merovingici [4.]*, 675n1. In her translation, McNamara presumed the text referred to chrism reliquaries.

[726] Regarding the connection between sweet odors and sanctity, see Béatrice Caseau, "Syméon Stylite Entre Parfum et Puanteur," *Revue Des Études Byzantines* 63 (2005): 71–96. Caseau states that in Christian literature: "L'odeur devient alors le révélateur de la quintessence d'un être, un révélateur de la vie spirituelle et morale, voire du salut ou de la perdition. Dans la littérature chrétienne ancienne, on trouve ainsi une vaste utilisation du champ olfactif qui passe de la métaphore à la réalité. Dans les *Vies* de saints qui insistent sur le travail ascétique, et qui font du corps un lieu du combat et de la victoire du saint, les références olfactives ne sont pas rares et montrent le progrès spirituel du saint." Ibid., 4. Looking at the example of Syméon Stylites, Caseau notes that not all redacteurs of the saint's life handled odor identically: "La question se pose de savoir si la sentibilité aux odeurs est plus particulièrement affirmée dans certaines sphères

of God's bounty, loudly weeping, he blessed Christ the faithful rewarder, who never fails those who hope in him, from the bottom of his heart.[727]

Since bishops were not anointed with oil on their heads prior to the ninth century, this miracle may have been a Carolingian interpolation. The Latin text described the liquid flowing from the reliquaries as "guttas suavissimas" – translated here as "softest drops" of chrism. The word *gutta*, however, also appears in Psalm 44, as "aloes" along with myrrh and cassia, the spices that make the royal bridegroom fragrant: "Therefore God, your God, has anointed you with the oil of gladness beyond your companions; your robes are all fragrant with myrrh and aloes and cassia..."[728] Like later Frankish kings and Latin bishops, Eligius received the oil on his head, ostensibly ahead of his time. Eligius, whose name bears a resemblance to the Latin verb "to choose" or "to elect," became like the Hebrew kings, the elect of God, through this anointing. Later in the *vita*, during a procession of relics, Dado directly compared Eligius to King David, "exulting and dancing before the ark with the relics like David of yore..." creating an even stronger parallel between a bishop and a king, especially

---

linguistiques ou culturelles. Ces variantes sont-elles le fait d'un choix personnel de ces auteurs ou recoupent-elles des différences culturelles?" Ibid., 5.

[727] Quo nimirum in loco, cum ex more quadam in nocte in oratione prostratus super cilicium incumberet, somno inguente obpressus, veluti transeundo in momento obdormivit, visumque est ei adstetisse repente quendam atque dixisse: 'Ecce, Eligi, exauditae sunt praeces tuae indiciaque olim quaestia nunc tibi concessa!' Mox ille excitatus odorem hausit gratissimum, sensit etiam ex gerulo reliquiarum guttas suavissimas supra suum lenissimae defluere caput. Ex eo nimis attonitus surrexit velociter, et sollicite conspiciens, vidit quasi balsamum distillare de crismario et pallio quo erat opertus. Tanta quippe flagrantia odoris suavissimi totum illud repleverat cubiculum, ut etiam ipse vix ibi subsistere quivisset. Tunc memor suae petitionis nimiumque largitatem bonitatis Dei miratus, altius ingemescens, fidelem retributorem ex intimo corde benedicebat Christum, qui numquam derelinquit sperantes in se." Krusch, *Passiones vitaeque sanctorum aevi Merovingici [4.]*, 675. English translation from McNamara, Medieval Sourcebook: "The Life of St. Eligius, 588-660."

[728] "Unxit te Deus, Deus tuus, oleo laetitiae, prae consortibus tuis. Myrrha, et gutta, et casia a vestimentis tuis..." Psalm 44:8. Cassia is a variety of cinnamon. See "Cassia, n.1," *OED Online* (Oxford University Press), accessed October 21, 2015, http://www.oed.com/view/Entry/28492. Aloe here refers to aromatic bark or resin, not the succulent tropical plant, which incidentally also oozes a salve often used on cuts or burns. "Aloe, N.," *OED Online* (Oxford University Press), accessed October 21, 2015, http://www.oed.com/view/Entry/5630.

given the references to David's anointing in the eighth and ninth-century prayers for ecclesiastical and royal consecrations.[729]

Several chants from the office proper for Eligius' feast day on December 1st told of the chrism being poured onto the head of the bishop-to-be, firmly establishing a correlation between Eligius and miraculous oil in the minds of medieval Christians. An early twelfth-century antiphoner from St. Maur-des-Fossés, a monastery founded in 640 on the Marne outside of Paris, contains 53 chants for this saint's office, several of which tell of Eligius' nocturnal anointing.[730] Vespers began by praising Eligius' love for the poor, using a common antiphon sung at the feasts of a number of saints: "Saint Eligius, you sweetness of the poor, you tender consoler of the miserable, pray for us."[731] Another common antiphon followed, which praised the saint for his intercessions on behalf of the dead.[732] The third antiphon, however, was peculiar to Eligius' office and told of the fragrant chrism dripping on the future bishop's head: "Over the haircloth blanket, Eligius prayed to God. An aroma like balsam filled that house. Euouae!"[733] The next antiphon likewise alluded to the flowing chrism, which was a sign that God heard the saint's prayers: "The angel of the Lord said to Eligius, 'Your supplication was heard.'"[734] Later in the office, a matins responsory picked up the theme of the angelic messenger appearing to Eligius, telling him his prayers were heard, saying God responded by giving the saint an extraordinary sign.[735] The responsory verse which followed then reintroduced the oil theme; while on his bed, Eligius was awoken from deep prayer and fragrant chrism was poured

---

[729] See McNamara, "Medieval Sourcebook: The Life of St. Eligius, 588-660." "Cum ergo Eligius, veluti quondam David ante archam exultans atque trepudians, cum reliquiis et praefato agime in voce exultationis praeteriret..." Krusch, *Passiones vitaeque sanctorum aevi Merovingici [4.]*, 684.

[730] For a more detailed discussion of the founding of St. Maur-des-Fossés, see Chapter 6.

[731] "Sanctae Eligi tu dulcedo pauperum tu pius consolator miserorum ora pro nobis." BnF Lat.12044, fol.218v. Can. 204411. For a detailed description and analysis of this antiphoner, see Andre Renaudin, "Deux Antiphonaires de Saint-Maur: BnF Lat 12584 et 12044," *Etudes Gregoriennes* 13 (1972): 53–150.

[732] " Orante sancto Eligio pro homine mortuo qui erat in patibulo anima deo reditta in corpore est reuersa." BnF Lat.12044, fol.218v. Can. 203713.

[733] "Supercilicium Eligius ad dominum orabat odor quasi balsami domum illam repleuit | euouae." Ibid. Can. 204806.

[734] "Angelus domini Eligio dixit exaudita est deprecatio tua." Ibid. Can. 200282.

[735] " Sanctus vir dei Eligius dum in oratione prostratus obdor misset in momento visum est ei dimitus quondam repote astitisse et dixisse ecce eligi exaudite sunt preces tuae concessaque indicio quesita hoc ergo suit inicium virtutum ejus." There is several inaccuracies with this transcription from Cantus. BnF Lat.12044, fol. 219r. Can. 602171.

upon his head: "Then having been roused, that man sensed the pleasing fragrance and the softest drops flowed over his head."[736] The office emphasized how the saint's wish to quell his carnal, youthful longings led to his divine election. The oil was a sign of the efficacy of the youth's prayers and God's responsiveness. God forged an intimate bond with the saint, anointing him as if to be a king or bishop, effectively foreshowing his clerical role later in life.

The miraculous anointing was simply the beginning of Eligius' ministry, in which he sanctified the medieval Christian community during his life and after death. During his life he faced the challenges of simony within the church, pagans within his bishopric, barbarian invasions from the north, and confusion about the location of holy remains.[737] Like in the *passio* of Reverianus, Eligius' *vita* told of how God revealed the location of holy relics with a blinding light and fragrance reminiscent of chrism. One night when Eligius feverishly dug for saints' remains, the discovery of a dead body was suddenly accompanied by a radiant light and sweet odor:

> ...as the middle of the third night flowed by, Eligius grabbed the hoe and, throwing off his cloak, began with all his strength to dig at the holy ground with his hands by the light of candles and lamps. And soon at the bottom of the ditch, to the side, he began to scratch at the earth and uncovered the wrapping of the holy body. Then filled with great joy, he opened the tomb with the hoe he held in his hand and a fragrant odor with a great light spread from it so that Eligius could barely sustain his strength in the power of that odor and that light. A globe of light proceeded from the tomb at the striking blow.[738]

Here again, we see the connection between dead bodies, the "odor of sanctity," and oil. Not only had Eligius discovered a sacred *fons olei,* but he himself would become one.

---

[736] "Mox ille excitatus odorem sensit gratissimum et guttas suauissimas supra suum defluere caput." BnF Lat.12044, fol. 219v.

[737] Bk II, 1-3.

[738] Bk.II,6. English translation from McNamara, Medieval Sourcebook "The Life of St. Eligius, 588-660."

O MIRA VIRTUS! OIL AS A HEALING BALM

In many myroblytes' lives, beginning with the precedent set by Martin of Tours, oil appeared as a healing balm - a holy liquid with power to restore health to the sick.[739] For centuries, people used oil to treat wounds. Christians believed oil had the power to cure illnesses of both the body and soul, making little distinction between physical and spiritual maladies. Beginning in the early church, clerics consecrated oils for the sick, *oleum infirmorum*. Like the other oils used in the Easter rites, by the mid-ninth century bishops consecrated the oil of the sick at Easter. These clerics, however, were not the only individuals producing holy oil. When oil first appeared in early medieval male myroblyte *vitae*, one of the most common uses was for healing. Reverianus' oil, which soaked his burial ground, wielded restorative powers: "Truly thereafter whoever among the faithful fell ill was immediately restored to perfect health."[740] The oil did not work on its own, but through the intercession of the saints: "...in every day and in every time, through the intercession of the precious martyrs, the blind were given sight, the paralyzed received movement, the deaf hearing, the mute eloquence and demons were ejected from besieged bodies. I am not strong enough to explain such powers and such miracles, so bountifully were so many sedulously granted in that place by the Lord."[741]

Bercharius (636-696), another early medieval male myroblyte, who was the abbot and martyr from the Dervo monastery in Hautvillers in Champagne likewise produced a prodigious amount of miraculous oil that healed the sick. The conclusion of his *vita*, written following his translation in

---

[739] On miraculous healings by saints in Gaul, see Raymond Van Dam, *Saints and Their Miracles in Late Antique Gaul* (Princeton, N.J.: Princeton University Press, 1993), 82–115. Van Dam argues that the miraculous healings performed by saints and bishops gave them an authority that rivaled that of kings and counts.

[740] "Quicumque vero ægrotantium fideliter exinde detulerint, statim pristinam recipiunt sanitatem." AASS, Jun. I, Dies 1, Col. 0041D.

[741] "omnibus diebus omnibusque temporibus, per intercessionem pretiosorum Martyrum, cæci illuminantur, paralytici gressum recipiunt, surdi auditum, muti eloquium, dæmones de obsessis corporibus ejiciuntur. Tantas virtutes tantaque miracula explicare non valebo, quantum in eodem loco sedule Domino largiente conferuntur." AASS, Jun. I, Dies 1, Col. 0041D.

686, states that "long ago" oil gushed from the saint's tomb, healing the sick.[742] The tomb of

Ragnebertus (d. circa 675) likewise produced a prodigious quantity of salutary oil.

> Among the other miracles that the Lord deigned to work through the merit of the glorious
> martyr Ragnebertus, for a long time he made oil flow from the tomb of the same, most holy
> soldier, in the lamps placed in that place. Everyone had whatever kind of illness kept away
> through the oil. Those wearied through sickness, immediately through the hands of the
> faithful of that place from the same liquid of oil, had the right to regain perfect health.[743]

Moreover, the author of the *vita* provided an exegetical exposition of the significance of the saint's

oil, linking the flowing oil to the oil used to anoint kings, priests and prophets:

> And because Ἔλεος in Greek is called Misericordia in Latin, divine rights are established
> through dispensation, such that the works of piety may be administered through the unction
> of oil. In the Old and even in the New Testament, King and Priests and Prophets were
> shown to have been consecrated through the oil of benediction: because the lessons of the
> wise demonstrate all the more what is signified allegorically. Hence even it is written by the
> ancient Israelite people, they sucked honey from a rock and oil from a solid rock [Deut.
> 32:13]. Hence Paul said: But the rock was Christ. [1 Cor. 10:3]. If therefore the rock is
> Christ, then oil from a solid rock. That ancient people of God drank a miracle, that for the
> glory of his martyrs, Christ deigned to show [himself] from the oil produced by the rock of
> the tomb.[744]

---

[742] "Ex cujus sepulcro longo post tempore oleum pullulans in vas ad hoc paratum visum est defluxisse, cunctis morbo obsessis nimium salubre." AASS, Oct. VII, Dies 16, Col.1018B.

[743] "Inter cetera miracula, quæ Dominus ob meritum gloriosi Martyris Ragneberti operari dignatur, plurimo tempore de sepulcro ejusdem sanctissimi sui Militis fluere oleum fecit, in lampadibus ibidem constitutis; de quo oleo quisquis in quacumque infirmitate detentus fuit, ægritudine fatigatus, statim ut per manus fidelium loci illius ex ipso olei liquore contactus est, pristinam meruit recipere sanitatem AASS Jun. II, Dies 13, Col. 0696A-B.

[744] "Et quia Ἔλεος Græce, Latine Misericordia nuncupatur, recte divina dispensatione actum est, ut pietatis opera per olei unctionem exercerentur. In veteri enim & novo Testamento, benedictionis oleo Reges & Sacerdotes atque Prophetas consecratos esse, manifestum est: quod quid allegorice signet, plura Doctorum documenta demonstrant. Hinc namque de antiquo Israëlitico populo scriptum est, Suxerunt mel de petra & oleum de firma petra. [Deut. 32, 13] Hinc Paulus ait: Petra autem erat Christus. [1 Cor. 10, 3] Si igitur petra Christus, atque de firma petra oleum; antiquus ille Dei populus suxit miraculum, quod ad gloriam Martyris sui Christus ex oleo de petra sepulcri producto demonstrare dignatus est." AASS Jun. II, Dies 13, Col. 0696B-C.

Eligius' *vita* told of the bishop, like Martin, healing people with his oil. While still alive, Eligius freed a woman from a demon and then restored her to life by having her drink oil mixed with water that he had blessed. The demon spoke through the woman's mouth, and through the woman's mouth she was saved by the oil. Eligius ordered the demon to leave "that vessel" (the woman) after which:

> ...immediately at his word, the spirit struck the woman to the ground and she seemed like the dead; then by the great power of the demon, blood from her very guts poured out the woman's mouth and the demon was poured out from her and fled from the face of the man of God. Then holy Eligius ordered the woman to be relieved and gave her a blessing with water and oil in a cup and when she had tasted it her spirit was rekindled and she was well without harm from that hour.[745]

The demon's dwelling in the woman's interior (*ex internis visceribus*) corresponds to the consecration prayers for oil, in which the power of the oil was said to penetrate all the way to the viscera.

Dado recorded how, in another instance, Eligius raged against Christians engaging in magical pagan practices, including those intended for healing, urging them instead to use oil consecrated by clerics. The Church alone was to be the source of remedies for physical as well as spiritual ills. Oil was one of the sanctioned means for restoring health:

> Above all, should any infirmity occur, do not seek incantators or diviners or sorcerers or magicians, do not use diabolical phylacteries through springs and groves or crossroads. But let the invalid confide solely in the mercy of God and take the body and blood of Christ with faith and devotion and ask the church faithfully for blessing and oil, with which he might anoint his body in the name of Christ and, according to the apostle, 'the prayer of the faith will save the infirm and the Lord will relieve him.' And he will not only receive health for the

---

[745] "Et confestim ad eius verbum conlisit spiritus mulierem in terram, et fact est velut mortua: sicque vim maximam patiens daemon et sanguinem per os mulieris ex internis visceribus egerens, confusus exiit ab ea et aufugiit a facie hominis Dei. Tunc sanctus Eligius iussit allevari mulierem et benedicens aquam cum oleo dedit ei in potu, et cum gustasset, refocillata est anima eius et sana facta est ex ea hora." Krusch, *Passiones vitaeque sanctorum aevi Merovingici [4.]*, 701–2. English translation from McNamara, "Dado of Rouen, Life of St. Eligius of Noyon."

body but for the soul and what the Lord promised in the Gospel will be fulfilled saying: 'For whatever you shall ask, you will receive through believing prayer.'[746]

Since God heard Eligius' own prayers and granted him a sign in the form of miraculous oil, we see the bishop urging the Christian population to likewise place their faith in the power of the Church when facing physical mortality.

Not only did Eligius heal the sick with oil he blessed as bishop. Once dead, the saint continued to heal with his own miraculous oozing. When the wife of a very old man fell prey to an illness, the saint's oily liquid was the best remedy. Thanks to an abbot's ministrations, the wife of the old man arose from her bed refreshed and rosy cheeked:

> ...one morning when the abbot entered the basilica of blessed Eligius for prayer, he met the husband weeping and wailing over his wife. He said that his mate was dead and asked pleadingly that she be buried in the basilica. And when he asked him if she was truly dead: 'It remains the same whether she is or soon will be, when now she lies mute and all her body dying.' But he hastened swiftly to the sepulchre of the confessor and taking up from it the oily liquor which had poured from it he hurried to the house of mourning. For in the night he had had a vision of Saint Eligius who had ordered him that he should heal the woman of her disease by means of that oily liquor. So entering the house, he saw the corpse lying swollen and cold, among the mourners. And approaching, confident in the saint's order, he anointed the corpse with the oil he brought and said: 'This saint Eligius ordered that by the virtue in the name of Christ you shall arise healed of this illness.' And immediately the holy oil penetrating her guts, she began to move her eyes and as though waking from a deep sleep she sighed. And then wonderfully, the swelling went down all over her body and she regained her strength and the woman sat up. Without delay, after that all pain fled from her body and not the least swelling remained on her skin and her face became rosy and she arose

---

[746] "Praeterea quotiens aliqua infirmitas supervenerit, non quaerantur praecantatores, non divini, non sortilogi, non caragi, nec per fontes aut arbores vel bivios diabolica filacteria exerceantur; sed qui aegrotat, in sola Dei misericordia confidat et eucaristiam corporis ac sanguinis cum fide et devotione accipiat oleumque benedictum fideliter ab ecclesia petat, unde corpus suum in nomine Christi ungeat, et secundum apostolum *oratio fidei salvabit infirmum et allevabit eum Dominus;* et non solum corporis, sed etiam animae sanitatem recipiet, conplebiturque in illo quod Dominus in euangelio promisit dicens: *Omnia enim quaecumque petieritis in oratione credentes, accipietis.*" Krusch, *Passiones vitaeque sanctorum aevi Merovingici [4.],* 707. English translation from McNamara, "Dado of Rouen, Life of St. Eligius of Noyon."

from her bed blessing and glorifying her creator who had recalled her from death.[747]

In addition to healing the sick with oil that seeped from his own body, a saint could heal
with oil that was merely in close proximity to his tomb or relics. Such was the case when a monk in
Dado's own abbey fell ill with a pustule like the one that afflicted the centenarian's wife:

> One of the brothers was hurt in the face with a terrible ulcer which the vulgar call a pustule.
> In that same monastery, there was an oratory in which relics of Saint Eligius had been
> deposited. Therefore, when the brother lay on his sickbed and the doctor prepared to treat
> the ulcer by heating an iron, the brother was overcome with fear and urged him to give up
> that operation with red hot iron. Confiding in the merits of the confessor, he asked that
> some of the healing oil that hung before the said antistes' relics be brought to him. As soon
> as it was brought he smeared it on his face and neck with the swelling pustule and, oh
> wondrous power! After the infusion of that liquor the cancer dried up at the root without
> the application of any fire and was removed at once so that no vestige or scar remained on
> the monk's face.[748]

---

[747] "Modelenus quidem centenarius, oppidi Noviomagensis colonus, habebat uxorem bonam, honestam valde atque
devotam, quae quodam tempore dum quietam ageret vitam, nefanda pustula nequiter est percussa. Quo tabo increscente,
iacebat tumida toto corpore, et paulatim plaga adolescente, sola iam sepultura maritum reddebat sollicitum. Uno itaque
mane cum abbas basilicae beati Eligii tenderet ad orationem, obvius ei factus flens et eiulans mulieris maritus moretm
coniugis suae indicat sepulturamque ei in basilicam suppliciter postulat. Cumque ab eo, utrum veraciter esset mortua,
interrogaretur: 'Unum,' inquit, 'constat, utrum sit factum an mox futurum, cum iam muta et toto corpore decumbat
praemortua.' Tunc ille festine valde ad confessoris sepulchrum contendit, et sumens ex eo qui ibi funditur olei liquore, ad
domum funeris cito accedit. Dicebat enim hoc sibi in nocturna visione a sancto Eligio praeceptum fuisse, ut, allato olei
liquore, sanaret ab incommodo mulierem. Ingressus ergo domum, vidit corpus inter lamenta adfinium iacere tumidum et
gelidum. Et ocius accedens, confidenter ex iussione sancti perunxit oleo quod detulerat corpus et ait: 'Haec mandat
sanctus Eligius, ut in virtute nominis Christi exsurgas modo sana ab hac peste.' Et confestim, oleo sancto viscera eius
penetrante, coepit palpebras oculorum commovere, ac veluti ex gravissimo somno evigilans, suspirare. Deinde mira
celeritate detumescente corpore et virium iam amplius resumens, femina resedit. Nec mora, post haec et omni dolore
fugiente de corpore nec ullo tumore remante in cute, facie etiam decorata robore, surrexit de lectolo, benedicens et
glorificans creatorem, qui se revocasset a morte." Krusch, *Passiones vitaeque sanctorum aevi Merovingici [4.]*, 731–32. English
translation from McNamara, "Dado of Rouen, Life of St. Eligius of Noyon."
[748] "Operae praetium est, ut non solum eas quae ad sacratissimum corpus eius efficiuntur virtutes, sed et eas quoque
quae per reliquias eius procul aut prope, ubicumque delatae fuerint, declarantur, huic operi vel pauca pro multis intexere.
Itaque res haec quae marro in meo nuper gesta est monasterio. Frater quidam ex monachis nostris ulcere pessimo, quod
vulgo pustula dicitur, percussus in faciem pessime laborabat. Erat autem in eodem monasterio oratorium quoddam, in
quo reliquiae beati Eligii depositae erant. Cum ergo praedictus frater in lecto aeger decumbert et medicus quoquendi
ulceris congruum ferri opificium praepararet, formidolose valde id frater ferens, rogat mox relinquere igniti illius ferri
operationem, et confidens de merita confessoris, rogat sibi deferri ex eo oleo quod medendi gratia ante pignora praefati
antestitis dependebat. Quo mox allato, faciem sibi et pustulam turgentemque perunxit cervicem, et o mira virtus! post
illius liquoris infusionem ita cancer ille absque ulla foci appositione radicitus exsiccatus atque extimplo deletus est, ut nec
vestigium quidem cicatricis ullius in faciem monachi relinqueret." Krusch, *Passiones vitaeque sanctorum aevi Merovingici [4.]*,
734. English translation from McNamara, "Dado of Rouen, Life of St. Eligius of Noyon."

Oil placed on an altar in a basilica dedicated to Eligius, and thus containing the saint's relics,

likewise healed a man's lame foot: "a man...stricken with a lame foot was healed when he was

anointed with the oil which had been placed on the altar before worship. The bonds of his nerves

were loosened and he was healed."[749] Oil from Eligius' tomb healed yet another man who had tried

to exact a payment from a devout follower of Eligius, who had petitioned for one of Eligius' relics in

order to dedicate an oratory to the bishop-saint. The man who gave the relic asked for a payment,

only to have the sum burn his chest:

> Avidly grabbing the offering, without hesitation, he hid it within his pocket. Immediately
> glowing with divine fire, it suddenly began to burn his breast and his clothing with an intense
> conflagration compelling him to cry out in a loud voice, 'Spare me, Saint Eligius, because
> miserable I should never have presumed to act as I have!' Soon the bystanders hastily pulled
> off his smoking clothes and restored the gift he had accepted to the traveller. Then they led
> the penitent weeping many tears to the tomb of the confessor, where, rubbing him with oils,
> they soon sedated the burns and he was freed from torment.[750]

Dado then deftly added a comment regarding how efficacious oil was for warding off

simony: "I don't doubt that this happened so that those of similar greediness might be more easily

attacked and their rapacity confounded, at least those who are not respectful of them perversely

accepting money to sell the relics of saints. Therefore cease, I beg, this contagium in all places, lest it

---

[749] "In alia nihilominus basilica, quae ad eius honorificentiam in regione Aquitanica miro eligantique opere fuerat aedificata, similiter vir quidam pede claudicans medendi gratia advenerat; qui cum ex oleo quod ante venerandum altare consuevit ardere fuisset perunctus, nervorum vinculis resolutis, et ipse sanatus est." Krusch, *Passiones vitaeque sanctorum aevi Merovingici [4.]*, 737. English translation from McNamara, "Dado of Rouen, Life of St. Eligius of Noyon."

[750] "At ille avidissime oblate praeripiens, sine aliqua tarditate intra gremium sibi abscondit. Nec mora, et inmisso divinitus igne, coepit subito pectus eum vestimentis eius vasto incendio conflagrare, ita ut prontinus conpelleretur inmensis vocibus clamare, dicens: 'Parce, sancte Eligi, qui ego miser numquam iam deinceps tale quid agere praesumam! Mox autem circumstantes praepropere ei vestimenta fumigantia auferunt munusque acceptum viatori restituunt; ipsum etiam paenitentem multaque deflentem ad confessoris tumbam reducunt, ubi oleo delibitus, vix tandem sedato incendio a tormento est liberatus." Krusch, *Passiones vitaeque sanctorum aevi Merovingici [4.]*, 736–37. English translation from McNamara, "Dado of Rouen, Life of St. Eligius of Noyon."

kindles the same fire."[751] Thus bishops continued to wield power over the faithful from the other

side of the grave via their holy oils.

LUX ETERNA: OVERFLOWING OIL LAMPS

Toward the end of Eligius' *vita*, the final oil miracle involves an overflowing oil lamp. After

telling of this miracle, the author admitted that he himself was overflowing the limits of his tale with

too many words and had to stop:

> Many other similar things, by order of the Lord, were achieved by the virtues of [Eligius']
> merits, among which a lamp overflowed, exuding an excess of oil from which many by that
> holy liquor were anointed here and healed of diverse disabilities and were blessed in the
> name of the savior our Lord. And all this was done in Compiègne. But likewise his bed,
> situated in the monastery on his estates called Vitry-en-Artois, announced similar virtues and
> effected diverse cures. All of which would lead us to proceed away from the order of our
> words and therefore about them we complete but a few syllables because now we must
> hasten to cease from this overlong locution.[752]

Eligius' lamp was not the only lamp in Gaul to overflow.[753] Tillo Paulus (d.703), a

Benedictine monk, chose to demonstrate his power through a great abundance of oil overflowing

the bounds of its lamp. First the saint caused a great quantity of oil to gush from a small vessel sent

to a woman to heal her illness:

---

[751] "Hoc autem idcirco evenisse non ambigo, ut per haec facilius obtundatur immoque confundatur rapacitas cupiditasque similium, eorum dumtaxat qui non verentur inportune, pecunia accepta, sanctoram pignora venundare. Cesset ergo, quaeso, iam hoc in omni loco contagium, ne contingat a facientibus simile incurrere incendium." Krusch, *Passiones vitaeque sanctorum aevi Merovingici [4.]*, 736–37. English translation from McNamara, "Dado of Rouen, Life of St. Eligius of Noyon."

[752] "Multae et aliae ibidem, iubente Domino, eius meritis operantur virtutes, inter quas etiam et cecindillus, exundante ubertim oleo, superfunditur, ex quo sancto liquore multi illic peruncti a diversis sanantur incommodis et benedicentur ibi iugiter nomen Domini salvatoris. Haec omnia quidem in Conpendio geruntur. Sed et aliud nihilominus eius lectum, quod situm est in monasterii sui praedio, loco nuncupante Victuriaco, virtutes similiter declarantur et diversae sanitates efficiuntur. Quae omnia ex ordine onerosum ducimus verbis prosequere et idcirco ea his paucissimis syllabis conpleximus, quia magnopere iam a locutione cessare festinamus." Krusch, *Passiones vitaeque sanctorum aevi Merovingici [4.]*, 739. English translation from McNamara, "Dado of Rouen, Life of St. Eligius of Noyon."

[753] In the Hebrew Scriptures, 2 Kings 4 tells of the prophet Elisha miraculously increased the oil in the jar of a poor widow so that she might sell the abundance of oil to repay her debts.

.... Almanna the wife of the companion of Lantarus, whose first husband was named

Acronem, sent a glass ampoule (that was far from full) to the holy man because of the

adversity of sickness so that he might bless the necessary oil. Because the holy blessing so

increased the oil, when the boy returned the small vessel to the wife, the vessel overflowed

between his hands, staining his clothes with a stream of liquid. Seeing this the wife...gave her

property to the Church and commended herself to the saint with prayers.[754]

The *vita*, like others, concludes with an eternal flow of oil, this time also from a lamp:

> By the command of the Lord and the merits of Tillo, many mighty works are accomplished.
> Among them, moreover, by the oil lamp copiously overflowing with oil poured out. From
> this holy liquid of oil, many anointed in that place were healed of diverse sicknesses, through
> our outstanding Lord Jesus Christ...[755]

While the majority of the myroblytes from the Merovingian period were male clerics, one

female myroblyte surfaced at the time. Oil also gushed from the oil lamp of Segolena (d. circa 769),

the abbess of Troclar in the Pyrenees. She was the only female Gallic myroblyte from the early

medieval period. Rather than having chrism drip on her head, like Eligius, she humbly provided oil

for her church's custodians. Nevertheless, like the oil of Andrew, Martin and Eligius, Segolena's oil

cured many ills.

> Once when the custodian of the church had prepared a glass vessel at the head of the tomb,
> the lamp was gushing beyond measure, more than the vessel was able to catch. By the gift of
> grace, the next day the oily liquid returned, with double profit for the custodians....For by the
> merit of those offering divine service, the overflowing vessel of oil gushes continually.

---

[754] "Alio namque tempore cum Almanna vxor Lantarij Comitis, quæ primum maritum habuit nomine Acronem, misisset
ad sanctum virum, vt aduersus morborum caussas, necessarium oleum benediceret, ampulla, quam miserat, vitrea
nequaquam fuerat plena. Quod Sancto benedicente ita creuit, vt dum ad matronam vasculum reportaretur, inter manus
portantis pueri sic exabundaret, vt omne illius vestimentum liquoris vnda inficeret. Hoc videns matrona, ipsa quoque
eum videre properauit, rebusque suis ecclesiam ditauit, & Sancti orationibus se commendauit." AASS, Jan. I, Dies 7,
380.

[755] "Multæ ibi, iubente Domino, & S. Tillonis meritis operantur virtutes. Inter quos etiam & cincentillus [cicindelis]
exabundante vbertim oleo perfunditur. Ex quo sancto olei liquore, multi peruncti illic a diuersis sanantur infirmitatibus,
præstante Domino nostro Iesu Christo, cui est omnis honor, gloria, & imperium, in sæcula sæculorum, Amen." AASS,
Jan. I, Dies 7, 380.

Where the body is buried, the lamp flashes with daily miracles: the sick come and are cured; the possessed come and are liberated; the lepers come and are cleansed; the mute come and speak; the feverish come and are healed.[756]

Aunemund, the seventh-century bishop of Lyon similarly caused the oil in a lamp near his tomb to overflow. The *Acta Aunemundi* stated: "There was a vessel which was placed before his tomb with oil for burning: it was never depleted, but very often overflowed and provided light everlastingly."[757] Praejectus (d. 676), the bishop of Clermont in Auvergne, likewise had encounters with miraculous oil. Once when the saint left a vessel outside of a church while praying, he returned to find the vessel full of oil.[758] Ursio, one of the saints' offenders, was later injured in a hunting accident; in his beneficence, Praejectus healed the man's wound with oil from the lamp hanging near his tomb: "...when several doctors and other rivals had gathered for the purpose of healing, to make [Ursio] better, by no effort of the doctors nor of the sayers of charms could he be cured. Having been left alone, he began to speak urgently to his wife that she might send to the tomb of the blessed Praejectus and that having taken oil from his lamp it should be brought back to him. Wonderful to say, when he was anointed with the oil, he won back his old health."[759] Having undergone a sort of conversion, Ursio then developed a devotion to the saint he had helped to kill. Ursio made a pilgrimage to the homestead of the young Praejectus and witnessed oil miraculously multiply in what had once been the boy's bed chamber, a miracle reminiscent of Eligius:

---

[756] "Cum semel ad sepulcri caput vas vitreum custos ecclesiæ aptasset, ultra mensuram exuberans, quam vas capere poterat; dono gratiæ liquorem olei reddidit die crastina custodibus fœnore duplicato. Exstat per tempora cunctis ad gaudium, fidelibus ad præmium, ægrotis ad remedium. Nam illius merito divinum munus oblatum, vas olei perfusum jugiter exuberat, ubi sepulta corpore quotidianis miraculis coruscat, Ægri veniunt, & sanantur; dæmoniaci veniunt, & liberantur; leprosi veniunt, & mundantur; muti veniunt, & loquuntur; veniunt febricitantes, & sanantur. Quæ & in eo tugurio, in quo prius habitavit, nunc usque, si petentium fides exigit, miraculis coruscat." AASS Jul. V, Dies 24, Col. 0636F.

[757] English translation from Paul Fouracre and Richard A Gerberding, *Late Merovingian France: History and Hagiography, 640-720* (Manchester; New York; New York: Manchester University Press, 1996), 190. Regarding the *Acta Aunemundi*, see Ibid., 166–79. Also AASS, Sept.VII.

[758] Fouracre and Gerberding, *Late Merovingian France*, 297.

[759] Ibid., 299.

When...the aforementioned Ursio kept vigil in the bedchamber, he asked one of the servants

to bring down a vessel with a little oil with which to adjust the lights. As he himself

positively swore afterwards, it held no more than a pound or two of oil, but went as far as to

affirm that it had filled up as many lamps as he had there, and he found the vessel brought

back fuller. Furthermore, indeed, he tells of how in the other churches that he had founded

in his honor it also filled twenty or thirty lamps and still he always found more in that vessel

and thence he liberally sent it to other holy places.[760]

While Praejectus' miracle was not particularly original, it explains the development of a particular

saint's cult and the extent to which the male cleric distributed his oil within a particular region, even

after death.

CONCLUSION

Oil, whether seeping from the ground where ancient martyrs lay buried or from lamps

hanging near the tombs of the more recent blessed dead, evidenced the power of male clerics, both

living and dead. In Merovingian Gaul, as the power of bishops increased and oil became a stable

feature of ordination and coronation rites, oil featured more prominently in male myroblyte *vitae*.

Chrism in particular was associated with a bishop and his elect status. Living and dead, bishops were

responsible for providing oil for their people except when, in rare cases, the oil of dead saints

supplanted the oils provided by living bishops.

---

[760] Ibid., 299–300. Other potential Merovingian myroblytes include: Sulpicius, Desiderius, Columbanus (notably Babolenus' poem about him), Gall, Sigiramnus, Virtutesque Fursei, Bavonis, and Gunde of Sas-van-Ghen.

CHAPTER 6

HIGH MEDIEVAL MYROBLYTES:

MALE AND FEMALE, HE CREATED THEM

INTRODUCTION

According to legend, in the late eleventh century a pilgrim's desire for holy oil was so ardent

that he lowered himself into the tomb of Saint Nicholas, the former Bishop of Myra. In the tomb,

the pilgrim bathed his body in holy liquid. A man describing himself as "the lowest of the clerks of

Bari" recorded the story, ostensibly just after the translation of Nicholas' relics from Myra to Bari in

1087.

> Bravely taking the hammer from his fellows, [Matthew, the pilgrim] struck savagely. When
> the tomb was open he found the whole coffin full of holy liquid up to the umbilicus of the
> saintly body...Immediately such a wave of perfume arose that everyone thought himself to be
> standing in God's paradise. This scent not only permeated the sanctuary where they were,
> but it was borne on the breezes that played around about the way to the sea, nearly three
> miles away, to the other company. As they breathed it in, each was at once overwhelmed
> with joy, knowing that the holy confessor of Christ had consented to join their company.
> After this, Matthew conducted himself even more rashly. In the whole episode, he had
> daringly stopped at nothing, so to speak. Now, still clad in shoes, he impetuously lowered
> himself into the sacred sarcophagus. Once down, he bathed both hands in the liquid. He
> found the holy relics swimming in an envelopment of all perfumes, which licked at the
> venerable priests as if in insatiable embrace.[761]

A nearly identical account appeared in the office of Catherine of Alexandria, the erudite virgin

whose bones spilled milk when Romans decapitated her for refusing to apostatize in the fourth-

century. Catherine's oil was as appealing to pilgrims as Nicholas'. An account of a pilgrim's zeal for

Catherine's holy oil appeared in a text from 1217 written by a man named Thietmar:

---

[761] Charles Williams Jones, *Saint Nicholas of Myra, Bari, and Manhattan: Biography of a Legend* (Chicago: University of Chicago
Press, 1978), 182.

209

...desiring with a most desirous desire to visit the body of blessed Catherine, dripping with
holy oil – the more ardently because I had for an excessively long time debated the question
in my own mind – not shrinking from any perils or mishaps, I submitted the whole of me
to the ministration of the body of blessed Catherine.[762]

The pilgrim immersed himself in Catherine's tomb, which according to Thietmar, was full of
fragrant oil. The narrator observed that her limbs and bones were swimming in the liquid.[763] This
version of the crusader's encounter with Catherine's relics was evidently drawn from the description
of Nicholas' wondrously oily tomb recorded in Nicholas' liturgy.[764] These nearly identical accounts
of the male and female myroblytes' oil reveal how, during the High Middle Ages in the Latin West,
medieval Christians no longer strictly associated holy oil with male clerics. Beginning with the spread
of Catherine of Alexandria's cult, oil would become a sign of exceptional sanctity for men and
women alike.

While the majority of myroblytes in the early medieval period were male, in the High Middle
Ages a shift occurred. Biographers began to circulate stories about both male and female saints'
miraculously oozing tombs. If stories about male clerics' miraculous oil circulated in early medieval
Europe in order to more firmly establish a correlation between holy oil and clerical authority, why
did producing holy oil become a gender-neutral miracle in the High Middle Ages? This chapter
argues that due to increased travel, trade, and pilgrimage to the Near East, holy oil assumed a new
significance in the Latin West in the High Middle Ages. Beginning in Italy and then Bavaria, the
fame of Nicholas, the Bishop of Myra (4th c.), began to spread. New accounts of his life and
miracles resulted from his translation of 1087, which itself was likely brought about by trade wars on
the Italian peninsula. In late tenth-century Bavaria, however, prior to the translation, Reginold, the
Bishop of Eichstätt (r. 966-991) composed a Germanic version of Nicholas' office that included

---

[762] Ibid., 152.
[763] "membra et ossa natant." Ibid.
[764] Ibid.

accounts of the bishop's miraculous oil. As the popularity of Nicholas' cult spread, and monks travelled from Bavaria to France, they took with them the stories about Nicholas' miraculously oily tomb. Once in France, rather than confining miraculous oil to a male bishop, a Germanic monk transposed the stories about the oily tomb to the office of a woman: Catherine of Alexandria (4th c.), a virgin martyr. Catherine's cult gained prominence in the Latin West in the eleventh century as interest in the Near East and crusading fervor increased. Once Catherine acquired renown for a desirably oily tomb, oil began to appear in the *vitae* of other women saints. Although her tomb had been a place of pilgrimage since the late Carolingian period, in the eleventh century Walburga (c. 710-779), the abbess of the Heidenheim monastery near Eichstätt, also gained fame for her miraculous oil and curative water. By the eleventh and twelfth centuries, oil was beginning to be a sign of sanctity for both holy men and women alike.

MYRRH FROM MYRA: THE CULT OF NICHOLAS

The cult of Nicholas, who was ostensibly a fourth-century bishop of Myra, became one of the most popular cults in Europe in the High Middle Ages. By the early twelfth century, Nicholas' feast (6 December) was such a prominent moment in the liturgical year that religious communities often celebrated with an octave rather than a single feast day.[765] Scholars have attempted to determine the origin of Nicholas' cult in the Latin West, a difficult task given the legendary nature of Nicholas' personage and the enormous source-base for his cult.[766] As one of the most widely celebrated saints in Christendom, an immense number of manuscripts relate to Nicholas' feast or cult.[767] According to *The Golden Legend,* the patriarch Methodius first wrote Nicholas' *vita* in Greek,

---

[765] Charles Williams Jones, *The Saint Nicholas Liturgy and Its Literary Relationships (Ninth to Twelfth Centuries)* (Berkeley: University of California Press, 1963), 4.
[766] Nicholas has over a hundred BHLs. See *Bibliotheca hagiographica Latina antiquae et mediae aetatis [2.]* (Bruxellis, 1900).
[767] 350 manuscripts in France alone contain material pertaining to Nicholas' office. See Jones, *The Saint Nicholas Liturgy and Its Literary Relationships (Ninth to Twelfth Centuries),* 5n13.

which a man named John the Deacon of Naples later translated into Latin.[768] John the Deacon's *vita*

(BHL 6104) said nothing about miraculous oil flowing from Nicholas tomb.[769] The only miracle

involving oil described how Nicholas foiled the devil's plot to burn down the basilica in Myra by

casting a vial of flammable oil into the sea. The source-base for the origin of Nicholas' cult in

Bavaria is thus unknown. Bishop Reginold of Eichstätt (966-991) composed an early *vita et miracula*

(BHL 6127) as well as Nicholas' office, prior to the saint's translation from Myra to Bari in 1087.

Although Nicholas' body had not yet landed on the shores of continental Europe, his fame already

extended across the Alps.

Christopher Hohler argued that the manuscript witnesses that explain the origin of the

proper office of Nicholas fall into two distinct groups: Anglo-French and Germanic.[770] The most

thorough manuscript witness of the Nicholas liturgy in the Anglo-French tradition appears in two

manuscripts produced at the abbey of St. Maur-des-Fossés, just outside of Paris,[771] and in a third

---

[768] See BHL 6104-6109. A bewildering number of John the Deacons appear to have existed in Naples in from the ninth through eleventh centuries. Ostensibly the early author of Nicholas' *life* is not to be confused with his namesake, John the Deacon (d. after 910) of the Church of St. Januarius in Naples. This is, however, the reputed author of the *life* according to Falcone, perhaps drawn from De Voragine. See Jacobus De Voragine, *The Golden Legend: Readings on the Saints*, trans. William Granger Ryan (Princeton: Princeton University Press, 2012), 21; Niccolò Carminio Falcone, *Sancti confessoris pontificis et celeberrimi thaumaturgi Nicolai acta primigenia nuper detecta, & eruta ex unico & veteri codice membranaceo Vaticano: per Nic. Carminium Falconium ... Ab eodem Latine reddita, et cum recentioribus aliis S.Nicolai Actis Graeco-Latine, cum suis notis edita ..* (typis Josephi de Bonis publici typographi, 1751), 112.

[769] BHL 6104. Falcone, *Sancti confessoris pontificis et celeberrimi thaumaturgi Nicolai acta primigenia nuper detecta, & eruta ex unico & veteri codice membranaceo Vaticano*, 131–39; Angelo Mai, *Spicilegium Romanum. Patrum ecclesiasticorum Serapionis, Ioh. Chrysostomi, Cyrilli Alex., Theodori Mopsuesteni, Procli, Diadochi, Sophronii, Ioh. Monachi, Paulini, Claudii, Petri Damiani scripta varia. Item ex nicetae thesauro excerpta, biographi sacri veteres, et asclepiodoti militare fragmentum Tomus IV* (Romae: Typis collegii urbani, 1840), 323–39.

[770] The proper of the office for a saint is also known as the *historia:* "*Historia* is the name given to the whole series of antiphons and responsories for the Canonical Office, or *cursus*, of a single day, especially when any, or all, of these musical pieces are given in metrical form or adorned with rhyme. *Historia*, in other words, indicates the musical skeleton of the *cursus*, to the exclusion of the psalms and *lectiones*, the musical pieces being more or less versified...From the tenth century onward, *historiae* of this sort were composed in very large numbers, especially for honoring particular saints or patrons." See Karl Young in Jones, *The Saint Nicholas Liturgy and Its Literary Relationships (Ninth to Twelfth Centuries)*, 71. Harper, however, defines *historia* as " books of the Old Testament and Apocrypha read at Matins during the summer months; i.e. Kings, Wisdom, Job, Tobias, Judith, Maccabees, Ezekiel, Esther." See John Harper, *The Forms and Orders of Western Liturgy from the Tenth to the Eighteenth Century: A Historical Introduction and Guide for Students and Musicians* (Oxford; New York: Clarendon Press; Oxford University Press, 1991), 301.

[771] See Jones, *The Saint Nicholas Liturgy and Its Literary Relationships (Ninth to Twelfth Centuries)*, 259–63.; BnF Latin 12584, fol. 383v-385v, and BnF Latin 12044. This same abbey produced the biographical dossier of another myroblyte, Babolenus, a seventh-century abbot whose remains were translated in 839 or 840, but whose *vita, acta miraculorum* and

manuscript, MS Cotton Nero E 1, which also contains a near-complete version of Nicholas'
office.[772] Scholars disagree, however, about whether this manuscript serves as the best prototype for
Nicholas' liturgy.[773] The manuscript witness for the Germanic version of Nicholas' office, which is
apparently older than the Anglo-French, is slightly more problematic and has not been readily
reproduced in modern printed editions, unlike the Anglo-Norman texts.[774] According to Hohler,
Reginold, the Bishop of Eichstätt, is the known author of the Germanic version of Nicholas' office,
including the ubiquitous *Confessor Dei*, the opening responsory. Reginold evidently also transformed
his benefactor, Pia, into a myroblyte: in her *vita* she bears a resemblance to a widow in another
account of Nicholas' life.[775]

Hohler argued that Reginold was not only responsible for Nicholas' office within the
Germanic tradition, but also engendered the Anglo-French version of the proper: Isembert, a
Germanic monk at St. Ouen-de-Rouen who became the founding abbot of St. Cathérine-au-Mont
(c.1031-c.1054), adapted Reginold's version of Nicholas' office for his monastic community in Gaul,
thus becoming the author or adaptor of Nicholas' office for the Anglo-French tradition. Similarly,
Ainard, another German monk at St. Cathérine-au-Mont, was the author of Catherine's office,
which was largely an adaptation of Nicholas' office.[776] Hohler speculated that even though Reginold
of Eichstätt was the author of the Germanic version of Nicholas' office, the author of Nicholas'
original office was more likely of Italian origin; Reginold in Bavaria may have simply been the first

---

laudatio, which record miraculous oil-production, were not composed until the eleventh and twelfth centuries. The cult
of Babolenus and his identity as a myroblyte will be discussed later in Chapter 6.

[772] Jones claims that this manuscript first carried the *historia* for Nicholas' office to England, where Wulfstan, a prior and
later a bishop, "intensely cultivated the patronage of Nicholas." Ibid., 120 et alii.

[773] Ibid., 6–41; Christopher Hohler, "The Proper Office of St. Nicholas and Related Matters with Reference to a Recent
Book.," *Medium Ævum* 36 (1967): 40–41.

[774] Hohler, "The Proper Office of St. Nicholas and Related Matters with Reference to a Recent Book.," 41.

[775] Jones, *The Saint Nicholas Liturgy and Its Literary Relationships (Ninth to Twelfth Centuries)*, 46. Text from Monumenta
Germaniae Historica Scriptores, VII, 256: "Unde hodieque ex sarcaphago venerabilis eius cineres continente vivae instar
aquae, ut oleum de tumba sancti Nicolai, iugiter manat, multosque languidos mira efficacia sanat." See also Johannes
Frey, *Heiligenverehrung und Familiennamen in Rheinhessen* (Giessen, 1938), 90.

[776] Christine Walsh, *The Cult of St Katherine of Alexandria in Early Medieval Europe* (Aldershot, England; Burlington, VT:
Ashgate, 2007), 76.

transalpine adaptor of the office which originated in Italy and was then handed on to the Anglo-French tradition by the Germanic monks Isembert and Ainard in France.[777] Incidentally, in the early fourteenth century by Philipp of Rathsamhaüser, another bishop of Eichstättt (1306-1322), embellished the *vitae* of Walburga and her brother Willibald with ecstatic accounts of the holy woman's oil.[778]

Two disparate accounts of the origin of Nicholas' office complicate all explanations of authorship. One account claims that choristers chanted Nicholas' *historia* (office) throughout Latin Christendom, but not in a church that had became part of the Cluniac network in 1059. According to this account, Nicholas' office was absent from the liturgy "because of the sloth of the inmates" and a prior who preferred to keep to "ancient custom" rather than adopting liturgical innovations, of which Nicholas' office was one.[779] This text exists in two manuscripts belonging to the thirteen and fourteenth centuries; the text itself, however, may date to the late eleventh or twelfth century.[780] By the mid-eleventh century, the cult of Nicholas had spread from France across the English Channel. Charles Jones observed that the feast of Nicholas first appeared in liturgical calendars from southwest England in the mid-eleventh century, prior to the Norman Conquest of 1066.[781] By the early twelfth century, Nicholas' feast day was ubiquitous.[782]

The account of the translation of Nicholas' relics exists in two texts, one by Nicephorus of Bari (BHL 6179) and another by John the Archdeacon of Bari. A second account of the origin of Nicholas' office was supposedly written in Bari following the translation of Nicholas' relics in 1087. Charles Jones argued that the translation of Nicholas' relics from Myra to Bari may have been either

---

[777] "I suspect (but cannot prove) that the Office for St. Nicholas will turn out to be, ultimately, Italian, and to have been adapted by bishop Reginold just as bishop Reginold's version of it was adapted by abbot Isembert." Hohler, "The Proper Office of St. Nicholas and Related Matters with Reference to a Recent Book.," 42.

[778] See Chapter 7.

[779] Jones, *The Saint Nicholas Liturgy and Its Literary Relationships (Ninth to Twelfth Centuries)*, 48.

[780] Ibid., 47.

[781] Ibid., 10.

[782] Ibid., 12.

the cause of the spread of the saints' cult in the West or the result of his increasing popularity.[783] The eleventh century witnessed a rise of interest in, and pilgrimage to, the Near East as well as political tensions between the Latin and Byzantine churches.[784] Moreover, trade between Europe and the Near East across the Mediterranean influenced Christian devotional practices in both regions. Myra's geographical position as a key seaport for trade may account for the growth and spread of Nicholas' cult; the translation of the saint's relics to Bari were perhaps the result of power plays between the rival port cities of Bari and Venice.[785] Such rivalries may also explain why the remains of Andrew the Apostle, the protomyroblyte, were translated from Constantinople to Amalfi in the thirteenth century.[786] Following the sack of Constantinople in 1204, Cardinal Peter Capuanus, the papal legate, transferred Andrew's oil producing remains to Amalfi, in spite of (or perhaps on account of) the fact that Andrew was the chief patron of the Byzantine church and its supposed founder.[787]

A thirteenth-century manuscript, likewise, contains the account of the 1087 translation as an addendum to John the Deacon's life of St. Nicholas. While the date and authorship of this text are uncertain, Jones observed that the style is characteristic of twelfth-century transalpine romances.[788] The story itself locates the composition of the Nicholas office in Bari, where a love-sick bard became infatuated with a beautiful widow who was a devotee of Nicholas. While discussing Nicholas' miracles on his feast day, the lady expressed dismay that no *historia* honored him. In order to please the lady and win her favor, the young man supposedly composed the office: "Hope of her favor therefore directed him; his spirit revived in hope, and from joy of mind his whole flesh tingled...summoning up within him the whole inspiration of poets and prophets, he set to music in

<hr>

[783] Jones, *The Saint Nicholas Liturgy and Its Literary Relationships (Ninth to Twelfth Centuries)*, 2.
[784] Ibid.; R. W Southern, *The Making of the Middle Ages* (New Haven: Yale University Press, 1973), 51–53.
[785] Jones, *The Saint Nicholas Liturgy and Its Literary Relationships (Ninth to Twelfth Centuries)*, 4.
[786] See Chapter 5 regarding the cult of Andrew the Apostle.
[787] Paul Oldfield, *Sanctity and Pilgrimage in Medieval Southern Italy, 1000-1200* (New York, NY: Cambridge University Press, 2014), 117.
[788] Jones, *The Saint Nicholas Liturgy and Its Literary Relationships (Ninth to Twelfth Centuries)*, 57.

neumes and rhythm that prose which begins *Congaudentes* and the response *Confessor Dei Nicolaus.*"[789]

Whatever the origin of Nicholas' office, the bishop's cult rapidly grew in popularity, spawning new

cults of male and female myroblytes throughout the Latin West.

Singing About the Bishop's Oil

As a widely celebrated feast, Nicholas' office includes numerous variations. At least 217

different chants were sung in celebration of Nicholas' feast day throughout the Latin West.[790] One

single manuscript contains 87 chants for Nicholas' feast.[791] Many more contain more than forty

chants. Several chants that commonly appear on Nicholas' feast day refer to oil or anointing. The

most common chants making reference to oil were two sets of responsories and responsory verses

sung at Matins, usually during the third nocturn. These include *Ex ejus tumbae*, *Catervatim ruunt populi*,

Dum Myrensium, and *Tamdiu quippe salutaris*. Following a reading from the lectionary, choristers

chanted the responsory *Ex ejus tumbae*, which told of how the oil flowing from Nicholas' tomb had a

Christ-like power to heal: "From his marble tomb holy oil perspires, oil by which the besmeared

blind are cured, hearing is restored to the deaf and any crippled person will rebound safe and

sound."[792] Another, slightly different version of the chant stated: "From his marble tomb holy oil

perspires, oil with which the besmeared sick are cured and any crippled person will rebound safe and

sound."[793] The responsory verse then told of throngs of people descending upon Nicholas' tomb:

---

[789] Ibid., 59.

[790] This analysis is based on the contents of the CANTUS chant database, which inventories, at present, over 130 medieval Latin chant manuscripts. See Debra Lacoste (Project Manager and Principal Researcher) and Jan Koláček (Web Developer), "Cantus Database: Inventories of Chant Sources | CANTUS Database," accessed July 31, 2015, http://cantus.uwaterloo.ca/. 69 manuscripts contain the feast of Nicholas.

[791] "I-Far Firenze (Florence), Arcivescovado - Biblioteca, S.c." 12th c.

[792] Another possible translation of *resudat* is "perspires." "Ex ejus tumbae marmore sacrum resudat oleum quo liniti sanatur caeci surdis auditus redditur et debilis quisque sospes resiliet." Can 006679.

[793] "Ex ejus tumbae marmore sacrum resudat oleum quo liniti sanantur infirmi et debilis quisque sospes resiliet." Ibid., Can 002744.

"People run in swarms eager to see what miracles were accomplished through him."[794] Another

feature of Matins for Nicholas' office was a Prose, which might have been composed by Isembert,

that combines many of Nicholas' miracles. The author even appears to have borrowed from the

legend about oil from Andrew's tomb being an indicator of agrarian yield. Not only was Nicholas' oil

a salve for the body, but an indicator of agricultural fecundity.[795]

> A profusion of oil restores the sick to health.
> Nicholas watches over the shipwrecked....
> O how the holy one of God sanctions an increase of grain.
> Let this sermon sing the praise of Nicholas...[796]

At the conclusion of Nicholas' feast day, at second vespers, choristers sang the nearly

ubiquitous antiphon *O Christi pietas omni*, which described how oil from Nicholas' tomb healed the

sicknesses of many: "O tenderness of Christ, which should be pursued with all glory, the glory

which proclaims far and wide the merits of Christ's servant, for from his tomb oil flows and heals all

the sick."[797] This antiphon appears mainly at Second Vespers, but also occasionally at Lauds. A few

eleventh-century manuscripts contain this chant, including one that dates to circa 1075 from the

Saint-Taurin, an abbey named after Taurinus, the first bishop of Evreaux, suggesting that perhaps

this antiphon was one of the earliest elements of Nicholas' office.[798]

While describing the wide appeal of Nicholas' oil and his miracles, one chant included the

word "to see", "to distinguish," or "to discern" (*cernere*) – as if the people were not simply gawking at

the tomb, but searching to comprehend the miracles. Again, a text referred to the ardor of the

---

[794] "Catervatim ruunt populi cernere cupientes quae per eum fiunt mirabilia." Ibid., Can 006679a. Jones includes the following variation: "Catervatim ruunt populi cernere cupientes que per eum fiunt mirabilia et debilia [lis] [Surdis]." Jones, *The Saint Nicholas Liturgy and Its Literary Relationships (Ninth to Twelfth Centuries)*, 30.

[795] Jones, *The Saint Nicholas Liturgy and Its Literary Relationships (Ninth to Twelfth Centuries)*, 120.

[796] "Sospitati reddit aegros olei perfusio | Nicolaus naufragantum affuit praesidio | Revelatur a defunctis defunctus in bivio | Baptizatur auri viso Judaeus indicio | Vas in mari mersum patri redditur cum filio | O quam sanctum dei probat farris augmentatio | Laudans ergo Nicolaum concinat haec concio | Nam qui corde quaerit illum propulsato vitio." Can 00679Pa. This text appears to be a fragment, since the last sentence appears truncated.

[797] "O Christi pietas omni prosequenda laude qui sui famuli merita longe lateque declarat nam ex tumba ejus oleum manat cunctosque languidos sanat." Can 004008.

[798] "F-Pn Lat. 12601" c 1075. See also Can 004008.

people. They were filled with desire (*cupientes*) not simply for the things of the flesh, but to behold

the miracle. The miraculous pouring of oil from Nicholas' tomb was a wonder that defied the laws

of nature. The composer of the office evidently conveyed people's great faith in the bishop's power,

even while dead. The oil seeping from Nicholas' tomb was not simply a miracle that emerged

spontaneously, independent of concrete social, political and religious forces at play in medieval

European society. The next responsory and responsory verse in Nicholas' office tells of the

correspondence between the deposition of an unjust ruler and oil flowing from Nicholas' tomb. The

responsory states: "When a certain Bishop of Myra was pushed from his throne on account of

hatred, immediately the stream of holy oil ceased to flow."[799] Nicholas continued to withhold his oil

until justice was accomplished: "Of course that healing liquid ceased to flow until that same prelate

recovered his throne."[800] In this chant we see that Nicholas' oil was not just a matter of popular

adulation, but reflected the potential for political instability if anyone removed the legitimate

ecclesiastical authority from his post. Considering these two chants in tandem, *Dum Myrensium* and

Tamdiu quippe, we see that perhaps the composer of Nicholas' office wished to convey the

connection between the *vox populi* and the authority of ecclesiastical rulers. A great number of people

expressed their devotion to a saint who had the power to bestow or withhold his support of a

particular ruler. Though indirect, these chants reveal how an interest in Nicholas' oil manifests the

widespread popular support of a saint who had the ability to intervene in matters of Church

governance. While the people may have been incapable of deposing an unjust bishop, the saint they

revered might intervene on their behalf to reestablish justice. Bishops were secular as well as

religious rulers who were often targeted by agitators instigating uprisings. The clergy may have thus

---

[799] "Dum Myrensium quidam antistes pulsus ob invidiam esset de sede sua stillicidium manare statim olei sacri desivit." Can 006550.

[800] "Tamdiu quippe salutaris ille liquor manare cessavit quousque praesul idem cathedram suam reciperet." Can 006550a.

been particularly interested in conveying the power of bishops through the liturgy and through

cultivating popular devotion to iconic bishops.

The theme of legitimate rulership arose elsewhere in Nicholas' office in a common versicle

and respond that invoked King David as the Lord's anointed: "I found my servant David. I anointed

him with my holy oil."[801] This chant was not particular to the office of Nicholas, but was widely used

for other feast days, including the feasts days of other saints and martyrs. If the saint and martyrs

were the "Lord's anointed" the reverse was also potentially true: those anointed by the Church were

among the immortal elect. Another variation on this chant text embellished the theme of God

bestowing power and authority on the divinely chosen one: "I found my servant David. I anointed

him with my holy oil. Indeed, my hand will help him and my arm will fortify him."[802] Other related

chants likewise spoke of the divine origin of the anointed's authority, which existed in perpetuity:

"My truth and my mercy will be exalted in him and in my name his horn will be exalted and I will

establish his seed for ever and ever and I will establish his throne like the days of heaven."[803] Yet

another chant elaborated on the theme of divine authority by including a statement about the elect

being chosen from among the people: "Lord, you are powerful and your truth encircles your own.

You said: 'I placed [my] help upon the powerful and I exalted [my] elect from my people.'"[804] Oil,

whether poured on a kings' head or drawn from a saint's tomb, signaled the ongoing presence of a

supreme authority, who bestowed power on leaders, making them his representatives on earth.

The inclusion of the *Inveni David servum meum* chant on Nicholas' feast day effectively

performed the subtle work of scriptural exegesis in the context of the liturgy. Rather than

---

[801] "Inveni David servum meum. R. Oleo sancto meo unxi eum." Can 800223. Only two manuscripts in the CANTUS database show this chant as having been sung for the feast of Nicholas. The same text, however, appears for other feast days.
[802] Can g01272, Can g01288.
[803] "Veritas mea et misericordia mea cum ipso et in nomine meo exaltabitur cornu ejus et ponam in saeculum saeculi semen ejus et thronum ejus sicut dies caeli" Can g01288b.
[804] "Potens es domine et veritas tua in circuitu tuo tu dixisti posui adjutorium super potentem et exaltavi electum de plebe mea." Can g01288a.1.

foreshadowing Christ, the anointed Hebrew king was a *tupos* for an oil-producing saint. The saint became the new servant of God, the new beloved, the Anointed One. In the medieval Church, the saints were God's anointed elect (metaphorically speaking) and thus resembled secular anointed kings. By comparing Nicholas to King David, the composer of this liturgy suggested that saints, including bishop saints, possessed a kingly authority. The people had the ear of their dead bishop who continued to work, after death, as an intermediary between the people and God. These saints responded to the peoples' needs, which the people expressed in prayers of petition. Here we see a kind of mystical aristocracy at work; the leaders, as divinely chosen intermediaries, were in communion with the people and willingly intercede on their behalf, curing wounds and deposing a illegitimate pontifex.

Nicholas' Influence in the High Middle Ages

After the spread of the cults of Nicholas in the eleventh century, more myroblytes began to appear in liturgical calendars. The *vitae* of holy men and women who lived long ago became suffused with stories of miraculously oozing tombs and biographers began imputing oil miracles to their saintly contemporaries. Although oil was said to flow from the tomb of Venerius the Hermit in the seventh century, no account of the miraculous oil exists prior to the High Middle Ages. As a result of Nicholas' cult, Babolenus (d. 670), the founding abbot of St. Maur-des-Fossés on the Marne River near Paris, also became a myroblyte in the eleventh century, as did Willibrord (658-739), the seventh-century Northumbrian missionary and first bishop of Utrecht.

The earliest textual evidence of a myroblyte on the Italic peninsula appears in an eighth century account of the life and miracles of Sabinus, the Bishop of Canosa (c. 461-566), whose miraculous oil might have rivaled that of Nicholas of Bari in the High Middle Ages. John the Archdeacon of Bari, appears to have eliminated accounts of Sabinus' miraculous oil once Nicholas' fame as a myroblyte had reached great heights. The earliest text to refer to Sabinus is Gregory the

Great's *Dialogues,* which tells of Sabinus visiting Benedict of Nursia (c. 480-543) and speaking,

among other things, of the destruction of Rome by the Ostrogoth King Totila (r. 541-552). Benedict

argued that natural disasters, rather than foreign invaders, would destroy the city.[805] Gregory later

told of how King Totila visited Sabinus when the bishop was advanced in age. Although blind,

Sabinus was able to sense the presence of the enemy king but nevertheless accepted a cup of wine

he offered. Sabinus later showed prophetic awareness when he sensed a rival bishop trying to poison

him with tainted wine; knowing full well that the cup was poisoned, the bishop drank it to no effect.

His rival, however, was devastated by consciousness of his own sinfulness, which brought about his

own death.[806] Neither of these pericopes from Gregory the Great mentions oil or miracles

accomplished at the bishop's tomb, suggesting that in the sixth century, Sabinus had not yet

acquired a reputation for producing miraculous oil. The first reference to miraculous oil flowing

from Sabinus' tomb appeared in an anonymous eighth-century account of the life and translation of

Sabinus (BHL 7443).[807]

The eighth-century account of Sabinus' translation offers a clue about when oil seeping from

saints' tombs may have first appeared on the Italic peninsula. The translation account described

fragrant oil dripping from the bishop's tomb as a "new and stupendous miracle." According to the

anonymous author, a large group of people gathered for the translation, eager to see "the holy

treasure of Christ."[808] Nevertheless, the heroic figure at the center of the narrative was not the holy

Bishop Sabinus, but his successor:

> Truly when people were standing outside the tomb, the bishop entered into the tomb with a
> choir of singers, as if needing to receive the Christ. They then removed the marbles of the

---

[805] Gregorius Magnus, *Dialogues* II, 15. PL LXVI. 162.

[806] Gregorius Magnus, *Dialogues* III, 5.

[807] AASS Feb. II, Dies 9. BHL 7443.

[808] "Hic videlicet in solenniis Apostolorum SS. Petri & Pauli cum omni populo vtriusque sexus, ad istud magnum &
laudandum spectaculum venerant, omnes cupientes Christi sacrum thesaurum reperire." AASS Feb. II, Dies 9.

tomb and approached the holy and venerable body, such a great smell of perfume erupted, as if from diverse blossoming flowers, that everyone's nostrils were satisfied. Nevertheless, the body was not translated at that time, but the bishop arranged for the body to be transferred the next day and left behind the seal with the episcopal ring. On the day of the translation, when the bishop came with a crowd of people, removed the seal and advanced toward the venerable corpse, God marvelously manifested a new and stupendous miracle to his priests. From the marbles of the tomb little drops of balsam started to drip in such a way that a liquid with an indescribably fragrance flowed. Anyone who was present, believing an angelic retinue to be there prayed zealously, filled with fear and jubilation.[809]

The corpse not only emitted oil, but also radiant light. The bishop alone, however, saw the light, which flowed over the corpse in brilliant abundance. The author may have played on his readers' knowledge of the Song of Song, using the word *effusuum* to draw a parallel between light flowing over the saint's body and the name of the beloved, which Solomon describes as being like flowing oil: "Thy name is as oil poured out [*effusum*]."[810] The light about the saint's body illuminated the entire church, but curiously enough did not endure:

> What else? They carried off the body, with hymns and heavenly songs and with all the
> people glowing with the light of various lamps, to the place that the bishop himself had
> prepared for Sabinus. Nevertheless, Sabinus rested there, placed for some time in the church
> and not yet transferred to the altars. During this time, when the venerable Bishop Peter,
> before the time of prayer in the dead of night, entered the church alone to sing psalms to the
> Lord, he found that so great a light was pouring out on the body of the servant of God, that
> every place in the church shone, as if in the middle of the day. But nevertheless after a little

---

[809] "Iis vero foris stantibus, Episcopus cum choro psallentium, quasi Christum suscepturus, ad sepulchrum ingressus est. Remotis igitur marmoribus ad sanctum ac venerabile corpus peruenerunt: sed tanta fragrantia odoris illico erupit, vt omnium nares, ac si ex diuersis virentibus floribus, satiaret. Non tamen eadem hora translatum est, sed in crastinum ferendum seruauit, & annulo episcopali signatum reliquit. Sed dum ad ferendum die altera Episcopus cum frequentia venisset populorum, remoto signo, cum ad venerabile corpus ingrederetur, mirabiliter Deus nouum suis & stupendum Sacerdotibus manifestauit miraculum. Ex marmoribus namque, quemadmodum balsami stillare solent guttulæ, inenarrabili odore liquor emanabat. Cuncti qui aderant, Angelica ibi esse obsequia credentes, cum exultatione pauoreque intenti impensius orabant." AASS Feb. II, Dies 9.

[810] ""Osculetur me osculo oris sui; quia meliora sunt ubera tua vino, fragrantia unguentis optimis. Oleum effusum nomen tuum; ideo adolescentulae dilexerunt te." Cant. 1:1-2.

while, what he had seen was quickly extinguished, as if so great a clarity was entirely absent from the church.[811]

While the eighth-century account of Sabinus' translation recorded the miraculous oil and light emanating from the bishop's tomb, two texts from the late eleventh century were curiously silent about Sabinus' oil. According to the Bollandists, in 1091 John the Archdeacon of Bari composed two texts relating to the life of Sabinus: a *vita metrica,* a metrical version of Sabinus' life (BHL 7444), as well as a prose *historia* (BHL 7445), both of which were contained in codices belonging to the Church of St. Nicholas of Bari.[812] Neither the metrical *vita* nor the *historia* mentioned oil seeping from Sabinus tomb, effectively erasing his reputation as a myroblyte, likely in light of Nicholas' greater glory. In the late eleventh century, John the Archdeacon of Bari may have sought to preserve Nicholas' reputation as the paramount producer of oil on the Italic peninsula.[813]

Venrius the Hermit

Prior to the late eleventh century, a bishop questioned the legitimacy of oil produced by Venerius, a seventh-century hermit who had lived on the island of Palamaria in the Gulf of Genoa.

---

[811] "Quid plura? Tulerunt corpus cum hymnis & cælestibus canticis, & omni populo exultante, diuersisque lampadibus refulgente, ad locum, quem illi ipse parauerat, venerunt. Aliquamdiu tamen in ecclesia positus, altaribus nondum mancipatus, quieuit. Inter hæc dum venerabilis Episcopus Petrus, ante tempus orationis, in ipsa intempesta nocte, vt Domino solus psalleret, ecclesiam intraret, super corpus Dei famuli tantum lumen effusum reperit, vt omnia illius ecclesiæ loca, ac si meridiano tempore, lucerent: sed post paullulum tamen, quod viderat, subito extinctum est, ac si in ea tanta claritas minime fuisset." AASS Feb. II, Dies 9.

[812] AASS Feb. II, Dies 9.

[813] Sabinus was not the only Italic saint whose fragrant body produced an abundance of bright light, like an oil lamp. The body of Fantinus (c. 927-1000), the confessor at Tauriano in Calabria, also emitted light, fragrance and curative oil: "Fantinus' cadaver was illuminated by such a great light and splendor, that for two hours, indeed no one was able to distinguish anything. The sweetest odor, moreover, filled the church for an entire thirty days and from the tomb oil began to overflow with such great power that resisted not only every kind of sickness, but also all the temptations of the soul." "Ejus cadaver tanta luce, ac splendore lustratum est, ut per duas horas ne cerni quidem ab ullo posset. Odor autem, triginta integros dies, ecclesiam suavissimus perfudit: & ex sepulcro cœpit oleum redundare quoddam tantæ virtutis, ut cum omni morborum generi, tum universis etiam animæ tentationibus occurreret." AASS Jul.V, Dies 24. I have yet to determine exactly when this account was composed or when Fantinus' cult grew in popularity.

Venerius was a rather obscure hermit, left out of some of the earliest martyrologies.[814] His cult, however, began to flourish in the seventh century, when oil was said to flow from his tomb.[815] On November 3rd, sometime in the ninth century, Venerius' relics were translated. According to the Bollandists, Venerius' *vita* was not written before the ninth century or after 1085. The hermit, who led a life of solitary fasting and prayer, was ostensibly buried "by angelic hands long ago" and so remained *incognito*. At some indefinite point in time, however, oil began to flow from the hermit's grave, revealing the presence of the holy man's body: "...he gave back his soul to heaven. His body, buried by angelic hands, remained incognito for a long time. In the place where his body rested, however, oil began to flow, which does so up until today. Anyone anointed with the oil immediately felt solace from labors and pains, provided that the oil was received with faith."[816] The author of Venerius' *vita* described how a bishop was skeptical about the hermit's holy oil and attempted to verify for himself that oil in fact flowed from the tomb.

The author of Venerius' *vita* described the willingness of people to believe in the saint and his miracles. A bishop, however, needed to see for himself whether or not the saint's body produced oil. The Lord was said to have commanded Lucius, the Bishop of Luna in Genoa, to build a church over Venerius' grave and appoint custodians to the holy place.[817] The bishop, leaving his ship in the harbor, sought the grave of the hermit to verify the source of oil; like the people who flocked to Nicholas' tomb, the bishop wanted to see the miraculous hermit with his very own eyes:

> The Lord appeared in a vision to Lucius the Bishop of Luna (in Genoa), commanding him
> to build a church in the place where the saint rested and place guardians there, who might
> show deference to the same Holy Man. Lucius, bringing the news of the revelation of

---

[814] *Commentarius Praevius*, AASS Sept. IV, Dies 13.

[815] Ibid.

[816] "...cælo animam reddidit: cujus corpus angelicis sepultum manibus longo tempore mansit incognitum. Cœpit autem in loco ubi sanctum corpus jacebat, oleum fundere, quod usque hodie fit; & quicumque ex eo ungitur, statim laboris & doloris se invenit percepisse solamen, dummodo cum fide percipiat." AASS Sept. IV, Dies 13.

[817] "Apparuit etiam in visione Dominus Lucio episcopo Lunensi, mandans, ut in loco, ubi Sanctus jacebat, ecclesiam fabricaret, & custodes poneret, qui eidem sancto Viro obsequium exhiberent." AASS Sept. IV, Dies 13.

Venerius' body to the clerics and to the people...arrived at the revealed place. Searching for the place at last, he found out for himself where the oil poured forth. Wanting to know the truth, he came to the tomb and became the first digger. When he began to dig, he discovered the body on the first of May and thus discovered the untouched and entire body, as if Venerius had been buried that same hour.[818]

Not only was Venerius' body perfectly intact, but he emitted a heavenly odor which, as we have seen, often accompanied a profusion of miraculous oil: "Such a great fragrant perfume emanated from that place, that appeared to equal the odors of paradise."[819] Bishop Lucius of Luna (whose name literally means *Light of the Moon*) ordered the grave to be covered and a beautiful church built over Venerius' resting place. The author of the *vita* then described how, when the custodians were in want of water to drink, they turned to the saint, whose tomb erupted with water in addition to oil. Not surprisingly, the water, as well as the oil, cured the faithful:

> ...ordering the grave to be covered over, the bishop built a very beautiful church there and established guardians, who cared for Venerius' body with diligent care. When the guardians did not have sweet water to drink, by the merits of this saint, below his church, near to the altar, an everlasting fountain of water (*fons aquae*) erupted, which up until today flows and heals the feverish, who drink from the fountain with faith by the merits of the Holy One of God.[820]

---

[818] "Apparuit etiam in visione Dominus Lucio episcopo Lunensi, mandans, ut in loco, ubi Sanctus jacebat, ecclesiam fabricaret, & custodes poneret, qui eidem sancto Viro obsequium exhiberent. Qui clero & populo hoc referens, & cum eis navim ascendens, ad locum revelatum pervenit, & quærens locum sibi demum reperit, ubi oleum fundebatur. Volens cognoscere veritatem, venit ad sepulchrum, & primus ipse episcopus terræ fossor accessit: & cum cœpisset fodere, pervenit ad corpus Kalendis Maji, & ita intactum & integrum invenerunt, acsi eadem hora fuisset sepultum..." AASS Sept. IV, Dies 13.

[819] "tantaque odoris fragrantia ex illo loco emanavit, ut paradisi odoribus videretur æquari." AASS Sept. IV, Dies 13.

[820] "Et jubens operiri sepulchrum, perpulchram ecclesiam ibi fabricavit, & custodes instituit, qui diligenti cura suum corpus custodierunt qui cum aquam dulcem non haberent ad bibendum, meritis Sancti hujus infra ipsam ecclesiam juxta altare erupit fons aquæ perennis, qui usque hodie manat, qui febricitantes, ex eo cum fide potantes, sanat meritis Sancti Dei." AASS Sept. IV, Dies 13.

Venerius' church stood over a miraculous spring of water, just as Santa Maria in Trastevere stood over a miraculous fountain of holy oil.[821] The Bollandists noted the parallel between a line of text in Venerius' *vita* and a liturgical verse describing flowing liquid as a sign of charity: "Thus his body rests and the liquid flows in testimony that he knew how to live with charity."[822] Did the Bishop of Luna wish to build his church over the oily hermit's grave in order to regulate popular devotion to a saint who produced oil? Despite the fact that the bishop questioned the legitimacy of the holy hermit's oil, Venerius obligingly produced numerous signs of his sanctity, including quantities of fragrance, oil, and water.

BABOLENUS, THE OOZING ABBOT

The number of oil-producing saints in France also increased when Nicholas' cult spread in the eleventh century. The St. Maur-de-Fossés monastery was ostensibly built on the ruins of a Roman encampment in the third century after a battle purportedly raged between the Roman Emperor Maximian Hercules (285-305) and a local population of brigands known as the *bagaudes*.[823] The remains of a Roman fortress, the *Castrum Bagaudarum*, became the foundation of the monastery three centuries later.[824] The site of the fortress in question was a piece of land located on the Marne River on the outskirts of Paris. Queen Nanthilde (610-642), regent of the Franks and mother of the young Clovis II, donated the land to Blidegisile, a local deacon, in order that he might found a monastery under the Benedictine rule dedicated to the Blessed Virgin Mary and the Apostles Peter and Paul. In 640 the Bishop of Paris, Audebert, installed a virtually unknown Irish monk named Babolenus as abbot of the new monastery. According to legend, Audebert discovered Babolenus

---

[821] See Chapters 8-10.

[822] "Cujus latet corpusculum, fluitque Dei munere / Liquor notans, quod noverat cum caritate vivere." AASS Sept. IV, Dies 13, n.F.

[823] Andre Renaudin questions the historicity of this claim made in *Vita Baboleni*, citing the absence of historical evidence and noting such an event would not have entered the annals of history. Renaudin suggests that such a telling of the place's past is likely lore perpetuated by the popular imagination of locals. See Renaudin, "Deux Antiphonaires de Saint-Maur: BN Lat 12584 et 12044."

[824] Renaudin observes it is unlikely that the Romans would have built a fortress so far from Rome. Ibid., 63.

praying in the church of Notre Dame in Paris following the death of the monk's *magister*, Saint

Columbanus (543-615), the late Irish abbot of the Luxeuil and Bobbio monasteries. The bishop was

so moved by the monk's piety that he made Babolenus abbot.[825]

From its inception, monks identified the monastery according to a geographical peculiarity in

its proximity. At the site of the old castle, a deep depression cut across the Marne. On May 15, 643

the Archbishop Audebert granted the abbey exemption from the region's Ordinary and allowed the

monks to freely elect their own abbot. From as early as 768, the monastery was referred to as "the

ditches": *cella quae dicitur fossatis*.[826] By the beginning of the eighth century, the Fossés had become

prosperous but lax, prompting reform.[827] In 816, the abbey was granted immunity, protecting its

assets from taxation by secular authorities, a privilege attributable to the reforms instituted by Louis

the Pious.[828] Beginning around 817, under the direction of the monastery's fourth abbot, Benedict,

the Fossés became the recipient of substantial donations from throughout the region, including

Paris, Maine, Anjou and Aquitane. The increase in the monastery's wealth allowed for the

reconstruction of its edifices, during which time Babolenus' remains were translated.

Little is known about the development of the cult of Babolenus. Modern historians have all

but neglected the abbot, consigning the origin and development of his cult to near obscurity.[829] The

abbot was also nearly forgotten by his near successors. In 839, during the dedication of a

reconstructed church, Babolenus' remains are reported to have miraculously translated themselves

---

[825] *Vita Baboleni* in Bede and Pierre-François Chifflet, *Bedæ presbyteri: et Fredegarii scholastici Concordia ad senioris Dagoberti definiendam monarchiæ periodum, atque ad primæ totius Regum Francorum stirpis chronologiam stabiliendam ...* (Parisiis: Apud Garbielem Martinum ..., 1681), 362-64.

[826] Pépin the Short referred to the monastery in this way in a charter of 768. Renaudin, "Deux Antiphonaires de Saint-Maur: BN Lat 12584 et 12044," 64.

[827] Ibid.

[828] Ibid.

[829] The two modern studies of Babolenus do not address the development of his cult, but rather the history of the monastery based on falsified charters and Roman archeology. See K Voigt, "Die Vita S. Baboleni Und Die Urkunden Fur St.-Maur-Des-Fosses," *Neues Archive Der Geselleschaft Fur Altere Deutsche Geschichtskunde* 31 (1906): 289–334; Lellia Cracco Ruggini, "Etablishements Militaries, Martyrs Bagaudes Et Traditions Romaines Dans La 'Vita Baboleni," *Historia: Zeitschrift Fur Alte Geschichte* 44, no. 1 (1955): 101–19.

from his burial place outside the original church into the interior of a new basilica.[830] Although

Babolenus died in 670 and was translated in the mid-ninth century, when his cult may have gathered

force.[831] The saint's biographical dossier was not composed, however, until the eleventh century.

The ascension of Babolenus' popularity and the importance attributed to his relics might

have derived in part from a rivalry with Saint Maur, which could have resulted from the Fossés'

coalescence with another monastic community, the Glanfeuil abbey on the banks of the Loire River

in Anjou.[832] Like the Fossés monastery, Glanfeuil was founded in a Roman locale in the sixth

century.[833] According to Eudes of Glanfeuil, an eleventh-century author of saints' lives, the founder

of the Glanfeuil abbey was Saint Maur, a companion of Saint Benedict. In the ninth century, when

the abbey had suffered a decline, Rorigon, the Comte of Maine and Anjou, placed Glanfeuil under

the auspices of the Fossés.[834] After a series of Viking invasions in the Glanfeuil region and a period

of peregrination, the monks of Glanfeuil took refuge at the Fossés. On November 13, 868, they

translated Saint Maur's relics with great ceremony to the main altar of the Fossés church.[835]

November 13th became the anniversary for the dedication of "St. Pierre-de-Fossés," but the

monastery remained dedicated to the Blessed Virgin Mary and the apostles Peter and Paul rather

than to Saint Maur. The peaceful repose of Saint Maur at the Fossés was short-lived. In 878, the

---

[830] Renaudin gives two dates for the translation: "On procède le 7 décembre 839, sans changement de vocable, à la dedicace de l'église reconstruite; les restes vénérés de Babolein sont à cette occasion transporté dans le nouvel édifice." See Renaudin, "Deux Antiphonaires de Saint-Maur: BN Lat 12584 et 12044," 64. Later Renaudin states: "translation de saint Babolein: la fête est liée à l'histoire du monastère des Fossés; elle commémore le transfert interne des reliques du fondateur de l'abbeye le 7 Décembre 989. C'est donc une fête de meme nature que celle rappelant le transfert également interne des reliques de saint Maur à l'abbeye de Glanfeuil le 12 Mars 845, première translation de saint Maur inscrite au Calendrier." See Ibid., 83. These two dates might suggest Babolenus was translated twice, once in 840 from outside the church to the interior of the basilica and a second time in 989, perhaps within the church itself. The *miracula*, however, only refers to one translation. 989 was the date when the wayward abbot Maynard was sent to Glanfeuil to do penance for his misdeeds; Renaudin makes no mention of this event coinciding with an "internal transfer" of Babolenus' relics, suggesting the abbot was only transferred once, in 830/40. Moreover, this is the date given by Baudot-Chaussin for the translation. See Jules Baudot, Léon Chaussin, and Benedictines, *Vies des saints et des bienheureux selon l'ordre du calendrier: avec l'historique des fêtes* (Paris: Librairie Letouzey et Ané, 1935), 440–41.
[831] Baudot, Chaussin, and Benedictines, *Vies des saints et des bienheureux selon l'ordre du calendrier*, 441.
[832] Glanfeuil means "acorn leaf."
[833] Renaudin, "Deux Antiphonaires de Saint-Maur: BN Lat 12584 et 12044," 65.
[834] Ibid.
[835] Ibid., 67.

Vikings drove the Fossés monks from the abbey on Marne.[836] After a series of sojourns at monasteries in Champagne region, notably at Fleury-la-Rivière and near Reims, the monks returned to the Fossés on the Marne in 920, where Saint Maur's reliquary was amicably installed in a third church.[837] In 996, the monastery joined the Cluniac network and entered into a period of prosperity.[838] This era witnessed the creation of a library as well as the increase of literary and intellectual productivity, including the writing of the monastery's history.[839] In this context, the monks of Fossés composed Babolenus' *vita* and *acta miraculorum* as they returned *ad fontes* to their monastery's inception.

Babolenus' biographical dossier consists of three texts: a *vita, acta miraculorum* and *laudatio*. The Bollandists argued that the *laudatio* was the oldest of the three texts, likely dating to the early eleventh century. The text is part of a *legendarium* from St. Maur-de-Fossés (BnF Latin 5607).[840] The *vita* and *acta* were likely not composed earlier than the mid-eleventh century.[841] The earliest extant copies of the *vita* and *acta miraculorum* appear in Troyes MS 2273, a twelfth-century *legendarium* that was copied in three stages between 1100 and 1130.[842] These texts, as well as the celebration of

---

[836] Ibid.

[837] Ibid.

[838] Ibid.

[839] Ibid.

[840] The Bollandists identify the *Vita Baboleni* [BHL 886] as dating from the mid-eleventh century and the *laudatio* [BHL 888], BnF Latin 5607, as older and more refined: "Celle-ci [the *vita Baboleni*] ne date pas d'avant le milieu du XIe siècle. Mais l'éloge BHL 888 est plus ancien et de meilleur aloi." See *Analecta Bollandiana*, vol 25 (Brussels: Société des Bollandistes, 1906), 343.

[841] Regarding the rise of Babolenus' cult in the ninth century, see Baudot, Chaussin, and Benedictines, *Vies des saints et des bienheureux selon l'ordre du calendrier*, 441. The earliest extant copies of the *vita* and *acta miraculorum* appear in Troyes MS 2273, a twelfth-century *legendarium* that was copied in three stages between 1100 and 1130. See Charlotte Denoël, Saint-Maur-des-Fossés (Abbey: France), and Médiathèque de Troyes, "Vie et miracles de saint Maur Life and miracles of Saint Maurus." (Réunion des Musées Nationaux ; Médiathèque de l'agglomeration troyenne, 2005). The *laudatio*, BnF Latin 5607, is also an eleventh-century text contained in a *legendarium* from St. Maur-de-Fossés; it may be an older text than the *vita* and *miracula*. The Bollandists identify the *Vita Baboleni* [BHL 886] as dating from the mid-eleventh century and the *laudatio* [BHL 888], BnF Latin 5607, as older and more refined: "Celle-ci [the *vita Baboleni*] ne date pas d'avant le milieu du XIe siècle. Mais l'éloge BHL 888 est plus ancien et de meilleur aloi." See *Analecta Bollandiana*, vol 25 (Brussels: Société des Bollandistes, 1906), 343.

[842] Ibid. This may have been the manuscript Pierre François Chifflet used for his 1681 edition of the *vita* and *miracula Baboleni*. Chifflet's introduction to the *vita* and *miracula* states: "vitam S. Baboleni ex manuscripto codice Fossatensi descriptam, ad me tunc in Collegio nostro Dolano commorantem transmisit R.P. Michaël *Rabardeau*, junctis litteris quae datae erant Parisiis ix. Aprilis 1630." See Bede and Chifflet, *Beda presbyteri*, 356. The manuscript is said to have come

Babolenus' translation in the monastery's liturgy, suggest the saint's cult was well established in the Fossés by the first half of the twelfth century. The founding abbot was not nearly as popular, however, as Benedict's companion, Saint Maur, who became the monastery's patron by popular acclaim when, after a period of intense draught, a procession of Maur's relics induced the "miracle de la pluie" after all other prayers had failed.[843]

The monks who composed Babolenus' dossier were likely from the Fossés. They drew their inspiration from various sources, including the *Life and Miracles of Saint Maur* by Odo of Glanfeuil and texts relating to Nicholas of Myra, whose cult would have newly spread across France.[844] The most thorough manuscript witness of the Nicholas liturgy appears in two manuscripts produced at the abbey of St. Maur-des-Fossés.[845] This same abbey produced not only the Nicholas' liturgy, but elaborately celebrated the feast of Eligius. The monks of St. Maur-des-Fossés tried to establish the authority of their founding abbot by borrowing oil miracles from the more famous St. Nicholas and by strategically surrounding Babolenus with other myroblytes in the liturgical calendar. The relics of Babolenus were said to have translated themselves at the time of the dedication of the new basilica, which was celebrated on November 13th. Nevertheless, other liturgical codices record the translation as occurring on December 7th, at a particularly oil-rich moment in the liturgical year.

While Babolenus' biographical dossier might have been composed in the eleventh century, various liturgical manuscripts and calendars suggest that the celebration of his feast day and translation were still tenuous until the first quarter of the twelfth century. Indeed, Babolenus' *acta miraculorum* tells of disputes within the choir regarding the singing of chants for his office. In MS Latin 5607, the earliest manuscript witness of Babolenus' feast, the abbot's *laudatio* appears just after

---

from Saint-Germain-de-Prés. Renaudin notes that much of the St. Maur-de-Fossés library was given over to Saint-Germain-de-Prés in 1716. Renaudin, "Deux Antiphonaires de Saint-Maur: BN Lat 12584 et 12044," 72.

[843] Ibid.

[844] See Denoël, Saint-Maur-des-Fossés (Abbey : France), and Médiathèque de Troyes, "Vie et miracles de saint Maur Life and miracles of Saint Maurus."

[845] See Paris BnF Latin 12584 (11th century), fol. 383v-385v, and Paris BnF Latin 12044 (12th century).

Nicholas' *vita*. This would suggest that beginning in the eleventh century, his translation was celebrated on December 7th, following Nicholas' feast day on December 6th.[846] A late eleventh or early twelfth century (1075-1100) graduale and antiphoner from St. Maur-des-Fossés (BnF MS Latin 12584), however, shows no indication of the celebration of either Babolenus' or Eligius' feast days.

A missale from 1075-1125 (BnF MS Latin 12054) presents contradictory evidence that is rather telling of just when the feasts of these two myroblytes were established at St. Maur-des-Fossés. A calendar in a gothic hand at the beginning of the codex lists both the feast and translation of Babolenus as well as Eligius' feast.[847] The body of the manuscript, written in an earlier, pre-gothic hand, contains the chants and texts for the liturgical year. This portion of the codex shows the celebration of the feast of the dedication of the church on November 13th, situated between the feasts of two well-known Gallic saints: Martin of Tours on November 11th and Brice, Bishop of Tours on November 13th. This part of the codex also contains the feasts of Andrew and Nicholas, but not Eligius' feast day or Babolenus' feast or translation, despite the fact that these feasts were recorded in the calendar, which was evidently a later interpolation.

BnF MS Latin 12044, another antiphoner from St. Maur-des-Fossés dating to 1100-1125 includes the feast of Babolenus in June, on either on the 25th or 26th. Here too Babolenus was strategically placed between the feast of John the Baptist (June 24th) and the feast of the fourth-century martyrs John and Paul (June 26th). This codex contains the feasts of the string of myroblytes including Andrew the Apostle (November 30); Eligius, Bishop of Noyon (December 1); Nicholas, Bishop of Myra (December 6); the translation of Babolenus, Abbot of St. Maur-des-Fossés (December 7), which coincided with the end of the octave of Andrew. Furthermore, in Troyes MS 2273, the legendarium from St. Maur-des-Fossés that was copied in the first half of the twelfth century, contains the earliest texts for Babolenus' *vita* and *acta miraculorum,* which follow

---

[846] BnF Latin 5607. *Vitae Sancti Nicholai* fol. 62v-88v and *Laudatio Sancti Baboleni,* fol. 89r-91v.
[847] BnF Latin 12054, fol. 4r, fol.6v. Gallica, accessed on April 12, 2017, http://gallica.bnf.fr/ark:/12148/btv1b8422976g.

directly after the life of Nicholas of Myra.[848] Likewise in Sacramentary from St. Maur-des-Fossés that

dates to 1134-1150, the feast of Babolenus is present in June, as is his translation on December 7,

directly following the feast of Nicholas.[849]

The monks of St. Maur-des-Fossés did not only try to bolster their founding abbot's

reputation as a myroblyte by surrounding him with other oozing prelates in the liturgical calendar.

Accounts of miraculous oil seeping from Babolenus' tomb embellished his *acta miraculorum*. When

Robert of Le Mans, a medieval prior of the St. Maur-de-Fossés abbey, answered the call of nature

one day, the "vengeful right hand of the Lord" inflicted a rare form of punishment that was both

painful and humiliating.[850] After a bout of extreme constipation, the prior's bowels unexpectedly fell

out: "When…the prior had just gone to the necessities of nature and had struggled more than usual

in this customary work, suddenly (I thus say) the doors of the belly opened and nearly all the

intestines gushed out."[851] Robert did not survive long but died "with excessive anguish" within a few

days.[852] The unfortunate man's transgression had been grave indeed; he had opposed the celebration

of Babolenus' translation. The founding abbot had become a divisive figure within the community.

While some monks faithfully reverenced their founder, others voiced dissent regarding the man's

holiness. A major bone of contention was the oil that seeped from the abbot's tomb. Some believed

that a holy salve had flowed from the sepulcher for years. Skeptics, however, questioned the veracity

of the claim and sought to abolish Babolenus' feast from the liturgical calendar. Divine intervention

settled the dispute.

The evisceration of Robert of Le Mans was simply one incident in the history of the abbey

that revealed conflict among the monks and instability within the abbey's hierarchy. Babolenus' *acta*

---

[848] Denoël, Saint-Maur-des-Fossés (Abbey : France), and Médiathèque de Troyes, "Vie et miracles de saint Maur Life and miracles of Saint Maurus."

[849] BnF Latin 12072, fol.42r-v, fol.56v.

[850] The vague chronology of Babolenus' *acta miraculorum*, from which this incident is drawn, makes it difficult to say when Robert of Le Mans was prior, though it was likely sometime in the eleventh or early twelfth century.

[851] AASS Jun. V, Col. 0183A.

[852] AASS Jun. V, Col. 0183A.

miraculorum disclosed a world in which saints of God were under constant attack from impious

monks, who numbered among the community's leaders. Babolenus' chief adversaries included a

priest, a prior, a deacon and a cantor; all displayed passionate hatred for the founding abbot and

sought to abolish his cult from the monastery. The troubles appear to have begun with a dispute

over the oil seeping from Babolenus' tomb. At an earlier time, the tomb had been a veritable

fountain of healing liquid:

> Long ago in the aforementioned church of the Mother of God, in which the same
> outstanding Confessor laid buried, oil flowed for many days and over a course of years from
> the stone of his sacred mausoleum where the sick, oppressed with varying illnesses, were
> smeared with oil and immediately returned to health.[853]

The explanation of Babolenus' flowing oil functions in part as a backward glance to an idyllic

period when the community was less beset with turmoil than in subsequent years. The author of

Babolenus' *acta miraculorum* depicted one of Babolenus' opponents as cruel and volatile. The negative

depiction of blisteringly unkind speech conveys the perception of holy individuals as people who

were able to control both their words and their actions. Self-control was evidently highly prized

among the monks and associated with holiness itself, in keeping with centuries of an ascetic

monastic tradition, as also seen in Eligius' *vita*.[854] Evidence of this tradition surfaces elsewhere in the

miracula, when the author describes Babolenus as someone who had been able to bring his physical

person "into his service through most strong affliction."[855] Self-control, however, did not apply

simply to the body; the narrator conveyed that the rancorous speech ought not flow freely like oil

---

[853] AASS Jun. V, Col. 0182C. Sigal notes that miracles involving holy oil were akin to miracles "du vinage" in which
relics were soaked in liquid which then was used as a salve. See Pierre-Andre Sigal, *L'homme et le miracle dans la France
medievale : XIe-XIIe siècle* (Paris: Cerf, 1985), 51–53.
[854] For studies on medieval monasticism see Lowrie John Daly, *Benedictine Monasticism, Its Formation and Development through
the 12th Century* (New York: Sheed and Ward, 1965); Ivan Gobry, *Les Moines En Occident* (Paris: Fayard, 1985); Noreen
Hunt, *Cluniac Monasticism in the Central Middle Ages*, Readings in European History (London: Macmillan, 1971).
[855] AASS Jun. V, Col. 0181F.

from the tomb. Babolenus' opponent exhibited an unholy lack of self-control by lashing out against

the saint's oil, claiming it was contrary to the will of God and Babolenus himself:

> That distinguished minister of the altar, inflamed with the stings of rage, who did not know
> how it was possible to hold back, soon brought forth a useless word from his malicious
> mouth: 'This was evidently not the will of kindest Jesus Christ and of his holy mother and of
> Babolenus the famous Confessor – that a more ample amount of his own liquid oil was
> flowing from hence and hereafter into eternity.'[856]

The drama increased when Babolenus made known he was listening and exercised power from the

other side of the grave. The scene replicated a miracle from the life of Nicholas of Myra, who

stopped his flow of oil when a bishop was unjustly deposed. Here too, oil ceased to flow as a protest

against an injustice: "This effect followed his most miserable voice: now the oil stood still and the

stone dried up."[857] Just as the munificent outpouring of the holy substance had been a sign of divine

favor, the cessation of oil was a sign of divine judgment or wrath.[858] The saint first manifested his

favor by generating an abundance of oil. Later he exhibited his discontent by making the flow of oil

cease. For some within the Fossés community, the abrupt change dramatically demonstrated the

presence of the saint at the tomb. Not all the monks, however, were persuaded of the abbot's

supernatural powers. To defeat a minority of skeptics, a trial took place in which witnesses were

brought forward to attest to the fact that Babolenus' holy oil had in fact flowed for generations.[859]

The conflict over Babolenus' salve was just the beginning of the strife surrounding the

abbot's cult. Several incidents illustrate how questioning the authority of the former abbot was met

---

[856] AASS Jun. V, Col. 0182C.

[857] AASS Jun. V, Col. 0182C.

[858] Regarding the role of monsters as signs of God's wrath and auguries of punishments that inspired horror, anxiety and fear, see Lorraine Datson, *Wonders and the Order of Nature, 1150-1750* (New York : Cambridge, Mass: Zone Books ; MIT Press, 1998), 51.

[859] Regarding the formalization of a process of verifying miracles, see André Vauchez, *La sainteté en Occident aux derniers siècles du Moyen Age: d'après les procès de canonisation et les documents hagiographiques* (Rome; Paris: Ecole française de Rome ; Diffusion de Boccard, 1981). Regarding skepticism about miracles among saints' contemporaries, see Clare Stancliffe, *St. Martin and His Hagiographer: History and Miracle in Sulpicius Severus*, Oxford Historical Monographs (Oxford: Clarendon Press, 1983).

with equally divine retaliation.[860] A rector "called Robert by baptism" was such a vehement

opponent of Babolenus's cult that in a fit a rage he overturned an altar dedicated to the saint. Divine

punishment was swift and collaborated with a secular authority: "…the vengeful right hand of God

did not long endure the insults about the saint. For from that year Robert was captured and

entangled with chains and by the order of King Henry was enclosed in prison."[861] The disreputable

rector was said to have "shamelessly destroyed the pastoral honor" and brought mockery on the

community; the subsequent grief he suffered became an example for posterity, such that further

outrages against the saint might be avoided.[862]

An untimely end befell another opponent of Babolenus. This time the adversary was

Hilduardus, a cantor, who attempted to prevent the choir from singing Babolenus' responsory

during the celebration of the translation. The choir, in contrast to the cantor, was an image of unity

and peace: "four brothers, according to custom, sang standing before the altar and in joyful voice

with the organ loftily resounding the responsory *Sanctus Domini Confessor*."[863] Hilduardus attempted to

intervene by singing a responsory not associated with Babolenus, but the choir succeeded in out-

singing him.[864] Hilduardus retreated to his room only to receive a nocturnal visitation by a revenant

Babolenus. Babolenus gently questioned the cantor about why he had not respected the celebration

and then announced that the cantor would soon die. To deliver the death sentence, Babolenus

appeared in human form with a divine radiance pouring forth from his body in beams of light. He

appeared, "like the glimmering sun."[865] In the night, the myroblyte radiated light like a brilliant oil

---

[860] Carlos Eire observed that in waging spiritual war against evil, Martin Luther sometimes similarly resorted to fighting fire with fire since the "Evil One could be attacked with his own weapons." According to Eire, Luther's diabology was deeply rooted in the medieval monastic tradition, which was based on dualities and the primal struggle between good and evil. See Carlos M.N. Eire, "'Bite This, Satan!' The Devil in Luther's Table Talk," in *Piety and Family in Early Modern Europe: Essays in Honour of Steven Ozment*, ed. Marc R Forster and Benjamin J. Kaplan (Aldershot: Ashgate, 2005).
[861] AASS Jun. V, Col. 0182E.
[862] AASS Jun. V, Col. 0182E.
[863] AASS Jun. V, Col. 0183B.
[864] In this portion of the *miracula,* the translation of the saint is said to take place on the sixth day of Kalends, or 26 June.
[865] AASS Jun. V, Col. 0183B.

lamp. Despite the cantor's best efforts to atone for his wrong by throwing himself into the

myroblyte's service, the damage was irrevocable. Hilduardus "met death's way, the entry of all

flesh."[866] Through his miracles, Babolenus showed himself to be a formidable presence in his abbey

long after his death. He was capable of both healing the faithful and inflicting pain or even death on

the unfaithful. Like Nicholas of Myra, Babolenus expressed his discontent with the community by

withholding his holy oil. In Babolenus' cult, the presence of oil thus became a sign of divine favor

and the willingness of the saint to succor the wounds or illnesses of the faithful.

FONS MISERICORDIAE: WILLIBRORD, BISHOP OF UTRECHT

Willibrord (658-739), the first Bishop of Utrecht, was a Northumbrian missionary whose

reputation as a myroblyte began in the late eleventh century. At the request of Pepin, King of the

Franks, Willibrord was sent on a missionary campaign with eleven companions to Frisia. In 695,

Pope Sergius I (687-701) consecrated Willibrord as Bishop of the Frisians, afterwhich the new

bishop established his see in Utrecht. In 698 Willibrord founded the Abbey of Echternach, where he

was buried after his death in 739. Alciun (735-804) first composed Willibrord's *vita,* which he

dedicated to the then Bishop of Echternach. Alcuin enumerated the great miracles that occurred at

the former bishops' tomb, including healing miracles accomplished by oil from the lamps that

illuminated the sepulcher. Alcuin never mentioned, however, any miraculous oil flowing directly

from Willibrord's tomb. On October 19, 1031 Willbrord's remains were translated to the altar of a

new basilica.[867] When Thiofrid, the Bishop of Echternacht (d. 1110) rewrote the founder's life in the

late eleventh or early twelfth century, miraculous oil was not only found in Willibrord's lamps, but

flowing from his tomb.

---

[866] AASS Jun. V, Col. 0183C.

[867] If a *translatio* exists recording this event, I do not know of it.

Thiofrid's version on Willibrord's life is preserved in a twelfth-century *legendarium* (BnF Latin

9740). The first folio contains a *Genealogia Francorum Regum,* followed by John the Deacon's Life of

Saint Nicholas, Bishop of Myra.[868] This version of Nicholas' *vita* has some curious editions, not

found in BHL 6104.[869] The author of Nicholas' life compared Nicholas' election as bishop to King

David's election by Samuel as king and described how Nicholas' consecration as bishop included the

new bishop being anointed on the head with oil.[870] This same text appears in MS Cotton Nero E 1,

an eleventh-century *legendarium* from Worcester Cathedral, which may be one of the earliest and

most complete versions of Nicholas' office.[871] The compiler of the codex (possibly Thiofrid of

Echternach) evidently wished to draw a parallel between a geneology of bishops as the Lord's

anointed and heirs of Hebrew kings. The appearance of a story about Nicholas' consecration as

bishop directly after the *Genealogia Francorum Regum* could not have been coincidental. Moreover, the

codex also contains the life of Pope Sergius I (d. 701), who consecrated Willibrord as bishop as well

as Willibrord's own *vita,* which contained accounts of his miraculous oil.[872]

When Thiofrid first referred to the oil lamp hanging by Willibrord's tomb, he spoke of its

miraculous abundance of oil. The lamp became, like the saint himself, a fountain of mercy *(fons*

emanavit misericordiae). According to Thiofrid, "the effusion of oil grew and boiled up and having been

received in ampullae and given and sent to the sick for salubrious unction, Willibrord restored

---

[868] BnF Latin 9740. Gallica, accessed on April 12, 2017, http://gallica.bnf.fr/ark:/12148/btv1b9067063n.

[869] Mai, *Spicilegium Romanum. Patrum ecclesiasticorum Serapionis, Ioh. Chrysostomi, Cyrilli Alex., Theodori Mopsuesteni, Procli, Diadochi, Sophronh, Ioh. Monachi, Paulini, Claudii, Petri Damiani scripta varia. Item ex nicetae thesauro excerpta, biographi sacri veteres, et asclepiodoti militare fragmentum Tomus IV,* 323–39.

[870] "Mira prorsus, mira et stupenda sunt quae narrantur et si fas est . antiquis per omnia comparanda quondam enim samuheli prophaetae sanctis precepit spiritus ut ad domum isai pergeret unumque ex enis filius placitum domino regem inungeret ; modo autem isti ex intimo episcopo precanti effectu . vox de caelo iussit ut coram templi foribus ex cubaret ; quatenus ibidem domino dignum {est} aecclesiae suae {proficuimi?} reperiret antistitem. Illi quamquam uidenti locus tantum non regis praedicitur nomen ; huic et locus et nomen presulis declaratur . ille capud regium cornu roborauit olei . iste super capud nicolai virtutem invocavit spiritus sancti sed tamem et praesul et rex uterque electus a domino est." BnF Latin 9740, 5v–6v.

[871] The British Library's note on this manuscript says that this version of Nicholas' life has no BHL number.

[872] BHL 7597. BnF Latin 9740, fol. 22v-26r.

soundness of mind and body."[873] Willibrord's holy oil not only cured physical and mental ills, but moral ones as well. Thiofrid recounted how the bishop's tomb saved a Magdalene-like figure: "The ever-flowing fountain of mercy flowed, which a certain dissolute woman, thirsting for seven years for good health, was carried there by her nearest blood relations."[874] Thiofrid likened the bishop to the prophet Elijah, who also accomplished miracles involving oil:

> Trusting in the aid of his powerful ampulla,
> Through which the faith of the widow, the vessel, full of flower, flowed.
> At his nod, the flowing oil, earlier having disappeared,
> having been poured out, flowed at intervals into spiral vessels,
> Elijah paid the debts acquired by the mother.[875]

Later in the same poem, Thiofrid compared the oil burning near Willibrord's tomb to the sun that conquered night, thus depicting oil as a force in the cosmic battle between light and darkness: "The oil, hanging in the lamps before the tomb of the father, conquered night / Night was not able to darken the oil..."[876] Then, in what appears to be an allusion the oil running to the edge of Aaron's robe in Psalm 132, Thiofrid claimed Willibrord's oil overflowed the lamp, running to the edge, presummably of the tomb: "The oil bubbled up and soaked the ground, pouring to edge."[877] The flowing oil was a sign, according to Thiofrid, of the former bishop's power and prosperity. Choosing words that denoted both manly strength, fecundity and wealth, Thiofrid presented Willibrord's oil as a manifestation of the saint's endless power and vitality: "There the ever-flowing fountain pours

---

[873] "Nulla id nox interpolare valuit; in die inter missarum solempnia usque ad effusionem excrevit ac efferbuit et excaeptum in ampullulis et datum et missum egrotantibus unctione salubri salutem et incolumitatem mentis et corporis restituit." AASS Nov. III, Dies 7, Col.0476E.

[874] "Iugis ibidem fons emanavit misericordiae, quem sitiens quaedam faemina septenis annis paralysis dissoluta valitudine, illo delata est a propinquis sibi sanguine." AASS Nov. III, Dies 7, Col.0476E.

[875] "Auxilio fisus, cuius virtute lechytus, / Per quem spes viduae manet hydria plena farinae / Ad cuius nutum manans oleum prius haustum / Infusum typicis fluit ad spiricula vasis. / Persolvit meritis Helysei debita matris." AASS Nov. III, Dies 7. See 3 Kings 17: 12-16; 4 Kings 4: 2-6.

[876] "In lychnis oleum pendens patris ante sepulchrum / Noctem devicit, nox id fuscare nequivit." AASS Nov.III, Dies 7, Col. 0494E.

[877] "Ebullivit, humum madefecit margine fusum." AASS Nov.III, Dies 7, Col.0494E.

forth, a rich vein of prosperity / The living fountain, I say, the lively strength (*virtus*) of Willibrord."[878] In Willibrord's miraculous oil, we see again how oil appeared as an affirmation of male bishop's sanctity and authority, akin to that of King David and Nicholas of Myra.

MYRON FROM THE HAGIASMA: DEMETRIUS OF THESSALONIKI

Although some of Europe's most famous myroblytes, like Nicholas and Catherine, lived in the Near East in the Late Antique period, no myroblyte *vitae* appeared in Byzantium prior to the twelfth century. Nicholas' influence as a myroblyte thus appears to have extended eastward in the High Middle Ages, spawning the cults of myroblytes in Greek East as well as the Latin West. Demetrius of Thessaloniki (circa 270 – 306) may be the first Byzantine myroblyte; the earliest accounts of his tomb miraculously flowing with oil, however, date to the High Middle Ages. Like Menas of Egypt, Demetrius was a soldier who converted to Christianity and died a violent death during the Roman persecution of Christians during and following the emperor Diocletian's reign (284-305). Some mystery surrounds Demetrius' early life, including when and where he was born and died. He or his cult may have started in Sirmium, northwest of Thessaloniki, in present-day Serbia.[879] Demetrius belonged to the senatorial class. Once a Christian, he held religious assemblies in the Roman baths, where he was subsequently martyred.[880] Demetrius' biographical dossier consists of two passions, *Passio prima* and *Passio altera*,[881] numerous *Encomia*[882], a collection of *Miracula* composed by Bishop John of Thessaloniki in the seventh century, and a couple of collections of

---

[878] "Manat ibi iugis fons, dives vena salutis / Fons inquam vivus Wilbrordi vivida virtus." AASS Nov.III, Dies 7, Col. 0494F.

[879] Charalambos Bakirtzis, "Le culte de saint Démétrius," in *Akten des XII. Internationalen Kongresses für Christliche Archäölogie, Bonn 1991* (Münster, Germany: Aschendorffsche Verlagsbuchhandlung, 1995), 66n51. See also Walter, *The Warrior Saints in Byzantine Art and Tradition*, 69–70.

[880] On early Christian assemblies taking place in bathhouses, see Chadwick, *The Early Church*.

[881] BHG 497.

[882] For a description of *encomia* genre, see René Aigrain, *L'hagiographie; ses sources, ses méthodes, son histoire* (Mayenne: Bloud & Gay, 1953).

miracula, whose authorship is unknown.[883] The anonymous *miracula* collections may have been composed about seventy years after Bishop John's seventh-century *miracula* collection.[884] These texts likely appeared after the advent of Demetrius' cult and sanctuary at his basilica in Thessalonika, where the faithful gathered around his ciborium, the locus of miracles, including healing miracles.[885]

In the fifth century, Demetrius' devotees may have moved his remains to Thessaloniki, where the saint's cult centered on the basilica, which now contained his tomb.[886] Demetrius's original shrine was a simple martyr's sanctuary. In the fifth century, a larger basilica replaced the simple sanctuary; two centuries later, the basilica underwent renovation. The basilica was built over Roman bathes, which were common in the Thessaloniki region.[887] The basilica's crypt occupied the ruins of the bathes themselves, which had once been at ground level. Ostensibly the site of the crypt was once a nymphaeum, a shrine or temple for pagan nymphs, particularly nymphs associated with springs.[888] Under Christian auspices, the nymphaeum became a hagiasma, a holy spring or well.[889] In addition to the crypt, another prominent feature of Demetrius' basilica was the ciborium, the alleged site of the saint's miracles by at least the late sixth century.[890] The locus of Demetrius' miracles

---

[883] Walter, *The Warrior Saints in Byzantine Art and Tradition*, 70. For the texts, see Paul Lemerle, *Les plus anciens recueils des miracles de Saint Démétrius et la pénétration des Slaves dans les Balkans*, Le Monde byzantin (Paris: Éditions du Centre national de la recherche scientifique, 1978).

[884] Walter, *The Warrior Saints in Byzantine Art and Tradition*, 71. Also see Lemerle, *Les plus anciens recueils des miracles de Saint Démétrius et la pénétration des Slaves dans les Balkans*.

[885] Walter, *The Warrior Saints in Byzantine Art and Tradition*, 67.

[886] Bakirtzis, "Le culte de saint Démétrius"; Charalambos Bakirtzis, "Pilgrimage to Thessaloniki: The Tomb of St. Demetrios," in *Dumbarton Oaks Papers. Number Fifty-Six, 2002*, Dumbarton Oaks Papers, no. 56 (2002) (Washington, D.C: Dumbarton Oaks Research Library and Collection, 2003), 175–92.

[887] Bakirtzis, "Le culte de saint Démétrius," 65.

[888] "(νυμφαῖον), a monumental fountain set against a wall articulated with niches, often decorated with columns and statuary. The *nymphaeum* was adopted from Roman architecture, though its original association with pagan nymphs was lost by the late 4th C., when the term meant no more than a fountain." "Nymphaeum - Oxford Reference," accessed August 31, 2015, http://www.oxfordreference.com/view/10.1093/acref/9780195046526.001.0001/acref-9780195046526-e-3886.

[889] Walter, *The Warrior Saints in Byzantine Art and Tradition*, 2003, 73. See also Alice-Mary Talbot, "Pilgrimage to Healing Shrines: The Evidence of Miracle Accounts," *Dumbarton Oaks Papers* 56 (2002): 153–73; Alice-Mary Talbot, "Constantinople: City of Miraculous Healings," in *Life Is Short, Art Long: The Art of Healing in Byzantium* (Istanbul: Perma Museums Publication, 2015).

[890] See D.I. Pallas, "Le ciborium hexagonal de St. Démétrios de Thessalonique" *Zograf* 10 (1974): 44-58.

appears to have shifted in the High Middle Ages; rather than the ciborium, the cult centered on the hagiasma, in the crypt that had formerly housed the Roman baths.[891] In this place, *myron* flowed.

Charalambos Bakirtzis argued that Demetrius' miraculous liquid did not begin to flow until the eleventh or twelfth century and that the hydraulic apparatus in the basilica's crypt indicates the movement of large quantities of liquid (water), not the slow seepage of a much smaller quantity of oil or myrrh associated with the martyr's relics.[892] Christopher Walker concurs with Bakirtzis, stating that Demetrius' oil did not appear prior to the eleventh century, even though the earliest written account of the flowing oil appears to be John Kaminiates' Chronicle of the sacking of Thessaloniki in 904.[893] The authenticity of the text is questionable, making the earliest account of Demetrius as a myroblyte uncertain.[894] Symeon the Metaphrast, the tenth-century compiler of Greek saints' lives, did not mention miraculous oil in his version of Demetrius' *passio*.[895] In the thirteenth and fourteenth centuries, John of Stauracus, a cleric from Thessaloniki from circa 1250-1300 and Demetrius Chrysoloras (c. 1350-1416), an imperial scribe, both wrote extensively about Demetrius' oil.[896] One synaxary (an account of a saint's life read within the context of the liturgy) described how a great quantity of perfumed oil emanated from the saint himself.

> Every day a perfumed oil flows, which heals those who accept it with faith, particularly on the feast of St Demetrius. That day, in fact, it flows more copiously than others, even from the walls and columns of the church. The people in great numbers wipe it from the walls and put this oil in flasks. This miracle will endure until the end of time. Virtuous priests who

---

[891] Walter, *The Warrior Saints in Byzantine Art and Tradition*, 75.

[892] Bakirtzis, "Le culte de saint Démétrius," 65n46. When Christopher Walker refers to myron that "descended through pipes into basins in the refurbished *hagiasma*" it's not clear if he intends the hydraulic machinery cited by Bakirtzis as the means for transporting water, not oil.

[893] For additional, later account of Demetrius' myron, see Walter, *The Warrior Saints in Byzantine Art and Tradition*, 81n54.

[894] Ibid.

[895] AASS Oct. IV, Dies 8, Col. 0096A-0103D.

[896] AASS Oct. IV, Dies 8, Col.0198A-0209F. Further analysis of Demetrius' miraculous oil is beyond the scope of this study.

have seen this have spoken of it and given witness to it.[897]

Demetrius' oil did not, however, flow forever. When Turks converted Demetrius' basilica into a mosque and stopped up the hagiasma, Demetrius' myron ceased to flow.[898] Demetrius was not the only saint to withhold his oil as a sign of rebellion against injustice; Nicholas similarly ceased to produce oil when one of his successors had been unjustly deposed.

The Thessaloniki crypt, according to Bakirtzis, had little to do with the flow of miraculous oil. Rather, the appearance of Demetrius' oil marked a shift in the character of the saint's cult, from localized, collective veneration to dispersed, individual intercession. Prior to the appearance of oil, the saint's role was primarily as protector of the city from enemies and famines, as was characteristic of many saints of Late Antiquity.[899] After the appearance of oil, Demetrius came to resemble the ascetic saints who humbled themselves to provide succor to widely dispersed individuals in need, suffering from pain or misfortune.[900] Demetrius' oil was perceived as so powerful that it rivaled oil consecrated by ecclesiastical authorities. According to a 1361 text, Demetrius' oil, combined with the oil of another saint, Barbarus, was used in lieu of baptismal chrism.[901] Soldiers anointed their bodies with Demetrius' oil before going into battle and defeating their enemies.[902] The market for Demetrius' oil led to fashioning of *encolpia*, small reliquaries for oil.[903] Christopher Walter has

---

[897] Walter, *The Warrior Saints in Byzantine Art and Tradition*, 81n55.

[898] Ibid., 81. See Franz Miklosich and Joseph Müller, *Acta et Diplomata Graeca Medii Aevi Sacra et Profana* (Athenai: Ch. I. Spanos, 1961), 175; 441.

[899] Christopher Walter notes: "...during these early centuries, the saint's interventions were almost entirely limited to granting favours to citizens of Thessaloniki or to safeguarding the city against marauders." Walter, *The Warrior Saints in Byzantine Art and Tradition*, 67.

[900] Bakirtzis, "Le culte de saint Démétrius," 65–66. Regarding saints of Late Antiquity as patrons of cities, see Brown, *The Cult of the Saints*, TBD.

[901] Walter, *The Warrior Saints in Byzantine Art and Tradition*, 2003, 81n56.

[902] Ibid., 82n57.

[903] See "Un nouveau reliquaire de saint Démétrius" by A Frolow – in *Revue des grecques*, 66, 1953, p.105. Cited in Ibid., 82n57-8.

suggested that Demetrius' *myron* accounts for the saint's universal veneration in Byzantium and Slavic lands, but gives little explanation for why he was not more popular in the Latin West.[904]

Anastasius Bibliothecarius (c. 810 – c. 878), the papal archivist and librarian during the reign of Pope Nicholas I (r. 858-867) and abbot of the Santa Maria in Trastevere monastery, translated Demetrius' *passio* in Rome in circa 876-82.[905] This text, however, makes no mention of oil. If Demetrius had a reputation as a myroblyte in the ninth century, surely Anastasius would have mentioned such a miracle given that he presided over an abbey in a region of Rome that was famed for its miraculously oily fountain.[906] Anastasius' knowledge of Greek allowed him to translate many Byzantine works into Latin for his contemporaries in Rome and elsewhere in the Occident.[907] Anastasius' translation of the martyr's life appears to have political purpose; he dedicated his work to Charles the Bald (823-877), the grandson of Charlemagne (circa 747-814) and son of Louis the Pious (778-840).[908] Anastasius composed and translated in the wake of Charlemagne's coronation as emperor in Rome, a ceremony that included anointing with oil.[909] Based on Anastasius' other writings, Karin Einaudi suggested that the papal librarian saw oil as a clear sign of legitimate authority among the Hebrew kings, Roman emperors and, by extension, Carolingian emperors.[910]

---

[904] Ibid., 67.

[905] Ibid., 68.

[906] See Chapter 8.

[907] Maximus, *Epistula ad Anastasium discipulum: (textus latinus servatus in collectione quae "Collectanea" nuncupatur - CPG 7701)*, trans. Anastasius Bibliothecarius (Turnhout: Brepols Publishers, 2013); Anastasius, *Epistula ad monachos Calaritanos*. CPG 7725, trans. Anastasius Bibliothecarius (Turnhout: Brepols Publishers, 2013); Apocrisiarius Anastasius, *Epistula ad Theodosium Gangrensem*, trans. Anastasius Bibliothecarius. CPG 7733. (Turnhout: Brepols Publishers, 2013); Spudaeus Theodorus and Anastasius Bibliothecarius, *Hypomnesticum*. CPG 7968. (Turnhout: Brepols Publishers, 2013); Germanus, *Il commentario liturgico*, ed. Nilo Borgia, trans. Anastasius Bibliothecarius, Studi liturgici, fasc. 1 (Grottaferrata: s.n., 1912); the Confessor Maximus and Anastasius Bibliothecarius, *Mystagogia: (excerpta)* (Turnhout: Brepols Publishers, 2013); Anastasius Bibliothecarius, *Relatio factae motionis inter dominum Maximum [Confessorem] monachum et socium eius coram principibus in secretario: (textus latinus secundum interpretationem quam fecit Anastasius Bibliothecarius.* CPG 7736. (Turnhout: Brepols Publishers, 2013).

[908] Bollandists, *Bibliotheca hagiographica latina antiquae et mediae aetatis* (Bruxellis: Socii Bollandiani, 1898), 320. BHL 2122. Acta SS Oct. IV, 87-89. See also Jones, *The Saint Nicholas Liturgy and Its Literary Relationships (Ninth to Twelfth Centuries)*, 45.

[909] Karin Einaudi, "'Fons Olei' E Anastasio Bibliotecario," *Rivista dell'Istituto Nazionale d'archeologia e storia dell'arte* 3, no. s.13 (1990): 179–222.

[910] "Il tema dell'olio santo ricorre ripetutamente come il segno della consecrazione imperiale e della legittimazione del potere, quale risuscitazione dell'impero romano in chiave cristiana. Il simbolismo dell'unzione ritorna anche nel famoso parallelo che Anastasio vi istituisce fra Samuele=pontefice, il quale ripudia Saul=imperatore greco, per ungere re

The absence of references to oil in Anastasius' translation of Demetrius life would suggest that, indeed, Demetrius' reputation as a myroblyte was a product of the High Middle Ages. Nevertheless, Anastasius recorded the presence of fragrance and light if not oil: "Truly, as I experienced in Thessalonika, where Demetrius' precious embalmed body emits a fragrance with splendor and shines brightly from miracles, which I made known for him through setting the miracles in order."[911] Given that the papal librarian signed at least one letter with an epithet that made reference to Trastevere's *fons olei,* he would have likely included any stories of a miraculously oozing tomb in Demetrius' *passio.*

THE AMBIGUITY OF OIL

While in the early Middle Ages, the miraculous oil seeping from saint's bodies was predominantly a sign of male ecclesiastical authority and sanctity, in the High Middle Ages, oil assumed an ambivalent character that began to transcended gender binaries. When Catherine of Alexandria's cult began to spread in the eleventh century, the composer of her office drew directly on Nicholas' of Myra's liturgy, firmly establishing the holy virgin's reputation as a myroblyte. Oil that was once primarily emblematic of male secular and ecclesiastical authority became a sign of sanctity among holy women, including the Virgin Mary and Mary Magdalene.

Within the medieval liturgy, the highest concentration of chants about oil and anointing appear on the feast days of women, namely the Virgin Mary, other virgins, Mary Magdalene, and occasionally on feasts commemorating married women.[912] Furthermore, a hymn that infrequently appeared in Nicholas' office raises questions about the polysemous nature of oil for medieval

David=Carlo Magno. L'argomento dell'olio santo, dell'unzione pontificia, sostituisce nel testo di Anastasio qualunque argomentazione di natura politica o giuridica, per restare l'unica prove che legittimava l'esistenza dell'impero franco." Ibid., 216–17.
[911] "Ego vero, sicut expertus sum apud Thessalonicam, ubi preciosum corpus ejus conditum redolet splendore et miraculorum refulget, innotui ei per ordinem." Acta SS, Oct. IV, Col. 0088B.
[912] See Chapters 3 & 9 regarding the association of oil and unguent with women and Marian feasts, which explains in part the connection between the *fons olei* and Marian devotion.

Christians. The hymn *Cujus tumba fert oleum matris* does not correlate oil with ecclesiastical leadership but rather with maternity and giving birth. The full text of the hymn reads: "The one whose tomb bears the oil of the mother olive, which does not know that marble by sweating brought forth what nature did not bring forth [i.e. oil]."[913] The sense of this text is rather confusing. It appears to suggest that the oil from Nicholas' tomb was, strangely enough, not conscious of having overturned the natural order of things by emanating from a substance (marble) that did not naturally produce oil. What the tomb could not accomplish naturally, the saint accomplished supernaturally. The chant suggests that the saint's tomb is like a mother sweating in childbirth. Just as "the mother olive" gives birth to oil (like a mother giving birth to a child), the marble tomb also gives forth oil. Moreover, the use of the future passive participle *sudando,* from the verb *sudare,* which means to sweat or to perspire, anthropomorphizes the tomb, making the "sweating" marble into a woman sweating in labor. This image of oil seeping from the tomb like sweat from the human body resonates with the depiction of oil in Nicholas' other chants, where the verb *sudare* also describes the emission of oil used to cure the sick and wounded.[914] While the mother olive births olive oil, the marble tomb births holy oil. At the risk of pushing the parallel too far, one might ask: is the saint within the tomb like a child in the womb?[915] Is the oil that proceeds from the tomb like the child that is born of a mother? Perhaps the chant points ever so vaguely to the birth of the Messiah: the Virgin Mary, as the paradigmatic mother, gave birth to the Anointed One.[916] One cannot help but wonder if in the mind of the liturgist who composed this chant, the marble tomb was a symbol for the Church itself, like Jacob's anointed stone which was widely interpreted as a symbol for *mater ecclesia.* The Church gives

---

[913] "Cujus tumba fert oleum matris olivae nescium quod natura non protulit sudando marmor parturit." Aachen, Aix-la-Chapelle, Domarchiv, G 20, fol.203r. See Can 830118c.

[914] See notes above for *Ex ejus tumbae,* Can 006679 and Can 002744.

[915] The comparison could just as easily correlate the saint within the tomb to the pit within the olive.

[916] I will further explore this parallel in Part Three, with respect to Santa Maria in Trastevere and the oil imagery within the church, as the site of the *fons olei.*

birth to Christians, as Mary gave birth to Christ and as Santa Maria in Trastevere gave forth a stream
of flowing oil.

A Virgin's Oil: Catherine of Alexandria

In the High Middle Ages, as the cult of Nicholas of Myra spawned the cults of a number of
other male myroblytes, the cult of a prominent female myroblyte also emerged: Catherine of
Alexandria, who became one of the most popular saints in Europe.[917] The spread of Catherine's cult
and her fame as a myroblyte are key to understanding the widespread proliferation of female
myroblytes in the Later Middle Ages. An examination of the biographical dossier and office chants
of Catherine reveals the peculiar nature of oil as a symbol for the sanctity of both men and women
in the High Middle Ages. The likeness between the miracles associated with Catherine and Nicholas
demonstrates the ambivalent potential of oil to convey the holy power of male and female figures
alike. While scholars have partially explored the connection between Nicholas and Catherine's
reputations as myroblytes, this analysis argues that in the eleventh century, oil became a gender-
neutral miracle, which then led to a proliferation of female myroblytes. In the life and office of
Nicholas of Myra, oil revealed the power of the bishop to not only cure the sick, but also to exert his
authority over ecclesiastical maters, including successors to his episcopal throne. Although Catherine
did not intervened in matters relating to the church hierarchy, she helped bring peace during a
political conflict by strengthening a weak duke. While Catherine performed many healing miracles
commonly associated with male myroblytes, such as curing physical and mental illnesses, she also

---

[917] For recent studies of Catherine's cult, see Christine Walsh, *The Cult of St Katherine of Alexandria in Early Medieval Europe*,
Church, Faith and Culture in the Medieval West (Aldershot, Hampshire ; Burlington, Vt: Ashgate, 2007); Jacqueline
Jenkins and Katherine J. Lewis, eds., *St. Katherine of Alexandria: Texts and Contexts in Western Medieval Europe*, Medieval
Women 8 (Turnhout, Belgium: Brepols, 2003); Katherine J. Lewis, *The Cult of St Katherine of Alexandria in Late Medieval
England* (Woodbridge, Suffolk: Boydell, 2000); Anne Simon, *The Cult of Saint Katherine of Alexandria in Late-Medieval
Nuremberg: Saint and the City* (Burlington: Ashgate, 2012).

accomplished miracles of a peculiarly feminine in nature, including miracles relating to childbirth, infertility, and a quintessential feminine ailment: the chronic flow of blood.

Catherine was one of the earliest virgin-martyrs in the Christian tradition. According to legend, she was famed for her beauty, nobility and erudition. She distained the idea of marrying a mortal man, preferring instead to marry Christ through martyrdom. When the Roman Emperor Maxentius held a pagan festival in Alexandria, Catherine publically denounced pagan worship, drawing on her erudition and skills as an orator. Catherine used a full arsenal of rhetorical weapons to persuade the Emperor Maxentius of the error of his ways: "Standing at the temple entrance, she argued at length with the emperor by syllogistic reasoning as well as by allegory and metaphor, logical and mystical inference."[918] When Maxentius was unable to defend himself against Catherine's more powerful arguments regarding the single Omnipotent Creator, he invited the empire's fifty wisest philosophers, "masters of logic and rhetoric" to debate her.[919] Rather than suffering defeat, Catherine succeeded in converting the pagan philosophers and further inflaming the ire of the Emperor Maxentius, who ordered her torture and execution.

When the executioner chopped off the young virgin's head, milk gushed out instead of blood. In *The Golden Legend* (c.1260), Jacob de Voragine claimed that centuries later oil continued to flow from Catherine's bones: "When the saint had been beheaded, milk flowed from her body instead of blood, and angels took up the body and carried it from that place a twenty-days' journey to Mount Sinai, where they gave it honorable burial. (An oil still issues continuously from her bones and mends the limbs of all who are weak.)"[920] De Voragine told of a pious monk who traveled from Rouen, France to Mount Sinai, spent seven years in faithful service to the virgin and received a relic as a reward: "He prayed insistently that he might be worthy to have a relic from her body, and

---

[918] Jacobus de Voragine, *The Golden Legend: Readings on the Saints*, trans. William Granger Ryan (Princeton: Princeton University Press, 2012), 721.
[919] Ibid., 722.
[920] Ibid., 725.

suddenly one of the fingers broke off from her hand. The monk joyfully accepted God's gift and carried it back to his monastery."[921] According to eleventh-century sources, however, a Greek monk named Simeon, who hailed from Mount Sinai, transport Catherine's relics to Rouen in Normandy.[922]

Owing to her extraordinary intellect and powers as an orator, Catherine does not fit the mold of most virgin-martyrs. Jacqueline Jenkins and Katherine J. Lewis observed that Catherine's miracles prior to her execution had little to do with traditionally "female" attributes or her female body; the Emperor Maxentius ordered that his own wife's breasts be torn off rather than Catherine's.[923] Yet, the appearance of milk rather than blood issuing from her neck was distinctly feminine, given that lactation, the natural flow of milk from the body, is a phenomenon found only among females. The *Maria lactans* depictions of Mary nursing the baby Jesus became a familiar image in Christian iconography in the Latin West during the High Middle Ages.[924] Mary's milk not only nourished Jesus but also, perhaps most famously, Bernard of Clairvaux (1090-1153), the renowned preacher whose lips the Blessed Virgin squirted with milk.

Although milk from Mary's breasts nourished a male preacher, milk also flowed from the body of a woman who herself possessed the gift of oratory. While Catherine's intellectual and rhetorical powers set her apart from other female saints, she was not the only woman known for her preaching abilities. Mary Magdalene, known as the *apostolorum apostola,* was likewise renowned for preaching and sometimes appeared along Catherine in frescos.[925] Skill at preaching was not, however, the only common bond uniting these two female saints. Both women were associated with oil, another symbol for flowing speech and Christ's teachings. In his *Moralia in Job,* Gregory the Great claimed that Christ's teachings were like "rivers of oil" which "flow quickly and anoint."[926]

---

[921] Ibid.
[922] Walsh, *The Cult of St Katherine of Alexandria in Early Medieval Europe,* 73.
[923] Jenkins and Lewis, *St. Katherine of Alexandria,* 10.
[924] See Chapter 8.
[925] Walsh, *The Cult of St Katherine of Alexandria in Early Medieval Europe,* 20.
[926] See Chapter 2.

The Gospels themselves, according to Gregory, were rivers of oil that flowed from the mouths of the apostles. Thus both Catherine and Mary Magdalene possessed verbal capacities often associated with men and, perhaps not coincidentally, were likewise both sources of oil. In the case of Catherine of Alexandria, the oil flowed from her bones long after she had ceased to speak.

Just when and where Catherine's bones began to ooze is unclear.[927] Christine Walsh has argued that Catherine may have acquired a reputation as a myroblyte when her shrine was established on Mount Sinai, in proximity to Mena's shrine in Abu Mina, on the north coast of what is now Egypt.[928] One of the extant *Menas ampullae,* which could date to the late sixth or seventh century, bears an image of a feminine (if not female) figure, which some scholars have argued is Catherine herself.[929] This single piece of evidence alone, however, does not demonstrate Catherine was reputed to be myroblyte in the early medieval period. Although Catherine's *passio* was first written in Greek, the earliest extant manuscript with this text is a Latin manuscript dating to circa 800-840.[930] Greek manuscripts dating from the tenth century onward are numerous.

The earliest text that, to my knowledge, imputed miraculous oil to Catherine appeared prior to the translation of Nicholas of Myra's relics from Myra to Bari in 1087. Alfanus, Archbishop of Salerno (1058-85), who had been a monk at Montecassino, composed three odes to Catherine, each of which mention the healing liquid that seeped from her tomb. While the archbishop may have first encountered Catherine's cult in Constantinople, the question remains as to when and where he first heard of her tomb producing miraculous oil.[931] Alfanus' first hymn spoke of the angels transporting

---

[927] I have not yet examined the earliest manuscript witnesses of Catherine's cult (some of which are in Greek) to determine whether or not they contain oil miracles.

[928] See Appendix A in Walsh, *The Cult of St Katherine of Alexandria in Early Medieval Europe,* 24. Also, A. P. Orbán, ed., *Vitae Sanctae Katharinae,* Corpus Christianorum 119–119A (Turnholti: Brepols, 1992).

[929] Walsh, *The Cult of St Katherine of Alexandria in Early Medieval Europe,* 23–24.

[930] Ibid., 162–68.

[931] Paul Oldfield, *Sanctity and Pilgrimage in Medieval Southern Italy, 1000-1200* (New York, NY: Cambridge University Press, 2014), 115–16.

Catherine's body to Mount Sinai where, "the body poured forth healing drops."[932] The second hymn

likewise concluded with praise to the miraculous oil that continued to pour from Catherine's body

long after her decapitation: "The wound pours forth a white liquid. / The virgin's bones buried by a

heavenly host / give out a healing balm."[933] The third hymn elaborated on the curative powers of

Catherine's oil, which seeped from her body on Mount Sinai: "The right hands of those who dwell

in heaven place / the body on a mountain peak, from which the liquid flows, / giving back strong

limbs to the weak."[934] These hymns to Catherine present a curious combination of saintly

characteristics and supernatural powers: maidenly virtue, intellectual prowess, and miraculous liquids

(milk and oil). Just as the Blessed Virgin Mary was paradoxically a virgin mother, Catherine was a

maiden who produced milk, a phenomenon usually reserved for new mothers. If prior to the spread

of Catherine's cult, producing oil had been solely a male attribute, oil flowing from a woman's body

could have struck Christians as yet another wondrous paradox.

Although Catherine's primary relics were scarce, in both the Latin West and Greek East her

cult burgeoned, perhaps on account of the appearance of a replenishing sacred commodity: holy oil.

In the early eleventh century, Catherine's primary relics consisted of only three small bones, but in

Sinai and Rouen, the virgin provided plentiful oil, which the faithful stored in small phials.[935] In

explaining why Catherine's cult grew and became a universally celebrated feast day within the Latin

West, Christine Walsh overlooked the potential influence of oil as a highly desirable, moveable and

replenishing sacred commodity.[936] Although a local nobleman had established the Holy Trinity

monastery of Rouen with a sizable endowment, revenue from pilgrims visiting a saint's shrine

---

[932] Alfanus, Archbishop of Salerno, "Three Odes to St. Katherine," in *The Cult of St Katherine of Alexandria in Early Medieval Europe*, trans. Christine Walsh, Church, Faith and Culture in the Medieval West (Aldershot, Hampshire ; Burlington, Vt: Ashgate, 2007), 169.
[933] Ibid., 170.
[934] Ibid., 171.
[935] Ibid., 5.
[936] Ibid.

became necessary for economic sustainability.[937] According to Walsh, since no local saint was associated with the monastery, Catherine was a viable patron; she hailed from a geographically remote yet desirable place and her cult had not yet taken root in the Latin West.[938] Catherine's reputation for healing the sick and the monastery's immediate need for an income-generating saint partially explain the proliferation of the cult of a Byzantine saint in northern France. The presence of Catherine's relics at Holy Trinity was key to its growth and prosperity; the oil seeping from Catherine's relics had the power to attract pilgrims in need of succor.

The fraternal exchange of legends between Isembert and Ainard, German monks who migrated from Southern Germany, where Reginald of Eichstätt had composed the Office of Nicholas of Myra, to Rouen, France, appears to have amplified Catherine's fame for producing miraculous liquid.[939] Isembert, as discussed above, had adapted Nicholas' office for his community in St. Ouen-de-Rouen; when he became the first abbot of Holy Trinity, he brought with him the legends of Nicholas' miraculously oozing tomb. During Isembert's time as abbot of Holy Trinity, Catherine's relics purportedly produced oil to great effect. An account of the miracles accomplished by Catherine during Isembert's abbacy, testified to the virgin's power to heal the sick with her oil:

> So after divine grace directed to us the remains of the Blessed Catherine this place never
> lacked for signs of miracles, even for a short time. Here, the blind recovered sight, the deaf
> hearing, the lame movement, paralytics were cured and others burdened with infirmities

---

[937] Walsh, *The Cult of St Katherine of Alexandria in Early Medieval Europe*, 75.

[938] Ibid.

[939] Walsh claimed that Isembert himself was the author of Nicholas' Office without providing evidence and without addressing the argument set forth, first in Hohler and then Jones. She references Jones's earlier work (1963) but not his subsequent book (1978) that included a revised thesis, published after Hohler's substantive critique (1967). See Ibid., 75; Christopher Hohler, "The Proper Office of St. Nicholas and Related Matters with Reference to a Recent Book.," *Medium Ævum* 36 (1967): 40–48; Charles Williams Jones, *Saint Nicholas of Myra, Bari, and Manhattan: Biography of a Legend* (Chicago: University of Chicago Press, 1978); Charles Williams Jones, *The Saint Nicholas Liturgy and Its Literary Relationships (Ninth to Twelfth Centuries)* (Berkeley: University of California Press, 1963).

were returned to health…Almost the whole of Neustria rejoices and exults, being suffused with the oil of so great a virgin…[940]

In a dream, the Abbot Isembert was instructed to anoint himself with Catherine's oil in order to cure himself of a toothache: "He, trusting in the vision, when day broke, asked for some of the precious treasure to be brought to him by the sacristan of the church. And when he had been anointed with the holy liquid, he took a draught of it, and immediately his pain was put to flight, and so he marvellously proved the merit of the blessed martyr by this one test of her virtues in himself."[941] The abbot was not the only individual miraculously cured by Catherine's oil. Her *miracula* told of how holy oil cured many members of the laity, who suffered from much graver illnesses than a toothache: a cancerous tumor, an ulcer, tremors, blindness, and paralysis.[942] A woman suffering from "an excessive flow of blood" drank Catherine's "health-giving oil" and was immediately cured: "at the command of the healing liquid, she was freed from her flow of blood."[943] Curiously enough, the narrator noted that the woman suffering from hemorrhaging was "joined in legal marriage" and that her husband was seeking to divorce her on account on her ailment. Such a story would have naturally brought to mind the biblical pericope in which Jesus healed a woman who had bled for twelve years.[944] In the Gospel narrative, Jesus' "power" (*virtus*) leaves him when the hemorrhaging woman touches his robe. Catherine's oil was said to likewise possess a divine power.

Catherine's oil not only had the power to remove physical ailments, but to restore mental health. When a young man "lost his mind," being anointed with Catherine's oil restored his sanity.[945] A baker, terrorized by demonic visions, was ordered to lie down near an altar displaying Catherine's

---

[940] Anonymous, "The Miracles of St. Katherine: A Translation of BM, Rouen, MS U.22. Fols 112v-115v," in *The Cult of St Katherine of Alexandria in Early Medieval Europe*, trans. Christine Walsh, Church, Faith and Culture in the Medieval West (Aldershot, Hampshire ; Burlington, Vt: Ashgate, 2007), 173.

[941] Ibid., 174.

[942] Ibid., 174, 177, 179.

[943] Ibid., 181.

[944] Mark 5:25-34; Matt 9:20-22; Luke 8:43-48.

[945] Anonymous, "The Miracles of St. Katherine: A Translation of BM, Rouen, MS U.22. Fols 112v-115v," 178.

relics. While meditating on an image of Catherine as a "girl of still tender age," which was painted on

the reliquary box, the baker had another vision: "When he concentrated more intensely on her, she

seemed to administer to him, with little fingers extended, the oil that he was to take and to tell him

in a sweet and cheerful voice not to be afraid."[946] The baker was soon anointed with the "life-giving

oil" and immediately "returned to his senses cured" and "lived out the rest of his life in happiness

and good health."[947] Another lunatic, described as a "madman" who was raving during "the waning

of the moon" regained his senses after drinking "the oil of the blessed virgin."[948]

Catherine's relics not only had the power to bring peace and sanity to individuals. The

miracula concluded by recounting how a procession of the relics brought peace to a warring realm,

drawing a symbolic parallel between a tormented human being and the body politic, which was also

in need of peace and succor. Normandy was "raging one part against another," like a madman, on

account, apparently, of the duke who needed to "regain his strength."[949] The weak ruler (and by

extension his realm) was akin to a mentally unstable man. Given that Catherine's miraculous oil

restored strength and health to those ailing in body and spirit, we see how the presence of her relics

could similarly strengthen political leaders, as chrism anointed and strengthened bishops and kings.

By the late eleventh or early twelfth century, the Holy Trinity monastery came to be known as

Sainte-Catherine-du-Mont-de-Rouen. The monastery had skillfully aligned itself with a mighty

patroness who was capable of succoring the sick in mind and body as well as strengthening the

politically powerless with her holy oil. Instead of relying on oil flowing from the tomb of a bishop,

the community in Rouen believed in a woman's capacity to produce holy oil.

An examination of Catherine's office reveals how liturgists adapted the legend of Catherine's

miraculous oil to the office of a virgin. As noted above, Isembert's fellow monk Ainard composed

---

[946] Ibid.
[947] Ibid.
[948] Ibid., 181.
[949] Ibid.

Catherine's office, which no longer exists. Later versions of her office, however, were replete with oil imagery, which may have been present in her original office. The 1217 account of the zealous pilgrim lowering himself into Catherine's tomb on Mount Sinai emphasized the great quantity of oil dripping from the body of the virgin. The chants of Catherine's office also feature her miraculous oil, which was said to flow from the body of the virgin and possess the power to cure the sick. Since in some manuscripts, chants from Nicholas' office also appeared on Catherine's feast day, we can see how oil was a malleable miracle that characterized male and female sanctity alike. A fourteenth-century manuscript containing Catherine's office includes the antiphon *Ex ejus tumbae*, which more commonly appears in the Office of Nicholas. In CH-E 611, a monastic antiphoner from Einsiedeln, Switzerland, includes *Ex ejus tumbae* as an antiphon in the third nocturn of matins, proceeded by *O Christi pietas* and *Ave Virgo speciosa*.[950] Directly following *Ex ejus tumbae*, chants appear that describe how liquids other than oil flowed from Catherine's body. The chant *Percussa gladio* refers to Catherine's bones spilling milk instead of blood.[951]

The early thirteenth-century compendium of liturgical material from Worcester (MS F.160), which included a chant invoking the "virgin of virgins" on Nicholas' feast day, also includes the chant listed as *Unguentum*, an antiphon for second vespers on Catherine's feast day.[952] This chant commonly appeared for the feast *Commune Virginum*, the Common of Several Virgins. The chant text draws on a line of text from Song of Songs, in which the bride asks her beloved to kiss her, compliments him on his fragrant oil, and compares his name to precious unguent: "Let him kiss me with the kisses of his mouth! For your love[953] is better than wine, your anointing oils are fragrant,

---

[950] Einsiedeln CH-E 611, fol.249r. Debra Lacoste (Project Manager and Principal Researcher) and Jan Koláček (Web Developer), "Cantus Database: Inventories of Chant Sources | CANTUS Database," accessed July 31, 2015, http://cantus.uwaterloo.ca/.
[951] "Percussa gladio dat lac pro sanguine collo quam manus angelica sepelivit vertice Sina." Can 601783.
[952] Worcester GB-WO F.160, fol.270r. Can 005273.
[953] In the Vulgate, *ubera* = literally, breasts.

your name is perfume [*unguentum*] poured out; therefore the maidens love you."[954] The chant sung on

Catherine's feast day and the *Commune Virginum*, included only the mention of the man's name being

like unguent: "Your name is perfume [unguentum] poured out; therefore the maidens love you."[955]

In this chant, we see how devotion to a saint (symbolized by the spouse), whether male or female,

was attributed to the saint's flowing oil. Although medieval exegetes widely interpreted the

bridegroom of the Song of Songs to be Christ, we see how the inclusion of such a chant on a

myroblyte's feast day suggests the parallel between the myroblyte and Christ as the anointed ones.

Even women, like Catherine, were akin to Christ, the Anointed One who healed the sick and

redeemed humanity.

Other chants sung for Catherine's office suggest a parallel between virginal purity and

physical as well as spiritual health. Since in the medieval period, physical illness was sometimes

explained as the result of sin, it's only fitting that the oil of a virgin had the power to heal an

assortment of physical ailments. A responsory verse for Matins on Catherine's feast day emphasized

how oil flowed from the virginal body of the saint: "A salubrious stream of oil flows from virginal

members."[956] A responsory attributes the healing power of Catherine's oil to Christ, who was

conceived without sin and who worked through the virgin's holy body to heal: "O goodness of

Christ, O strength and power of the virgin from whose limbs a sacred stream of liquid flows,

whence the faith pours the gift of health on the sick."[957] Another Matins Antiphon for the second or

third Nocturn likewise emphasized the virginal and sacred nature of Catherine's body as the source

of healing oil: "From the virgin's oil, which flows from the sacred body, comes a certain cure, and

---

[954] "Osculetur me osculo oris sui; quia meliora sunt ubera tua vino, fragrantia unguentis optimis. Oleum effusum nomen tuum; idea adolescentulae dilexerunt te." Cant. 1:1-2. Translation from the NSRV.

[955] "Unguentum effusum nomen tuum ideo adolescentulae dilexerunt te nimis." Can 005273.

[956] "Membris virgineis olei fluit unda salubris." Ibid., Can 601783a. 33 manuscripts in the CANTUS database contain the feast of Catherine. Of those 33 MSS, 20 contain this chant.

[957] "O Christi pietas o virtus atque potestas virginis ex membris sacri fluit unda liquoris unde fides aegris infundit dona salutis." Can 601551.

every kind of sickness is driven away."[958] An antiphon from Lauds emphasized the divine (i.e. non-material) origin of Catherine's oil, stating that God, though in heaven, worked through Catherine's body to heal faithful Christians: "Blessed Lord king of heaven, who through the merits of the blessed virgin Catherine, offers a healing cure for the weak who are happily anointed with oil of her own body."[959] The power imputed to Catherine as a myroblyte reveals how medieval Christians perceived the presence of a non-corporeal, invisible God who manifested through the bodies of male and female saints alike. The body of the virgin became, in a sense, the instrument through which God incarnated, and cured the world of sin and illness. Oil from Catherine's own body possessed the divine presence that was necessary to remedy the material world, including human bodies.

In his *Dialogue of Miracles*, Caesarius of Heisterbach (1180-1240) included a discussion of Catherine's miraculous oil within a larger discussion of virginity.[960] In the dialogue, a novice mentioned to a monk that Catherine's bones endlessly produced oil, to which the monk replied that the oil was a sign of Catherine's virtues.[961] The monk later said that a great abundance of oil filled Catherine tomb and that a drop of her oil resided in their very own monastery. Although Catherine's tomb lay a great distance from rural Westphalia, as her fame increased and her primary relics remained few, her oil was capable of multiplying and, since the oil was portable, her cult could also spread. Furthermore, in his account of the life and miracles of Elizabeth of Thuringia (1207-1231), Caesarius bolstered his argument for Elizabeth's sanctity by explaining that in producing miraculous oil, she joined the ranks of three other famous myroblytes from the east, including Demetrius of Thessaloniki, Nicholas of Myra and Catherine of Alexandria: "No one doubts that oil flows from

---

[958] "Virginis ex oleo quod manat corpore sancto certa medela datur morbi genus omne fugatur." Can 205244.

[959] "Benedictus dominus rex caelestis qui per merita beatae Catharinae virginis medelam languidis praestat sanitatis ipsius corporis oleo feliciter perunctis." Can 200662.

[960] Walsh, *The Cult of St Katherine of Alexandria in Early Medieval Europe*, 86–87.

[961] Christine Walsh, *The Cult of St Katherine of Alexandria in Early Medieval Europe* (Aldershot, England; Burlington, VT: Ashgate, 2007), 87.

the tombs and bones of Saint Catherine, virgin and martyr."[962] In the imagination of Caesarius at least, Catherine served as the female prototype for later female myroblytes. Although Catherine of Alexandria set the precedent for subsequent female myroblytes, their numbers did not increase dramatically until after 1200.

WALBURGA, THE VIRGIN OF EICHSTÄTT

In the eleventh century, Walburga (c. 710-779), the Abbess of the Heidenheim monastery in Bavaria acquired a reputation for an oozing tomb, with one author even comparing her curative water to Nicholas' oil. In 720, following the lead of the Anglo-Saxon missionary Boniface (d. 754/5), a family of West Saxons left England for continental Europe, as missionaries and pilgrims. King Richard (d.722), his sons Willibald (d.787) and Wunebald (d.761), as well as his daughter Walburga (c. 710-779) were destined for southern Bavaria, where they would establish two monasteries in the wilderness. In 740 Willibald founded a monastery in Eichstätt, shortly after being ordained by Boniface. In 752, Wunebald established a neighboring monastery in Heidenheim, where he remained until his death in 761. After her brother's death, Walburga brought nuns to Heidenheim and presided over the double monastery until her own death in 779.[963] Wunebald's relics were translated to Eichstätt in 776, followed by Walburga's relics in the 893, after which her relics were circulated elsewhere in the Latin West as her cult grew.

According to Andeas Bauch, by the late Carolingian period, Walburga's tomb, with its oil lamps, was a destination for pilgrims.[964] Wolfhard von Herrieden (d. circa 902) composed Walburga's *miracula* (BHL 8765) in 895 but never mentioned oil flowing from the abbess' tomb,

---

[962] "De sepulchro etiam et ossibus sancte Katherine virginis et martiris oleum emanare nemo dubitat." Caesarius, *Die Wundergeschichte des Caesarius von Heisterbach Bd. 3*, ed. Alfons Hilka (Bonn: Hanstein, 1937), 388. For further discussion of Elizabeth of Thuringia, see Chapter 7.

[963] David Parsons, "Some Churches of the Anglo-Saxon Missionaries in Southern Germany: A Review of the Evidence.," *Early Medieval Europe* 8, no. 1 (1999): 36.

[964] Andreas Bauch, *Quellen zur Geschichte der Diözese Eichstätt: Ein bayerisches Mirakelbuch aus der Karolingerzeit : die Monheimer Walpurgis-Wunder des Priesters Wolfhard* (Pustet, 1979), 118.

despite his repeated use of the adjective *liquidus*, meaning "clear, pure, smooth, without interruption."[965] Adelbold, Bishop of Utrecht (c.970-1026), who composed Walburga's *vita* (BHL 8766) in the late tenth or early eleventh century, also did not mention miraculous oil flowing from the abbess' tomb, nor did the eleventh-century anonymous author(s) of some letters (BHL 8767) written in Tiel, a town southeast of Utrecht.[966] Stefan Weinfurther, however, cites an anonymous text from 1075/1078, which testifies to Walburga's curative water and compares the liquid to the oil flowing from Nicholas' tomb:

> When the body of our Holy Mother Walburga...was elevated during the reign of Bishop Erchanbald, the sacrosanct remains were saturated with so much moisture that the moisture could almost be squeezed out of the relics. Since then, from the sarcophagus there flows incessantly until today, that which her venerable relicts contain, something like living water, like the oil from the tomb of Saint Nicholas, which heals the sick with a miraculous power.[967]

The author of this account of Walburga's miraculous liquid anticipated his male readers' surprise at such a miracle and commented on the fact that while the bodies of Willibald and Wunebald remained untouched, the body of their sister Walburga was a locus of devotion. Medibard, an eleventh or twelfth century poet, who might have composed texts during the reign of Pope Eugene III (r. 1145-53), mentioned liquid flowing from Walburga's tomb (BHL 8770). The bard, however, referred to the liquid as water: "From her sacred tomb thus water flows, by which any of the

---

[965] AASS Feb.III, Dies 25: "Idem namque sanus & valens in ministerio eiusdem vsque hodie deseruit Ecclesiæ, vt cunctis liquido demonstretur, qualis cuiusue meriti apud Deum hæc sancta sit Virgo, quæ huiusmodi & similia impetrare meretur." Col.0526D; "...Virginem quoque, cuius in loco hoc suffragia requisiui, cum omnibus Sanctis testem adhibeo, me non quidquam verisimile, aut falsa prodere ratione, verum vt contigit, liquidissimo narrare sermone..." Col.0531C; "Verum numquam ad eamdem cellam peruenire potuisse, vt cunctis liquido clareat, quantum in se iram Domini prouocasset..."Col.0532B; "ab ara liquidissimi pectoris mitterent polo..." Col.0533A etc. See also Bauch, *Quellen zur Geschichte der Diözese Eichstätt.*

[966] In the eleventh century, however, Thiofrid of Echternach claimed miraculous oil flowed from the tomb of his predecessor, Willibrord, Bishop of Utrecht.

[967] English translation based on German translation of Latin. See Stefan Weinfurter, "'Überall Unsere Heiligste Mutter Walburga': Entstehung, Wirkkraft Und Mythos Eines Europäischen Heiligenkults," in *Female Vita Religiosa between Late Antiquity and the High Middle Ages: Structures, Developments and Spatial Contexts.* eds., Gert Melville and Anne Müller, Vita Regularis: Ordnungen Und Deutungen Religiosen Lebens Im Mittelalter, 47 (Münster: LIT Verlag, 2011), 187.

anointed sick attain the effect of the swift medicine through the merits of the Holy Mother."[968] Had

Medibard referred to the liquid as oil, one might conclude he drew directly from the office of

Nicholas, which was evidently known in Bavaria in the late eleventh century. Andreas Bauch noted

that Walburg's oil (not water) attained widespread notoriety as a remedy for illness in the eleventh

century.[969] Nevertheless, the first author (to my knowledge) to explicitly identify the liquid seeping

from Walburga's tomb as oil was Philipp von Rathsamhausen, bishop of Eichstätt (r. 1306-1322).

After the rise of the cults of Elizabeth of Thuringia and Hedwig of Silesia in Germania in the

thirteenth century, Philipp von Rathsamhausen (1240/45-1322), the Bishop of Eichstätt, saturated

Walburga's *vita* (BHL 8771) with oil, claiming that oil rather than water flowed from the abbess'

tomb.[970] Rathsamhausen was not the last cleric to reach rapturous heights in discussing Walburga's

holy oil. In 1620, the German Jesuit Jacob Gretser (1562-1625) published a monumental work

entitled *Fons olei Walpurgini apud Eystettenses explicatus atque defensus.*[971] Thus, by the early seventeenth

century, Santa Maria in Trastevere was not the only feminine figure famed for her *fons olei.*

Rathsamhausen was a former Cistercian monk who entered the Cistercian monastery of

Pairis in Alsace in 1260 and later studied theology in Paris. In 1301 he was elected abbot of Pairis

and in 1306 Pope Clement V appointed Rathsamhausen as Bishop of Eichstätt, where he remained

until his death in 1322.[972] As bishop, Rathsamhausen effusively praised the power of Walburga's

---

[968] "Nam ex eius sacra tumba / Aqua manat igitur, Qua infirmi quoque uncti / Medicinae celeris / Per merita sanctae Matris / Effectum consequuntur." AASS Feb.III, Dies 25, Col. 0551A.

[969] Bauch, *Quellen zur Geschichte der Diözese Eichstätt*, 220–22, 248, 66. According to Bauch, miraculous oil from lamps near the tombs of saints first appeared in Tours. Ibid., 67n17.

[970] For a discussion of the cults of Elizabeth of Thuringia and Hedwig of Silesia, see Chapter 7.

[971] Jakob Gretser, *Fons olei Walpurgini apud Eystettenses explicatus atque defensus. A Jacobo Gretsero Societatis Jesu theologo. ... Accessit appendix recentium quorundam miraculorum quae Deus per oleum S. Vvalpurgis patravit* (ex typographeo Ederiano, apud Elisabetham Angermariam, Viduam, 1620).

[972] Bayerische Akademie der Wissenschaften, "Philip von Rathsamhausen in Repertorium 'Geschichtsquellen Des Deutschen Mittelalters,'" accessed August 24, 2016, http://www.geschichtsquellen.de/repPers_100958427.html. See also Stefan Weinfurter, *Die Geschichte der Eichstätter Bischöfe des Anonymus Haserensis: Edition-Übersetzung-Kommentar* (Regensburg: F. Pustet, 1987).

miraculous oil to cure the sick, even going so far as to drink the woman's holy oil himself.[973]

Naturally, the oil was swift in working its miraculous cure. In his account of Willibald's life,

Rathsamhausen described in detail the manner in which the oil flowed from Walburga's tomb and

how one was to collect it; he claimed that if the place where one collected the oil was not clean or if

the vessel used to collect the oil was dirty, the said vessel would froth, boil over, or shake

feverishly.[974] Although Walburga's oil had the power to heal physical ailments, instead of driving

away moral sins, sins caused the oil to evaporate. If someone carried the oil off to a place where

people committed sins, the oil disappeared.[975]

Walburga's oil did not simply react to sins committed by private individuals, but to political

injustices as well. In a scene reminiscent of Nicholas' office, in which Nicholas stopped the flow of

oil from his tomb in response to the unjust deposing of his successor, Rathsamhausen described

how Walburga's oil ceased to flow when the city and Diocese of Eichstätt was placed under

interdict.[976] The similar behavior of Nicholas' and Walburga's oil was in no way coincidental.

---

[973] "Hanc etiam gratiam curationis ipsi experti sumus. Nam graui infirmitate aegrotantes ad excidium vitae peruenimus; et rememorantes gratiam, quam B. Walpurga suis dilectoribus indesinenter ostendit, praecepimus de oleo sacro sanctae suae emanationis nobis copiosius afferri, et desiderabili haustu philiam plenam ebibimus, orantes in haec verba. *B, Walpurgis Virgo, ob reuerentiam B. Willibaldi fratris tui dilectissimi, cuius successor indignus sum ego Philippus peccator; interpella pro me ad Dominum, pro condonatione peccatorum meorum, et ut respirem à grauamine huius agritudinis, ad laudem Dei omnipotentis, et intemeratae matris eius Virginis Mariae.* Vt quid plura? eadem die creticauimus; et breui pòst in tempore, sanitati omnimodè restituti sumus." Jakob Gretser, *Philippi Ecclesiæ Eystettensis XXXIX. Episcopi: De eiusdem ecclesiæ diuis tutelaribus. S. Ricardo, S. Willibaldo, S. Wunibaldo, S. Walpurga. Commentarius nunc primum evulgatus; Unâ cum duobus Observationum libris & catalogo Historico, omnium Episcoporum Eystettensium* (Ex Typographia Ederiana, apud Elisabetham Angermariam, 1617), 113–14.

[974] "Hoc quoque sciendum, quod hora celebratinis Missarum, cùm Sacramentum corporis et sanguinis Iesu Christi in altari conficitur, in quo recondita est, frequentius, nec non vberius oleum de sacro corpore eius distillat; vnde haec hora pro receptione eiusdem olei diligentissime obseruatur: et si philiae, in quibus sacrum oleum recipiendum est non directè et perpendiculariter destillationi supponantur, guttae eiusdem olei sibi cohaerent, dependentes ad modum botri, vel saui mellis, nequam in alium locum decidentes. Sed postquam negligentia corrigitur, et vasa, in quibus mundè sacrum oleum recipi debet, destillatini aptantur, eisdem fine omni cooperatione illabitur; per quod apertè monstratur, vt in vasa munda recipi debeat; quia ab immundis locis vel vasis omnino se praeferuat." Ibid., 114–15.

[975] "Et saepe compertum est, quod receptum etiam in vase mundo, si immundè vel irreuerenter teneatur, vel ad loca, vbi peccati illecebrae perpetrari consueuerunt, deportetur, omnino euanescit; vel per orificium vasis nequaquam ad effectum sanationis egreditur." Ibid., 115.

[976] "Ex scriptis etiam collegimus, et certa relatione fide dignorum intelleximus, quòd ciuitas Eystettensis, vnà cum tota Dioecesi Ecclesiastico interdicto quodam tempore supposita fuerat, propter quasdam domnosas iniurias, quas Episcopus, qui tunc praeerat, à Baronibus terrae et incolis sustinuit. Ex tunc liquor sacrae emanationis stillare cessauit, vsque in diem, quo Ecclesia restituta esset indemnitati. Et idem Venerabilis Episcopus, cum universitate ciuitatis indicto ieiunio, nudipes, et absque lineis, ad monasterium B. Walpurgis ascendit, deuotè ac submixè cum vniuersitate populi sui supplicans, ne effectu tantae benignitatis, sicut est manatio sacri liquoris, in amplius priuarentur. Et accedens ad altare

Rathsamhausen himself invoked the oil of both Nicholas and Catherine as the precedent for

Walburg's miraculous oozing.[977] According to the Bishop of Eichstätt, the saints whose tombs

produced the greatest quantities of oil had demonstrated the greatest mercy and holiness while alive.

These myroblytes' reputations for sanctity, and their fame for curing illnesses, spread "on the river

of their sacred emissions to the ends of the earth."[978] Riffing virtuosically on the idea of the

reputation of the myroblyte spreading like a fragrant aroma, Rathsamhausen alluded, in a single

sentence, to Psalm 51,[979] Ecclesiastes[980] and the Songs of Songs:[981] "Thus the blessed virgin

Walburga, like a fruitful olive in the house of the Lord, and like a beautiful olive tree in the fields of

the Church, spread His name through oil poured out."[982] Although the Song of Songs referred to the

bridegroom's oil, the unguent was sufficiently ambiguous and could likewise describe the oil of the

virgin abbess.

---

distus Pontifex Missarum solemnia, astante populo, deuotè peregit, et in confectione Sacramenti, et eiusdem perceptione, sacratissimus liquor, qui infra spatium vnius anni nequaquam destillauerat, nec vllo modo se ostenderat, adeò abundanter erupit, vt ampullam dimidiae *pintae,* capacitatis, vel vnius serici ad impleret. Quod Pontifex videns cum plebe deuota, plusquam narrari potest, gaudio repletus, immensas gratiarum actiones Deo ac B. Walpurgae, pro concessione tanti beneficii persoluit. Notendum etiam, quod idem sacrum oleum tantae munditiae ac meracitatis exiflit {sic}, vt sine omni corruptione, et foeda maculationis seculentia per ducentos annos seruatum, consimilis puritatis inuenitur, cum illo, quod hodierna die de stillicidio eiusdem sacrae emanationis susceptum est." Ibid., 115–16.

[977] "Nunc videamus, qui sibi vult per significationem emanatio olei in beata Walpurga, vel aliis sanctis, puta in B. Nicolao, vel B. Catharina, vel quibuscunque sanctis concessum est, ex speciali praerogatiua meritorum, et ostensione magnitudinis praemiorum. Iuxta quod sciendum, quod oleum cuicunque liquori infusum supernata: vnde misericordiam ex similitudine designat: superexalat enim misericordia iudicium. Et item: Misericordia eius, super omnia opera eius. Oleum nihilominus magnae est lenitatis, et multae vtilitatis; nam illuminat, pascit, et sanat. Sic pietas secundum B. Apstolum, ad multa proficiendo valet; habet enim promissionem vitae, quae nunc est, et vitae futurae. Hinc etiam est, quod oleum cordialem pietatem sua proprietate exprimit. Et ideo de Sanctorum corporibus sacri olei emanatio plenitudinem exuberantis misericordiae, ac redundantiam viscerosae pietatis, ac lenitiuae mititatis praetendo figurat. Fuerunt namque hi sancti, qui habent scaturiginem emanationis sacri olei, misericordissimi ac piissimi in vita: et ideo misericordiam consecuti per signa misericordiae et pietatis hominibus post mortem laudabiliter innotescunt." Ibid., 117-18.

[978] "Riuulo enim suae sacrae emanationis, notitia sanctitatis eius derivata est in fines terrae, oleo misericordiae et pietatis illuminans caecos, spiritualiter et corporaliter pascens esurientes, in bonis pro affectu sancti desiderii, ac corpore sauciatos sanans, contritis corde medetur." Ibid., 118–19.

[979] "Ego autem, sic oliva fructifera in domo Dei; speravi in misericordiae Dei, in aeternum et in saeculum saeculi." Psalm 51:10.

[980] "quasi oliva speciosa in campis, et quasi platanus exaltata sum juxta aquam in plateis. Sicut cinnamom et balsamum aromatizans odorem dedi; quasi myrrha electa dedi suavitatem odoris...quasi balsamum non mistum odor meus." Ecclesiastes 24:19-21.

[981] "Fragrantia unguentis optimis. Oleum effusum nomen tuum; ideo adolescentulae dilexerunt te." Cant. 1:2.

[982] "Sic beata Walpurgis Virgo, tanquam oliua in domo Domini fructuosa, et quasi oliua in campis Ecclesiae speciosa, per oleum effusum dilatauit nomen suum." Gretser, *Philippi Ecclesia Eystettensis XXXIX. Episcopi*, 118.

Although Rathsamhausen composed Willibald's *vita* and *miracula* (BHL 8934), he imputed no oil miracles to the male bishop.[983] The bishop's tomb healed a boy through direct contact with the tombstone, but not through oil.[984] Likewise, Rathsamhausen told of how the tomb of the bishop's father, Richard (d.722), cured illnesses, but not by oozing oil.[985] According to accounts composed by Henry of Rebdorf,[986] during the translation of Wunebald's relics in 1363 to a new tomb, the brother's physical proximity to his sister caused her to produce an even greater quantity of oil, while the brother's relics remained dry: "...a copious amount of oil flowed from the bones of St. Walburga, as if the Virgin felt the presence of her brother and, in his grace and honor, discharged a plentiful amount of sacred liquid.[987] Jacob Gretser (1562-1625) expressed misgivings about the reliability of the manuscript containing this account but argued that one could nevertheless not interpret the text as suggesting that oil flowed from Wunebald's relics instead of Walburga's.[988] Even though Rathsamhausen imputed no oil miracles to Willibald and Wunebald, he may have authored the *miracula* of Gundechar (r.1057-1075), a former Bishop of Eichstätt, whom he claimed was a myroblyte like Walburga.[989] According to the *miracula*, during Gundechar's translation, oil began to seep from the dead bishop's bones; Rathsamhausen claimed he sometimes collected as much as two cups full of oil, which cured illnesses.[990] Just after the feast of St. Michael (September 29), the oil started to bubble up and flow everywhere, furnishing the monastery with plenty of oil to cure the

[983] AASS Feb. III, Dies 25.

[984] "Illico tactu sanctuarii, adolescens pristinæ restitutus est sanitati." AASS Jul.II, Dies 7, Col. 0518B.

[985] AASS Feb.II, Dies 7, Col. 0081A-C. Bynum lists both Richard and Wunebald as myroblytes, but I have yet to locate texts that attest to their oil.

[986] Rebdorf was a monastery founded in the eleventh century in Eichstätt, Bavaria.

[987] "Reliquias [sic] S. Wunibaldi allatas esse in stillicidium, hoc est, ad sepulchrum B. Walpurgis, seu ad locum illum, in quem stillae olei ex lipsanis S. Walpurgae decidunt, et mox ad Reliquiaru [sic] praesentiam oleum copiosius ex ossibus S. Walpurgis fluxisse; quasi Virgo fratris praesentiam senserit, et in eius gratia et honorem sacrum liquorem largius effuderit." Gretser, *Philippi Ecclesiæ Eystettensis XXXIX. Episcopi*, 286.

[988] "Hic si non sit legitimus sensus tum fateor me nullum alium ex tam corruptis verbis extundere posse: nam ex ipsius Reliquiis S. Wunibaldi copiosum oleum manasse ad exemplum S. Walpurgis, verisimiliter non affirmatur, cum id à nullo veterum sit memoriae mandatum, neque Henrici verba huc nos necessariò trahant." Ibid.

[989] For BHL 3700, the Bollandists say: "Auctore, ut putamus, Philippo episcopo Eystettensi." AASS Aug. I, Dies 2.

[990] "Antequam ossa ipsius in secundo essent sepulchro recondita, oleum tam de eisdem ossibus, quam de superiori lapide sepulchri marmoreo adeo visibiliter emanavit, quod per venerabilem patrem Philippum, hujus loci episcopum XXXIX, cum duobus calicibus captum interdum extitit, & pro infirmorum debilitate servatum." AASS Aug.I, Dies 2, Col. 0184E.

illnesses of the many people who sought succor there.[991] While in the eleventh century, Walburga had acquired a reputation for producing a miraculous liquid like the liquid of Nicholas and Catherine, her status as a myroblyte was more firmly established in the early fourteenth century, as biographers increasingly attributed the miraculous production of oil to holy women rather than men alone.

CONCLUSION

In the early medieval period, when almost all myroblytes were male clerics, the spread of Nicholas of Myra's cult across Europe led to an increase in the number of female myroblytes, beginning with Catherine of Alexandria. An eighth-century account of miraculous oil from the tomb of Sabinus, Bishop of Canosa appears to have had little direct influence on the emergence of Nicholas' cult in Bavaria in the tenth century. By the eleventh century, however, when Nicholas' popularity had spread and his relics had been translated to Bari in the late eleventh century, the Archdeacon of Bari eliminated Sabinus' oil from accounts of the bishops' miracles. The clerics of Bari may have perceived the miraculous oozing of other myroblytes as a threat to Nicholas' cult (more precisely the economic benefit of pilgrimages to his tomb). Elsewhere in Europe, however, Nicholas' fame as an oil-producer fertilized the *acta miraculorum* of other saints. The cults of saints such as Babolenus and Eligius, also drew on Nicholas' popularity. The monks of St. Maur-des-Fossés in particular helped establish the cult of Babolenus within their monastery by borrowing miracles from Nicholas' office and by strategically surrounding the founding abbot with other myroblytes within the liturgical calendar. The miracles associated with Willibrord's oil also increased in tandem with the spread of Nicholas' cult in the eleventh century. Although Alcuin claimed that oil from Willibrord's lamps cured the sick, Thiofrid greatly embellished the quantity and force of the

---

[991] "Feria quarta post Michaëlis festum, ab hora matutinarum usque post meridiem, de superiore lapide sepulchri marmoreo oleum in diversis hinc inde locis sursum cœpit visibiliter ebullire." AASS Aug. I, Dies 2, Col. 0185B.

former bishop's holy liquid, which he claimed overflowed the bounds of the lamps and manifested how the saint was a great source of mercy and manly virtue.

While most of the new myroblytes in the eleventh and twelfth centuries were male prelates, it was just a matter of time before more female myroblytes appeared. The similarity of the offices of Nicholas and Catherine demonstrate that in the eleventh century, liturgists began to viewed oil production as a gender-neutral miracle that evidenced the extraordinary sanctity of male and female figures alike. The rise of Catherine's cult, the appeal of her oil, and the spread of her fame derived in part from increasing interest in pilgrimage to, and trade with, the Near East, which was the source of incense and exotic spices that were lauded in the Psalms and Song of Songs; these same spices also lent their fragrance to unguents, such as chrism, used in rituals in the Latin West. Her cult also spread due to belief that a virgin's oil had the power to heal physical and mental illness. Female myroblytes, whose numbers would eclipse male myroblytes in the late medieval period, resulted from the rise of the cults of both Nicholas of Myra and Catherine of Alexandria and later, in the thirteenth century, of Mary Magdalen, revealing the ambivalent nature of oil as representative of polarities: virgin and sinner as well as male and female.

INTRODUCTION

Although nearly all of the myroblytes from the early medieval period were male, after the

appearance of Catherine of Alexandria's cult in the eleventh century, a high number of female

myroblytes emerged in the Latin West. After 1200, at least eighteen new myroblytes appeared in

Europe, only seven of them men. This chapter argues that this shift was largely due to the rise of the

cults of several key female figures: Catherine of Alexandria, the Blessed Virgin Mary and Mary

Magdalene. The cults of these three women led to the rise of female saints more generally and, in the

case of Mary Magdalene, emphasized the connection between a women's devotion and the

outpouring of holy oil, since the Magdalene famously anointed Jesus' feet with an abundance of

costly unguent. The corporeal generation of miraculous oil eventually became a predominantly

feminine expression of sanctity, often appearing in the lives of laywomen who were Dominican,

Franciscan and Cistercian tertiaries. In the thirteenth century, a series of women myroblytes

appeared in the Low Countries and Germania; the authors of their *vitae* were often Dominicans and

Cistercians. The cult of Rolendis (d. 774) supposedly gathered force in the eighth century, although

no one composed her *vita* until the thirteenth century; the composition of her *vita* coincided with

Thomas de Cantimpré (1201-1272) authoring two highly unusual myroblyte *vitae* that emphasized

the importance of penance: Christina Mirabilis (1150-1224) and Lutgard of Aywières (1182-1246). In

the mid and late thirteenth century, the cult of Elizabeth of Thuringia (1207-1231) emerged shortly

after the noblewoman's death. During her life, Elizabeth was a model of charity and penance; after

death, according to some, her tomb oozed oil. Conrad of Marburg (1180-1233), the infamous papal

inquisitor, spearheaded Elizabeth's canonization inquest and authored her *vita* (BHL 2490) in 1232, although he did not list miraculous oil among the wonders worked at her tomb.[992] Other authors of her *vitae* included both Caesarius of Heisterbach (1180-1240) a Cistercian abbot, who claimed she produced oil, and Detrich von Apolda (1228-1298), a Dominican who also authored a *vita* for Domingo de Guzmán (1170-1221), the founder of the Order of Preachers (Dominicans).[993] According to an early fourteenth-century biographer, Elizabeth of Thuringian's niece, Hedwig of Silesia (1174-1243) also produced oil that cured the sick; the sweet oil flowed from the noblewoman's head. Not far from Andechs, the Cistercian monastery that was the epicenter of Hedwig's cult, another bishop of Eichstätt, Philipp of Rathsamhausen, claimed Walburga produced a great quantity of holy oil, which he himself imbibed. Given that Walburga's earlier biographers had claimed that water, but not oil, seeped from Walburga's tomb (which they said was like the oil from the tomb of Nicholas) perhaps Rathsamhausen's praise of Walburga's oil was an attempt to divert pilgrims from Andechs to Eichstätt.[994]

During the late-medieval period, the number of female myroblytes likewise increased in Italy, where Franciscans and Dominicans helped proliferate the cult of Mary Magdalene. Prior to the eleventh century, the cults of mostly male myroblytes emerged in the southern half of the peninsula, in Nola, Canossa, Naples, and Calabria, with one exception in the north, on the Island of Palmaria in the Gulf of Genoa. In contrast, between the early thirteenth and late fifteenth century, myroblytes appeared mainly in northern Italy, where biographers composed the *vitae* of seven or eight female myroblytes but no male myroblytes. The last male myroblyte to appear on the Italic peninsula was Fantinus (c. 927-1000), a confessor at Tauriano in Calabria. Northern and central Italy were likewise

---

[992] For English translations of the miracle depositions from the canonization trials as well as Conrad of Marburg's *vita* of Elizabeth of Thuringia see Kenneth Baxter Wolf, *The Life and Afterlife of St. Elizabeth of Hungary: Testimony from Her Canonization Hearings* (Oxford; New York: Oxford University Press, 2011).

[993] For recent critical editions, see Caesarius of Heisterbach, *"Vita S. Elizabeth Lantgrafie": = Das Leben der Heiligen Elisabeth, Landgräfin von Thüringen*, trans. Aloys Finken (Siegburg: Rheinlandia-Verl, 2007); Theodoricus, *Die Legende der heiligen Elisabeth*, ed. Werner Heiland-Justi, Orig.-Ausg (Freiburg, Br. Basel Wien: Herder, 2015). For older editions, see Albert Huyskens, *Quellenstudien zur Geschichte der hl. Elizabeth: Landgräfin von Thüringen* (N.G. Elwert, 1908); Caesarius of Heisterbach, *Die Wundergeschichte des Caesarius von Heisterbach Bd. 3*, ed. Alfons Hilka (Bonn: Hanstein, 1937).

[994] Weinfurter, "'Überall Unsere Heiligste Mutter Walburga,'" 187.

the loci of Franciscan and Dominican penitents.[995] The female myroblytes in Italy include Franca

Visalta (1170-1218), a Cistercian Abbess; Rose of Viterbo (1233-1252); Zita of Lucca (1212-1272);

Humility, founder and abbess of the Vallombrosians of Florence (1226-1310); Agnes of

Montepulciano (1268-1317); Margaret of Città di Castello (1287-1320), a Dominican tertiary;

Eustochia of Padua (1444-1469) as well as the anomalous Candida the Younger of Naples (d. 586),

whose cult likely emerged in the late medieval or early modern period. These holy, oil-producing

Italian women, like Christina and Lutgard, were often connected to the Dominican or Franciscan

orders, which invoked Mary Magdalene as an ideal of lay piety.[996] In late medieval Italy, the

production of holy oil by saints had become a distinctly feminine expression of sanctity because

rather than being associated with male clerical authority, oil increasingly signified the laity, especially

women, as a result of the cult of Mary Magdalene, whose broken alabaster jar symbolized mercy and

an active apostolate: good works, charity, care of the poor.[997]

MYROBLYTES IN THE LOW COUNTRIES

In the thirteenth century, some of the most remarkable transalpine myroblytes surfaced in

the Low Countries. Although the cult of Rolendis (d. ca 774) gathered force in the eighth century,

no one composed her *vita* until the thirteenth century. Christina Mirabilis (1150-1224) and Lutgard

of Aywières (1182-1246) had the exceptional distinction of having oil flow from their bodies while

still alive. Thomas de Cantimpré, a former Augustinian canon, who became a Dominican in 1232,

authored both these holy women's lives and recorded their miraculous oozings as being new

---

[995] Maiju Lehmijoki-Gardner, Daniel Ethan Bornstein, and E. Ann Matter, *Dominican Penitent Women* (Mahwah, N.J.: Paulist Press, 2005), 2.

[996] Katherine Ludwig Jansen, *The Making of the Magdalen: Preaching and Popular Devotion in the Later Middle Ages* (Princeton, N.J: Princeton University Press, 2000).

[997] Regarding the symbolic or mystical meaning of Mary Magdalene's alabaster jar, see Ibid., 97, 99, 108–9, 230, 243, 291.

miracles, never before seen in Christendom.[998] By the thirteenth century, we see that oil in a

myroblytes' *vita* was associated much more closely with female piety, including virginity and

repentance, rather than with male ecclesiastical power and authority. In the *vitae* of Christina,

Lutgard and Rolendis, oil became a symbol for divine grace that precipitated repentance and

conversion. The oil exuding from these holy women coincided with their extraordinary asceticism

unlike their male predecessors. Caroline Walker Bynum's argument that oil was the result of extreme

asceticism thus corresponds with these thirteenth-century holy women of the Low Countries in a

way that it does not with the episcopal Gallic myroblytes of the early medieval period.

ROLENDIS, BRIDE OF THE GUSHING FONT

Unlike the *vitae* of the episcopal myroblytes who dominated early medieval Gaul, Rolendis'

vita emphasized the virginal character of the myroblyte, alluding to the Song of Songs and the

virgin's mystical marriage to Christ who, as the Anointed One, was the source of purity itself:

> The true spouse, himself a gushing font of all purity, in order to make the sanctity of the
> most beloved Rolendis known as much through presence as through future absence,
> compelled a man deprived of sight to go to the body of the great virgin, imagining hopefully
> that he would regain sight and be restored to the light. The same man prostrated on bended
> knee before the saint....[999]

---

[998] Regarding Thomas de Cantimpré, see Barbara Newman's introduction to his collected saints' lives: Thomas de Cantimpré, *Thomas of Cantimpré: the Collected Saints' Lives : Abbot John of Cantimpré, Christina the Astonishing, Margaret of Ypres, and Lutgard of Aywières*, ed. Barbara Newman, trans. Margot H King (Turnhout, Belgium: Brepols, 2008), 3–51.

[999] "Ipse verus Sponsus totiusque puritatis fons exuberans, ut dilectissimæ sibi Rolendis sanctitas tam præsentibus quam absentibus & futuris innotescat, virum quempiam orbatum lumine, ad tantæ Virginis corpus ire compulsum, spe luminis recuperandi concepta, ante ipsam flexo genu prostratum restituit claritati. Hujus miraculi veritate percepta, hospes, tantæ congratulans hospitæ, eum qui cæcus fuerat ad matrem ecclesiam, Gerpiniensem videlicet, cum multis eum intueri admirando gaudentibus, delegavit. Prænominata vero ecclesia, cum signis hujus miraculi novitate resultantibus & resonantibus, filios ejusdem ecclesiæ, tunc temporis militia & probitate insignes & admodum florentes, convocavit ad se, & devotissime adunavit. Urgo veritate prorsus discussa, cum omni reverentia & lacrymarum devotione atque nudis pedibus, ad sanctissimæ Virginis corpus venerabiliter deportandum, a Clericis & Militibus atque honestissimis viris, quibus hæc villa tunc florebat, properatum est." AASS, Maii. III, Dies 13, Col. 0244B-C.

Although the author of the *vita* described Christ as a "gushing font," Rolendis herself produced a great quantity of oil, albeit through Christ's power:

> To this tomb glittering with many kinds of miracles, endless people - even from remote regions - avidly ran, needing to be cleansed, not only of physical defect but also mental blindness. The virginal body dripped with a copious transcendence of holy oil, by whose gentle touch wounds were healed.[1000]

The healing miracles that occurred at Rolendis' tomb, however, were not extraordinary; they were akin to the miracles of other myroblytes, such as Nicholas and Catherine. The author gave emphasis, however, to the virginity of the saint, perhaps in imitation of Catherine of Alexandria, whose "virgin members" were imputed with the power to ooze and heal. When Thomas de Cantimpré composed the *vitae* of two other holy women from the Low Countries who were his own contemporaries, he told of oil miracles that surpassed those other virgins and myroblytes in novelty.

Christina Mirabilis, The Astonishing Virgin

Christina Mirabilis (1150-1224), also known as Christina the Astonishing, was a liminal character, more at home in the wilderness than society. Although later in life she became affiliated with a religious order, she never became a nun. Christina was born in the town of St. Trond, the same town where her fellow myroblyte Lutgard of Aywières (1182-1246) spent forty years as a nun at St. Catherine's Benedictine monastery. The youngest of three daughters, Christina became her older sisters' charge after the death of their parents. The two sisters delegated Christina to be the

---

[1000] "Quod honorifice a majoribus & reverendis hominibus delatum, in præfata ecclesia, parte templi dextra, venerabili mausoleo consecratum & conservatum est. Ad cujus tumulum multimodo miraculorum genere coruscantem, gens infinita, etiam a remotis regionibus, tum pro labe corporis tum pro mentis cæcitate purganda avidissime cucurrit. Corpus autem virgineum stillabat olei sacri transcendente copia; cujus leni tactu languentium curabantur vulnera. Contigit quemdam importunum virum & duræ cervicis, de tanta multitudine gentium pro temporis adstrictione conquestum, sacrum in terra cum phyala fudisse oleum: cujus effusionis pœna in ipsum & posteros ipsius originis, nodis in manibus eorum innatis redundavit, oleumque ipsum in Virgine nullatenus comparuit. Christus tamen, pro fidei meritis digna dignis rependens præmia, electæ suæ loculum miraculorum non privavit gloria." AASS, Maius III, Dies 13, Col. 0244C-D.

family's shepherd and, although the Lord allowed Christina to assume this humble office, he also granted her "the grace of an inward sweetness and very often visited her with heavenly secrets."[1001] After some time herding in the pasture, Christina "grew sick in body by virtue of exercise of inward contemplation and she died."[1002] Her death proved the beginning of her ministry in the world. After dying, Christina saw souls suffering in purgatory and conversed with God. God gave Christina the choice to remain dead and enjoy life with Him or "return to the body and suffer there the sufferings of an immortal soul in a mortal body without damage to it, and by these your sufferings to deliver all those souls on whom you had compassion in that place of purgatory…"[1003] Christina opted for the latter and dedicated herself to "the improvement of men."[1004]

Thomas de Cantimpré composed Christina's *vita* in 1232, more than 15 years before writing Lutgard's *vita*. While de Cantimpré based Lutgard's *vita* on sixteen years of friendship with the nun, he never met Christina. Christina died (for the second time) eight years before de Cantimpré recorded her miracles as a myroblyte, causing him to rely entirely on second-hand accounts of "the unforgettable virgin."[1005] De Cantimpré was supremely concerned with veracity; he swore he learned the truth about Christina from "many straightforward witnesses" and further defended his narrative by stating that "these things were not done in narrow corners but straightforwardly among people."[1006] The events in the life of Christina the Astonishing myroblyte were only possible with God (and a little imagination).

All the miracles recorded in Christina's *vita* took place post-mortem, after she returned to earth to bring lost souls into Christ's fold. De Cantimpré conveys Christina's dislike for fallen humanity. Like one of the desert fathers, Christina abhorred "the stench of men" and fled "into

---

[1001] Thomas de Cantimpré, *The Life of Christina Mirabilis*, trans. Margot H. King (Toronto, Ont.: Peregrina, 1989), 12. This and subsequent English translations of this text are by Margot King.
[1002] Ibid.
[1003] Ibid., 14.
[1004] Ibid.
[1005] Ibid., 10.
[1006] Ibid.

deserts, or to trees, or to the tops of castles or churches or any lofty structure."[1007] As a result,

people thought Christina was possessed by demons. They captured her and put her in "chains and

fetters."[1008] According to de Cantimpré, with God's help Christina escaped her imprisonment and

returned to the wilderness where "she desired to remain alone with God."[1009] Despite this blessed

and peaceful union, Christina eventually got hungry. While she was an immortal soul, she suffered

the pains of a physical body. To remedy the one pain she could not abide, Christina prayed to God

for food. In turn, her body produced a great quantity of liquid: milk.

> …pouring forth a prayer to the Lord, she humbly begged that He gaze on her anguish with
> the eyes of His mercy. Without delay, when she turned her eyes to herself, she saw that the
> dry paps of her virginal breasts were dripping with sweet milk against the very law of
> nature…Using the dripping liquid as food, she was nourished for nine weeks with the milk
> from her fruitful but virginal breasts.[1010]

This mammalian miracle was the template for the myroblytic miracle that followed.[1011]

Although God provided for Christina in the wilderness, "her own people" discovered her wild

lifestyle and imprisoned her. After a series of imprisonments and liberations, Christina took

communion and fled again into the wilderness, crossing a wide and rapid river, from which she

emerged "untouched."[1012] After this baptism of sorts, Christina "began to do those things for which

she had been sent back by the Lord."[1013] Those things include astonishing, penitential miracles in

which she subjected her body to torture by creeping into a fiery furnace, immersing herself in icy

water, stretching her arms and legs on the rack, tearing her flesh with thorns and brambles, hanging

herself in the gallows and lying in the graves of the dead. Rather than successfully reconciling

---

[1007] De Cantimpré, *The Life of Christina Mirabilis*, 15.
[1008] Ibid.
[1009] Ibid.
[1010] Ibid.
[1011] According to Bynum: "…the female body was seen as powerful in its holy or miraculous exuding, whether of breast milk or of blood or of oil." Bynum, *Holy Feast and Holy Fast*, 274.
[1012] De Cantimpré, *The Life of Christina Mirabilis*, 16.
[1013] Ibid.

humanity with God, Christina's shenanigans ruffled the feathers of her sisters and their friends. Christina's two older sisters bribed "a most wicked man" to capture and bind her; the man had to break her leg with a cudgel to do so.[1014]

After the wicked man crippled the virgin, the sisters put a physician in charge of healing their sister and of ensuring she was adequately secured: "The physician knew her strength so he bound her firmly to a pillar in a dungeon where chains hung on all the walls and he locked the doors securely."[1015] Ostensibly the physician tried to heal Christina's wounds, but Christina would have no physician except Christ:

> After the physician had left, she drew off the bandages since she thought it shameful to have any doctor for her wounds but Jesus Christ, and the Almighty did not fail her. One night when the Spirit came upon her, the chains with which she was bound were loosed and, healed from all hurt, she walked around the dungeon and danced and praised and blessed Him for whom alone she had chosen to live or die.[1016]

The liberation, however, proved only temporary. Before long Christina found herself bound and unable to eat: "The hardness of the wooden yoke which lay heavily on her neck and rubbed her shoulders caused festering wounds and she was so wasted by these pains that she could not eat her bread."[1017] The remedy in this instance was "that great miracle, unheard of in all previous centuries." Thomas de Cantimpré knew myroblyte miracles well. For the first time ever, a woman's breasts were filled with oil.

> Her virginal breasts began to flow with a liquid of the clearest oil and she took that liquid and used it as a flavouring for her bread and ate it as food and smeared it on the wounds of her festering limbs as an ointment. And when her sisters and friends saw this, they began to weep and they struggled no more against the miracles of the Divine Will in Christina and

---

[1014] Ibid., 19.
[1015] Ibid.
[1016] Ibid., 19-20.
[1017] Ibid., 20.

they released her from her chains and knelt down begging for mercy for their injuries to her and let her go.[1018]

De Cantimpré was well-versed in miracle literature; no longer did a saint have to be dead for oil to flow from his or her body. Never before had oil flowed from the body of a living saint. The first time Christina escaped from the dungeon, the Holy Spirit freed her.[1019] The second time she escaped oil liberated her. The idea was reminiscent of Gregory the Great's *Moralia in Job*, which imputed to oil the power to liberate captives from the yoke of tyranny, citing Isaiah 10:27: "the yoke decays through the presence of oil."[1020] The first liberation, which resulted in ecstatic dancing, was the action of the invisible Spirit; the second liberation was sacramental: the oil which acted as a conduit for the Spirit. The liberator, oil, was visible and made evident the Divine Will. The unguent which flowed from Christina's breasts fed her, healed her wounds, converted her sisters and loosened the dungeon's bonds so she could fulfill her earthly mission: the holy oil finally allowed Christina to free others from sin and suffering.

After becoming a myroblyte, Christina was reconciled with humanity. During her new-found freedom, Christina became more "moderate"; she immersed herself in a baptismal font: "It is said that when this event occurred, thereafter her manner of life was more moderate with regard to society and she behaved more calmly and was more able to endure the smell of men and to live among them."[1021] When Christina was able to abide humanity, she attached herself to a religious

---

[1018] Ibid., 20–21.

[1019] "Her spirit then felt itself to be shut up in a narrow dungeon, and she took a stone from the dungeon floor and in her impassioned spirit she threw it with such force that she made a hole in the wall. To use an example, it was like an arrow which is more forcefully released the harder it is pulled in the bow. Thus her spirit, which had been restrained more than was just, flew with her body in its weak flesh through the empty air like a bird because 'where the Spirit of the Lord is, there is liberty' (2 Cor 3:17)." Ibid., 20.

[1020] See Chapter 2 regarding the interpretation of this text in the *Glossa Ordinaria*.

[1021] De Cantimpré, *The Life of Christina Mirabilis*, 21. Strangely enough, Christina's life reverses the traditional order of sacraments. She is "anointed" with oil and then is "baptized." Also, earlier, when God provides milk (like manna) in the desert, this event preceeds Christina's captivity (a clear reversal of the order found in Exodus).

order.[1022] She became the instrument of divine intercession in her community; she begged, warned, prophesied, advocated on behalf of a sinful apostate, and prayed for people on pilgrimage. Margot King argued that Christiana's *vita* demonstrated how characters such as Christina, though devoted to God and more or less socialized, were still problematic for clergy in the thirteenth century.[1023] In de Cantimpré's life of Christina, the appearance of oil marks the seminal moment in which the woman ceased to live on the fringes of society as a savage and became an instrument of spreading the Dominican call to repentance. Once she became a living source of holy oil, Christina assimilated into the Christian community. Once a myroblyte, Christina was no longer a specimen of demonic possession but an example of holiness and devotion.[1024] The oil in Christina's breasts made her Christ-like; she was not only like the "Anointed One" who suffered the "pains for the sins of men" but she became an example for others to imitate as a model of grace, servitude and repentance.[1025]

While Christina worked and suffered fervently on others' behalf, de Cantimpré stated that sinners were nevertheless responsible for taking their salvation into their own hands. At the conclusion of Christina's *vita*, de Cantimpré returned to the oil theme, urging other Christians to imitate the myroblyte and not be caught like the foolish virgins:

> Certainly a day will come – it will come and there will be no delay! – when we would gladly do much more than [Christina did] if a place of penance were given to those who would ask for it and thereby make up for lost time. Woe to those who want to buy the oil of mercy

---

[1022] Caroline Walker Bynum notes: "…Christina the Astonishing (Christina Mirabilis) – despite later efforts to claim her as Benedictine, Cistercian, or Premonstratensian – was simply a laywoman seeking to follow Christ and the saints." Bynum, *Holy Feast and Holy Fast*, 24.

[1023] "The poverty espoused by the thirteenth-century practitioners of the *vita apostolica* stood in sharp contrast to the monastic poverty of the period. Up to the eleventh century the official church had recognized only two forms of religious life: the priesthood and religious orders. With the appearance of a heightened lay religious enthusiasm, however, which was based on a literal interpretation of the poverty of Christ and His apostles, the Church was faced with a dilemma.…Thomas [de Cantimpré] is at pains to emphasize that Christina did, in fact, show due regard for the official Church." De Cantimpré, *The Life of Christina Mirabilis*, 45n11.

[1024] Of the medieval *exemplum*, King notes: "…the end [of the *exemplum*] is not good behaviour nor entertainment nor even the earthly well-being of the listener. Rather, the *exemplum* is characterized by its emphasis on the last things and by a preoccupation with eternal salvation. There is no question that the life of Christina is eschatological in nature and that this is the *raison d'être* of the work." Ibid., 48n24.

[1025] Ibid., 21.

after the time of trading has passed! With empty lamps they will beat on the door and will

not be able to enter. Rather, He will say, 'Amen, I say to you I know you not. Watch ye

therefore, because you know not the day nor the hour.' (Mt 25:12-13).[1026]

According to de Cantimpré, the oil of gladness and the oil of mercy could not be bought but

only won through God's favor and through repentant suffering. In Christina Mirabilis' *vita*, we see

that oil had the power to transform a laywoman, who was a marginal and wild creature, into a holy

servant of God, who was closely aligned with the Order of Preachers.

Lutgard of Awyières, Lamp of Wisdom

Unlike Christina Mirabilis who ran with the dogs and sang with the nuns, Lutgard of

Awyières devoted herself exclusively to solitary prayer and mystical encounters with God.

Born in 1182 in Tongres, a city in the Flemish region of Belgium, Lutgard was the daughter

of a noblewoman and a burgher. In an attempt to secure his daughter's future, Lutgard's

father entrusted silver to a merchant during her childhood, hoping the investment would

increase and become the young woman's dowry. The Lord, however, had other plans for

Lutgard. The merchant spent the investment unwisely and lost the dowry. Lutgard's mother

offered the girl a second dowry on the condition that she agree to enter religious life. At the

age of twelve, Lutgard entered the Benedictine monastery of St. Catherine in the town of St.

Trond, where she met Thomas de Cantimpré, who would become her biographer. It was

likely no coincidence that Lutgard's renown as a myroblyte began in a monastery named

after the most famous female myroblyte in the Latin West: Catherine of Alexandria, whose

miraculous oozing rivaled and imitated that of the Nicholas of Myra.

[1026] Ibid., 41.

De Cantimpré composed the *Vita Lutgardis* shortly after the Lutgard's death in 1246,

following a sixteen-year friendship with the woman. De Cantimpré addressed the *vita's* prologue to

Hadewijch, the abbess of St. Catherine's, where Lutgard spent forty years as a nun. De Cantimpré

told of how when the nuns at St. Catherine's unanimously elected Lutgard prioress of St.

Catherine's, she eschewed the administrative role, opting instead to transfer to the Cistercian

convent at Aywières, seeking a more ascetic and solitary atmosphere than she found among the

Benedictines.[1027] Lutgard's *vita* records a miraculous incident that took place at neither convent but at

the home of a recluse in the town of Looz:

> …Once when she had been staying with this woman for a fortnight it happened that after
> the contemplation of her prayers, she was so filled up with sweetness of spirit that she called
> the recluse and showed her the fingers of her hand. Squeezing them, she said, 'Look, sister,
> how the Almighty deals with me! I am so filled up inwardly by the grace of His
> superabundance that even now my fingers are outwardly dripping a kind of oil as a
> manifestation of grace.' Saying this as if she were drunk – indeed she *was* drunk – she ran
> rapidly to and fro through the reclusorium with wondrous movement and dancing.[1028]

While oil only slipped from Lutgard's person once, oil as a leitmotif recurred throughout her

vita, which included a series of miracles such as levitation and miracles of light.[1029] According to

Cantimpré, on account of Lutgard's arduous fasting, a brilliant luminescence filled Lutgard (instead

of food, presumably): "a heavenly radiance of light, more brilliant than the sun and which lasted for

most of the night, was seen above her by the nuns."[1030] The light, which was "poured inwardly into

her," greatly benefited Lutgard's companions; they experienced an increase in "grace of their

---

[1027] Thomas de Cantimpré, *The Life of Lutgard of Aywières*, trans. Margot H King (Toronto, Ont.: Peregrina Pub. Co., 1991), 123n23.

[1028] Ibid., 35–36.

[1029] "On the holy day of Pentecost when the *Veni creator spiritus* was being chanted in choir by the nuns, it was most manifestly seen by those who were in choir that Lutgard was elevated two cubits from the earth into the air." Ibid., 29.

[1030] Ibid., 30. Caroline Walker Bynum observes: "…myroblytes were often miraculous fasters." Bynum, *Holy Feast and Holy Fast*, 274.

spiritual life."[1031] The myroblyte, who had been filled with the "oil" of spiritual grace, became a kind

of lamp for her sisters. On account of this divine illumination, Lutgard desired to learn Latin, which

she apparently did, "since she was even more enlightened by the radiant light" than before making

this request of God.[1032] Her desire for knowledge of Latin and further illumination led to some of

the most curious incidents in the story, which include the exchange of various liquids.

Unlike other myroblytes who accomplished miraculous healings after death, Lutgard

possessed the power to heal the sick while alive, either through touch or through her spittle. So great

a number of people asked Lutgard for healing miracles that she felt distracted from her pursuit of

contemplative prayer. The saint therefore asked God to exchange the grace of healing for the grace

to understand the Psalter. God answered Lutgard's desire to know Latin by granting her knowledge

of his own heart: "And so a correspondence of hearts occurred from that time on or, rather, the

union of an uncreated with a created spirit through a surplus of grace."[1033] As a result of this union

or divine knowledge, Lutgard was continually accompanied by Christ and even drank his blood. In

one instance, Lutgard made up her mind to miss Matins because of excessive "sweating."[1034] After

feeling distraught about her indulgence and laziness, she rushed to church, where she unexpectedly

met Christ at the entrance:

> Lowering His arm which was nailed to the Cross, He embraced her who was standing
> opposite and pressed her mouth against the wound in His right side. She drank in so much
> sweetness from that place that always afterwards she was stronger and quicker in the service
> of God. Those to whom she revealed this event have reported and even certified that then
> and for a long time afterwards the saliva in her mouth tasted mellower than the sweetest
> honey.[1035]

[1031] De Cantimpré, *The Life of Lutgard of Aywières*, 30.
[1032] Ibid., 31.
[1033] Ibid.
[1034] Ibid., 32.
[1035] Ibid., 33.

After filling her body with Christ's blood, Lutgard was again filled with light. This time the

beak of a bird, representing not the Holy Spirit but John the Evangelist, illuminated Lutgard. In a

vision, Lutgard imbibed from the one who "drank from the streaming fountain of the Gospel which

flowed from the sacred breast of the Lord."[1036] De Cantimpré narrated the vision as follows:

> An eagle appeared to her in the spirit, his wings brightly shining with such luster that all the
> universe could have been enlightened by the dazzling clarity of its rays…When the manner
> of the vision moderated, she saw in contemplation that the eagle was placing its beak on her
> mouth, filling her soul with a flashing from such an ineffable light so that no secrets of the
> Divinity lay hidden from her insofar as is possible for mortal people…[1037]

After having been filled first with the blood of Christ and then with an "ineffable light" it

should come as no surprise that in the next scene, Lutgard's fingers are dripping with oil. She had

become a kind of oil lamp. Like an ampulla of Menas of Egypt, Lutgard's living body became a

vessel of holy liquid.[1038] Lutgard's encounter with the oil of gladness was also, in a sense, a moment

of anointing. Afterwards she was overcome by the Spirit and gave way to a boundless ecstasy, like

Saul after her anointing as king. When the moment of euphoria passed, Lutgard was committed to

God and the religious life; she entered into a "mystical marriage" and was consecrated by the

bishop. Just as Jesus' baptism in the gospels marked the beginning of his public ministry, and the

baptism and anointing of an ordinary Christian marked the beginning of their lives in the Christian

community, so too did the encounter with holy oil change Lutgard irrevocably. After her anointing

at Looz, Lutgard "began to gasp to be more perfectly joined to one husband, the Lord Christ, by the

---

[1036] Ibid., 34.

[1037] Ibid.

[1038] Margot King notes the appearance of oil from Lutgard's hands is: "A clear reference to Cant 5:5: 'My hands dropped with myrrh, and my fingers were full of the choicest myrrh.' This visible sign of invisible grace – a popular definition of the term of the sacrament, attributed to Augustine by Berengar – is paralleled in *The Life of Chistina* when Christina's breasts drip a kind of oil…This oil would seem to be 'the oil of gladness' (Ps 44:8), 'the unction of the Holy Spirit which teaches, the taste of the divine sweetness, the perfume of eternity, the powerful experience of the spiritual sense' " (William of St Thierry, Exposition of the Song of Songs…)…" Ibid., 142n98.

ceremony of consecration through the hands of a bishop…"[1039] The mystical bride of Christ

required consecration by a bishop; consecrated oil sealed the mystical union.

Rather than emphasizing oil as a symbol for charity and corporeal works of mercy, as other

authors would do, Thomas de Cantimpré presented oil as characteristic of monastic piety: excessive

fasting, seclusion and *lectio divina*.[1040] The theme of a virgin bearing oil (or becoming an oil lamp), in

reference to Matthew's parable of the Wise and Foolish Virgins, extended through Lutgard's *vita* as

an ideal of monastic life and an *exemplum* addressed to the women of St. Catherine's. De Cantimpré

exhorted the nuns of St. Catherine's to greater piety and explained Lutgard's election as abbess by

stating: "…since it was not fitting that such a lamp be concealed under a bushel, she was placed

upon a lamp stand (*cf.* Mt 5:15) so that the resplendence of its grace might appear to all."[1041] Without

overtly criticizing the nuns of St. Catherine's for their lax spirituality, de Cantimpré attributed the

success of the convent to the prayers Lutgard made on its behalf; she raised up St. Catherine's amid

a general decline in the Benedictine order.[1042] De Cantimpré exhorted the nuns at St. Catherine's to

aspire to greater spiritual heights through discipline and penance. He urged them to imitate the one

who fasted and prayed so fervently that God filled her living person with the oil of gladness.

ROYAL MYROBLYTES: ELIZABETH OF THURINGIA & HEDWIG OF SILESIA

Shortly after de Cantimpré recorded Christina's miraculously oily breasts, but before he told

of Lutgard's dripping fingertips, Caesarius of Heisterbach, prior of the Cistercian monastery in

Heisterbach, in the North Rhine-Westphalia region of Germany, authored a *vita* of Elizabeth of

---

[1039] Ibid., 36.

[1040] Margot King observed: "Having been occupied in the *lectio divina*, Lutgard has 'fingered and touched the inner sense of scripture and the strength of the mysteries and secrets of God with the hand of experience'…This is the result of Lutgard's mystical and experiential union with Christ and the miracle of the oil marks, as it did with Christina, the turning point in her spiritual ascent." Ibid., 142n98.

[1041] Ibid., 39.

[1042] "…without doubt we see this [spiritual advancement] up to the present day in the convent of St. Catherine's, while almost everywhere else the discipline of that Order has become tepid." Ibid., 29.

Thuringia (1207-1231) as well as a sermon about her translation that told of oil flowing from the

noblewoman's tomb. If Lutgard was filled with the oil of gladness, Elizabeth was filled with the oil

of mercy. Elizabeth of Thuringia was a noble laywoman who, once widowed, devoted herself

entirely to asceticism and care for the poor. The cult of Elizabeth gained force following her death

and canonization proceeding, which was led by Conrad of Marburg (1180-1233), Elizabeth's

confessor and guardian. Marburg was also a papal inquisitor who combatted heretics in Germania

during the reigns of Popes Innocent III, Honorius III and Gregory IX.[1043] In 1232 Conrad authored

Elizabeth's *vita* to accompany miracle depositions sent to the papal commission for her canonization

trial. Nowhere, however, did Conrad mention oil oozing miraculously from her tomb, although he

did say that "On the day after her burial, the Lord began to work miracles through his handmaid."[1044]

According to Conrad, Elizabeth's extraordinary sanctity manifested in her humility, her love for the

poor, and her works of corporeal mercy, including caring for sick and hungry.[1045] Caesarius of

Heisterbach's *vita* and *sermo*, which appeared a few years after Conrad of Marburg's *vita*, were likely

the first accounts to claim Elizabeth was a myroblyte. Caesarius may have drawn inspiration from

the Office of Catherine of Alexandria. In his *Dialogus Miraculorum,* two interlocutors discussed the

endless emission of oil from Catherine of Alexandria's relics, which one interlocutor interpreted as a

sign of the holy woman's virtues.[1046] Detrich von Apolda (1228-1298), not only wrote an account of

Elizabeth's life and miracles in the 1280s, but was also authored a *vita* (BHL 2226) of the founder of

the Order of Preachers (Dominicans), Domingo de Guzmán (1170-1221), which incidentally did not

include miraculous oil. Although closely tied to the Order of Preachers, Elizabeth's love of poverty

also led her to cultivate relations with the Franciscans, whom she installed in a chapel in Marburg. In

---

[1043] Wolf, *The Life and Afterlife of St. Elizabeth of Hungary,* 7n20.
[1044] Ibid., 95. One boy is cured with dirt from her tomb, but not oil.
[1045] Wolf, *The Life and Afterlife of St. Elizabeth of Hungary,* 91–95.
[1046] See Chapter 6. Also Walsh, *The Cult of St Katherine of Alexandria in Early Medieval Europe,* 2007, 87. In this same work, Caesarius also discussed oil oozing continually from an icon in Cistercian monastery in France. See Caesarius of Heisterbach, *Caesarii Heisterbacensis ... Dialogus miraculorum* (sumptibus J.M. Heberle (H. Lempertz & Comp.), 1851), 35.

imitation of Francis of Assisi, Elizabeth renounced her worldly goods and chose to live in extreme

poverty.[1047]

In the early fourteenth century, Elizabeth of Thuringia's niece, Hedwig of Silesia, likewise

gained fame for the miraculous oil that flowed from her tomb. Hedwig's *Vita Major* (BHL 3766),

composed circa 1300, recounted the marvelous events surrounding Hedwig's translation at the time

of her canonization by Pope Clement IV (r. 1265-1268) in 1267. The *vita* described how a

mellifluous odor as well as an oil-like liquid flowed from Hedwig's tomb: "With the earth having

been dug away from the tomb and the upper slab removed from the sarcophagus in which the

sacred body rested, the sweetest and liveliest aroma flowed outward, so the minds of everyone

appearing in that place might be transformed by wonderment and delight."[1048] After being buried for

twenty-five years, oil as well as a marvelous fragrance, flowed from Hedwig's tomb. A liquid, which

the biographer described as either "like oil" or "in the form of oil" did not ooze amorphously from

the noblewoman's relics, but from her head in particular: "The day before a certain liquid, pure and

clear as the sweetest and most marvelous olive oil, perspired from her head; the liquid completely

soaked the muslins and cloths covering her head, as if they had been drawn from a river and needed

to be wrung out to dry."[1049] The author of this miracle borrowed a word from the Nicholas' liturgy,

which describes oil perspiring from the marble of the bishop's tomb: *resudare*. One chant from

Nicholas' liturgy spoke of the oil oozing from Nicholas' tomb being like the sweat pouring from the

body of a woman in labor, evidencing the gender-neutral nature of oil seeping from a saint's tomb.

Furthermore, although she was a laywoman, Hedwig belonged to the political and religious elite. The

---

[1047] Wolf, *The Life and Afterlife of St. Elizabeth of Hungary*, 93.

[1048] "Nam ejecta humo de tumulo remotaque superiori tabula de sarcophago, in quo corpus sanctum jacebat, odor tanti vigoris et tam suavissimus emanavit, ut omnium illic existentium mentes in admirationem commutaret et gaudium." AASS Oct. VIII, Dies 17, Col. 0263F.

[1049] "Præterea quidam liquor purus et clarus ad instar olei olivarum suavissimi mirandique odoris de ipso capite resudabat, qui sindones et pannos, quibus involvebatur ipsum caput, reddebat totaliter madidos, quasi de flumine tracti essent et ad desiccandum extorti." AASS Oct. VIII, Dies 17, Col. 0263F-0264A. "ad instar" could also be translated as "in the likeness" or "in the form of."

author of Hedwig's *vita* claimed Hedwig's oil flowed from her head, highly symbolic of Christ himself, the head of the Church. A laywoman's head thus became a source of oil used to anoint the sick, in lieu of the "oil of the sick" consecrated by bishops. Did the people who flocked to Hedwig's tomb have greater faith in a laywoman's power to heal than a bishop's hallowed oil? Whether the people loved the saint or her oil, they arrived in droves to celebrate Hedwig's translation. The pilgrims who sought oil from Hedwig's tomb were not only peasants, but the nobles and ecclesiastical elites of the Holy Roman Empire.[1050]

FEMALE ITALIAN MYROBLYTES

In late medieval Italy, miraculous oil flowing from saints' tombs became a miracle exclusively associated with holy women. The Italic female myroblytes of the late thirteenth and fourteenth centuries crossed social boundaries, comprising both noble women and servant-girls alike. The most remarkable trend in the myroblyte *vitae* from Italy in this period, however, is the distinct absence of male saints producing oil. The last male cisalpine myroblyte appears to have been Fantinus the Confessor (c.927-1000), who lived as a hermit and monk in Taurino in Calabria. Beginning in the early fourteenth century, a series of female myroblytes emerged in northern Italy. These women stemmed from both powerful, noble families as well as peasant families; they were abbesses of wealthy convents but also lay women tertiaries and servants. Almost invariably, the women were associated with the Franciscans, Dominicans, or sometimes Cistercians, whose members authored the *vitae* and fostered devotion to the myroblytes. In the *legendae* of these Italian holy women, oil did not simply reveal the saint's sanctity or her power to heal the sick. Oil flowing from women's tombs

---

[1050] "Ad prædictam autem festivitatem de diversis mundi regionibus confluxit populi multitudo quasi innumerabilis. Principes quoque et domini terrarum, prælati et rectores plurimi Ecclesiarum cum religiosarum multitudine personarum Ordinum diversorum sua solemnizaverunt præsentia festum illud, in quo fuit hæc translatio celebrata." AASS Oct. VIII, Dies 17, Col. 0264A.

demonstrated the power and authority of women within their own communities and within the

Church.

Lay women, including both tertiaries and domestic servants with humble origins, became

increasingly popular saints in the late medieval period, when they were also reputed to produce oil.

Michael Goodich argued that greater numbers of *ancillae Domini,* female servant-saints, appeared in

late medieval Italy as a result of the mendicants orders, which tried to bring an increasingly urban,

servant class within the fold of the Church.[1051] Mendicants viewed women as particularly susceptible

to heretical sects and thus promoted the cults of female saints who would appeal to women,

particularly women belonging to the servant class.[1052] In some instances these female saints reversed

social conventions and appropriated quintessentially male roles during life and after death. Bishops

were no longer the only sources of holy oil which had the power to cure the illnesses of the general

medieval population. Poor lay women also proved to be powerful saints and intercessors whose

tombs could produce the powerful, desirable healing liquid, without the aid of bishops. Male

hagiographers were needed, however, to record and legitimize the myroblytes' miraculous activity,

whether the holy woman was a poor servant or a famed abbess.

AN OILY ABBESS: FRANCA VISALTA

Franca Visalta (1170-1218), the Cistercian Abbess of Piacenza, acquired a reputation for

producing miraculous oil-like water that healed many. Her first vita, composed by a priest named

Lanfranc[1053] shortly after her death, recorded no miracles at the abbess' tomb. A century later,

however, in 1326, a Cistercian monk named Betramo Reoldo (dates unknown) recorded a

---

[1051] Michael Goodich, "Ancilla Dei: The Servant as Saint in the Late Middle Ages," in *Lives and Miracles of the Saints: Studies in Medieval Hagiography,* ed. Michael E. Goodich, Variorum Collected Studies Series, 798 (Aldershot: Ashgate, 2004), 120–22.

[1052] Ibid., 121.

[1053] Not Lanfranc of Bec (c.1005-1089).

prodigious amount of liquid flowing from the abbess' dead body (BHL 3093). According to

Betramo, on the feast of Bernard of Clairvaux in 1266, water with the color of oil (*acqua, quasi olei

colorata*) flowed from Franca's relics.[1054] Betramo also claimed that in 1306, lamps near Franca's

tomb miraculously replenished themselves, burning endlessly.[1055] As discussed above, the prominent

Cistercian Caesarius of Heisterbach had authored Elizabeth of Hungary's *legenda* in the mid 1230s,

comparing Elizabeth's oil to that of Catherine of Alexandria, which he discussed in the *Dialogus

Miraculorum*. One could surmise, therefore, that nearly a century later, these works would have been

known to Cistercians living and composing biographical texts in northern Italy. Although Franca

Visalta's biographer may have not been so bold as to claim that actual oil flowed from her tomb

(only an oil-like liquid), later authors would claim oil more precious than balsam flowed from the

tombs of female saints.

An Accident or a Miracle? Humility of Faenza's Oil

The early life of Humility the Vallombrosian (1226-1310), born Rosanese Negusanti, fits one

prototype of Italian holy women: she was born to a noble family, married a wealthy man in her

youth, lost her children, and later persuaded her husband to enter religious life.[1056] Humility's life was

unlike that of other Italian holy women, however, in several ways. Humility distinguished herself

---

[1054] "Quam capsam cum aperuissent, viderunt et invenerunt eam aqua, quasi oleo colorata, plenam; et ossa S. Franchae superenatantia. Super quo mirabiliter obstupescentes, fecerunt apportari vasa plura vitrea et vacua, in quibus aquam ipsam collegerunt, ac in sacrario devote reposuerunt: et sic altari parvo condito, capsellam, ossa reliquiasque continentem, cum reverentia reposuerunt in altari illo, quod est in oratorio dicto prope altare S. Michaelis, cujus devota tam hic quam & in S. Syro fuit." AASS Aprilis III, Dies 25. BHL 3093.

[1055] "In primis, cum anno Domini millesimo trecentesimo sexto, quadam die propter suam solicitudinem Conventu præsente lampadem extinxisset, quæ coram altari S. Franchæ solet ardere, pariter ibidem consistens cum Sociabus pluribus; viderunt eamdem lampadem per seipsam reaccensam. Quod quidem factum non tantum tunc et semel, sed multoties accidisse clamatur per Conventum, ita quod etiam divulgatum sit apud seculares. Ex quibus cum plures viderint id ipsum, sæpe de oleo dictæ lampadis requisiverunt, devoteque quandoque perceperunt, quasi pro reliquiis perfruendo. Propter quod statutum est, ut numquam extinguatur, et sic ardet continue diebus noctibusque, mirantibus plurimis; quia in ea vix vix oleum consumatur." AASS Aprilis III, Dies 25. BHL 3093.

[1056] E. Ann Matter, "Italian Holy Women: A Survey," in *Medieval Holy Women in the Christian Tradition C. 1100-C. 1500*, Brepols Essays in European Culture, v. 1 (Turnhout, Belgium: Brepols, 2010), 536. Michael Goodich presents the *ancilla domini* as another type of Italian holy woman. See Goodich, "Ancilla Dei."

through her preaching. As noted above, the cults of Catherine of Alexandria and Mary Magdalene

had previously established a correlation between preaching and dispensing oil.[1057] In Humility's *vitae*,

we see another holy woman whose speech flowed during her earthly life and whose tomb flowed

after death.

Humility's actions as well as her words departed from the social and religious norms of her

day. Catherine Mooney argued that Humility' *vitae* emphasized the saint's authority and her

independent, persuasive power.[1058] She defied established monastic convention by fleeing her

monastery to seek a more contemplative life as a secluded hermit. When various powerful

authorities beseeched her to return to her monastery, she did so as an anchorite, spending the next

decade in relative isolation. As a result of her extreme lifestyle and ascetic devotion, Humility'

reputation for sanctity grew. Holy men and women were drawn to the eremetical figure, particularly

women. Like Lutgard of Aywières, Humility had mystical tendencies and cultivated a particular

devotion to John the Evangelist. She refused to live according to either the Benedictine or

Franciscan rule, prompting her to forge a new path for religious women in northern Italy.[1059] As the

result of a vision she received from the Blessed Virgin Mary, Humility founded two Vallombrosian

convents for women, one in Faenza and one in Florence. Following her death in 1310, numerous

miracles occurred at her tomb, including the appearance of oil, which astonished many.

Two *legendae* composed shortly after Humility' death recorded her life and post-mortem

miraculous activity.[1060] A Vallombrosian monk by the name of Biagio likely authored Humility' Latin

vita, which dates to circa 1332. In 1345, Silvestro Ardenti, another Vallombrosian monk, composed a

---

[1057] Matter, "Italian Holy Women: A Survey," 537; Catherine M Mooney, "Authority and Inspiration in the Vitae and Sermons of Humility of Faenza.," in *Medieval Monastic Preaching,* ed. Carolyn Muessig, Brill's Studies in Intellectual History, 90 (Leiden: Brill, 1998), 123–44.

[1058] Mooney, "Authority and Inspiration in the Vitae and Sermons of Humility of Faenza," 125.

[1059] For a summary of Humility's life and a critical edition of her biographical dossier, see Adele Simonetti, ed., *Le Vite di Umiltà da Faenza: agiografia trecentesca dal latino al volgare* (Florence: Edizioni del Galluzzo, 1997).

[1060] Ibid.; Lea Montuschi, "Voci e storie ei monache del medio evo Italiano: Umiltà da Faenza (1226-1310). Il racconto della sua vita nella spiritualità Vallombrosna," *Studia Monastica: commentarium ad rem monasticam investigandam* 55, no. 1 (2013): 157–67.

vernacular version of the saint's life, based largely on the Latin version. The narrative appears to be tailored to a female audience, likely the Vallombrosian nuns themselves. The Bollandists presented what they claimed to be a composite version of the two texts.[1061] Adele Simonetti, however, published both texts in critical edition, based on numerous redactions, arguing the two texts must be examined separately. In fact, a comparison of the Biagio's and Ardenti's texts reveals significant discrepancies in the post-mortem miracle accounts, particularly with respect to Humility's holy oil.

In the Latin version of Humility's life, Biagio described the miraculous oil flowing from the abbess' tomb as her first miracle post-mortem. When throngs of people, lay and clerical alike, came to venerated Humility's body, her tomb began to work miracles:

> The stone placed above the tomb suddenly began to appear to emit oil. When another of the sisters saw this (it was no illusion), she began to prudently wipe the edge [of the tomb] many times. While [the sister] observed the [oil] to be something divine, everyone approaching [the tomb] said that it was so. With the stone having been wiped, every experience attested to [the miracle's] truth and on account of this, everyone gave avid care to [Humility's] translation to Florence.[1062]

According to Biagio, on June 6, 1311, just a year after Humility's death, the Bishop of Florence, various abbots, prelates, clerics and a multitude of laity gathered around the oil-producing body for the saint's translation. Curiously enough, however, the *vita* makes no further mention of oil seeping from Humility's tomb. Although the saint cured the illnesses of many who sought succor at her tomb, she did so through means other than oil, such as through prayer or by raising a cross above the afflicted. Ardenti, in contrast, omits the discussion of oil flowing just after her death, in the presence of those gathered to mourn her. Instead, the vernacular *vita* gives the back story to her

---

[1061] AASS Mai V, Dies 22. BHL 4045.

[1062] "Cepit interea lapis superpositus tumulo emictere oleum apparenter. Quod altera sororum attendens, ne foret illusio, cepit tergere sepe sepius et prudenter; quod dum quid divinum fore conspexit, ut erat dixit omnibus accedentibus. Facta extersione, omni experientia verifice patuit, et ob id de ipsius translatione Florentinis avidam curam dedit." Biagio, "Vita Sancte Humilitatis Abbatisse Ordinis Vallisumbrose," in *Le Vite di Umiltà da Faenza: agiografia trecentesca dal latino al volgare* (Florence: Edizioni del Galluzzo, 1997), 16.

translation, offering an elaborate narrative of how skeptical monks questioned the veracity of the

miraculous oil. The vernacular *vita* described how faith in Humility's oil depended on one's gender.

The Vallombrosian sisters and lay women first recognized and believed in the copious amount of oil

flowing from Humility's tomb, while male monks questioned the oil's legitimacy, only to eventually

be proven wrong.[1063]

In his *Vita di Umiltà*, Ardenti did not claim that oil flowed from Humility's tomb just after

her death, when lay and clerical admirers surrounded her tomb. Instead, Ardenti described how

Humility's tomb began to spontaneously ooze on a more ordinary day, in more ordinary company

sometime after her initial burial.

> After the venerable saint was buried in the space between the wall and the left side of the
> altar of the aforementioned church [St. John the Evangelist], a carved marble stone was
> placed over her sepulcher. And after some time, one day the aforementioned stone began to
> sweat and spill the purest clear oil…certain monks from the choir above, having no respect
> for the miracle, thought that it was oil carelessly spilled there by some minister of the altar or
> by the rupture of a lamp or another vessel and pointing it out to a very old sister, she replied
> to them: 'Be silent and let us await the work of the Lord and we will see what will be.' "[1064]

Following this rather cryptic admonition, the clerics of the monastery gathered to assess the miracle

and investigate its legitimacy:

> After a few days, the church's cleric noticed this miracle but since he did not see, nor could
> he imagine, how this oil could have shot out, so powerfully miraculous. Completely
> stupefied, he ran to announce the aforementioned mishap to the sisters of the place. The
> abbess then sent the aforementioned elderly sister to him to attest to so great a novelty. The

---

[1063] Silvio Ardenti, "Vita di Umiltà," in *Le Vite di Umiltà da Faenza: agiografia trecentesca dal latino al volgare* (Florence: Edizioni del Galluzzo, 1997), 54–57.

[1064] "Poi che fu sopellita la venerabile santa nello spazzo tra 'l muro e 'l sinistro altare della Chiesa predetta, fu messa una lapida di marmot lavorata sopra la sua sopoltura. E dopo alquanto tempo cominciò un giorno la detta lapida a risudare e a spandere olio purissimo e chiaro. Della qual cosa acorgendosi certe monache del coro di sopra, nonn-avendo rispetto al miracolo, pensarono che fosse olio che quivi per alcuno ministro della Chiesa incautamente fosse versato, o per rottura di lanpana o d'altro vasello, e manifestando ciò ad alcuna molta antica suora, disse a llor: 'Tacete e attendiamo l'operatione del Signore, e vedremo quel che sarà.' " Ibid., 55–56.

sister, knowing with certainty that it was a miracle, in reverence placed a piece of cloth over the aforementioned stone, such that no one would step on it with their feet. She returned to the other sisters and said to them: 'Behold, about this deed, let no one be bothered to reason with anyone, and we will see what the Lord will do again before us.'[1065]

In Ardenti's narrative, the tension between incredulous men and enlightened women further played out when a monk from nearby Florence paid a visit to Humility's tomb "to see the miracle."[1066] When the monk saw the oil on the tomb, he could not believe what he saw and, like the other monks, opined a vial of oil must have fallen on the tomb by accident.[1067] The elderly sister testified to veracity of the miracle by showing the skeptical monk her veil and saying she used it to wipe up the myroblyte's oil. Then, she invited the monk to witness the miraculous oil flowing from the tomb with his own eyes. Humility's tomb began to ooze as if on cue:

> A moment later, the said stone began little by little to perspire and to throw off the thickest drops, bright and clear like the purest oil, abundantly spreading out over the said stone. The monk, seeing such a thing, so powerfully miraculous, and being convinced of the miracle, returned to his monastery with great faith, praising God and commending himself to the saint.[1068]

Why, one might wonder, were these northern Italian clerics so skeptical about Humility's oil if the oil of the saints was an entrenched tradition of the Church by the early fourteenth century? Surely

---

[1065] "Dopo alcun giorno il chierico della Chiesa s'accorse di questo miracolo, e però ch'egli non vedeva né immaginare poteva come quell'olio vi potesse essere sparto, si maravigliò fortissimamente, e tutto stupefato corse incontanente ad nunziare il detto accidente alle suore del luogo. Allora la badessa vi mandò la predetta antica suora per certificarsi di tanta novitade, la quale conoscendo certamente che quello era miracolo, puose per reverenza sopra la detta lapida un pezzo di <bancale>, acciò ch'altri non vi montasse co'piedi. E ritornata a l'atre suore disse a lloro: 'Vedete, di questo fatto niente vi travagliate di ragionare con persona, e vedremo quello che farà ancora lo Signore per inanzi." Ibid., 56.
[1066] "In questo mezzo, venendo alcuno Monaco del munistero di Santo Pancrazio di Fiorenza al detto luogo per vedere lo miracolo, aprossimossi alla sua sepoltura…" Ibid.
[1067] "…e veduto ch'ebbe il detto licore, guatando innalto fe' segno di sospitione, quasi stimasse che dalla parte di sopra vi fosse potuto cadere per alcuno accidente." Ibid.
[1068] "E poco stante cominciò la detta lapida a poco a poco a sudare e gittare gocciole grossissime, lucide e chiare in similitudine d'olio purissimo, stendendosi sopra la detta lapida abondevolmente: la qual cosa vedendo il Monaco, si maravigliò fortissimamente, e certificato del miracolo, laudando Iddio e racomandandosi alla santa, con gran fiduzia si ritornò al suo monasterio." Ibid.

the monks had sung an antiphon or two about the oil of Nicholas of Myra or Catherine of Alexandria. In fact, the verb Ardenti used to describe the oil seeping from Humility's tomb *(sudare)* is the same verb that appears in Nicholas of Myra's Office. The Vallombrosian nuns were surely not the only choristers familiar with myroblyte legends. Were the monks perplexed that oil should flow from the tomb of a woman or someone who lived in their own age or? Surely they too were familiar with the legends of ecstatic pilgrims finding oil seeping from the relics of Nicholas and Catherine. Was Ardenti simply presenting the well-worn trope of a show-down between a saint and her skeptics? Was he perhaps tailoring his narrative to the Vallombrosian sisters, who emerged triumphant from the conflict between those who believed and those who disbelieved in Humility's sanctity?

In his retelling of Humility's *miracula,* Ardenti further addressed the skepticism about the miracle by alluding to the Gospel scene in which Mary Magdalene and other myrrh-bearing women approach Jesus' tomb to anoint his body after death.[1069] In the Gospel, when the women discover Jesus' tomb to be empty, they return to the disciples, proclaiming Jesus was the Christ, the Anointed One, the Messiah who resurrected. In Ardenti's replaying of the biblical scene, a group of women from Florence visit Humility's tomb, only to discover, to their great surprise, the tomb oozing oil:

> After a few days, certain Florentine women, who went to visit [Humility's] tomb in order to commend themselves [to the saint] with great fervor of devotion, lifted the said cloth, knowing nothing of the things mentioned above. Seeing the stone underneath bathed with oil and opining that it was a sign of [Humility's] sanctity, silent no longer, they ran to the city and, announcing what they had seen, roused all the townspeople to go and see so wonderful a thing, saying: 'Run, run and see the saint of Faenza: oil spouts from her tomb!'[1070]

[1069] In all four Gospel accounts, the first witnesses of Jesus' resurrection are women. The Gospels differ, however, about who the women were, except they all agree that Mary Magdalene was present. See Mark 16:1-8; Matt 28:1-10; Luke 24:1-8; John 20:1-13.

[1070] "E dopo alquanti dì, essendo certe donne fiorentine andate a visitare la sua sepoltura, e per racomandarlesi per più fervor di devotione alzarono il predetto bancale, non sapiendo niente delle cose predette, e vegendo bagnata d'olio la lapida ch'era di sopra, stimando che fosse segno della sua santitade, incontanente senza più corsono alla cittade e,

In Ardenti's narrative, the women possess the capacity to recognize the oil as miraculous and announce, the good news. Furthermore, Humility became another Christ. By juxtaposing the biblical scene of the myrrh-bearers discovering the empty tomb with the Florentine women discovering the oily tomb, Ardenti drew a symbolic parallel between Christ and Humility. The author also did so by alluding to a chant based on the Song of Songs, in which young women show adoration for "the King" the anointed Christ by running after him. Ardenti played off his audience's knowledge of the chant, *In odore unguentorum tuorum,* which was sung during the Divine Office on the Feast of the Assumption and the Commune of Virgins. The allusions turns around the word "run" (*correte*): "We run in the scent of your unguents, the young women love you exceedingly."[1071] In Humility's *vita,* a Florentine woman urges the townspeople to "Run, run and see the saint of Faenza: oil spouts from her tomb!"[1072] Through this allusion, Ardenti strengthened the parallel between Humility and Christ, showing that a holy woman could be the Anointed One and the anointer.

In Ardenti's narrative, the nuns claimed a privileged status and knowledge about their foundress' oil not accorded to either male clerics or the laity. After the Florentine women had announced the miracle and encouraged all the people of Florence to run to Humility's tomb, the townspeople unanimously wished to see the oil and circulate news of the miracle. In essence, they wanted to play a role in declaring Humility a saint. The elderly nun stepped in again, however, to admonish the people to not overstep their bounds and appropriate a role that only rightfully belonged to the nuns themselves. Addressing the townspeople, the elderly nun gently reestablished their appropriate role as the laity: "My children, God advises you: what you are saying would be neither suitable nor legal for you laity. Since we live according to a rule and have a superior over

---

manifestando ciò che veduto avieno, commossono tutti i cittadini ad andare a vedere cotanto mirabile cosa dicendo: "Correte, correte a vedere la santa da Faenza: gitta olio sopra la sua sepoltura." Ardenti, "Vita Di Umiltà," 56–57.
[1071] "in odore unguentorum tuorum currimus adolescentulae dilexerunt te nimis." See above.
[1072] Ardenti, "Vita Di Umiltà," 57.

us…it is not for you to do this."[1073] The people quickly acquiesced to the gentle words of the elderly

sister and returned to their houses "with great consolation."[1074] Ardenti's narrative then returned to

the storyline found in Biagio's text. According to Ardenti soon after this confrontation between the

nuns and the townspeople, important clerics gathered at the tomb to translate Humility's body, with

due ceremony, to Florence. The members of the ecclesiastical hierarchy included the Bishop of

Florence, three abbots, prelates, religious and secular clerics, as well as a great multitude of the laity.

Ardenti makes no mention, however, of oil flowing from the tomb at that point in time or

thereafter. In Ardenti's version of the story, the oil allowed the nuns to showcase their superiority

over both male clerics and the laity. The Vallombrosian nuns demonstrated their ability to recognize

legitimate miracles and announce that a saint lived among them.

THE IMMACULATE MYROBLYTE: AGNES OF MONTEPULCIANO

Approximately two decades after Ardenti embellished Humility's *vita*, Raymond of Capua

(1330-1399) tried his hand at composing a myroblyte's *vita*. Although Agnes of Montepulciano

(1268-1317) died before Raymond was born, he composed the prioress' life in 1365-1366, claiming

among other miracles, that a beautiful fragrance and abundance of holy oil emanated from her tomb.

Agnes spent her entire life in women's religious houses and achieved fame as a miracle-worker and

mystic. At the age of nine, Agnes joined a group of religious sisters known as Sister of the Sackcloth

who resided near her hometown of Montepulciano in southern Tuscany. At fourteenth years old,

Agnes founded a new convent for women in Proceno, a town in the Province of Viterbo, roughly 30

miles south of Montepulciano. A year later, the sisters of Proceno elected Agnes to be their abbess.

In 1298, Agnes returned to Montepulciano to found a new convent for women. The convent,

---

[1073] "Figliuli miei, Dio vi consigli: questo che dite non saria convonevole né licito a voi secolari, inperò che noi semo a
regula e avemo maggiore sopra noi, si che ad altrui s'aspetta, e non a voi, di fare queste cose." Ibid.
[1074] "con molta consolation." Ibid.

dedicated as Santa Maria Novella, was loosely affiliated with the Dominican order and later attempted to adopt a more definite Dominican identity, in part, through having a young Dominican, Raymond of Capua, compose the foundress' *vita*.[1075]

Although Raymond of Capua never met Agnes of Montepulciano, he played a central role in establishing her fame for holiness and miraculous oozing. Raymond studied law at the University of Bologna, entered the Order of Preachers, and became the rector of the convent in Montepulciano, where he composed Agnes' *legenda* almost a half century after the saint's death. In 1380, he became Master General of Dominicans, a role he retained until his death in 1399. Working in tandem Catherine of Siena (1347-1380), whose disciple he became, Raymond had sought to bring the papacy back to Rome during the period of the "Babylonian Captivity."[1076] Raymond's life of Catherine of Siena contains a rapturous praise of Agnes, whom Catherine also revered.

Raymond crafted the biography of a woman he had never met by weaving together various legends that circulated in the monastery or by recording stories from elderly sisters who had known the saint in their youth.[1077] According to Silvia Nocentini, Raymond likely expanded and embellished the established legend of Agnes in order to meet the needs of the community, which viewed Agnes as their patron.[1078] Maiju Lehmijoki-Gardner has argued that the nuns of Montepulciano, like other Dominican nuns and penitents in Italy, essentially enlisted a male cleric's services as a hagiographer to strengthen their convent's association with a religious order and in so doing, gain legitimacy as a religious institution. Although the convent originally bore the name Santa Maria Novella, the sisters' devotion to their foundress led them and others to refer to the convent as Saint Agnes. Raymond's

---

[1075] Regarding the somewhat tenuous affiliation of this convent with the Dominican Order, see Maiju Lehmijoki-Gardner, "The Women behind Their Saints: Dominican Women's Institutional Uses of the Cults of Their Religious Companions," in *Images of Medieval Sanctity: Essays in Honour of Gary Dickson*, ed. Debra Higgs Strickland, Visualising the Middle Ages, 1 (Leiden: Brill, 2007), 5–24.

[1076] For a brief introduction to Raymond's life and works, see Silvia Nocentini, "Introduzione," in *Legenda Beate Agnetis de Monte Policiano* (Tavarnuzze (Firenze): SISMEL edizioni del Galluzzo, 2001), ix – lix.

[1077] Ibid., xiii.

[1078] Ibid., xiv.

vita may have served in part to justify such an irregular rededication, whether formal or informal. A

formal renaming would not have been licit according to canon law, especially given the non-beatified

status of the patroness.[1079]

Raymond established Agnes' sanctity, in part, by presenting the foundress as being another

Christ. Like Ardenti's portrayal of Humility of Faenza, Raymond's *legenda* illustrated the likeness

between Agnes and Christ by recounting the miracles she accomplished while alive, including

multiplying bread and turning water into wine.[1080] Agnes also miraculously replenished an empty oil

jar, making her like Elijah, the forerunner of Christ, according to the *Glossa Ordinaria.*[1081] In the

Proceno convent, money did not flow in abundance. Neither did oil. One day, the sister in charge of

the *officium temporalia* (the non-sacred duty of cooking) discovered there was no more oil to be found.

Agnes urged the sister to see with the eyes of faith that the oil jar was full. As if referring to the

parable of the Wise and Foolish Virgins, Raymond referred to Agnes as "the holy virgin" (*virgo*

sancta), who urged the disbelieving sister to have faith: " 'Believe, daughter, that this vessel is not

empty. Go back, therefore, and look again, because indubitably you will discover the oil of God

Omnipotent in the vessel for service.' The disciple, humbly obeying the voice of faith, proceeded to

the vessel itself, and she discovered the vessel full with oil all the way to the top."[1082] Agnes' miracle,

naturally, led to a great increase of faith within the convent. The sisters rejoiced and Raymond noted

that the oil lasted abundantly throughout Lent. Before the miracle, there had been barely enough oil

for cooking. After the miracle, there was plentiful oil for "every necessity."[1083] An abundance of oil

---

[1079] Although her canonization process began in 1705, she was only canonized in 1726 by Benedict XIII (r.1724-1730).
See Lehmijoki-Gardner, "The Women behind Their Saints," 10.

[1080] Nocentini, "Introduzione," xxv.

[1081] See Chapters 2, 6, & 8.

[1082] " 'Crede, filia, quod vas vacuum non est. Redi igitur, & iterum videas: quia indubitanter omnipotentis Dei munere
oleum in vase invenies.' Ad cujus vocem fidelis discipula humiliter obediendo, ad vas ipsum perrexit ipsumque plenum
oleo usque ad summum invenit." Raymond of Capua, *Legenda Beate Agnetis de Monte Policiano*, ed. Silvia Nocentini
(Tavarnuzze (Firenze): SISMEL edizioni del Galluzzo, 2001), 28.

[1083] "quod vas parvum olei, quod prius vix paucis diebus ad cotidianum victum sororum solebat sufficere, tunc per totam
Quadragesimam in omni necessitate monasterii copiose impensum abundanter suffecit." Ibid.

during Lent would have been particularly miraculous, given that the supply of holy oil would have

also been at its lowest; bishops only consecrated and distributed holy oil once a year, on the

Thursday before Easter.

Agnes' ability to miraculously produce prodigious amounts of oil, whether for sacred or

profane purposes, continued after her death on April 20, 1317. Although he never made the parallel

entirely explicit, Raymond portrayed Agnes as the Anointed One in so far as oil saturated her body

and tomb.[1084] In the opening lines of Agnes' *legenda,* Raymond referred to the woman as "herself a

fountain of purity and grace."[1085] After her death, Agnes became a fountain of fragrance and holy oil.

Raymond's allusions to Agnes being "the aroma of Christ to God" throughout her *legenda*

culminated in a description of the saint's tomb emitting a sweet fragrance and an abundance of holy

oil.[1086] Shortly after Agnes' death, a devoted sister who was weeping near her deathbed took the

rosary which Agnes had held in her hands, and kissing it, suddenly smelled a fine odor. The sister's

sorrow and anguish suddenly turn into wonder and joy.[1087] Soon the fragrance filled the entire room:

"so quickly the odor filled the cell where the holy body laid, that one could have believed that a

vessel of all the aromatic spices rested there, not a dead body."[1088] The fragrance not only emanated

from the holy corps, but from everything the virgin had ever touched while dead or alive.[1089]

In describing Agnes' marvellously fragrant body, Raymond claimed that such a miracle

should not have surprised his readers given the sanctity of the holy woman while alive: "It's not

surprising, because a soul, so filled with the good fragrance of Christ and the virtues, had inhabited

---

[1084] Nocentini does not list miraculous oil as typical of saints' legends or Dominican hagiography in particular, in contrast with miraculously lovely fragrance which appeared more frequently in saints' lives. Nocentini, "Introduzione," xxvii.
[1085] "ipsum fontem puritatis et gratie."Capua, *Legenda Beate Agnetis de Monte Policiano*, 3.
[1086] 2 Cor. 2:15.
[1087] "subito sensit odorem, quod statim luctus et dolor in admirationem et gaudium sunt conversi." Capua, *Legenda Beate Agnetis de Monte Policiano*, 69.
[1088] "tantus subito odor cellam implevit, ubi sacrum corpus iacebat, quod putasses non corpus mortuum, sed omnium aromatum vasculum ibi repositum." Ibid.
[1089] "Nec solum de virgineo corpore odor ille prodibat, sed de omnibus que ipsum corpus in vita vel in morte tetigerant." Ibid.

that body, such that in the fragrance of her unguents, she drew a multitude of maids."[1090] In

describing the *odorem unguentorum suorum*, Raymond alluded to the bride of the Song of Songs who

loved the unguents of the bridegroom: "Draw me: we will run after you in the odor of your

unguents."[1091] Just as the young women (*adolescentulas*) in the Song of Songs loved the bridegroom, so

too did the sisters of Montepulciano adore Agnes, who thus became more Christ-like through her

profusion of fragrance. Given the allusion to the bridegroom's unguents, Raymond was one step

away from describing flowing oil: "your name is like oil poured out."[1092] As in Ardenti's account of

the women discovering Humility's oil, when the sisters of Montepulciano discovered the

magnificent fragrance of their foundress, they disseminated the good news. Setting up the narrative

for Agnes' next miracle, Raymond compared Agnes' corpse to a lamp (i.e. a vessel filled with oil).

Just as a lamp could not be concealed but needed to be raised on a lampstand, so too did the news

of Agnes' miraculously scent-filled body spread. With her fragrant body, she drew the sisters to

herself as she had drawn them, while alive, with "spiritual light."[1093]

Following the discovery of the fragrance emanating from Agnes' corps, she quickly acquired

a reputation for being able to heal the sick. Those who were ill or tending to the sick received

visions admonishing them to seek succor at Agnes' tomb. Raymond tells us that according to

custom, the nuns sought to preserve Agnes' body through embalming and sent envoys to a

neighboring city to retrieve balsam, the aromatic oil or tree resin which, when mixed with olive oil,

makes chrism, the holiest of holy oils. Raymond recounted how, in a moment of dearth, Agnes

herself became a source of balsam: "The Most Almighty Lord, who through his miraculous deeds no

creature wants, in one and the same miraculous sign at once and only once, appeared to not bring

---

[1090] "Nec mirum, quia corpus illud inhabitaverat anima tam plena bono Christi et virtutum odore, quod in odorem
unguentorum suorum adolescentularum multitudinem traxerat." Ibid.

[1091] "Trahe me, post te curremus in odorem unguentorum tuorum." Cant.1:3.

[1092] "Oleum effusum nomen tuum." Cant.1:2.

[1093] "Dantur ergo duplicate laude Altissimo et currunt undique populi circumstantes ad tam mirum miraculorum initium,
nec potest occultari lucerna sub modio, quin sicut in vita fideles traxerat luce spirituali, eos etiam post mortem odore
attrahat corporali." Capua, *Legenda Beate Agnetis de Monte Policiano*, 69.

balsam to Agnes' relics for embalming and, on account of the audible grumblings, was able through

an exchange of lesser balsam, to give balsam by extracting a yet more precious liquid."[1094] Agnes'

body began to produce a prodigious amount of fragrant, holy oil:

> For after the mission of the aforementioned messengers, the body of the sacred virgin began
> to ooze around the extremities of the hands and feet and to discharge numerous drops of
> precious liquid and to saturate cloths underneath with the liquid itself, such that it was clearly
> understood that the body did not need any balsam, because the body itself produced a liquid
> more precious than balsam.[1095]

Soon after Agnes began to ooze, "thinking carefully" the sisters placed vessels beneath the body to

catch the dripping liquid and called the monks to the tomb to witness the miracle. Like Ardenti,

Raymond addressed the possibility of skepticism regarding the authenticity of the holy oil: "all

together they openly gaze on Agnes' miracles without ambiguity."[1096] Agnes' oil, like the oil of other

myroblytes, cured many illnesses. Throngs of people, of all genders and ages, afflicted with a variety

of disabilities, flocked to Agnes' tomb and found the cures they sought. Moreover, Raymond

explicitly recorded the fact than men as well as women sought succor at the tomb: "The sick run,

male and female, and devoutly beg to be anointed with holy oil. Many are anointed and are liberated

without any delay."[1097] Agnes' service as a healer extended to the wider population, beyond the

women of the convent. Not only men, but married women as well as virgins sought the oil. Making

a rather original contribution to the myroblyte phenomenon, Raymond argued that, as the bride of

---

[1094] "Sed omnipotentissimus Dominus, qui in factis suis mirabilibus nulla indigent creatura, uno et eodem signo mirabili simul et semel ostendit et Agnetis reliquias, pro incorruptione, balsam non egere, et de se ipsis balsamum querentibus absque auri commutatione posse nedum balsamum, sed pretiosiorem adhuc liquorem educendo donare." Capua, *Legenda Beate Agnetis de Monte Policiano,* 71.

[1095] "Nam post missionem nunciorum supradictorum cepit corpus sacre virginis desudare circa manuum extremitates et pedem, ac frequentes guttas pretiosi liquoris emittere, suppositosque pannos ipso liquore replere, ut clare daretur intelligi quod balsamo non egebat corpus, quod de se ipso liquorem, pretiosiorem balsamo, producebat." Ibid.

[1096] "Quod perpendentes sorores , vasa supponunt, fratres advocant, miraculum monstrant et, congregatis ad cratem terrigenis, cuncti Agnetis mirabilia absque ambiguitate patenter aspiciunt..." Ibid.

[1097] "Currunt languentes, mares et femine, petuntque devote sacro inungi oleo et quotquot inunguntur, absque dilatione temporis liberantur..." Ibid., 71–72.

Christ, Agnes' body was "intact" (*integrum*) during her life, which accounted for the incorruptibility

of her corpse after death. Thus, since her body was pure, no balsam was needed to preserve her

corpse from decay. In fact, on account of her virginal sanctity, she produced oil that surpassed

balsam. Agnes' oil was thus a product of her virginal purity and a preservative of her corporeality, an

innovation on Raymond of Capua's part.

MARGARET OF CITTÀ DI CASTELLO

Following Raymond of Capua's lead, other Dominican biographers produced *legendae* of

Italian holy women producing holy oil. Margaret of Città di Castello (1286/7-1320), a Dominican

tertiary of sorts, became the subject of several hagiographical compositions, including two Latin

legendae composed by anonymous authors sometime in the 1300s and a vernacular version of her life

composed by the Dominican Tommaso Caffarini (c.1350-1434) in 1400.[1098] Born blind and

unusually small, Margaret faced many trials in her infancy and youth. Margaret's parents, who were

nobles, tried first to hide their daughter away in their home. They later tried to cure Margaret's

blindness at the tomb of a Franciscan saint, Brother Jacob of Città di Castello.[1099] When the

Franciscan was unable cure Margaret, her parents left their daughter with the nuns of the convent of

St. Margaret, where Margaret worked as their servant until they expelled her for her extreme

asceticism. A married couple, described as "pious citizens" (*piis civibus*), took Margaret into their

home, where she lived and worked as a servant. This couple would later promote her cult.[1100] During

her life with the married couple, Margaret frequented the church of St. Dominic and eventually took

---

[1098] Daniele Solvi, "Riscritture agiografiche: le due 'legendae' latine di Margherita da Città di Castello," *Hagiographica: Rivista di Agiografica e Biografia della Società Internazionale per Lo Studio Del Medio Evo Latino / Journal of Hagiography and Biography of Società Internazionale per Lo Studio Del Medio Evo Latino* 2 (1995): 253.
[1099] Goodich, "*Ancilla Dei*," 130.
[1100] Ibid.

a penitent's habit.[1101] Though blind, Margaret showed a great capacity for learning. She memorized

the Office of the Blessed Virgin and the Cross, which she recited daily. Moreover, she interpreted

the Psalms "beautifully and elegantly, like a professed theologian" and corrected her host-parents'

children when they returned from school. Margaret astonished everyone with her uncanny

"knowledge of letters" since she had never received an education.[1102]

After her death on April 13th, 1320, in the home of her employers (or adoptive parents) the

Dominicans carried Margaret's body to their cloister, where they intended to bury her. A great

"multitude of people," however, demanded that the "holy virgin" be buried in the church, not in the

cloister or cemetery.[1103] Moreover, a girl whom Margaret miraculously healed at her tomb

immediately assumed the Dominican habit.[1104] Just as in the *legenda* of Agnes of Montepulciano, soon

after Margaret's death, the question of embalming soon presented itself, leading to an outpouring of

holy oil from the saint. As in Raymond of Capua's account of Agnes' holy oil, the author

emphasized the virginal nature of the myroblyte. When the Dominican brothers gathered around

Margaret's naked body to embalm her, she modestly covered her private parts with her hands before

a stream of oil flowed from her severed corps.

> Since the stream of people descending on the church increased, and different healing
>
> benefits were being obtained there, the Brothers, who had thought to embalm the body and
>
> thus accepted money from the magistrate of the city for balsam and aromatic spices. With
>
> Master Manno Eugubino and Master Vitali of Castello and with many other religious and
>
> seculars, the Brothers gathered together to disembowel the holy cadaver, with extended
>
> hands and arms, before the altar. Without delay, with everyone examining [the cadaver]

[1101] "In quorum domo cum pietatis ac religionis operibus semper incumberet, continueque dum liceret ecclesiam S. Dominici frequentaret, in ea etiam sanctum habitum, qui Pœnitentiæ dicitur, religiose suscepit; solita quotidie Sacramentali confessione purgare [animam] etiam non peccantem." AASS Aprilis II, Dies 13.

[1102] "quasi Theologiam professa, interpretaretur; ac filios hospitis Venturini, a grammaticali schola revertentes, examinaret & corrigeret; mirantibus cunctis scientiam litterarum, quas non didicerat." AASS Aprilis II, Dies 13.

[1103] "Defertur corpus ad ecclesiam Fratrum Prædicatorum, quod ipsa mandaverat: dumque ibi communis humatio in claustro praeparatur, insurgit multitudo populi, qui ad funus et ecclesiam convenerat, et impeditur opus, dicentibus cunctis, sanctam Virginem in ecclesia, non in claustro vel coemeterio, sepeliendam esse." AASS Aprilis II, Dies 13.

[1104] "statimque recta sanaque prosiliens, inter astantem populum conclamare coepit, B. Margarita me curavit, et illico S. Dominici habitum sumpsit." AASS Aprilis II, Dies 13.

together, the extended arms bend back over the body itself with its own strength and with both hands folded like a cross, cover the secrets of nature. While cutting into the thigh to remove the vitals, suddenly the church and convent were struck by an earthquake and an abundance of oil like balsam flowed from the body, from which indeed many ampullae were filled."[1105]

In Margaret's *legenda*, the "body of Christ" metaphor took on new life when the author drew a parallel between the dead body of the saint and the Dominicans' edifices. The prodigious shaking of buildings by an earthquake heralded the great outpouring of oil. Moreover, the brothers found "a precious treasure within her heart" which they discovered having been "captured by a desire" while embalming her: "searching for the internal heart buried among the viscera, on which the heart itself depends, at once they cut into three stones, like carved globes…in which certain small images representing Christ's nativity with the Blessed Virgin and the crèche and Joseph no less, with a white dove, were observed."[1106] The body of the virgin became a corporeal symbol of the Church, which contained the mystery of Christ's birth and functioned as the font of grace and healing, which is to say, as a fountain of holy oil.

In advancing the canonization of Catherine of Siena, Tommaso Caffarini, a Dominican, presented both Agnes of Montepulciano and Margaret of Città di Castello as Catherine's precursors.[1107] Why, one might ask, did Catherine of Siena not ooze when she fit the profile of a late medieval Italian myroblyte nearly perfectly? Around the time of Catherine of Siena's death, Zita of

---

[1105] "Dum populi concursus augetur ad ecclesiam, et varia ibi sanitatum beneficia impetrantur, Fratres qui de corpore condiendo cogitaverant, ac propterea a magistratu civitatis pro balsamo et aromatibus pecuniam receperant, convocatis peritis, Magistro Manno Eugubino, et Magistro Vitali de Castello, multisque aliis religiosis ac secularibus, sanctum cadaver exenterandum ante altare extensis manibus et brachiis collocant. Nec mora, cunctis inspicientibus, extensa brachia vi propria in ipsum corpus reflectuntur, ambaeque manus in modum crucis complicatae, naturae secreta cooperiunt. Dumque inciso femore praecordia extrahuntur, repentino terræmotu ecclesia & conventus concutitur, oleique quasi balsami copia fluxit e corpore, ex quo etiam nonnullæ ampullæ completæ sunt." AASS Aprilis II, Dies 13.
[1106] "cor inter sepulta viscera quæritantes, intestinum, a quo cor ipsum dependet, incidunt; tresque statim lapides, quasi sculpti globi mespisorum magnitudine, mirabiliter erumpunt: in quibus imagunculæ quædam, Christi nativitatem cum beata Virgine ac præsepe, nec non S. Josephum cum alba columba representantes inspiciebantur." AASS Aprilis II, Dies 13.
[1107] Nocentini, "Introduzione," xix.

Lucca (c.1218-1272), another servant-saint like Margaret of Città di Castello, purportedly produced

an oleous healing liquid. Zita was a lay women of humble origins. Leaving the poverty of her village

of Montesagrati in the Province of Lucca at the age of twelve, Zita became a domestic servant in the

household of the wealthy Faytinelli family of Lucca.[1108] After Zita's death, the family collected

statements about their servant's sanctity, although her canonization process did not advance until

1380, the year of Catherine of Siena's death. Zita's biographer did not specify if the liquid from her

tomb was oil or water.[1109] Nevertheless, the liquid had the power to heal, like oil from the tombs of

other myroblytes. Zita's reputation as a myroblyte might have thus been a late fourteenth century

innovation that drew inspiration directly from the fame surrounding Agnes of Montepulciano and

Margaret of Città di Castello following Catherine of Siena's death. By the end of the fourteenth

century, the miraculous appearance of oil at saint's tomb was predominantly associate with female

virgins, particularly laywomen or tertiaries. According to Dominican hagiographers, the oil signaled

the women's sanctity, which coincided with virginal modesty. In some instances, these lay female

myroblytes appropriated roles previous reserved for male clerics, including the role of preacher.

ROSE OF VITERBO

Few women preached in medieval Europe; those who did so and were unaffiliated with a

convent or religious order were often highly suspect. In several instance, female myroblytes such as

Catherine of Alexandria and Humility of Faenza, were renowned for both their ability to preach and

to produce oil. Rose of Viterbo (1233-1252) was known for both her rhetorical skills and her oil

---

[1108] For a discussion of Zita of Lucca and other holy women servants in Italy, see Goodich, "Ancilla Dei."

[1109] "Post dies siquidem paucos, cœpit de tumba, in qua sacrum corpus manebat, liquor emanare salubris, quo debilium & ægrotorum quorumlibet membra inuncta reddebantur sanitati: & sicut ab omni carnali inquinatione virgineum illud corpus exstitit illibatum, sic huc usque in hodiernum diem a consueta dissolutione & corruptione aliorum cadaverum permanet alienum, ac integrum perseverat; nisi quod aliquantulum apparet corpulentiæ siccioris." AASS April III, Dies 27, Col.0508A.

production. Her words flowed during her life and her tomb oozed after her death.[1110] Born to

impoverished but devout parents, Rose became a street preacher who may have remained a lay

woman her whole life, becoming only loosely affiliated with the Franciscans.[1111] Preachers populated

the streets of thirteenth-century Viterbo, including the Waldensians and Humiliati, whose voices

criticized the papacy.[1112] Anna Benvenuti Papi suggested that Rose's image as a holy woman resulted

in part from political conflicts in thirteenth century Italy, particularly anti-imperial, anti-Ghibelline,

and anti-Cathar sentiment among the mendicant orders.[1113] In Rose's *vitae*, for example, the Holy

Roman Emperor Frederick II (1194-1250) assumed the role of the enemy, the *fautor ereticorum*,

protector of the heretics, while Rose defended the true faith.[1114]

Rose's canonization trial began during the papacy of Alexander IV (r.1254-1261) and

continued under Calixtus III (r. 1455-1458) but never resulted in canonization. A text (BHL 7339)

interpolated into the canonization documents for Rose's trial in 1457 claimed her tomb oozed oil:

"Truly after the exhumation of the sacred body, many asserted that manna in the form of sweet-

smelling oil was found in her tomb."[1115] Rose's *miracula* (BHL 7347) and an appendix (BHL 7345),

however, only recount how Rose's curative water, not oil, healed many.[1116] Although Rose never

reached canonical sainthood, her biographers evidently attempted to bolster her legitimacy as a saint

by suggesting her tomb oozed. Rose's oil attested to her being among the Church's anointed and

akin to some of the Church's great saints, such as Nicholas of Myra and Catherine of Alexandria, as

well as other well-established holy women on the Italic peninsula, such as Humility, Agnes, and

---

[1110] Regarding Rose of Viterbo's preaching, see Darleen Pryds, "Proclaiming Sanctity through Proscribed Acts: The Case of Rose of Viterbo," in *Women Preachers and Prophets through Two Millennia of Christianity*, eds. Beverly Mayne Kienzle and Pamela J. Walker (Berkeley: University of California Press, 1998), 159–72.

[1111] Scholars disagree about Rose's status as tertiary. See Ibid., 161, 167n8; Anna Maria Vacca and Rosa Viterbensis Sancta, *La menta e la croce* (Roma: Bulzoni, 1982); Ernesto M Spigone, *S. Rosa da Viterbo, terziaria francescana, 1235-1252* (Padova: Messaggero di S. Antonio, 1945).

[1112] Pryds, "Proclaiming Sanctity through Proscribed Acts," 162.

[1113] Anna Benvenuti Papi, *"In castro poenitentiae": santità e società femminile nell'Italia medievale* (Roma: Herder, 1990), 138.

[1114] Ibid., 154.

[1115] "Post vero exhumationem sacri corporis fuit assertum a multis, quod in sepulcro ejus fuerat inventum manna in modum olei redolentis." AASS Sept. II, Dies 4, Col. 0439D-E.

[1116] AASS Sept. II, Dies 4.

Margaret. Not only did the oil flowing from Rose tomb manifest her personal sanctity, but also her legitimacy as a preacher within the Church, like other women myroblytes before her.

CANDIDA THE YOUNGER OF NAPLES

In the early sixteenth century, Italy produced the last known myroblyte by reviving the cult of a Late Antique saint known as Candida the Younger of Naples (d. 586). No trace of Candida's cult exists prior to 1525. Candida shared a feast day with Candida the Elder, a first-century martyr whom Saint Peter himself healed and converted. In *Napoli Sacra* (1623), Cesare d'Engenio Caracciolo describes Candida the Elder as "the first Neapolitan Christian."[1117] Curiously enough, Candida the Younger shared a feast day with Rose of Viterbo, who acquire fame as a myroblyte in the early fifteenth century. The Roman Martyrology lists Candida the Younger just before Rose of Viterbo, making no mention of Candida the Elder. Candida the Younger was supposedly a married, noble laywoman, praised for her prayers and works of charity. Her *vita* claims she healed many through the oil that oozed from her tomb. Although Candida the Younger ostensibly died in the late sixth century, the earliest extant manuscript containing her life dates to 1525.[1118] Candida the Younger is curiously absent from De Voragine's *Golden Legend*, perhaps suggesting that her cult had disappeared by the thirteenth century, or had not yet appeared. Since no early-medieval evidence of her cult exists, she may reflect the late medieval and early modern tendency to impute oil miracles to holy women rather than men.

Several historians discussed Candida's piety, including Cesare Baronius as well as Cesare d'Engenio Caracciolo in *Napoli sacra* (1623). The account of Candida's oozing tomb appears in the third reading of Office for her feast day.[1119] According to the *vita*, after her death the faithful

---

[1117] Cesare D'Engenio Caracciolo, *Napoli sacra di d. Cesare d'Engenio Caracciolo, Napolitano* (per Ottauio Beltrano, 1623).
[1118] *Commentarius Praevius*, AASS Sept. II, Dies 4.
[1119] AASS Sept. II, Dies 4. BHL 1538.

deposited her body in a marble tomb in the Basilica of Saint Andrew the Apostle in the Nido region

of southern Naples.[1120] Candida's burial was supposedly by the command of Pope Mauritio and the

Emperor Augustus, errors the Bollandists point out.[1121] According to the Office Proper of Candida

the Younger, she was herself a noblewoman of the Brancaccio family.[1122] In *Napoli sacra*, Cesare

d'Engenio Caracciolo describes how Candida's tomb lay in the Basilica Sant'Andrea, where the

faithful celebrated her feast day.[1123] A shrine in the Chiesa Sant'Angeli a Nido, built by the

Brancaccio family in 1384, supposedly also contained a shrine bearing an inscription claiming

Candida hailed from the Brancaccio line.[1124]

Directly following the account of her burial, the Office describes the healing miracles

Candida accomplished at her tomb: "Since long ago, a certain liquid issued from the same marble

tomb in which the body of the blessed Candida reposed. Devout Christians, assembling together,

anointed the pained or weakened parts of human bodies in the name of the Lord and the bodies

were healed, whatever the illness."[1125] This description of the miraculous oil oozing from Candida's

tomb emphasized the collective nature of the anointing and the fact that the group consisted of

apparently lay-Christians, not clerics. Directly following this description of popular devotion,

however, the author of the *vita* describes how an elite figure also sought succor from Candida. He

bypassed the crowd, however, and sought divine intercession directly at the woman's tomb rather

than through her oil.

Thus a certain nobleman, a citizen of the same Naples, named Philipp, whose surname was

Brancaccio, suffered the greatest sickness, what doctors call paralysis: the members, namely

---

[1120] "Corpus vero ejus honorifice cum hymnis & laudibus repositum fuit in monumento marmoreo in basilica sancti Andreæ apostoli, quæ sita est infra eamdem civitatem Neapolitanam in loco, ubi dicitur, Ad Nidum." AASS Sept. II, Dies 4. Andrew the Apostle was himself a myroblyte. See Chapter 5.

[1121] AASS Sept. II, Dies 4, notes b & c.

[1122] *Commentarius Praevius*, AASS Sept. II, Dies 4.

[1123] Caracciolo, *Napoli sacra di d. Cesare d'Engenio Caracciolo, Napolitano*, 299–300.

[1124] "Sacellum sanctae Candidae Neapolitanae ex familia Brancatia." AASS Sept. II, Dies 4.

[1125] "Igitur post multa curricula temporum, quidam liquor de eodem marmoreo sepulchro, in quo corpus ejusdem beatæ Candidæ repositum fuerat, exibat. Quod religiosi Christiani colligentes, loca dolentia vel infirma humanorum corporum in nomine Domini ungebant; sanique fiebant, a quocumque languore detinebantur." AASS Sept. II, Dies 4.

at the center of his body, were so lethargic or dry that he was unable to perform any functions. Naturally the aforementioned man, thoroughly despising bodily healings on account of the inconvenience of so great a malady, devoutly sought instead to beg for divine assistance. The faithful man thus proceeded to the tomb of the aforementioned venerable woman. Prostrate before the tomb in prayer, exactly as the man knew how, with copious prayers, moving deep sighs and groans, he suppliantly entreated the same Lady [Candida], to such a point that through her holy intercession, he was freed from infirmity. Without doubt, the healing was thus brought about through divine mercy, as if the man, with such great health, had never been held back by such an illness.[1126]

Rather than being anointed with the oil proffered by Candida's followers, the nobleman sought the saint's non-corporeal intercession. The woman healed the paralyzed man without pouring out oil on his paralyzed body. Prayers alone elicited the woman's response and proved sufficient to restore the man to health. In the early sixteenth century, Candida's oil was evidently still popular among Christian's. Nevertheless, Candida's *vita* points ever so slightly toward a decline in faith in holy oil. The nobleman chose to bypass the oil and seek healing from directly from the saint at her tomb.

CONCLUSION

Following the emergence of the cult of Catherine of Alexandria in the eleventh century, biographers increasingly recorded miraculous oil flowing from the living bodies and tombs of female saints. Rather than being a miracle that exclusively represented male ecclesiastical authority and power, holy oil became a sign of female sanctity. In the late medieval period, the women whose bodies oozed miraculous unguent were often women associated with Dominicans, Franciscans and

---

[1126] "Unde quidam nobilis vir, civis ejusdem Neapolis, nomine Philippus, cui cognomen erat Brancatius, maximam patiebatur infirmitatem, quam medici paralysim vocant: membra enim medietatis corporis ejus adeo torpentia seu arida erant, ut nihil operis facere posset. Præfatus quippe vir carnalem medicinam propter nimiæ infirmitatis incommodum penitus despiciens, petere cæleste potius devote quæsivit auxilium. Perrexit itaque fidus ad sepulchrum præfatum venerabilis Feminæ; prostratusque ante illud in oratione, prout melius scivit, prolixis precibus, mœstisque suspiriis & gemitibus eamdem Dominam suppliciter deprecatus est, quatenus per sanctam ejus intercessionem a sua, qua tenebatur, infirmitate liberaretur. Is nimirum divina misericordia ita sanus effectus est, acsi numquam tali valetudine detentus fuisset." AASS Sept. II, Dies 4.

Cistercians. Oil became a sign of corporeal works of mercy and penance, which were characteristic forms of devotion among women of this period. This shift in the perception of oil occurred as Dominicans and Franciscans disseminated the cult of Mary Magdalene, whose oil and alabaster jar symbolized good works and an active apostolate among the laity. Not coincidentally, from the thirteenth through fifteenth centuries, new female myroblytes were as often lay tertiaries as religious sisters. While a handful of male myroblytes (including bishops) continued to appear in the late medieval period, they were a minority. After 1200, the saints who produced holy oil were predominantly women. Their oil signified the potentially powerful role of women within the Church as female myroblytes, not clerics, cured the sick and sanctified their communities.

CHAPTER 8

THE BIRTH OF A MYROBLYTE:
OUR LADY OF THE FLOWING OIL

INTRODUCTION: A PRODIGIOUS ERUPTION

In the Latin West prior to 1200, saints' biographers predominantly associated miraculous oil

with male ecclesiastical authorities, as the *vitae* of myroblytes show. After 1200, authors began to

attribute miraculous oil to female saints, particularly laywomen. A similar shift occurred during the

eleventh and twelfth centuries vis-à-vis the *fons olei* when chroniclers and biblical commentators

circulated a legend about miraculous oil flowing from a Roman church dedicated to Mary, Santa

Maria in Trastevere. According to the oldest known version of the legend, in the first century

B.C.E., oil burst from the ground in Trastevere, a neighborhood across the Tiber River from the city

walls and thus outside Rome's city limits. Although this version of the legend began to circulate in

Europe in the second century C.E., little evidence suggests that any authors located the fountain

within Santa Maria in Trastevere before the twelfth century.[1127] Chronicles and Gospel commentaries

from the late antique and Carolingian period mentioned the *fons olei*, but invariably said the oil

flowed from a *taberna meritoria*, a lodging house for Roman soldiers. Only one piece of evidence,

which dates to the late ninth century, potentially suggested early medieval Romans associated the *fons*

olei with Santa Maria in Trastevere. The majority of extant sources demonstrate that this shift

---

[1127] Dale Kinney, "S. Maria in Trastevere from Its Founding to 1215" (Ph.D., New York University, 1975); Karin
Einaudi, "'Fons Olei' E Anastasio Bibliotecario," *Rivista dell'Istituto Nazionale d'Archeologia e Storia dell'arte* 3, no. s.13
(1990): 179–222; L. J. Engels, "Fons Olei: Abelard, Sermon 4 et Hymne 34," *Festoen*, 1976, 235–47.

occurred in the eleventh or twelfth century.[1128] This chapter expands on the work of previous

scholars by examining a wider source-base of early medieval texts, including biblical commentaries

and chronicles which mention the *fons olei*. These sources reveal that even in the Carolingian period,

the legend of the *fons olei* was quite separate from Marian devotion. Carolingian authors interpreted

the miraculous eruption of oil in Trastevere mainly as portent of Christ's birth, which they said

occurred, by divine arrangement, during the reign of Caesar Augustus. While remaining silent about

Mary, these authors argued that the eruption of oil coincided with the *Pax Romana*, which paved the

way for the Prince of Peace.

ANCIENT LEGENDS ABOUT FLOWING OIL

The ancient Greeks established a precedent for legends about oil flowing before a shrines

dedicated to women in the Mediterranean world. According to Pausanius (c. 115-180 C.E.), the

Greek traveler and geographer, olive oil once flowed before a temple dedicated to Athena. While

Greeks associated Aphrodite with oil suffused with perfume (unguent), they associated Athena

simply with the olive because of the founding myth of the city of Athens.[1129] Athena, the goddess of

war and wisdom, vied with Poseidon, the god of the sea, for the honor of being patron of the city

that would become Athens. Poseidon tried to win people's favor by striking the ground with his

trident, leaving behind a saltwater spring. Athena, in contrast, bequeathed an olive tree, a symbol of

peace and prosperity, to the people. In *Description of Greece* (160-180 C.E.), Pausanius recounted how

olive oil flowed before the temple of Athena following a man's ardent prayer to the goddess:

"...Epopeus...forthwith offered sacrifice for his victory and began a temple of Athena, and when this

was complete he prayed the goddess to make known whether the temple was finished to her liking,

---

[1128] Dale Kinney observed that by the eleventh century, the appellation *fundens oleum* was attributed to the church. See
Kinney, "S. Maria in Trastevere from Its Founding to 1215," 190–91.
[1129] Martin Dudley and Geoffrey Rowell, eds., *Oil of Gladness: Anointing in the Christian Tradition* (London; Collegeville,
MN: SPCK; Liturgical Press, 1993), 27-29, 31.

and after the prayer they say that olive oil flowed before the temple."[1130] While Athena expressed her

favor by producing a great quantity of flowing oil, another goddess expressed her wrath by causing

olive oil to erupt from the earth. Ancient pagan myth bequeathed an idea to medieval Christians:

flowing oil revealed divine favor.

According to a legend recorded by Cassius Dio (c. 164 – c. 229 C.E.), a native Greek speaker

and Roman statesman, in the 30s B.C.E., oil exploded from the ground in Trastevere as a portent,

warning Romans of divine retribution. Following the assassination of Gaius Julius Caesar (100 – 44

B.C.E.) in 44 B.C.E. civil wars beset the late Roman Republic until Gaius Octavianus (63 B.C.E. –

A.D. 14), the nephew and adoptive son of Caesar, defeated Mark Antony in the battle of Actium in

31 B.C.E., reestablishing control of Rome and by extension, the wider Mediterranean.[1131] In 27

B.C.E. Octavian assumed the title 'Augustus,' signaling the end of the Roman Republic and the

advent of imperial rule as well as a period of unprecedented stability known as the *Pax romana*. Circa

200 C.E., when internal strife once again beset the Roman Empire, Cassius Dio began composing

his *Roman History*, an eighty-book narrative of Rome's past, from its founding in 753 B.C.E. to 229

C.E in Greek.[1132] Writing during the period of civil war, Dio described the development of Rome's

imperial government, in which he played a part, with the aim perhaps of pointing the way back to

---

[1130] Pausanias, *Description of Greece*, trans. W. H. S Jones (Cambridge, Mass.: Harvard University Press, 1998), 277.

[1131] According to Jerome, the eruption occured in 39 B.C.E. See Paulus Orosius, *Seven Books of History against the Pagans*, trans. A. T. Fear, Translated Texts for Historians, v. 5 (Liverpool: Liverpool University Press, 2010), 305n283.

[1132] Dale Kinney notes that Dio is the earliest source of the legend. "No earlier context recorded the event: How Dio, writing in the early third century, could have known of the event is not clear. It is not mentioned by Suetonius, and the pertinent books of Livy, Dio's other chief source for the period, are lost. The *Prodigiorum Liber* of Julius Obsequens, drawn ultimately from Livy, is unfortunately also lacunary at just the same point. The question of the primary authority for the *fons olei* must therefore remain unanswered, at least temporarily." Kinney, "S. Maria in Trastevere from Its Founding to 1215," 172. Mary Beard observed that one must read Roman historical works, such as Dio's, with a critical eye, given Roman authors' tendency to project present concerns on the past: "...with these later writers we constantly face the possibility of anachronism: in referring to the Augustan period, they inevitably reflect the concerns of their own day. In fact Dio sometimes slips into the present tense when discussing religious changes of the Augustan principate (as well as more strictly constitutional reforms); and he highlights festivals and ceremonies...that are still practised in his own day." Mary Beard, *Religions of Rome*, vol. 1 (Cambridge ; New York: Cambridge University Press, 1998), 170.

stability and peace.[1133] Dio's narrative constitutes the first textual reference to the *fons olei*, the

miraculous eruption of oil on the banks of the Tiber that later Christian authors interpreted as

heralding the birth of Christ.

In his *Roman History*, Dio described the tumultuous atmosphere of Rome in the early 30's

B.C.E., prior to the reign of Caesar Augustus. The fabric of society was unraveling; discord

abounded among the Roman citizens and civic authorities: "...the populace revolted against the tax-

gatherers, who oppressed them severely, and came to blows with the men themselves, their

assistants, and the soldiers who helped them to collect the money."[1134] In Dio's narrative, the

anxieties of the Roman people were palpable as they looked to omens to understand what the future

might bring.[1135] The social unrest was accompanied by divine wrath, which manifested in prodigies,

which Romans interpreted as warning signs. When such prodigies – or 'unnatural' events – occurred,

the senate would seek the counsel of diviners (*haruspices*) to understand how best to avoid the

imminent danger.[1136] Dio interpreted the prodigious eruption of oil as a portent of impending doom:

> Now many events of a portentous nature had occurred even before this, such as the
>
> spouting of olive oil on the bank of the Tiber, and many also at this time. Thus the hut of
>
> Romulus was burned as a result of some ritual which the pontifices were performing in it; a
>
> statue of Virtues, which stood before one of the gates, fell upon its face, and certain persons,

---

[1133] See Josiah Osgood, *Caesar's Legacy: Civil War and the Emergence of the Roman Empire* (Cambridge, UK ; New York: Cambridge University Press, 2008), 9–10. See Cassius Dio Cocceianus, *Dio's Roman History*, The Loeb Classical Library 82 (Cambridge, Mass: Harvard University Press, 1954). For scholarly studies of Cassius Dio, see Fergus Millar, *A Study of Cassius Dio* (Oxford: Clarendon Press, 1964); Benedikt Simons, *Cassius Dio Und Die Römische Republik: Untersuchungen Zum Bild Des Römischen Gemeinwesens in Den Büchern 3-35 Der Rhomaika*, Beiträge Zur Altertumskunde, Bd. 273 (Berlin: De Gruyter, 2009).

[1134] Cassius Dio, *Dio's Roman History*, 311.

[1135] Regarding the intersection of Roman religion and civic affairs, see Beard, *Religions of Rome*; John North and S. R. F Price, *The Religious History of the Roman Empire: Pagans, Jews, and Christians* (Oxford; New York: Oxford University Press, 2011).

[1136] Mary Beard defines prodigies as: "Prodigies were events, reported from Rome or in its territories, which the Romans regarded as 'unnatural' and took as dangerous signs or warnings – monstrous births, rains of blood, even strokes of lightning. These had to be considered by the senate, who took priestly advice and recommended action to avert the danger." Beard, *Religions of Rome*, 1:19–20. Regarding the role of omens, portents and prodigies in ancient Roman culture, see also Franklin Brunell Krauss, "An Interpretation of the Omens, Portents, and Prodigies Recorded by Livy, Tacitus, and Suetonius" (1930); Bruce MacBain, *The Function of Public Prodigies and Their Expiations in Furthering the Aims of Roman Imperialism in Italy down to the Period of the Social War* (Ann Arbor, MI: University Microfilms International, 1985).

becoming inspired by the Mother of the Gods, declared that the goddess was angry with them.[1137]

For Romans, such prodigies did not necessarily suggest that the gods were directly interfering in the human sphere, but rather that something had gone awry between the city of Rome and the gods.[1138] The senate, the priests and citizens as a whole bore the responsibility of turning the tide of events or averting the goddess' anger. While Roman citizens may have perceived the oil spouting from the banks of the Tiber as an ominous prodigy that heralded a breakdown between the gods and the city, other religious groups at the time may have interpreted the portent in a less negative light.

Josiah Osgood suggested that the legend of the *fons olei*, as recorded by Dio, may have originated with the Jewish population of Trastevere, who would have seen Messianic significance in the miraculous fountain of oil.[1139] In the first century B.C.E, the appearance of oil in Trastevere could have been a sign of the imminent arrival of the long-awaited Messiah of the Jewish people when they were imperiled by the civil war. Messianic prophecies circulated in Rome during this period and may have even made their way into Roman literature, such as Vergil's Fourth Eclogue, which spoke of the Sibylline prophecy regarding the birth of a Messianic figure and the return of a "Golden Age."[1140] Vergil suggested that the Messianic figure, whom the Sibylline oracle predicted, was to be a child:

[1137] Cassius Dio, *Dio's Roman History*, 311.

[1138] Beard, *Religions of Rome*, 1:37–39.

[1139] Osgood, *Caesar's Legacy*, 194–96.

[1140] Ibid., 193–95. The historiography on the Sibylline prophecy is extensive, including the role of Sibylline prophecy in the medieval Latin West. See J. L. Lightfoot, ed., *The Sibylline Oracles: With Introduction, Translation, and Commentary on the First and Second Books* (Oxford ; New York: Oxford University Press, 2007); Anke Holdenried, *The Sibyl and Her Scribes: Manuscripts and Interpretation of the Latin Sibylla Tiburtina C. 1050-1500*, Church, Faith, and Culture in the Medieval West (Aldershot, Hants, England ; Burlington (VT): Ashgate, 2006); D. S. Potter, *Prophecy and History in the Crisis of the Roman Empire: A Historical Commentary on the Thirteenth Sibylline Oracle*, Oxford Classical Monographs (Oxford [England] : New York: Clarendon Press ; Oxford University Press, 1990); Sarolta A. Takács, *Vestal Virgins, Sibyls, and Matrons: Women in Roman Religion*, 1st ed (Austin, TX: University of Texas Press, 2008); H. W. Parke and B. C. McGing, *Sibyls and Sibylline Prophecy in Classical Antiquity* (London ; New York: Routledge, 1988); Luisa Breglia Pulci Doria and Phlegon, *Oracoli*

The last stage of the Cumaean Sibyl's song has come
a great sequence of centuries is born anew.
Now also the Virgin (i.e. Justice) returns, Saturnian rule returns,
now new offspring comes down from high heaven.[1141]

According to Osgood, the Sibylline prophecy was "sufficiently vague" – such that Christians could interpret the Messianic child to be the Christ.[1142] Perhaps as a result of this ambiguity, the story of oil spouting on the banks of the Tiber made its way into early Christian narratives of Rome's history.

During the reign of Augustus and the *Pax Romana*, Jesus was born in a distant outpost of the Roman Empire. Eusebius of Caesaria (c. 260 – 339) mentions the oily portent in his *Chronological Table* (Χρονικοὶ κανόνες or *Chronici canones*), a "Christian world chronicle" initially composed in 308-311.[1143] The *Chronological Table* was a synthesis of an earlier work, which aimed to record a complete world history, beginning with the birth of the Hebrew patriarch Abraham in 2016 B.C.E. and ending with the festival celebrating twenty years of Constantine's rule in 325 C.E.[1144] According to Dale Kinney, Jerome interpolated the story of the *fons olei* in his 380/1 Latin translation of Eusebius' text.[1145] Since Eusebius' original Greek text no longer exists, however, scholars cannot say with certainly if Jerome's inclusion of the *fons olei* prodigy was an interpolation or if Jerome glossed

sibillini tra rituali e propaganda: (studi su Flegonte di Tralles), 1. edizione (Napoli: Liguori, 1983); J. Schleifer, *Die Weisheit der Sybille. Ein kritischer Beitrag* (Wien: A. Höhler, n.d.); Susan Boynton, "An Early Notated 'Song of Sibyl,'" in *Hortus Troporum: Florilegium in Honorem Gunillae Iversen. A Festschrift in Honour of Professor Gunilla Iversen on the Occasion of Her Retirement as Chair of Latin at Stockholm University*, Acta Universitatis Stockholmiensis: Studia Latina Stockholmiensia, 54 (Stockholm: Stockholms Universitet, 2008), 47–56; Bernard McGinn, "*Teste David Cum Sibylla*: The Significance of the Sybilline Tradition in the Middle Ages.," in *Women of the Medieval World. Essays in Honour of John H. Mundy*, ed. Julius Kirshner and Suzanne F. Wemple (Oxford: Basil Blackwel, 1985), 7–35; Annick Waegeman, "The Medieval Sibyl," in *The Pagan Middle Ages*, ed. Ludo J.R. Milis (Woodbridge, Suffolk: Boydell & Brewer, 1998), 83–107; Wilhelm Hoffmann, "Wandel und Herkunft der Sibyllinischen Bücher in Rom," in *La Patria Dell'imperatore Publio Elvio Pertinace*, ed. Filippo Noberasco (Savona, 1933); Madeleine Le Merrer, "Des Sibylles à la sapience dans la tradition médiévale," *Mélanges de l'École Française de Rome. Moyen Âge - Temps Modernes* 98, no. 1 (1986): 13–33.

[1141] Osgood, *Caesar's Legacy*, 193.

[1142] Ibid., 195.

[1143] R. W. Burgess and Witold Witakowski, "Studies in Eusebian and Post-Eusebian Chronography," in *Periclitans Res Publica*, Historia. Einzelschriften, Hft. 135 (Stuttgart: F. Steiner, 1999), 21.

[1144] Ibid.

[1145] "Dio says merely that the oil spouted on the Tiber bank; he does not even specify which bank. Considerably more information is provided by St. Jerome: 'From an inn (*taberna meritoria*) across the Tiber oil erupted from the ground and flowed the whole day without cease, signifying the grace of Christ [born] of mankind.' The passage is one of Jerome's interpolations into the *Chronici Canones* of Eusebius, which he translated into Latin around the year 381." Kinney, "S. Maria in Trastevere from Its Founding to 1215," 174.

Eusebius' account of the *fons olei* by describing it as a portent of Christ's birth.[1146] Osgood observed

that since the account of this portent is also found in Paulus Orosius (c. 385 – post 418), the original

source is likely to have been Livy (Titus Livius) (59 B.C.E –17 C.E.), whose *History of Rome* served as

the basis for much of Orosius' work. Livy's *History,* like Orosius', narrated the city's history from its

founding to the reign of Augustus and included many prodigies.[1147] A search of Livy's text, however,

reveals only two mentions of oil, neither of which pertains to the oil in Trastevere.[1148] The account

of Trastevere's *fons olei* might have appeared in one of the now-lost books of Livy's *History of Rome,*

which were only partially preserved in Julius Obsequens *A Book of Prodigies after the 505th Year of

Rome.*[1149] The only mention of oil in Obsequens' work, however, is a prodigy in which oil and milk

rained from the skies.

Jerome's description of the *fons olei* is the earliest extant text to impute Christological

significance to the miraculous liquid in Trastevere. Later medieval and early modern authors would

often closely replicate Jerome's text, although sometimes with significant variations. Jerome wrote:

"From the *taberna meritoria* across the Tiber oil erupted from the earth and flowed for a whole day

without ceasing, signifying the grace of Christ born for the sake of humankind."[1150] For Jerome, the

miraculous appearance of oil had little to do with the wrath of a pagan goddess, as recorded by Dio,

or the need of the Roman people to seek reconciliation with the gods. Rather, the oil portended the

birth of the Anointed One and heralded the incarnation of God "ex gentibus" – for the sake of

---

[1146] Kinney further notes: "Congruences and differences with Dio's account suggest that Jerome was describing the same miracle, but drawing on an independent source – most likely a Latin source, and not improbably the same source used by Dio himself." Ibid. Whether the inclusion of the miracle is attributable to Eusebius or Jerome remains, nevertheless, unclear. See Burgess and Witakowski, "Studies in Eusebian and Post-Eusebian Chronography," 21–23.

[1147] Osgood, *Caesar's Legacy,* 197n143. Sections 25-32 of Orosius' *Historiarum aduersum paganos* are drawn from Livy 129. The miraculous oil appears in Section 34, however, making the exact source uncertain. See Orosius, *Seven Books of History against the Pagans,* 305n280.

[1148] Livy, "History of Rome 21," trans. B. O. Foster (Harvard University Press, 1929); Livy, "History of Rome 25," trans. Frank Gardner Moore (Harvard University Press, 1940).

[1149] Jeffrey Henderson, "Livy, Julius Obsequens, History of Rome, Volume XIV: Summaries. Fragments. Julius Obsequens. General Index," *Loeb Classical Library,* accessed February 10, 2016, http://www.loebclassics.com/view/LCL404/1959/volume.xml.

[1150] "E taberna meritoria trans Tiberim oleum terra erupit fluxitque tota die sine intermissione significans Xpi gratiam ex gentibus." PL 27, Cols. 431-32. See Kinney, 174.

humankind. An identical retelling of the prodigy appears in Prosper of Aquitaine's (c. 390 – c. 455)

Chronicum Integrum, though he said the oil appeared after Anthony began to wage war against

Augustus, emphasizing that the oil, which signified "the grace of Christ," appeared during

tumultuous political circumstances.[1151]

While Augustine made no reference to the prodigious appearance of oil in Trastevere, his

student, Orosius, was a key figure in the transmission of the legend.[1152] Augustine may have

commissioned Orosius to write *Histories Against the Pagans* (*Historiarum aduersum paganos*) (pre 418), as

a continuation of the argument set forth in the third book of *The City of God*.[1153] Augustine asserted

that the calamities besetting the Roman Empire after the adoption of Christianity were not greater

than before, thus countering the pagan argument that the gods punished Rome for forsaking them

in favor of Christianity. Unlike previous pagan historians, Orosius narrated the disasters that beset

the Roman Empire from a peculiarly Christian perspective.[1154] In his retelling of Rome's history,

Orosius claimed that oil erupted in Trastevere when Augustus triumphantly entered Rome after

having suppressed a military and slave revolt. When the oil flowed, Augustus assumed permanent

---

[1151] "Antonius adversus Augustum bellum movet. E Taberna meritoria trans Tiberim oleum terra erupit, fluxitque toto die sine intermissione, significans Christi gratiam ex gentibus. Antiochus superatus ab Augusto, in amicitiam ejus, interveniente senatu, redit." *Patrologia Latina the Full Text Database* (S.l.: Chadwyck-Healey, Inc, 1996), Vol. 51, Cols. 0548B-0549A.

[1152] Fear describes Orosius' *Histories* as "a standard reference work on antiquity for the medieval world." A. T. Fear, "Introduction," in *Seven Books of History against the Pagans*, Translated Texts for Historians, v. 5 (Liverpool: Liverpool University Press, 2010), 24–25.

[1153] Augustine did use the term *fons olei* to refer to an empty flask of oil that became miraculously full and never became empty again, revealing God's providential care. This term appeared in *City of God*, in Augustine's discussion of the miracles accomplished by Elijah in 1 Kings 17:8-16, drawing a parallel between the Hebrew prophet and Christ, emphasizing how a fountain of oil signified richness and abundance in contrast to poverty. The flowing oil, like an abundance of bread or grain, was a sign of God providing abundance through Christ, who was poor: "A little flask of oil was made into a fountain of oil [*fons olei*], a little flour superseded the greatest abundance of grain. If Elijah lacked nothing, did Christ lack anything? Therefore, my brothers, Holy Scripture admonishes us that God is generally able to feed any of his servants…Let no one be haughty, because Christ gives to the poor one. Christ became poor." "…laguncula olei facta est fons olei, farina parua uberrimas segetes superauit. si elias non indigebat, christus indigebat? ideo, fratres mei, admonet nos scriptura sancta, quia plerumque seruos suos quos potest pascere deus, ideo facit indigentes, ut inueniat operantes. nemo superbiat, quia dat pauperi: christus pauper fuit." LLT: Sermo 239; PL 38, Col.1128, linea 26.

[1154] Fear, "Introduction," 7.

rulership and ushered in the era of peace known as the *Pax Romana*.[1155] Orosius described a large

river of oil flowing from the *taberna meritoria,* which he interpreted as a symbol for the Church: "In

those days, across the Tiber, a fountain of oil gushed from the earth of a lodging house (*taberna*

meritoria) and flowed in a abundant river for a whole day."[1156] Within the context of Orosius'

narrative, the oil appeared in tandem with Augustus' reign, signifying the reestablishment of order

and peace that also accompanied Christ's birth. Throughout his narrative, Orosius sought not just to

illustrate the error of the pagans in religious matters, but also to depict the horror of war, which for

Romans had been a great source of glory.[1157]

In his *Histories,* Orosius elaborated on the signs and wonders that accompanied the advent of

Augustus' reign in order to explain how the secular ruler's presence and power coincided with

Church, which was also responsible for establishing peace and order, despite the fact that Augustus

was not a Christian emperor. According to Orosius, Augustus' reign was part of God's providential

plan and "had been ordained in advance entirely to prepare for the future coming of Christ."[1158]

According to Orosius, Augustus' triumphal entry into Rome and his accession as emperor occurred

on January 6th, the day that would become the feast of the Epiphany. On this day, two signs

appeared as prefigurations of Christ's birth – one in heaven and one on earth.

> …when [Augustus] entered the city…at around the third hour, a circle of light like a rainbow
> surrounded the sun in a clear, serene sky as if to mark him as the one, mightiest man in this
> world and by himself the most glorious man on the earth in whose days would come He
> Who by Himself made and rules over the sun and whole world.[1159]

[1155] "He entered the City to an ovation and the Senate decreed that he should have the power of a tribune permanently. It was at this time that a spring of oil came out of the earth in a lodging house across the Tiber and flowed copiously for the whole day." Orosius, *Seven Books of History against the Pagans*, 305. English translation by Fear.

[1156] "His diebus trans Tiberim e taberna meritoria fons olei terra exundauit, ac per totum diem largissimo riuo fluxit..." LLT: Cl. 0571, vol. II, lib.:6, cap.:18, par.:34, linea:3.

[1157] Fear, "Introduction," 22–23.

[1158] Orosius, *Seven Books of History against the Pagans*, 309.

[1159] Ibid.

The sign in heaven resembled the image of celestial light in a Sibylline prophecy, in which a woman appears in the sky holding a child, foretelling the birth of the Messiah. While the light encircling the sun was the heavenly sign of the imminence of Christ's birth, the terrestrial sign was the fountain of oil. Carolingian authors consistently paired the miraculous light encircling the sun with the *fons olei,* such that these two signs became the twin portents heralding the birth of the Prince of Peace. The wondrous signs alerted people to the eternal reign of Augustus, the author of the *Pax Romana*, as well as the birth of the Prince of Peace, drawing a clear parallel between these two rulers, one temporal and one spiritual. In his retelling of the *fons olei,* Orosius explained the correlation between a pagan emperor's rule and the advent of Christ.

> At that time, as I have already mentioned, a spring of oil flowed all day out of a lodging house. What could be more obvious than that this sign declared that the birth of Christ would occur when Caesar ruled the whole world? For Christ in the language of that race into which and from which he was born, means 'the anointed.' So at that time when permanent tribunician power was granted to Caesar, a spring of oil flowed all day in Rome. These clearest of signs were set forth in heaven and on earth for those who did no heed the voices of the prophets."[1160]

Orosius interpreted the miraculous oil of the past as if he were writing an exegetical commentary of scripture. The purpose of his narrative, after all, was to illustrate how pagan authors who preceded him had failed to grasp the "underlying message" of history, since they failed to see God's providential plan to save the world through Christ.[1161] Pagans who had failed to "heed the voices of the prophets" could now learn from Orosius' own words. The oil held a meaning beyond the literal; one had to read this miraculous event in Roman history as a sign of what would occur in the future, just as the people and the events of the Hebrew

---

[1160] English translation from Ibid., 310. See LLT: Cl. 0571, vol. II, lib.:6, cap.:20, par.:6, linea:1. Fear points out the oddity of Orosius' statement that Christ was born among Greek-speaking people (i.e. those for whom *christos* meant 'anointed.') Orosius, *Seven Books of History against the Pagans*, 310n309.
[1161] Fear, "Introduction," 8.

Scriptures foreshadowed Christ. Orosius noted that the oil appeared in tandem with the beginning of Augustus' rule, which according to Orosius, also coincided with Christ's birth. Since Christ's name meant "Anointed One" the oil heralded the eternal reign not just of Augustus, but the Christ. According to Orosius, the river of oil flowing for an entire day manifested the eternality of Christ' rule. The Church, symbolized by the *taberna meritoria*, was the source of the oil. Orosius did not, however, mention Mary or the presence of a Marian shrine in Trastevere whence the oil flowed.

> They tell us that in the principate of Caesar in the Roman Empire for a whole day – interpreted this means that as long as the Roman Empire endures – Christ and, after him, the Christians – that is the oil and those anointed by it – will march from a lodging house – that is the welcoming and bountiful Church – in great and inexhaustible numbers to restore, with Caesar's aid, all slaves who acknowledge their master and hand over the rest who are found to have no master to death and punishment. The debts from their sins are to be redeemed in Caesar's reign in that city whence the oil flowed of its own accord.[1162]

In Orosius' reading, the flowing oil symbolized not just Christ, but all anointed Christians, whom Christ sent out into the world to bring those who were slaves to sin back into the fold, returning them to their one true master, God. Orosius may have intended to play on the feminine character of the *taberna*, interpreting the lodging house as a *"hospita larga"* – a bountiful hostess. Orosius may have been alluding to the fact that in ancient Rome, an inn or lodging house was often a brothel where the hostess or innkeeper acted as a kind of pimp or *madam* for the women

---

[1162] "Itaque cum eo tempore quo Caesari perpetua tribunicia potestas decreta est, Romae fons olei per totum diem fluxit: sub principatu Caesaris Romano que imperio per totum diem, hoc est per omne Romani tempus imperii, Christum et ex eo Christianos, id est unctum atque ex eo unctos, de meritoria taberna, hoc est de hospita larga que Ecclesia, affluenter atque incessabiliter processuros restituendos que per Caesarem omnes seruos, qui tamen cognoscerent dominum suum, ceteros que, qui sine domino inuenirentur, morti supplicio que dedendos, remittenda que sub Caesare debita peccatorum in ea urbe, in qua spontaneum fluxisset oleum, euidentissima his, qui Prophetarum uoces non audiebant, signa in caelo et in terra prodigia prodiderunt." See LLT: Orosius – Historiarum aduersam paganos libri vii (CPL 0571) vol.II, lib.: 6, cap.:20, par. 5, linea: 7. English translation by Fear. See Orosius, *Seven Books of History against the Pagans*, 310.

working at the inn.[1163] The clients were often soldiers. Since many prostitutes were also slaves,

Orosius' discussion of slaves returning to their masters and having their sins forgiven takes on a

peculiar significance with respect to the *taberna meritoria*. The birth of Christ caused sinners (slaves)

to return to their true master, Christ. Orosius effectively took pagan history and transposed it

into a key amenable to Christian ears, as so many early Christian exegetes before him had done

with the Hebrew Scriptures. The oil flowing from the *taberna meritoria* marked the conversion of

humanity from sin to sanctity. Roman slaves returned to their masters in the same way sinners

repented and returned to Christ. According to Orosius, Augustus' reign was part of God's

providential plan; his rule was "predestined by the secret ordering of events" that would

prepare for the Incarnation. The Incarnation, however, was no secret and only surprised those

who had not learned to heed the voices of the prophets, who had been speaking for ages

through the veiled symbols of the Scriptures.

FONS MARTYRIS: CHRISTIAN WORSHIP IN ANCIENT ROME

Although Christians were present in Rome beginning at least circa 50 A.D., their status was

tenuous.[1164] Romans expected Jews and Christians to sacrifice to gods for the sake of the emperor;

failure to invoke divine protection and support for the emperor himself was the source of tension in

imperial Rome, not the fact that Jews or Christians had fundamentally different relationships with

divinity.[1165] While their numbers increased over the course of the first century A.D., early Christians

often met in small groups in private, domestic dwellings such that no identifiable Christian gathering

place exists that dates prior to the fourth century A.D. Since early Christians believed that "no object

---

[1163] For further discussion of prostitution in ancient Rome, see Chapter 9. Regarding the *taberna* as a brothel see also
Kinney, "S. Maria in Trastevere from Its Founding to 1215," 354n2; Thomas A. McGinn, *Prostitution, Sexuality, and the
Law in Ancient Rome* (New York: Oxford University Press, 1998).
[1164] Beard, *Religions of Rome*, 1:267–71, 368–69.
[1165] Ibid., 1:361.

or building could or should enclose the majesty of god," they had little need for fixed, public

sanctuaries. By the third century, this attitude had begun to shift, resulting in the construction of

explicitly Christian churches, none of which survive.[1166] In the fourth century, when Christianity

became the official state religion under Constantine, the Christian population grew and became

more prominent. By the fifth century, churches were built in all the residential quarters of Rome,

such that all people could readily worship in these places.[1167]

In ancient Rome a fixed boundary, the *pomerium,* designated the city limits. During the

Republican period, Trastevere, which lay outside the *pomerium,* was home to mainly foreigners and

marginalized populations, including Jews, Christians and Syrians, among others.[1168] For ancient

Romans, Trastevere was a remote region, separated from the rest of the city.[1169] The land beyond the

Tiber was made up of small farms, woods and groves, where Syrian, Jewish and freeborn Romans

worked as artisans, manual laborers and foreign traders and where they tended "squalid houses and

small industries."[1170] Archeological remains reveal the presence of these marginalized populations in

ancient Trastevere, including seven synagogues, the earliest known Jewish catacomb, and a Syrian

sanctuary dedicated to the gods of Palmyra.[1171] Jews in Rome may have been emancipated slaves

from the eastern Mediterranean, who were brought to Rome following the conquest of Jerusalem in

63 and 37 B.C.E.[1172] In the first and second centuries A.D., Trastevere was also likely the locus of

the Christian population.[1173]

[1166] Ibid., 1:267–68.

[1167] Ibid., 1:376.

[1168] S. M. Savage, "The Cults of Ancient Trastevere," *Memoirs of the American Academy in Rome* 17 (January 1, 1940): 26–56; Robert E. A. Palmer, "The Topography and Social History of Rome's Trastevere (Southern Sector)," *Proceedings of the American Philosophical Society* 125, no. 5 (1981): 368–97; Beard, *Religions of Rome*; North and Price, *The Religious History of the Roman Empire.*

[1169] Savage, "The Cults of Ancient Trastevere," 28.

[1170] Ibid.

[1171] Beard, *Religions of Rome,* 1:269–70, 272.

[1172] Ibid., 1:272.

[1173] Ibid., 1:269.

The early Christian shrine that would one day become Santa Maria in Trastevere was

originally dedicated to an early Christian martyr, Pope Callixtus (r. 217 – 222), rather than Mary.[1174]

The *Liber Pontificalis* credits Callixtus with founding the church, which Pope Julius I (r. 337 – 352)

later enlarged.[1175] According to the Bollandists, Callixtus' *passio,* recorded in the *Acta martyrii* (BHL

1523), was the work of an anonymous author from Late Antiquity, who might have composed the

text as late as the fifth or sixth century.[1176] Callixtus' *passio* told of prodigies in Rome, reminiscent of

the signs and portents described by Dio, who would have been a near contemporary of Callixtus.[1177]

Following some destructive fires, diviners and priests informed Emperor Severus Alexander (r. 222

– 235) that sacrifices were needed to placate the gods. As the priests were offering their sacrifices,

lightning from a clear blue sky struck four priests and fire consumed an altar dedicated to Jove. The

sky turned black and Romans fled the city, going beyond the city walls. When people scattered

throughout Trastevere, some arrived at what the author of the *passio* referred to as the temple of

Ravenna – *"venerunt trans Tiberim in Urbem ad templum Ravennatium."*[1178] Extant sources offer few clues

about the region or temple designated as *"in urbe Ravennatium"* or *"in Urbem ad templum Ravennatium"*

since these terms only appear in Callixtus' *passio* and the entry on Callixtus in the *Liber Pontificalis.*[1179]

The term *"castra Ravennantium"* appears in one ancient source and may have referred to the

headquarters of Ravennian sailors stationed at Rome; the *urbs Ravennatium* may have also been the

area surrounding the *castra.* Some scholars have argued the area would have encompassed the

location of Santa Maria in Trastevere; Dale Kinney argued this was not necessarily so.[1180]

[1174] For the biographical dossier of Calixtus, see BHL 1523-1525 (Callistus).

[1175] Regarding the founding of Santa Maria in Trastevere, see Kinney, "S. Maria in Trastevere from Its Founding to 1215," 1–36.

[1176] AASS Oct. VI, Dies 14.

[1177] AASS Oct. VI, Dies 14, Col.0439C.

[1178] Ibid.

[1179] Kinney, "S. Maria in Trastevere from Its Founding to 1215," 11–12.

[1180] Ibid., 12. Regarding the potential dimensions of the *urbs Ravennatium,* see Ibid., 13n25.

Callixtus' *passio* contains one of the earliest accounts of a Christian community in Trastevere. In a *coenaculum*, an upper room of the temple, Christians, the bishop Callixtus and an old priest, Calepodius, gathered to sing psalms. Palmatius, a Roman consul, reported the Christian gathering to the Emperor, saying that the city was filthy and needed to be purified of Christians in order to placate the wrathful gods. The Emperor gave Palmatius authority to eradicate the Christians, after which Palmatius gathered an army and marched to Trastevere, to the temple where the Christians gathered. Instead of destroying the Christians, however, the Romans converted to Christianity.[1181] Calepodius catechized Palmatius and blessed water from a nymph's spring, ostensibly located within Callixtus' *domus* (house), to use for his baptism.[1182] According to S.M. Savage, numerous Latin inscriptions confirm the existence of springs within ancient Trastevere, including dedications to the guardian spirit (*genius*) or divinity (*numen*) of the springs. Evidence also suggests the existence of a *nymphaeum* – a sacred well or spring – in Trastevere in the second century A.D.[1183] Situated at the base of the Janiculum, one of the seven hills of Rome, several streams may have converged in Trastevere, possibly in stagnant pools.[1184] The hill itself bore the name of the god Janus, who was associated with running water.[1185] Indeed, the god Janus was said to be father to another god named *Fons*.[1186] According to Cicero, an altar to this god – an *ara Fontis* – was somewhere near the

---

[1181] When the soldiers entered the temple, they lost their sight. When they begged to see again, the old priest Calepodius answered: "God, who sees everything, has blinded your eyes himself." "Deus qui videt omnia, ipse cæcavit oculos vestros." AASS Oct. VI, Dies 14, Col.0440A. Later, after other Romans argued about whose magic was stronger – the pagan gods' or the Christian God's and the need for more sacrifices, a demon from a virgin named Juliana announced that Callixtus' God, who was "living and true," was incensed by the pollutions of the Roman Republic itself. Palmatius, persuaded by this oracle, fled to Trastevere and asked to be baptized. AASS Oct. VI, Dies 14, Col.0440B-C.

[1182] "Respondit Calepodius senex & dixit ad beatum Episcopum: Beatissime Pater, petenti baptismum noli denegare. Eodem tempore indixit Jejunium ei uno die, & catechizavit eum: & allatam aquam de lympha putei, qui erat in eadem domo, benedixit..." Oct.VI, Dies 14, Col.0440C-D.

[1183] Savage, "The Cults of Ancient Trastevere," 27.

[1184] Ibid.

[1185] Ibid., 30. According to Orosius, when August assumed power, he "closed the temple of Janus for the first time in 200 years." Orosius, *Seven Books of History against the Pagans*, 310. I have yet to determine the significance of this gesture or how it might relate to an altar to Janus in Trastevere or the *fons olei*.

[1186] Savage, "The Cults of Ancient Trastevere," 30.

Janiculum hill.[1187] In 1914, the shrine to *Fons* was discovered, replete with waterspout and an inscription suggesting the shrine was dedicated as early as A.D. 70.[1188]

The great irony of Callixtus' *passio* lies in the fact that, after baptizing a Roman consul with water from a spring or well, the bishop himself was martyred in one. After Callixtus converted one too many Romans, the Emperor had the bishop thrown out of a window and into a well, with a heavy stone tied around his neck. The stone, supposedly a phallus-shaped donation made to pagan deities, was long kept in Santa Maria in Trastevere.[1189] The mythic as well as the real presence of water or springs could perhaps explain, in part, how or why a legend about a fountain of oil flowing from Trastevere could have circulated among the Roman Jewish and Christian population or why a fountain – be it water or oil – was associated with an early Christian shrine across the Tiber. Just as the baptismal font was said to impart eternal life to initiates, so Callixtus experienced his own "rebirth" through a *fons* in Trastevere.

MARIAN DEVOTION IN ANCIENT ROME: FROM ANGRY GODDESS TO PACIFIC MOTHER

The cult of the Virgin Mary was not the first religion in the Mediterranean basin to associate flowing, life-giving liquid with a woman or a motherly figure. The people of the ancient Mediterranean did not live in isolation from one another, but experienced an exchange of cultural influences, which led to a blending of religious ideas or forms of devotion.[1190] Marian devotion within the Christian tradition was a natural outgrowth of non-Christian devotional practices directed toward goddesses or the divine feminine in manifold manifestations.[1191] The roots of Roman

---

[1187] Ibid.

[1188] Ibid.

[1189] "The seemingly phallic donation to Jupiter Best and Greatest of Damascus was kept in Santa Maria in Trastevere because it was thought to have been the weight dragging St. Callixtus to his drowning in the well of his house in Trastevere." Palmer, "The Topography and Social History of Rome's Trastevere (Southern Sector)," 374.

[1190] Stephen Benko, *The Virgin Goddess : Studies in the Pagan and Christian Roots of Mariology* (Leiden; New York: E.J. Brill, 1993), 21.

[1191] Ibid., 21.

goddess worship extended far back into ancient Asia Minor and North Africa, where in several locations centuries later, Mary was associated with sacred springs.[1192] Goddesses were often associated with water, since reproduction involved liquids of several kinds. The fertility of the body, like the fertility of a field, was dependent on the presence of life-giving moisture.[1193] Egyptians in particular imputed great potency to water, which signified both fertility and purification.[1194] The veneration of figures such as Caelestis, Isis, the Syrian Goddess, and Cybele all contributed to Marian devotion as it emerged in the early centuries of the Christian church.[1195] The roots of the cult of the Blessed Virgin are to be found in the cult of Isis, who was not only depicted as a goddess holding her infant son, but who evidenced a clear link between maternity, salvation and flowing liquids – be they water or oil.[1196] The cult of Isis, with its ritual ablutions and sprinklings, reveals an intimate link between water, femininity and fertility in the ancient Mediterranean world, which was later transposed to Marian devotion with Christianity. While in these ancient fertility cults the mother was the divine figure rather than the child, Christianity inverted the order and presented the child as divine, not the mother. In the eastern Christian tradition, Mary was the *theotokos,* the God-bearer. Neveretheless, within medieval Christianity, Mary attained a quasi-divine status.

[1192] Alice-Mary Talbot, "Pilgrimage to Healing Shrines: The Evidence of Miracle Accounts," *Dumbarton Oaks Papers* 56 (2002): 153–73; Alice-Mary Talbot, "Constantinople: City of Miraculous Healings," in *Life Is Short, Art Long: The Art of Healing in Byznatium* (Istanbul: Perma Museums Publication, 2015).

[1193] As we saw in Paulinus of Nola's *carmen*, on the Italic peninsula, water was tantamount to live, blessing and divine presence.

[1194] Benko, Stephen. *The Virgin Goddess: Studies in the Pagan and Christian Roots of Mariology* (Leiden; New York: E.J. Brill, 1993), 50.

[1195] Benko, *The Virgin Goddess*, 20–82.

[1196] According to Stephan Benko, "This was a cosmic religion which held out the hope of personal salvation by an intimate reintegration into a totality. In the mysteries of Isis this totality was represented by the primordial waters." Ibid., 52–53.

Until 502, the church in Trastevere bore the name *Basilica Juli*, after Pope Julius I (r. 337 –

352), who was credited with expanding the dwelling founded by Callixtus a century earlier.[1197] By the

late sixth century, most churches in Rome were dedicated to saints. Dale Kinney argued that an

exception was the church formerly known as *Basilica Juli*, which was dedicated to the Blessed Virgin

Mary, despite the fact at least one document from this time still associated the church with Julius

and Callixtus.[1198] Two other exceptions were other Marian churches in Rome: Santa Maria Maggiore

and Santa Maria Antiqua. A pilgrimage itinerary entitled *De locis sanctis martyrum quae sunt foris civitas*

Romae, which may date to circa 625 – 638, mentioned a basilica named Santa Maria Transtiberis,

where there was an *imago* of Mary.[1199] This text, however, said nothing about the *fons olei* or the

taberna meritoria. Dale Kinney argued that this itinerary referred to the icon known as *Madonna della*

Clemenza, which still hangs in a side chapel of the church today, or to another icon now lost.[1200]

Kinney rejected C. Bertelli's argument that the itinerary's reference to Santa Maria in Trastevere was

a Carolingian interpolation. Bertelli argued that the icon was anterior to the mid-seventh century, as

a commission by Pope John VII (r. 705 – 707), a thesis Per Jonas Nordhagen subsequently

upheld.[1201] If the reference to the Marian icon at the church of Santa Maria in Trastevere is a later,

possibly Carolingian interpolation to the seventh-century pilgrim itinerary, as Bertelli argued, we can

be less certain about precisely when Marian devotion in Trastevere took hold and exactly when the

---

[1197] Kinney, "S. Maria in Trastevere from Its Founding to 1215," 60. Valentini and Zucchetti note that textual references from the fourth and fifth centuries always referred to the church by Pope Julius' name until 595, when it was referred to as the *titulus* of both Callixtus and Julius: "tituli Sancti Iuli et Calisti." Roberto Valentini and Giuseppe Zucchetti, *Codice topografico della città di Roma,* vol. 2, Fonti per la storia d'Italia 88 (Roma: Tipografia del senato, 1942), 123.

[1198] Kinney, "S. Maria in Trastevere from Its Founding to 1215," 60. Valentini and Zucchetti, *Codice topografico della città di Roma,* 2:123.

[1199] "Basilica quae appellatur s(an)c(t)a Maria transtiberis [sic] ibi est imago s(an)c(t)ae Marie quae per se facta est." Also, Kinney, "S. Maria in Trastevere from Its Founding to 1215," 65n11.

[1200] Ibid., 66–67.

[1201] Per Jonas Nordhagen, "Icons Designed for the Display of Sumptuous Votive Gifts," *Dumbarton Oaks Papers* 41 (1987): 453–60.

fons olei was first located within Santa Maria in Trastevere.[1202] The emergence of Marian devotion in

Trastevere and the legend of the *fons olei* appear to have been distinct religious or cultural

phenomena in early medieval Rome. These two strands of belief only merged much later, in the

eleventh or twelfth century, as the next chapter will demonstrate.

With the rise of Marian devotion and churches dedicated to Mary, the Christian perception

of worship spaces transformed. Prior to the construction of Hagia Sophia in 537, the buildings in

which Christian worship took place were of little significance; no symbolic meaning was imputed to

the physical edifice in which Christians gathered.[1203] The church as a building was viewed as a house

of prayer and was significant only insofar as it was the gathering place for the Christian assembly.

The Christians themselves, and not the space in which they gathered, was the locus of the holy.

From the time of Justinian, however, Byzantine liturgical descriptions and commentaries focused on

what happened in the church, the church itself, and its symbolic meaning. The building was no

longer simply a building, but became an image of the cosmos, providing the faithful with a glimpse

of heaven.[1204] The Christian church was not originally a temple; the community, not the material

shrine, was the dwelling place of God's presence. In time, however, Christians viewed the church

building as a symbol for the mysteries celebrated within it.[1205] Byzantines imagined Hagia Sophia to

be a New Temple and Justinian as a supreme ruler who surpassed Solomon.[1206] The church, with its

resplendent dome, was also an image of the Platonic idea of the cosmos, from God's throne in

heaven, down to Cherubim, and down to the lower realm where human beings dwelt.

While Hagia Sophia may have been the first house of Christian worship consciously

constructed to convey a reality beyond its physical reality, for centuries Christian authors had

---

[1202] Kinney, "S. Maria in Trastevere from Its Founding to 1215," 67.
[1203] Robert F. Taft, *The Byzantine Rite : A Short History* (Collegeville Minn.: Liturgical Press, 1992), 35.
[1204] Ibid.
[1205] Ibid.
[1206] Ibid., 36.

envisioned the Virgin Mary as representing the universal Church. One of the earliest descriptions of Mary as an image of the Church appeared in an Easter hymn by Ephrem of Syria (d. 373), in which the author characterized Mary as the source of life-giving bread and as the first to witness the resurrection of Christ: "The Church gave us the Living Bread instead of that unleavened bread which Egypt gave. Mary gave us the Bread of Refreshment instead of the Bread of Weariness, which Eve gave."[1207] In describing the appearance of angels at the tomb of Jesus on Easter morning, Ephrem observed that Mary was present, saw the angels, and understood their significance: the Christ had arisen. Similarly, the Church was a witness not only to Jesus's life but to his crucifixion and resurrection: "Three angels were seen by the grave: that he would arise – on the third day, the three announced. Maria, who saw him, is the symbol of the Church, which will be the first to see the sign of his Second Coming."[1208] Ephrem is also one of the earliest authors to have spoken of Mary as the Bride of Christ.[1209] Ambrose of Milan[1210] and Augustine of Hippo also elaborated this Marian symbology,[1211] firmly establishing the interpretation of Mary as an image of the Church within ecclesiastical tradition of the Latin West. Nevertheless, when Late Antique and Carolingian authors explained that the *fons olei* in Trastevere flowed from the *taberna meritoria* in Trastevere, they made no mention of Mary. Even though some explained that the *taberna* represented the Church, they did not suggest that the *fons* flowed from a particular shrine dedicated to the Mother of God or the church now known as Santa Maria in Trastevere.

[1207] Translations based on Edmund Beck's German translation from Syriac. "Die Kirche gab uns das lebendige Brot – statt jenes ungesäuerten, das Ägypten gab. Maria gab uns das Brot der Erquickung – statt des Brotes der Ermüdung, das Eva gab." See Ephraem, *Des heiligen Ephraem des Syrers Paschahymnen.* Vol. 248; Tome 108/109 (Louvain: Secrétariat du Corpus SCO, 1964), 11.

[1208] "Drei Engel sah man bei dem Grab: dass er erweckt werde – am dritten (Tag) verkündeten die drei. – Maria, die ihn sah, ist das Symbol der Kirche, die zuerst – sehen wird das Zeichen seiner (zweiten) Ankunft." Ephrem, *Des heiligen Ephraem*, 47.

[1209] Hymns on the Nativity, CSCO, 186 & 187, XVI, 9-11.

[1210] See De inst. Virg 98, PL 16, 328 and IV, 3,4; PL 17, 876.

[1211] See De sancta virginitate 6, PL 40, 399; CPL 368.

By the eighth and ninth centuries, the legend of the *fons olei* had spread across Europe but

was in no way associated with Marian devotion, apart from the fact that the *taberna meritoria* was a

symbol for the Church. Nearly every mention of the *fons* referred to the *taberna meritoria* without

explicitly mentioning Mary. Rather than stressing the Marian origin of the miraculous oil,

Carolingian authors were more concerned with explaining the correlation among the oil, the reign of

Augustus, and the advent of the Prince of Peace. In the eighth and ninth centuries, Roman emperors

became models for Carolingian rulers, including both Pippin and Charlemagne.[1212] Charlemagne in

particular implemented Roman law (or some version of it) within his own kingdom, assumed the

title of Emperor in Rome on Christmas day, and minted coins bearing an image of Augustus.[1213] In

commenting on the lives of early Christian emperors, Carolingian clerics often praised those

emperors who showed a willingness to submit to the bishops of the early Church, a theme that

would recur throughout medieval discourse well into the High Middle Ages.[1214] When Carolingian

authors retold the history of Rome and its empire for their contemporary audiences, they included

the legend of the *fons olei*, drawing directly on Orosius' *Histories*. The miraculously flowing oil was a

sign of Christ's birth and the reign of peace that accompanied the rule of Augustus. No Carolingian

authors, however, correlated the flowing oil with Mary or a shrine devoted to the Mother of God.

While Karen Einaudi rightly suggested that Anastasius Bibliothecarius was the first author to

associate the *fons olei* with Santa Maria in Trastevere, no evidence suggests the papal librarian was

---

[1212] Janet L. Nelson, *The Frankish World, 750-900* (London: Hambledon, 1996), 89–98. See also Rosamond McKitterick, "Transformations of the Roman Past and Roman Identity in the Early Middle Ages," in *The Resources of the Past in Early Medieval Europe*, eds. Clemens Gantner, Rosamond McKitterick and Sven Meeder (Cambridge: Cambridge University Press, 2015), 225–44; Georges Duby, *The Three Orders: Feudal Society Imagined* (Chicago: University of Chicago Press, 1980).

[1213] Nelson, *The Frankish World*, 90–91.

[1214] Ibid., 89–90.

referring to the church in particular rather than simply to the part of Rome associated with the ancient legend.[1215]

At least three eighth-century sources maintained that the *fons olei* flowed from the *taberna meritoria* while saying nothing about the location also being the shrine or basilica dedicated to Mary. The *Commentarius in Lucam*, an anonymous commentary on Luke's Gospel, which was likely written by a Celtic author in the Salisbury region circa 780-785, preserved the elements of the *fons olei* legend found in both Jerome and Orosius.[1216] Some of the text from this commentary appeared in what Ernst Kantorowicz referred to as the "Celtic Catecheses."[1217] As discussed earlier, a pilgrim itinerary from the same region, the Itinerary of Salisbury (circa 682), recorded the presence of an image of Mary in Trastevere (*transtiberis*), but said nothing about the *fons olei*. Thus, even though the *fons olei* and a Marian shrine in Trastevere were known to Christians in Salisbury in the late eighth century, conceptually the *fons olei* and Marian devotion remained separate. An eighth- or ninth-century collection of homilies, the *Homiliarium Veronense,* which may have been composed by a Hibernian, also contains a reference to the *fons olei* in its first sermon.[1218] The homily draws largely on Orosius, referring to the oil as a sign of Christ's birth, which occurred during the reign of Augustus, thus juxtaposing the rule of the secular leader with that of Christ.[1219] This homily also described the source of oil simply as a *taberna meritoria* that foreshadowed the *ecclesia*.[1220]

[1215] Einaudi, "'Fons Olei' E Anastasio Bibliotecario."

[1216] See LLT background notes to Anonymous – Commentarium in Lucam.

[1217] Ernst H. Kantorowicz, "Oriens Augusti. Lever Du Roi," *Dumbarton Oaks Papers* 17 (1963): 150n183. I have yet to determine if this anonymous commentary is in fact the text in MS Vatican 1933.

[1218] The LLT notes: "Eleven brief homilies make up this Homilarium Veronese. They are found in a single manuscript preserved in Verona, which probably dates from the beginning of the ninth century. These sermons relate to the liturgical period from Christmas to Pentecost. Even though it is impossible to confirm that the author of this collection was an Irishman, the Irish stamp is undeniable."

[1219] "In diebus ipsis fons olei 'sponte ' <de taberna> meritoria' Rome terra prorupit fluxit que tota die sine intermisione, significans Christi gratiam ex gentibus. Quibus signis, 'quid euidentius quam in diebus Cessaris toto orbe regnantis futura Christi natiuitas declarata est." LLT: Homiliarium Veronense Homilhom.: 1, pag.: 4, linea: 110.

[1220] "Quibus signis, 'quid euidentius quam in diebus Cessaris toto orbe regnantis futura Christi natiuitas declarata est? Per totum' enim 'diem, hoc est per omne Romani imperii tempus, Christum et ex eo Christianos, id est, unctum' et 'ex eo unctos, de taberna meritoria, hoc est, de hospita larga que ecclesia, affluenter' et 'incessabiliter processuros restituendos que per Cessarem omnes seruos, qui' tunc 'cognoscerent Dominum suum; caeteros, | qui sine Domino inuenirentur,

Drawing on Orosius' *Histories,* the author of the *Commentarius in Lucam* explained the significance of Christ having been born during the reign of Augustus. Christ, who was "Lord of all the world" was born in the forty-second year of Augustus' reign, just as Abraham was born during the forty-second year of the reign of Ninus.[1221] This passage from Orosius, cited by the Celtic commentator, spoke of Abraham as one "to whom divine promises were given and from whose seed Christ was promised to come forth."[1222] Orosius' discussion of divine succession, of Christ from Abraham, related directly to the creation of the Roman Empire. While Augustus was the first Roman emperor, he descended from a father [albeit adoptive] who, according to Orosius, distinguished himself "rather as the architect of the empire than as an emperor."[1223] Rather than emphasizing the creation of an empire or the fact that Jesus was born from a woman, the commentator prioritized the timing of Christ's birth. While Abraham, a "creature among creatures," was born in the middle of the year, Christ was born "at the end and at the beginning" of the year since Christ himself "is the beginning and the end."[1224] Without mentioning Mary, the commentator went on to explain the meaning of the signs and wonders that accompanied the savior's birth.

The author of the *Commentarius in Lucam* referred to the heavenly sign of the light encircling the sun as well as the terrestrial sign of oil flowing from the *taberna meritoria.*[1225] Evidently writing for a Christian audience, the biblical commentator's main concern appears to have been to explain how, with the appearance of the oil, wars ceased: "According to the history, the wars ceased such that it

---

morti suplicio que dedendos, remitenda que sub Caessare debita peccatorum in ea urbe in qua spontaneum fluxit oleum, euidentissima his, qui profetarum uoces non audierunt, signa in celo et in terra prodigia prodiderunt'." LLT: Homiliarium Veronense, hom.:1, pag.:4, linea: 112-14.

[1221] Orosius, *Seven Books of History against the Pagans*, 322.

[1222] Ibid.

[1223] Ibid.

[1224] "Sed Abraham in medio anni nascitur, quia creatura in creaturis erat Abraham. Iesus autem christus in fine et in initio anni nascitur, quia ipse est initium et finis." LLT: Anonymous, Commentarius in Lucam, cap.2, linea: 7-8.

[1225] "In diebus illis: adfuerunt magna miracula in aduentu saluatoris: circulus lucem solis supereminens, oleum in taberna meritoria promens, in terra flumen tiberis prorumpens in ciuitatem ueniens, serui in potestatem dominorum redacti." LLT: Anonymous, Commentarius in Lucam, cap.2, linea: 9.

was said: removing wars all the way to the end of the earth."[1226] The author was also intent on

clarifying the meaning of the name "Caesar Augustus" for his Christian audience. Caesar Augustus

was the one whose most intimate familiars referred to him as "Lord": "Not even by son nor wife

nor his companions did he concede to not be called 'Lord.' Augustus, stands solemnly. Caesar,

possessio principalis "[1227] While presenting an image of an ideal ruler, the author of the commentary also

described this ideal ruler as the Christ: "These two names [Caesar Augustus] are harmonized by

Christ, who solemnly possesses all things and [*possessio principalis*] because he holds fast the rulership

of the present and of the future and of the past."[1228] Describing Christ, the Anointed One, as the

ruler of the universe could have effectively put any temporal leader in check while simultaneously

introducing the image of a perfect, all-powerful sovereign for mortal men to emulate.

The *Liber questionum in evangelis,* an anonymous eighth-century commentary on the Gospels,

contained in an eleventh-century manuscript of French provenance and attributed to the Pseudo-

Alcuin, did not speak explicitly about the cessation of war, but saw the heavenly sign, which

accompanied the *fons olei,* as a symbol for divine power circumscribing or encompassing temporal

power. The commentary presented exegesis of Jesus's birth, as recorded by the Gospel of Matthew,

comingled with interpretations of the miracles from Orosius' *Histories.*[1229] Like the *Commentarius in

Lucam,* the *Liber questionum* noted that Christ was born during the forty-second year of Augustus'

reign, but then explicated the various aspects of Orosius' narrative including the rainbow-like light

surrounding the sun and the oil flowing from the *taberna meritoria.* The commentator found a

---

[1226] "Id, qui dominos agnouerunt non cognoscentes puniti erant, et bella cessauerunt secundum historiam ut dicitur: auferens bella usque ad finem terrae. Exiit edictum: dictio inter propinquos, aedictio inter populos et plebes currit." LLT: Anonymous, Commentarius in Lucam, cap.2, linea: 9.

[1227] "A caesare augustuo: ipse est octauianus, qui nec filio, nec uxori, nec socio suo, uocari dominum non concessit. Augustus sollemniter stans. Caesar possessio principalis." LLT: Anonymous, Commentarius in Lucam, cap.2, linea: 17-19. "Possessio principalis" is evidently an epithet for 'Caesar.'

[1228] "Haec duo nomina christo conueniunt, qui omnia sollemniter possidet et possessio principalis <conuenit> quia principatum praesentium et futurorum et praecidentium optinet." LLT: Anonymous, Commentarius in Lucam, cap.2, linea: 20.

[1229] See background notes in LLT for *Liber questionum in evangelis.*

common element in the two miracles. Oil, like the radiance surrounding the sun, signified the

presence of light: "the oil flowing from the *taberna meritoria*" signified that "the grace of faith began

to shine in the church."[1230] The radiant light encircling the sun in turn represented the divine

circumscription of temporal power: "The true light encompassed all remaining powers."[1231] Here

again the commentator made no mention of a Marian church in Trastevere being the source of oil.

Rather, the commentator simply emphasized that these signs accompanied the birth of Jesus, who

was born in Bethlehem during the time of Herod, perhaps to distinguish between the wondrous

signs that occurred in Rome during the reign of Augustus and historical events that occurred some

years later far off in the Near East.[1232]

The legend of the miraculous *fons olei* was not just retold for Carolingian audiences in

anonymous biblical commentaries. In his *Roman History (Historia Romana)* (c. 763) Paul the Deacon

(720 – c.799) recounted how a great quantity of oil spouted from the ground in Trastevere and

flowed for an entire day.[1233] As a young man, Paul visited the court of the Lombard king Ratchis

(744-749) and dedicated an early poem as well as his *Roman History* to Adalperga, the king's daughter

and later duchess of Benevento.[1234] Paul spent four years in Charlemagne's court but returned to

Italy, where he became a monk at Monte Cassino and composed his most famous work, the *History

of the Lombards (Historia Langobardorum)*, which would become a foundational narrative for later

medieval and Renaissance chroniclers.[1235] Paul dedicated his *Roman History* to Adalperga, whom he

---

[1230] "Oleo de taberna meritoria fluente, gratia fidei in 'ecclesia' lucescit." LLT: Cl. 1168, cap. (s.s.): 2, pag.: 41, linea: 3.
[1231] " 'Circulo' praeclaro 'solem ambiente', Lux uera omnes potestates circumambit, reliqua." LLT Cl. 1168, cap. (s.s.): 2, pag.: 41, linea: 4. One might also translate "omnes potestates…reliqua" as "all future powers."
[1232] "NATUS EST IESUS. Hic persona Iesu et tempus Herodis et locus Bethlem inuenitur." LLT: Cl. 1168, cap. (s.s.): 2, pag.: 41, linea: 6.
[1233] "His diebus trans Tiberim de taberna meritoria fons olei e terra exundavit ac per totum diem largissimo rivo fluxit significans ex gentibus gratiam Christi."
[1234] Walter A Goffart, *The Narrators of Barbarian History (A.D. 550-800): Jordanes, Gregory of Tours, Bede, and Paul the Deacon* (Princeton, N.J.: Princeton University Press, 1988), 329.
[1235] Ibid. See also Sharon Dale, Alison Williams Lewin, and Duane J Osheim, *Chronicling History: Chroniclers and Historians in Medieval and Renaissance Italy* (University Park, Pa.: Pennsylvania State University Press, 2007), x.

claimed was capable of equaling her husband, Duke Arichis of Benevento, in wisdom.[1236] For her

edification, Paul recommended the Duchess read Eutropius' *Breviarum Historiae Romanae,* a

condensed history of Rome from its founding until 364. The Duchess, however, found the fourth-

century text too brief and wanting in explanation of spiritual matters, including "divine history and

our religion."[1237]

While Paul's aim was ostensibly to bring to light the Christological significance of events

relating to Rome's ancient history, his explanation of the legendary *fons olei* was succinct and lacked

the extensive exegetical embellishments found in Orosius. Paul the Deacon reproduced only

Orosius' first mention of the *fons olei,* which simply stated the oil flowed from the *taberna meritoria* for

a whole day: "[Augustus] entered the city to an ovation, and the Senate decreed that he should have

the power of a tribune permanently. It was at this time that a spring of oil came out of the earth in a

lodging house [*taberna meritoria*] across the Tiber and flowed copiously for the whole day."[1238] Paul

appears to have been more concerned with recounting Augustus' military maneuvers than disclosing

the hidden workings of divine providence, the mystical significance of the oil and whence it flowed

or how the oil foreshadowed the advent of Christ. Instead, Paul omitted the passage from Orosius

that mentioned the *fons olei* for the second time, when Orosius explained that the oil heralded the

immanent arrival of the Christ, the significance of the oil flowing for a day (as long as the Roman

Empire endured), that the *taberna meritoria* was a symbol for the Church and all Christians,

manifesting the intricate, hidden workings of divine providence.[1239] Instead, with his Beneventan

---

[1236] Goffart, *The Narrators of Barbarian History (A.D. 550-800),* 347.

[1237] Ibid.

[1238] "*Ovans urbem ingressus, ut in perpetuum tribunitiae potestatis esset, a senatu decretum est. His diebus trans Tyberim e taberna meritoria fons olei de terra emanavit, ac per totum diem largissimo rivo profluxit. His diebus trans Tyberim e taberna meritoria fons olei de terra emanavit, ac per totum diem largissimo rivo profluxit.*" English translation from Orosius, *Seven Books of History against the Pagans,* 305. PL entitled this work *Historia Miscella.* An ambrosian manuscript referred to the text as "Eutropii Breviarum Historiae Romanae." See PL 95, Col. 0854A.

[1239] Ibid., 310-11.

audience in mind, Paul the Deacon proceeded ahead to Augustus' military conquests, without a

single mention of the oil flowing from a church dedicated to the Blessed Virgin.

The omission of a lengthy discussion of the *fons olei* and the total absence of a reference to

Mary is significant given the fact that Paul composed the *History* for a married laywoman. Walter

Goffart observed that Paul often tailored his narratives, not just the *Historia Romana*, to a female

audience, providing numerous examples of devious women engaging in folly or wreaking

destruction.[1240] Paul recommended Adalperga read Eutropius' narrative in particular, in which,

according to Goffart, "the female presence…is enlarged."[1241] The women who appear in Paul's

Roman History evidently served to influence Benevento's Duchess through cautionary tales or by

negative example. Had the legend of the *fons olei* been associated with a church dedicated to Mary in

the mid-eighth century, surely Paul would have emphasized this aspect of the legend for the

Christian wife of an Italic ruler.

Paul the Deacon was not the only Carolingian historian to proliferate the legend of the *fons

olei*. Frechulf of Lisieux (d. 850/52), a Carolingian bishop and historian, composed a universal

chronicle, the *Historiarum libri XII* (829/30), during the reign of Charles the Bald (823-877) included

the *fons olei* in his story, though he omitted Orosius' exegetical interpretation of the oil.[1242] Frechulf

dedicated Books I-VII of the chronicle, which recounted all of human history from God's creation

of Adam to the reign of Augustus, to Elizachar (dates unknown), the Chancellor of Louis the Pious

and Books VIII-XII to Louis the Pious' second wife, Judith of Bavaria (802-43).[1243] Frechulf's

reference to the *fons olei* appeared in Book VII of the chronicle, just after Augustus' triumphal entry

to Rome. More so than Paul the Deacon, Frechulf minimized the emphasis on the oil as a

---

[1240] "The taste for history in which women play a part may have been as much Paul's own, or the wider public's, as
Adalperga's." Goffart, *The Narrators of Barbarian History (A.D. 550-800)*, 351.
[1241] Ibid.
[1242] Nelson, *The Frankish World*, 91.
[1243] See LLT background notes for Frechulf of Liseux, *Historiarum libri XII*.

prodigious sign of Christ's birth and manifestation of God's providential plan. Rather, Frechulf used

the *fons olei* as a temporal reference point for other historical developments, mainly the military

advances of Augustus and Anthony.[1244] In contrast with Frechulf, Ado de Vienne (d. 875), the

Archbishop of Vienne from 860 onwards, included Orosius' explanation of the mystical significance

of the oil and the *taberna meritoria* from which it flowed. His *Chronicon sive Breviarium chronicorum de sex

mundi aetatibus de Adamo usque ad annum 869* (c. 869) recounted how the *fons olei* coincided with

Augustus' reign and emanated from the *taberna meritoria*. Ado reproduced the portion of Orosius text

that interpreted the *taberna* as a "bountiful" (*larga*) Church from which Christ and Christians, like the

oil, were "advancing abundantly and ceaselessly."[1245]

A number of other ninth-century authors also mentioned the *fons olei* in their biblical

commentaries, without making any direct reference to oil flowing from a church dedicated to Mary.

Writing in the mid-ninth century Sedulius Scotus (circa 848-874), an Irish poet in Liège, used *fons olei*

to reflect on the coexistence of powerful temporal and spiritual leaders. His patrons included the

bishops of Liège as well as Lothar I (d. 855). As the author of *On Christian Rulers* (*De Rectoribus

Christianis*), one of the earliest texts in the "mirror of princes" genre, Sedulius sought to influence

his audience's understanding of the role and function of a ruler vis-à-vis Christ. Sedulis omitted

Orosius' discussion of the heavenly sign, of light encircling the sun, mentioning only that the *fons olei*

flowed when Caesar Augustus ruled "over the whole earth."[1246] Moreover, Sedulius emphasized that

---

[1244] "His diebus trans Tiberim e taberna meritoria fons olei terra exundauit ac per totum diem largissimo riuo fluxit. Antonius uero postquam Araxim transmisit, omnibus undique malis circumuentus, uix tandem." LLT: Frechulfus Lexouiensis, Historiarum libri XII, pars: 1, liber: 7, cap.: 14, pag.: 410, linea: 120.

[1245] "in diebus ipsis fons olei largissimus de taberna meritoria, per totum diem fluxit; quo signo quid evidentius quam sub principatu Caesaris Romanoque imperio per totum diem, hoc est per omne Romani tempus imperii, Christum, atque ex eo Christianos, id est unctum atque ex eo unctos, de meritoria taberna, hoc est de hospita largaque Ecclesia, affluenter atque incessabiliter processuros, restituendosque per Caesarem omnes servos, qui tamen cognoscerent dominum suum, caeterosque qui sine domino invenirentur, morti supplicioque dedendos, remittendaque sub Caesare debita peccatorum in ea urbe in qua spontaneum fluxisset oleum?" PL 123, Col.0074C-D.

[1246] "Octauiano regnante Augusto, fons olei largissimus de taberna meritoria per totum diem fluxit. Quo signo quid euidentius quam, in diebus Caesaris toto orbe regnantis, futura Christi natiuitas declarata est?" LLT: Sedulius Scotus, *Collectaneum Miscellaneum*, diuisio : 22, linea : 120.

among the people into which and from which Christ was born, his name meant, "anointed."[1247]

Then, Sedulius added a statement not found in other retellings of the *fons olei* legend. He suggests,

potentially, that pagans not understanding the miraculous oil as a sign of Christ's imminent birth was

akin to flagellants not feeling the whip: "The wicked one is flogged and does not feel."[1248]

Christianus of Stavelot (d. post 880), a priest who taught at the Stavelot-Malmédy monastery

in the Low Countries, mentions the *fons olei* in his biblical commentary, known as the *Expositio super*

Librum generationis (Expositio in euangelium Matthaei), which dates to circa 864 or 865.[1249] In this work,

like previous authors, Christianus drew a parallel between Abraham and Christ, stating that Abraham

prefigured Christ by being born in the forty-second year of the reign of Nini, who was "the

foremost king in the world."[1250] Christ, according to Christianus, was born in the forty-second year

of the reign of Caesar Augustus, "who was called the foremost emperor."[1251] Christianus situated the

eruption of oil within the context of August's reign, claiming that appearance of the oil revealed the

power of God, a male Creator, rather than the anger of the Mother of Gods, as recorded by Cassius

Dio.

> And on that day itself, many prodigies appeared, which revealed Him, the creator of the
> earth. On that day itself an enormous fountain of oil flowed for a whole day from the *taberna*
> *meritoria,* revealing that He was born who was called 'Christ,' that is anointed with spiritual oil
> and moreover from his church 'Christians' were named.[1252]

[1247] "Octauiano regnante Augusto, fons olei largissimus de taberna meritoria per totum diem fluxit. Quo signo quid euidentius quam, in diebus Caesaris toto orbe regnantis, futura Christi natiuitas declarata est? Christus enim lingua gentis eius, in qua et ex qua natus est, unctus interpretatur." LLT: Sedulius Scotus, *Collectaneum Miscellaneum*, diuisio 22, linea 120.

[1248] "Impius flagellatur et non sentit." Ibid.

[1249] See notes in LLT for Christianus Stabulensis.

[1250] "Et sicut Abraham, qui in figura domini precessit, quadragesimo secundo anno Nini, qui primus rex in mundo fuit, natus est, sic Christus quadragesimo secundo anno Octauiani, qui primus 'imperator' appellatus fuit, natus est."

[1251] Ibid.

[1252] "Et ipso die multa prodigia exstiterunt quae eum creatorem orbis ostenderunt: ipso die fons olei largissimus de taberna meritoria per totum diem fluxit ut ostenderet quia is nascebatur qui Christus diceretur, id est unctus oleo spiritali, atque ex eius aecclesia 'Christiani' essent dicendi." LLT: Christianus Stabulensis, *Expositio super Librum generationis (Expositio in euangelium Matthaei)* cap. (s.s.): 2, pag.: 91, linea: 23.

Christianus went further than previous authors in characterizing the period in which the *fons olei* appeared as one of peace rather than tumult. The *fons olei* heralded the advent of Anointed One, the Prince of Peace, foretold by the prophets. When he appeared, the Christ excelled secular rulers in establishing peace:

> On the same day, angels sang 'Glory to God in the highest and on earth peace to people of good will' and that voice was so perfect that peace was established in the Roman world for twelve years, peace that no king could make in one province. Thus, just as the prophet said, 'they beat their swords into plowshares and their spears into pruning hooks'[1253] and the psalmist had said, 'in those days an abundance of peace shall arise.'[1254]

Rabanus Maurus (c.780/83-856), the Benedictine Abbot of Fulda and Archbishop of Mainz, included the legend of the *fons olei* in his *Expositio in Matthaeum,* where he drew a parallel between Augustus and Christ while also emphasizing how the earth, rather than the *taberna meritoria,* was the source of the miraculous oil.[1255] Without explicitly interpreting the earth as a symbol for Mary, Rabanus quoted Isaiah's prophecy to explain how the earth brought forth oil in the same way it brought forth the Messiah.[1256]

> Truly with Augustus entering the city, the Senate decreed that he should have the power of a tribune permanently and in those days across the Tiber, a fountain of oil gushed from the earth in the *taberna meritoria* and flowed for a whole day in an copious river, which evidently

---

[1253] Isaiah 2:4: "He shall judge between the nations, and shall arbitrate for many peoples; they shall beat their swords into ploughshares, and their spears into pruning-hooks; nation shall not lift up sword against nation, neither shall they learn war any more."

[1254] "Eodem die angeli cantauerunt gloria in excelsis deo et in terra pax hominibus bonae uoluntatis, et ut ista uox conpleretur tanta pax in orbe Romano facta est per XII annos, quantam nullus rex potuit facere in una prouintia, ita ut, sicut propheta dixit, conflarent gladios suos in uomeres et lanceas suas in falces, et psalmista dixerat orietur in diebus eius abundantia pacis." LLT: Christianus Stabulensis, *Expositio super Librum generationis (Expositio in euangelium Matthaei)* cap. (s.s.): 2, pag.: 91, linea: 28. Christianus cited Psalm 72:7: "In his days may righteousness flourish and peace abound, until the moon is no more."

[1255] Regarding Rabanus Maurus' use of the past and parallels between the empire and the Church, see Mayke De Jong, "The Empire as Ecclesia: Hrabanus Maurus and Biblical Historia for Rulers," in *The Uses of the Past in the Early Middle Ages* (Cambridge, UK; New York: Cambridge University Press, 2000), 191–226.

[1256] "Shower, O heavens, from above, and let the skies rain down righteousness; let the earth open, that salvation may spring up, and let it cause righteousness to sprout up also; I the LORD have created it." Isaiah 45:8.

signified Christ entering the world (from which is was written: let the earth sprout forth a savior and he will rule over the house of Jacob forever and his kingdom will have no end).[1257]

Rabanus not only characterized the earth as the source of both oil and the Messiah, but correlated the source of that oil, the *taberna meritoria*, with the Church, as Orosius had done, although without mentioning Mary by name or a shrine dedicated to her. Rabanus included Orosius' interpretation of the oil flowing for a whole day as a symbol for the entirety of the Roman Empire, but then Rabanus went further. While the Roman Empire ended, Christ's presence (or reign) extended eternally: "for a whole day, that is for the entire time of the Roman Empire, more correctly all the way up to the end of the world - Christians were made by Christ, that is the anointed ones by the Anointed One, themselves from the *meritoria taberna*, that is a large and hospitable church, advancing abundantly and unceasingly."[1258] Just as the power of Augustus' legions spreading over the empire, the power of Christ spread outward from the church, like oil in a river from the *taberna,* flowing into the Tiber.[1259] Rabanus' student, the Bavarian monk Otfrid of Weissenberg (800 – 870), also circulated the legend of the *fons olei* in his *Gloss on Matthew* (*Glossae in Mattheum*). Otfrid presented the legend in abbreviated form, mentioning briefly the miraculous appearance of light around the sun and oil flowing for a

---

[1257] "Hoc uero, quod Augusto Vrbem ingresso in perpetuum illi tribunicia potestas manere a senatu decretum est, et his diebus trans Tiberim e taberna meritoria fontem olei terra exundauit ac per totum diem largissimo riuo fluxit, quid euidentius in eo significatur, quam quod Christo mundum intrante (de quo scriptum est: Terra germinet Saluatorem, et Regnabit in domo Iacob in aeternum, et regni eius non erit finis)." LLT: Rabanus Maurus, *Expositio in Matthaeum*, CM 174, lib.1, p. 52, linea 40. Isaiah 45:8 & 9:7: "His authority shall grow continually, and there shall be endless peace for the throne of David and his kingdom. He will establish and uphold it with justice and with righteousness from this time onwards and for evermore."

[1258] "…per totum diem, hoc est per omne tempus Romani imperii, immo usque ad finem mundi a Christo Christianos fieri, id est unctos ab uncto, et ipsos de meritoria taberna, hoc est de hospita larga que ecclesia, affluenter et incessabiliter processuros." Ibid.

[1259] "Illud quoque, quod Augustus legiones suas ad tutamen orbis terrarum distribuisset ouans que omnia superiora populorum debita donanda, litterarum etiam monumentis abolitis, censuisset, significat, quod Christus ipsis temporibus natus praedicatoribus suis orbem terrarum contra perfidiam tuendum distribuit et iussit praedicari in nomine eius paenitentiam et remissionem peccatorum in omnes gentes." Ibid., CM 174, lib.1, p. 52, linea 50.

whole day, mentioning neither the *taberna meritoria* or other details included in Orosius, apart from the fact that the signs foretold the birth of Christ.[1260]

The first evidence to potentially correlate the *fons olei* with a Marian shrine in Trastevere appears in a letter by Anastasius Bibliothecarius (c.810 – c.879), the papal librarian and abbot of Santa Maria in Trastevere's monastery. In a letter addressed to Ursus, the physician of Pope Nicholas I (r.858 -867), Anastasius Bibliothecarius closed his letter with the following signature: "humble abbot of the monastery of the Holy Mother of God, the Virgin Mary, situated across the Tiber, where formerly around [the time of the] birth of the Lord, a fountain of oil flowed."[1261] A twelfth-century manuscript (Vat.lat.5696) containing Anastasius' Latin translation of the Greek *Acta miraculorum* of Basil the Great, includes the same epithet in its authorial attribution.[1262] Karin Einaudi argued that following Charlemagne's coronation in Rome in 800, oil was increasingly viewed as a sign of legitimate authority. The ancient, anointed figures of the Hebrew Scriptures, including Samuel, Saul and David were reincarnated in Carolingian personages, with Charlemagne as David, the rightful anointed ruler.[1263] The papal librarian might have wished to capitalize on the *fons olei* legend to lend legitimacy to his status and that of Pope Nicholas. As a deposed cardinal and anti-pope during the reign of Pope Benedict III (r. 855-58), perhaps Anastasius intended to invoke the ancient image of August as the triumphant, enduring ruler, whose reign coincided with the appearance of oil flowing from the very place where Anastasius was abbot. Given the fact that up

---

[1260] "Tunc circulus apparuit circa solem et fons olei totum emanauit diem, Christum nasciturum praesignantes. Ipse autem Augustus X'X'X' seruorum dominis reddidit et V'T' dominis non expectantibus cruci subegit, id est qui fidem obseruando se Trinitati manciparint, uite+ dabuntur aeterne+, condemnentes autem omnes per VI aetates mundi morti subiguntur aeternae." LLT: Otfrid Weissenberg, *Glossae in Matthaeum*, cap.2, par.1, linea 20-22.

[1261] "Anastasius exiguus abbas monasterii sanctae dei genitricis mariae virginis siti trans tiberim, ubi olim circa domini nativitatem fons olei fluxit, in domino salutem." See Kinney, "S. Maria in Trastevere from Its Founding to 1215," 165n202.

[1262] Vatican City, Biblioteca Apostolica Vaticana, MS Vat.lat. 5696, fol. 183vB.

[1263] "'Il tema dell'olio santo ricorre ripetutamente come il segno della consecrazione imperiale e della legittimazione del potere, quale risuscitazione dell'impero romano in chiave cristiana. Il simbolismo dell'unzione ritorna anche nel famoso parallelo che Anastasio vi istituisce fra Samuele=pontefice, il quale ripudia Saul=imperatore greco, per ungere re David=Carlo Magno. L'argomento dell'olio santo, dell'unzione pontificia, sostituisce nel testo di Anastasio qualunque argomentazione di natura politica o giuridica, per restare l'unica prove che legittimava l'esistenza dell'impero franco." Einaudi, "'Fons Olei' E Anastasio Bibliotecario," 216–17.

until the late ninth century, the legend of the *fons olei* invariably invoked either the reign of Augustus

or Christ or both, the abbot of Santa Maria in Trastevere evidently sought to associate himself with

those rulers, rather than somehow promote his church as the source of oil. A few centuries would

pass before authors would claim the oil gushed from the church dedicated to a woman. In the

twelfth century, or possibly as early as the eleventh century, rather than being primarily a sign of

enduring male rulership, oil became deeply intertwined with Marian devotion and eventually

symbolized both female virginity and motherhood.

CHAPTER 9

SPONSA CHRISTI:

THE WISE VIRGIN OF VIRGINS

INTRODUCTION: HINC OLEUM FLUXIT

In the early Middle Ages, the legend of the *fons olei* appeared mainly in biblical commentaries and chronicles as a sign or portent of the birth of the savior, whose advent coincided with the reign of Caesar Augustus. Although the authors who disseminated the legend never suggested that the miraculous oil flowed from Santa Maria in Trastevere, the symbolic framework was in place for Mary to become the myroblyte of myroblytes. Orosius had compared the *taberna meritoria* to the universal Church, and Patristic authors, whose works circulated widely in the medieval period, presented Mary as a symbol for the Church. Prior to the eleventh century, the legend of the *fons olei* often emphasized how the miraculous oil presaged the birth of the savior. Authors never explicitly mentioned Mary or discussed the Blessed Virgin being the source of the oil, which symbolized Christ. As Marian devotion and the cults of myroblytes grew in the eleventh and twelfth centuries, the legend of the *fons olei* also transformed; miraculous oil denoted female as well as male sanctity.[1264] Rather than associating the flowing liquid with the enduring reigns of male rulers, namely Augustus and Christ, authors attributed the oil to a woman: the Mother of God. Once the *fons olei* became an element of Roman Marian devotion, oil no longer symbolized the enduring rulership of a secular emperor or Christ. Instead, oil signified the spousal bond between the pope and the Church. Mary, as the Bride of Christ, became a virgin bearing oil, like the wise virgins of Matthew's parable, who gained entrance to the wedding feast.

Extant evidence suggests this shift began sometime in the eleventh century, at the time of the Investiture Controversy. As ecclesiastical leaders vied with kings and emperors for claims to

---

[1264] Engels observed that the twelfth century witnessed the proliferations of any number of legends. See Engels, "Fons Olei: Abelard, Sermon 4 et Hymne 34," 236.

legitimate authority, a church dedicated to the *regina caeli* became a source of holy oil – the very substance that signaled political and ecclesiastical legitimacy. Increasingly, medieval authors cited Santa Maria in Trastevere, rather than the *taberna meritoria*, as the source of the legendary oil, giving emphasis to the connection between Christ, the 'Anointed One' and the oil-producing *mater ecclesia*. The oil flowing from the church, which became a symbol for the universal Church, testified to the presence of legitimate papal authority.

When Innocent II rebuilt the edifice of Santa Maria in Trastevere in the mid twelfth century (1140-43), following the end of the papal schism with Anacletus II, he commissioned mosaics that indirectly gestured towards oil and anointing. This era marked a dramatic reinterpretation of the *fons olei* legend and holy oil. Instability and infighting among Rome's noble families dominated the political, social and ecclesiastical landscape of medieval Rome.[1265] In the twelfth century in particular, a fierce rivalry between the Pierleoni, Frangipane and Papareschi families shaped Santa Maria in Trastevere's development within Rome and the Latin West more generally. Although Nicholas II (r. 1058-1061) issued a decree in 1059 intended to regularize papal elections, a culture of discord prevailed.[1266] In the century spanning the mid eleventh to the mid twelfth century, the See of Peter changed hands ten times. Anti-popes opposed all but three of the "legitimately" elected popes. Thus, when Honorius II (1124-1130) joined the choir of angels on February 13, 1130, tumult ensued once again. On the morning of February 14, following Honorius II's death, the cardinal-bishops of Rome elected Gregory Papareschi (d. 1143), the cardinal-deacon of S. Angelo, as pope. Within a few hours, another faction of cardinals in Rome elected a member of one of Rome's wealthiest merchant and banking families, Pietro Pierleoni (d. 1138), as pope. The Pierleoni family had risen to power in part through financial gains made by the traditionally Jewish family, prior to their conversion to

---

[1265] For a detailed discussion of the social, economic and political structures of medieval Rome, see Chris Wickham, *Medieval Rome: Stability and Crisis of a City, 900-1150* (Oxford: Oxford University Press, 2015).
[1266] Regarding the Roman synod of 1059, see John A. F. Thomson, *The Western Church in the Middle Ages* (London ; New York : New York: Arnold ; Oxford University Press, 1998), 82–84.

Christianity in the eleventh century.[1267] On February 23, the rivals were both consecrated as pope in different churches. Gregory was anointed as Innocent II in the church of Santa Maria Nuova, the stronghold of the Frangipane family, archrivals of the Pierleoni. Pietro Pierleoni was anointed Anacletus II in Saint Peter's. Both men claimed to be the rightful heir to the throne of St. Peter. When the majority of cardinals, wealthy elites and the general Roman population sided with Anacletus II, Innocent II fled Rome, finding refuge in transalpine Europe and establishing alliances with Bernard of Clairvaux (1090-1153), Peter the Venerable (1092-1156), Abbot of Cluny and Suger (c.1081-1151), Abbot of Saint-Denis.

The conflict between Innocent II and Anacletus II played out in Trastevere, the stronghold of Pierleoni and Papareschi families. Before fleeing Rome, Innocent II returned to his native Trastevere, taking refuge in his father's home. The neighborhood, however, was also the bastion of the Pierleoni. Indeed, Anacletus II had been Santa Maria in Trastevere's cardinal priest before being elected pope. When the Frangipani family reconciled with the Pierleoni, they no longer offered Innocent II protection within Trastevere, necessitating his escape.[1268] Certain authors tried to plead Innocent II's cause by spreading rumors about Anacletus II's immoral conduct and indicting him for being Jewish.[1269] They never succeeded, however, in ousting Anacletus II from power. Although Innocent II continued to conduct himself as pope while abroad, he could not return to Rome and claim the role of Bishop of Rome until Anacletus II's death in 1138. Upon returning, Innocent II began reconstruction of Santa Maria in Trastevere, putting his own image within the distinct apse mosaic, which depicted Christ and Mary enthroned as husband and wife. Innocent II symbolically

---

[1267] Regarding the role of Anacletus II's Jewish heritage in the schism, see Mary Stroll, *The Jewish Pope: Ideology and Politics in the Papal Schism of 1130* (Leiden; New York: E.J. Brill, 1987).

[1268] For an account of the election and its aftermath, see John Doran, "Two Popes: The City vs the World," in *Pope Innocent II (1130-43): The World vs the City*, Church, Faith, and Culture in the Medieval West (London ; New York: Routledge, Taylor & Francis Group, 2016), 5–26.

[1269] Stroll, *The Jewish Pope*, 156–68.

reclaimed the Church that he viewed as rightfully his.[1270] *Ecclesia* had once again supplanted *Synagoga*.

Santa Maria in Trastevere's interior reflected the juxtaposition of the Judaic and Christian traditions, including the Hebrew prophets Isaiah, bearing a scroll declaring the virgin will conceive and bear a son (Isaiah 7:14), and Jeremiah, likewise bearing a scroll alluding to Christ being made a captive because of human sinfulness (Lamentations 4:20). Other allusions to Christianity's Judaic roots appeared in the form of miniatures within the apse mosaic of Bethlehem and Jerusalem, which are dwarfed by the immense image of Jesus embracing Mary, the Church, the source of the *fons olei*.

Since by the mid twelfth century oil was a well-established symbol of royal and ecclesiastical authority, Santa Maria in Trastevere, as home of the *fons olei*, was a particularly rich venue for Innocent II's reassertion of his papal authority. Santa Maria in Trastevere's mosaics, including the apse mosaic of Jesus and Mary seated together on a throne and the thirteenth-century exterior mosaic of *maria lactans* surrounded by the wise and foolish virgins (Matt. 25:1-13), alluded to a biblical tradition that associated holy oil with the conjugal union of spouses, a ruler's divine election and perpetual kingship. The church – both particular and universal – was a source of oil, which was an instrument for establishing legitimate authority figures, be they popes, bishops, kings or emperors. Ordinary Christians too acquired their status as Christians through the anointing that followed their baptisms or through their willingness to repent on Holy Thursday, when bishops consecrated holy oils.

Drawing on a biblical tradition that was saturated with oil imagery, Santa Maria in Trastevere's interior and exterior mosaics played on themes of kingship, election, and the eternal nature of God's fidelity to his 'chosen one' – whether the elect was a *rex* or a *sponsa*. Rather than invoking the ancient Roman dimension of the legend of the *fons olei*, the mosaics pointed toward the

---

[1270] Ibid., 26; Jérôme Croisier, "I Mosaici dell'abside e dell'arco trionfale di Santa Maria in Trastevere," in *La Pittura medievale a Roma, 312-1431. Corpus. Vol. IV, Riforma E Tradizione, 1050-1198* (Milan: Jaca Book, 2006), 305–11; Dale Kinney, "S. Maria in Trastevere from Its Founding to 1215" (Ph.D., New York University, 1975).

harmonic juxtaposition of the Judaic and Christian traditions, in which miraculous oil played a

seminal role as a sign of God's eternal fidelity. In the High Middle Ages, Christian authors in the

Latin West were not only aware of how their tradition was rooted in an ancient classical civilization,

but also conscious of how Christianity was the fulfillment of beliefs and rituals of ancient Judaism

and the *terra sancta*, where the Anointed One was born. Perhaps as a result of the Investiture

Controversy and the clashes between the papacy and the rulers of the Holy Roman Empire,

ecclesiastical authors and Innocent II sought to distance the *fons olei* from the image of the eternal

emperor, as depicted by Orosius. Instead, to establish an image of the enduring nature of the Bishop

of Rome, ecclesiastical writers invoked God's fidelity to Hebrew kings instead. Mary, as a

multivalent symbol, represented both the Church and eternity. By establishing his "throne" with the

Church (i.e. Mary), the pope (representing Christ) established himself in an eternal line, reminiscent

of Davidic kingship. Just as a man established a legitimate heir through a nuptial union with his

spouse, the papacy brought the mystical body of Christ into being through his presence within the

Church. The creation of Christ's mystical body did not pertain only in the earthly, temporal realm.

The pope's embrace of his spouse, the Church, had a heavenly parallel: the soul enjoying eternity in

heaven. Before Mary could represent the heavenly realm, however, she first had to appear to

medieval Christian audiences as an ordinary woman who gave birth to a child.

Oleum Effusum : The Fons Olei Legend in the Eleventh Century

By the eleventh century, Santa Maria in Trastevere acquired the epithet *fundens oleum*. Dale

Kinney observed that a land donation given to the church in 1073 attributed this epithet to Santa

Maria in Trastevere.[1271] Exactly when during the course of the eleventh century the Marian church

acquired this appellation is unclear. An eleventh-century codex, British Library Add MS 14801, that

---

[1271] Kinney, "S. Maria in Trastevere from Its Founding to 1215," 191.

once belonged to the monastery of Santa Maria in Trastevere, which Gregory IV (827-844)

established adjacent to the church in the mid-eighth century, contains no reference to oil or the *fons*

olei.[1272] This composite manuscript consists primarily of Jerome's *Martyrology*, but contains curious

additions that attest to the devotional life of monks in Trastevere in the eleventh century. The scribe

included in his description of each month of the liturgical year notes indicating the corresponding

signs in the western zodiac as well as the months in the Hebrew calendar. Furthermore, for each

month the scribe indicated the number of days and nights, the number of hours for each day and

night (*luna*), on which days one should not let blood, as well as what foods or herbs to eat or to

avoid. In the margins of this manuscript, the monks of Santa Maria in Trastevere indicated the

"obits" or passing of their brother monks. They also indicated the days that were of import to Santa

Maria in Trastevere's history, such as the feast days of Pope Julius and Pope Calixtus, whose bodies

was translated to the church.[1273] Later marginal interpolations also indicate the anniversary of

Innocent II's death as well as the Feast of the Immaculate Conception of Mary.[1274] No marginalia in

this manuscript, however, make any references to the *fons olei*, not even on the Feast of the

Epiphany, when, according to Orosius, the oil first flowed.[1275] Neither do the numerous colophons

at the end of the codex, which refer to the church of "*sancte Marie transtiberim*" but never with the

epithet *fons olei* or *fundens oleum*.[1276] The martyrology text does, however, include the feast of Nicholas

of Myra for December 6th, with a later marginal note in a Gothic hand indicating that an altar was

---

[1272] Einaudi, "'Fons Olei' E Anastasio Bibliotecario," 181; Guy Ferrari, *Early Roman Monasteries; Notes for the History of the Monasteries and Convents at Rome from the V through the X Century* (Città del Vaticano: Pontificio Istituto di archeologia cristiana, 1957), 228–29.

[1273] London, British Library, Add MS 14801, 43v.

[1274] "Anno domini incarnationis .m.cxliii In diem .vi. dominus papa innocentius sedundus hobiit in pace qui ecclesiam sancte marie trans tyberim a fundamentis renouauit." Ibid., 34v. "Et conceptio beate virginis mariae." Ibid., 43r.

[1275] The manuscript contains a marginal note for this feast day, but it appears to be unrelated to the *fons olei*. BL Add MS 14801, 7r.

[1276] BL Add MS 14801, 211v. There are also indications in the colophon that the codex was once associated with the monastery of Cosme and Damian. A later colophon, in a late twelfth or early thirteenth-century hand, reads: "Constat me {valone} subdiaconum et monachum sanctorum cosime et damiani" and "Constat me gregoris et monachum sanctorum cosme et damiani." London, British Library, Add MS 14801, 211v.

dedicated to the saint on his feast day.[1277] The martyrology likewise includes the feast of Catherine of

Alexandria, although her name appears at the end of a list of other martyrs who died on that day in

Alexandria, namely bishops who also suffered decapitation.[1278] If her inclusion on that feast day was

a later interpolation (as it appears to be) it could not have been at a much later date than the

composition of the main body of the text since her name appears in a similar, if not the same,

hand.[1279]

Pilgrimage & the Fons Olei

One of the earlier texts to definitively associate the fons olei with the church of Santa Maria

in Trastevere was the *Mirabilia Romae*, a twelfth-century pilgrim itinerary of Rome's marvels.[1280] In

the eleventh and twelfth century, pilgrimage to distant shrines became a dominant expression of

Christian devotion in the Latin West. A triad of holy places emerged, which drew pilgrims from far

and wide: Rome, Jerusalem and Compostela. The rise of pilgrimage led to economic developments

in Europe, including the growth of infrastructures and cottage industries designed to accommodate

travelers.[1281] Merchants were ready to sell food, cloth, shoes, medicine and religious paraphernalia.

Pilgrim traffic also lead to the construction of additional churches, chapels, bridges, inns, hospitals,

baths, fountains, and other amenities.[1282]

At the end of the tenth century, an overland route opened between Europe and Jerusalem,

making travel to the Near East more feasible. When the Normans conquered southern Italy, they

also assumed control of shipping routes across the Mediterranean, which facilitated the safe

---

[1277] "viii.id.dece. Nat. sci. nicolai epi. et confessoris. In africa…" The marginal note reads: "et dedicatio altaris sci nicolai." BL Add MS 14801, 42v–43r.

[1278] Ibid., 41r.

[1279] See image below.

[1280] Maria Accame and Emy Dell'Oro, eds., *I "Mirabilia Urbis Romanae"* (Rome: Tored, 2004).

[1281] Debra J Birch, *Pilgrimage to Rome in the Middle Ages: Continuity and Change* (Woodbridge, Suffolk; Rochester, NY: Boydell Press, 1998), 118–49; William H. Swatos and Luigi Tomasi, eds., *From Medieval Pilgrimage to Religious Tourism: The Social and Cultural Economics of Piety*, Religion in the Age of Transformation (Westport, Conn: Praeger, 2002).

[1282] Birch, *Pilgrimage to Rome in the Middle Ages*, 123–49.

transport of goods as well as pilgrims.[1283] The presence of Muslims in the Holy Land and their

destruction of Christian churches, including one near the Holy Sepulchre in 1009, incited fervor

among Christians to travel to, and eventually recapture, Jerusalem. Beginning with Urban II's (r.

1088-1099) proclamation of the First Crusade in 1099, waves of crusading pilgrims sought material

enrichment as well as absolution from their sins by visiting the Holy Land. The Christian zeal to

attain salvation through conquering Muslim "infidels" did not just play out, however, in Jerusalem.

In the ninth-century, Galicians sought to drive the Muslims from Iberia under the patronage of Saint

James the Greater. The shrine of Saint James in northwestern Spain, known as Santiago de

Compostela, consequently became a locus of pilgrimage and crusading fervor in the eleventh

century, when it enjoyed more pilgrim traffic than Rome.[1284] Saint James acquired the epithet

"Matamoros" – "the killer of Moors" and became the protector of Christian knights. Jerusalem,

however, as the site of Jesus' crucifixion and resurrection, surpassed the other cities in claims to

holiness.[1285] Moreover, Jerusalem symbolized the New Jerusalem, the heavenly homeland for

Christians.[1286] To compete with Jerusalem and Compostela, Rome had to offer comparably holy

attractions to pilgrims. Rome could claim the tombs of saints Peter and Paul as well as the sites of

other early Christian martyrs. Moreover, for many Latin Christians, Rome was more accessible than

Jerusalem.

Rome lay at the center of network of pilgrimage and trade across the Mediterranean.[1287]

While some pilgrims were drawn to saints' shrines in Rome or elsewhere on the Italic peninsula,

other pilgrims were simply passing through the Eternal City on their way to the holier shrines in

---

[1283] Paul Oldfield, *Sanctity and Pilgrimage in Medieval Southern Italy, 1000-1200* (New York, NY: Cambridge University Press, 2014), 182.

[1284] Horton Davies and Marie-Hélène Davies, *Holy Days and Holidays: The Medieval Pilgrimage to Compostela* (Lewisburg, Pa: Bucknell University Press, 1982), 18–19; Oldfield, *Sanctity and Pilgrimage in Medieval Southern Italy, 1000-1200*, 183.

[1285] Davies and Davies, *Holy Days and Holidays*, 17.

[1286] Regarding Jerusalem in the imaginations of medieval Europeans and their "mental pilgrimage," see Lucy Donkin and Hanna Vorholt, eds., *Imagining Jerusalem in the Medieval West*, Proceedings of the British Academy 175 (Oxford: Published for the British Academy by Oxford University Press, 2012).

[1287] Oldfield, *Sanctity and Pilgrimage in Medieval Southern Italy, 1000-1200*, 181–89.

Jerusalem and Bethlehem.[1288] Some so-called pilgrims travelled to Rome to attend to ecclesiastical

business as much as to visit the holy shrines.[1289] Nevertheless, in the twelfth century, Rome enjoyed

fewer pilgrims than either Compostela or Jerusalem, potentially due to the political turbulence

within the city and ongoing conflicts with the Holy Roman Emperor.[1290] Some popes, such as

Innocent III, tried to remedy the deficit of pilgrims by introducing processions of relics that would

simultaneously draw pilgrims and reinforce papal power and presence. When Innocent III claimed

the epithet "vicar of Christ," he also instituted a procession of the Veronica, a cloth bearing Christ's

"true image," making the parallel between Christ's presence in Rome and that of the pope all the

more evident.[1291] Although the Veronica drew large crowds, Rome did not surpass Compostela and

Jerusalem as a destination for pilgrims until 1300, when Boniface VIII (r. 1294-1303) declared a

Jubilee year and offered plenary indulgences to anyone who visited the Eternal City.[1292] As Boniface

VIII's power diminished through his conflicts with Philip IV of France (r. 1285-1314) as well as his

own bishops and cardinals, he used pilgrimage to reassert his own authority and that of Rome as the

epicenter of Christianity in Europe.

Prior to the Jubilee of 1300, pilgrim itineraries, like the *Mirabilia*, helped to boost Rome's

renown as a holy destination, drawing on Christians' desire to see ancient Roman as well as Christian

sites. A canon of St. Peter's named Benedetto may have authored the *Mirabilia Romae*, which dates to

1140-1143. The *Liber Polypticus,* a liturgical-administrative book of the Roman curia, contains the

oldest version of the text, which refers to the *fons olei* twice. The *fons olei* would have appealed to

pilgrims who were interested in miraculous landmarks as well as individuals seeking healing at a

shrine. At the beginning of the second part of the *Mirabilia*, which recounts the marvels of the city,

---

[1288] Ibid., 182.

[1289] Diana Webb, *Medieval European Pilgrimage, c.700-c.1500*, European Culture and Society (Basingstoke, Hampshire ; New York, N.Y: Palgrave, 2002), 1.

[1290] Ibid., 24–25. See also Birch, *Pilgrimage to Rome in the Middle Ages*, 150–73.

[1291] Webb, *Medieval European Pilgrimage, c.700-c.1500*, 25–26.

[1292] Davies and Davies, *Holy Days and Holidays*, 51.

the first account tells of Augustus seeking the Sibyl's counsel regarding whether he should assent to

the senate's wish for him to rule as caesar. While the Sibyl was in her prophetic ecstasy, Augustus

had the following vision: "…heaven opened, and a great brightness shown on him, and he saw in

heaven a virgin exceedingly fair standing on an altar holding a man-child in her arms. Octavian

marveled greatly at this, and he heard a voice from heaven saying: 'This is the Virgin who shall

conceive the Saviour of the World.'"[1293] After this vision, according to the *Mirabilia,* Octavian agreed

to become emperor. Later in the narrative, the author described Trastevere as the region where the

oil flowed in the time of Octavian, distinguishing between when the oil flowed (*tempore Octaviani*)

and the presence of Mary or her shrine in Trastevere (*nunc est Santa Maria):* "Across the Tiber, where

Santa Maria is now, there was the Temple of Ravenna, where oil flowed from the earth in the time

of the Emperor Octavian, and there was the public inn (*domus meritoria*) where soldiers, who served

without payment in the senate, earned money."[1294] What were the unpaid soldiers doing at the inn

near the Temple of Ravenna? Possibly consorting with prostitutes (*meretrices*) or collecting taxes from

them.[1295] Since ancient Roman prostitutes were excluded from the religious cults that more

respectable women participated in, alternative cults sprang up outside the pomerium – outside the

city wall in regions such as Trastevere.[1296] Prostitutes could be found working at inns or lodging

houses (tabernae) as well as other public places of entertainment, including under the arcades of the

---

[1293] Francis Morgan Nichols, trans., *The Marvels of Rome - Mirabilia Urbis Romae,* 2nd ed. (New York: Italica Press, 1986), 17–18.

[1294] "Trans Tiberim, ubi nunc est Sancta Maria, fuit templum Ravennantium, ubi terra manavit oleum tempore Octaviani imperatoris, et fuit ibi domus Meritoria, ubi merebantur milites qui gratis serviebant in senatu. Sub Ianiculo templum Gorgonis. Ad ripam fluminis, ubi naves morantur, templum Herculis. In Piscina templum Fortunae et Dianae. In insula Licaonia templum Iovis et templum Aesculapii. Foris portam Appiam templum Martis et triumphalis arcus." Accame and Dell'Oro, *I "Mirabilia Urbis Romanae,"* 176. See also Dale Kinney, "S. Maria in Trastevere from Its Founding to 1215" (Ph.D., New York University, 1975), 354n2.

[1295] "As Suetonius indicates, the collection of the prostitute tax…was at first entrusted to the *publicani* but later transferred to the officers of the Praetorian Guard 'quia lucrum exuberabat.' Outside Rome the tax appears to have been collected…by regular army troops in the military areas, and elsewhere by legionary soldiers serving on detached duty as *beneficiarii* and *curiosi,* where these were available." Thomas A. McGinn, *Prostitution, Sexuality, and the Law in Ancient Rome* (New York: Oxford University Press, 1998), 256–57.

[1296] Ibid., 25.

Circus Maximus and the Coliseum, where other goods, including food, were sold.[1297] Suetonius (b. circa 11 C.E.) used the euphemism "fast food" to refer to prostitution, potentially because both were on offer in taverns; a similar statement is also found in Cassius Dio.[1298] While pimps were excluded from both the senatorial order and the army, soldiers sometimes collected the tax on erotic transactions.[1299] If some milites served in the senate without remuneration, they may have supported themselves through collecting taxes in places like Trastevere on behalf of the state.

While in the twelfth century some authors elaborately embellished the legend of the *fons olei,* others continued to circulate the legend of *fons olei* as it appeared in Orosius with little variation. Still others simply alluded to Mary as a fountain of oil without directly discussing Trastevere's *fons olei.* Given the central role of oil in ecclesiastical ordinations and royal coronations by the High Middle Ages, oil became an indelible element of political discourse. And, since oil featured so prominently in Scriptural passages about marriage or conjugal love, oil easily fused these two spheres of Christian existence. Marriage became a metaphor for political and ecclesiastical governance. In the twelfth century, like in the Carolingian period, some authors referenced the *fons olei* within a larger discourse on temporal and spiritual power, without discussing the relationship between oil and the Blessed Virgin or the *terra sancta.* These authors were chiefly concerned with questions of divine election and kingship. Otto of Freising (c.1111/1114 – 1158), the chronicler and bishop of Freising in Bavaria, cited Rome's *fons olei* in his world chronicle, the *Historia de duabus civitatibus,* giving emphasis to the fact that Jesus, as the Anointed One, possessed a spiritual power that made him superior to all temporal kings: "In those days a large rivulet of oil was discovered to flow in the Trastevere region

---

[1297] Ibid., 127, 137, 297.
[1298] Ibid., 250.
[1299] Ibid., 138, 249–50, 256, 266–87.

of the city, to show Jesus was born in the flesh, who was anointed with the oil of gladness and the Holy Spirit of exaltation above all kings."[1300]

John of Salisbury's (1115 – 1180) discussion of the *fons olei* in his *Policraticus* (1159) presented a variant interpretation of the relationship between anointing and kingship. According to John, tyrants sometimes existed through God's providential design.[1301] Anointing a man as king did not preclude a tyrannical reign: "Yet the same man [Saul] was called the anointed of the Lord and, exercising tyranny, he did not lose the honour of kingship."[1302] According to Salisbury, among the Gentiles the Lord's anointed were so called "not because they were holy men but because they carried out the will of the Lord against Babylon."[1303] Nevertheless, the oil of the *fons olei* signaled the advent of Augustus' just reign and that of God's justice: "...in those very days the greatest fountain of oil flowed from the *taberna meritoria* for a whole day. ...that certainly revealed the imperial rule to be near, announcing that through the just dominion of God, He came to subdue the sinful slaves of the Devil and to have mercy on the poor."[1304] In his retelling of the *fons olei* legend, John of Salisbury, like other authors before him, referenced the *fons olei* as part of a larger discourse on the nature of spiritual and political authority without making a statement about Marian devotion or the place of the Blessed Virgin in salvation history.

While the *Mirabilia Romae* itinerary could potentially explain how the legend associating Santa Maria with the *fons olei* spread across Europe, L.J. Engels argued that two texts by Peter Abelard (1079 – 1142) that predated the *Mirabilia Romae* located the *fons olei* within Santa Maria in Trastevere. According to Engles, Abelard's Sermon 4, a sermon for the feast of the Epiphany, and Hymn 34,

---

[1300] "Illis diebus largus olei rivulus in Transtyberina Urbis regione fluxisse invenitur, ut nasciturus in carne, qui super omnes reges oleo laeticiae et exultationis spiritu sancto unguendus foret, monstraretur." Otto of Freising, *Chronik oder die Geschchte der zwei Staaten,* trans., Adolf Schmidt, ed., Walther Lammers, Ausgewählte Quellen zur deutschen Geschichte des Mittelalters, Bd. 16 (Berlin: Rütten & Loening, 1960). See Engels, "Fons Olei: Abelard, Sermon 4 et Hymne 34."
[1301] John of Salisbury, *Policraticus* (Turnholt: Brepols, 1993), 201–5.
[1302] Ibid., 202.
[1303] Ibid.
[1304] "in diebus ipsis fons olei largissimus de taberna meritoria per totum diem defluxit." LLT: tom. II, lib.: 8, cap.: 18, pag.: 361, linea: 4.

one of the four hymns for the Epiphany in *Hymnarius Paraclitensis,* a collection of hymns intended for

Héloïse and her nuns in the Convent of the Paraclete, date to sometime after 1129/30 but before

1135/6. This dating of Abelard's texts suggests that Santa Maria in Trastevere's fame as an oil-

producer potentially predated the pilgrim itinerary by five years. At least one copy of Abelard's

Sermon 4 derives from a manuscript from Einsiedeln, which also produced an eighth-ninth century

pilgrim itinerary that, in its section entitled *De locis sanctis,* lists the *basilica quae app[ellatur] sca maria*

transtiberis…ibi est imago scae mariae quae per se facta est.[1305] Why did Abelard mention the *fons olei* in a

hymn and sermon for the Epiphany? Evidently he was drawing inspiration from Orosius'

Histories.[1306] Orosius had, after all, claimed that the oil erupted on January 6th, presaging the feast of

the Epiphany before Christ's birth:

> 725 years after the foundation of the City…Caesar Augustus returned in triumph from the
>
> east. On the sixth of January, he entered the city in a triple triumph…This day was the first
>
> day on which he was called Augustus…No believer, nor even anyone who opposes the faith,
>
> is ignorant of the fact that we keep on this same day, the sixth of January, the feast of
>
> Epiphany, that is the appearance or manifestation of the Lord's sacrament.[1307]

In his Hymne 34, Abelard presented a metric distillation of the miracles that appeared on

the Epiphany, prior to Christ's birth, when Augustus began his reign.[1308] In Sermon 4, however,

Abelard significantly glossed Orosius' version of the legend and mentioned Santa Maria in

Trastevere by name. Like Orosius, Abelard observed that the oil was indicative of the arrival of a

---

[1305] The version of the text in PL derives from a manuscript from Einsiedeln. Regarding the pilgrim itinerary, see
Kinney, "S. Maria in Trastevere from Its Founding to 1215," 65–66.

[1306] Engels, "Fons Olei: Abelard, Sermon 4 et Hymne 34," 235.

[1307] Orosius, *Seven Books of History against the Pagans,* 308–9.

[1308] Engels, "Fons Olei: Abelard, Sermon 4 et Hymne 34," 237. The text for Hymne 34 reads: "Nasciturum sive natum /
Caeli regem et terrae / Miris signis eo dignis / Praedicarunt utraque. / Veniente redemptore / Servis datur libertas, /
Servitutis iugum tollis / Et, quem nescis, praesignas. Iani portas tenet clausas / Pax a Christo praemissa, / Quae
prophetae quondam voce / Mundo fuit promissa. / Nam, Auguste, te florente / Solem cinxit corona, / Inundavit, quod
manavit, / Oleum de taberna. / Interdicis nec permittis / Te dominum vocari, / Ut venturo possit Christo / Decus hoc
reservari. / Pax in terris, in excelsis / Sit gloria, sit summa / Regi summo, patri, verbo, / Spiritui per saecula." Clemens
Blume and Guido Maria Dreves, eds., *Analecta Hymnica Medii Aevi,* vol. 48 (New York: Johnson Reprint Corp, 1961).

monarch: "from that day ultimate power was vested and remained in the hands of one individual – a system the Greeks call monarchy."[1309] According to Abelard, the sign in heaven and on earth (i.e. the halo around the sun and the fountain of oil), demonstrated which realms were subject to the rule of the monarch, Christ: "What did these signs suggest, if not that at the same time he was born who maintained absolute rule of heaven and earth to so great an extent? What did the aforementioned halo around the sun and the unction flowing from the earth promise, if not a king equally of heaven and earth?"[1310] Setting aside the rhetorical question for a moment, Abelard indulged in a bit of exegesis, borrowing directly from Augustine's *City of God* as well as his commentary on Psalm 44, which was reproduced in the *Glossa Ordinaria* for the pericope of Jacob anointing the stone at Bethel as well as Psalm 44.[1311] Abelard stated: "Naturally the Savior himself is the sun of justice to such an extent that he is called 'Christ' from 'chrism,' that is 'anointed' from 'anointing.'"[1312] Abelard then advanced an idea that Innocent III would also circulate: the anointing was a sign of Christ's human nature.[1313]

Gesturing towards Orosius' description of the *taberna meritoria* or the Church as a "plentiful hostess" (*hospita larga*), Abelard claimed that Christ's lavish (*larga*) anointing corresponded to his

---

[1309] Orosius, *Seven Books of History against the Pagans*, 309.

[1310] "Quae profecto quid aliud praetendebant, nisi eum eodem tempore nasciturum esse, qui tam coeli quam terrae monarchiam obtineret? Quid enim praedicta corona solis, aut de terra unctio profluens, nisi coeli pariter ac terrae promittebat regem?" PL 178, Col.0411B-C.

[1311] ""*Dilexisti iustitiam, et odisti iniquitatem: propterea unxit te, Deus, Deus tuus.* Propterea unxit te, ut diligeres iustitiam, et odires iniquitatem. Et vide quomodo ait: *Propterea unxit te, Deus, Deus tuus.* O tu Deus, unxit te Deus tuus. Deus ungitur a Deo. Etenim in latino putatur idem casus nominis repetitus: in graeco autem evidentissima distinctio est, quia unum nomen est quod compellatur, et alterum ab eo qui compellat: *Unxit te, Deus.* O tu *Deus, unxit te Deus tuus.* quomodo si diceret: Propterea unxit te, o tu Deus, Deus tuus. Sic accipite, sic intellegite, sic in graeco evidentissimum est. Ergo quis est Deus unctus a Deo? Dicant nobis Iudaei. Scripturae istae communes sunt. Unctus est Deus a Deo: unctum audis, Christum intellege. Etenim Christus a chrismate: hoc nomen quod appellatur Christus, unctionis est. Nec in aliquo alibi ungebantur reges et sacerdotes, nisi in illo regno ubi Christus prophetabatur et ungebatur, et unde venturum erat Christi nomen: nusquam est alibi omnino, in nulla gente, in nullo regno. Unctus est ergo Deus a Deo: quo oleo, nisi spiritali? Oleum enim visibile in signo est, oleum invisibile in sacramento est, oleum spiritale intus est. Unctus est nobis Deus, et missus est nobis: et ipse Deus, ut ungeretur, homo erat: sed ita homo erat, ut Deus esset; ita Deus erat, ut homo esse non dedignaretur: verus homo, verus Deus; in nullo fallax, in nullo falsus; quia ubique verax, ubique veritas. Deus ergo homo, et ideo unctus Deus, quia homo Deus, et factus est Christus." Augustine, *Enarrationes in Psalmos*, Psalm 44, accessed on February 18, 2015. http://www.augustinus.it/latino/esposizioni_salmi/esposizione_salmo_059_testo.htm.

[1312] "Ipse quippe Salvator tam sol justitiae, quam Christus a chrismate, id est unctus ab unctione, nuncupatus est." PL 178, Col.0411C.

[1313] See Chapter 10.

human nature: "His plentiful anointing, moreover, is according to human nature, full of spiritual gifts and seven-fold grace and a perfect comparison can be made between Christ and the one about whom it is said: 'God your God anointed you with the oil of gladness before your companions.'"[1314] Abelard then moved on to nuptial imagery, arguing that the oil which flowed from the *taberna meritoria* was akin to the name of the *sponsus* of the Song of Songs: "We accept everything that is written regarding this abundance of unction, such as that oil exuberantly flows from the inn, such that it is said of Christ: *Your name is oil poured out.*"[1315] But Abelard's discourse regarding the oil and the *taberna larga* was far from straightforward. Responding, potentially, to concerns regarding simony, Abelard turned over the meaning of the lodging house or inn being "for sale" (*meritoria*) or up for hire. Was he potentially suggesting a parallel between the Church and prostitutes who frequented public, commercial spaces in ancient Rome, including taverns, where soldiers collected the taxes on such amorous transactions?[1316] Could Abelard have been responding to Héloïse's bold claim that she would prefer to be his prostitute than the emperor's wife: "God is my witness that if Augustus, Emperor of the whole world, thought fit to honor me with marriage and conferred all the earth on me to possess forever, it would be dearer and more honourable to me to be called not his Empress but your whore."[1317] Curiously enough, Héloïse statement touches on all the major themes of the legend of the *fons olei's* connection to the Emperor Augustus, namely his being ruler of the whole world for eternity.

[1314] "Haec autem secundum humanam naturam larga ejus unctio est, illa spiritalium donorum et septiformis gratiae plena et perfecta ei facta collatio, de qua ipsi dicitur: *Unxit te Deus Deus tuus oleo laetitiae prae consortibus tuis* (Psal. XLIV, 2)." PL 178, Col. 0411C.

[1315] "De hujus plenitudine unctionis, sicut scriptum est, omnes accepimus (Joan. I, 16), tanquam de taberna exuberanter oleum manat, secundum quod ei dicitur: *Oleum effusum nomen tuum* (Cant. I, 2)." PL 178, Col. 0411C.

[1316] Regarding Roman soldiers as the collectors of taxes on prostitution and taverns as loci of this economic activity, see McGinn, *Prostitution, Sexuality, and the Law in Ancient Rome*, 138, 249–50, 256, 266-87, 137, 297.

[1317] Peter Abelard and Heloise, *The Letters of Abelard and Heloise*, ed. Michael Clanchy, trans. Betty Radice, Revised edition (London, England ; New York, N.Y., USA: Penguin Books, 2003), 51.

Engels dated the Sermon 4 text to circa 1130-1135, almost a decade prior to Santa Maria in Trastevere's reconstruction by Innocent II from 1140-43.[1318] If the text postdates the reconstruction, can it be read as a dig at Innocent II and his backer Bernard of Clairvaux, Abelard's foe?[1319]

> Moreover that house was considered a hired inn (*meritoria…taberna*), where unpaid soldiers (*emeriti milites*) were kept warm. However much the *taberna* was able to provide for their daily necessities, by how much more did the portico overflow (*abundabat*) with things for sale. In this place, the Basilica Santa Maria, whose outpouring of oil therefore having given honor to Rome until now, was considered famous.[1320]

For Abelard, however, the house that opened up its door for a price was not entirely a bad thing. In that place, God joined himself with humanity: "But rightly that house, which existed well through the earnings of atonement, was established by the Lord assuming humanity, through which God was made favorable to all the faithful."[1321] For this reason, Abelard urged his readers to humble themselves, in a spirit reminiscent of those participating in the *Ad mandatum* rite, which included imagery of Mary Magdalene, the repentant prostitute with the flowing oil.[1322]

[1318] Kinney noted that Innocent II's family, the Papreschi, were established in Trastevere, which may have precipitated the reconstruction of Santa Maria in Trastevere. Kinney, "S. Maria in Trastevere from Its Founding to 1215," 207–8.

[1319] Regarding Bernard's support of Innocent II's papacy, see G. R. Evans, *Bernard of Clairvaux*, Great Medieval Thinkers (New York: Oxford University Press, 2000), 6, 13–18, 95, 110, 121, 141, 158. "In backing Innocent II against Anacletus II, Bernard supported the side which he thought best represented the spirit of the reforms of the period of Gregory VII." Ibid., 14.

[1320] "Meritoria autem taberna illa domus aestimatur [*leg.* existimatur], ubi emeriti milites fovebantur. Quae tanto magis eorum necessitatibus quotidianis sufficere poterat, quanto amplius ejus porticus venalium rerum abundabat copia. Hoc in loco, basilica S. Mariae, quae ideo fundentis oleum agnominata Romae adhuc ostenditur, celebris habetur." PL 178, Col. 0412A.

[1321] "Merito autem domus illa, quae propitiationis bene merentibus existebat, assumptae a Domino humanitati comparatur, per quam universis fidelibus propitiatus est Deus." PL 178, Col. 0412B.

[1322] "Quis enim Spiritu sancto suggerente factum esse non videat, cum in tanta sublimatus gloria Augustus praemineret, se dominum vocari omnino interdixerit, nec vel joco id se appellari, sed solummodo Augustum permitteret; quasi quadam divina dispositione venturo Christo hujus appellationis decus reservaret, qui discipulis ait: *Vos vocatis me, Magister et Domine, et bene dicitis; sum etenim* (Joan. XIII, 13). Unde et ejus humilitatem Dominus ipse respiciens, cum ait: *Qui se humiliat exaltabitur* (Matth. XXII, 12,) ipsum Augusti nomen proprium adeo extollere decrevit, ut deinceps Romani imperatores se generaliter Augustos vocitari gloriarentur: et quod prius proprium atque personale, factum est generale vocabulum et imperiale. Patenter eum avunculo suo Julio Caesari in humilitate contrarium videmus, cum ille, ut Lucanus quoque meminit, omnium dignitatum gradus in se retinens, jam non se numero singulari, sed plurali proferri

Over the course of the twelfth century, the idea that holy oil flowed from the Virgin proliferated, creating sundry interpretations of the *fons olei* legend, as Engels noted. One such variation appeared in a text by Rupert of Deutz (c.1075/6 – 1129), Abelard's contemporary. In *On the Holy Trinity and His Works (De sancta Trinitate et operibus eius)*, Rupert also emphasized, when he wrote about the nativity, how Jesus was born of the Virgin. Instead of discussing how the sign of Christ's advent coincided with the beginning of Augustus' reign, however, Rupert explained that Jesus was born in Bethlehem, giving priority to the connection between Christ and the *terra sancta* rather than Rome. The juxtaposition of Bethlehem and the Virgin created a symbolic parallel between the Mother of God and the Holy Land. Deutz, possibly drawing on the *Glossa Ordinaria,* said the name 'Christ' derived from Christ having been anointed by the "oil of gladness" (Psalm 44:8).

> Therefore rightly and venerably when the Lord Jesus Christ was born in Bethlehem of Judea from the Blessed Virgin, before all the saints, he was anointed with the oil of gladness, whence in those days Romans called him 'Christ,' such that the stories relate that the greatest fountain of oil flowed from the *taberna meritoria* for a whole day.[1323]

Instead of saying simply that the anointing of the king occurred before his companions - *prae consortibus tuis* – Deutz suggested that the companions of the king (Christ) were the saints. Deutz did not pick up on the fact that *christos* was Greek, not Latin but nevertheless tried to explain why ancient Romans, living so far from the *terra sancta,* believed in the *fons olei.* While Deutz was less concerned with probing into the terrestrial aspects of the savior's birth, his interest in the correlation between Bethlehem as the source of Christ and Rome as a source of oil was a theme that would appear in the writings of later authors.

---

permitteret, non se jam quasi unum hominem, sed plures juxta dignitatum multitudinem considerans." PL 178, Col. 0412B-C.

[1323] "Bene ergo et uenerabiliter quando in bethleem iudae de beata uirgine natus est dominus iesus christus oleo laetitiae prae omnibus sanctis unctus unde et dicitur christus in diebus illis romae ut historiae tradunt fons olei largissimus de taberna meritoria per totum diem fluxit." LLT: CM 24, lib. : 41, De operibus Spiritus Sancti VIII.

Honorius of Autun (1080 - 1154), supposedly a native of Autun in Burgundy, who may have

spent his most prolific years in southern Germany or Canterbury, England, mentioned the *fons olei* in

his *Elucidarium* (c. 1100) a *summa* of Christian theology in a question and answer format. His chapter

on the circumstances and miracles surrounding Christ's birth (*De nativitatis Christi circumstantiis, et

patratis in ea mirabilibus*) delved into the reality of God having been born of a woman. Referring to

Mary as "a sinful woman" (*peccatrix*), Honorius discussed Mary's body as well as her virginity, posing

the question: "How could he be born without sin from the burden (*massa*) of a sinful woman

(*peccatrice*)?"[1324] Regarding Mary's virginity, Honorius invoked nuptial imagery: "How did she give

birth to him? Without filth, without pain. Indeed He entered the bridal chamber (*thalamus*) of the

womb with the door closed. He united human nature with himself and with the door closed, so the

true bridegroom came forth from the bridal chamber."[1325] Unlike previous Carolingian authors,

Honorius showed no concern for the political or military developments in the Roman Empire when

the savior was born. Rather, he was concerned with questions about Mary's maternity and Christ's

infancy: could Christ walk and talk for instance, when he was born?[1326] Within this context,

Honorius discussed the prodigies associated with Christ's birth, including the legend of the *fons olei*.

Without mentioning Augustus, Honorius simply stated: "A fountain of oil erupted from the earth.

There was great peace."[1327]

In recounting the heavenly and earthly prodigies that accompanied Christ's birth, Honorius

altered the legend, giving a new interpretation to the oil as representing mercy, which he said flowed

---

[1324] "Quomodo potuit nasci sine peccato de massa peccatrice?-- Ab initio Deus quosdam qui se familiarius colerent de aliis segregavit, de quibus Virgo quasi de linea producta pullulavit; quae velut olim virga arida sine humore protulit florem, ita sine concupiscentia mundo edidit Salvatorem." PL 172, Col. 1123C.

[1325] "D. Qualiter genuit eum? M. Sine sorde, et sine dolore. Clausa enim janua thalamum uteri introivit, humanam naturam sibi conjunxit, et clausa porta, ut verus sponsus de thalamo processit." PL 172, Col. 1123C.

[1326] "Potuit ambulare vel loqui, mox ut natus est?-- Secundum potentiam utrumque potuit; sed humanam naturam per omnia absque peccato imitari voluit." PL 172, Col. 1123D.

[1327] "Fons olei de terra erupit. Pax maxima fuit." PL 172, Col. 1124A.

from the Virgin. While still discussing the nature of Christ's rulership and the people's relationship to their ruler, Honorius focused on the Virgin as the source of oil, mercy and Christ:

> A golden or purple circle glowed around the sun for the Sun of Justice to show the Church his divinity with gold and that he came to crown with the purple of his passion. Oil signifies mercy. The fountain of oil flowed from the earth because a fountain of mercy emanated from the Virgin. Momentous peace came forth because the true peace appeared on earth. The world was enrolled in the census, because the human race was marked for the heavenly kingdom through anointing.[1328]

Honorius's *Speculum Ecclesiae,* a collection of sermons, contains a Christmas sermon (*de nativitate domini*), which explicitly associates the *fons olei* with the Virgin Mary, again saying that she was not only a source of oil but also mercy. Like earlier Carolingian authors, Honorius explained how the appearance of oil was like the advent of Christ the Saviour, but unlike other authors (apart from Abelard), Honorius claimed that the Virgin Mary herself was the source of oil. Here too Honorius was concerned with explaining the implication of this miracle for "the people" or the relationship of people to the miraculous oil. Rather than correlating the advent of Christ with Augustus' reign, Honorius explained that the fountain of mercy flowed among human beings, symbolized by the water of the Tiber.

> The fountain of oil in Rome erupted from the ground and ran in an abundant stream (*vena*) into the Tiber River, because that day the pure Virgin produced a fountain of mercy that flowed abundantly among human beings. The angels with their own great radiance of light and with the voice of praise revealed for human beings that they prefigured praise to the eternal light and perpetual Creator today through the future king's birth.[1329]

[1328] "Circulus aureus vel purpureus circa solem fulsit; quia Sol justitiae auro suae divinitatis Ecclesiam illustrare, et purpura suae passionis coronare venit. Oleum significat misericordiam. Fons olei de terra fluxit, quia fons misericordiae de Virgine emanavit. Pax ingens exstitit, quia pax vera in terris apparuit. Mundus ad censum est descriptus, quia ad supernum regnum chrismate est praesignatum humanum genus." PL 172, Col. 1124A-B.

[1329] "Fons olei in Roma de terra erupit, et in flumen Tyberim larga vena cucurrit, quia fontem misericordiae munda Virgo hodie produxit qui largiter in humanum genus profluxit. Angeli se cum magno fulgore luminis et omniloga voce laudis hominibus demonstrabant, quia eos ad aeternam lucem et perpetuam Conditoris laudem per Regem hodie natum futurum praesignabant." PL 172, Col. 0818D-0819A.

To my knowledge, Honorius d'Autun was the first author to say both that the oil from the *fons olei*

flowed into the Tiber River, and interpret the river to represent human beings.[1330] This addition to

the legend would circulate in subsequent variations. Honorius was perhaps embellishing Jerome's

comment that Christ was born "ex gentibus" – of human kind. The oil mixing with the water, of

course, would have also suggested the comingling of water and wine in the Eucharistic rite, which

represented the mingling of human and divine natures. Honorius further amplified the sacramental

nature of the *fons olei,* by clarifying how the oil flowed from Mary, who was a symbol for the Church,

the source of all the sacraments, including anointing with oil: "These are the sacrosanct mysteries

that the holy Church with the angels honors today according to what pleases the Lord. Because

today three masses are celebrated, this signifies that human beings, for three ages – of course the

patriarchs before the law, the prophets under the law, the faithful under grace – are saved through

Christ's birth."[1331] The emphasis that Honorius gave to Mary being the *fons olei* is particularly

noteworthy given that the frontispiece to a collection of Honorius' works, including his commentary

on the Song of Songs, contains an image of Mary and Christ seated on a throne as husband and

wife. Carlo Cecchelli noted a resemblance of these figures to those in Santa Maria in Trastevere's

apse mosaic, which will be discussed in turn.[1332] Given the fact that the frontispiece postdates the

apse mosaic, however, the image from Honorius' collection could not have served as inspiration for

the apse mosaic.[1333]

[1330] See PL 172.

[1331] "Haec sunt sacrosancta mysteria quae hodie in Domino jocundando cum angelis sancta veneratur Ecclesia. Quod hodie tres missae celebrantur, significat quod homines per tria tempora, scilicet patriarchae ante legem, prophetae sub lege, fideles sub gratia, per Christi nativitatem salvantur." PL 172, Col. 0818D-0819A.

[1332] The manuscript is a southern German manuscript (Munich, Bayerische Staatsbibliothek MS Lat. 4450, fol.1v). Carlo Cecchelli, *Mater Christi 1. 1.* (Roma: Ferrari, 1946), 95; Ernst Kitzinger, "A Virgin's Face: Antiquarianism in Twelfth-Century Art," *The Art Bulletin* 62, no. 1 (March 1, 1980): 9.

[1333] Kitzinger, "A Virgin's Face," 9.

An anonymous sermon for the Nativity of Christ advanced the legend of the *fons olei*, by probing even further than Honorius d'Autun did into the human nature of the infant and mother who bore him. The Bollandists originally attributed the text to Peter Damian (1007-1072) but since the sermon referred to Bernard of Clairvaux (1090-1153), who was born almost two decades after Peter Damian's death, the Bollandists later attributed the text to Bernard's secretary, Nicholas of Clairvaux (12th century – dates unknown).[1334] If Nicholas composed the sermon after Bernard's death, the date of composition would be sometime in the second half of the twelfth century, after the reconstruction of Santa Maria in Trastevere by Innocent II. The sermon not only mentioned the *fons olei* as coinciding with the birth of Christ but continually alluded to the flow of oil, which runs like a *leitmotiv* throughout the sermon. The word "effusion" appeared twelve times, along with several instances of the verb *effundere* – to pour out. Apart from delighting in his oil theme, the author played with paradoxes and the incomprehensible tension between marvelous prodigies and ordinary human existence.

> One will not be able to explain in a sermon what I conceived in my mind, for the torpor of miracles overwhelms me and as I unfold everything, everything is folded up again: "Who can think of the day of his coming?" Therefore let the tongue be speechless, memory forgetful, feeling insensible. All shines forth the usual nativity and all yields to a birth from a virgin.[1335]

Among the paradoxes that filled the narrator's mind were the coexistence of great destruction and great peace. After first narrating the portents of doom and cataclysmic events befalling ancient Rome (blending the spirit of Cassius Dio with narrative details from Orosius) the author turned to the most extraordinary and incomprehensible miracle of all: the birth of a child.

[1334] PL 144, Col. 0847 ff.

[1335] "Non poterit explicari sermone quod mente concepi, stupor enim miraculorum opprimit me, et dum omnia replico, omnia complicantur: «Quis poterit cogitare diem adventus ejus?» (Malach. III.) Ideo fit elinguis lingua, memoria immemor, insensibilis sensus. Insueta nativitate relucent omnia, et omnia partui Virginis obsequuntur." PL 144, Col. 0848B.

The author set up a geographic (and potentially political) dichotomy between the great epicenters of

civilization and a humble village. The author appears to have conflated a number of historical

events: the destruction of the Second Temple in Jerusalem in 70 C.E., when the Roman Emperor

Vespasianus (r. 69-79) suppressed the Jewish rebellion in what has come to known as the Roman-

Jewish Wars (66-136 CE); the destruction of Vespasianus' Temple of Peace (*templum pacis*), which the

emperor built in 71 C.E. following the destruction of Jerusalem,[1336] when Alaric sacked Rome in 410;

the eruption of the *fons olei* in Rome circa 30s B.C.E.; the birth of Jesus in Bethlehem. According to

the sermon's author, while Rome and Jerusalem were both rattled by violence and mayhem,

Bethlehem was an oasis of peace. When Rome began to crumble, the *fons olei* appeared. The

apocalyptic events in Rome included the collapse of the Temple of Peace, which fell into ruins after

the Virgin gave birth to the true Prince of Peace in fulfillment of the Sibylline oracle.

> The star is born on high and God on earth, whose possession is from sea to sea. The kings
> of Tarshish prepare themselves, so that with the newness of gifts, they may see the new
> mother, the new birth of a son. The fountain of oil (*fons olei*) gushed from the earth. The
> Temple of Rome, which was called eternal, collapsed, with everyone immoderate of both the
> city and the earth, miraculously destroyed. For when the Romans had decided to make a
> memorial temple with a singular design in victorious antiquity, they searched by all those
> things of the gods, no indeed by the multitude of daemons. How long could the painstaking
> construction, built with such excellent care, endure? The response is: Until the virgin gave
> birth. Turning back to the impossible oracle, the Romans called that eternal sacred temple a
> mere scheme. Moreover, during that night, when from the virginal bridal chamber the
> virginal flower of Mary emerged, then that walled and pillared work fell and was shattered,
> so that scarcely any vestige of the ruins was visible.[1337]

[1336] Not to be confused with Augustus' *Ara Pacis,* which the emperor dedicated in 9 BC. See Erika Simon, *Ara Pacis Augustae* (Greenwich, Conn: New York Graphic Society, 1968), 8.

[1337] "Nascitur stella in excelsis, et Deus in terris, cujus possessio a mari usque ad mare. Praeparant se reges Tharsis, ut cum novitate munerum videant novam matrem, filii novam nativitatem. Fons olei de terra erumpit. Templum Romae, quod vocabatur aeternum, corruit, omnibus impensis et Urbis et orbis mirabiliter consummatum. Cum enim Romani in victoriosae antiquitatis memoriam templum singulari schemate facere decrevissent, ab omni illa deorum, imo

The temple that shattered was evidently the temple of false belief. Peter Comestor, in his own sermon on the nativity, also retold the story of the Temple of Peace shattering at the time of the *fons olei* and Christ's birth. In Comestor's narrative, the cataclysmic destruction heralded the salvation of God's people from their sin.

> And from the east of Rome he gave a sign, not only that the fountain of oil erupted and flowed all the way to the Tiber, but also in that, because in the same night, in which a virgin gave birth, the Temple of Peace inwardly collapsed. Indeed the Romans, with a blossoming monarchy (*monarchia*) encircling the globe, built the Temple of Peace with great labor, with great expenses and much ambition because it was admirable in the eyes of onlookers. Moreover, consulting Apollo concerning the Temple's duration, the response to them was that it would last until a virgin gave birth. Rejoicing over this, they inscribed above the doors ETERNAL TEMPLE OF PEACE. Consequently that same night, in which the virgin gave birth, the temple miraculously and miserably collapsed as if it was openly said to the Romans: "The Saviour was born, the living and true God in whose presence the deaf and mute idols will fall down: 'For He himself saved his people from their sins.'"[1338]

Peter Comestor and the anonymous author (possibly Nicholas of Clairvaux) were evidently working from the same source, or Comestor was borrowing from Nicholas. Both mentioned the oil flowing all the way into the Tiber and interpreted the fall of the Temple of Peace as coinciding with Christ's birth, which fulfilled the Sibylline prophecy and displaced the pagan version of a Temple of Peace with a new temple: the Christ child.

---

daemoniorum multitudine quaesierunt, usquequo durare posset tam excelientis operis operosa constructio. Responsum est: Donec Virgo pareret. Illi ad impossibilitatem oraculum retorquentes, templum aeternum solemnem illam machinam vocaverunt. Nocte autem ista, cum de virginali thalamo virgineus flos Mariae egressus est, ita cecidit, et confractum est illud murale et columnatum opus, ut vix appareant vestigia ruinarum." PL 144, Col. 0848C-0849A.

[1338] "Occidentalibus etiam Romae signum dedit, non solum, quod fons olei erupit et fluxit usque in Tiberim; sed etiam in hoc, quod in eadem nocte, qua virgo peperit, templum Pacis penitus corruit. Romani enim, in monarchia orbis florentes, templum Pacis aedificaverunt multo labore, grandibus expensis et ambitione multa, quod erat admirabile in oculis intuentium. Consulentes autem Apollinem de ejus diuturnitate, responsum est eis, ipsum permansurum donec virgo pareret. Super hoc gavisi, titulum prae foribus inscripserunt: TEMPLUM PACIS AETERNUM. Eadem itaque nocte, qua virgo peperit, mirabiliter corruit, et miserabiliter, ac si aperte diceretur eis: Natus est Salvator, Deus vivus et verus, ante cujus faciem corruent idola surda et muta: *Ipse enim salvum faciet populum suum a peccatis eorum* (Matth. I)." PL 198, Col.1723A

By juxtaposing the destruction of the Roman temple with the perfect virginal birth of the

child, the anonymous author of the nativity sermon also commented, indirectly, on the destructive

nature of childbirth. The parallel of the temple's destruction would have been the destruction of the

virgin's body, had the author not been discussing miraculous paradoxes. As such, while the sacred,

well-constructed temple (akin to a human body) was ripped apart, the virgin's body gave birth as if

to a flower, in all gentleness and delicacy. But surely the author was not simply reflecting on the

violent nature of how a human being entered the world. The birth of Jesus in Bethlehem

represented the peace and joy that coexisted with violent destruction. While Rome and Jerusalem

were in ruins, Bethlehem was a new realm where peace reigned. As the *locus* of Christ's birth,

Bethlehem was also home to the most incomprehensible miracle: God in the form of a human child.

> O Bethlehem! City (*civitas*) of the Highest God! In you and in your suburbs today miracles
> are seen. God hanging from the breasts, is placed in the manger, is swaddled in the cradle,
> wrapped in cloth, and the little bandages having been loosened, the happy hands and holy
> little arms extend beyond the smallness of the cradle. He plays with the virgin, he smiles at
> the mother, and throws pleasing glances at Mary. The Queen of Heaven stands before such
> terrifying miracles, carrying in her heart the salutation of the archangel, the conception of
> God, the birth of the boy, and she wonders that He, who was able to come to us in such a
> way, that He wished to rescue us in such a way.[1339]

After a brief discourse on how Joseph, along with the shepherds and angels, likewise adored

the infant Jesus, the author of the sermon created a dichotomy between the chaos of Jerusalem and

the marvelous peace of Bethlehem. Since Orosius, Santa Maria in Trastevere's *fons olei* was associated

with the universal reign of peace. Using the present tense to describe the miracles that attended

Christ's birth, the author created the sense that the events of the distant past extended into his own

---

[1339] "O Bethleem! civitas Dei summi, et in te, et in suburbiis tuis visa sunt mirabilia hodie. Deus pendet ab uberibus, ponitur in praesepe, ligatur in cunis, pannis involvitur, et laxatis fasciolis, felices manus, et sancta brachiola per cunarum parvitatem expandit. Alludit virgini, matri arridet, et blandientes oculos ad Mariam intorquet. Stat perterrita tantis miraculis regina coelorum, confert in corde suo salutationem archangeli, conceptionem Dei, nativitatem pueri; et miratur quod ille, qui sic potuit ad nos venire, sic voluit subvenire." PL 144, Col. 0849A.

present. The author paradoxically juxtaposed oil bubbling up in Trastevere, as a sign of peace, with the chaos in Jerusalem.

> Herod is tormented, Jerusalem is thrown into confusion, the scribes are sought, the place foretold, the deceit introduced, the feigner leads to nothing, the inventions of trickeries are uncovered. The magi return by another way, peace unheard of through the ages reigns, the entire world is enrolled in the census, the stream of oil gushes from the earth, and the sanctified liquid bubbles in a fertile vein.[1340]

In this sermon, the author used language to describe the *fons olei* that was not present in other texts, suggesting that he was inventively reinterpreting the legendary oil and giving it new meaning within his twelfth-century context. Moreover, he used words that appeared, not in Jerome or Orosius, but in the lives and offices of myroblytes. While most authors used words such as *fluxit*, *emanat*, *exundavit*, *erupit*, or *defluxit*, this anonymous author, potentially Nicholas of Clairvaux, introduced a verb that appeared in no other account of the *fons olei*. The verb *persudare* – from *sudare* – to sweat or perspire – never before appeared with respect to the *fons olei* – but in the hymn for the feast of Nicholas of Myra, the potential author's namesake. The hymn, *Cujus tumba fert oleum matris*, described the saint's marble tomb perspiring oil: "The one whose tomb bears the oil of the mother olive, which does not know that marble by sweating brought forth what nature did not bring forth [i.e. oil]."[1341] Curiously enough, the hymn for Nicholas' feast day contains maternal imagery, which would have been applicable, of course, to the feast of Christ's nativity. Playing with paradox, the author of the sermon also used a word that appeared in a myroblyte *vita* to describe the manly strength of a bishop. In the sermon, the word "vein" (*venam*) described the river of oil, a word that

---

[1340] "Cruciatur Herodes, Hierosolyma turbatur, requiruntur Scribae, locus praedicitur; inducitur simulatio, simulator ad nihilum deducitur, deteguntur commenta fraudum. Magi per aliam viam revertuntur, pax inaudita a saeculo regnat, universus orbis ad censum describitur, rivus olei de terra persudat, et in divitem venam liquor sanctificatus ebullit." PL 144, Col. 0849B.

[1341] "Cujus tumba fert oleum matris olivae nescium quod natura non protulit sudando marmor parturit." Aachen (Aix-la-Chapelle), Domarchiv, MS G 20, fol. 203r. See Can 830118c. See Chapter 6 for further discussion of this hymn and its significance within Nicholas' liturgy.

also appeared in the *Life of St. Willibrord*, composed by Thiofrid (d. 1110), the Bishop of Echternacht: "There the ever-flowing fountain pours forth, a rich vein (*vena*) of prosperity / The living fountain, I say, the lively strength (*virtus*) of Willibrord."[1342] Questions of gender aside, in explaining the Incarnation, the author of the anonymous nativity sermon was not speaking about a minor event, but rather something that shook the entire known universe. He interpreted the fountain of oil as evidence of the extreme nature of change brought about by God's birth. The effects of the Incarnation, symbolized by the oil gushing everywhere, were limitless.

Working within the precedent set by Abelard and Honorius d'Autun, the author of the anonymous nativity sermon wove bridal imagery into his discussion of the *fons olei*. Alluding to Canticles 1:2, the author repeated that Mary's fountain of oil was a fountain of mercy, like the oil of the Bridegroom. The vision of the Bridegroom and his oil appeared as if in a dream – from which the author of the sermon tried to rouse his readers or listeners, to make them understand the magnitude of the feast being celebrated. More importantly perhaps, the author exhorted his audience (and tried to wake them from sleep) to recall the august words of his predecessor, Bernard of Clairvaux, whose works on the Canticles would have been familiar to monks in Clairvaux.

> Why is this if not because the true peace appeared on earth, if not because the citizens (*cives*) are enrolled in the heavenly kingdom (*regnum*), if not because the fountain of mercy (*fons misericordiae*) flows from the Virgin, 'your name is oil poured out'? The Holy Spirit, the singular and sole maker of that Scripture of yours, left behind the considerable sweetness of his oiliness (*pinguedinis*) in this chapter of the Scriptures.[1343]

[1342] "Manat ibi iugis fons, dives vena salutis / Fons inquam vivus Wilbrordi vivida virtus." AASS Nov.III, Dies 7, Col. 0494F.

[1343] The author tried to rouse his readers from the torpor of sleep by conveying the immensity of the Incarnation. "Quid est hoc, nisi quia vera pax in terris apparuit, nisi quia ad supernum regnum cives ascribuntur, nisi quia fons misericordiae de Virgine emanat, oleum effusum nomen tuum? (Cant.1:2) Spiritus sanctus Scripturae istius unus, et unicus fabricator, nonnullam suae pinguedinis dulcedinem sub hoc capitulo dereliquit. Sed vos nocturnis vigiliis ita defatigati estis, ut vix possitis somnum ab oculis removere. Evigilate tamen paulisper, et somni torporem excutite. Aderit ille, de cujus nativitate loquimur, ut illuminet oculos nostros, ne obdormiamus. Totus autem sententiae sensus ex illius arca mutuabitur, cujus consilium est quasi consilium Dei. Ipse ille est Dominus videlicet Claraevallensis, cujus religio et

Praising first the mellifluous, honey-tongued Abbot of Clairvaux and then the Holy Spirit,

the author delved into the ineffable nature of the Trinity, in which oil played a salient part: "That

kind Spirit, from whose secret fountain of songs a river escapes, in these three words he left us

seeking three things – evidently the name of the bridegroom, because he is like oil and how he is

poured out, because even the name is silent. Nothing speaks of the comparison, nothing tells of the

effusion."[1344] The author then spoke of the great effusion of God's love that was poured out on the

day of Christ's birth – giving a distinctly human quality to God's need to release his great quantity of

compassion for humankind. The discourse was replete with liquid imagery, including an allusion to

Psalm 132, in which oil ran down the beard of Aaron, the High Priest:

> Let us see which of these names was poured out, whether the name of power (*potentiae*) in
> the name of grace or the name of compassion in the vocabulary of majesty (*majestatis*). God
> forbid that mercy should be imprisoned in power (*potentia*), because "his mercies are over all
> his works." (Ps 144) Therefore he is trustworthy, because the power of God was poured out
> in great tenderness (*pietatem*) today, when the skies were dripping through the presence of
> God and the ancient one of days comes out from the virginal members. Is it not He who
> hides himself in that passion, because a more plentiful effusion of oil descended from the
> head to the beard, which even abundantly sprinkled the outer edge of the garment? So great
> is the abundance of compassion, that not only under the name of profusion (*effusionis*), but
> even emptying might be thought of. 'He emptied himself' the Apostle said 'in the form of a
> servant.' Today divinely 'accepting' and with all the greatness of his compassion he gushed
> (*prosiliit*) from the virginal bridal chamber. For he did not have a pleasant way to bring us
> back from an abyss [i.e. absence] of God's councils, because whatever of divinity was found

---

discretio, sapientia et eloquentia, vita et fama per totam Latinitatem non immerito decurrit; libenter enim illius sarcinas
adoro." PL 144, Col. 0849B-D.

[1344] "Benignus ille Spiritus, de cujus secretiori fonte canticorum flumen evadit, in his tribus verbis tria nobis requirenda
reliquit, videlicet nomen sponsi, quare oleo comparetur, et quomodo effundatur, quia et nomen tacet, de comparatione
nil loquitur, nihil dicit de effusione." PL 144, Col. 0849D.

in the treasure chamber of compassion, everything was accumulated in the womb of the virgin.[1345]

Following this meditation on the great outpouring of oil (or love), which was an instrument of salvation, the author made a direct allusion to antiphons sung primarily for the feast of the Assumption or the Commune of Virgins: "We run in the scent of your unguents, the young women loved you exceedingly" (*in odore unguentorum tuorum currimus adolescentulae dilexerunt te nimis*) and "Draw me after you in the scent of your unguents, your name is oil poured out." (*Trahe me post te in odorem curremus unguentorum tuorum oleum effusum nomen tuum*).[1346] The author then discussed the parable of the Good Samaritan, who used oil and wine to heal a man's wounds. Instead of addressing the sermon to the young women (*adulescentulae*) mentioned in the antiphon, Nicholas directed his discourse to his brother monks, drawing a distinction between mercy and justice:

> Therefore let us run, brothers, in the scent of those unguents. Let us run to the oil from the beautiful olive, pressed out in the plains, no infected watery olive fluid, none of the natures with bitterness, the oil that gladdens the face of men, that heals wounds, removes pains, restores sweetness. Is it not our Samaritan who brings to our wounds, inflicted by the worst robber, oil and wine for the cleansing and soothing the greatest wound? So much oil, little of wine, so much mercy, of justice little.[1347]

[1345] "Videamus quod horum nominum effundatur, utrum nomen potentiae in nomen gratiae, vel nomen pietatis in majestatis vocabulum. Absit, ut misericordia in potentia includatur, quia «miserationes ejus super omnia opera ejus (Psal. CXLIV)» Certum est ergo, quia potestas Dei in majorem hodie pietatem effusa est, cum coeli distillaverunt a facie Dei, et de virgineis membris vetustus dierum exoritur. Non est, qui se abscondat a calore isto; quia largior olei effusio a capite descendit in barbam, quae etiam extremam vestimenti fimbriam largius irroravit. Tanta est abundantia miserantis, ut non solum sub nomine effusionis, sed et exinanitionis censeatur: «Exinanivit semetipsum, «ait Apostolus,» formam servi» hodierna die «accipiens» (Philip. II), et cum tota multitudine miserationum suarum de thalamo prosiliit virginali; non enim habuit dulciorem modum ad redimendum nos abyssus illa consiliorum Dei, quia quidquid divinitatis in thesauro pietatis inventum est, totum in utero Virginis est aggestum." PL 144, Col. 0850B-C.

[1346] These antiphons were also sung at the feasts of Mary Magdalen, as well as a few other female saints and diverse Marian feasts. See Can 003261, Can 005170.

[1347] "Curramus ergo fratres, in odorem unguentorum istorum. Curramus ad oleum de oliva speciosa in campis expressum, nulla infectum amurca, nulla substantiarum amaritudine, oleum quod exhilarat faciem hominis (Psal. CIII), quod sanat vulnera, dolorem tollit, reddit suavitatem. Nonne Samaritanus noster nobis a latrone pessimo vulneratis attulit oleum et vinum ad purgandum, et mitigandam vulneris magnitudinem? Sed multum olei, parum vini; multum misericordiae, justitiae parum." PL 144, Col. 0851D-0852A.

Through his discussion of oil in the parable of the Good Samaritan, the author of the

nativity sermon wove together two disparate conceptual threads into a single piece of exegeis. By

combining the Songs of Songs with the Good Samaritan, the author showed the interconnectedness

of nuptial imagery and charity in medieval Christian thought. Oil, which represented love as well as

mercy, was not confined to voluptuous enchantment of the mystical bridal chamber. Oil also

expressed a selfless, self-sacrificing compassion for the strangers or the marginalized, pointing

towards the great commandment to love one another, a commandment that, in the minds and

memories of medieval Christians was inextricably bound up with oil and anointing. Those who

would be like Christ, the Bridegroom and head of the Church, would have to empty themselves in

humble servitude, let their oil flow like the bridegroom's oil (*oleum effusum nomen tuum*) or the oil

spreading outward across Aaron's robe.[1348]

SPONSA CHRISTI: THE WISE VIRGIN OF VIRGINS

Twelfth-century authors, including Bernard of Clairvaux, elaborated the symbolic depiction

of Mary as the Bride of Christ. During the twelfth-century reconstruction of Santa Maria in

Trastevere, when Innocent II commissioned the apse mosaic, a debate was emerging in the Latin

West regarding clerical celibacy and marriage as a sacrament. By examining the images in Santa

Maria in Trastevere, we can see how the interior of the church reflected the concerns of the

ecclesiastical authorities in the Latin West regarding both marriage and papal primacy. The apse

mosaic of the bride and groom looms above the high altar, where the priest consecrates the

---

[1348] John of Forda's (1140/50 – 1214) sermon on the Canticles also characterized the Bridegroom, not the Bride (i.e. Mary) as the *fons olei*: "Nempe et nomen sponsi sui oleum effusum sponsa non immerito ideo nuncupauit, quod percepta coelitus miseratio auaros refugiat sinus et concludi nescia uel cohiberi, uelut fons olei indeficiens erumpere gestiat et ebullire, uasorum tantum copiam capacitatem que requirens ut deriuari queat ex hoc in illud....uelut quidam fons olei primum ad proxima et deinde in ea, quae procul sunt, ubertim dilatari. Quod nobis precibus ac meritis sponsae suae uberrimus unctionis fons Christus Iesus donare..." LLT: Iohannes de Forda, *Super extremam partem Cantici canticorum sermones*, cxxCM 18, sermo : 74.

Eucharist. Placing the conjugal image above the altar emphasized the Eucharist as a symbol for the heavenly wedding banquet.[1349]

The texts associated with the dedication of medieval churches often alluded to the bride-like nature of the Church, to whom Christ unites himself in a quasi-conjugal union.[1350] A late eleventh or early twelfth-century collection of sermons of either Roman or Tuscan origin reveals how in the medieval Church, marital imagery was intertwined with altars, the Eucharist and the church building itself.[1351] In Vat.lat. 6451, which dates from 1076 – 1125, among the sermons listed for the dedication of a church (*Sermones in dedicatio aecclesiae*), several contain nuptial imagery, including references to the Lord's altar (*altare domini*) as the table of the wedding banquet (*convivium nuptiale*). The first sermon for the dedication of a church is Caesarius of Arles' Sermon 227, although the manuscript mistakenly attributes the text to Augustine.[1352] In this sermon, Caesarius cited the parable from the Gospel of Matthew, in which a man shows up at a wedding feast without a wedding garment and is subsequently thrown into the outer darkness.[1353] Caesarius explained that the wedding feast was the altar of the Lord, from which drunks, adulterers and those with hatred in their hearts were prevented from entering.[1354] The altar of the Lord was, in turn, a symbol for the Church and heaven itself. The "wedding garment," which permitted one to enter the heavenly realm, consisted of penance and almsgiving:

[1349] Phillip J. Long, "The Origin of the Eschatological Feast as a Wedding Banquet in the Synoptic Gospels: An Intertextual Study" (Andrews University, 2012).

[1350] The existing body of historiography on the rituals and theology of medieval church dedication is extensive. A starting point is Didier Méhu, ed., *Mises en scène et mémoires de la consécration de l'Église dans l'Occident médiéval* (Turnhout: Brepols, 2007).

[1351] Vatican City, Biblioteca Apostolica Vaticana, MS Vat.lat. 6451. The MS dates to 1076 – 1125 and contains sermons for the liturgical year from Easter to Advent.

[1352] Vat. lat. 6451, fols. 241r – 242r. This same text, with a few variations, is found in the Library of Latin Texts: Caesarius Arelatensis - Sermones Caesarii uel ex aliis fontibus hausti Cl. 1008, SL 104, sermo: 227, cap.: 1.

[1353] Matt 22:1-14.

[1354] "sic enim habet textus evangelicae lectionis, quod quidam fecerit nuptias filio suo, et intraverit simul recumbentes; ut videret et videns ibi hominem non habentem vestem nuptialem dixit ad eum: amice, quomodo huc intrasti non habens vestem nuptialem? et illo obmutescente dixit ministris: ligate illi manus et pedes, et proicite eum in tenebras exteriores: ibi erit fletus et stridor dentium. Ecce qualem sententiam merebitur audire, qui ad convivium nuptiale, id est, altare domini aut ebriosus aut adulter aut odium in corde retinens praesumit accedere." Vat. lat. 6451, fol. 241v.

May God turn us away from this, dearest brother, and grant that we may never wish to permit this evil, or if we are cast into this evil, that without any delay we may strive to heal through penance or peace and by great almsgiving may we hasten to be purified. Truly if by chance we come before the tribunal of the eternal judge with the wounds of sin, through excommunication may we be separated from the eternal Church and from the everlasting heavenly Jerusalem.[1355]

Caesarius then waxed eloquent about the sorrows befalling those who were excommunicated from the heavenly Jerusalem and its *mediatrix,* the Church. By approaching the table where a priest celebrated the Eucharist, a medieval Christian protected him or herself from exclusion from the heavenly table.[1356]

Another sermon for the dedication of a church discussed the parable about entering, or being excluded from, the wedding banquet. The sermon text, drawn from Isidore of Seville's *Etymologies,* cities the parable of the wise and foolish virgins.[1357] For the virgins, their sins did not determine the fate of their souls or their entrance to the heavenly banquet. The presence or absence of oil in their lamps, as they await the return of the Bridegroom, determined if they would enter the wedding banquet – if their souls would be saved. According to Isidore, the wedding feast – or the Eucharistic celebration within a church – was an instance when God descended from heaven, when

---

[1355] "Avertat hoc deus a nobis fratres karissimi .et concedat. ut mala ista aut numquam uelimus admittere.aut si ad missa fuerint.sine ulla mora per paenitentiam vel pacem studeamus sanare. et largioribus elemosinis festinemus abluere. ne forte, si cum peccatorum vulneribus ante tribunal aeterni iudicis venerimus, ab illa aeterna ecclesia et ab illa caelesti hierusalem perpetua excommunicatione separemur." Vat. lat. 6451, fol. 241v.

[1356] "...qui enim ab illa caelesti hierusalem excommunicatione meruerit, non solum hoc paene[1356] habebit, quod nec manducare nec bibere poterit, sed etiam flammas infernales sustinebit, ubi est fletus et stridor dentium, ubi ululatus lamentatio et paenitentia sine ullo remedio; ubi est vermis ille qui non moritur, et ignis quinunquam extinguitur; ubi mors quaeritur, et non invenitur. Quare in inferno mors quaeritur, et non invenitur? quia quibus in hoc saeculo vita offertur, et nolunt accipere, in inferno querent mortem, et non poterunt invenire: ubi erit nox sine die, amaritudo sine dulcedine, obscuritas sine lumine: ubi nec divitiae nec parentes nec coniuges nec filii nec vicini poterunt subvenire: ubi nichil peccator inveniet, nisi quod de hoc saeculo caste et iuste vivendo per helemosinarum[1356] largitatem transmiserit. Haec ergo cogitantes, fratres carissimi, tam casti et tam sobrii et tam pacifici ad istud altare deo auxiliante studeamus accedere, ut ab illo aeterno altari non mereamur excludi." Vat. lat. 6451, fol. 241v–242r.

[1357] For the text in LLT, see Isidorus Hispalensis - Etymologiarum siue Originum libri XX, Cl. 1186, lib.: 7, cap.: 2.

Christ and the Church became one flesh: *duo in carne una.*[1358] Isidore's sermon described the union of

Christ with the Church as being like the conjugal union of a wife and husband: "The Bridegroom,

descending from heaven, united to the Church, so that two might be one in flesh, in accordance

with the peace of the New Testament."[1359] This statement appears after a statement about the

forgiveness of sins.[1360]

Just as biographers of female myroblytes sometimes described the holy women as fonts of

oil, certain authors described Mary as being a *fons olei.* Without referring directly to Santa Maria in

Trastevere's *fons olei,* in a sermon for the feast of the Annunciation (Sermon 25), Peter Cellensis

(1115-1183) presented Mary as full of the Holy Spirit or full of grace, which he equated with oil.

Cellensis juxtaposed the *fons olei* with the *fons gratiae,* alluding to the parable of the wise and foolish

virgins, substituting the word *sapida* for *prudens* or *sapiens,* the words used by the Vulgate to describe

the virgins with oil in their lamps. Offering exegesis of every line Gabriel's annunciation speech to

Mary, Peter drew a parallel between Mary and the wise virgins or the lamps they carried: "Ave Maria,

full of grace. Therefore we exchange the empty vessels that are not small. Today we carry them to

the fountain (*fontem*) of oil, presupposing that if water from the fountain of water was so prudent,

how prudent will be the oil be from the fountain of grace?"[1361] By the twelfth century, the term *fons

gratiae* was a stable feature of the Holy Thursday liturgy, when bishops consecrated holy oils. The

Sermo generalis de confectione chrismatis spoke of the baptismal font as a *fons gratiae caeliestis,* since bishops

hallowed the font by smearing it with oil: "Truly the water of baptism is made holy through the oil

---

[1358] Vat. lat. 6451, fols. 241vA & fol. 248vB.

[1359] "Sponsus, quia descendens de caelo adhesit Ecclesiae, ut pace Noui Testamenti essent duo in carne una." Vat. lat. 6451, fol. 248v.

[1360] "Quod nomen et Filio et Spiritui sancto ascribitur, iuxta quod et Dominus in Euangelio ait: 'Rogabo Patrem, et alium paraclitum dabit uobis.' Intercessor autem ideo uocatur, quia pro culpa nostra remouenda curam gerit, et pro abluendis nostris criminibus curam impendit." Vat. lat. 6451, fol. 248v.

[1361] "Ave Maria, gratia plena. Mutuavimus ergo vasa vacua non pauca; et hodie deferimus ad fontem olei, praesumentes quod si tam sapida fuit aqua de fonte aquae; quale oleum erit de fonte gratiae?" LLT: Petrus Cellensis – Sermones, sermo: 25 (in annuntiatione dominica IV), col.: 715, linea: 8.

of chrism and the fountain of heavenly grace is produced."[1362] In Sermon 28, another Annunciation sermon, Peter made a reference to Mary pouring out unguent and being the Seat of Wisdom, a term which will be discussed in turn, since it was an image that would proliferate in the iconography of Santa Maria in Trastevere.[1363]

The theme of Mary as the seat of wisdom is further elaborated in the exterior mosaic, which depicts Mary as *maria lactans* – Mary nursing the child Jesus – surrounded by the wise and foolish virgins who appear in the parable of Matthew 25:1-13. Mary is shown as both *sedes sapientiae* and *maria lactans* – a seated Mary with the child on her knee, nursing at her breast. If Mary is the seat of wisdom, who would be the seat of folly? The exterior mosaic of Santa Maria in Trastevere presents a paradoxical juxtaposition of feminine images. The Virgin Mary sits in the middle of the wise and foolish virgins, bearing their oil lamps, which are lit or oil-less. The image of Mary is a *maria lactans* – Mary as the mother, offering her breast to the child Jesus who sits on her lap and as *sedes sapientiae* – the seat of the Jesus, the wisdom of God. The virgins represent the moment before the wedding feast, to which the wise with their oil will enter and from which the unwise, wanting oil, will be excluded. Mary with the baby, however, represents the natural consequence of the wedding and its subsequent conjugal union: new life in the form of a child. The virgins await the arrival of the bridegroom and yet, Mary sits nursing him on her lap. The mosaic as a whole thus represents both the anticipation and fulfillment of the wedding banquet. Christ, as the Bridegroom, is the still absent, long-awaited one and yet as the nursing child, is already the divine presence Incarnate.

[1362] Regarding the *fons gratiae*, see Chapter 3; Peter Damians' *Epistola XVIII. Ad Ubertum Presbyterum*, PL 144, Col.0369C-0372A; Cyrille Vogel, Reinhard Elze, and Michel Andrieu, *Le Pontifical romano-germanique du dixième siècle* (Città del Vaticano: Biblioteca apostolica vaticana, 1963).

[1363] "O Maria, ecce unguentum exinanitum omnia vasa tua implevit; ecce dolia tua plena sunt vino meracissimo; ecce scrinia tua referta sunt vestibus valde bonis; ecce in arca tua est panis vivus qui de coelo descendit; ecce lectulus tuus floridus; ecce domus tuae ligna cedrina, laquearia cypressina; columnae portantes quatuor parietes, prudentia, fortitudo, justitia, temperantia: ecce sedes Sapientiae parata, quae docet facienda et non facienda, intellectus legit et intelligit omnia in Scriptura divinitus inspirata." LLT: Peter Cellensis – Sermones, sermo: 28 (in annuntiatione dominica VII), col.: 722, linea: 51.

Given that the *fons olei* was located beneath the high altar, where the Incarnate God was celebrated in the Eucharist, how did oil fit into this symbolic schema? A chrism tabernacle by Mino Reale dating to 1400 gives us a clue: beneath a *ciborium,* an edifice-like structure that usually stands over the high altar of a church, a golden door bears the words *olea sancta* – holy oils. Instead of an altar for consecrating the Eucharist, there is only a door concealing the holy oils. Angels swoon as they hold up the golden portal, itself a symbol perhaps for the *janua* – the door leading to the heavenly banquet, as recorded in Matthew 25:10: "[The virgins] that were ready went in with [the Bridegroom] to the marriage and the door was shut." The passage to heaven, at least according to the image of the chrism tabernacle, involves oil – not bread and wine. Behind the door were kept the consecrated oils. Opening the golden door, one would have found oils in place of heavenly food kept in Eucharistic tabernacles.

THE ETERNAL WEDDING BANQUET

A defining characteristic of Santa Maria in Trastevere is the twelfth-century apse mosaic, which depicts the Virgin Mary as the *sponsa christi,* the Bride of Christ. Seated together on a *synthronon* [throne] Christ embraces Mary, his right arm encircling her, with his hand resting upon her right shoulder. According to Ernst Kitzinger and Jérôme Croisier, this image is peculiar to Santa Maria in Trastevere, presenting an innovation, not just within the context of Roman mosaics, but within all of European iconography.[1364] The apse mosaic of Santa Maria Maggiore, Santa Maria in Trastevere's long-standing rival, similarly depicts Mary and Jesus seated on a throne next to each other, although

---

[1364] Jérôme Croisier, "I Mosaici Dell'abside E Dell'arco Trionfale Di Santa Maria in Trastevere," in *La Pittura Medievale a Roma, 312-1431. Corpus. Vol. IV, Riforma E Tradizione, 1050-1198* (Milan: Jaca Book, 2006), 309; Kitzinger, "A Virgin's Face," 7. A no longer extant apse mosaic in the church of Santa Susanne apparently also placed the Virgin in a place of prominence within the apse, alongside Christ. See Cäcilia Davis-Weyer, "Die Mosaiken Leos III. und die Anfänge der Karolingischen Renaissance in Rom: Richard Krautheimer Zum Siebzigsten Geburtstag in Verehrung Gewidmet," *Zeitschrift Für Kunstgeschichte* 29, no. 2 (1966): 125.

the two face each other as Jesus crowns his mother.[1365] Since the apse mosaic of Santa Maria

Maggiore was constructed close to a century and a half after the mosaic in Santa Maria in Trastevere,

the earlier mosaic likely served as an influence upon the later, which in a sense elaborates on the

themes presented in Santa Maria in Trastevere. Other apse mosaics in Rome, such as the ninth-

century apse mosaic of Santa Maria in Domnica, present the Virgin alone as the central figure.[1366]

Since Santa Maria in Trastevere's apse mosaic represented Jesus, the Anointed One, and his mother

Mary in such an unusual fashion for the time, and since Santa Maria in Trastevere alone among

Marian churches claimed to be the source of miraculous oil, a discussion of the apse mosaic and its

relationship to the *fons olei* will help us further understand the significance of holy oil among

medieval Christians in Rome and within a larger discourse on papal authority in the High Middle

Ages.

The apse mosaic in Santa Maria in Trastevere was likely installed during the church's

reconstruction under Innocent II, between 1139/40 – 1148.[1367] Innocent II's reconstruction of the

church may have been motivated by a desire to supersede his former rival Anacletus II, who had

challenged his claim to the papacy by creating a schism. Innocent II chose to reconstruct a church in

which a *fons olei* was said to have flowed. In the first half of the twelfth century, Anacletus II

renovated another edifice dedicated to a producer of miraculous oil: the Oratory of St. Nicholas of

Myra in the Lateran Palace. Although the interior decoration of the oratory no longer exists,

seventeenth-century watercolors and an engraving preserve the image.[1368] The 1638 engraving by an

artist named Caetani shows Nicholas of Myra as a bishop with his crosier in one hand and a book

---

[1365] This rivalry played out, in part, through each church's claims to the *praesepio*, relics of the cradle in which the Christ child lay. The reconstruction of a *praesepium* (manger) was meant to imitate the manger in Bethlehem; Sant Maria in Trastevere's *praesepium* was meant to replicate S. Maria Maggiore's. See Kinney, "S. Maria in Trastevere from Its Founding to 1215," 110.

[1366] Kitzinger, "A Virgin's Face," 7.

[1367] Croisier, "I Mosaici dell'abside e dell'arco trionfale di Santa Maria in Trastevere," 308. See also Kinney, "S. Maria in Trastevere from Its Founding to 1215".

[1368] Jérôme Croisier, "La Perduta decorazione dell'oratorio di San Nicola al patriarchio lateranense," in *La Pittura Medievale a Roma, 312-1431. Corpus. Vol. IV, Riforma e Tradizione, 1050-1198* (Milan: Jaca Book, 2006), 290.

with three purses, from the legend of his *vita*, in which the bishop supposedly gave three purses

filled with gold to three young women without dowries. No aspect of the iconography alludes to

Nicholas' reputation as a myroblyte. By the early and mid twelfth century, however, when Anacletus

II undertook the renovations of the Oratory of St. Nicholas, the Bishop of Myra's reputation as a

myroblyte would have been well established.

MARY'S SCROLL

Why would a Marian church, with a reputation for a *fons olei*, present Christ as a husband,

embracing Mary, his spouse? Not only the mosaic image, but the epigraphy within the mosaic refers

to a conjugal union.[1369] In Santa Maria in Trastevere's apse mosaic, Mary holds a scroll, which

represents the Hebraic rather than the Christian Scriptures, which are represented by the book Jesus

holds. Mary's scroll bears a quote from Canticles 2:6; 8:3: "His left hand under my head, and his

right hand shall embrace me."[1370] (*Laeva eius sub capite meo et dextera illius amples abitur me*). Jesus' book,

in contrast, contains the phrase: "Come, my chosen one, and I will place my throne within you."[1371]

(*Veni electa mea et ponam in te thronum meum*). Kitzinger noted that the texts displayed by Jesus and

Mary, on their book and scroll respectively, were drawn from chants sung for the feast of the

Assumption (15 August).[1372] While this is certainly true, the chants were not peculiar to the

Assumption, but were sung on various feast days, including the feast of Mary Magdalene and other

female saints.

Laeva eius chant was frequently sung at feasts other than the Assumption, including Marian

feasts such as the Visitation (2 July), the Nativity of the Blessed Virgin (8 September), and, notably,

---

[1369] Stephano Riccioni refers to the epigraphy within a mosaic as 'epiconography.' Stefano Riccioni, *The Mosaic of S. Maria in Trastevere in Rome: The Visual Rhetoric of Triumphant Church* (forthcoming).

[1370] The epigraphic text reads: "Leva eius sub capite meo et dex[t]era illius amples abitur me." See Croisier, "I Mosaici dell'abside e dell'arco trionfale di Santa Maria in Trastevere"; Riccioni, *The Mosaic of S. Maria in Trastevere in Rome: The Visual Rhetoric of Triumphant Church*.

[1371] "Veni electa mea et ponam in te thronum meum."

[1372] Emile Mâle, *The Early Churches of Rome* (London: E. Benn, 1960); Kitzinger, "A Virgin's Face," 8.

for the feast of Mary of the Snows (Mariae ad Nives) (5 August), which was the feast of the dedication of Santa Maria Maggiore, Santa Maria in Trastevere's rival. The chant also appeared for the Common of Several Virgins (various dates), the feast of Mary Magdalene (22 July), and on the feasts of other women saints, including the virgins Agnes (21 January) and Agatha (5 February), as well as the married lay woman Elisabeth of Hungary (19 November), who incidentally was also one of medieval Europe's most popular myroblytes. Bernard of Clairvaux, who might have influenced Innocent II during the reconstruction of the basilica, quoted the *Laeva eius* chant in his commentary on the Song of Songs.[1373] The chant was an established feature of the Divine Office for the Cistercian order, of which Bernard of Clairvaux was a part.[1374] While the *Laeva eius* chant was a feature of the Assumption feast, it appears to have been relatively rare.[1375] Notably, however, one manuscript containing *Laeva eius* for the feast of the Assumption is an eleventh-century Roman manuscript (Bibliotheca Vallicelliana, C.5), suggesting that even if the chant were not widespread in the Latin West for the Assumption, Roman Christians would have been familiar with it.

What was the iconic significance of this chant within the apse mosaic? The words in Mary's scroll (*Laeva eius sub capite meo et dextera illius amplexabitur me*) refer to the gesture Jesus makes in the mosaic itself. This gesture of embrace, according to Ernst Kitzinger, was indicative of a married couple. In several twelfth-century miniatures for the opening verse of the Song of Songs (*Osculetur me osculo oris sui* – Let him kiss me with the kiss of his mouth), the capital letter "O" corresponding to the first word of the Canticles (*Osculetur*) shows a couple enthroned, with the *sponsus* embracing the *sponsa* as Jesus embraces Mary in Santa Maria in Trastevere's apse mosaic.[1376] The next line of text in the Song of Songs, which would have appeared on the same page as the image of the

---

[1373] See Kitzinger, "A Virgin's Face," 9; LLT: Bernardus Claraeuallensis, *Sermones super Cantica Canticorum*, Sermon 27.
[1374] Vitaliano Tiberia, *I mosaici del XII secolo e di Pietro Cavallini in Santa Maria in Trastevere: restauri e nuove ipotesi* (Todi, Perugia: Ediart, 1996).
[1375] Of the 130 manuscripts cataloged in the CANTUS database, eighty-three contain chants for the feast of the Assumption, and yet only four of these manuscripts contain the *Laeva eius* chant.
[1376] Kitzinger, "A Virgin's Face," 10.

embracing spouses or just after, contained an oft-quoted reference to oil and unguent: "...for thy

breasts are better than wine, smelling sweet of the best ointments. Thy name is as oil poured

out..."[1377] This line of text "thy name is as oil poured out" which appeared in tandem with the image

of the embrace of *sponsus* and *sponsa,* appeared in references to the *fons olei,* suggesting a conceptual

link in the minds of medieval Christians between oil, conjugal union and the birth of a child, as

evidenced in Nicholas of Clairvaux's sermon.

Jesus' Book

Since the memorization of biblical texts played such a central role in the devotional life of

literate Christians in the medieval period, viewers of Santa Maria in Trastevere's apse mosaic would

have likely recalled the verse following the one on Mary's scroll: "I adjure you, O daughters of

Jerusalem, that you stir not up, nor awake my love til she please."[1378] But Jesus, as the Bridegroom,

presented another verse as a counterpoint to the text in Mary's scroll. Jesus' epigraphical text is a

variation of Canticles 4:8, as it appeared in the Assumption liturgy as well as other feast days.[1379] The

Vulgate reads: "*Veni de Libano, sponsa mea: veni de Libano, veni, coronaberis...*" (Come from Libanus, my

spouse, come from Libanus, come: thou shalt be crowned...).[1380] The mosaic text, however,

reproduced the text as it appears in the chant on the feast of the Assumption as well as other feasts:

"*Veni electa mea et ponam in te thronum meum...*" (Come, my chosen one, and I will place my throne

within you...). The mosaic text is in fact only the first half of the chant that medieval Christians sang.

[1377] "Osculetur me osculo oris sui; quia meliora sunt ubera tua vino, fragrantia unguentis optimis. Oleum effusum nomen tuum." Cant. 1:1-2.

[1378] Jerome attributes this verse to the Bridegroom, but not everyone agrees, arguing that this could be the voice of the Bride, speaking to her fellow maidens, asking them to allow her to dwell in her reveries about her beloved for as long as possible. Translation from the Douay-Rheims. Vulgate: "Sponsus: Adjuro vos, filiae Jerusalem, ne suscitetis, neque evigilare faciatis dilectam, donec ipsa velit." Regarding the role of memory and memorized texts, see M. T Clanchy, *From Memory to Written Record, England, 1066-1307* (Cambridge: Harvard University Press, 1979); Beryl Smalley, *The Study of the Bible in the Middle Ages* (Notre Dame: University of Notre Dame Press, 1964).

[1379] Croisier, "I Mosaici dell'abside e dell'arco trionfale di Santa Maria in Trastevere," 306.

[1380] Cant. 4:8.

The full text alludes to the desire of the royal *sponsus*: "Come, my chosen one, and I will place my throne within you because the king greatly desired your beauty."[1381] (*Veni electa mea et ponam in te thronum meum quia concupivit rex speciem tuam*). This chant text is an amalgamation of phrases from the Hebrew Scriptures, including Canticles 4:8, Psalm 44:11-12, Psalm 88 and 3 Kings.[1382] The phrase extracted from Psalm 44, "because the king greatly desired your beauty (*speciem*)" – *quia concupiuit rex speciem tuam* – is a variation of "the king shall greatly desire your beauty (*decorem*)" – *concupiscet rex decorem tuum.* The full line in Psalm 44 reads: "Hearken, O daughter, and see, and incline thy ear: and forget thy people and thy father's house. And the king shall greatly desire thy beauty; for he is the Lord thy God, and him they shall adore."[1383] In Psalm 44, this verse appears just after one of the most frequently quoted phrases in biblical glosses relating to oil: "God, thy God, hath anointed you with the oil of gladness above thy fellows."[1384] Thus, while the epigraphy in the apse mosaic of Santa Maria in Trastevere does not refer directly to oil, it invokes a well-known psalm that described God's elect being anointed with the "oil of gladness" (*oleo laetitiae*) before his companions. Moreover, this phrase appeared in several texts on the *fons olei,* including Abelard's Sermon 4. Just as the king was the elect and anointed beloved of God, so was the bride whom the king (as symbol for God) desired or chose as his spouse. The king was, of course, a symbol for both God and the pope while the bride represented the Church.

CORONABERIS ELECTA MEA: THE CROWNING OF THE BRIDE

While the Vulgate text and the epigraphic text within the apse mosaic both refer, directly or indirectly, to the crowning of the Bride, curiously enough no such imagery appears in the Hebrew

---

[1381] "Veni electa mea et ponam in te thronum meum quia concupivit rex speciem tuam." Can 007826, Can 007828a.
[1382] "Veni electa mea et ponam in te thronum meum." See Canticles 4:8; Psalm 88:30; 3 Kings 1:24.
[1383] "Audi, filia, et vide, et inclina aurem tuam: et obliviscere populum tuum, et domum patris tui. Et concupiscet rex decorem tuum, quoniam ipse est Dominus Deus tuus, et adorabunt eum." Psalm 44:11-12.
[1384] Psalm 44:8. For a discussion of the prevalence of this line in biblical glosses, see Chapter 2.

text of the Canticles. No Hebrew verb in this verse corresponds to crown – *coronare*. In his translation of the Hebrew text, Jerome interpreted the verb *tashuri* – "to walk" or "to come" as meaning "to crown" although the word does not carry this meaning in Hebrew. Perhaps Jerome's translation of *tashuri* for Canticles 4:8 took into account the appearance of the same verb in Isaiah 57:9, in which a maiden, anointed with oils, approached or walked toward, a king: "you have adorned yourself with ointment for the king and have multiplied your pigments."[1385] The Hebrew verb *tashuri* only means to "approach" or "come towards" – which is consistent with the Hebrew text of Canticles 4:8: "Come from Libanus" – although there is no inherent meaning of "crowning" or "adorning" in the Hebrew.[1386] Nevertheless, the image of the crowning of the bride or young woman is central to the chant text shown in the mosaic as well as in the Vulgate text from which the chant derived. In Santa Maria in Trastevere's mosaic, Mary acquiring royal status – potentially nearly equal to that of her spouse – is represented by the fact that she sits on the throne beside Jesus and has become, in a certain sense, his wife or queen.

The chant *Veni electa mea*, which appeared in Jesus' book, appears to have been a far more widespread chant than *Laeva eius*, which appeared on Mary's scroll.[1387] Kitzinger noted that the text inscribed on Jesus' book was drawn not only from the Canticles, but also the liturgy for the feast of the Assumption. He did not take into account, however, the chant's appearance on other feasts, including the Common of Virgins as well as the feast days of other virgins and female saints, including Lucy, Felicity, Agnes and Cecilia, in addition to feasts for the Blessed Virgin, including the Nativity of the Virgin in addition to the Assumption. Moreover, the antiphon was also an antiphon

---

[1385] "ornasti te regi unguento, et multiplicasti pigmenta tua." Isaiah 57:9.

[1386] Thanks to Yair Zakovitch of the Hebrew University in Jerusalem for his help with identifying the corresponding verses in the Hebrew texts.

[1387] *Veni electa mea* appears 307 times as a Responsory Verse among the CANTUS manuscripts, indicating that this antiphon was considerably more popular than *Laeva eius*, which only appears 48 times among the same manuscripts. See Lacoste (Project Manager and Principal Researcher) and Koláček (Web Developer), "Cantus Database: Inventories of Chant Sources | CANTUS Database," Can 007826, Can 007828a.

for the feast of Mary Magdalene.[1388] Both Jesus' text in the apse mosaic, which is based on the liturgical chant and the original text of the Vulgate, allude to the royal status of the bride, but with significant variations. First, the Vulgate (Canticles 4:8) refers to the beloved as *sponsa* – "spouse," while the mosaic and chant refer to her as *electa mea* – "my chosen one." While according to the Vulgate, the bridegroom promises to crown the bride (*coronaberis*), the mosaic text follows the chant, which includes a promise to place the throne "within."

By quoting the text about the throne of Christ dwelling with Mary, Santa Maria in Trastevere's apse mosaic made an indirect reference to the Eucharist. Even though most Christians took communion only once a year, the Eucharist was a central aspect of medieval Christian devotion, particularly for women, as Caroline Walker Bynum demonstrated.[1389] By the mid twelfth century, the Eucharistic devotion had taken hold; the faithful venerated the host and wished to be present at the moment of consecration.[1390] The Fourth Lateran Council (1215) decreed that Christians take communion at least once a year. In the late thirteenth century, however, William Durand the Elder said that because of their sinfulness, ordinary Christians should take the Eucharist no more than three times a year while priests were entitled to take the Eucharist each day.[1391] According to Bynum, by the late Middle Ages, "deep ambivalence" permeated the Christian community regarding the frequency of communion; some theologians and canon lawyers favored frequent consumption of the Eucharist while others feared such practices would lead to irreverence, carelessness or profanation.[1392]

The Eucharist would nevertheless have been the most tangible way for Christ to dwell within an observant Christian, given the belief in the real presence of Christ within the host. The

---

[1388] See Can 005323, Can 005322.
[1389] Caroline Walker Bynum, *Holy Feast and Holy Fast: The Religious Significance of Food to Medieval Women* (Berkeley: University of California Press, 1987).
[1390] Ibid., 54–55.
[1391] Ibid., 57.
[1392] Ibid., 58.

Eucharistic wafer or host was, in a sense, a symbolic throne containing Christ – or the real presence of God. Through the consumption of the consecrated host, each faithful Christian could internalize the throne of God. Christians could thus become Christ's bride if, like Mary, God's throne dwelt within them. The epigraphic text of Santa Maria in Trastevere's apse mosaic referred to a multiplicity of means of assuming royal power. Instead of sitting on a royal throne or wearing a crown upon one's head, a Christian received the divine presence within his or her person. The king of kings could dwell within, on his metaphorical throne (the Eucharist), the body of Christ within the body of each Christian.

We can further understand the significance of the epigraphic text *Veni electa mea et ponam in te thronum meum* by considering that the Eucharistic celebration took place within the building of the church, which was also a metaphor for the human body or, more specifically, the body of a woman: the Virgin Mary. In Santa Maria in Trastevere, the apse mosaic depicting the conjugal union hung directly over the high altar, where priests consecrated the Eucharist. Within the Christian tradition, the Eucharistic celebration was seen as a wedding banquet.[1393] The wedding banquet was itself a metaphorical heavenly banquet – or the afterlife – when the soul of the just was united with God. Thus, consuming the Eucharist foreshadowed heavenly feasting while also bringing the Christian one step closer to the actual feast. Participating in the Eucharist enabled the soul to gain entrance to heaven, depicted as either a heavenly banquet or the heavenly Jerusalem. The church, as the place where the Eucharistic celebration took place, was the portal to the divine realm. The *ecclesia*, represented by the Blessed Virgin, contained the Eucharist and its divine presence within her, like a child in its mother's womb before birth. In this sense, the Virgin was like a tabernacle.[1394]

[1393] Long, "The Origin of the Eschatological Feast as a Wedding Banquet in the Synoptic Gospels."
[1394] Regarding Mary as a kind of Tabernacle, Margot Fassler observes: "Through the use of familiar Marian imagery and allusions to the Song of Songs...the Virgin becomes architectural symbol with many attributes. Mary, as type of the

The symbolic meaning of the throne dwelling within Mary, like the Eucharist dwelling within

the Christian, is perhaps both complicated and clarified by the fact that in the medieval period, Mary

herself was widely referred to as the *sedes sapientiae* – Seat of Wisdom or Throne of Wisdom.[1395] By

the mid and late twelfth century, the depiction of Mary as a *sedes sapientiae* had become a central

feature of Marian devotion, at least in Northern Europe. Small wooden statutes represented Mary as

a mother holding the child Jesus on her lap.[1396] Medieval iconography depicted Mary with the Christ

child on her lap, thus herself becoming the seat or throne for Christ, the Logos – or Divine Wisdom

Incarnate.[1397] Sometimes, the child Jesus was even depicted with a crown.[1398] The depiction of Mary

as the Throne of Wisdom proliferated in the Carolingian period when authors began to cast Mary as

"Queen of Heaven," imputing to the Virgin a royal character and authority.[1399] Statues depicting the

Virgin as the Throne of Wisdom are also known as *Maiestas*, since Mary appears in majesty – on a

royal throne or herself the royal throne. In these depictions Mary herself, not the Eucharistic host,

was the king's throne. In their analyses of Santa Maria in Trastevere's apse mosaic and the

significance of the presence of text *Veni electa mea et ponam in te thronum meum*, scholars have neglected

to take into account this perception of Mary as the Throne of Wisdom. Understanding the symbolic

dimensions of Mary as the *sedes sapientiae* is particularly relevant to understanding the conceptual link

---

church, is a 'throne without blemish,' whom Christ calls 'my resting place throughout all ages.' The resting place for all
the ages is also the Mercy Seat found within the Temple of Solomon, an architectural setting for the Holy of Holies.
Both testaments locate the Godhead there, within the sanctuary and in the midst of worship." Margot Elsbeth Fassler,
The Virgin of Chartres: Making History Through Liturgy and the Arts (New Haven: Yale University Press, 2010), 205.
[1395] On the difference between "seat" and "throne" see Ilene H. Forsyth, *The Throne of Wisdom: Wood Sculptures of the
Madonna in Romanesque France* (Princeton, N.J: Princeton University Press, 1972), 1.
[1396] Fassler, *The Virgin of Chartres*, 207. The devotion was prominent in Northern Europe, particularly Gaul.
[1397] For studies of Mary as the *sedes sapientia*, see Forsyth, *The Throne of Wisdom: Wood Sculptures of the Madonna in Romanesque
France*.
[1398] Fassler, *The Virgin of Chartres*, 208.
[1399] Forsyth states that Carolingians "ascribed to Mary the character of a sovereign, developing this subject as a favorite
theme in their literature, and that such an ascription involved a transfer to her of the regalia of imperial office including
the royal insignia, particularly the throne and orb, so that they referred to her as *regina nostri orbis* or Queen of Heaven,
indicates a frame of mind receptive to a more vivid representation of Mary enthroned than had theretofore been
provided by painting." Forsyth, *The Throne of Wisdom: Wood Sculptures of the Madonna in Romanesque France*, 6-7.

between the conjugal union depicted in the apse mosaic and the *fons olei*, which lay beneath the apse

and the high altar where the Eucharist was consecrated.

The term *sedes sapientiae* appears in the writings of both patristic and medieval authors. Some

of the earliest texts described the seat of wisdom as the "soul of the just" which was then interpreted

as the Church, though these texts make no direct reference to the Blessed Virgin Mary. The term

sedes sapientiae appears to be Augustine's commentaries on the psalms, where in several instances, the

Bishop of Hippo referred to the soul of the just as the *sedes sapientiae*.[1400] In his commentary on Psalm

34, Augustine alluded to the Wisdom of Solomon, which said the souls of the just were in the hands

of God: "Behold, David, the psalmist said the soul of the just is the spear of God. Again he says the

soul of the just to be the seat of God. The soul of the just is the seat of wisdom."[1401] Later authors

attributed the expression to Solomon, even though this expression did not appear in his writings, as

preserved in the Vulgate: "the soul of the just one is the seat of wisdom."[1402]

Ilene H. Forsyth traced the use of the epithet *sedes sapientiae* to Guilbert of Nogent's (d.1125)

exegesis of 1 Kings 10:18-20, in which he interpreted the Throne of Solomon to be a symbol for the

Church, which is in turn a symbol for Mary.[1403] Peter Damian's (d.1072) sermon for the Nativity of

the Virgin further elucidated the meaning of the chant and epigraphic text. In this sermon, Damian

refered to Mary as "the one...in whom God placed his throne." The words themselves are strikingly

similar to the texts of the Assumption chant and the apse epigraphy: "*Hodie nata est illa...in qua Deus

posuit thronum suum.*"[1404] Note the similarity with *ponam in te thronum meum*. As Ilene H. Forsyth noted,

Damian drew a parallel between the Virgin and Solomon's throne, interpreting the throne to be the

---

[1400] Augustine, Enarrationes in Psalmos 34, 46, 96, 98, 121, accessed on April 13, 2017,
http://www.augustinus.it/latino/esposizioni_salmi/index.htm

[1401] "ecce animam iusti dixit frameam dei; iterum dicit animam iusti esse sedem dei; anima iusti sedes sapientiae. ergo
quidquid uult, facit de anima nostra. cum in manu eius est, utatur ea quemadmodum uult." LLT: Augustine, *Enarrationes
in Psalmos*, Psalm 34. See Wisdom 3:1: "justorem autem animae in manu Dei sunt."

[1402] "Solomon ait: anima iusti sedes sapientiae."

[1403] Forsyth, *The Throne of Wisdom*, 24-25.

[1404] PL CXLIV, 736-740. See also Forsyth, *The Throne of Wisdom*, 25n62.

Virgin's womb: "She herself is that wondrous throne about which in the Book of Kings it is written in these words: 'King Solomon made a great throne of ivory and covered it with exceedingly brilliant gold.' Our Solomon, not only wise, but even the wisdom of the Father, not only peaceful, but even our peace, which makes both one, made the throne, evidently the womb of the undefiled Virgin, in which that majesty sat, who shakes the earth with a command...Blessed throne, in which the Lord Ruler sits, in which and through which not only everyone but everything is renewed!"[1405]

Sedes Caelestis: Mary as a Heavenly Throne

Augustine encouraged Christians to imagine that their own hearts could be the royal thrones of God. In his discourse on Psalm 46, Augustine introduced the idea that the seat of God was not only heaven, but also the heart of every Christian and the soul of every just person:

> 'God sits upon his holy throne.' What is his holy throne? Perhaps the heavens – one understands well. For Christ ascended, just as we knew, with the body in which he was crucified, and he sits at the right hand of the Father. Thenceforth we expect his coming to judge the living and the dead. He sits upon his holy throne. Are the heavens his holy throne? Are you also willing to be his throne? Do not think that you cannot be; prepare a place for him in your heart. He comes and sits willingly. Certainly he is himself the power of God and the wisdom of God and what does scripture say about wisdom herself? The soul of the just is the throne of wisdom. Therefore if the soul of the just is the throne of wisdom, let your soul be just and you will be a royal throne (*sella*) of wisdom.[1406]

[1405] PL CXLIV, Col.736C-737C. See also Forsyth, *The Throne of Wisdom*, 25.

[1406] "deus sedet super sedem sanctam suam. quae sedes eius sancta? forsitan caeli; et bene intellegitur. adscendit enim christus, sicut nouimus, cum corpore in quo crucifixus est, et sedet ad dexteram patris; inde eum uenturum exspectamus ad iudicandos uiuos et mortuos. sedet super sedem sanctam suam. caeli sunt sedes sancta eius? uis et tu esse sedes eius? noli putare te esse non posse; para ille locum in corde tuo; uenit, et libenter sedet. ipse certe est dei uirtus et dei sapientia. et quid dicit scriptura de ipsa sapientia? anima iusti, sedes sapientiae. si ergo anima iusti sedes est sapientiae, sit anima tua iusta, et eris regalis sella sapientiae." Augustine, *Enarrationes in Psalmos*, Psalm 46.

Augustine continued this basic theme, with variations, in his commentaries on Psalms 96, 98, and 121.[1407] Nowhere did Augustine suggest, however, that the soul of the just, as the *sedes sapientiae,* was a symbol for the Church or the Virgin Mary. Nor did Cassiodorus, who like Augustine, interpreted the soul of the just to be the seat of wisdom. Cassiodorus contributed to the discourse by introducing the idea of *maiestatis,* in his gloss on Psalm 88:37: "...the throne of God must be understood here to be the soul of the faithful, in which he will actually sit, when he will have filled the soul with the glory of his majesty (*maiestatis*)."[1408] The first characterization of the *sedes sapientiae* as *ecclesia* appears to derive from Caesarius of Arles' *Expositio in Apocalypsim:* "But at any time, you must understand the holy soul to be the throne, just as it was written: the soul of the just is the seat of wisdom; at anytime you must understand the throne to be the church, in which God has a seat."[1409] This would explain the significance of Jesus' book bearing the inscription *Veni electa mea et ponam in te thronum meum* in Santa Maria in Trastevere's apse mosaic. One of Caesarius of Arles contemporaries, Fulgentius of Ruspe (467-533), the bishop of Ruspe in what is now Tunisia, likewise discussed the

[1407] Augustine, *Enarrationes in Psalmos,* Psalm 96: "sedem eius dicit eos ipsos qui in eum crediderunt; de ipsis enim sibi fecit sedem, quia in eis sedet sapientia; filius enim dei, sapientia dei est. audiuimus autem ex alia scriptura magnum huius intellegentiae documentum. anima iusti, sedes sapientiae. ergo quia isti facti sunt iusti, qui in eum crediderunt; iustificati ex fide, facti sunt sedes ipsius: sedet in ipsis, iudicans ex ipsis, et dirigens eos."; Psalm 98: "qui sedet super cherubim regnauit; commoueatur terra. cherubim sedes dei est, sicut scripturae tradunt, caelestis quaedam sedes sublimis, quam nos non uidemus; sed uerbum dei nouit illam, nouit tamquam sedem suam, et ipsum uerbum dei et spiritus dei dixit seruis dei ubi sedeat deus. non quia sic sedet deus, quomodo homo: sed tu si uis ut sedeat in te deus, si bonus eris, sedes dei eris; sic enim scriptum est: sedes sapientiae, anima iusti. thronus enim, latine sedes dicitur. nam et ipsum cherubim interpretati sunt quidam quid diceretur latine, qui nouerunt linguam illam hebraeam; quia hebraea lingua dictum est cherubim; et dixerunt esse cherubim plenitudinem scientiae. ergo quia superat deus omnem scientiam, super plenitudinem scientiae sedere dicitur. sit in te ergo plenitudo scientiae, et eris et tu sedes dei. sed forte dicturus es: et quando in me erit plenitudo scientiae?"; Psalm 121: "si ergo caelum sedes dei, apostoli autem caelum; et ipsi facti sedes dei, ipsi sunt thronus dei. dictum est alio loco: anima iusti, thronus sapientiae. magna res, magna res dicta est: thronus sapientiae anima iusti; id est, in anima iusti sedet sapientia tamquam in sella sua, tamquam in throno suo, et inde iudicat quidquid iudicat. ergo erant throni sapientiae, et ideo dixit illis dominus: sedebitis super duodecim thronos, iudicantes duodecim tribus israel. sic et ipsi sedebunt super duodecim sedes, et ipsi sunt sedes dei; de illis quippe dictum est: ibi enim sederunt sedes. quoniam ibi sederunt sedes. qui sederunt? sedes. et qui sunt sedes? de quibus dictum est: anima iusti, sedes sapientiae."
[1408] "Thronus autem dei hic intellegendus est anima fidelis, in qua reuera insidet, quando eam maiestatis suae illuminatione compleuerit; sic enim scriptum est: sedes sapientiae anima iusti." LLT: Cassiordorus, *Expositio psalmorum,* Psalm 88.
[1409] "Sed aliquando et animam sanctam intellege thronum, sicut scriptum est: ANIMA IUSTI SEDES SAPIENTIAE; aliquando ecclesiam, in qua sedem habet deus. ET IN MEDIO THRONI QUATTOR ANIMALIA, id est, in medio ecclesiae evangelia." LLT: Caesarius of Arles, *Expositio in Apocalypsim,* Pars 3.

sedes sapientiae as the soul of the just, where Christ dwells.[1410] Another sixth-century African bishop,

Primasius of Hadrumentum (d. post 552) also discussed the *sedes sapientiae* as the soul of the just in

his *Commentarius in Apocalypsin,* in which he told readers that God dwelt within those who dwelt on

his throne:

> The Church is the thrones of God…for which he places ascensions in the heart, in the valley
> of prayers, in the place in which he places them, serving him day and night, that is, in
> prosperity and in adversity. They themselves are to be understood as a temple, which are
> remembered to serve in the temple just like the throne…the one who sits in the throne, he
> will inhabit them. For the soul of the just is the seat of wisdom, wisdom and moreover
> Christ, Christ truly God.[1411]

These late antique authors indicate that prior to the High Middle Ages there was an

established tradition of seeing the Church as the seat of wisdom or the soul of the just in heaven. A

seventh-century glossed psalter made an explicit parallel between the seat of wisdom, the soul of the

just and heaven itself as being where God resides: "You sit on the throne. 'Throne' is Greek, in

Latin it is called 'seat' because every holy person is a seat of God, such that God himself says:

'Heaven is a seat for me' and elsewhere 'the soul of the just is the seat of wisdom.'"[1412] Later, in his

exposition of Psalm 44:7, the author of the same glossed psalter explicitly interpreted the Seat of

Wisdom to be the Church: "Your seat, O God, is forever and ever: the seat of God is the Holy

---

[1410] "Verbum utique caro factum est in eo quod est una in christo dei hominis que persona: habitauit autem in nobis, quia in christo uera tota que permanet diuina humana que substantia. Verbum enim habitans in homine, non est mutatum in hominem. Vbi autem maxime uerbum potuit habitare, quam in illa substantia quam ad suam imaginem fecit, hoc est, in anima illius hominis quem suscepit? quod prophetice per salomonem spiritali gratia cernimus intimatum, cum dicitur: anima iusti sedes sapientiae. Ecce et animam nominat et cor appellat, ubi christum habitare confirmat." LLT: Fulgentius of Ruspe, *Ad Trasamundum* Book III.

[1411] "Propter hoc sunt in conspectu throni dei et deseruiunt ei die ac nocte in templo eius. In conspectu throni dei ecclesia est, cui ascensiones in corde disposuit in conualle plorationis, in locum quem disposuit, seruiens ei die ac nocte, hoc est et in prosperis et in aduersis. Ipsi autem intelleguntur templum, qui seruire memorantur in templo sicut et thronum. Denique sequitur: Et is qui sedet in throno inhabitabit in eis. Anima enim iusti sedes sapientiae, sapientia autem Christus, Christus uero deus." LLT: Primasius Hadrumentinus, *Commentarius in Apocalypsin,* lib.2, cap.7.

[1412] "SEDES SUPER THRONUM. 'Thronum' Graecum est, Latine sedes dicitur, quia unusquisque sanctus sedes dei est, ut ipse ait: Caelum mihi sedes est; et alibi: Anima iusti sedes sapientiae." LLT: Anonymi Glosa Psalmorum ex traditione seniorum, Psalm 9.

Church, because the soul of the just is the seat of wisdom."[1413] The same author also referred to the church as the *sedes sapientiae* in his gloss of Psalm 88: " 'Your seat' that is your Holy Church, where God sat, such that: the soul of the just is the seat of wisdom."[1414]

Ernst Kitzinger noted the danger of inverting the "in" and "te" in order to read the text to suggest that Jesus' text was intended to mean he would place Mary on his throne (*ponam te in thronum meum*), as the mosaic suggests pictorially.[1415] Kitzinger observed that a reference found in Bernard of Clairvaux partially explains what *ponam in te thronum meum* could have meant: Mary, as the bride, was a symbol for heaven – the "holy city, new Jerusalem" according to the Book of Revelation (Rev. 21:2).[1416] We can corroborate Bernard's interpretation by examining Psalm 88, which likewise speaks of God's throne – and seed – being placed in heaven or enduring forever. The chant text for the feast of the Assumption – *ponam in te thronum meum* – appears nearly verbatim in Psalm 88:30, which speaks of David's lineage enduring forever, as the anointed king of Israel. Psalm 88:21 states: "I have found David my servant; with my holy oil I have anointed him." The subsequent nine verses attest to the fidelity of God and the steadfast nature of his covenant with David. In Psalm 88:30, among the promises God makes to his elect, we find the line: "And I will make his seed to endure for evermore and his throne as in the days of heaven" – *Et ponam in saeculum saeculi semen eius et thronum eius sicut dies caeli.*[1417] The forgers of the liturgical chant for the Assumption thus appear to have engaged in a poetic rearrangement of words and ideas, playing on their audience's knowledge of this psalm. Instead of *ponam in saeculum saeculi* (I will place his seed in the age of ages) the chant became: *ponam in te* – substituting the literal expression "in the age of ages" (i.e. forever) with "you" – meaning Mary or medieval Christians who heard or sang the chant and internalized eternity or divine

---

[1413] "SEDES TUA DEUS IN SAECULUM SAECULI: sedes dei sancta ecclesia est, quia anima iusti sedes sapientiae." LLT: Anonymi Glosa Psalmorum ex traditione seniorum, Psalm 44.

[1414] 'Sedem tuam' hoc est ecclesiam tuam sanctam, ubi deus sedit, ut illud: Anima iusti sedes sapientiae." LLT: Anonymi Glosa Psalmorum ex traditione seniorum, Psalm 88.

[1415] Kitzinger, "A Virgin's Face," 11.

[1416] Ibid. See Bernard of Clairvaux, Sermon 27.9.

[1417] Ps 88:30.

presence within them. This rearrangement suggested, as Bernard of Clairvaux noted, that the one

(i.e. Mary) in whom the seed was placed, was – or was like – eternity. Surely the presence of this

divine seed also engendered a divine quality in a human being, thus having a divinizing effect.

The idea of the eternality of the recipient of God's seed, which for medieval Christians could

be interpreted as God's Word – the Logos – or Christ himself – is repeated in the second part of the

Psalm 88 verse with a slight variation: instead of the seed *(semen eius)*, the psalmist speaks of the

throne being placed "as in the days of heaven" – i.e. in eternity or the heavenly Jerusalem: "*Et ponam

in saeculum saeculi semen eius et thronum eius sicut dies caeli.*"[1418] The original psalm verse thus juxtaposed

two parallel or synonymous images: the seed being planted in eternity and the throne being placed in

the heavenly realm. Within the context of Christian devotion, the metaphors become unstable. As

multivalent symbols, the seed, throne, Eucharist, Word or Logos are placed within the soul, body,

heaven, Mary or every pious medieval Christian hearing or singing or beholding this text. But what

does all this have to do with oil?

The Eucharist was one means by which God placed his throne with medieval Christians or

within the medieval Christian community, as the Church. The other means was through anointing –

bestowing on individuals not jus the Holy Spirit, but the name of *Christian,* "the anointed." The

epigraphic text in Jesus' book in the apse mosaic of Santa Maria in Trastevere presented only the

first half of the liturgical chant *Veni electa mea.* The second half, which would have been implied but

not explicitly stated, would have been left to the viewer to remember. Recalling the second half of

the text – *quia concupivit rex speciem tuam* – would have brought Psalm 44 to mind with its attendant oil

imagery: "therefore God, your God has anointed you with the oil of gladness above your

companions" and "myrrh and stacte and cassia perfume thy garments."[1419] Early Patristic authors

conceived of oil as symbol for the Holy Spirit and oil became the means by which God put his spirit

---

[1418] Ps 88:30.
[1419] Ps 44:8-9.

within the human being. Thus, the Christian, in receiving God's spirit, was divinized – or rather

divinity – divine presence – *praesentia divina* – or heaven itself, dwelt within human beings while they

live on earth. Their interior beings belonged to heaven. God placed his throne (i.e. heaven) within

them through anointing. Thus perhaps we can read the apse mosaic and its inscriptions, as a kind of

elaboration on what it meant to be anointed with holy oil.

The idea that God placed his throne in the heavenly realm also appears in the writings of

several Patristic authors, including Tertullian (c.150/170-c.230), Cyprian of Carthage (r. 248/9-258),

Ambrose of Milan (c.340-397), Origen (c.185-254) and Augustine (354-430), all of whose writings

were widely reproduced and disseminated in the medieval Latin West. Several of these texts refer to

how God, speaking through a prophet said he would place his throne in the sky among the clouds,

above the clouds or above the stars. In *Against Marcion,* Tertullian wrote: "I will place my throne in

the clouds" – *ponam in nubibus thronum meum.*[1420]

The Latin expression *ponam in thronum meum* appears in Jerome's Latin Vulgate in 3 Kings,

within the context of a discussion of who will inherit David's throne. Nathan, the prophet,

approached Bathsheba, drawing her attention to the fact that the rightful heir of David's throne was

Solomon, not Adonias, who was in fact ruling in his stead. Nathan urged Bathsheba to approach

David and request that her own son be placed "upon his throne." Jerome's translation of the

Hebrew text alternates between two words for "throne" – *solium* and *thronus. Solium* appears

numerous times, while *thronum* only appeared once. Nevertheless, the verbal construction in this one

appearance was close to the phrase as it appeared in Psalm 88, the Assumption chant, and the

epigraphic text in Santa Maria's apse mosaic. Instead of the verb *ponere (ponam)*, 3 Kings uses *sedere*

(sedeat) – to sit. Nathan posed a rhetorical question to David, asking him if he said that Adonias

should sit on his throne: "Nathan said: My lord O king, hast thou said: Let Adonias reign after me,

---

[1420] LLT: Tertullianus – *Adversus Marcionem* (CPL 0014) lib.:5, pag. CSEL: 613, linea: 18; CSEL: 634, linea 27.

and let him sit upon my throne?"[1421] When David agreed that Solomon and not Adonias should be

king, the author of 3 Kings recounted how David ordered that Solomon to be placed on a mule

(*mulam*), not a throne, and to be anointed with oil.[1422] Sitting on a mule fulfilled the prophecy of

Zephaniah, which held that the ideal future king of Jerusalem would ride a donkey or mule.

Moreover, the ancient Hebrews associated horses with war; Deuternomy warned the Hebrews not

to own too many horses.[1423] The same verb (*imponere*) which appears in Psalm 88 and the

Assumption chant appears in this chapter of the 3 Kings: "...set my son Solomon upon my mule:

and bring him to Gihon. And let Sadoc the priest, and Nathan the prophet anoint him there king

over Israel..."[1424] Thus in the Latin Vulgate, the expression *thronum tuum* would have evoked the idea

of the transfer of power between kings, between father and son – and the idea that the successor

was to be mightier than the predecessor.[1425]

CONCLUSION

If God's throne was in heaven, and heaven was the destination of human souls at the end of

time, medieval authors would naturally discuss the significance of the *sedes sapientiae* in commentaries

on the Book of Revelation – or apocalyptic literature.[1426] In the High Middle Ages, authors

continued to explore the connection between the throne of wisdom and the Virgin, and by

extension the Church, as the *sedes sapientiae*. The Assumption and the Book of Revelation

corresponded theologically since both represented the ascent from the earthly to the heavenly realm.

[1421] "Dixit Nathan: Domine mi rex, tu dixisti: Adonias regnet post me, et ipse sedeat super thronum meum?" 3 Kings 1:24.

[1422] The mule signified the humility of the king.

[1423] Deut. 17:14-20. Thanks to Yair Zakovitch for this explanation of the donkey's significance in the Hebraic tradition.

[1424] "...imponite Salomonem filium meum super mulam meam: et ducite eum in Gihon. Et ungat eum ibi Sadoc sacerdos, et Nathan propheta, in regem super Israel..." 3 Kings 1:33.

[1425] The Hebrew for *imponare* would have meant "cause Solomon my son to ride upon my own mule." See Biblehub, accessed on October 2, 2016, http://biblehub.com/interlinear/1_kings/1-33.htm.

[1426] Several early medieval commentaries on the Book of Revelation reference the *sedes sapientiae*, including Caesarius of Arles (469/70-542), Julian of Tolentino (Toletanus) (c.652-690), and Ambrosius Autpertus (c.652-690).

The predominant interpretation of the *fons olei* legend in the Carolingian period conveyed how the oil was a sign of enduring rulership: Augustus and the Christ. In the High Middle Ages, authors were no longer so concerned with explaining how or why a pagan emperor had established a reign of peace or the extent to which that emperor was paving the way for the true Prince of Peace. As Marian devotion became increasingly popular in the twelfth century, authors such as Abelard, Honorius and Nicholas of Clairvaux interpreted the *fons olei* as reflecting Mary, the Church, as the source of oil, the Christ. Instead of the *fons olei* representing the eternal reign of an emperor, the *fons olei* heralded the eternal rule of Christ or his representative – the pope. God's throne – his eternal seat – was within the Church: Mary, his royal *sedes*.

INTRODUCTION

By the early thirteenth century, when Innocent III consecrated Santa Maria in Trastevere,

the legend of the *fons olei* no longer declared that oil heralded the triumphant reign of Augustus, the

pagan Roman Emperor. Rather, the oil flowed from a church dedicated to Mary, who symbolized

the Church, the *sedes sapientiae*. In her, the pope enjoyed everlasting power. During the Fourth

Lateran Council, which was arguably the most important ecclesiastical council of the medieval

period, Pope Innocent III made a visible gesture that revealed his vision of the expansive nature of

papal power, Roman primacy, and oil's potency. On November 15, 1215, fifteen days after the

convocation of the council, which was the largest in the history of the Church, the Bishop of Rome

led a procession to Santa Maria in Trastevere, where he, as Vicar of Christ, consecrated the *domus

dei*.[1427] Innocent III was no stranger to liturgical pageantry or to the holy appeal of oil.[1428] A few days

prior, at a Mass in the Lateran Basilica, Innocent III had stated his reason for convening the council:

"Not for the sake of earthly convenience or temporal glory, but for the sake of the reform of the

universal church and the complete liberation of the Holy Land – it is for these two causes that I

have principally and especially convoked this holy council."[1429] By entering the church of Santa

Maria in Trastevere, the source of the *fons olei,* Innocent III put himself, physically and symbolically,

in proximity to the sacred font of oil that by the High Middle Ages represented Christ himself. The

oil permeated biblical texts with nuptial imagery and the texts for medieval church dedications.

[1427] For an account of this event, see Stephan Kuttner and Antonio García y García, "A New Eyewitness Account of the Fourth Lateran Council," *Traditio* 20 (January 1, 1964): 115–78.

[1428] See Brenda Bolton, *Innocent III: Studies on Papal Authority and Pastoral Care* (Aldershot; Brookfield: Variorum, 1995).

[1429] John C Moore, *Pope Innocent III (1160/61-1216) to Root up and to Plant* (Leiden; Boston: Brill, 2003), 231. See also Kuttner and García, "A New Eyewitness Account of the Fourth Lateran Council," 124, 132.

Moreover, ecclesiastical officials bestowed legitimate authority on rulers through anointings and gave

Christians their identity as 'Christian' through post-baptismal anointings. Santa Maria in Trastevere

was itself a source of this sanctifying oil, which played a salient role in defining both Christians and

the Christian community. At the start of the thirteenth century, Santa Maria in Trastevere's *fons olei*

could represent the Church universal, which was a source of the anointing – physical and spiritual –

that defined Christian identity and membership within medieval Christian society.

In the late 1140s or early 1150s, just after the reconstruction of Santa Maria in Trastevere by

Innocent II, Bernard of Clairvaux first used the term *vicarius Christi* to refer to Pope Eugenius III (r.

1145-1153). Prior to Bernard's appropriation of the term for the Roman pontiff, Byzantine

emperors and the Holy Roman Emperor Henry III (1017-1056) had referred to themselves as vicars

of Christ.[1430] In the Latin West, the term appeared only semi-privately within papal circles until

Innocent III publically identified himself as Christ's vicar.[1431] The pope himself anointed the Church

which possessed the miraculous source of oil, *prae consortibus suis,* during the council at which he

would, among other things, establish canons regarding the number of sacraments, marriage as a

sacrament, the persecution of heretics and the papacy's intent to recapture the Holy Land.

Scholars have presented various arguments regarding why Innocent III chose to process to

and consecrate Santa Maria in Trastevere. Dale Kinney first argued that Innocent III's choice to re-

consecrate Santa Maria in Trastevere stemmed from his legal inclination for a written record of a

consecration and his willingness to assent to a request from Johannes Crassus (dates unknown), a

canon of Santa Maria in Trastevere, as well as a descendent of Innocent II, Guido of Praeneste in

Palestrina, who was both bishop of Palestrina and the titular cardinal of Santa Maria in

Trastevere.[1432] Kinney further argued that a factor in play was likely Innocent III's desire to impress

---

[1430] Jane E Sayers, *Innocent III : Leader of Europe, 1198-1216* (London; New York: Longman, 1994), 16.
[1431] Ibid.
[1432] Kinney, "S. Maria in Trastevere from Its Founding to 1215," 339–41.

his *confreres*, given that the ceremonial consecration or re-consecration took place within the context

of the largest gathering of prelates in the medieval period.[1433] The size of the gathering was

unprecedented for the time.[1434] Brenda Bolton interpreted the consecration during the Fourth

Lateran Council as revelatory of Innocent III's tendency to capitalize on Roman "legend, folklore

and the continuity of popular devotion" to bolster the primacy of Rome and the successor of St.

Peter.[1435] Innocent III was evidently familiar with the legend that associated the appearance of the

fons olei with the advent of the reign of Augustus and the imminent birth of Christ, as retold by

Orosius.[1436] Innocent III viewed Rome as the *caput mundi,* the divinely chosen see of the Church in

the Latin West; like his namesakes (Innocent I & Innocent II), Innocent III sought to establish

Roman primacy within the Latin Church and to assert the Church's dominance over secular

kingdoms.[1437] Since Innocent II had commissioned the reconstruction of Santa Maria in Trastevere

following the papal schism with Anacletus II, but had not seen the project through to the

consecration on account of his death, Innocent III continued the work begun by his predecessor,

consecrating the church during the Fourth Lateran Council.[1438] Dale Kinney also argued that

Innocent III sought to establish Roman primacy by emphasizing the spiritual axis between Rome

and the Holy Land, particularly Bethlehem.[1439]

[1433] "For him, the consecration of S. Maria in Trastevere was legally proper, historically apt, and a spectacular way to impress the delegates to the Fourth Lateran Council." Ibid., 343.

[1434] Brenda Bolton claimed there were 1,200 "archbishops, metropolitans, bishops and abbots attending the Council." Bolton, *Innocent III : Studies on Papal Authority and Pastoral Care*, XVII:129. John C. Moore, however, quoted a different figure: "It was surely the most peaceful invasion that Christian Rome had ever seen. In addition to the multitude of representatives of the cathedral chapters and monasteries, there were over four hundred bishops, archbishops, patriarchs, and cardinals, representing over eighty ecclesiastical provinces. The kings of France, Hungary, Jerusalem, Cyprus, and Aragon sent representatives, as did Frederick, the emperor elect of the west, and Henry, the emperor of Constantinople. Other princes came in person, especially those concerned with the disposition of lands conquered by the Albigensian crusade." Moore, *Pope Innocent III (1160/61-1216) to Root up and to Plant*, 229–30.

[1435] Bolton, *Innocent III : Studies on Papal Authority and Pastoral Care*, 8–13.

[1436] See Kinney, "S. Maria in Trastevere from Its Founding to 1215," 344–46.

[1437] Bolton, *Innocent III : Studies on Papal Authority and Pastoral Care*, I:5.

[1438] Ibid., 10–13.

[1439] Kinney, "S. Maria in Trastevere from Its Founding to 1215," 345–46.

Scholars have overlooked two additional related factors that arguably influenced Innocent III's decision to consecrate Santa Maria in Trastevere at the opening of the Fourth Lateran Council: his wishes to combat the Cathar heresy and to bring marriage more firmly within the purview of the Church. The Cathars' dualistic theology entailed an abnegation of the human body as well the institutional Church, the "body of Christ."[1440] Their resistance to the Church did not originate in the early thirteenth century. During the 1120s, the dualist heretics denied the necessity of the Church and its priests as necessary to salvation.[1441] They proclaimed that sex and marriage were inherent evils that prevented Christians from attaining spiritual purity; the carnality of marriage, in their view, precluded its sacralization.[1442] Given the Cathars' rejection of the carnal body, marriage, offspring and the institution that presided over these aspects of Christian existence, Innocent III's choice to process to a church containing an apse mosaic depicting Christ and the Church as regal spouses could not have been coincidental.

At the consecration of Santa Maria in Trastevere during the Fourth Lateran Council, the theme of marriage played out in a twofold manner. First, the Pope, as the Vicar of Christ, was uniting himself to Santa Maria in Trastevere through the consecration of the church. Innocent III effectively enacted a kind of marriage in the consecration ceremony, which involved anointing the church's altar with oil, accompanied by readings with nuptial imagery. Second, within the church

---

[1440] Regarding the Cathars and the Church's movement against them see: Arno Borst, *Die Katharer.* (Stuttgart: Hiersemann, 1953); Aubrey Burl, *God's Heretics: The Albigensian Crusade* (Thrupp, Stroud, Gloucestershire: Sutton, 2002); Carol Lansing, *Power & Purity: Cathar Heresy in Medieval Italy* (New York, N.Y.: Oxford University Press, 1998); Catherine Léglu, Rebecca Rist, and Claire Taylor, eds., *The Cathars and Albigensian Crusade: A Sourcebook* (London: Routledge, 2014); Sean McGlynn, *Kill Them All: Cathars and Carnage in the Albigensian Crusade* (Stroud, Gloucestershire: The History Press, 2015); Mark Gregory Pegg, *A Most Holy War: The Albigensian Crusade and the Battle for Christendom,* Pivotal Moments in World History (Oxford ; New York: Oxford University Press, 2008); Steven Runciman, *The Medieval Manichee, a Study in Christian Dualist Heresy.* (New York: Viking Press, 1961); Jonathan Sumption, *The Albigensian Crusade* (London ; Boston: Faber, 1978).
[1441] Georges Duby, *The Knight, the Lady, and the Priest: The Making of Modern Marriage in Medieval France*, 1st American ed (New York: Pantheon Books, 1983), 107–8.
[1442] Ibid., 109–11.

itself, the apse mosaic above the high altar depicted precisely the marriage Innocent III was ritually

reenacting with great pageantry. Innocent III anointed Santa Maria in Trastevere *prae consortibus suis*,

to quote Psalm 44:8, which the pope himself quoted on several occasions in discourses on marriage

and its natural consequence, the birth of a child. Psalm 44 served as the basis for the second half of

his discourse on the four types of marriage, *De Quadripartita Specie Nuptiarum*, which Innocent III

likely composed in 1197, the year before his election as pope.[1443] The "marriage" that Bishop of

Rome symbolically enacted during Lateran IV sent a message to the furthest reaches of

Christendom, via the prelates and courtly representatives present at the council. Innocent III

transformed the symbolism of the mystical marriage between Christ and the Church into a social

and political reality.[1444] By symbolically wedding himself to Santa Maria in Trastevere, Pope Innocent

III affirmed the sanctity and sacramentality of the conjugal union between Christian spouses as well

as the rights of the ecclesiastical "body" to preside over such unions. Within Christendom the power

of the Bishop of Rome was as enduring as the conjugal bond between husband and wife or God's

union with the human soul.[1445]

While the Cathars rejected human flesh and reproduction, Innocent III affirmed the human

body as the locus of the holy. Christians' bodies, as well as the souls that dwelt within them, fell

within the purview of the Church. By affirming the sacrament of marriage, Innocent III reinforced

the Church's role as *mediatrix* of salvation.[1446] The Church defined what constituted a valid marriage

as well who had the right to marry.[1447] Regardless of social rank, every marriage involved a contract

---

[1443] PL 217, Col. 922-968. See also Richard Kay, "Innocent III as Canonist and Theologian: The Case of Spiritual Matrimony," in *Pope Innocent III and His World* (Brookfield, Vt.: Ashgate, 1999), 37–40.

[1444] D.L. D'Avray observed: "Thus Innocent III took the exalted idea of indissolubility out of the ivory tower and into the world of power politics." D. L. D'Avray, *Medieval Marriage: Symbolism and Society* (Oxford ; New York: Oxford University Press, 2005), 104.

[1445] Regarding the indissolubility of marriage in the medieval period, see Ibid., 74–130.

[1446] D'Avray notes that at Lateran IV Innocent III did not attempt to regulate the marriage ceremony. The decree regarding the need for marriage banns "was not about sacralizing the ritual entry into marriage, which varied from one part of Europe to another." Ibid., 105.

[1447] Sayers, *Innocent III*, 115–18.

regarding the couple's property.[1448] Before the spread of lay literacy, clerics were largely responsible

for composing these marriage contracts.[1449] The transfer of property often did not take place after

the betrothal, but after the nuptials, when the status of the woman changed from *sponsa* to *uxor*.[1450]

The Church's authority in matrimonial matters included the right to judge the legitimacy of an heir,

thus abrogating the laity's rights regarding succession and the transfer of property, including land.[1451]

In the late twelfth century, when Innocent III became the Bishop of Rome, discontent

among medieval Christians was on the rise. Groups the papacy deemed heretical challenged the

Church's teachings as well as the life-styles of clerics. With the eleventh-century Gregorian Reforms,

which more clearly delineated the boundaries between the clergy and the laity as well as the

distinction between the spiritual and material worlds, the sacraments were accorded greater and

greater significance.[1452] By the High Middle Ages, the tenor of Christian spirituality had also changed.

In the eleventh and twelfth centuries, instead of depicting Christ as an omnipotent king and judge,

theologians and artists emphasized Christ's humanity and cultivated greater devotion to his mother,

the Virgin Mary.[1453] In this atmosphere of religious transformation, ordinary Christians asked what it

meant to live a truly Christian life. They began to see the opulence and power of ecclesiastical

authorities as distortions of Christian teachings. Groups such as the Waldensians, the Humiliati and

the Cathars sought to establish purer or more authentic forms of Christianity. These groups'

critiques of the ecclesiastical hierarchy brought them into conflict with the wealthy, worldly

---

[1448] Duby, *The Knight, the Lady, and the Priest*, 95.

[1449] Ibid., 98.

[1450] Ibid., 96–97.

[1451] Sayers, *Innocent III*, 116–17.

[1452] Caroline Walker Bynum, *Jesus as Mother: Studies in the Spirituality of the High Middle Ages*, Publications of the Center for Medieval and Renaissance Studies, UCLA 16 (Berkeley: University of California Press, 1982), 12.

[1453] Ibid., 16–19; Moore, *Pope Innocent III (1160/61-1216) to Root up and to Plant*, 145; Herbert Grundmann, *Religious Movements in the Middle Ages: The Historical Links between Heresy, the Mendicant Orders, and the Women's Religious Movement in the Twelfth and Thirteenth Century, with the Historical Foundations of German Mysticism* (Notre Dame, Ind.: University of Notre Dame Press, 1995).

clergy.[1454] In this spiritual climate Innocent III processed to Santa Maria in Trastevere, making

marriage a sacrament *prae consortibus suis*. He also wrote his Second Sermon on the Nativity, in which

he presented the *fons olei* as a spectacularly new sign of the birth of the Anointed One, the Christian

of Christians.

Innocent III himself was acutely critical of clerics for their ignorance, greed, lust and general

worldliness.[1455] Nevertheless, with Innocent III at the helm, *mater ecclesia* attempted to assert herself

as the *mediatrix* of salvation through the sacraments. In order to establish the full reign of the Prince

of Peace, Innocent III decided to wage war against those whom he perceived to be Christ's enemies.

The Cathars became a central target of this crusading fervor when in 1208, papal legates began to

use the weapons of war to eliminate spiritual or political foes.[1456] The Cathar beliefs led them to

reject, among other things, the Christian doctrine of the Incarnation.[1457] The name 'Cathar' derived

from "Cathari" or purified ones, the spiritual leaders who had purified themselves of material

existence.[1458] While little extant evidence suggests the Cathars were direct descendants of the

Manichaeans, whom Augustine encountered in North Africa in the fourth century, they espoused

similar beliefs.[1459] The dualist heresy may have reached southern France via the Bogomils, ninth and

tenth-century Bulgarian converts who showed a proclivity for dualism, causing Byzantine clerics to

suggest they were witnessing a revival of Manichaeism.[1460]

[1454] R. I Moore, *The Formation of a Persecuting Society: Authority and Deviance in Western Europe, 950-1250*, 2nd ed (Malden, MA: Blackwell Publishing, 2007), 146; Grundmann, *Religious Movements in the Middle Ages*.

[1455] Joseph R. Strayer, *The Albigensian Crusades* (Ann Arbor: University of Michigan Press, 1992), 16-21.

[1456] Sayers, *Innocent III*, 160-63.

[1457] For scholarly literature on the Cathars and their beliefs, including their connection to Manichaeism, see Pegg, *A Most Holy War*; Borst, *Die Katharer.*; Burl, *God's Heretics*; McGlynn, *Kill Them All*; Lansing, *Power & Purity*, 1998; Grundmann, *Religious Movements in the Middle Ages*; Sumption, *The Albigensian Crusade*; Léglu, Rist, and Taylor, *The Cathars and Albigensian Crusade*; Runciman, *The Medieval Manichee, a Study in Christian Dualist Heresy*.

[1458] Strayer, *The Albigensian Crusades*, 26. "Cathari" is based on the Greek word καθαρίζειν to purify, whence our word *catharsis*. "'Catharist, N.," *OED Online* (Oxford University Press), accessed April 25, 2016, http://www.oed.com.proxy.library.georgetown.edu/view/Entry/28922.

[1459] Strayer, *The Albigensian Crusades*, 26.

[1460] Edward Peters, *Heresy and Authority in Medieval Europe: Documents in Translation*, The Middle Ages (Philadelphia: University of Pennsylvania Press, 1980), 103-4.

According to the Cathar dualist cosmology, there were two gods in the universe: one good

god who created spiritual things, and one evil god who created material things. Some Cathars

believed in the ultimate supremacy and omnipotence of God, who had merely allowed Satan to

create the material world, which God would one day vanquish.[1461] Thus, for the Cathars, all

materiality, including human flesh, was evil. This belief was a direct contradiction to Christian

doctrine, which held that God himself assumed human flesh in the Incarnation. The Cathars'

rejection of the body led to the belief that giving birth perpetuated evil. Cathars believed that human

souls, which had either been previously free in the realm of the spirit or created anew through

conception, were trapped in a prison of flesh.[1462] Furthermore, the Cathars denied the existence of

sexual difference or genders, which they viewed as external projections which bore no relation to a

person's internal reality.[1463]

The Cathar's rejection of the body and the material world coincided with a rejection of the

institutional church and its hierarchy.[1464] For these heretics, the ecclesiastical hierarchy's involvement

in the secular, political sphere was unholy.[1465] Priests, who distributed the 'body of Christ' in the

form of the Eucharist and sacralized Christian bodies through baptisms and anointings, were

dispensable. According to the Cathars, sanctification and salvation depended on the abnegation of

flesh and human desire. Austerity and restraint, not ritual pageantry, promised salvation. For

Cathars, Jesus, the central salvific agent in Christian belief, was neither God nor a human being, but

a kind of emanation of God and a spiritual being without materiality.[1466] The non-material nature of

the savior obviated the need for the Eucharist or the other sacraments. In the twelfth and thirteenth

centuries, the religious orders that disseminated myroblyte biographies were also in hot pursuit of

---

[1461] Strayer, *The Albigensian Crusades*, 27. This form of Catharism is known as "mitigated" dualism. See Peters, *Heresy and Authority in Medieval Europe*, 106.
[1462] Strayer, *The Albigensian Crusades*, 28.
[1463] Carol Lansing, *Power & Purity: Cathar Heresy in Medieval Italy* (Oxford ; New York: Oxford University Press, 2001), 10.
[1464] Lansing, *Power & Purity*, 5-6.
[1465] Ibid., 159.
[1466] Strayer, *The Albigensian Crusades*, 29.

heretics. Several notable Cistercians preached against or persecuted the Cathars in southern France. When their efforts failed, the Dominicans succeeded them.[1467] In 1145 Bernard of Clairvaux embarked on a preaching tour of Languedoc to no avail.[1468] In the early thirteenth century Arnald Amaury (1160-1225), abbot of Cîteaux and Innocent III's legate, ostensibly incited troops to massacre Cathars throughout the Languedoc region.[1469]

THE INCARNATION OF PLENITUDO POTESTATIS

In the late twelfth and early thirteenth century, Innocent III's nativity sermons extolled the Incarnation and furthered the conceptual link between oil and the birth of the savior of the world. Innocent III's first sermon on the nativity unfurled the meaning of John 1, which presented the paradox of the Incarnation, God becoming human flesh: "And the Word was made flesh and dwelt among us."[1470] What better way to confront a dualist heresy than to reassert the dual nature of Christ? The Church not only claimed exclusive sovereignty over Christian salvation via the sacraments, but also presented herself as the mystical body of God. The image of the Church as the body of Christ with the pope as the head was fundamental to medieval political and ecclesiastical discourse on power and authority.[1471] In *Policraticus,* John of Salisbury envisioned society as a 'body politic' in which the king ruled as the head rules over the body: "It is first of all required that the prince evaluate himself entirely and direct himself diligently to the whole body of the republic, whose condition he enjoys. For a republic is, just as Plutarch declares, a sort of body which is…ruled by a sort of rational principle."[1472] For Salisbury, the individuals responsible for the

---

[1467] Peters, *Heresy and Authority in Medieval Europe*, 105–6.

[1468] Ibid., 105.

[1469] Sayers, *Innocent III*, 160.

[1470] "Verbum caro factum est et habitavit in nobis." John 1:14.

[1471] Joseph Canning, *A History of Medieval Political Thought, 300-1450* (London ; New York: Routledge, 1996), 31.

[1472] John of Salisbury, *Policraticus: Of the Frivolities of Courtiers and the Footprints of Philosophers*, trans. Cary J. Nederman, Cambridge Texts in the History of Political Thought (Cambridge [England] ; New York: Cambridge University Press, 1990), 66. See also 14, 33, 49-50, 63, 66-67, 189-90, 200-201.

practice of religion in society were like the soul of the body, giving it life: "Indeed those who direct the practice of religion ought to be esteemed and venerated like the soul in the body. For who disputes that the sanctified ministers of God are his vicars? Besides, just as the soul has rulership of the whole body so those who are called prefects of religion direct the whole body."[1473] According to Salisbury, the head of the republic, as the vicar of God, was subject to God alone but received his power through the Church.[1474]

In his understanding of the interrelationship between the human body and soul, "corruptible flesh" drew life from the soul, whose ruler was God. Quoting Augustine, Salisbury wrote: "God is the life of the soul, the soul the life of the body; the one dissolves when the other flees, lost when it is undermined by God."[1475] Thus Salisbury imagines a hierarchy: the human body depends on the soul, which in turn depends on God. God acts as an omnipotent ruler of the soul (and by extension the body): "God occupies totally the soul that lives perfectly; He possesses it totally; He rules and vitalizes it in total."[1476] In the same way God rules over the human soul and body, God also rules within the body politic, according to Salisbury. God's power manifests in the prince, who is the image of the divine majesty: "…the prince is the public power and a certain image on earth of the divine majesty."[1477] When a prince exercises authority, he manifests "divine virtue."[1478] The authority is not the prince's own but God's, whom Salisbury characterized as the source of all power: "For all power is from the Lord God, and is with Him always, and is His forever. Whatever the prince can do, therefore, is from God, so that power does not depart from God, but it is used as a substitute for His hand, making all things learn His justice and mercy."[1479] The prince thus acts as God's

---

[1473] Ibid., 67.
[1474] Ibid.
[1475] Ibid., 14.
[1476] Ibid.
[1477] Ibid., 28.
[1478] Ibid.
[1479] Ibid.

instrument on earth. As God's vicar, however, the prince was subordinate to the Church, through

whom the prince received God's power.

Salisbury imagined a prince, as God's vicar, being an extension of the Church's power as the

hand is part of a human body. Using the metaphor of a sword, Salisbury characterized the prince's

power as being like a sword handed to the prince by the Church: "…while [the Church] has this

sword, yet it is used by the hand of the prince…reserving spiritual authority for the papacy."[1480] The

secular prince, according to Salisbury, ruled as a "sort of minister of priests," establishing justice in

the worldly, and thus inferior realm, while leaving the higher sacred duties to priests.[1481] In so far as

the secular prince ruled as God's proxy, he did so through the authority given to him by the pope,

who in turn received his power a single, divine source.

Innocent III claimed the role of God's vicar within the Christian *corpus,* expressed in

numerous decretals as *plenitudo potestatis* – fullness of power. This power, which came directly from

God, belonged the pope alone, who was the sole source of power and authority bestowed on other

prelates.[1482] What better symbol could there be for the pope's *plenitudo potestatis* than the *fons olei*? In

Policraticus, John of Salisbury referred to Socrates as establishing a political system in which all

precepts were said, "to emanate from that purity of wisdom which is like a sort of font of

nature."[1483] The *fons olei* readily symbolized the divine source of all earthly power. Over the course of

the thirteenth century secular rulers including Holy Roman Emperors and kings of France

appropriated the idea of fullness of power to express the nature of their own authority.[1484]

In his second sermon on the Nativity of Christ, Innocent III referred directly to the *fons olei*

without making a reference to Santa Maria in Trastevere. He said instead that the oil flowed from

---

[1480] Ibid., 32.

[1481] Ibid.

[1482] Canning, *A History of Medieval Political Thought, 300-1450,* 142–43.

[1483] Salisbury, *Policraticus,* 137.

[1484] Canning, *A History of Medieval Political Thought, 300-1450,* 118–19.

the *taberna emeritoria*, like Carolingian authors before him. Nevertheless, Innocent III's sermon for

the nativity explored the mystery of God's humanity, expressed in the Incarnation. The pope

broached the great paradox of the union of divinity with flesh via dichotomies, including the male –

female binary.[1485] Presenting Christ as the combination of opposites (human and divine), Innocent

III also suggested that Christ united both the male and female genders in one person: he was both

bride and bridegroom. The combination, reconciliation or unification of opposites in one person

was, according to Innocent III, representative of Christ's anointing: he was a human being and yet

imbued with the Holy Spirit. Christ was not alone in this capacity: all Christians shared in this dual

nature, which the Church bestowed on people by anointing them with holy oil.

In the *Sermo in nativitate* (II), Innocent III presented an extended discourse on a verse from

Jeremiah 31, in which God promised to restore Israel to her former glory. Innocent III chose the

second half of a verse, which spoke of the birth of a child, as the basis for his sermon: "The Lord

will make something new on the earth. A woman will encompass a man in the womb of her

belly."[1486] Innocent III's citation from Jeremiah was remarkable in two respects. First, he omitted the

first half of the verse, which addressed the wayward nature of the mother: "How long will you be

dissolute in delights, O wandering daughter?" Second, he presented a significantly altered Vulgate

text for Jeremiah 31, which included no mention of "the womb of her belly." The Vulgate simply

reads: "For the Lord created a new thing upon the earth: A woman will encompass a man."[1487] The

variation, however, that Innocent III chose was not his own innovation. This same phrase appeared

in both Peter Abelard's *Sic et Non* as well as Peter Lombard's *Collectanea in omnes Pauli apostoli*

Epistulas. Innocent III's phrasing of the line from Jeremiah was closer to Abelard and Lombard's

---

[1485] Regarding Innocent III's Mariology, see Wilhelm Imkamp, "Virginitas Quam Ornavit Humility: die Verehrung der Gottesmutter in den Sermones Papst Innocenz III," *Lateranum* 46 (1980): 344–78. Regarding the image of the Church as *mater ecclesia*, see Karl Delahaye, *Ecclesia Mater chez les pères des trois premiers siècles: pour un renouvellement de la pastorale d'aujourd'hui* (Paris: Éditions du Cerf, 1964).

[1486] "Novum faciet Dominus super terram. Femina circumdavit virum gremio uteri sui." PL 217, Col. 455C.

[1487] "quia creavit Dominus novum super terram: femina circumdabit virum." Jerome 31:22.

texts than the Vulgate. Abelard cited Jerome's discourse on Jeremiah: "Jerome on Jeremiah, Book VI: The Lord created something new on the earth, without the seed of man, without intercourse and without conception. A woman encompassed a man in the womb of her belly."[1488] A verbatim version of Peter Lombard's text appeared in Innocent III's sermon: "The Lord will make something new on the earth. A woman will encompass a man in the womb of her belly."[1489] Innocent III thus began his sermon on the nativity with a meditation on the meaning of "new":

> "For the Lord made a new thing upon the earth: A woman will encompass a man in the womb of her belly."[1490] New in Holy Scripture is understood in multiple ways. For 'new' means 'innovating' and 'new' means 'innovated.' 'New' means 'recent' and 'new' means 'unused.' 'New' means 'latest' and 'new' means 'miraculous.' 'New' means 'innovating', for example: 'I give you a new commandment, that you should love one another as I have loved you.'[1491] 'New' means 'innovated,' for example: 'I saw a new heaven and a new earth' – 'And the one who was sitting in the throne said: Behold! I make all things new!'[1492]

The power to create something new, according to Innocent III, belonged to the one occupying the throne – the *sedes sapientiae*. This all-powerful creator could communicate his power through the newness of miracles, which were signs and wonders attesting to his presence and fidelity. A woman giving birth to a child who would "renew Jerusalem" was a sign of God's omnipotence.

> *New* means *miraculous*, for example: 'Renew your signs and work new miracles.'[1493] The Lord therefore makes a new thing on earth. For 'this was done by the Lord and is miraculous in

---

1488 "Hieronymus super Jeremias, Libri VI: Novam rem creavit dominus super terram absque viri semine, absque coitu atque conceptu. Femina circumdabit virum gremio uteri sui." LLT: Petrus Abaelardus, *Sic et Non*, quaestio: 72; sententia:1; linea:3.

1489 "Unde Jeremias: Novum faciet Dominus super terram. Femina circumdavit virum gremio uteri sui." LLT: Petrus Lombardus, *Collectanea in omnes Pauli apostoli Epistulas*, PL 192, ad Ephesios, cap.: 4; versus: 23+; col. 205; linea: 29.

1490 Jeremiah 31:22.

1491 John 13:34-35.

1492 Rev. 21:5. "*Novum faciet Dominus super terram. Femina circumdabit virum gremio uteri sui* (Jer. XXXI). Novum in sacra Scriptura multis modis accipitur. Nam novum dicitur innovans, et novum dicitur innovatum; novum dicitur recens, et novum dicitur insuetum; novum dicitur ultimum, et novum dicitur miraculosum. Novum dicitur innovans, secundum illud: «Mandatum novum do vobis, ut diligatis invicem, sicut dilexi vos (Joan. XIII).» Novum dicitur innovatum, secundum illud: «Vidi coelum novum et terram novam (Apoc. XXI).»----«Et dixit qui sedebat in throno: Ecce nova facio omnia (ibid.)." PL 217, Col.0455D.

1493 Eccl. 36:6.

our eyes.'[1494] The Lord made something new on earth in all these ways, because *a woman encompassed a man in the womb of her belly.* 'For then a great prophet came and he himself renewed Jerusalem.'[1495] Then the Lord completed the New Testament over Jerusalem, over the house Israel, and over the house Judah.[1496]

Innocent III then explained that God renewed Israel by means of paradoxical generation. The Incarnation was unlike any miracles God had previously accomplished. An unfathomable inversion of the natural order characterized the advent of Christ.

> For then the Lord made something new in a person (*in persona*), he made something new in nature, he made something new in grace. In a person, because he made something new in a mother, he made something new in a descendent; in nature, because he made something new in a sign, he made something new in a way; in grace, because he made something new in the marriage contract, he made something new in an offering. He made something new in a mother, because a virgin bore a son, a star brought forth the sun, a daughter conceived [her] father, a creature gave birth to the Creator: in one at the same time mother and daughter, birthmother and slave, who gave birth in chastity, who conceived in virginity, because the fire in the kindling, the fruit in the sprig, because the dew in the clouds [lit. fleece] were all prefigured: 'For he will descend just like the rain in the clouds, like drops dripping upon the earth.'[1497]

[1494] Psalm 117:23.

[1495] Jeremiah 38.

[1496] "Novum dicitur miraculosum, secundum illud: «Innova signa, et immuta mirabilia (Eccli. XXXVI).» *Novum* ergo *faciet Dominus super terram.* Nam «a Domino factum est istud, et est mirabile in oculis nostris (Psal. CXVII).» His omnibus modis *novum* fecit *Dominus super terram;* quoniam *femina circumdedit virum gremio uteri sui.* «Tunc enim venit propheta magnus, et ipse renovavit Jerusalem (Jer. XXXVIII).» Tunc consummavit Dominus testamentum novum super Jerusalem, domum Israel, et super domum Juda; non secundum testamentum quod dedit patribus eorum, cum exirent de terra Aegypti. Tunc illud impletum est: «Vetustissima veterum comedetis, et novis supervenientibus vetera projicietis (Levit. XXVI).»" Leviticus 26:10. PL 217, Col. 456D.

[1497] "Tunc enim novum fecit Dominus in persona, novum fecit in natura, novum fecit in gratia. In persona, quia novum fecit in matre, novum fecit in prole; in natura, [Col.0457A] quia novum fecit in signo, novum fecit in modo; in gratia, quia novum fecit in foedere, novum fecit in munere. Novum fecit in matre, quia virgo peperit virum, stella protulit solem, filia concepit patrem, creatura Creatorem genuit: simul in unum mater et filia, genitrix et ancilla, quae cum integritate peperit, cum virginitate concepit: quod ignis in rubo, quod fructus in virga, quod ros in vellere praesignaverant. «Descendit enim sicut pluvia in vellus, et sicut stillicidia stillantia super terram (Psal. LXXI)." Ps 71:6. PL 217, Col. 0456D.

Innocent III suggested that what appears unnatural to us is simply hidden in nature as potential that had not yet manifested.[1498] God descending from heaven like a life-giving liquid signified salvation or God imparting new life to earth. This life existed in potentiality but not in actuality until the birth of Christ. The miraculous newness required an earthly abode. The body of a woman became the vessel of God, bringing the all-powerful ruler into the world as well as into time. Like other authors who circulated the *fons olei* legend, Innocent III said the appearance of the omnipotent ruler ushered in an era of unprecedented peace. Unfathomable reversals and unnatural paradoxes accompanied the advent of this new ruler's reign.

> This door in the House of the Lord is closed and man does not enter through it.[1499] This is she who was the first and only one to escape the reproach of the law, which said: Cursed is the sterile one in Israel![1500] And He fulfilled the plan for her virginity, because 'before they came together, she was discovered to have the Holy Spirit in her womb.'[1501] He made something new in the offspring, because the Eternal Lord was made a servant boy, the most exalted was made lowly, the boundless was made local, the singular was made composite, the immortal was made mortal, father was made from his mother, the son from his daughter. He descended into the mother but remained with the father. He assumed humanity but retained divinity…his name will be Prince of Peace[1502]…the Highest himself will establish himself in her.[1503]

[1498] This idea appears in Augustine's explanation of the monstrous. See Augustine, *Concerning the City of God against the Pagans* (Harmondsworth: Penguin Books, 1972), 982–83.

[1499] Ezek 44:2. Innocent III presents a variation of the idea presented in Ezekiel, speaking of the door in the present rather than future tense, as if the fact of God (Jesus) having passed through the door has already happened: "Et dixit Dominus ad me: Porta haec clausa erit: non aperietur, et vir non transibit per eam, quoniam Dominus Deus Israel ingressus est per eam: eritque clausa."

[1500] Exod. 23:26.

[1501] Matt 1:18. The Douay-Rheims translates this phrase as: "…before they came together, she was found with child, of the Holy Ghost."

[1502] Isaiah 9:6.

[1503] Psalm 86. "Haec est porta in domo Domini clausa, et vir non est ingressus per eam (Ezech. XLIV). Haec est illa, quae prima et sola maledictum legis evasit, qua dicitur: Maledicta [sit] sterilis in Israel (Exod. XXIII)! et propositum virginitatis implevit; quoniam 'antequam convenirent, inventa est in utero habens de Spiritu sancto (Matth. I).' Novum fecit in prole, quia Dominus servus, aeternus factus est puer, excelsus factus est factus est parvulus, immensus factus est localis, simplex factus est compositus, immortalis factus est mortalis, matris suae Pater, et filiae suae filius. Descendit in matrem, sed remansit cum patre. Suscepit humanitatem, sed retinuit Divinitatem. Nam 'cum in forma Dei esset, non rapinam arbitratus est esse se aequalem Deo,' etc. (Philip. II.) 'Puer natus est nobis, et filius datus est nobis, et vocabitur nomen ejus Admirabilis, Consiliarius, Deus, Fortis, Pater futuri saeculi, Princeps pacis (Isa. IX).' Matri 'Sion dicet: Homo, et homo natus est in ea, et ipse fundavit eam Altissimus (Psal. LXXXVI)." PL 217, Col.0457A-C.

Innocent III emphasized that these signs and wonders, these inversions and paradoxes occurred not only in ancient Israel but also in Rome, affecting even the sphere of political authority. The birth of Christ, according to Innocent III, fundamentally altered how the emperor understood his role within the hierarchy of powerful beings. Innocent III referred to the legend told of Augustus consulting the Sibyl at Santa Maria in Ara Caeli, Santa Maria in Trastevere's rival.[1504]

> Behold that new thing, miraculous and unusual, that the Lord made on earth, when *a woman encompassed a man in the womb of her belly*. Therefore 'Sing to the Lord a new song, because the Lord did wonders.'[1505] He made something new in a sign, because with Christ being born, a great star appeared, according to the prophet Balaam: 'It is said a star will be born of Jacob, and a shoot will rise from Israel.'[1506] Octavius Augustus is said to have seen a virgin bearing a son, according to the Sibyl's vision and from then on, he forbid anyone to call him Lord because 'the King of Kings and the Lord of Dominions' was born. Thus the poet [Vergil] said: 'Behold! A new progeny is sent from high heaven.'[1507]

Innocent III's invocation of the Sibyl for the feast of Christ's nativity was nothing new. Beginning as early as the fifth century, verses from the Sibylline oracles appeared in churches on Christmas Day, sometimes in miracle plays, in which Vergil and the Sibyl appeared as prophets announcing Christ's birth.[1508] Curiously enough, Vergil also appeared in another mystery play about the foolish virgins who wanted oil.[1509]

[1504] Nichols, *The Marvels of Rome - Mirabilia Urbis Romae*, 17–18; Domenico Comparetti, *Vergil in the Middle Ages* (Princeton, N.J: Princeton University Press, 1997), 313.

[1505] Ps 97:1.

[1506] Num. 24:17.

[1507] "Ecce novum illud miraculosum et insuetum, quod fecit Dominus super terram, quando *femina circumdedit virum gremio uteri sui*. Ergo 'cantate Domino canticum novum, quia mirabilia fecit Dominus (Psal. XCVII).» Novum fecit in signo; quia, Christo nascente, stella magis apparuit, secundum vaticinium Balaam: «Orietur, inquit, stella ex Jacob, et exsurget virga ex Israel (Num. XXIV).' Octavianus Augustus fertur in coelo vidisse virginem gestantem filium ad ostensionem Sibyllae, et extunc prohibuit ne quis eum dominum appellaret, quia natus erat 'Rex regum, et Dominus dominantium (Apoc. XVII).' Unde poeta: *En nova progenies coelo dimittitur alto* (VIRG., Buc. eclog. IV, 7.)." PL 217, Col. 0457C.

[1508] Comparetti, *Vergil in the Middle Ages*, 309–10.

[1509] Ibid., 311.

In his Christmas sermon, Innocent III was not showing complete partiality to any one

Marian church in Rome. In addition to mentioning the legend about the founding of Santa Maria in

Ara Coeli, Innocent III also mentioned a legend associated with Santa Maria in Trastevere: the *fons*

olei. When God descended from heaven, oil bubbled up from the earth. Like Nicholas of Clairvaux

(potentially), Innocent III connected the flowing oil with the destruction of a pagan emperor's

temple, which buckled at the birth of a more powerful prince:

> For an entire day a fountain of oil flowed from the *taberna emeritoria*, revealing that he was
> born on earth who was anointed with oil before his companions.[1510] The Temple of Peace
> completely collapsed. The Romans had constructed a wonderful temple of peace, if such a
> thing were possible, on behalf of the perfect peace that spread over the whole earth during
> Augustus' reign. When people asked how long the peace would remain, the answer was:
> "Until a virgin gives birth." Who rejoicing answered: "Therefore he will be eternally, because
> a virgin will never give birth." But God destroyed the wisdom of wisdoms and rejected the
> prudence of prudences,[1511] because in the hour of the Lord's birth, he completely destroyed
> the temple.[1512]….He himself is our peace, who made two one…[1513]

The temple only remained as long as the peace and the peace only as long as the temple. Innocent

III's language was ambiguous, creating a parallel between the ephemeral peace and the instability of

Augustus' temple. When one disappeared, so did the other. What lasting temple corresponded to

Christ's peace? The church where oil flowed.

[1510] Ps 44:8.

[1511] 1 Cor. 1:19

[1512] Luke 2:14. "Fons olei per totum diem de taberna emeritorum largissimus emanavit; signans quod ille nasceretur in terris, qui unctus erat oleo prae consortibus suis (Psal. XLIV). Templum Pacis funditus corruit. Romani siquidem pro pace perfecta, quae toti orbi sub Augusto imminebat, templum Pacis mirificum construxerant. De quo consulentes quandiu deberet durare, responsum est: 'Donec virgo pariat.' Qui gaudentes responderunt: 'Ergo erit aeternum, quia nunquam virgo pariet.' Sed perdidit Deus sapientiam sapientium, et prudentiam prudentium reprobavit (I Cor. I); quoniam in hora Dominicae nativitatis funditus corruit. Cum enim plena pax et perfecta per totum orbem universaliter abundaret, quod nunquam ante contigerat, nec diu post unquam [Col.0458A] evenit, natus est Deus, Fortis, Pater futuri saeculi, Princeps pacis. Unde Propheta: 'Orietur in diebus ejus justitia et abundantia pacis, donec auferatur luna (Psal. LXXI).' Et alius item propheta: 'Pax erit in terra nostra cum venerit (Mich. V).' --- 'Ipse enim est pax Dei, quae exsuperat omnem sensum (Philip. IV).'-- 'Ipse pax nostra, qui fecit utraque unum (Ephes. II)' in cujus ortu coelestis militiae multitudo psallebat: 'Gloria in altissimis Deo, et in terra pax hominibus bonae voluntatis (Luc. II).' PL 217, Col.0457D-0458A.

[1513] Eph. 2:14.

In observing that the oil flowing from the *fons olei* signaled the birth of the Anointed One, Innocent III was not saying anything remarkably new. Other authors before him had interpreted Rome's fountain of oil as a symbol for the Anointed One. Innocent III embellished the legend, however, by describing how in Christ the old and the new coalesced, like humanity and divinity. The flowing oil was a new wonder and prodigy God had never showed before and yet this sign evoked an old and familiar image: Christ was the king whom God anointed before his companions (*prae consortibus suis*). The symbols of marriage, coronation, and the birth of a child coalesced in Innocent III's nativity sermon.[1514] The old order (represented by the temple) collapsed and yet oil not only remained but flowed. The Anointed One was new and yet, paradoxically, existed and would exist for all eternity. Perhaps this was Innocent III's hope for his papacy.

Observing that Christ, the bringer of peace, made two one (He himself is our peace, who made two one[1515]) provided Innocent III with an opening for a discourse on gender when heretics denied gender distinctions. Christ was "new" by virtue of the peculiar combination of genders that led to his generation and a new modality of existence.

> He made something new in modality, because in his birth, he assumed the modality of the human condition. For the first modality was a human being made neither from male nor from female, like Adam. The second modality was truly a human being made from male, not female, like Eve. The third modality was a human being made from male and female, like Abel. The fourth modality was a human being made from female, not from male, like Christ, in such a way that the astonished virgin had said to the angel: "How will this be done, since I do not know a man?"[1516]

[1514] The second part of his treatise on marriage, *De Quadripartitia specie nuptiarum* is an exegetical discourse on Psalm 44. See Kay, "Innocent III as Canonist and Theologian: The Case of Spiritual Matrimony," 37. See PL 217, Col.949-68.
[1515] Eph. 2:14.
[1516] Luke 1:34. "Novum fecit in modo, quia in sua nativitate modum humanae conditionis implevit. Primus enim modus fuit, ut homo fieret nec de masculo, nec de femina, sicut Adam; secundus vero fuit, ut homo fieret de masculo, non de femina, sicut Eva; tertius fuit, ut homo fieret de masculo et de femina, sicut Abel; quartus fuit, ut homo fieret de femina, non de masculo, sicut Christus, quemadmodum admirans Virgo dixerat ad angelum: 'Quomodo fiet istud, quoniam virum non cognosco?' " PL 217, Col.0458B.

Having completed the last possible modality or gender combination for generation, God had done something new. Innocent III, however, was drawing on an older idea that years later Jacob de Voragine (c. 1229-1298) presented in the *Legenda Aurea* in his chapter on the Nativity of Christ and attributed to Anselm (presumably of Canterbury).[1517] What arose from this discussion of the genders at play during Christ's conception was a vision of the human being as being in possession of a rational soul, like divine presence dwelling within human flesh. The bursting of the oil from the ground marked, in a sense, the anointing of Christendom, allowing the divinity of God to dwell within humanity. Once anointed human beings, now Christians, possessed rational souls that allowed them to see the extent to which God's divine presence dwelt within them: "…a trinity of substances cannot not differ in person because just as a human being is rational soul and flesh in one, so Christ is God and human being in one. Behold that new thing, fresh and last, that the Lord made on earth, because a woman encompassed a man in the belly of her womb."[1518] According to Innocent III, in the same way Christ was both God and human being, he was both male and female: a man encompassed in the womb of a woman. One can discern, in this depiction of the male-female binary, hints of Aristotelianism: the male as the rational principle and the female as the flesh.[1519] Innocent III's rather abstract meditation on gender and divine substance was not, however, divorced from earthly concerns, but directly related to the question of marriage as a sacrament, marriage from whence Christian children were to be born. Whether Innocent III was concerned with literal, physical children whose souls would be the care of the Church or children in another, mystical sense remains to be seen.

[1517] Eamon Duffy, "Introduction," in *The Golden Legend: Readings on the Saints* (Princeton: Princeton University Press, 2012), 39.

[1518] Ps 97:1. "Et sicut tres sunt personae in unitate substantiae, ita fecit ut tres sint substantiae in unitate personae: ut sicut trinitas personarum non distinguit substantiam, ita trinitas substantiarum non distinguat personam. Quoniam sicut anima rationalis et caro unus est homo, ita Deus et homo unus est Christus. Ecce novum illud recens et ultimum, quod fecit *Dominus super terram, quoniam femina* circumdedit *virum gremio uteri sui.* Ergo 'cantate Domino canticum novum; quia mirabilia fecit Dominus (Psal. XCVII).'" PL 217, Col.0458B-C.

[1519] Aristotle, *On the Generation of Animals.*

What we can say with more certainty, however, is that oil was at the center of both the

pope's discussion of conjugal union (spiritual and physical) and the birth of a salvific offspring. In

the woman's womb, God united with human materiality, like oil with the flesh of the anointed.

Again, Innocent III was not introducing an idea that was entirely new, but reproducing one Abelard

had touched on in his Sermon 4, in which he suggested that Mary or Santa Maria in Trastevere was

like a *taberna meritoria* through which God united himself with humanity.[1520] For Innocent III, Christ,

the Anointed One, was two: groom and bride, God and human being. This dual nature was evident

in another appellation, Emmanuel (God with us), which described the presence of heavenly divinity

in the earthly realm. In this nativity sermon, the citations from the Song of Songs even suggested the

divine character of human sexuality, since he compared the comingling of the human and divine in

Christ to a conjugal union.[1521] Nevertheless, within Christ a hierarchy existed between the divine and

human elements, which in turn corresponded to masculine and feminine figures who, perhaps not

surprisingly, had political counterparts.

In his discussion of Christ being both bridegroom and bride, Innocent III altered a quote

from the prophet Isaiah, so that instead of wearing a crown, the bridegroom wore a mitre. Instead

of wearing necklaces (*monilibus*) the bride wore a crown: "He made a new thing in a marriage

covenant (*foedere*), because God joined human nature to himself in the virginal womb, representing in

one person bridegroom and bride, with the prophet saying: 'He put the mitre (*mitram*) on me like on

a groom and he adorned me with a crown (*corona*) like a bride.'"[1522] Then Innocent III turned to the

theme of the eternal rule of Christ, established forever in the heavens, his bride and *sedes sapientiae*.

[1520] See Chapter 9.

[1521] For Innocent III's less positive view of human sexuality, see Constance M Rousseau, "Pregnant with Meaning: Pope Innocent III's Construction of Motherhood," in *Pope Innocent III and His World* (Brookfield, Vt.: Ashgate, 1999), 108–12.

[1522] "Novum fecit in foedere, quia Deus in utero virginali naturam sibi conjugavit humanam. In una persona sponsum repraesentans et sponsam, dicente propheta: 'Sicut sponso imposuit mihi mitram, et tanquam sponsam decoravit me corona (Isa. LXI)." Isaiah 61:10. The Vulgate reads: "…quasi sponsum decoratum corona, et quasi sponsam ornatam monilibus suis."

The union of God and humanity was the marriage of marriages. Human marriage was simply a symbol pointing toward a greater reality:

> "'For he placed his tabernacle in the sun and he, like a groom coming out of his bridal chamber....'[1523] Hence that nuptial song resounds: "Let him kiss me with the kiss of his mouth" and "Your breasts are better than wine, smelling sweet of the best ointments."[1524] The sacrament of this marriage signifies this name, because the prophet (Isaiah) foretold: "His name will be called Emmanuel."[1525]

The unity of seeming opposites, the living paradox, was according to Innocent III, salvific. Having been anointed with holy oil was a defining characteristic of the one who accomplished the miraculous combination of opposites. Oil was a sign of the comingling of humanity and divinity. Human flesh assumed a new quality in being anointed with oil, in being suffused with the Holy Spirit. Borrowing largely from Augustine, Innocent III reiterated that Christ, the Messiah, was synonymous with oil.

> Christ is interpreted as *anointed*, and he himself, because a human being 'is anointed with the oil of gladness before his companions' whence in the Song of Songs: 'Your name is oil poured out.'[1526] For Christ is so called by anointing. The principle chrism is made from oil, whence his name means oil. And thus all faithful Christians are so called through Christ, on account of this oil poured out.[1527]

[1523] Psalm 18:6.

[1524] Cant. 1:1-2.

[1525] " 'In sole namque posuit tabernaculum suum, et ipse tanquam sponsus procedens de thalamo suo (Psal. XVIII).' Hinc illud resonat epithalamicum canticum: 'Osculetur me osculo oris sui;' et: 'Meliora sunt ubera vino, fragrantia unguentis optimis (Cant. I).' Hujus conjugii sacramentum illud nomen significat, quod propheta praedixit: 'Vocabitur nomen ejus Emmanuel (Isa. VII).' Ipse namque vocatur Jesus, vocatur Christus, vocatur Emmanuel. Jesus secundum naturam divinam, Christus secundum naturam humanam, Emmanuel secundum utramque." PL 217, Col.0458C-D. The full verse from Isaiah 7:14 reads: "Propter hoc dabit Dominus ipse vobis signum: ecce virgo concipiet, et pariet filium, et vocabitur nomen eius Emmanuel."

[1526] Cant. 1:1-2.

[1527] "Christus interpretatur *inunctus*, et ipse, secundum quod homo, 'unctus est oleo laetitiae pro consortibus suis:' unde in Cantico canticorum: 'Oleum effusum nomen tuum (Cant. I).' Christus enim a *chrismate* dicitur, chrisma vero principaliter fit ex oleo: unde nomen ejus dicitur oleum. Et quoniam a Christo cuncti fideles Christiani dicuntur, ob hoc oleum effusum." PL 217, Col.0458D.

If Innocent III saw oil as the essential source of Christian identity, Santa Maria in Trastevere,

with her *fons olei* would have been the natural location to establish himself as Christ, the head of the

Church. The 'Lord of the World,' however, could not act alone. At the very end of his sermon,

Innocent III emphasized Mary's role. For all time, the Virgin held eternity itself in her womb:

"Behold that new thing, renewed and renewing, that the Lord made on earth, when a woman

enveloped a man in the womb of her belly, enveloping him in the womb, by which he was

enveloped forever. The female virgin, the intact wife, enveloped true God, perfect man, she who

'reaches from end to end mightily and arranges all things sweetly.'"[1528] Innocent III's vision of

Christ's nativity was a far cry from a chubby child lying on dirty straw in the dark squalor of a stall.

In a sense, the Bishop of Rome appears to have lost touch with human reality. He could speak of

God only through an elaborate symbolism. The pope even drew a distinction between Mary and

ordinary, run-of-the-mill women: "Other wives conceive infants, but this woman enveloped a man

in the womb of her belly. Then time produced eternity, place conceived vastness, a number

produced infinity. Therefore 'Sing to the Lord a new song, he has done wonderful things.'"[1529] While

Innocent III's sermon ostensibly extolled the corporeal origin of the savior and carnal marriage as a

locus of the holy, the lingering impression is the opposite. The two central figures of Innocent III's

homiletic drama – Mary and Jesus – appeared as pieces of a symbolic framework rather than actual

human beings. Whether he successfully persuaded listeners (or Cathars) of the beauty and truth of

Incarnation remains to be seen.

[1528] Wisdom 8:1. "Ecce novum illud innovatum et innovans, quod fecit *Dominus super terram, quando femina*
circumdedit *virum gremio uteri sui;* circumdans illum in utero, a quo circumdabatur in saeculo. Femina virgo, mulier illibata
circumdedit Deum verum, virum perfectum, qui «attingit a fine usque ad finem fortiter, et disponit omnia suaviter." PL
217, Col. 0460A.

[1529] Psalm 97:1. "Caeterae mulieres concipiunt infantes, haec autem femina circumdedit virum gremio uteri sui. Tunc
tempus produxit aeternitatem, locus concepit immensitatem, numerus comprehendit infinitatem. Ergo 'cantate Domino
canticum novum, quia mirabilia fecit Dominus.'" PL 217, Col.0460A-B.

In Rome, processions were essential expressions of Christian devotion, especially during the

celebration of increasingly popular feasts such as the Assumption of the Virgin (15 August). During

one such procession, to celebrate the Virgin's bodily entrance into heaven, an image of Christ, the

Uronica, also called the Acheropita, made its way through the city, departing from the Holy of

Holies, the *sancta sanctorum* of the Lateran Palace, processing through the city and paying visits to

various churches.[1530] The icon was said to be an *acheiropoieta*, an icon made miraculously without

hands or by angels. The Uronica's final destination was Santa Maria Maggiore, where Christ

encountered his mother, so to speak, in the form of a Marian icon, known as the *Salus Populi Romani*.

The icons encountered one another in prayerful adoration on the eve of Mary's bodily assumption

into heaven.[1531] Throngs of Rome's faithful reverently witnessed the holy encounter.[1532] If we recall

Bernard's interpretation of the bride as heaven, then strangely enough the Christ symbolically

entered heaven (Santa Maria Maggiore) on the feast of her own entrance into the heavenly realm.[1533]

Once again, Christ was "encompassed" in a woman as she prepared to depart from the earth. In the

thirteenth century, the apse mosaic of Santa Maria Maggiore would reproduce the central theme of

Santa Maria in Trastevere's apse mosaic: the coronation of the Virgin and her marriage to Christ.

Pope Nicholas IV (r. 1288-1292), the first Franciscan pope, commissioned one of his fellow

Franciscans, Jacopo Torriti (13th century), to create a new apse mosaic. In this mosaic, Jesus and

Mary are again depicted sitting side by side on a synthronum. Rather than embracing Mary as his

---

[1530] According to Kristin Noreen, the stops along the way were "strategic locations associated with the ancient and Christian history of the city." See Noreen, *Re-Covering Christ*, 119.

[1531] Kitzinger, "A Virgin's Face," 11.

[1532] According to Noreen, the procession of the *Uronica* was part of a complex interplay of religious images, papal power, and social divisions: "the interaction of image and public was highly structured through ritual stops and a processional movement that reconfirmed the hierarchy of Rome's class structure." See Kristin Noreen, "Re-Covering Christ in Late Medieval Rome: The Icon of Christ in the Sancta Sanctorum." *Gesta* 49, no. 2 (January 1, 2010): 119.

[1533] Literature on the development and meaning of the Assumption.

spouse, however, the Christ placed a crown upon her head, invoking the themes of royal and

ecclesiastical authority.

Innocent III was keenly aware of the power of images. For this reason, he ordered that the

Uronica be covered in gold and silver so that the eyes of viewers might be protected from the

'fearsome image' which was kept in the papal chapel of St. Laurence, known as the 'Holy of Holies,'

the sancta sanctorum of the Lateran Palace.[1534] While such coverings were common in the

Byzantine Empire, they were rare in Italy.[1535] Pope Alexander III (r. 1159 – 81) covered the face of

Christ with veils, believing the image could "lead to blindness or even death" according to the

English chroniclers Gervase of Tilbury and Gerald of Wales.[1536] The gilded silver covering which

Innocent III added not only protected viewers from a potentially destructive sanctity, but intensified

the mystery and the appeal of Christ's image.[1537] Kristin Noreen suggests the revetment nonetheless

heightened viewer's awareness of the limits of corporeal vision since "the viewer can perceive

Christ's divinity only indirectly through the materiality of the image on the icon."[1538] The Uronica

image was unlike other images, not only because of the extraordinary visual power emanating from

the wood and paint. The hands of angels, rather than human hands, painted this image that exuded

oil as well as divinity. When Innocent III ordered the Uronica to be covered with a gold and silver

sheath to protect, not Christ's modesty, but the eyes of viewers, the goldsmith and silversmith left a

small opening over the right knee, from which unguent flowed.[1539] Innocent III had evidently

recognized the popular appeal of oil within the city of Rome. Oil flowed in the Holy of Holies, a

place largely beyond the reach of ordinary medieval Christians. While heretical groups like the

---

[1534] Brenda Bolton, *Innocent III: Studies on Papal Authority and Pastoral Care*, 120.

[1535] Noreen, "Re-Covering Christ," 124.

[1536] Noreen, "Re-Covering Christ," 122.

[1537] "By the late twelfth century, the original Lateran icon was thus encased in multiple layers that concealed, restructured, or revitalized Christ's miraculous representation...Although the gilded cover permanently disembodied the image of Christ, it also replaced his body with new imagery and iconographic significance." Noreen, Re-Covering Christ, 122.

[1538] Noreen, "Re-Covering Christ," 127.

[1539] See Gerald of Wales, *Speculum Ecclesiae*, 278; Noreen, "Re-Covering Christ," 117–135.

Cathars and Waldensians critiqued the ecclesiastical hierarchy for straying too far from the essence of Christ's teachings (poverty, simplicity, abstaining from worldly matters), Innocent III made Christ yet more inaccessible, creating an even greater mystique of a divine power that had to be mediated (or shielded) from humanity more generally.

The openings in the metal sheath covering the Uronica allowed a select few direct access to the Anointed One, Christ himself: one opening led to his knee, another to his feet, which "allowed for the ritual washing of the icon" as well as the pope's kisses.[1540] The pope, in kissing the feet of the Jesus icon, becomes like the Magdalene, who washed and kissed the feet of Christ. And naturally oil would trickle down from the knee, anointing the feet, recalling perhaps the time when Mary anointed Jesus' feet with nard from the alabaster jar. Why would Innocent III have left an opening for holy oil? And why did oil flow from the knee of Christ? The Gospel tells of blood and water flowing from the side of Christ; there is no mention of oil from the knee. Again, during Innocent III's reign, Christ appeared more divine that human: rather than exuding blood as all mortals do, the body of the Christ oozed holy oil.

The Temple of Solomon: Gregory IX & Corpus Domini

The perception of holy oil continued to evolve over the course of the thirteenth century. The battle for Roman primacy did not end with the reign of Innocent III in 1216. Nor did the ecclesiastical hierarchy's struggle to assert the Latin Church's centrality as *mediatrix* of salvation through the sacraments, particularly the Eucharist. Textual and iconographic sources from the thirteenth century demonstrated how Santa Maria in Trastevere and her *fons olei* continued to figure prominently in the ongoing discourse about papal primacy and *mater ecclesia* as a source of oil that sanctified or legitimized the anointed. On June 22, 1232, in the sixth year of his pontificate and at the ripe age of 87, Pope Gregory IX (r. 1227-1241) promulgated a letter from Spoleto for the feast

---

[1540] Noreen, "Re-Covering Christ," 122, 124.

of the dedication of Santa Maria in Trastevere. In this letter, Gregory IX compared Santa Maria in

Trastevere with the Temple of Solomon in Jerusalem.[1541] Gregory IX alluded to the most notable

phases of Santa Maria in Trastevere's history: her reconstruction by Innocent II and later

consecration by Innocent III. Gregory IX compared the two popes to Kings David and Solomon,

respectively. According to Gregory IX, the work that the father began, the son completed. The

theme of the son completing the work begun by the father is poignant give that Gregory IX was

Innocent III's nephew – a euphemism, perhaps, for the pope's own son.[1542] Even if not a direct

descendent of Innocent III, Gregory IX expressed concern for the continuity of the family's *casa*.

Given the power and influence of medieval popes within the secular and ecclesiastical

realms, papal succession would have been foremost in the minds of these leaders. Although the

Second Lateran Council in 1139 condemned marriage and concubinage (Canons 6,7,11), the

problem persisted to the extent that the rule was reinforced again at the Third Lateran Council in

1179 (Canon 11) and the Fourth Lateran Council in 1215 (Canon 6). Bishops of Rome were known

to have strategically elevated their nephews or close relatives (potentially their own sons) to the

status of Cardinal. Thus, only the sons of Rome's most powerful families ascended to the See of

Peter. For medieval kings, preserving one's *casa* was a central concern and appears to have been no

less so for medieval popes. If the Bishops of Rome were equally concerned with their descendants

or family members securing the See of Peter, this would have been a concern they could not express

openly, but only in veiled allegories, such as the one of David and Solomon.

Gregory IX's letter expressing his concern for his family reigning in perpetuity surfaced in

Vat. lat. 8429, a manuscript entitled *Acta Consecrationis* that dates to the late seventeenth or eighteenth

---

[1541] To my knowledge, there are two extant manuscript copies of the letter. One in the Archivum Secretum Vaticanum (SAV Reg. Vat. 16, fol. 15v-16r) and a copy in a seventeenth century composite manuscript housed in the Biblioteca Apostolica Vaticana (BAV Vat. lat. 8429). See Appendix II for a transcription of the letter.

[1542] Agostino Paravicini Bagliani, *Cardinali di Curia e familiae cardinalizie dal 1227 al 1254*, Italia Sacra, 18-19 (Padova: Antenore, 1972).

century. The original letter, or at least a thirteenth century copy, is preserved in the Archivio Segreto

Vaticano.[1543] This composite manuscript contains a few folios of what appear to have been excerpts

from the liturgical readings for the feast of the dedication of Santa Maria in Trastevere.[1544] In a

preface to Gregory IX's letter an anonymous author argued for the authenticity of the historical

evidence that testified to Innocent II's having reconstructed Santa Maria in Trastevere and Innocent

III's consecration.[1545] The author reminded readers that Innocent II's successor, Innocent III,

liberated Christian lands from the hands of the infidels.[1546]

Gregory IX's letter for the feast of the dedication of Santa Maria in Trastevere opened with a

discussion of King David's desire to build the Ark of the Covenant and in so doing, to expand

God's cult. In his discourse, the pope appeared less concerned with connecting the Church of the

present day with Rome's ancient pagan past, including its emperors. Rather, Gregory IX sought to

depict Rome as the New Jerusalem. The pope retold the church's history using Jewish figures from

the past – and not just ordinary people – but the most celebrated kings. The layering of symbolic

parallels in Gregory IX's letter is not surprisingly fluid. King David could represent Innocent II who

wanted to build the temple but only began the work completed by his successor, Solomon. King

David, however, as the *vir bellator* could have equally represented Innocent III who waged war on the

Albigensians and in the Holy Land. If Innocent III represented David, Gregory IX would fill the

role of Solomon, who continued the work begun by the "father." Like Innocent III, Gregory IX

[1543] SAV Reg. lat. 16, fol.15v-16r. See also Brepols Papal Letter Database. No. 000809 for a summary.

[1544] Roman numerals appear next to the passages.

[1545] "…testantur antiqui, ac moderni rerum Ecclesiasticarum Scriptores Vide Martinum Polonum in Chronico, Panuinium de VII: urb: Ecc: Ciacconium in Vita Innoc. III {?} Sed tempus modus, et sollemnitas ex sequentibus authenticis documentis apertius demonstrantur. Excerpta De perantiquo lectionaris MS: in pergameno composito ab Auctore Innocentis III Coaeuo, quod asseruatur Archivo S⁻ Mariae, quodque premittit narrationi de consecratione historiam aedificationis Basilicae sub Innocentio II." BAV Vat. lat. 8429, fol. 160r.

[1546] "Is cùm pacem Urbi Romanae caeterisque orbis Christianae Prouinciis restituisset deliberationem suscepit de Terra Sancta ex manibus Infidelium liberanda sed quoniam arouum/s negocium, ardua requirit consilia, et quod omnes tangit ab omnibus debet comprobari, ideò prudentissimus Pontifex de Terrae Sanctae Liberatione consilia cum uniuersa Christianitate communicare volens." BAV Vat. lat. 8429, fol. 160v.

continued the crusade against heresy. Any good work of literature or liturgy, however, plays with

meanings on multiple levels.

> David, the most pious of kings, wanting to expand the cult of the Lord, thought to build a
> house in which he might place the Ark of the Covenant of the Lord and prepared everything
> for its construction. But having been heard by the Lord, since for Him he was a warlike man
> and had poured forth much blood, he did not build the house in the Lord's name. King
> Solomon, his son, whom the father himself had chosen to make the house, with God
> commanding and helping, finished the Temple, with the altar and the vessel fulfilling the
> divine cult, he solemnly consecrated the Temple.[1547]

Gregory IX's letter then continues with an account that mirrors closely the description of Innocent

III's procession to Santa Maria in Trastevere during the Fourth Lateran Council, as recorded in the

Eyewitness Account.[1548]

> And so with all the sons of Israel seeing how greatly the majesty of the Lord had filled the
> Temple and fire had come from the heavens and the glory of the Lord had come over them
> and how they celebrated sacrificing offerings in the presence of the Lord, then similarly the
> King Solomon therefore made solemnity at that time for seven days and all the Israelites
> processed vigorously with him to the great church…[1549] He dedicated the House of the
> Lord, shut by him and the altar in seven days and all the days were celebrated with solemnity.
> On the twenty-third day he sent the people away to their tabernacle rejoicing and delighting
> over the good the House of David had done and by his people of Israel.[1550]

[1547] "David Regum Pyssimus uolens cultum Domini amplicare cogitauit edificare domum, in qua arcam foederis domini collocaret et ad edificandam eam omnia preparauit, sed audito à Domino, quod pro eo quod fuerat vir Bellator, et multum sanguinis fuderat, non edificaret nomini suo Domum, Salomon Rex filius eius, quod Pater ipsius facere optaverat, iubente Deo, et auxiliante perficiens Templum cum Altari, et vasis ad diuinum cultum explendum fecit solempniter consecrare…" SAV Reg. lat.16, 15v.

[1548] Kuttner and García, "A New Eyewitness Account of the Fourth Lateran Council."

[1549] The text appears to be a variation on the account of Salomon building the Temple in 2 Chron 5:3: "And all the men of Israel came to the king in the solemn day of the seventh month." The Vulgate reads: "Venerunt itaque ad regem omnes viri Israel in die solemni mensis septimi."

[1550] "…tàm idem Rex, quàm omnes filii Isrhaelis videntes quod Maiestas Domini [domum] repleuisset eandem, venissetque ignis de C[a]elo, et gloria Domini super eam, et immolantes victimas coram Domino [in tubis ymnis et organis diem sollempnem domino] celebrarunt, fecit ergo Salomon sollempnitatem in Tempore illo septem diebus, et omnis Isrhaeliticus cum eo magna Ecclesia ualde ab introitu Emath, usque ad Torrentem Egypti, fecitque die VIIIᴬ: collectam, eo quod dedicasset domum Domini, et altare septem diebus, et sollempnitate diebus totidem celebrata, in

After drawing a close analogy between Roman Christians and ancient Israelites, Gregory IX delineated the distinction between Christianity and Judaism. In keeping with the Christian exegetical tradition (and potentially to the dismay of contemporary readers) Gregory IX explained how Christianity surpassed Judaism to become a more perfect and divine religion.

> If therefore in the Old Testament the temple and altar had a famous consecration, how much more now ought the more famous temple to have a new consecration, when there is not less difference between this temple and that temple than between light and darkness? For in that temple, which was made from carved stone, the Ark of the Covenant of the Lord rested.[1551] But in that temple [Santa Maria in Trastevere] which was prefigured [*designabatur*] in the other temple [in Jerusalem] and which was constructed from living stones, Christ stands, the High Priest [*pontifex*] of future good things...[1552]

Having established the preeminence of the Christian church over the Judaic temple, Gregory IX offered an extended meditation on the difference between Jewish and Christian sacrifice, characterizing Christian sacrifice as superior since God himself was both the priest and the offering.

> Evidently on that carnal altar, the unreasoning sacrificial victims were slaughtered. Truly on that [Christian] altar, that single and life-giving holocaust is always offered, because once on the altar of the cross, for the redemption of humankind, He stood sacrificed, evidently the Only-Begotten Son of God, Jesus Christ, himself likewise the sacrifice and the priest...[1553]

Gregory IX addressed the centrality of the Eucharist in medieval Christian devotion, following Innocent III's establishing the doctrine of transubstantiation at the Fourth Lateran

---

uigesimo tertio die dimisit Populum ad Tabernacula sua laetantes, atque gaudentes super bono quod fecerat dominus Dauid, ac Populo suo Isrhaelis." SAV Reg. lat.16, fol.15v.

[1551] God is in the ark and the ark is in the Temple. See 2 Chronicles 7:1 "salomon fundens preces."

[1552] "Si ergo in veteri Testamento tàm celebris habebatur Templi consecratio, et altaris, quanto magis nunc in nouo debet haberi celebrior, cum non minus inter illud, et istud Templum, quam inter lucem distet et umbram? In illo enim Templo, quod erat de sectis lapidibus arca foederis domini, acquieuit, in isto autem quod designabatur in illo, quod ex uiuis lapidibus est constructum Christus assistit Pontifex futurorum bonorum..." SAV Reg. lat.16, fol.15v.

[1553] "In illo quippe altari Carnales, et irrationabiles hostiae mactabantur, in isto uero illud unicum, et uiuificum holocaustum semper offertur quod pro redemptione humani generis semel in ara Crucis extitit immolatum, Unigenitus uidelicet Dei filius Jesus Christus, idem ipse Sacrificium, et Sacerdos..." SAV Reg. lat.16, fol.15v.

Council but before the institution of Corpus Christi (also called Corpus Domini) as a universal feast.

Pope Urban IV (r. 1261-1264) first promulgated the feast in 1264, from Orvieto, which had become

a hotbed of Cathar heresy.[1554] Pope John XXII (r. 1316-1334) later made the celebration of the feast

universal, such that by the early fourteenth century, the feast of the Lord's Body was celebrated

throughout the Latin West.[1555]

Establishing a distinction between carnal sacrifice taking place on the altar of the Israelites

and the spiritual sacrifice within the altars of Christian churches, Gregory IX discussed Santa Maria

in Trastevere as *mater* and *dei genitrix* and as the gathering point of the ecclesiastical hierarchy during

the Fourth Lateran Council. Gregory IX expressed the wish that not just Roman Christians, but that

all Christians (*christianus populus*) would venerate Santa Maria in Trastevere and offered an indulgence

to all who visited her. Nowhere in his letter did Gregory IX refer to the legendary *fons olei* – perhaps

to avoid evoking the reign of Augustus who had long been the model for secular emperors and

kings in the Latin West.

> Truly do great and lofty is the sacrament of this kind, everywhere far and great, that we may
> prevail to imitate Pope Innocent, of happy memory,[1556] our predecessor who solemnly
> consecrated your church in honor of the Mother of God with Patriarchs, Archbishops,
> Bishops, Cardinals and with Prelates of other churches, who came to the General Council in
> his time 17 Kalends of December. We, therefore, desiring that the Christian people might
> venerate the most Glorious Virgin, Blessed among women, with all the power of the intellect
> and, with suitable honors, frequent the same church consecrated to the virgin herself and the
> station we are establishing on the day of the her consecration, in herself, Mercy of the
> Omnipotent God and of his blessed Apostles Peter and Paul.[1557]

[1554] Lansing, *Power & Purity*, 2001.

[1555] Miri Rubin, *Corpus Christi: The Eucharist in Late Medieval Culture* (Cambridge [England] ; New York: Cambridge University Press, 1991), 164–85.

[1556] The abbreviation in Reg. lat.16, fol.16r: "fe.re.I.pp." Vat. lat. 8429, fol.163r, partially expanded the abbreviation: "felic.record."

[1557] "Quia uero tàm magna et arduum est huiusmodi sacramentum, ubique longe maius, quàm nos exprimere ualeamus feliciter recordantibus Innocentius Papa predecessor noster Ecclesiam vestram in honorem dei Genitricis assistentibus sibi Patriarchis, Archiepiscopis, Episcopis, Cardinalis, et aliis Ecclesiarum Prelatis, qui uenerunt ad Concilium generale

The anonymous author who transcribed Gregory IX's letter in the *Acta Consecrationis* testified once again to the authenticity of the sources and explained their origins. He verified that the Congregation of Holy Ritual had given its approval regarding the authenticity of the documents: "A cleric of Santa Maria in Trastevere now reads aloud the proper readings for the day of dedication, compiled from several ancient contracts, not just one, which were approved by the Congregation of Holy Rituals, which we here attach, having been especially expressly approved in the year 1687."[1558] Although in his letter Gregory IX had made no direct reference to Santa Maria in Trastevere's fountain of holy oil, the fourth reading for the dedication (Lectio IV) which directly followed the pope's letter, mentioned the *fons olei* as a desirable destination for devotion: "Among the special temples of the city, the Basilica of Santa Maria in Trastevere rightly shines with every kind of ornament. The place in which the fountain of oil erupted at the Lord's advent is foremost in attracting veneration."[1559] Thus Vat. Lat. 8429, dating from the late seventeenth or eighteenth century, testified to the *fons olei* being a popular place for pilgrimage long after the reigns of Innocent II, Innocent III and Gregory IX.

A Slippery Legend: the Fons Olei in the Legenda Aurea

In the 1260's, the Dominican Friar Jacobus de Voragine composed *The Golden Legend* (*Legenda Aurea*), a trove of miraculous tales about the saints, including tales about oil miraculously

---

tempore ipsius XVII: Kale: Decembris solempniter consecravit: Nos igitur cupientes ut populus Christianus gloriosissimam virginem in mulieribus Benedictam toto mentis conamine uenerentur, et congruis frequentetur honoribus eadem Ecclesia in honorem ipsius virginis consecrata, et stationem constituentes in die consecrationis eius in ipsa de omnipotentis dei misericordia, et Beatorum Petri, et Pauli Apostolorum eius, ac ea, quam nobis Dominus indulsit authoritate confisi omnibus vere paenitentibus, et confessis, qui Ecclesiam ipsam in die dedicationis eiusdem, et usque ad octauas ipsius uenerabiliter uisitauerint annum unum de iniuncta sibi paenitentia misericorditer relaxamus." SAV Reg. lat.16, fol.16r.

[1558] "Clerus Sanctae Mariae Transtyberim recitat nunc proprias lectiones diei dedicationis ex antiquioribus contractis conflatas, non semel approbatas à sacram Congregatione rituum, et impressas praesertim anno MDCLXXXVII quas hic annectimus." BAV Vat. lat. 8429, fol.163v.

[1559] "Inter praecipua Urbis Templa merito numerator Basilica S. Mariae Transtyberim omni ornamentorum genere maxime illustris. Venerationem in primis conciliat locus, in quo olei fons aduentante Domino erupit." BAV Vat. lat. 8429, fol.163v.

seeping from their tombs. The compilation included a combination of narrative and expository

chapters, which Eamon Duffy called an "encyclopedic handbook of doctrine, clearly designed to

provide material for instruction and preaching" in contrast with the narrative accounts of the lives of

saints.[1560] In one of these expository chapters, "The Birth of Our Lord Jesus Christ according to the

Flesh," Jacobus de Voragine discussed Santa Maria in Trastevere's legendary *fons olei*, giving slightly

new twists to an old story. His primary sources for the legend appear to have been Orosius, Peter

Comestor, and Innocent III. Contextualizing the birth of Christ within the larger history of the

Roman empire, Voragine emphasized the reign of peace that accompanied the Incarnation, like

other authors before him: "When the Son of God became incarnate, the universe enjoyed such

peace that the emperor of the Romans reigned alone and peacefully over the whole world. It was the

Lord's will that since he was coming to give us peace in time and in eternity, temporal peace should

lend luster to the time of his birth."[1561] Then, however, Voragine drew directly on Innocent III's

Second Sermon on the Nativity – perhaps it lay open before him as he composed – since the

parallels are evident. Like Innocent III, Voragine described the four ways God generated human

beings or the four modalities of human existence (i.e. from neither man or woman, from man alone,

from man and woman together and from woman alone). Apparently inspired by an Aristotelian or

Scholastic text, Voragine delineated how the Christ was "made manifest through every level or class

of creatures."[1562] The hierarchy of creatures included those with mere existence (such as stones) as

well as creatures with reason and understanding (human beings and angels, respectively). The

creatures enjoying existence but without reason or understanding were "simply material or

corporeal, like stones."[1563]

[1560] Eamon Duffy, "Introduction," in *The Golden Legend: Readings on the Saints* (Princeton: Princeton University Press, 2012), xiii.

[1561] Jacobus de Voragine, *The Golden Legend: Readings on the Saints*, trans. William Granger Ryan (Princeton: Princeton University Press, 2012), 37.

[1562] Ibid., 39.

[1563] Ibid.

Even creatures with mere existence could herald the birth of a savior, irrational though they were. Voragine appears to have borrowed a legend from the *Mirabilia Romae* or another source to describe how even inanimate idols could proclaim a savior's birth. The *Mirabilia Romae* recounted how Romulus placed a golden image between two temples on the Via dei Fori Imperiali, which stretched from the Colosseum past Trajan's column. Romulus claimed that the image would remain until a virgin bore a child: "Romulus set his golden image saying: 'It shall not fall until a virgin bears a child.' And as soon as the Virgin bore a son, the image fell down."[1564] This story was akin to the one Nicholas of Clairvaux told regarding the Temple of Peace, which he misattributed to Augustus. The idol in Voragine's story bore a close resemblance to the *Sedes sapientiae*, which by the mid-thirteenth century would have been a well-established form of devotion, particular in France:

> ...we read in [Peter Comestor's] *Scholastic History* that the prophet Jeremiah, going down to Egypt after the death of Godolias, indicated to the Egyptian kings that their idols would fall to pieces when a virgin bore a son. For that reason the priests of the idols made a statue of a virgin holding a male child on her lap, set it up in a secret place in the temple, and there worshiped it. When King Ptolemy asked them the meaning of this, they told him that it was a mystery handed down by the fathers, who had received it from a holy man, a prophet and they believed that what was foretold would really happen.[1565]

Although the worship of an idol, even of a virgin and her child, may have appeared misdirected, Voragine explained how a messianic prophecy coincided with an oppressed people throwing off the yoke of tyranny. The stone-like idols were not the only heralds of Christ's birth. Within the category of non-rational creatures, three subdivisions of creatures existed: opaque, transparent or pervious, and lucid or luminous creatures. In his discussion of transparent or pervious beings, Voragine retold the legend of the *fons olei*.

[1564] Nichols, *The Marvels of Rome - Mirabilia Urbis Romae*, 9.
[1565] De Voragine, *The Golden Legend*, 40.

Now regarding transparent or pervious corporeal beings: in the night of the Lord's birth the darkness of night was turned into the brightness of day. In Rome, it also happened (as attested by Orosius and Pope Innocent III) that a fountain of water turned to oil and burst into the Tiber, spreading very widely all that day; and the Sibyl had foretold that when a fountain of oil sprang up, a Saviour would be born.[1566]

Saying nothing about the *taberna emeritoria* or Santa Maria in Trastevere in particular, Voragine focused instead on invoking established authorities, who had also testified to the veracity of the legend. Voragine's embellished the legend, however, by saying the gushing liquid transformed from water to oil. Like Innocent III, Voragine presented the oil as the fulfillment of the Sibyl's prophecy.

While Voragine never mentioned Santa Maria in Trastevere by name in connection with the *fons olei* or Christ's birth, he cited the foundation legend of Santa Maria Nuova as miraculous proof of Mary's virginity. Voragine gave five proofs for the virginity of Mary, perhaps in imitation of Anselm of Canterbury's five proofs for the existence of God. The first proof was the prophecy of Isaiah (7:14): "Behold the virgin will conceive and bear a son..." which incidentally appeared in the apse mosaic of Santa Maria in Trastevere.[1567] The second and third proofs were prefigurations from the Hebrew Scriptures.[1568] The third proof was an account of divine intervention when a woman tried to examine Mary to verify her virginity. The fifth and final proof was the collapse of the Temple of Peace in Rome (*Ara Pacis*), which Voragine proffered as miraculous evidence of Mary's purity. This is the same temple the Nicholas of Clairvaux said collapsed at the moment of Christ's birth – when the virgin gave birth to a flower, juxtaposing the ruin of Rome and Jerusalem with the peace of Bethlehem. Again, Voragine was drawing on the authority of Innocent III:

As Pope Innocent III testifies, during the twelve years when Rome enjoyed peace, the Romans built a Temple of Peace and placed a statue of Romulus in it. Apollo was asked how

---

[1566] Ibid.

[1567] See Chapter 9.

[1568] Aaron's staff and Ezechiel's gate.

long the temple would stand, and the answer was that it would be until a virgin bore a child. Hearing this, the people said that the temple was eternal, for they thought it impossible that such a thing could happen; and an inscription, TEMPLUM PACIS AETERNUM, was carved over the doors. But the very night when Mary bore Christ, the temple crumbled to the ground, and on its site the church of Santa Maria Nuova stands today."[1569]

In Voragine's retelling of the Temple of Peace legend, the destruction of the temple coincided with foundation of Santa Maria Nuova but not the appearance of the *fons olei*. Also, according to Voragine, the Romans consulted Apollo rather than the Sibyl, who by the High Middle Ages enjoyed a reputation as a prophet of Christ.

Voragine's legend about the founding of Santa Maria Nuova was reminiscent of the founding legend for Santa Maria in Ara Coeli which, according the *Mirabilia Romae,* was the location where Augustus consulted the Sibyl and received the vision of the virgin in the sky holding a child, announcing to Octavian that he would rule the world as Augustus. Voragine used this legend to discussion the third and final subcategory of existential creatures who manifested Christ's birth: "luminous corporeal creatures, such as the super-celestial."[1570] God made Christ's birth known to the super-celestial creatures, who in turn announced the birth to others. These super-celestial beings included the star which appeared in Bethlehem, and the marvelous celestial occurrence which long ago Orosius had paired with the *fons olei* legend: a halo around the sun. Voragine, however, explicitly connected the usual celestial occurrence with Santa Maria Ara Coeli without making any reference of Santa Maria in Trastevere or her *fons olei*.[1571] Voragine even quoted Orosius' account of the celestial spectacle that throughout the medieval period authors had juxtaposed with the bursting of oil from

---

[1569] De Voragine, *The Golden Legend*, 38-39.
[1570] Ibid., 40.
[1571] De Voragine, *The Golden Legend*, 40.

the Tiber.[1572] The author of the *Golden Legend* was again, however, curiously silent about the gushing

oil.

THE FONS OLEI IN THE MIND OF GOD: BONAVENTURE'S TAKE ON THE LEGEND

Voragine was not the only mendicant friar responsible for disseminating the legend of the

fons olei in the thirteenth century. Bonaventure (c.1221-1274), the Franciscan philosopher and author

of the *Journey of the Mind into God* (*Itinerarium Mentis in Deum*) (1259), which charts the movement of

the mind and spirit toward God, including how to perceive the signs or vestiges of divine presence

in the material and spiritual realms, referred to the *fons olei* in two of his sermons. Sermon 88, The

Nativity of the Lord, addressed the question of celestial wonders at the moment of Christ's birth,

including the radiant rainbow that appeared around the sun and how divinity was masked in flesh as

if in a cloud. Some themes of this sermon parallel those of Gregory IX's letter, particularly an

oblique reference to the theme of a father rebuilding a temple, which echoed Gregory IX's

discussion of Innocent II's rebuilding of Santa Maria in Trastevere. If Bonaventure's reference to

these popes was intended, however, it was masqued. Furthermore, it is unclear how Bonaventure

would have been familiar with Gregory IX's letter. If the text had in fact been incorporated into the

liturgy of the feast of the dedication (15 November) by the late thirteenth century, Bonaventure may

have potentially encountered these ideas via the liturgy.

Although Bonaventure was born in Lazio in the town of Bagnoregio, he spent little of his

adult life on the Italic peninsula, since he received his scholarly and religious training at the

University of Paris. In 1273 Bonaventure was appointed bishop of Albano, a town some fifteen

miles southeast of Rome, but was consecrated bishop in Lyon. He may have thus spent little or no

---

[1572] "The emperor, understanding that the child he had seen was greater than he, offered incense to him and refused to
be called God. With reference to this Orosius says: 'In Octavian's day, about the third hour, in the limpid, pure, serene
sky, a circle that looked like a rainbow surrounded the orb of the sun, as if to show that One was to come who alone had
made the sun and the whole world and ruled it." Ibid., 40-41.

time in or near Rome given that after his consecration as bishop he became a leading figure at the second Council of Lyon, which opened on May 7, 1274. He died shortly thereafter – on July 15 of the same year.[1573] Although we cannot know with certainty if Bonaventure intended to refer to Gregory IX's letter for the feast of Santa Maria in Trastevere's dedication, beyond a doubt he knew about the *fons olei*, which he referred to as a sign of God's presence, abundant mercy and goodness, which coincided with Christ's birth.

The great mystery of the Incarnation, according to Bonaventure, was best understood through the metaphor of a heavenly rainbow, presumably the rainbow that appeared around the sun at the start of Augustus' reign and the rainbow that appeared to Noah after the flood in Genesis 9:11-17, which was a sign of God's covenant with his people. The Genesis passage and image of the rainbow (*arca*) may have appealed to Bonaventure for two reasons at least. First, the Genesis passage makes several references to God's fidelity to humanity's carnal existence. God's promise to preserve human flesh would have been Scriptural evidence contradicting the Cathars' dualist beliefs. Second, the rainbow in the sky would allow Bonaventure to pun on the word *arca*, which meant both arc (rainbow) and ark (the Ark of the Covenant), in which the presence of God dwelt for the Hebrew people.

In Genesis, God communicated his covenant to the Hebrew people through the miraculous display of light and color in the sky and promised never again to destroy "all flesh": "God said…I will establish my covenant with you, and all flesh shall be no more destroyed with the waters of a flood…I will set my bow in the clouds, and it shall be the sign of a covenant between me, and between the earth."[1574] The themes of this pericope echo the words of the apse mosaic in Santa Maria in Trastevere, where Jesus' book bore the words "I will place my throne within you." *Ponam in*

[1573] Christopher M. Cullen, *Bonaventure*, Great Medieval Thinkers (New York ; Oxford: Oxford University Press, 2006), 8-14.
[1574] Gen. 9:11-15.

te thronum meum. In the Genesis passage, the Vulgate translation of the Hebrew uses the same verb: *arcum meum ponam in nubibus.* Instead of God promising to place his throne within the Virgin Mary, in the Genesis passage, God promised to place his rainbow (*arcum*) in the clouds, which corresponded perfectly with Bernard of Clairvaux's *Commentary on the Book of Revelation,* in which he interprets heaven to be the Blessed Virgin Mary. In the Book of Revelation, the Bride who came down from heaven, adorned for her spouse was the heavenly city, Jerusalem. Thus, the movement for Christian was one towards heaven, toward Jerusalem, where God lived eternally and where his covenant (*foedus, foedaris*) rested. And yet, Bonaventure suggested that the covenant in heaven, represented by the rainbow or arc, was akin to the Incarnation, God's covenant with humanity on earth, in the flesh.

Bonaventure's sermon, knowingly or not, played on one of the central themes in Gregory IX's letter for Santa Maria in Trastevere: the arc and the ark. Bonaventure discussed the rainbow (arc) as if it were the Ark of the Covenant (*arca foederis*).[1575] One can easily see how Bonaventure made the conceptual leap from the rainbow of the Genesis to the Ark of the Covenant placed in the Temple in Jerusalem: "I will place my arc in the clouds, and it will be a sign of the covenant between me and the earth"[1576] (*arcum meum ponam in nubibus, et erit signum foederis inter me et inter terram*). For Bonaventure, the rainbow in the clouds became a symbol for the Incarnation, where the divinity of God was immersed and partially hidden in human flesh, symbolized by the clouds.[1577] The radiance of the sun represented the divinity of God which, when mixed with the dew or rain of the clouds, produced Christ the rainbow.

[1575] Bonaventure may have also been drawing on Hugh of St. Victor's *The Mystical Ark of Noah,* in which the Victorine canon delineated the various mystical meanings of Noah's Ark. See Conrad Rudolph, *The Mystic Ark: Hugh of Saint Victor, Art, and Thought in the Twelfth Century* (New York, NY: Cambridge University Press, 2014).

[1576] Gen. 9:11-15.

[1577] "Sub metaphora ergo iridis sive caelestis arcus Dei potentia nobis inclinata per humanitatem ostenditur, cum dicit sapiens: Vide arcum, id est, divinam maiestatem considera quasi per nubem humanitatis, se mundo inclinantem per incarnationis mysterium et condescendentem per novae nativitatis in carne sacramentum; et benedic, per recognitionem, qui fecit illum, hoc est Patrem aeternum qui sic eum incarnari et nasci ordinavit." LLT: Bonaventura, Sermones de tempore, Sermo 88, par. 2.

Perhaps Bonaventure had a sense of humor and wished to play with or pun on the word *arca*. One has to wonder too if Bonaventure was punning on the word 'cloud' (*nubes, nubis*) given that the Latin verb *nubo, nubere* means "to marry, to be married." Thus *in nube* could mean either 'in the cloud' or as the second-person imperative, "Marry!" "Clouds" (*nubis*) could also mean "You marry" (in the singular). Here again, the themes of marriage, fertility and moisture intertwine. In Bonaventure's metaphorical reading of the heavens, the cloud is concave (*nube concave*). Though he does not say so directly, the image of the concave cloud suggests the belly of the Virgin before giving birth. Pregnant with rain, the cloud brings forth a rainbow:

> Note, therefore, that Christ born means the rainbow (*arcus*) of heaven, on account of eight virtuous qualities, which are represented in the arc according and were in Christ's birth through every season according to truth. For how greatly the rainbow is begotten from the substance created from the flashing and rebounding of the rays of the sun in the concave cloud, bedewed and rainy. If the substance of Christ's birth was made as great in the body and in the soul from the reflection of the rays and of the virtues of the blessed Trinity, so also was the eternal sun in the glorious Virgin or in human nature made, as in the cloud, concave through profound humility, bedewed and rain-bringing through the arriving abundance of the Holy Spirit, as in Ecclesiastes 50: 'As the rainbow giving light in the bright clouds' means concerning Christ's birth.[1578]

Bonaventure's quotation from Ecclesiastes 50:8 was the second half of an analogy, in which the author of Ecclesiastes compared Simon, a high priest whose father repaired and strengthened the temple, to a star born of a cloud: "He shone in his days as the morning star in the midst of a

---

[1578] "Nota ergo, quod Christus natus dicitur arcus caelestis propter octo proprietates |55r| virtuales, quae sunt in arcu secundum repraesentationem et fuerunt in Christo nato per omne tempus secundum veritatem. Nam arcus quantum ad substantiam procreatur ex refulgentia et repercussione radiorum solarium in nube concava, rorida et imbrifera. Sic substantia Christi nati quantum ad corpus et animam procreata est ex reflexione radiorum et virtutum beatissimae Trinitatis tanquam solis aeterni in Virginem gloriosam sive in naturam humanam, tanquam in nube concava per humilitatem profundam, rorida et imbrifera per Spiritus sancti supervenientem abundantiam, Eccli. 50: Quasi arcus refulgens inter nebulas gloriae etc., dicitur de Christo nato." LLT: Bonaventura, Sermones de tempore, Sermo 88, par.3.

cloud, and as the moon at the full…And as the rainbow giving light in the bright clouds…"[1579] In

discussing a cloud giving forth life-giving, salvific liquid, Bonaventure was just one step away from

the *fons olei* dispensing its miraculous liquid. Santa Maria in Trastevere's legendary fountain was,

according to Bonaventure, the fulfillment of the Hebrew prophecy that God would reveal Himself

not in a drought, but amidst an abundance of life-giving liquid:

> The Lord of humility shows himself in the sky, because on his account Bede, the Master of
> History, says 'because for forty years before the judgment He will not appear in a sign of
> dryness or deficiency of elements.' Just as Christ's birth signified a predominance of
> goodness, compassion and grace were given to the world, as a sign of Christ's birth the
> Roman fountain of oil erupted and flowed in the Tiber, Ezechiel 1: 'Just like a rainbow,
> when it was in a cloud on a rainy day.'[1580]

Here again, Bonaventure was playing with words. His word-choice for "humility" as in "the

Lord of humility" (*Dominum humiditatis*) could also be read as the adjective "humid" (*humidus*).

Instead of choosing *humilitatis* – which bears nearly the same meaning as *humiditatis,* Bonaventure

chose the word that evoked moisture to say the God was the God not just of humility, but of

humidity. In so doing, the philosopher conveyed to his reader a perception of God as a God of

lightness and humor rather than a God of vengeance or violence. Bonaventure's God poured out an

abundance of joy as well as oil – the oil of gladness.

The theme of a peaceful and loving divine presence also permeated Bonaventure's Sermon

111. Bonaventure enumerated the historical instances in which miracles occurred heralding the

Christ's birth. He wrote: "According to various histories, these are the miracles revealed to the sinful

---

[1579] Eccl. 50:6-8.

[1580] "Dominium humiditatis in aere significat; propter quod dicit Beda et Magister in Historia, 'quod per quadraginta annis ante iudicium non apparebit in signum desiccationis et defectionis elementorum.' Sic Christus natus significavit praedominantiam pietatis et misericordiae et gratiae dandam mundo in cuius signum, nato Christo, Romae fons olei erupit et defluxit in Tyberim, Ezech. 1: Velut arcus, cum fuerit in nube in die pluviae." LLT: Bonaventura, Sermones de tempore, Sermo 88, par. 3.

people at Christ's birth."[1581] The fourth miracle was the fountain of oil. Bonaventure again affirmed

that the *fons olei* signaled the appearance of Christ who was compassion and love: "The Roman

fountain of oil erupted plentifully and flowed all the way to the Tiber, so that it might be revealed

that the fountain of tenderness and compassion was being born."[1582] In saying that Christ was

himself the fountain presented a variation among the interpretations of the significance of the oil. In

Bonaventure's reading, Christ supplanted Mary as the source of oil. He was himself not only the

Anointed, but the fountain – the source of the anointing oil itself.

MARY IN BETHLEHEM: THE CAVALLINI MOSAICS

While in Bonaventure's retelling of the *fons olei* legend, Christ may have eclipsed Mary,

relegating her to the clouds, the iconography of the late thirteenth century shifted her once again to

the foreground, making her the source of the legendary holy oil. In 1291, during the reign of the

Franciscan pope Nicholas IV (r.1288-1292), Cardinal Bertoldo Stefaneschi commissioned Pietro

Cavallini (1259-c.1330) to compose a series of mosaics, the Scenes from the Life of the Virgin, that

would encircle the nave just below the apse mosaic of Santa Maria in Trastevere. These mosaics

reflected the earlier shift in Latin Christendom toward Christ's humanity, shown through the life of

his human mother.[1583] The six scenes include the Nativity of Mary, the Annunciation, the Nativity of

Jesus, the Adoration of the Magi, the Presentation in the Temple, and the Dormition of Mary. The

mosaic of the Nativity of Jesus, which occupies a central position under the apse, depicts the *taberna*

meritoria with the river of oil flowing outwards into the Tiber River, alongside the Virgin who

reclines, having just given birth. The epigraphic text below the image referred to liquid gushing into

---

[1581] "Mirabilia autem ostensa genti peccatrici in Christi nativitate sunt ista, secundum historias varias." LLT: Bonaventura, Sermones de tempore, Sermo 111, par. 8.

[1582] "Quartus, Romae fons olei erupit largiter et usque in Tyberim fluxit diu, ut ostenderetur, quod fons pietatis et misericordiae nascebatur..." LLT: Bonaventura, Sermones de tempore, Sermo 111, par.8.

[1583] Vitaliano Tiberia, *I Mosaici del XII secolo e di Pietro Cavallini in Santa Maria in Trastevere : restauri e nouve ipotesi*, 1. ed. (Todi Perugia: Ediart, 1996), 40.

the Tiber.[1584] The epigraphic text presented several innovations. First, the verb "scaturire" appeared

for the first time in reference to the *fons olei*. This word, which means to "gush" or "bubble over"

suggests a greater degree of movement and energy than many of the other words commonly

associated with the movement of the oil from the font: *manare, emanare, fluere, profluere, effundere*. Some

words conveyed a sudden eruption or forceful emission of oil, such as *erumpere, exundare, prorumpere*.

Perhaps the artist chose *scaturire* because it best conveyed the natural bubbling of a spring and

suggested the flow of oil, which would fuse with the flow of the Tiber, was of like substance, just

like the two natures of God, the divinity and humanity.

Next to the mosaic of Jesus' Nativity, also in the central position under the apse, a mosaic

depicted the Adoration of the Magi and likewise contained a prominent representation of the *fons

olei*, this time flowing from the church, not the *taberna meritoria*. This shift, evidently signified that

with the birth of Christ, the pagan inn had transformed into a Marian church. The church rests on

what looks to be the top of a high mountain, despite the fact that in actuality Santa Maria in

Trastevere sits at the base of a high hill, the Janiculum Hill, rather than at the top. Effectively, the

building appears to float toward the upper portion of the panel, perhaps to suggest the

correspondence between the church and the heavenly Jerusalem. A river of oil flows from the

church, which bears a clear resemblance to the Santa Maria in Trastevere. The oily river then joins

with another stream flowing from the mountain. Since the mountain looks for all practical purposes

like a large rock, the mosaic may have been alluding to Numbers 20:11, when Moses strikes the rock

and an abundance of water gushes out. In addition to water gushing from the rock or mountain, a

small tree grows, likely representing an olive tree. The olive tree would have been an allusion to the

olive oil flowing from the *fons olei*, the olive branch offered to Noah after the Flood, and the Mount

of Olives in Jerusalem, where Christ prayed before the Crucifixion. From the highly positioned

---

[1584] "Iam puerum iam summe pater post tempore natum. Accipimus genitum tibi quem nos esse coeuum. Credimus hinc
{?} olei scaturire liquamina Tybrim."

church, the river of oil flows down to the lower part of the mosaic, where the three magi offer their gifts to the Christ child who sits on Mary's lap. The Church celebrated the encounter between Christ and the magi as the feast of the Epiphany, the day when, according to Orosius, the oil flowed in Rome.

In his mosaic Cavallini reinforced the depiction of Mary as the *sedes sapientiae* by positioning her on a throne. The Christ child, though in Mary's lap, lowers his hands as if he were already the priest, receiving the gifts brought to the altar during the Mass. Among the gifts, naturally, is myrrh, which would have been used to make oil fragrant. The epigraphical text below the image makes no mention of the oil but focuses instead on the appearance of the star and the gifts presented to the Prince of Peace.[1585] In these mosaics, we see a return to depictions of Mary and Christ's humanity. While in the early medieval period, authors predominantly associated the *fons olei* with the rule of the pagan emperor, Augustus, over the course of the High Middle Ages a distinct shift occurred. Boniface VIII strategy for making Rome a center for pilgrimage and Christian devotion emerged at a time when the papacy's authority tottered. Conflicts with Philip IV of France and certain cardinals within the Church had greatly diminished Boniface VIII's power, despite his continued claims to papal omnipotence. The papal bull *Unam sanctam* (1302) made inflated claims to the pope's *plenitudo potestatis* in the absence of actual power over either the spiritual or temporal realms, as both the King of France and the pope's bishops flagrantly defied Boniface.

The miraculous oil flowing in Rome no longer signified the eternal reign of a male secular ruler. Rather, the oil appeared from a woman, who gave birth to a son. In the midst of the conflict between the papacy and heretics or secular rulers, the image of the *fons olei* became a symbol for the pope's own power – the *plenitudo potestatis* – that flowed directly from God into eternity and which was the source of all other earthly power and authority. This perception of the fountain, however,

---

[1585] "Gentibus ignotus stella duce noscitur infans in presepe iacens celi terreque profundi conditor atque magi myrram thus accipit aurum."

ebbed over the course of the thirteenth century. In the hands of Franciscan artists and theologians, the miraculous fountain became once again the oil of gladness, a source of compassion and maternal mercy.

Although the number of myroblytes diminished in the Late Middle Ages, miraculous oil lingered in the imaginations of Europeans well into the Early Modern period. In particular, Rome's fascination with the *fons olei* only slowly waned. During the Babylonian Captivity, when the papacy moved to Avignon, Petrarch invoked the *fons olei* as a sign of Rome being the rightful home of Peter's see.[1586] In an *epistola metrica* addressed to Pope Clement VI, Petrarch, like Nicholas of Clairvaux, juxtaposed the destruction of pagan temples with the ruin of the Virgin's body during childbirth, both of which coincided with a torrent of olive oil flowing into the Tiber.[1587] Furthermore, tucked into the composite codex containing Santa Maria in Trastevere's *Acta Consecrationis*, which dates to the 1658-1688, a much older text languishes uncatalogued and virtually unnoticed: Antonine of Cremona's *Itinerarium* (1327), an itinerary for a pilgrimage to the Holy Land, which starts by detailing all relics in the basilicas in Rome and the many indulgences available to those who visit them. Composed at the time of the Avignon papacy (1309 – 1376) during the reign of John XXII (1316-1334), Cremona, a Franciscan, emphasized Rome as the *terra sancta*. According to the *Itinerarium*, in Saint John Lateran one could find the table where Jesus ate with his disciples as well as two ampullae of the blood and water that flowed from his side.[1588] As if the table and blood

---

[1586] In his *Epistola ad Johannem Columna*, Petrarca wrote: "Hic ninxit nonis Augusti; hinc rivus olei fluxit in Tiberim; hinc, ut fama est, monstrante Sibylla, senex Augustus Christum vidit infantem." Francesco Petrarca, *Epistolae de rebus familiaribus et variae*, ed., Joseph Fracassetti, Volume 1 (Florence: Typis Felicis Le Monnier, 1859), 1:313. A slightly different version of the text appears in Moretti: "Hinc vinctus Petrus nonis Augusti: hinc rivus olim (leg. olei) fluxit in Tyberim." Pietro Moretti and Antonio (Rome) Fulgoni, *De S. Callisto PP. et M. ejusque basilica S. Mariae Trans Tyberim nuncupata disquisitiones duae critico-historicae duobus tomis exhibitae ...* (Romae: ex typographia Antonii Fulgonii ..., 1752), 132.
[1587] In the *epistola metrica*: "Condita quin etiam supremo maenia monte / Aestivae nivis indicio, delubraque partu / Obruta virgineo, et fontes olivi, / Ac Tibridos commixta vadis nova flumina cernes, / Quasque dedit scaterbras Pauli sanctissima cervix / Dulcis aquae..." Francesco Petrarca, *Poëmata Minora*, Volume III (Milan: Società Tipografica de Classici Italiani, 1834), 14. In Moretti: "Condita quin etiam supremo moenia monte / Aestivae nivis indicio, delubraque partu / Obruta virgine, & fontes torrentis olivi, / Ac Tybridos commixta vadis sacra flumina cernes." Moretti, *De S. Callisto PP. et M. ejusque basilica S. Mariae Trans Tyberim*, 132.
[1588] Vatican City, Biblioteca Apostolica Vaticana, Vat. lat. 9832, fol.64r.

were not enough, one could also find Christ's cradle, the handkerchief that covered the Christ-child's head, the linen Christ later used to dry his disciples feet, the blood of St. John the Baptist as well as his hair shirt (*de pillis camelorum*).[1589] Beneath the altar of the Lateran, one could truly (*nempe*) find the Ark of the Covenant and two tablets Moses and Aaron carried down from Mount Sinai.[1590] The Holy Land lived in Rome in small pieces, making a pilgrimage to the cities' major basilicas effectively a pilgrimage through the *terra sancta*. Santa Maria in Trastevere did not number among the major basilicas of Rome, but nevertheless, her font functioned as a source of Christ's presence.

Well into the early modern period, perhaps due to the efforts of the Counter-Reformation, the legend of Santa Maria in Trastevere's *fons olei* continued to proliferate. Sometime during the eighteenth century, a *pluteo* beneath the high altar on the right side of the central aisle acquired the words *Fons Olei*, indicating where ages ago oil flowed. While Enlightenment philosophes in France called for breaking with the superstitions of the past, ecclesiastical historians in Rome mounted a robust defense of Santa Maria in Trastevere's prodigious, miraculous fountain. Material from Santa Maria in Trastevere's *Archivio Capitolare* demonstrates that the epithet *fons olei* appeared on all manner of church documents in the early modern period. Even the great wooden armoires that stand in the church offices today have the words 'Fons Olei' carved on their doors. A 1799 account of the translation of St. Bartholomew's relics from the island in the Tiber River to the high altar of Santa Maria in Trastevere includes white seal that shows, in relief, an image of a river of oil pouring forth from the church's front door.[1591] Lists of relics and indulgences for Santa Maria in Trastevere likewise identified the church as the *fons olei*.

Works of popular devotion, including John Capgrave's *Ye Solace of Pilgrims* (1450) and Onofrio Panvinio's *Le sette chiese romane* (1570) discussed the *fons olei* as a convergence point for

---

[1589] Ibid.

[1590] Ibid.

[1591] Rome, Archivio Storico Vicariato di Roma, Archivio Capitulare di Santa Maria in Trastevere, Palchetti 249-269, Armad. II 3B, Sante Reliquie e Indulgenze.

pilgrims and retold the history of the *fons olei* as it emerged within the context of the Roman Empire. Caesar Baronis likewise included the legend in his *Annales Ecclesiastici* (1589) as did Panciroli in his *Tesori nascoti* (1600). Panciroli altered the chronology slightly by saying the oil erupted in the third year of Augustus' reign and three years before Christ's birth. According to Panciroli, the oil flowed from a *taberna meritoria*, which he described as a hospital for old and infirm soldiers. Some catchy verses stood above the miraculous fountain, including the line "*Hinc oleum fluxit, cum Christus Virgine luxit.*" (From here oil flowed, when Christ shown (i.e. was born) from the Virgin).[1592] In addition to oil, the miraculous fountain offered forgiveness for sins: "And here an indulgence is given for whatever is asked."[1593] A canon Santa Maria in Trastevere named Ramoino recorded the miraculous *fons olei* in his *Diverse cose…per la Basilica di Santa Maria in Trastevere* (1658-88), when he gave a brief sketch of the church's history.[1594] According to Ramoino, the oil appeared during Augustus' reign and on the night of Christ's birth, not before, flowing into the Tiber River for an entire day. Like so many authors before him who borrowed from Augustine, Ramoino informed readers that "Christ in the Greek language means 'anointed.'"[1595] Like Panciroli, Ramoino claimed the *taberna meritoria* was a home for the poor and disabled war veterans.[1596] Pietro Moretti's *De S. Callisto PP. et M. ejusque basilica S. Mariae trans Tyberim* (1752) devoted an entire chapter to rejecting false opinions regarding the *fons olei* by cataloguing all the ancient and medieval sources which testified to the oily fountain's existence and power. Furthermore, Roman authors were not the only champions of the legitimacy of the *fons olei*. In *Histoire de l'église depuis la naissance de Jésus Christ, jusqu'à la fin du siècle* (1633) Antonius Godeau likewise retold the story of the appearance of a great quantity of oil, testifying to Christ's birth.

[1592] Ottavio Panciroli, *I tesori nascosti nell'alma città di Roma* (Roma: appresso L. Zannetti, 1625), 584.
[1593] "Hic & donatur venia quodcumque rogatur." Ibid.
[1594] BAV Vat. lat. 9832, fol.191r.
[1595] "Cristo in lingua greca vuol dire unto." Ibid.
[1596] "In detto luogo vi era una Taberna meritoria, la quale serviva per li Poveri, e quelli stroppiati, che aveano servito in guerra." Ibid.

Today Santa Maria in Trastevere is home to the Community of Sant'Egidio, a lay community founded in Rome in 1968 by Andrea Riccardi, who sought a new way for the laity to care for the poor and help establish peace. One of the guiding principles of the community is the non-violent resolution of conflict, since they maintain, "war is the mother of poverty."[1597] Every day of the week this community fills Santa Maria in Trastevere, gathering below the apse mosaic of Mary and Jesus as bride and groom. Above the *fons olei,* priests consecrate hosts during Mass. On Sundays, pews at the front of the church near the high altar are reserved, waiting for the elderly who slowly make their way to their seats. Further back, more places are reserved for the friends of the Sant'Egidio community – mentally and physically disabled children and adults of all ages. At Christmas, the members of the Sant-Egidio community clear away the pews from the church's nave, replacing them with tables and chairs. The homeless and the poor are invited in to share a meal and find solace, even if only for one night, in a human community gathered near the *fons olei.*

[1597] Community of Sant'Egidio, accessed on October 8, 2016, http://www.santegidio.org/pageID/16/Service-to-Peace.html.

Menedemus. All this is appropriate to religion.

Ogygius. Yes, and if you peered inside, Menedemus, you would say it was the abode of the
    saints, so dazzling is it with jewels, gold, and silver.

Menedemus. You make me impatient to go there.

Ogygius. You wouldn't regret the trip.

Menedemus. Is there no holy oil there?

Ogygius. Silly! That oil exudes only from the tombs of saints, such as Andrew and Catherine.
    Mary isn't buried.

Menedemus. My mistake, I admit. But finish your story.

~ *A Pilgrimage for Religion's Sake*, Desiderius Erasmus[1598]

As Erasmus' colloquy demonstrates, by the early sixteenth century, holy oil had become an

established element of the cult of the saints. Europeans seeking an encounter with the sacred, or the

intercession of a holy one, could turn towards the shrines of myroblytes. Although oozing saints

first emerged in the late antique period, their popularity burgeoned in the High Middles Ages,

beginning in the eleventh century, through the widespread popularity of Nicholas of Myra and

Catherine of Alexandria. The earliest myroblytes originated in the Near East, drawing pilgrims to

shrines in northern Africa and Anatolia, where pilgrims poured perfumed olive oil into saints'

sarcophagi, waited for the oil to drip down over the holy relics, and collected the hallowed oil from a

spout at the bottom of the tomb. This late antique practice may have given rise to the myroblyte

phenomenon in both the Greek East and Latin West. Pilgrims carried saints' oil back to their homes

as sacred souvenirs or for medicinal purposes. The archeological remains that attest to this practice,

---

[1598] Desiderius Erasmus and Craig R. Thompson, *Ten Colloquies* (New York; London: Macmillan, 1986).

such as the terracotta Menas *ampullae*, travelled as far as from Egypt to western England. People prized the saints' oil because they believed that anything that enjoyed physical proximity to a saint, acquired the saint's *praesentia* or invisible holy power.

Early medieval hagiographical texts reveal Europeans' nascent devotion to myroblytes. Gregory of Tours became one of Europe's first raconteurs of myroblyte tales when he told of oil miraculously spilling from the tombs of Andrew the Apostle and Martin of Tours. The earliest accounts of myroblytes' tombs claimed that the amount of oil flowing from a saint augured certain natural phenomena, such as how fecund a crop would be in a given year. The idea of a large or small quantity of fragrant oil flowing from the tomb of a saint captured the imaginations of medieval Christians. In several instances, biographers described how a saint could exercise authority from heaven by controlling how much oil flowed out of his or her tomb. An abundance of oil signaled divine favor. A dearth of oil reflected divine wrath. A saint withheld oil to communicate discontent with how Christians conducted themselves, usually with respect to a particular event, such as the usurpation of an episcopal see or the theft of a relic. Saints could also communicate with the living regarding the whereabouts of their corporeal remains by causing oil to saturate a plot of ground. As monasteries and their churches increasingly populated the European landscape in the pre-Carolingian period, the presence of saints' relics lent legitimacy to newly established Christian communities. In some instances, oil functioned as a substitute for primary relics when a desirable saint's tomb lay a great distance from Europe or when the saint was so ancient that obtaining a bit of bone or dried flesh was untenable.

When Christians no longer faced intense persecutions by pagans, biographers sought to explain the extraordinary sanctity of Christ's holy ones by describing the oil miracles they performed while dead and alive. The early medieval myroblytes in Europe were predominantly male clerics – bishops and abbots who struggled against a pagan population, admonishing inchoate Christians to ward off demons and illnesses with holy oil rather than amulets, incantations or magical springs and wells. Early medieval Christians saw oil as a powerful remedy for both mental and physical illness. The biographies of early medieval myroblytes tell of the saints' power to heal relatively minor illnesses, such as pustules, as well as more dire life-threatening conditions, through anointing. As early as the Patristic era, bishops consecrated oil to anoint the sick - *oleum infirmorum*. Centuries later, oil from myroblytes' tombs provided a salve for communities experiencing a dearth of consecrated oil. Oil from lamps hanging near saints' tombs also had the power to cure many. Several *vitae* recount how lamps endlessly replenished themselves or continuously overflowed with oil. Such local sources of holy oil occasionally obviated the need for oil to be brought from any other place, including the Mediterranean, where olive trees grew, or a cathedral, where a bishop consecrated holy oils and distribute them to distant parishes in exchange for a tithe.

In the High Middles Ages, an increase of trade and travel across the Mediterranean led to the wider dissemination of myroblyte legends in Europe. Crusaders and pilgrims sought the shrines of the holy ones in the *terra sancta* in greater numbers and sometimes returned to Europe with devotional souvenirs. As trade wars emerged on the Italic peninsula, saints became important sacred and economic commodities. The translation of Nicholas of Myra's relics from Myra to Bari in 1087 marked a turning point in European devotion to Nichols, who would become one of the most widely celebrated saints in all of Christendom. Nicholas' cult and his reputation for producing oil spread rapidly, spawning cults of other myroblytes in the Latin West. Clerics sometimes sought to strengthen the standing of their beloved saints by closely associating them with other universally celebrated myroblytes, such as Nicholas of Myra and the Andrew the Apostle. By positioning new myroblytes in liturgical calendars in close temporal proximity to more famous myroblytes, proponents of certain saints' cults tried to establish those saints' reputations as oil-producers, especially if there were disputes within the monastery regarding the person in question or his cult.

In the male myroblyte *vitae* of the early medieval period, miraculous oil often signified the male cleric's status as the beloved elect of God. Oil miracles solidified the power of bishops by explicitly associating them with miraculous oil or chrism. Eligius of Noyon, for example, knew he was God's elect when chrism miraculously dripped on his head one night as he prayed. Oil dripping on the head of the young man, who would become a bishop, evidently alluded to the Hebrew tradition of kings being anointed on their heads. Thus, the saints who were similarly anointed, and in turn produced oil from their own bodies or lamps, became part of the royal lineage that stretched back through time to the Hebrew prophets, patriarchs, and kings. In some instances, however, oil assumed a more ambiguous character with respect to gender. Although predominantly associated with male sanctity prior to the eleventh century, authors attributed oil miracles to both men and women, beginning in the High Middle Ages. In the cult of Nicholas, oil appeared with quintessentially feminine images. A chant from Nicholas' office, for instance, combined imagery of oil with maternity and childbirth: the oil seeping from the bishop's tomb was like sweat from a woman's body as she perspired in childbirth. The tomb of a male myroblyte was thus like the body of the Virgin Mary, who contained "the Anointed One." Since Mary symbolized the universal Church, she was like Santa Maria in Trastevere, pouring out the oil of gladness, which is to say, Christ.

When Germanic monks travelled from Bavaria to northern France in the late eleventh century, they took the stories of Nicholas' miraculously oozing tomb with them. In an effort to establish a community devoted to Catherine of Alexandria in Rouen, those same monks composed an office for Catherine in which they described the virgin's relics also swimming in fragrant oil and thus established oil as characteristic of female virginity as well as of male ecclesiastical authority. The rise of Catherine's cult marked the first widespread popularity of a female myroblyte. At Sainte-Catherine-du-Mont-de-Rouen in northern France, Catherine successfully healed the illnesses, both mental and physical, of clerics and the laity alike. Moreover, just as she restored sanity to a lunatic, she stabilized an entire realm by strengthening its weak ruler. The miracles wrought by Catherine's oil were thus not limited to peculiarly feminine conditions, such as hemorrhaging or problematic childbirths. The virgin's oil played a key role on the larger political stage, imbuing secular and ecclesiastical leaders with the power or strength they needed to govern effectively, thus functioning in a manner akin to the oil used to anoint both bishops and kings.

Subsequent biographers looked to the precedent set by Catherine when composing the *legendae* of other holy women. A handful of female saints, including Catherine of Alexandria, Mary Magdalene, Humility of Faenza, and Rose of Viterbo acquired fame for their eloquent speech and oily tombs. Gregory the Great's interpretation of the Book of Job, which appeared in the *Glossa Ordinaria,* established the correlation between oil and oratory. Gregory interpreted the oil flowing from the rock in the Book of Job as a symbol for the teachings of Christ flowing from the mouths of the Apostles. Gregory claimed that Christ's teachings anointed listeners. Certain female myroblytes, who were skilled at preaching, possessed the power to figuratively anoint listeners with their sermons and to literally anoint people's bodies with their oozing tombs, or in the case of Mary Magdalene, to anoint Jesus with oil from her alabaster jar.

In the thirteenth and fourteenth centuries, the number of female myroblytes increased dramatically thanks to Dominican, Franciscan, and Cistercian biographers, who promoted the cults of holy women affiliated with their religious orders. As the Church grew increasingly concerned about heresy among the laity, mendicants tried to bring women more firmly within the fold of the Church by recording the *legendae* of holy women. Mendicant biographers increasingly attributed the power miraculously to produce oil to these holy women, as a sign of both their extraordinary sanctity and their religious legitimacy. The *vitae* of these female myroblytes also often emphasized the importance of penance as a Christian devotion. Through the dissemination of Mary Magdalene's cult, mendicants called for the laity to atone for their sins through works of corporeal mercy. Mary

Magdalene, with her alabaster jar of fragrant unguent, became an emblem for all repentant sinners

and the active apostolate of the laity.[1599]

The mendicant propensity for composing female myroblyte *vitae* appears to have begun in

the Low Countries in the mid-thirteen century, and then to have spread to Italy in the early

fourteenth century. Thomas de Cantimpré's *vitae* of Christina Mirabilis and Lutgard of Aywières

marked major innovations in myroblyte hagiography. Not only did de Cantimpré attribute

miraculous oil production to his female contemporaries, but he claimed that oil flowed from their

living bodies, not their tombs. Christina the Astonishing's breasts wondrously produced oil, which

she used as unguent for her wounds and a condiment for her food. De Cantimpré himself was

conscious of the novelty of this miracle, claiming that the great miracle was "unheard of in all

previous centuries."[1600] De Cantimpré presented Lutgard of Aywières as a literal and figurative lamp

bringing light to her sisters. While visiting the home of a recluse, Lutgard experienced a mystical

ecstasy, after which she saw oil flowing from her fingertips. The saint herself interpreted the oil as a

"manifestation of grace."[1601] According to de Cantimpré, Lutgard later shone with divine radiance, as

if she herself were an oil-filled lamp dispensing light.

In the mid-thirteenth century, when Thomas de Cantimpré claimed that contemporary holy

women, rather than male clerics, produced holy oil, he heralded mendicants' interest in bringing

women and their devotional practices more firmly within the purview of religious orders. Christina

existed on the fringes of the Church, her family, and society more generally, engaging in wild, almost

savage, antics of penitential corporeal punishment. Christina's *vita* showed how a liminal holy

---

[1599] See Katherine L. Jansen, *The Making of the Magdalen: Preaching and Popular Devotion in the Later Middle Ages* (Princeton, N.J: Princeton University Press, 2000).

[1600] Thomas de Cantimpré, *The Life of Christina the Astonishing*, 2nd ed, Peregrina Translations Series (Toronto, Ont: Peregrina Pub. Co, 1999).

[1601] Thomas de Cantimpré and Margot H King, *The Life of Lutgard of Aywières* (Toronto, Ont.: Peregrina Pub. Co., 1991), 35–36.

woman became affiliated with a legitimate ecclesiastical institution. The miraculous virgin undertook astonishing corporeal feats in order that she might relieve souls in purgatory through her own bodily suffering. The Dominican urged his Christian readers to see in Christina's life a call to penance, lest they be caught like unwise virgins who, lacking oil in their lamps, never gained entrance to the wedding feast, which is to say, to eternal life. De Cantimpré presented Lutgard as another image of holiness that could draw women into greater penance and asceticism. Although Lutgard had entered a Benedictine convent dedicated to Catherine of Alexandria at a young age, she sought a more ascetic lifestyle among the Cistercians and experienced oil flowing from her body while secluded in a recluse's hermitage. In recounting the mystical ecstasies and corporeal miracles of both myroblytes, the Dominican biographer presented the holy women as being outliers in terms of their extraordinary devotion and yet well within the boundaries of the institutional church.

In late medieval Italy, the dramatic increase of female myroblytes appears to have also resulted from mendicant efforts to incorporate laywomen's spirituality into the institutional church. Like the myroblytes of the Low Countries, the female myroblytes of Italy crossed social boundaries and the lay-religious binary. Italic myroblytes of the thirteenth and fourteenth centuries included abbesses of wealthy convents as well as poor servant girls. In most instances, however, mendicant biographers promoted the cults of the holy women and reiterated the women's ties to religious orders or institutions. In Humility of Faenza's vernacular *vita*, the miraculous oil from the abbess' tomb manifested the saint's sanctity, other women's ability to discern miraculous activity and their power to overcome adversity when confronted by skeptical male clerics. In the case of Agnes of Montepulciano's *vita*, composed by Raymond of Capua, fragrant oil testified to the woman's holiness and virginity. Her intact body required no balsam for preservation. By virtue of the woman's holiness, her body was not only incorruptible, but also produced a large quantity of liquid more precious than balsam. Similarly, when male clerics tried to embalm Margaret of Città di Castello, her virginal dead body discretely covered her naked private parts and then gushed oil. The legends of

Agnes and Margaret, who were both affiliated with the Dominicans, urged women to become

tertiaries and take the penitential habit. Zita of Lucca and Rose of Viterbo were likewise

distinguished holy myroblytes despite (or as a result of) their gender, low social status, and tenuous

affiliations with mendicant orders. Although they were often poor laywomen, the myroblytes of late

medieval Italy performed miracles that in previous centuries had been reserved for male clerics and

which, in the Holy Roman Empire, were increasingly associated with noblewomen.

Poor, marginalized servants and mystics were not the only holy women to become

myroblytes in the later medieval period. In the thirteenth- and fourteenth-century Germania,

myroblytes tended to be more well-established noblewomen. In the mid-thirteenth century, the

Cistercian abbot Caesarius of Heisterbach attributed oozing oil to the tomb of Elizabeth of

Thuringian, a lay, married noblewoman. Elizabeth embodied the mendicant vision of charity by

renouncing her wealth and dedicating her life to serving the poor. She cultivated close relations with

the Franciscans and emulated Francis in her renunciation of worldly goods in exchange for a life of

poverty, humility, and corporeal works of mercy. Elizabeth's oil became a means of continuing to

serve impoverished and sick people after her death, as many sought succor at her tomb. Rather than

symbolizing her status as a powerful member of the elite, the noblewoman's holy oil manifested her

humility and elective poverty. Nevertheless, Caesarius of Heisterbach explained the noblewoman's

holy oil was indicative of her belonging to a royal succession of myroblytes, the rest of whom hailed

from the Late Antique Near East: Demetrius of Thessaloniki, Catherine of Alexandria, Nicholas of

Myra, and then Elizabeth of Thuringia. Caesarius argued that miraculous oil spilled from the tombs

of both clerics and married people alike, and that both wives as well as virgins could be crowned

with martyrdom and produce holy oil. In the development of Elizabeth of Thuringia's cult, we see

further evidence that in the late medieval period, oil became a sign of a holy woman. In the mid thirteenth century, a married laywomen became a notable myroblyte, whereas in previous centuries, the most famous myroblytes (according to Caesarius of Heisterbach) included a male bishop, a male martyr, and a female virgin.

In late medieval Germania, two other women with noble or elite affiliations became myroblytes following the growth of Elizabeth of Thuringia's cult. Hedwig of Silesia's *vita* correlated holy oil with nobility by describing how Hedwig's unguent flowed from her head in particular, not simply from her tomb. The noblewoman's head might have resonated with readers as a symbol for Christ, the head of the Church. The *Glossa Ordinaria* repeatedly interpreted the human head as being a symbol for Christ; the pope himself was the head of the Church. In fourteenth-century Bavaria, as the cult of Hedwig of Silesia grew, Philipp von Rathsamhausen, the Bishop of Eichstätt and former Cistercian, promoted the cult of Walburga by saturating her *legenda* with oil, arguing that the saints whose tombs produced the greatest quantities of oil after death had shown the most mercy while alive. While in previous centuries, the abbess of Heidenheim had enjoyed fame only for her curative water, in the early fourteenth century, the bishop lauded the virginal abbess for producing large quantities of curative holy oil, which he himself drank on one occasion. Throughout late medieval Europe, when biographers depicted women as sources of holy oil, they invariably linked the women's oil with members of the ecclesiastical hierarchy who composed the women's *vitae* and personally promoted the popular (and potentially economically lucrative) devotions surrounding the women's cults.

Although this study primarily examines myroblytes venerated in the Latin West, a comparative study of myroblytes in Byzantium and in medieval western Europe would allow us to determine the extent to which sacred biographers from these two regions traded stories about oozing tombs and holy bodies. Such a study could trace how legends about myroblytes travelled from Byzantium to medieval Europe and vice-versa, altering the devotional landscapes of both regions. The Byzantine saints who could be incorporated into such a study include Menas of Egypt

(3rd century), Demetrius of Thessaloniki (3rd-4th century), the martyr George (d. 303), Pantalemon

of Nicodemia (d. 305), Matrona of Perge, who distributed fragrant oil from the head of John the

Baptist (6th century), Elizabeth the Wonderworker (6th century), Athanasia of Aegina (circa 790-

860), Theodora of Thessaloniki (812-892), and Thomaïs of Lesbos (10th century). A study of these

saints and their correspondance with saints in medieval Europe would naturally entail an

investigation of questions regarding gender. Was the holy oil of Byzantine women fundamentally

different from that of men? Did their miracles differ in nature? Were male and female saints truly

loci of popular devotion or simply political ploys?

Unlike the lives of Latin myroblytes or their followers, Byzantine hagiographical texts tell of

women anointing the faithful with myroblytes' oil or distributing the oil to large crowds. Such

practices never appear (to my knowledge) in the hagiographical literature of the Latin West. By

examining such contrasting accounts of miraculous oil, one could determine the extent to which

saints' myron was in tension or harmony with ecclesiastical authorities. Demetrius' oil, for example,

was evidently sometimes used in lieu of baptismal chrism. Understanding how clerics responded to

the unauthorized use of oil by the laity or minor clergy in both the Byzantine and Latin churches

would greatly enhance our understanding of oil's power as sign of holiness and authority among

medieval Christians. The oil miracles of Byzantine saints would thus offer illuminative points of

comparison for the Latin West. One could explore, for example, the extent to which oil fell under

the purview of the ecclesiastical elite and if oil miracles in Byzantium and Europe similarly reflected

shifts in Marian devotion as well as liturgical and political developments.

The High Middle Ages proved a turning point, not only for myroblyte biographies, but also for the legend of the *fons olei*. The story of olive oil miraculously bursting from the banks of the Tiber River in Rome in the first century B.C.E. may have originated as a Messianic prophecy within the Jewish community in Rome, as the Roman Republic convulsed with political and social conflict. When Cassius Dio retold the story a few centuries later, in the second century C.E., the Roman Empire once again strove for stability during a civil war. Dio posited the oil gushing from the banks of the Tiber resulted from the wrath of the Mother of the Gods, who was incensed with the Roman population. Although Christianity was gaining a foothold in Rome at the time, Dio never suggested the *fons olei* occurred at the site of a Marian shrine in Trastevere. Jerome's translation of Eusebius' *Chronological Table* first interpreted the *fons olei* as a divine sign with Christological significance, but never mentioned a Marian church *transtyberim*. According to Jerome (or Eusebius), the oil augured Christ's birth, before the event occurred in Bethlehem. Rather than signifying the wrath of the pagan goddess, the oil heralded "the grace of Christ born for the sake of humankind."[1602]

Subsequent late antique and Carolingian authors who incorporated Jerome's gloss on Eusebius' chronical into their own narratives about the *fons olei* likewise never mentioned the Virgin Mary or a church dedicated to her. Prior to the twelfth century, authors almost universally discussed the *fons olei* miracle as a sign of Christ's birth, emphasizing how the oil flowed from the *taberna meritoria*, which prefigured the universal Church, but not an actual Marian shrine. Moreover, rather than interpreting the oil as having any maternal or feminine aspects, the authors of the early medieval period emphasized how Christ's birth and the miraculous oil coincided with the reign of Caesar Augustus and the *pax romana*. When secular rulers, like Charlemagne, sought to identify

---

[1602] "E taberna meritoria trans Tiberim oleum terra erupit fluxitque tota die sine intermissione significans Xpi gratiam ex gentibus." PL 27, cols. 431-32.

themselves with Roman Emperors, authors circulating the *fons olei* legend claimed the oil marked the

advent of the Prince of Peace and the reign of the most powerful of Roman emperors.

In the twelfth century, a shift occurred in the telling of the *fons olei* legend in medieval

Europe. Early medieval authors had established the symbolic framework for Santa Maria in

Trastevere to become the source of the *fons olei*. In early medieval texts, the Roman *taberna meritoria*

prefigured the universal Church as the source of grace. In the twelfth century, as cults of myroblytes

spread and the tombs of women as well as men were reputed to flow with holy oil, authors

interpreted the source of the *fons olei* as being peculiarly feminine, indeed, as being the Mother of

God herself. Abelard's Sermon 4 is the first known text to have named Santa Maria in Trastevere as

the source of the *fons olei*, which he claimed was a sign of the birth of a monarch, Christ, into whose

hands power was vested and remained, and who ruled both heaven and earth. According to Abelard,

Christ was so-called because of his anointing (from the Greek, *christos*), which was a sign of Christ's

human nature, and thus of the Incarnation. In discussing the ancient legend and the curious miracle,

the provocative philosopher also touched upon conflicts regarding the legitimacy of rulers in his

present day.

With the rise of Marian devotion in the Latin West in the twelfth century and an attendant

shift towards emphasizing Christ's humanity, authors reinterpreted the *fons olei* legend, giving

emphasis to Mary as a human mother giving birth to little baby. After Abelard pointed toward the

humanity of Christ and the correspondance between human nature and anointing, other twelfth-

century authors likewise explored the humanity of both Christ and Mary in their retellings of the *fons

olei* legend. Honorius of Autun's discussion of the miracles surrounding Christ's birth included a

meditation on the pain and filth normally associated with childbirth, explaining that in Mary's case,

her child's birth was both immaculate and pain-free on account of her virginity. Even though he

presented Mary as beyond human, Honorius had begun to explore the human dimension of the

Incarnation. Rather than claiming that the *fons olei* coincided with the reign of a powerful Roman emperor, Honorius stated "a fountain of mercy emanated from the virgin," placing an emphasis on Mary's role.[1603] Other authors went further in imaginatively presenting the coincidence of events that were at once colossal and absolutely ordinary. An anonymous sermon for the Nativity, possibly authored by Nicholas of Clairvaux, drew a parallel between the destruction of a woman's body in childbirth and the destruction of pagan and Jewish temples, in Rome and Jerusalem respectively. Peter Comestor likewise reproduced such an image, in which the pagan Temple of Peace (a false peace) shattered at the birth of the Prince of Peace, which coincided with the flowing oil. According to the anonymous nativity sermon, the "true peace" was not an abstract, divine entity, but a human child, grasping at his mother's breasts and smiling, small and vulnerable. Though the author characterized Christ's mother as the "Queen of Heaven" she nevertheless appeared as a human mother, subject to human joys and fears. When the oil erupted in Trastevere, strife and false belief ceased as divine peace spread over the globe, like oil spreading from the *fons olei*.

Although some twelfth century texts emphasized the humanity of Christ and Mary in their retelling of the *fons olei* legend, others presented the mother and child as symbols for abstract concepts that were both theological and political in nature. In twelfth-century visual and textual discourse, Santa Maria in Trastevere became the Bride of Christ, one of the wise virgins bearing oil and gaining entrance to the eternal wedding feast. As papal schisms destabilized the Roman papacy, popes created images to symbolically depict the omnipotent nature of papal authority over the Church. The apse mosaic within Santa Maria in Trastevere, in which Jesus sat enthroned next to Mary and embraced her as if she were his wife, represented the extension of papal power over the Church. Mary represented the Church, which provided the oil used to hallow Christians and to consecrate secular and ecclesiastical rulers. The source of oil, and all authority, was *mater ecclesia.*

[1603] PL 172, Col. 1124A-B.

When Innocent II reclaimed the church of Santa Maria in Trastevere following the papal

schism with Anacletus II, the image of Jesus' arm encircling Mary and claiming her as his wife (and

thus under his own authority) echoed as a symbol for legitimate papal authority more generally.

Since the time of the Hebrew prophets and kings, oil signified divine election, eternal kingship and

being the God's beloved "chosen one." The pope's throne (*sedes*) was the Church itself, with Mary as

the *sedes sapientiae,* the Throne of Divine Wisdom. Wooden images, particularly from northern

France, depicted Jesus sitting on his mother's lap as a king sits on the throne. In the apse mosaic of

Santa Maria in Trastevere, Jesus and Mary sat side-by-side on the throne, as husband and wife. Mary,

as the Bride of the Christ at the eternal wedding banquet, also represented heaven or eternity, in part

through the symbolic interpretation of the imagery of the Book of Revelation. Bernard of Clairvaux

in particular interpreted Mary's role as the Bride of Christ to mean she was also the "new

Jerusalem."[1604] A epigraphical inscription embedded in the apse mosaic of Santa Maria in Trastevere,

alluded to various biblical texts that spoke of the eternal lineage of God's anointed elect, based on

texts from the Song of Songs and psalms: *"ponam in te thronum meum"* – "I will place my throne within

you." God's throne, like God's spirit, entered the beloved through anointing. Oil designated the

beloved elect of God, whose rule would endure forever.

In 1215 when Innocent III processed to Santa Maria in Trastevere at the opening of the

Fourth Lateran Council, he sought to address issues such as the enduring nature of papal rule and

the ultimate source of secular and ecclesiastical authority. The pageantry surrounding the procession

to Trastevere and the symbolism of consecrating the church, which was itself the source of the *fons

olei,* can be understood in light of the conflicts surrounding the papacy in Innocent III's day as well

as his efforts to establish the pope as the *vicarius Christi,* who alone could claim *plenitudo potestatis* –

fullness of power. As Rome struggled to recapture Jerusalem after the failed Fourth Crusade and

---

[1604] Rev. 21:2.

faced heretical adversaries within Europe, Innocent III strategically consecrated a church that evoked the miracles of Christ's birth in the Holy Land and the reign of a powerful ruler in Rome. The nuptial imagery permeating the liturgy for the consecration of a church also conveyed the extent to which Innocent III united himself, as if in a marital bond, to the church (and Church) which was the source of all authority. The *fons olei* functioned as a symbol for *plenitudo potestatis* – the source of power from which all other power and authority flows. As Innocent III's predecessor, Innocent II, had done before in reclaiming Santa Maria in Trastevere as his own through its reconstruction, Innocent III claimed the church as his bride through the ritual anointing at the consecration. Innocent III ruled over the church and the Church universal, as a husband ruled over his wife.

In consecrating Santa Maria in Trastevere, with its apse mosaic presenting Jesus and Mary as husband and wife, Innocent III made a potent gesture of papal authority vis-à-vis human marriage and the offspring that issue from carnal unions. During Innocent III's reign, the Cathars rejected the institutional church, its clergy and sacraments. Moreover, the Cathars' dualist theology, which posited the existence of two gods – one good, which created the soul or spirit, and one evil, which created the flesh and all material things – led the Cathars to reject the humanity of Christ, the doctrine of the Incarnation, and the institutional Church, the "body of Christ." By extensions, the Cathars rejected human marriage, offspring and even ideas of sexual difference or genders. Amidst the Cathar presence in Italy and southern France, Innocent III included marriage as one of the Church's sacraments, reaffirming the sanctity of marriage, the dual nature of Christ, and the doctrine of the Incarnation. In one of his Nativity sermons, in which he discussed the wondrous signs at Christ's birth, including the *fons olei,* Innocent III presented Christ as having both two natures (human and divine) and two genders (male and female). Anointing characterized Jesus' human nature, since through anointing a human being was suffused with divinity. Thus, the outpouring of oil in Rome marked the anointing of the world, the merging of human and divine natures in the

Incarnation. God united with humanity in Mary's womb, just as God's spirit joined with human flesh through anointing.

Further study of the *fons olei* legend might include the role of miraculous oil in late medieval Rome and the Counter-Reformation. To my knowledge, scholars have not yet commented on how the Church continued to defend the legend of the *fons olei* during the Protestant Reformation, Counter-Reformation and the Enlightenment. Since the church of Santa Maria in Trastevere not only produced a great quantity of oil but also a prodigious amount of Baroque music, understanding the correspondance between these two phenomena would also substantially augment our understanding of the church's history as well as the relationship between music and marvels in the Baroque period.[1605] Further, to my knowledge, studies of Santa Maria in Trastevere's *fons olei* have been based entirely on Latin and Italian primary sources. Given that Trastevere was home to a substantial Jewish population, scholars with knowledge of Hebrew might look for evidence of popular devotions to the *fons olei* in any extant Hebrew sources authored by the medieval Jewish community living in Trastevere.

Ex Fontibus: The Sources of Medieval Ideas about Miraculous Oil

The legends of myroblytes and the *fons olei* in the medieval Latin West can be explained in part by understanding the significance of oil in pre-Christian pagan and Hebraic cultures, which directly influenced early Christian thought and ritual. In the ancient Near East and Mesopotamia, oil belonged to both daily life and sacred rituals. Oil was an integral part of the social and cultural fabric of early societies, which informed the character and trajectory of Christianity. Hosts showed hospitality by bathing their guests and anointing their bodies with holy oil. Oil protected the skin

---

[1605] A starting point for this would be Santa Maria in Trastevere (Church : Rome, Italy); Archivio storico del Vicariato di Roma. and Eleonora Simi Bonini, *Catalogo del fondo musicale di Santa Maria in Trastevere nell'Archivio Storico del Vicariato di Roma : Tre Secoli Di Musica Nella Basilica Romana Di Santa Maria in Trastevere* (Rome: IBIMUS, 2000).

from wear and tear and could heal open wounds. Men forged contracts by smearing oil into their skin and taking oaths, knowing that if they broke the oath, the oil that permeated their skin could release a curse. Female slaves were anointed with oil upon their heads at manumission and brides-to-be were similarly anointed before marriage. Women carried oil mixed with spices to the tombs of their beloved kin to anoint their bodies in preparation for burial. Wrestlers anointed their naked bodies with oil before matches. Kings and priests received the spirit of God when a prophet poured oil on their heads from a horn. Oil thus not only met the practical daily needs of people in early societies but also played a role in hallowing certain individuals and signaling crucial social bonds.

When Christianity emerged in the Near East in the first century C.E., it adapted ancient ideas and practices involving oil for new religious purposes. Oil, which often signified abundant life, health, and fecundity in ancient pagan and Hebraic culture, engendered new life for Christians through initiation rituals. Jesus of Nazareth was hailed as the Messiah, the Anointed One, who received God's spirit and was anointed as God's beloved son through a spiritual anointing. Christian ritual replicated Jesus' spiritual anointing with a literal, physical anointing with holy oil. In the early church, catechumens received full-body anointings prior to baptism, as if they were wrestlers preparing to battle their enemy Satan. Anointing oil marked the entrance of God's spirit into the Christian's body and strengthened him or her for a new life and mission. New Christians, like the king of Psalm 44, were anointed with the oil of gladness before their companions. Patristic exegetes established a precedent for interpreting oil symbolically. Often oil represented God's grace or mercy. Exegetes sometimes also interpreted Jesus as the "true olive" whose outpouring of oil bestowed salvation on the world. While Christ was anointed directly with God's spirit, human beings needed a visible, tangible sign of God's spirit and thus were anointed with oil.

Patristic ideas about holy oil entered medieval culture, in part, through the *Glossa Ordinaria,* which circulated widely in Europe from the twelfth century onwards. The compilers of the *Glossa* drew directly on the writings of Augustine, Isidore of Seville, Gregory the Great, Jerome, whose exegesis on the meaning of holy oil in the bible permeated medieval thought and ritual. Glossators and exegetes, for instance, referenced Augustine's interpretation of Psalms 44 and 132 in their glosses on other biblical pericopes involving holy oil. The phrase "Therefore God, your God anointed you with the oil of gladness before your companions" became so pervasive in the *Glossa Ordinaria* that glossators simply abbreviated this line of text, knowing medieval readers knew the verse by heart. Medieval exegetes invariably interpreted the oil that appeared in the bible as having a meaning beyond its literal meaning. Physical anointings represented spiritual or interior anointings, performed by the Holy Spirit, which had the power to liberate people enslaved by sin, illness, or ignorance.

Certain biblical scenes that involved oil and anointing, such as the anointing of Aaron in Psalm 132, the anointing of the king in Psalm 44, the anointing of David by Samuel, Jacob's anointing the stone at Bethel, and Mary Magdalene's anointing of Jesus with unguent from her alabaster jar, became iconic images in the minds and memories of medieval readers and practitioners of the liturgy. Such scenes found their place in medieval ritual through liturgical chant, as well as through ritual actions, including: the anointing of new Christians at Easter; the anointing of the sick; the consecration of churches, bishops and kings; and the *pedilavium* ritual on Holy Thursday, in which monks and other clerics replicated Jesus' washing the disciples' feet as choristers sang about Mary Magdalene washing and anointing Jesus' own feet in Bethany. Medieval authors saw in the literal outpouring of oil a metaphor for spiritual oil: God's grace, mercy or divine spirit poured out for the transformation and redemption of human kind. Oil became a symbol for love, which had the power to divinize a limited, mortal human being. Although bishops alone had the authority to consecrate oils, transforming the liquid of an olive into something sacred, the bodies of saints could also produce oil that had the power to heal and sanctify the sick or sinful, subverting the Church's established hierarchy. Santa Maria in Trastevere, with her legendary *fons oki,* became the myroblyte of

myroblytes, producing a flowing river of oil that brought peace and joy to a broken, wounded world.

The presence of oil transformed earth into a heavenly abode.

456

9 785960 598828